THINKING IN

# JAZZ

*Selected by the*

*Black Student Union of Menlo College*

*in Celebration of*

*Black History Month 1996*

**Chicago Studies
in Ethnomusicology**

Edited by
PHILIP V. BOHLMAN
and
BRUNO NETTL

Editorial Board
MARGARET J. KARTOMI
HIROMI LORRAINE SAKATA
ANTHONY SEEGER
KAY KAUFMAN SHELEMAY
BONNIE C. WADE

# Paul F. Berliner

## THINKING IN

# JAZZ

### The Infinite Art
### of Improvisation

**The University of Chicago Press**

**Chicago and London**

The University of Chicago Press, Chicago 60637
The University of Chicago Press, Ltd., London
© 1994 by The University of Chicago
All rights reserved. Published 1994
Printed in the United States of America

03 02 01 00 99 98 97 96 95          5 4 3

ISBN (cloth): 0–226–04380–0
ISBN (paper): 0–226–04381–9

Library of Congress Cataloging-in-Publication Data

Berliner, Paul.
    Thinking in jazz : the infinite art of improvisation / Paul F. Berliner.
       p.     cm. — (Chicago studies in ethnomusicology)
    Includes bibliographical references (p.   ), discography (p.   ),
filmography (p.   ), and index.
    ISBN 0-226-04380-0. — ISBN 0-226-04381-9 (pbk.)
    1. Jazz—History and criticism.   2. Improvisation (Music)   3. Jazz musicians—
Interviews.   I. Title.   II. Series.
ML3506.B475   1994
781.65'136—dc20                           93-34660
                                                     CIP
                                                     MN

*Pictured on overleaf, clockwise from left: Billy Bauer (guitar), Eddie Safranski (bass),
Charlie Parker and Lennie Tristano (piano).*

*To the Artists of the Jazz Tradition*

# CONTENTS

# PART V
## Music Texts
505

# FIGURES

xi

# MUSIC TEXTS

# ACKNOWLEDGMENTS

Any work of this kind, which has been in the making for many years and has depended on many different methods of data collection—each with its own demands on time and resources—owes its success to the cooperation and support of many individuals and institutions. I am indebted, foremost, to the musicians/interviewees named in appendix B, whose views inspired and challenged my own thinking about music throughout the study, constantly influencing its course. Readers who are not familiar with the artists by reputation will find short biographies of most in *The New Grove Dictionary of Jazz* (Kernfeld 1988d). Providing an invaluable background for the project was private study over the years with several other jazz musicians cited in the work: trumpeters Johnny Coppola, Julius Ellerby, and Herb Pomeroy; pianists Howard Levy and Alan Swain; and saxophonists Joe Giudice, Warren James, Charlie Mariano, and Makanda Ken McIntyre. (I did course work with McIntyre as well in graduate school at Wesleyan University.) Still others, artists Donald Byrd, Betty Carter, Dizzy Gillespie, Warren Kime, Don Sickler, Ira Sullivan, Art Taylor, Billy Taylor, and Dick Whitsell, shared ideas with me informally at nightclub and concert engagements and other venues.

Different aspects of the research were carried out under the auspices of a number of organizations. In 1978 Northwestern University's Office for Research and Sponsored Programs funded a pilot project, which crystallized many questions for further research. Two years later, a National Endowment for the Humanities grant supported comprehensive interviews with jazz musicians in New York City, and assistance from the United Church Board for Homeland Ministries helped with the interviews' transcription. Generous sponsorship by the Spencer Foundation subsequently provided the opportunity to analyze the interview data, to initiate a component of the project transcribing recorded improvisations, and to begin preparation of a manuscript based on the study's preliminary findings. I am especially grateful to Mr. H. Thomas James, the Foundation's former president, his wife, Mrs. Vienna James, and to Mrs. Marion M. Faldet, former Foundation vice-president and secretary, for their special interest in the research and commitment to its goals. My residence as a research fellow at the Rockefeller Foundation Bellagio Study and Conference Center in the spring of 1984 produced a major breakthrough in teasing out the themes of the oral history material, and, between 1988 and 1990, a partial research fellowship and supplementary assistance from Northwestern University's Center for Interdisciplinary Research in the Arts (under the directorships of Susan Lee and Dwight Conquergood) enabled me to integrate the oral history material with additional musicological data. The University's Center and School of Music helped subsidize a continuation of the transcription work and the preparation of musical examples for this book. I am especially appreciative of the personal encouragement I received throughout the study from the School's former dean, Thomas W. Miller, and his wife, Peggy Miller, and from the current dean, Bernard Dobroski.

A number of professional jazz musicians, composers, and music theorists with jazz performance experience collaborated with me in transcribing recorded improvisations and participated in the collective process of score revision described in the headnote to part 5 of this work. Bassist Larry Gray focused largely on transcribing bass and piano parts; drummer David Fodor, the drum set parts; guitarist Stephen Ramsdell and tuba player Richard Watson, the solo parts. Joining us in editing the transcriptions were music theorist–pianist James Dossa, pianist Michael Kocour, keyboardist Shawn Decker, and saxophonist Robert Fried. An overlapping team helped prepare computer-generated music copy. Ryan Beveridge, Shawn Decker, David Fodor, Arne Eigenfeldt, and Robert Fried worked with the "Finale" program; James Dossa, with "Score." Building on the herculean efforts of their colleagues, Fried and Dossa's skillful work is largely responsible for the professional appearance of the final examples. No challenge seemed beyond their virtuoso control of the music writing programs.

To broaden the base of this study's original transcription work, I also included short excerpts from published and unpublished musical examples of several other transcribers. Credited for their fine contributions throughout part 5 are Jamey Aebersold, David Baker, Todd Coolman, Bill Dobbins, Pat Harbison, Barry Harris, Kenny Kirkwood, Thomas Owens, Lewis Porter, Don Sickler, Ken Slone, Steven Strunk, Dick Washburn, and Robert Witmer.

Because of the study's interest in bridging such worlds as music theory, performance practice, composition, cognition, history, cultural interpretation, and so on, I sought criticism from colleagues with different specializations who kindly agreed to serve as readers. I am grateful to them for sharing their responses with me and raising various issues for consideration during the work's revision. At Northwestern University, sociologist Howard Becker, composer Michael Pisaro, music theorist Richard Ashley, historian Sarah Maza, and choreographer and dancer Lynne Blom read individual chapters. Giving an entire draft of the manuscript a thorough reading were jazz keyboardist–composer Joan Wildman at the University of Wisconsin, Madison; ethnomusicologist and jazz bassist Robert Witmer at York University, Toronto; ethnomusicologist and jazz trumpeter Ingrid Monson at the University of Chicago, and, at the same institution, Keith Sawyer, a doctoral candidate in the Department of Psychology; Stephen Ramsdell and James Dossa; and three participants in the original interviews, pianist Howard Levy, trumpeter Bobby Rogovin, and drummer Paul Wertico. Pianist Barry Harris also looked over many portions and made important recommendations for revision. Additionally, Christopher Rudmose brought her fine editorial eye to several chapters, and folklorist Linda Morley generously shared her talents by meticulously examining the last two drafts of the work and making sensitive editorial suggestions throughout.

Over the years, I have also derived inspiration from discussions with several associates with common interests in ethnographic research and in jazz. They include sociologist Howard Becker and performance ethnographer Dwight Conquergood at my own institution; musicologist Lawrence Gushee and ethnomusicologist Bruno Nettl at the University of Illinois; ethnomusicologist Christopher Waterman at the University of Washington; bassoonist and music history professor Joseph Urbinato at Roosevelt University; and composer T. J. Anderson, formerly at Tufts University. Additionally, many friends have consulted on one point or another or shared records and other pertinent materials with me. The limitations of space prevent my acknowledging each by name, but, at the very least, let me thank my colleagues Karen Hansen, Eddie Meadows, Thomas Owens, Lawrence Pinto, Lewis Porter, Don Roberts, Bob Welland, and fellow Barry Harris workshop members cited in this work, Franklin Gordon, Jeff Morgan, and Al Olivier. Also, I would like to express special gratitude to David Dann of station WJFF 90.5 FM in Jeffersonville, New York, who assisted me in tracking down essential discographical information; to David Pituh and Ruth Charloff, who brought great powers of concentration to proofing the final manuscript and made valuable editorial recommendations; and to Michael Kocour, who contributed the photograph that appears in example 3.5. Students in my improvisation courses at Northwestern University have also been a constant source of stimulation, expanding my own understanding of the subject.

As the project evolved, I often felt the supportive presence over my shoulder of three old friends who encouraged the research from its onset but, sadly, passed away before its conclusion. Robert Share, director at the Berklee College of Music, was a dedicated college administrator with an early inspirational vision for jazz education. Lynne Blom, associate professor of dance at Northwestern University, was an innovator in choreography and dance improvisation pedagogy. Klaus Wachsmann, my predecessor at the same institution, was an ethnomusiciologist and a gentleman who always raised the imaginative, challenging questions.

Finally, seeing me through the trials and tribulations that long-term projects inevitably encounter has been the unwavering support of my parents, Ann and Joseph, my sister, Nancy, and my brother, Carl. And, of course, I am greatly indebted to Gabriel Dotto, former music editor at the University of Chicago Press, and to T. David Brent, senior editor, for their belief in the work and for the respectful treatment it received in their hands.

# INTRODUCTION

## Picking Notes out of Thin Air?

Improvisation and Its Study

*I used to think, How could jazz musicians pick notes out of thin air? I had no idea of the knowledge it took. It was like magic to me at the time.* —Calvin Hill

Energized by its vitality, transported by its affective powers, and awed by its elegance and cohesion, listeners might well imagine that jazz was thoroughly composed and rehearsed before its presentation. Yet jazz artists commonly perform without musical scores and without a specialized conductor to coordinate their performances. They may never have met before the event nor played together in any other setting. Contributing further to the mystique surrounding jazz is the transient and unique nature of jazz creations; each performance's evolving ideas, sustained momentarily by the air waves, vanish as new developments overtake them, seemingly never to be repeated. That jazz performers improvise their music, a common explanation for these marvels, begs the more difficult question: Just what is improvisation? A popular general dictionary maintains that "to improvise is to compose, or simultaneously compose and perform, on the spur of the moment and without any preparation."[1] Similarly, a prestigious music dictionary has, until recently, asserted that improvisation is the "art of performing music spontaneously, without the aid of manuscript, sketches or memory."[2] Such definitions reflect the common view that the activity of improvisation comprises neither the faithful re-creation of a composition

1

nor the elaboration of prefigured musical ideas. In the absence of such models or goals, it follows that there is no music for improvisers to prepare for performance. Indeed, they *must* perform spontaneously and intuitively.

At times, remarks by musicians appear to support this argument. "I have no idea what I am going to do when I take a solo," Doc Cheatham says. "That's the thing that I don't understand myself, and I've been asked about it so many times. When I play a solo, I never know any more about what I am going to play than you do."[3] George Duvivier also does not "want to go into a solo with anything preconceived." He finds it "best to go in with an open mind and let it develop." Other veterans advised Kenny Washington as a youngster "not to think about playing—just play."

Faced with authoritative definitions that, in effect, describe improvisation in terms of what it is *not* rather than in terms of what it is, earnest young performers are amazed by the abilities of their idols. They ruminate over issues as fundamental as they are intriguing: Precisely what is the music that jazz groups perform, and where does it come from? To the young Arthur Rhames, the "cats" seemed to be "standing up and making something out of nothing." Resolving this paradox for himself at the time, he decided that jazz was "just something the fellas got together and played out of their heads."

Such explanations may temporarily satisfy observers, but continued probing soon presents new puzzles. Wynton Marsalis noticed early on that, although the things created by the artists changed from event to event, he could, nevertheless, recognize aspects of artists' styles in their new creations. How can performances embody these enigmatic qualities, and what is their significance for the artists themselves? In Marsalis's recollection, "all of these giants could play and sound different." His idols remain vivid in his mind's eye after years of experience. "Here's Miles," he says, and sings a phrase by Miles Davis.

> I'd say, "Damn, why did he play like that?"
> Here's Trane. [He sings a passage by John Coltrane.] He's playing just the exact opposite. Why is he playing like that?
> Here's Newk [Sonny Rollins] playing some rhythms that still nobody else can keep up with. Why is Newk doing that?
> Here's Diz [Dizzy Gillespie] and Clark Terry and Pops [Louis Armstrong]. . . . My father was a ridiculous [amazing] pianist. He can play. Damn, how does a cat play like that?
> When you're just learning jazz, everything is mystical.

For those outside the jazz community who discover improvisers as mature artists through their recordings, these issues remain mysterious. For prospective musicians who wish to follow in the footsteps of their idols, however, unraveling the mystery is essential.

## Studying the Learning of Improvisation

I have shared the artist's captivation with these issues since the fifties: initially as a classically trained, aspiring trumpeter trying to learn jazz, and over the past fifteen years as an ethnomusicologist carrying out formal research for this study of jazz improvisation. Roots of this research also lie in my work among the Shona people of Zimbabwe, which left me with a lasting appreciation for the depth of oral musical traditions, the rigors of composing music in performance, and the intelligence with which musicians articulate the subtleties of their art.

Influenced by my experience and earlier research, I approached this jazz project with the conviction that there is far more to improvisation than meets the ear. Still, every study is unique. For scholars entering a music culture not their own, the path to understanding is rarely clear-cut; it demands constant absorption, interpretation, and synthesis of bits of information obtained from different sources by various methods. Determining the appropriate methods invariably involves finding the benefits and limitations of each—often by trial and error. In some respects, the challenges are comparable to those faced by young artists seeking musical knowledge within the music community itself. To serve the needs of a preliminary study on the subject, I ultimately combined various approaches to data collection, analysis, and interpretation.

At the outset of the pilot study in 1978, I brushed up on my general knowledge of jazz from secondary sources, sampling articles, books, and dissertations. Jazz writing falls typically into several basic, sometimes overlapping, categories: autobiographies by major jazz figures, largely anecdotal biographies, compilations of interviews with different artists, bibliographies, discographies, and historical interpretations of the music's development chronicling successive style periods. Complementing these are works of jazz criticism, textbooks describing musical features, analytical studies of great solo styles, sociological accounts of the jazz community, philosophical speculation on the nature of improvisation in relation to composition, and improvisation method books representing various theoretical approaches. Despite the importance of all these sources, it seems to me that, taken together, they gave but discrete glimpses into the individual and collective processes of learning, transmitting, and improvising jazz.

Although welcome changes occurred in the general state of the jazz literature over the course of the larger study, there were no precise models to guide the research as I envisioned it. At one point or another, however, exceptional writings by a few scholars and authors confirmed my research goals or indicated some fruitful possibilities: critical, interpretative, and biographical writing about jazz in the broader context of the African diaspora and African

American culture by Richard Waterman (1948, 1967), Amiri Baraka (1963, 1970), and A. B. Spellman (1966); Charles Keil's early article on interactive aspects of jazz that argues for understanding "the [musical] system or style in action, music as a creative act rather than as an object" (1966b, 338); Thomas Owens's painstaking transcriptions and analyses of Charlie Parker's improvisations (1974); Frank Tirro's writing on the historical dimensions of improvised solos (1974); and the first volume of Gunther Schuller's history of jazz (1968). Additionally, there were phenomenological accounts of particular facets of learning and improvisation by Alfred Pike (1974) and David Sudnow (1978); John McKinney's study of Lennie Tristano as a teacher (1978); sociologist Howard Becker's work (1951; 1953) and that of Alan Merriam and Raymond Mack (1960) treating the jazz community as a community both implicitly and explicitly. Offering rich sources of data were Jelly Roll Morton's autobiography with Alan Lomax (Lomax, 1973), Dizzy Gillespie's autobiography with Al Fraser (Gillespie 1979), Baby Dodds's narrative recording (1946), and interview compilations appearing in works by Nat Shapiro and Nat Hentoff (1966) and Whitney Balliett (1971, 1977), and a few others.

From a comparative cultural viewpoint, other writings were also influential. Albert Lord's classic study of Serbo-Croatian epic sung poetry (1970), positing a theory of formulaic oral composition and re-creation, seems to me, as it has to several other scholars, to have relevance for the study of jazz. Bruno Nettl's comparative work on improvisation (1974) was also helpful in identifying important issues for research and in clarifying thorny problems concerning improvisation in relation to oral and written composition.

At the beginning of my research, I held what I thought was a reasonably clear notion of the distinction between improvisation and various other practices associated with composition. When, as an early exercise, I tried to draw up a precise list of their exclusive properties, however, I realized that my grasp of them was less strong than I had thought. In fact, their characteristics seemed to overlap hopelessly at the margins. Constant tautologies also plagued my thinking about the distinctions. Was a particular musical practice improvisation or not? If one defines improvisation in such a way as to include the practice, then, presumably, it is.

To extract myself from this quagmire, I decided to set aside such questions temporarily and return to them only at the end of my research. I decided to focus initially on close observation and description of the full range of musical activities that occupied active members of a community known for its expertise in improvisation. My hope was that this would eventually lead to an understanding of just what improvisation is in relation to other compositional processes. Moreover, given what is perhaps the most fundamental finding of ethnomusicology—that the bases for music and musical knowledge in aesthetic values, goals, and outlook can differ substantially from one culture to the next—understanding how the artists themselves viewed the issue, how they defined their own musical practices, was of central importance. My personal experience as a jazz learner before studying ethnomusicology left me with a certain feel for this matter, but my intention was to keep my own impressions in the background of the study. I wanted to begin anew, to make a more formal effort to understand the concepts of others and thereby extend my own understanding. The artists' view of the subject became a distinctive focus of this work, one that emerged as imperative for a serious analytical work on jazz improvisation.[4]

As I was reviewing the relevant literature, I initiated field research by seeking access to artists. It is still largely the case, as it was when I began this work, that if one wants to learn the intricacies of jazz improvisation, one must learn them directly from musicians. Initially, I had the opportunity to interact with several musicians in Chicago, studying privately with some individuals while performing and recording with others in a group I had organized.[5] I also carried out informal interviews during this period, testing the viability of talking about the elusive issues involved by asking particular questions, and found the early results to be encouraging. After working with several musicians in Chicago, I moved, in 1980, to New York City—the world's largest jazz community, made up of artists from all across the country—and began familiarizing myself with the setting I had selected for the larger study. Over the year, I devoted one component of the research to extensive interviews with the more than fifty musicians named in the acknowledgements and in the list of artists interviewed, located in appendix B. Whereas interviews have been a standard ethnomusicological method in the past, a unique feature of this study is its involvement with a large enough pool of participants to portray the diverse and complex texture of the larger community they represent. Most participants were individuals I approached in nightclubs after admiring a performance. Many were known to me by reputation; others I became acquainted with for the first time; a few were friends I had performed with years earlier and who had since become established in the field of jazz.

In each instance, I explained something of my own background and that of the study. I conveyed my interest in jazz education, in redressing such issues as stereotypes about improvisation and the lack of general understanding that limits potential audiences for jazz. Despite the contribution of jazz as a unique musical language—one of the world's most sophisticated—the marginal existence of jazz musicians and the negative feedback to their community from some of the writings about jazz leave many of its practitioners with the perception that their skills are poorly understood, even downright misunderstood, and their knowledge undervalued by outsiders. From the jazz community's viewpoint, the observations of even the most attentive of scholars and critics have periodically created offense by imposing outsider perspectives on jazz that are alien to the music and unsympathetic to the artists.[6] Discussions revealing this and similar lingering issues for jazz musicians helped me to resolve what had been an initial apprehension concerning the appropriateness of probing into the private inner world of jazz performance and making available to outsiders what has largely remained knowledge privileged within a close-knit community. The willingness on the part of musicians to participate reaffirmed for me the importance of the project's objectives.

Interviews took place in my apartment or in the homes of musicians and lasted typically from one and a half to three hours. As a way of showing participants my own scholarly approach to music, I began each session by giving the artist a copy of *The Soul of Mbira,* my book on Zimbabwean music, and one of its accompanying albums of field recordings.[7] In many instances, the artists themselves had a serious interest in African music, and if their schedules allowed, I played my Zimbabwean instruments for them before we turned our attention to jazz. In some instances, additional sessions, phone conversations, and informal meetings in between sets at nightclubs helped to clarify points raised in earlier discussions.

Because I was interested in many variables that potentially bore on learning, creativity, and the development of extraordinary skill, I had prepared a twenty-five-page set of diverse questions for artists. In my first interview, I decided to make a complete run through the questions. Although it was useful to collect such a comprehensive response from one participant, the approach turned out to be impractical; the questions required three sessions and nine hours to complete. After this experience, I drew selectively from the prepared questions during each interview: What were the earliest musical memories of the artists? When did they first encounter jazz, and how did they go about learning it? Jazz players, even the great masters, knew nothing about their subject at one time; yet, by their middle teen years, many had become proficient players—without the aid of formal educational institutions or instruction. How did the youngsters develop such exceptional ability and technical knowledge? Along other lines, I asked about activities of musical thinking and experiences associated with improvisation. Moreover, how do improvisers evaluate one another's performances?

The early interview data stimulated additional questions. Some concerned the dilemma of reconciling the notion of the artist's changing perceptions about improvisation with the long-standing popular definitions of improvisation. For example, Arthur Rhames stated that in the beginning he had not understood "that the motives, the riffs" jazz musicians performed "had any history behind them." Patience Higgins recalled that initially he had "no idea of the form of what [great artists] were playing," especially when they played "very fast." Nor could he figure out how older soloists could improvise with such "logic," a feature that "sounded easy" until Higgins himself "tried to do it." If the object of improvising is for performers to create music anew, I asked, then what did it mean that their phrases "had history behind them?" Moreover, if improvisers express personal feelings of the moment, what do considerations of form and logic have to do with this?

Equally important for the study was the posing of questions to artists of different backgrounds so that I could collect material that would provide a basis for comparison. Although most of the participants are African American, members of other ethnic groups are included as well; both men and women; performers of different instruments and singers; individuals at varying stages of development—beginners, young professionals, and veterans, some of whom are historic figures in jazz. Most of the performers developed their skills between the late thirties and early sixties and subsequently devoted their careers to bebop or related hard-bop styles. I had a special interest in these styles because they represent great periods of empowerment in jazz history, periods in which a concentration of virtuosos forged and refined many practices that have remained conventions of the language of jazz. The musicians also include a few representatives from the early jazz period and from the avant-garde, as well as some who perform multiple styles from New Orleans jazz to jazz rock. This diversity provides a representative sample of the professional artists and aspirants who make up the core of the jazz community. Art worlds consist not only of their most seasoned and single-minded members, but of a large support system made up of individuals with different interests and varying degrees of talent and knowledge.[8]

The interviews, once transcribed, produced over three thousand pages of material. It took about six months to complete a single careful reading. Because I had never before worked with such a huge mass of formal interview material, it was not immediately clear how to absorb the data. After several passes through the typescript—cutting, pasting, and collating—I found that I could begin to cross-reference musicians' remarks. The subsequent search for common themes and idiosyncratic patterns was like being host to a large meeting in which participants were engaged in a lively discussion. In a sense, this imagined discourse samples and re-creates the larger, ongoing discourse among artists that forms an essential part of the jazz community's intellectual life. "What do you listen to in other band members' performances when you improvise?" I had asked. "Your mind is basically on yourself," one musician had replied. "It takes everything you've got just to improvise your part because everything is happening so quickly." Another had said, "You have to listen to other people very closely. If you're not doing that, you're not playing jazz." According to a third, "It depends; sometimes you listen to other people, sometimes you don't." Through these questions, my role, as was inevitable, moved beyond collector and monitor of the discussion to interpreter of the data.

At such moments during research, when confronted with apparent inconsistencies in the data yet aware of the basic interconnectedness of ideas related to an issue, one can take various positions to reconcile seemingly contradictory statements. On the one hand, perceptions of the experience of improvising may differ, even significantly, from player to player. On the other hand, an individual may be mistaken in the information given during an interview. For example, if a player has not recently or previously reflected on a particular issue, impressions of performances recollected during an interview may differ from actual performance experiences. Still another interpretive position can be fruitful. When a scholar adopts complex and variable models for improvising and for learning, contradictions typically turn out to be more apparent than real. As suggested by the questions and answers sampled above, musicians contemplating variable processes of performance, out of an intricate web of possibilities, talk about those aspects that come to mind at the time. Collectively, their accounts provide insight into the multifaceted nature of improvisation. Similarly, performers of different ages are likely to remember different kinds of details about learning and to contribute insightfully on those issues with which they have recently been grappling. Collectively, their accounts chronicle broad developmental processes that occur over a career. By examining and piecing together the observations of various artists over an extended period, one gets a picture of what many musicians experience as a whole. Recognizing the necessity for flexibility in interpreting such comprehensive data, I generally adopted the viewpoint that every observation of the musicians was important for the understanding of improvisation.

The performers who participated in the interviews patiently fielded my questions during sessions that, at times lighthearted and at other times grueling, were always informative. To translate into words impressions of mental and physical activities, some of which are nonverbal in nature, is a demanding task; having to recall these activities outside the special contexts in which jazz is made compounds these difficulties. It was their own curiosity about the topics under study and their interest in educating audiences and young musicians that inspired artists to contribute the important data on which this work rests. As their comments indicate, there may be elements of creativity that are destined to remain mysteries, but it *is* possible to talk effectively about many aspects of the subject that previously had eluded articulation by scholars.

My approach in the presentation of this study's data has been to quote and paraphrase liberally from interviews, elucidating many salient issues by allowing artists to speak for themselves. Presenting artists' ideas from interview data necessarily requires the reductive process of extracting quotations from a larger body of recorded discussions. I found it interesting that, while artists shared common understanding, one or another was often exceptionally articulate on certain features of the music, thereby contributing multiple gems of insight on a subject. My selection of quoted material reflects this.

In preparing this manuscript, I became aware of the liabilities of translating oral discourse onto the page. Language that sparkles in conversation—enhanced by inflection and by various features of nonverbal communication—sometimes appears dull when printed. Moreover, the asides and redundancies of speech, normally filtered out cognitively in conversation, seem disproportionately weighted in print and can be distracting. For the sake of continuity and flow, I have deleted portions of longer quotations and, with general permission, made minor editorial changes. At times, when artists fielding difficult questions revised their own ideas over the course of discussions or supplemented earlier responses with afterthoughts in later portions of interviews, I have reassembled or condensed their remarks accordingly. In some instances, for aural and visual clarity, conversational markers or pieces of information not central or pertinent to the point of discussion have been deleted without ellipsis indicators. Repeated verification with musicians of my use and interpretation of interview excerpts has made it possible for this study to embody both the intent and the spirit of the artists' words. One of the goals of this work is to present artists in the light by which their own community has always appreciated them—as knowledgeable, articulate, exacting practitioners of a highly valued art form.[9]

Typically, I identify quotations by giving the speakers' names or by providing their initials in parentheses.[10] Most unidentified quotations or similar data represent references to formal interviews concerning information too personal or sensitive to ascribe to the individual, such as frank assessments of the musical abilities of other players on the scene. Some are frequently used expressions that suggest common agreement among artists about various aspects of jazz. A very few are memorable comments heard here and there from artists whom I encountered casually within the community.

In an effort to serve as an evenhanded interpreter of the data gathered from interviews, I engaged in several other activities during the project, both as participant and observer, standard methodological fare in ethnomusicology. To consider ideas expressed about music in light of the music itself, I routinely attended rehearsals and performances by jazz groups where I could collect data that would contextualize artists' remarks. I refer to these experiences throughout this study because they cast light on aspects of group interaction that a listener may not hear or recognize in a studio recording. They also added to my understanding of repertory and playing styles and suggested appropriate questions to raise during subsequent interviews. The interview data gave me cause to reflect on my own early learning experiences as well.

To keep comparable issues before me during this project, I resumed my former study as a jazz trumpeter and took periodic lessons with various artists. This allowed me to observe how different players evaluated my performance and the methods they adopted for correcting my mistakes and encouraging my progress. Using myself as a subject for the study—training myself according to the same techniques described by musicians—offered the kind of detail about musical development and creative process that can be virtually impossible to obtain from other methods. So, too, did reflection during my own performances on the experiential realm of jazz. Musical experiments in the practice room—for example, trying to invent and develop musical ideas—proved especially useful for testing different ideas about improvisation.

As my former experience had taught me, such activities as direct study with improvisers can present their own challenges. It is not always apparent to fluent improvisers who have grown up in the jazz tradition what, precisely, naive learners need from them. A trumpet player who once accepted me as student gave me a series of musical exercises to practice. Each time we met, he encouraged me to learn them more thoroughly. When I had finally developed the technical control to repeat them unerringly, he praised my efforts in a manner that seemed to say, "That's fine and that's what I have to teach you." The problem was that what I had learned did not sound like jazz to me. When he first sensed my disappointment, he seemed surprised. Then he picked up his instrument and added modestly, "Well, of course, you have to throw in a little of this here and there." To my ears, the lifeless exercises I had been practicing were transformed into a vibrant stream of imaginative variations that became progressively more ornate until I could barely recognize their relationship to the original models. This experience awakened me to my responsibility for effecting meaningful exchange between us as teacher and student.

In connection with the current project, inquiries in New York City about learning jazz inevitably led me to "Coach" Barry Harris, the man who became my principal mentor.[11] Harris, a pianist and disciple of Bud Powell and Thelonious Monk, is not only a great musician, he is a charismatic figure, renowned for his successful teaching of difficult and elusive matters. Old and young alike attended Harris's lively biweekly workshops, which attracted an international, multiethnic following. From the moment they set foot in his workshops, participants knew themselves to be in the presence of a true master teacher. His sessions were sometimes intimate, a small group in attendance; at other times they swelled to over a hundred participants. Harris handled the classes comfortably, with virtuosity. For a year and a few subsequent summers, faithful attendance not only provided a forum in which I could observe Harris's teaching methods and the gradual development of the skills of other participants but expanded my own understanding of bebop, Harris's specialty, a complex style of which I had only a basic grasp.

Amid the trials and tribulations of research, it is sometimes unclear which circumstantial features, even initially frustrating ones, may prove helpful in the long run. At the beginning of the jazz study, after many years of *mbira* playing, I returned to the trumpet only to discover considerable technical limitations.

Ultimately, however, my struggle to regain control over the trumpet elicited important advice from other performers and made me sensitive to the potential constraints that a musician's anatomy and relative mastery over instruments place upon improvisation.

To complete my immersion in the subject, I devoted time throughout the project to studying and transcribing jazz recordings, those precious resources of the oral tradition of improvisation. Although performances embedded in recordings are primarily useful for aural analysis, the painstaking work of transcription provides interpretive pictures of improvisers' thoughts. Allowing for the imprecision of translating sounds into visual representation, these images lend themselves to more conventional kinds of musical analysis. Consequently, this book includes numerous samples of improvisations—from published compilations, my own, and those solicited from musicians—amplifying some of the more subtle themes that emerge from the players' verbal accounts. Amid many examples by better known improvisers like saxophonist Charlie Parker, I include performance samples of artists like trumpeter Booker Little—as a tribute to the contributions of jazz prodigies. Little died at the age of twenty-three, of uremia. By that young age, Little had achieved what some spend a lifetime pursuing. An improviser, composer, and arranger, his was a unique voice whose recognition within the jazz community attests to his meaningful contribution to the tradition.

So that readers with musical training may refer to them in one place, transcriptions are in part 5 (Music Texts) at the back of the book. This allows the general reader to glean the essential points through the discussion in the main body of the text without the disruption of extensive musical notation. As transcribed, the musical examples range from basic building blocks for fashioning individual parts to extended group performances, presented in large score samples at the end of part 5.* The latter examples showing improvised group interplay have special importance insofar as they have been virtually unavailable to those interested in the serious study of jazz.[12]

I intend the transcribed examples to serve as the basis for a variety of analytical exercises. Some illustrate compositional materials and forms in and of themselves. Others provide the basis for speculation on the processes of musical transformation by comparing, for example, a hypothetical skeletal or lead sheet model of a composition to a solo or an accompaniment, or comparing variant improvised phrases to each other. Overall, the intention behind the selection and arrangement of examples is to show a variety of musical ideas in the ever-wider contexts in which jazz artists conceive and manage them.

---

*Background and explanatory information on the preparation and presentation of musical examples is found in the headnote to part 5. The trumpet and saxophone notation key (ex. I.1) and the drum set notation key (ex. I.2) also provide pertinent information.

Within individual parts, artists fashion gestures from small musical components, phrases from gestures, and complete solos or accompaniments from
phrases; within the ensemble, they interrelate their musical ideas.

Toward such ends, examples excerpted from the large score samples isolate particular features of the music for analysis. Readers can examine the
highlighted musical features per se or, by referring to the scores, pore over
them in the context of their extended settings. Ultimately, this work's analysis
and discussion of representative features of the scores are intended as guides
for readers who may wish to immerse themselves in the original recordings,
exploring yet other comparable features of the music.

## Putting It All Together

What I found most exciting at the project's outset was the prospect that
corroborating data from several approaches would clarify various elusive, inextricably interwoven issues connected with learning and improvisation, and that
each illuminated issue would, in turn, throw light on the others. I expected an
examination of the creative process to demystify artistic products and vice
versa. By looking at the aspirations and successes of learners when acquiring
their skills and at their struggles and frustrations through different stages of
development, I hoped to discover those skills most valuable to artists and their
criteria for judging standards of excellence in jazz performance. It seemed to
me that pinning down the interrelated features of jazz would demonstrate that
there is a functioning pedagogy of instruction within the tradition. It was a
great breakthrough for the project when, after several years, data obtained
through each of the approaches began to correlate, one facet reinforcing another: remarks in interviews began to tally with my own experiences in the
practice room; observing a master's approach to teaching enlarged my understanding of ideas expressed by musicians in a nightclub audience; and analysis
of transcribed improvisations verified described impressions of performance.

In this regard, my interpretation and categorization of creative processes
are based on data derived from the combination of the approaches described
earlier. In particular, experimental improvising with a set of known model
phrases reveals precise transformational processes at play, shedding light on
ruminations of the musical imagination and such potentially enigmatic matters
as the difference between intention and realization in the articulation of ideas.
Experience with this method guides my conjectures about possible musical
models and transformational procedures underlying related recurring ideas in
other artists' improvisations as discussed in this work and illustrated in its musical examples. My interpretation of the examples also relies on the orientation
I received from players concerning the features of jazz that they consider important.

Insight provided by such corroborative evidence found its way into the evolving manuscript as, over several years, I boiled down initial interview data, extracting salient material and arranging it in search of logical organization. The challenge became to create a structure appropriate for discussing the many aspects of improvisation revealed as essential to understanding the music, and for exploring their connections. After numerous revisions of the manuscript, I settled on a final structure based, in part, on the artist's musical life cycle. It begins with the relatively clean slate that new members of every culture initially bring to the task of learning music—regardless of innate talent—and proceeds by identifying different learning processes, stages of development, categories of knowledge, and other aspects of making music.

While reworking the data's presentation along these lines, it seemed to me that two tasks remained. The first was to update my review of the jazz literature because it had grown considerably since 1978, a development greatly encouraging to the future of jazz studies. An increasing number of scholars in different disciplines had become interested in specific issues that have bearing on particular aspects of the knowledge system that my study attempts to understand and define. Thus, having drawn conclusions from my own data, I took a fresh look at the secondary sources I had sampled initially and reviewed the work that had been published over the course of my research.

Of special relevance was research published in several Ph.D. dissertations, including fine data on the transmission of jazz by folklorist Al Fraser (1983) and on the collective aspects of improvisation carefully detailed by ethnomusicologist Ingrid Monson (1991). Additional studies by musicologists Lewis Porter (1983, 1985b), Barry Kernfeld (1981), Gregory Smith (1983, 1991), and others provided important analysis of the language of particular improvisers and speculation about processes underlying the improviser's formulation of solos. In this regard, Lawrence Gushee's exemplary article on Lester Young was heartening, demonstrating the value of applying "a versatility of analysis" to the interpretation of improvisation (1981, 151).

Broadening the scope of jazz research in still other areas were contributions in cognitive psychology by John Sloboda (1989), Jeff Pressing (1984, 1988), and Philip Johnson-Laird (1988), whose studies have aimed, in large part, to construct psychological models of improvisation from the individual's standpoint. Keith Sawyer (1991) extended such perspectives with consideration of the group aspects of improvisation. Additionally, musicologists Samuel Floyd Jr. (1991) and Gary Tomlinson (1991) and anthropologist Ann Beeson (1990) have contributed articles that, as does Monson's dissertation, interpret jazz in light of recent theories in such disciplines as anthropology, sociolinguistics, and literary criticism. Finally, *The New Grove Dictionary of Jazz,* edited by Barry Kernfeld (1988d), and the second volume of Gunther

Schuller's jazz history (1989) were helpful research tools, filling in gaps in my knowledge and providing useful historical sketches on the roles of different instruments that I drew upon when contextualizing my interview data.

Together with this review of the literature, perusing an additional sample of jazz biographies, autobiographies, and interviews has enabled me to compare my conclusions with those of other scholars and to compare the views expressed by artists in my study with a larger sample of artists of earlier generations, thereby broadening the project's historical dimensions. Ultimately, as data from other sources corroborated and amplified my own findings, I became convinced that, despite stylistic changes over time, jazz retains the continuity of certain underlying practices and values associated with improvisation, learning, and transmission. These factors of continuity, moreover, rest at the very core of the tradition, contributing to its integrity as a music system. Although I have periodically interwoven information from secondary sources into the fabric of my text, I have largely used endnotes for this purpose. For interested readers they present supplementary data and refer to additional technical studies by scholars and musicians that complement and expand upon this book's themes. Endnotes place analytical observations of practitioners next to scholarly analysis, which juxtaposition often highlights common concerns and overlapping perspectives.

My final task was to circulate a draft of the manuscript among a few of the participants in the study in order to check my representation and interpretation of the interview material. Just as methodological emphasis on the concepts and the values of artists leads scholars to interact with artists during various stages of data collection, thus it was important to me to solicit reactions from artists in the last stretch of the project, opening my work to criticism and treating their responses as additional data.

At every level of interpretation, as jazz musicians reacted to their own quoted material and to that of other musicians, their comments were invaluable. At times, they suggested alternative viewpoints on musical concepts or reflected in new ways on their own experience. At other times, they made significant editorial suggestions, questioning a word usage or grammatical construction or calling my attention to an unnecessary piece of jargon that had eluded my editorial eye. Especially reassuring were their reactions to the presentation as a whole. I had been concerned that, although every interview had been valuable, the relative length of artists' sessions and the particular issues on which the work had ultimately focused had resulted in some artists being represented more frequently than others. "What difference does that make?" one musician-reviewer asked. "We're not just speaking for ourselves in this book. It's like we're all speaking for each other." Said another, "You know what this book's really about? It's about all the things that we share in common—

the things that we know and care about but we don't necessarily ever say to one another." Several musicians made suggestions for revision, many of which have been incorporated into the final text, as has material from informal follow-up discussions clarifying or expanding original interview data.

An important aspect of the study generally missing from past research is its focus, not simply on the artworks produced by improvisation, but on the wide compass of practice and thought that improvisers give to music outside formal performance events. This includes group rehearsals, individual practice routines, and imaginative compositional play while away from an instrument. Jazz artists are among those who are especially attuned to the general soundscape of their environments, constantly assessing its features for musical value. Moreover, many periodically engage in their tradition through the subconscious ruminations of dreams that unfold explicitly in the language of music.

Based on a compilation of the materials described above, this book tells the story of the remarkableness of the training and rigorous musical thinking that underlie improvisation. It elucidates the creative processes that lie at the heart of the music culture of jazz. Intimate accounts of artistic growth from childhood to old age portray the deeply creative experiences that engage artists, revealing a serious, ongoing preoccupation with the music and music making that define their lives. The book's overall goal is to increase the abilities of readers to comprehend jazz in much the same terms as do its improvisers. Having a framework for interpreting the rich yet disparate nuggets of technical information divulged by artists through interviews and other public forums can greatly enhance the experience of listening to jazz.[13]

Although this work is not a practical manual, its documentation of traditional learning practices contains advice useful to young musicians. Moreover, as, sadly, so many of the field's major figures are passing away, educators also need to understand these practices if they are to be effective in supporting the jazz tradition. By emphasizing the larger, value-laden music culture of jazz, this study can supply background for the increasing number of improvisation method books, helping to guide the function and application of various individual techniques in jazz. The 100th United States Congress, in a telling symbolic gesture, passed a resolution recognizing jazz as "a rare and valuable American national treasure to which we should devote our attention, support and resources to make certain it is preserved, understood and promulgated."[14] In light of this mandate, it is important for educators to ensure that students gain early exposure to jazz and learn to appreciate its rich and varied practices, thereby fostering their continued contributions to the tradition as future artists and knowledgeable audience members.

Finally, while this book is a case study of jazz improvisation, its insights should also shed light on creativity across various disciplines. Its findings should have relevance not only for musicians and jazz aficionados but for readers interested in cultural studies generally and in African American and American studies specifically. Scholars in the fields of musicology, performance studies, folklore, anthropology, psychology, sociology, education, and linguistics may also find it pertinent. Within my own field of ethnomusicology, I hope it serves as a useful model for understanding comparable processes of learning and improvisation germane to music communities worldwide.[15]

In the overall design of this work, part 1 samples the contexts in which jazz musicians develop skill and considers the methods that assist them. Parts 2 and 3 explore the two major categories of understanding that comprise the artist's base of knowledge. One category, improvisation as an individual enterprise, includes those skills and conventions that enable performers to formulate a credible contribution of their own. The second, collective aspects of improvisation, discusses a complementary set of skills and conventions, social as well as technical, that enables band members to integrate their distinctive musical thoughts during performances.

Successive chapters within these sections identify different musical models that are integral to jazz, examine ways in which improvisers interpret and transform them, and discuss the improviser's relative success at these operations. In accord with this work's view of jazz as a language and its emphasis on traditional learning methods, the presentation of material emphasizes the aural absorption of jazz before the study of music theory, a relationship that, within the contemporary pedagogy of jazz, is sometimes reversed.[16] Part 4 looks at the effect on improvisation of factors external to the music, such as audience and concert setting. The epilogue presents reflections by performers on the challenge and satisfaction of a career in jazz and offers the study's conclusions about improvisation as a creative process. Part 5 contains musical examples and additional commentary.

Pondering the overlapping issues discussed above and sharing jazz musicians' sometimes harsh experiences in the throes of learning, lead one to realize that, for the improviser, there is a great distance between common misconceptions about improvisation and the reality of music making. In this regard, some earlier accounts by seasoned artists about their performance's intuitive nature are more incomplete than inaccurate. "Improvisation is an intuitive process for me now," Arthur Rhames asserts, "but in the way in which it's intuitive," he adds, "I'm calling upon all the resources of all the years of my playing at once: my academic understanding of the music, my historical understanding of the music, and my technical understanding of the instrument that I'm playing. All these things are going into one concentrated effort to produce something that is indicative of what I'm feeling at the time I'm performing."

Rhames's explanation makes clear that the popular conception of improvisation as "performance without previous preparation" is fundamentally misleading. There is, in fact, a lifetime of preparation and knowledge behind every idea that an improviser performs. As the following chapter reveals, this preparation begins long before prospective performers seize upon music as the central focus of their lives.

# PART

## I

**Initial Preparations for Jazz**

# ONE

## Love at First Sound

### Early Musical Environment

*Jazz was a street music in a sense, the kind of expression coming out of the black community. When I discovered jazz, it was like going to some part of the world where I hadn't actually studied the language, but finding out that I could understand certain things immediately, that it spoke to me somehow. I knew that I would have to travel a long and rocky road in my endeavor to play jazz, but I felt like I already understood the language.* —Curtis Fuller

Precisely when musical development begins is a matter for speculation. It depends on definitions of both music and development. Some consider that the earliest musical conditioning takes place in the womb, where the heartbeat of the mother accompanies her baby's growth. Late in its development the unborn child also responds to sounds outside the womb as they are transmitted through the mother's body, although it is impossible to know how the sounds are transformed in the process or what perception the unborn child has of them. The act of birth itself can be viewed as the newborn's first performance. Raised in the hands of the attendant, its flailing arms and kicking legs comprise its first dance; its expressive cry, its first song.[1]

Once out of the womb, the infant finds itself in a rich auditory world, many of whose elements are not easily differentiable. Intermittent bird song, episodes of thunder, and the patter of rain melt together, filtering into the infant's immediate setting. Sounds made by machines with their own specialized dialects of pitch and rhythm intermingle with nature's patterns and sometimes impose upon them forcefully. The playful voices of parents periodically assume the foreground within this kaleidophonic array to engage the infant in responsive exchanges. In part, the infant gains a sense of its identity by dis-

21

covering its own power as a sound producer and manipulator. Stirring on its mattress and extending its reach creates an entertaining counterpoint of escaping air, crinkling plastic sheets, and colliding toys. Vocal cords summon relatives to nurse it or pacify it with their company.

As infants make headway in sorting out the diverse patterns in their surroundings and defining their own relationship to them, they discover other sounds that, although differing from all others, bear a curious relationship to them, at times even mimicking their elements. The new sounds are called music, of course, and their precise characteristics can vary greatly from one part of the world to the next, from one community to the next, from one household to the next, and ultimately from one imagination to the next.

It is within the soundscape of the home and its environs that children develop their early musical sensibilities, learning their culture's definition of music and developing expectations of what music ought to be. Similarly, within the confines of their music community or music culture, children learn the aesthetic boundaries that define differing realms of performance, forming impressions of the most basic attributes of musicianship.

### Early Performance Models

In reflecting on their early childhoods, many jazz artists describe the process by which they acquired an initial base of musical knowledge as one of osmosis. They cultivated skills during activities as much social as musical, absorbing models from varied performances—some dramatic, others incidental yet profoundly effective—that attuned them to the fundamental values of African American music. Ronald Shannon Jackson remembers his father's infectious habit of humming the blues "around the house" while carrying out daily routines. Vea Williams's mother sang jazz "all the time" at home; she possessed a beautiful, powerful voice that passed easily through the apartment's screens and resonated throughout the courtyard.

The children of professional musicians receive a particularly intense exposure to performance. Tommy Turrentine fondly recollects his father's "saxophone section" that practiced regularly in their living room. Music literally "surrounded" Turrentine as a child. Lonnie Hillyer also describes much of his early musical education as "environmental"; his older brother "played jazz, and he always had guys in the house fooling around with their instruments." In Barry Harris's Detroit neighborhood, he and his young friends absorbed the intricate rhythms of the "ham bone"; its clever body percussion—slapping movements between the thigh and chest—accompanied improvised texts. Additionally, in the surrounding neighborhood, the "average black family had a piano and at least one family member who could play boogie-woogie." Kenny Barron used to anticipate eagerly the daily arrival of the neighborhood ice peddler, a blues player who routinely availed himself of the Barrons' piano after delivering the family's ice, fascinating the youngster with his musical prowess. After he left, Barron would try to pick out on the piano "the little melodies and chords" he remembered from the performance.

Within the larger community, hymnody at church services, marches at football games, and soul music at social dances contribute further to the children's education, as do concerts in performance halls and informal presentations in parks and at parades. During the thirties, Charli Persip was especially fascinated by a black orphanage's high-stepping marching band that performed jazz and by the swing bands that accompanied stage shows in the intervals between film showings at New York City's renowned Apollo Theatre. Moreover, in some neighborhoods "every corner bistro had a piano, and the pianists were sometimes joined by a bassist and a drummer and, sometimes, a horn player. There was live music all over the community" (MR). Sympathetic club owners in Detroit left their back doors open so that passersby and underage audiences who congregated in the alleyways could sample the music of featured artists. Performers in the "bars, weekend storefronts, and neighborhood jazz clubs" in other cities similarly made a deep impression upon youngsters, as did informal get-togethers by musicians. George Johnson Jr. was enticed by weekly jam sessions conducted in the apartment of his building superintendent.

Music provided by record players, radios, and jukeboxes complements live performances within the general soundscape.[2] People "could listen to jazz all day long" on the jukeboxes of Cleveland's neighborhood restaurants, cafés, and nightclubs in the forties: "You heard this music every place you went" (BB). Since the fifties, television has sometimes featured jazz as well. Record stores also offered places for young enthusiasts to gather and socialize, particularly when the stores provided listening booths for customers to sample the latest albums before deciding whether to buy them.

Some homes of musicians actually "looked like record stores" because the families owned so many recordings; they listened to music "constantly" (DP). In other instances, children participated in an "extended family" that shared and distributed recordings among adults. Patti Bown remembers private records circulating from house to house in the black community of Seattle. In another musician's neighborhood, few could afford records or record players; however, a neighbor whose generous spirit equaled his enormous collection made others welcome in his home. Evenings, everyone met there to listen to jazz.

Record collections of aficionados typically represented a wide range of popular jazz artists, including Louis Armstrong, Bessie Smith, Lester Young, Coleman Hawkins, Louis Jordan, Count Basie, Duke Ellington, Charlie Parker, Dizzy Gillespie, Ella Fitzgerald, Sarah Vaughan, Nat King Cole, Horace Silver, Art Blakey, Miles Davis, and John Coltrane. Ronald Shannon Jackson does not recall hearing the term *jazz* or such idiomatic designations as *New Orleans jazz* or *swing* when he was a youngster. In describing the music of "black dance bands" during the thirties as "jump music," his community simply viewed the music some called jazz as part of the larger family of African American musical traditions. The record collections of black families typically included examples of spirituals, gospel music, boogie-woogie, blues, and rhythm and blues, as well as selections of Western classical music and light popular classics. This discussion of early jazz musical education reminds us that exposure to their own community's music as well as that of the mainstream is one advantage commonly afforded minority children in America.

Musicians reflecting on their impressionable years tell insightful, touching stories of the importance of recordings in their childhoods. Melba Liston often contended with bouts of loneliness at home, for she had no siblings; early in life "music" became her "very dear friend," with the radio its primary vehicle. In another case, operating the record player was one of Kenny Washington's first manual skills. He often spent the day by himself listening to recordings while his father was at work. Family anecdotes attest to his emotional attachment to favorite recordings. As a toddler, Washington had learned to associate the designs on record jackets with their respective sounds. One day, he observed his father misfiling one of his albums. "I couldn't really talk yet," he explains, "but I started going through changes, trying to tell him that he'd put the record in the wrong case." His father was baffled, but his mother "insisted that he check it out. Sure enough, he'd put the record in the wrong case."

On another occasion, when Washington was intensely listening to recordings, his father interrupted him by placing a new one on the turntable. Noticing his son's agitation, he promised that he only intended listening to one cut. The younger Washington became increasingly upset as his father extended his promise, cut by cut on the album's first side, ignoring his son's appeals. When his father turned the disk to begin side two, Washington "went through a temper tantrum and ran down the hall," tripped over his pajamas and hit his mouth on a bed with enough force to knock a tooth up into his gums. "This was all over a record," he muses.

### Early Training and Performance Opportunities

As youngsters absorb musical materials from the performances of others, they simultaneously cultivate a few skills in formal settings. The church typically provides children with their first experiences as performers. Vea Williams participated in church choirs that made progressively greater demands upon their members. Music and religion "were always intertwined" in Carmen Lundy's background. She remembers that "all the women from grandmother to granddaughter" sang in church choirs, commonly three to five days a week, and her mother led a gospel group that met regularly in their home. Lundy attended every rehearsal and performance.

Ministers of fundamentalist Christian churches sometimes provide congregation members with musical instruments during services or encourage them to perform on instruments brought from home to add color and intensity to the choir's performances. Jimmy Robinson remembers Pentecostal churches in which instrumental performance was as "natural" as singing: "Everybody in the congregation would grab any instrument and play it—tambourines, guitars, banjos, drums, anything." Some churches also offer music instruction and organize small ensembles to accompany services or to provide youngsters with recreation. Art Farmer began his musical development as a brass player with the church's tuba before a cornet became available. Melba Liston made her debut in church as a trombonist; so did Max Roach, as a drummer.

The meaning that such experiences holds for learners became apparent to me when I attended a Holiness church service at the invitation of a jazz musician, a former congregant. Before the service began, a frail boy of seven years propped himself up amid the components of an enormous drum set arranged midway between the pews and the pulpit. As the congregation members sang and swayed—accompanying themselves by syncopated handclapping patterns and a collection of instruments—the child thrashed about on the drum skins, attempting to maintain a steady beat and to perform rhythms that fit the changing musical parts around him. Every eye was upon the young drummer, who beamed with tremendous pride as he performed. What greater inducement for the young musician's development could there have been than the warm approval and affection that the congregation showered upon him as he held center stage in this adult world?

While continuing to cultivate their skills in the nurturing environment of the church, young musicians also attended public schools, where they gained additional experience within various extracurricular performance situations. Moreover, schools commonly offered music appreciation classes devoted to the works of Western classical music composers; instrumental instruction programs typically taught groups of beginners how to read music. Schools also afforded them exciting access to a greater variety of instruments than many had ever seen. Arthur Rhames "hung around the band room" during all his free time in grade school and "fooled with every instrument I could get my hands on." Max Roach "dabbled" with trumpet and clarinet in elementary school as well as learning piano and drums, and Buster Williams studied drums and piano before taking up string bass. Whereas some youngsters cultivated multi-instrumentalist skills over their careers, most explored the band room's diverse options as a prelude to selecting an instrument of specialization.[3]

Factors beyond the control of students sometimes determined their initial courses. Some adopted the one instrument that had been passed down in the family or that band directors assigned them on the basis of the band's needs, the availability of instruments, or some, perhaps dubious, personal theory about the physical suitability of one instrument or another for a particular student. In other instances, youngsters selected instruments, thereby revealing their early tastes and sensitivities. Logically, an instrument's sound was the most impressive feature for many, although sometimes the physical features of an instrument had important bearing as well. The "beautiful way" the trombone and saxophone "looked in music store windows" immediately attracted Melba Liston and James Moody to their respective instruments. The "personal images" that performers of particular instruments projected in concert inspired others. The first time Curtis Fuller attended a performance by J. J. Johnson, "I fell in love with him," Fuller remembers, "just the way he stood there and played. He looked so elegant" compared to the behavior of other musicians on stage who were "crowd-pleasing."

Having determined the objects of their affections, students sought to convince their parents that they were serious enough about music to warrant their own instruments. Ronald Shannon Jackson convinced his parents of his earnestness and ingenuity by performing for them with a drum set that he fashioned from pots and pans. As parents succumbed to their children's pressure, youngsters become proud possessors of instruments borrowed, rented, or purchased from neighborhood schools, churches, and local music stores.

School bands, orchestras, and choirs allowed musicians to perform a diverse repertory that included marches, tunes from musical theater, and simplified arrangements of selected movements from operas and symphonies. Additionally, "every black school had its swing bands that played stock arrangements," orchestrated versions of jazz pieces that were initially popularized by Erskine Hawkins, Count Basie, and others (DB). Also known as stage bands, these groups performed in school concerts, assembly programs, and occasional dances.

The public school system fostered a "healthy sense of competition" among young artists that contributed to their musical development (RSJ). Junior high school graduates typically attended a central high school where, pitting their skills against those of the best performers from the larger community, they competed for positions in new band organizations. Some programs featured a succession of stage bands starting with more elementary bands and progressing to the most advanced stage band, in which membership was the object of great pride and considerable striving among teenagers. "All-city" and "all-state" honor concert bands, stage bands, orchestras, and solo competitions further motivated serious young musicians.

David Baker stresses the important role that "enlightened high school band leaders" played in African American communities across the country in developing the sensitivities and abilities of prospective jazz musicians. "Every community had its Walter Dyett," he says, referring to the renowned Chicago music educator who inspired young artists Gene Ammons, Richard Davis, Johnny Griffin, Clifford Jordan, Julian Priester, Harold Ousley, and many others. Similarly, in Indianapolis, Baker's early teacher and band director "also taught the Montgomery brothers, the Hampton boys, Jimmy Spaulding, Virgil Jones, and many others." Although the band leaders did not actually teach improvisation, their sympathy and respect for jazz encouraged students to apply the general skills they had acquired through more formal musical education to their practice of jazz.

Many serious young performers ultimately supplemented their training at school with coaching by relatives at home or in the neighborhood. In Vea Williams's household, her earliest "voice lessons" consisted of singing with her mother and sisters as they all washed dishes after meals and did other household chores. When Max Roach grew up in New York City, "there was always somebody's uncle next door or across the street who had a band, and when they took a break, the kids were allowed to fool with their instruments."

Alternatively, they received private lessons from professional musicians in community music schools and local music stores, where they could study instrumental performance technique, classical music repertory, and, in some instances, elementary music theory and composition. Strongly motivated students commonly learned musical instruments without formal instruction by synthesizing bits of knowledge from commercial method books, other young performers, and their own experimentation. Chuck Israels studied guitar and cello formally, then combined his knowledge of both instruments to teach himself bass. Doc Cheatham received a cornet and a few prepaid lessons as a gift from his father but chose to ignore the instruction in favor of copying the "ad-lib playing" of local jazz musicians. He subsequently learned the C melody saxophone on his own as well.

As a consequence of formal training, instrument selection, and performance participation, youngsters acquired different kinds of knowledge, including musical exercises, tunes, and different parts from band arrangements of compositions. Such knowledge reflected the youngsters' characteristically diverse, polymusical environment, spanning sacred and secular African American and Western classical traditions, among others. As was typical, while still a teenager, pianist Lil Armstrong had not only attained enough proficiency in jazz to be hired by Joe Oliver's Creole Jazz Band but felt confident performing Bach and Chopin during her impromptu meeting with Jelly Roll Morton.[4]

Moreover, such early knowledge commonly assumed different forms of musical representation from student to student. Singers without formal music education primarily learned their parts in choirs by ear, thinking of them as precise paths of rising and falling pitches, sometimes accompanied by imagined visualizations—graphic representations of their contours and rhythm. Many other self-educated performers also initially learned music by ear, as well as by hand and by instrument: memorizing the sounds of phrases together with their corresponding finger patterns and positions on an instrument. Having, in effect, formulated an internal tablature representation, the student can draw upon its visual and physical imagery to aid the ear in retrieving and rendering a part. Still others underwent successful training in reading and writing music, and they envision sounds in terms of symbols of conventional Western staff notation. Those with the extraordinary aptitudes of perfect pitch and photographic memories can translate sounds into notation almost instantly and store their images.

Attitudes toward the benefits of music literacy differed among youngsters, however. Youths with exceptional memories for sounds could recall pieces after hearing them demonstrated during lessons. A newspaper in Bix Beiderbecke's hometown described his ability at the age of seven to reproduce instantly, in any key, the melody and bass accompaniment to a piece after hearing his mother play the piece just once on the piano. Great artists like Louis Armstrong carried such gifts throughout their careers, evidencing the extraordinary ability to apprehend and remember tunes after a single hearing.[5] Several musicians I interviewed tell of teachers who were surprised indeed when their inability to perform a complex composition revealed that the students had all along resisted learning to read. They had simply pretended to follow the notation. For some of them, the subterfuge had gone on for a year or more.

On the other hand, some felt limited without written musical representation and, as early as grade school, invented personal notation systems or adapted those of instrument instruction manuals to assist them in recalling pieces. Melba Liston "wrote down tunes remembered from church and simple popular tunes" by assigning each pitch a different number according to her own construction of a seven-pitch scale. She vividly recalls puzzling over how to reconcile the chromatic pitches of tunes with her system—"sitting out on the back porch trying to figure out 'that's not a 4 and it's not a 5, but it's somewhere in between.'" Lonnie Hillyer "gave each trumpet valve a number" and recorded the sequence of valve combinations that produced the pitches of simple melodies. Some youngsters also approximated the rhythms of pieces within their notational schemes through varied spacing arrangements on the page. Others avoided the difficulties inherent in such practices and supplied the rhythms from memory during performances. Ultimately, different mixtures of representation colored each student's distinct world of musical imagination, whether engaged in remembering, performing, or inventing pieces.

## The Benefits of Cultural Milieu in Shaping Musical Development

Training received within the overlapping religious and secular musical domains enabled many learners to experiment with African American music performance at the same time as they gained control over instruments: re-creating,
if only on an elementary level, the sounds with which they had become intimate. They shaped melodies according to such models as a relative's habit
of humming the blues, fellow students' renditions of soul music on the school
bus, and patterns heard on household jazz recordings. They comfortably
placed intricate figures within a framework of rhythm and meter absorbed
through a succession of popular dances fashionable among their schoolmates
and the handclapping patterns that accompanied hymns. They endeavored
to imitate harmonic structures that reappeared in a local peddler's impromptu performance, in the improvisations overheard at the apartment manager's weekly jam sessions, and in the organist's accompaniment to religious
services. "Like most black musicians," Dizzy Gillespie explains, "much of
my early inspiration, especially with rhythm and harmonies, came from the
church."[6]

Moreover, they explored other musical implications of the church service,
a complex, integrated model for performance derived from the testimonial
cries of ministers and worshippers engaged in vocal exchanges, spirited ser-
mons that stand tantalizingly on the border between speech and song, and the
soulful musical interludes that enhance the service's emotional intensity and
its message. Max Roach explains that, in church, young musicians were judged
on the basis of "their abilities to stir the congregation's feelings" rather than
on the basis of "their technical proficiency" alone. The emotional intensity of
performances at black "hallelujah possession churches," where hymns build to
"fantastic climaxes" over forty-five minutes until "sinners shout and preach,"
epitomizes this value (LD). Don Pate first "heard talk about that spiritual feeling" from his mother in church. When he asked "why some of the old ladies
would get up and have fits and scream and holler," she answered that "they
were feeling the spirit, the spirit being Jesus Christ or the Holy Ghost." Pate
elaborates,

> The spirit would also be something that would be transmitted by the
> minister if he was an eloquent speaker. He could summon it with his
> message. Often times, it would also be the choir or the soloist in the
> choir, and occasionally, when the organ player or the piano player
> would be hot, it was like having Ray Charles in church. To me, that's
> where the spirituality comes in. If the music has spirit, you can feel
> it. If it's without feeling or without meaning, deep inner meaning,
> then it's spiritless.

Churches that encourage ecstatic singing, handclapping, and animated physical movement in the service of religious devotion hold inestimable value for young musicians in the congregation. These practices cultivate an expressive freedom in performance that is absent from churches where notions of dignified worship restrict movement and repress emotion. Nevertheless, musicians whose religious backgrounds are more moderate find the music of fundamentalist churches compelling. Many recall visiting such churches or tuning in to weekend radio broadcasts of such services and spending occasional mornings or evenings on the street outside these churches in their neighborhoods, listening to the performances, thereby expanding the range of their early musical influences.[7] Nat Adderley describes the "Gregorian chant style" of music heard in his own Episcopal church, as well as the lasting "musical impressions" generated by the "sanctified kind of feeling" of the Tabernacle Baptist Church "across the street." He goes on to say that "what one hears in his formative stages has a tendency to affect him. . . . [It] cause[s] you eventually to play what you play, the way you play it, with a particular feeling."[8]

The appreciation for impassioned musical expression carries over into the secular world of "musical situations . . . like the gospel pop field." Don Pate notes that the record store where he worked in Chicago "used to sell Savoy gospel pop records featuring groups like the Mighty Sounds of Joy right alongside the jazz records." Countless jazz performers also merge sacred and secular musical elements in their creations. Pate adds that the religious poem and chanted refrain on John Coltrane's album *A Love Supreme* served as a bridge between religious and secular music for some devout listeners who were generally mistrustful of the latter's social values. "My mother was amazed that a jazz musician would feel this way about God, and, she said, 'Well, he must have been all right if he felt this way.' I mean this was before she even heard the record! So I mean the cover of the album, everything else, prompted her to get into the music and listen to it." Altogether, the youngsters' early base of musical knowledge and its multilayered cultural associations provided solid ground for their specialized study of jazz.

The varied and subtle ways in which a music culture actually shapes the sensibilities and skills of its members are not always apparent to the members themselves until they encounter individuals whose backgrounds differ from their own. When young black musicians first encountered white audiences who, to their surprise, clapped to the "wrong beat" when listening to jazz, the musicians perceived an alien scheme of rhythmic organization imposed upon the music by the outsiders. Similarly, an African American singer recalled the occasion when a white, classically trained pianist substituted for her gospel choir's accompanist. After an introduction to the choir, the pianist asked the director for her "music." The director explained that they did not use "sheet music" and that the pianist should take the liberty to improvise her part in relation to the choir's. Taken aback, she replied apologetically that, "[without] music," she was unable to accompany them. She had never before faced such artistic demands. The choir members were equally astonished by the pianist's remark, never having met a musician who was dependent upon written music.

As these situations suggest, children who grow up around improvisers regard improvisation as a skill within the realm of their own possible development. In the absence of this experience, many view improvisation as beyond their ability. Moreover, music teachers in the schools can encourage the early inclinations of talented youngsters to embellish compositions assigned during lessons and improvise their own pieces, or they can inhibit such inclinations. Stories of the early abilities of prospective jazz artists to improvise within the diverse styles and structural forms of classical music, rock, polkas, and marches are common.[9]

Because of cultural differences that have generally distinguished white and black American communities in the past, the capacity for jazz improvisation and other musical skills has, at times, been confused with the benefits of different training and subject to racial stereotyping. Even though Red Rodney and his white peers played in swing bands in high school, they thought that improvising was something special that only the "black guys" did well. In contrast, the white players were the good readers, the good section players. It was an important turning point in Rodney's view of his own potential to become an improviser when Dizzy Gillespie took a personal interest in him and initiated his association with Charlie Parker.

## Different Paths of Commitment

In the face of the diverse musical options around them, learners decide to pursue jazz for reasons that are as different as their ultimate individual contributions to the field. Many prospective players are simply overwhelmed when they first hear jazz. The circumstances surrounding such encounters remain as vivid in the memories of performers as does the music's dramatic impact. For them, it was love at first sound. The bands at the Apollo Theatre "mesmerized" Charli Persip as a child; he walked around "in a cloud" after performances and "daydreamed" about them during school. Gary Bartz was stunned by the beauty and power of a Charlie Parker recording. The music made him euphoric, intoxicating him with the notion that "I just had to play that." This determination to play like Parker came even before Bartz had discerned which instrument it was that Parker was playing. Buster Williams was captivated by Oscar Pettiford's "intensely moving, personal sound" on recordings, an expressive representation of the person behind the music that revealed even "the sound of his thumb sliding up and down the neck of the bass."

This intimate identification with great artists can have an effect similar to religious conversion, in many instances transcending cultural boundaries.

When Howard Levy first heard John Coltrane, he had the inexplicable experience that he was hearing himself singing, as if he had known Coltrane's music all his life. Similarly dramatic was the experience of one young Japanese musician who, adjusting with difficulty to the loss of his sister, heard a Coltrane concert in Japan. Disarmed by the performance, he returned alone to his apartment and wept into the night. Rising at dawn from a restless sleep, he interpreted the experience as a sign that he was to become Coltrane's musical disciple.[10]

The pursuit of jazz is not always as visceral or direct for youngsters. Their commitment to the music sometimes reflects a variety of considerations, from the precise artistic challenges of jazz to such fluid issues as the personal identity of individual musicians and their relationship to society. Fred Hersch abandoned his early career as a classical pianist because he tired of the tradition's preoccupation with "the purely technical aspects of performance" and with the masterworks of composers. In contrast, jazz offered him the prospect of creating his own music. While touring the country with renowned soul bands, Keith Copeland became similarly discouraged by their lack of creativity. "The guys often wanted me to play just like the drummers on the records," he bemoaned, "instead of making up my own parts." Akira Tana became bored with the limitations rock bands placed upon collective improvisation; he found jazz to be "more sophisticated, more musical, more expressive."

Within the artists' own community, family and peer approval offers additional inducements. George Johnson Jr. remembers the pleasure that family friends displayed when hearing him sing jazz tunes from his father's record collection. They were touched and amused by the sight of a young boy performing their generation's music. "It's natural to want to be like your father when you grow up," Johnson reflects. Harold Ousley explains his decision to become a jazz saxophonist in terms of the warm relationship he developed with a favorite uncle who invited him to listen to Jimmie Lunceford recordings. The first instrument his uncle taught him to recognize on recordings, when Ousley was but six years old, was the saxophone. For the children of musicians, opportunity to meet leading artists intensifies the children's early involvement with jazz. Don Pate was thrilled the night his father, jazz bassist Johnny Pate, brought members of the Basie band home to join his family for dinner. One of the high points of Wynton Marsalis's childhood was the occasion when his father, pianist Ellis Marsalis, seated him between Al Hirt and Miles Davis at a New Orleans nightclub. The renowned figures had come to honor the elder Marsalis by hearing his band perform.

Economic incentives are also significant for performers, especially during crests in the waves of jazz's popularity. Regardless of cultural background, many players come from poor families in which each child feels a responsibility for contributing to the household income.[11] Those who evidence musical talent early begin playing professionally at the first opportunity. Conventional occupational role models viewed with great pride in particular communities can have the effect of channeling the talents of youngsters. In more adverse terms, patterns of job discrimination can also direct youngsters toward a musical career. When Curtis Fuller was a child, there were limited career opportunities for African Americans. Not everyone could be a sports hero like Jackie Robinson or Willie Mays, Fuller explains, so he took one of the other routes and became a jazz musician. Art Davis adds that racial barriers commonly discouraged talented black musicians of his and earlier generations from pursuing careers in Western classical music. Thus, for many, jazz held out the prospect of bettering their economic and social circumstances. The opportunity to travel with road bands and to see the world was an added attraction, one that took on special meaning for those who were ambitious to escape from the stifling confines of a small town's bigotry.[12]

Special aptitude for jazz provides young performers with an identity among their peers, a matter of considerable priority for teenagers. In Ronald Shannon Jackson's town, all the students were known for "what they could do." One person was "the greatest baseball player"; another "the greatest actor"; and Jackson "the greatest drummer." Sometimes musical skill compensates for the early shyness of youngsters. By enabling him "to play jazz at parties and be accepted by everyone," Walter Bishop Jr.'s ability "opened up a whole new world socially."

If in some communities jazz performance is a vehicle for social acceptance, in others—or in subgroups within them—it is a symbol of rebellion, a musical emblem distinguishing individuals from their contemporaries or from their parents. Don Pate's attraction to jazz reflected his rejection of black middle-class social values. In contrast to his peers, whose party socials included "Motown records and a lot of dancing," Pate, who was "never concerned with the crowd," used to sit on the floor on pillows in dimly lit rooms and listen to jazz. The music served likewise as a symbol for white performers' rebellion against middle-class values. Bobby Rogovin recalled troubled teenaged years aggravated by the tense family relationships in his household's cramped quarters. It was only within the world of sound created by his jazz recordings that he could preserve any sense of privacy. Within this world, he regarded the artists as "close friends" who spoke to him in a deeply personal language that eluded family members around him.

Changing self-perceptions also mark changes in the musical tastes of performers. Emily Remler initially loved to play rock, regarding it as "good-time partying music." In her mid-teens, however, she abandoned it for jazz, which, as epitomized by Pat Martino's work, she viewed as "introverted and serious." Remler wanted to become "that serious about music." Wynton Marsalis also traces his professional interest in jazz to his early teens, when he "questioned

everything about life" and became especially concerned with political and social issues integral to African American history. Although Marsalis had attained proficiency as a classical musician, the jazz tradition held increasing
attraction for him because of "culture heroes like Charlie Parker" with whom
he felt a special identification.[13]

A dynamic tension between musical and extramusical issues sometimes
permeates the learning programs of reflective students working through difficult periods of personal growth, changing social awareness, and self-definition.
Arthur Rhames grew up in a home where he felt torn between the cultural
values represented by African American music on the one hand and Western
classical music on the other. As an exceptionally gifted child, he received private piano training. Early church schooling and influences within his extended
family reinforced the personal esteem he developed for classical music.
Rhames adopted this preference so thoroughly that whenever his mother
played rhythm and blues recordings at home, he would retreat to his bedroom
with an obvious display of disdain and spend the time playing classical music
recordings, miming the conductor's role as he listened.

When Rhames was later transferred into the public school system, however, his musical tastes and prodigious talents so isolated him from his peers
that he led a relatively solitary existence. Ironically, the loneliness Rhames
suffered eventually led him to identify with the mournful sounds of the blues.
Enlarging the scope of his education, he adopted B. B. King as a musical
model and began learning the guitar. After acquiring a fundamental technique,
Rhames performed in teenage soul bands, eventually finding a place for himself among his contemporaries. Rhames's increasing proficiency as a blues guitarist laid the foundation for his eventual interest in jazz rock, or fusion music.
He adopted John McLaughlin as his next mentor and continued to grapple with
larger questions of personal identity. For several years he patterned not only
his performance style after McLaughlin but his lifestyle as well, looking
briefly into Indian spiritualism before joining a religious group with similar
interests, an attachment he maintained for several years.

These combined involvements prepared the way for Rhames's discovery of
John Coltrane. Identifying immediately with Coltrane's "Eastern orientation,
musically and spiritually," Rhames had the "profound revelation" that Coltrane's music comprised the culmination of everything he had studied over his
career. Subsequently, Rhames took up the saxophone and devoted himself to
learning jazz, which he had come to appreciate on its own terms. In the years
to follow, his concerts would feature Rhames on guitar, piano, and saxophone
and as vocalist, his then current preoccupation. The biographical details of
Rhames's story find parallels in the lives of other extraordinarily talented aspiring musicians and highlight the delicate interplay between social and musical

factors that can influence the interests, tastes, and knowledge of learners, ultimately shaping their interpretations of jazz.

As implied above, an appreciation for the role of cultural milieu in the development of improvisers would not be complete without considering their exposure to the diverse fabric of America's music culture and the particular demography of the villages, towns, and cities where improvisers grew up. Population and immediate musical environment vary from one part of the country to the next. In some cases, they may be distinctive and relatively uniform, but they are as often pluralistic, representing different kinds of ethnic mixtures. Within discrete locales, the character of musical knowledge is itself constantly subject to change. Innovative individuals produce new musical models, supplementing or supplanting older ones. New ideas transform the general soundscape as they pass through permeable community borders. Furthermore, differences in values and knowledge can distinguish particular neighborhoods and households, thereby influencing the chosen learning models and precise performance practices of their members. Even within households, the absorption of musical knowledge is a relative matter, varying with the talents of individuals, whose discovery of the importance of jazz occurs at different stages in their education.

Though aspiring artists may follow different paths initially, arriving at a commitment to jazz along direct or circuitous routes, they ultimately face the same basic challenge: to acquire the specialized knowledge upon which advanced jazz performance depends. Precisely how to pursue such knowledge is not always apparent to new enthusiasts. Traditionally, jazz musicians have learned without the kind of support provided by formal educational systems. There have been no schools or universities to teach improvisers their skills; few textbooks to aid them. Master musicians, however, did not develop their skills in a vacuum. They learned within their own professional community— the jazz community.

# TWO

## Hangin' Out and Jammin'

### The Jazz Community as an Educational System

*I tell people, "I was a high school dropout, but I graduated from Art Blakey College, the Miles Davis Conservatory of Music, and Charlie Parker University."*—Walter Bishop Jr.

Continually drawing sustenance from its fundamental ties to African American culture, the American jazz community cuts across boundaries defined by age, class, vocation, and ethnicity.[1] At its core are professional musicians and aspirants for whom jazz is the central focus of their careers. Overlapping with the core are accomplished improvisers who divide their professional energies and talents between jazz and other musics. Serious amateurs or semiprofessionals who earn their living outside of music sometimes play a significant, but less influential, part in the life of the field. Around its core of artists, the jazz community includes listeners with wide-ranging tastes. Their ranks include supporters with diverse national and cultural backgrounds who have adopted the community's music as their own—a trend reinforced since World War I by the movement toward greater social integration and by such factors in the music industry as international record distribution, the promotion of touring bands abroad, and the interaction among overseas performers with expatriate jazz artists and American military band personnel stationed abroad. It is their abiding devotion to the music that binds this diverse population together.

Regionally, aspiring players form relationships through a complex network of interrelated music centers that form the institutional infrastructure of the jazz community. Record shops, music stores, musicians' union halls, social clubs for the promotion of jazz, musicians' homes, booking agencies, practice studios, recording studios, and nightclubs all provide places where musicians interrelate with one another and, to some extent, with fans. Amateur discographers and other devotees with extensive holdings of recordings, books, magazines, newsletters, films, and, more recently, video documentaries about jazz, act often as informal archivists for all or part of the community. Throughout the country, participants in local networks of this sort—players and fans—are linked as members of major jazz institutes, subscribers to trade periodicals, audiences for national radio and television jazz programs, and participants in the nightclub, concert, and festival scene. Cities comprise the interstices of the jazz community's larger network. At its center is Manhattan, regarded both as "a finishing school" and a national stage where jazz artists can interact with the field's greatest talents (BH).

Young musicians typically find points of entry into their local community within the intersecting domains of neighborhood and public school where they seek out knowledgeable peers who share their musical passion. Aficionados who recognize the inclinations of prospective artists invite them into the fold by encouraging them to participate in the community's oral tradition of learning. "I hear what you're trying to do," a salesman once volunteered after overhearing a student's efforts to improvise while experimenting with an instrument at a piano store. "Now what you must do is get around the people who play this kind of music and learn everything you can from them." For almost a century, the jazz community has functioned as a large educational system for producing, preserving, and transmitting musical knowledge, preparing students for the artistic demands of a jazz career through its particularized methods and forums.

### Informal Study Sessions and Apprenticeships

One conventional way for young artists to share information is through informal study sessions, a mixture of socializing, shoptalk, and demonstrations known as hanging out. "Most of the guys were self-taught, but they really went at the academics, the mechanics of the music, so thoroughly," Tommy Turrentine says. "Other guys went to school, and they would pass their knowledge to one another." Turrentine himself learned largely "by asking about things I didn't understand."

Commonly, performers of the same instruments enjoy a special fraternity. "Drummers always seem to hang out together at drum shops. They're always sharing information and showing each other how to play different things" (CH). Melba Liston and her junior high school peers similarly followed the buses of the swing bands that performed in their town to locate the hotels where the bands put up musicians so that they could get tips from them. "They were nice. They knew we were in awe of them, and they might show us something or tell us how to clean our instruments," she recalls. Whenever friends couldn't locate Liston, her mother would say to them, " 'Oh, there must be another band in town; just look in the trombone section.' "

Complementing short-lived associations with transient musicians are more sustained relationships in which individuals pool their knowledge, each contributing in the area of his or her greatest expertise. Tommy Flanagan and his young peers were "always learning from one another." In some instances, one performer assumes primary responsibility for educating others by forming bonds of casual apprenticeship. "It's hard not to be a little envious of the environment in which some of the great players grew up," Don Sickler remarks. "Many jazz players grew up with other great players in their neighborhoods. Jackie McLean was telling me not long ago about how, when he was a young kid, Bud Powell was always dropping by the house and playing with him, encouraging him to develop, and inviting him along on gigs."

Barry Harris also recalls Detroit's rich learning environment, which produced so many great jazz artists. "Tommy [Flanagan] and Kenny Burrell were about the hippest as far as modern jazz was concerned, but there were other cats too." Among them were pianist Will Davis, who, together with Flanagan, was an important model for Harris; trumpeter Cleophus Curtis, "who could play so pretty"; and an alto player named Kokie, whose talent was so remarkable that Harris and his peers "thought he *was* Bird [Charlie Parker]." Some of the "cats could really play. And we're talking about teenagers!" Harris emphasizes. Saxophonist and composer Frank Foster was also a major figure as a teacher "for everyone" in the community after he settled in Detroit. Lonnie Hillyer remembers an extraordinarily "creative guy," Abe Whitley, a pianist and vibraphone player they called "the Thinker."

Exceptionally talented educators also emerge at a young age. While still a high school teenager, Barry Harris organized musical get-togethers at his home. Amid the activities of rehearsing and performing, whenever the young artists stopped to "discuss" and "learn about" the music, Harris shared his special gifts as a music theoretician and teacher with them, transforming sessions into seminars for the moment. At the same time as he was interacting collegially with peers like Donald Byrd and Pepper Adams, Harris served as a mentor for an increasing number of musicians. Within a few years, news of Harris's activities spread to other cities, drawing the attention of performers like John Coltrane, who traveled from Philadelphia to Detroit to investigate Harris's method. Harris once invited some of his protégés to perform for Coltrane at his home, where, Harris says, "I showed him my system and he wrote down all the stuff. He was really searching." A list of Harris's graduates reads like a *Who's Who of Jazz;* among them are Paul Chambers, Curtis Fuller, Joe Hender-

son, Lonnie Hillyer, Yusef Lateef, Hugh Lawson, Kirk Lightsey, Charles Mc-
Pherson, and Doug Watkins.

When the ambitions of performers lead them to New York, many maintain
their former relationships as they join new, closely knit study groups that form
within the remarkable pool of talent around them. When Kenny Barron left
Philadelphia for New York at the age of eighteen, he initially lived with his
brother, saxophonist Bill Barron, then moved next door to room with bassist
Vishnu Wood on East Sixth Street. Barron describes his neighborhood: "This
was 1961, and at that time, it was an incredible block. Elvin Jones and Pepper
Adams lived upstairs, the guys from Detroit. Across the street in one apartment
were all the guys from Philly—Reggie Workman, Lee Morgan, Percy Heath,
and somebody else. Up the street a few doors was Ted Curson. The Jazz Gal-
lery was around the corner. The Five Spot was three blocks away. There were
a lot of coffee shops and a lot of music out there. This was 1961."

Curtis Fuller views the same period as "the most beautiful in my life. I
stayed at 101st Street, and Coltrane was at 103rd Street, and every day I could
just take my horn and walk around there—stay over there all day. We'd have
some tea and we'd sit and talk, and we'd laugh and put on records." After this
ritual of social amenities, they would get down to the music. Fuller continues:

> Coltrane would say, "Hey Curtis, try to play this on the trombone,"
> and I would try to run something down. I'd struggle with it and he'd
> say, "You're getting it"—and so on and so on. Paul Chambers lived
> all the way in Brooklyn, and he would get in the subway and, gig
> or no gig, he would come over to practice. He got this thing from
> Koussevitsky—the Polonaise in D Minor—and he'd say, "Hey Cur-
> tis, let's play this one." It wasn't written as a duet, but we would run
> that down together for three or four hours. A couple of days later,
> we'd come back and play it again. The whole thing was just so beauti-
> ful, the camaraderie.

In addition to exchanging knowledge among peers, many young artists
also develop apprenticeships with jazz veterans outside their hometowns, occasionally at the latter's initiation. When a famous saxophone player briefly met
a jazz student at a midwestern saxophone store, he disarmed the student with
his ingenuousness, inviting him "to drop by" his apartment and "practice together" whenever he came to New York. Pursuing a similar arrangement, Curtis Fuller was not able to meet regularly with one of his mentors, J. J. Johnson,
so he wrote letters to him. Whenever Johnson came to town with Kai Winding,
however, Fuller would "run by" his hotel from school and "sit over there two
or three hours in his room and have a little session together."

Despite the disruption caused by touring, many relationships of this nature
endure over a musician's career. Calvin Hill describes a Max Roach concert in

which four generations of jazz drummers, including "Papa" Jo Jones, Louis Hayes, and a teenaged drum prodigy, appeared in the audience to show their appreciation and support. "Max treats Papa Jo with such concern and respect, the same way the younger drummers treat Max," Hill remarks. "They take him as a mentor and adviser and they look up to him."

From the student's side, these relationships sometimes verge on idolatry and, as in Arthur Rhames's earlier account, include emulation of the mentor's personal style. Lonnie Hillyer and his teenaged peers were so impressed by the "images" of artists like Miles Davis that they copied their dress.[2] George Johnson Jr. used to study Eddie Jefferson's "every move, the way he would gesture," eventually getting to the point where he "would sit up and be acting like him." Johnson still remembers the circumstances surrounding his first meeting with Jefferson, in 1976, as "a dream come true. For the past couple of years, I was practicing this cat day and night. I realized there was something very valuable in what he was doing—he was writing jazz lyrics and there wasn't many people doing it. So when I heard he was singing at Fort Dupont in the park, I went down there about two hours early and I practiced, boy! I knew this was my time to meet Eddie."

Although he had intended to maintain a semblance of reserve as he introduced himself, Johnson lost his composure the moment he recognized Jefferson on the concert grounds and "jumped up and hugged him." During their encounter, Johnson sang for Jefferson. As it turned out, Jefferson already knew of him because word had spread within the jazz community that a young performer was patterning his style after Jefferson and performing his material. The two became fast friends.

> We talked a lot, and we stayed with each other. Whenever he came to D.C., he stayed at my house, and whenever I came to New York, I stayed at his house. I would go to hear him perform whenever I wanted to. If he would be in Detroit, I would fly to Detroit. If he would be in Philly, I would go to Philly. I had stacks of eight-track tapes of his records in the car, and I would play them everywhere. He would get tired of me playing his songs, but he never got tired of me asking questions. We were like buddies. We talked about everything. Eddie was like a walking encyclopedia. This cat knew everything.

In the exciting atmosphere of exchanges between veterans and novices, the latter discover the disparity between their romanticized view of the jazz world and the stark social and economic realities with which performers actually contend. Equally enlightening is counsel about music copyright laws, potential exploitation by the recording industry, the insidious lure of commercial music, and the pressures students must be prepared to face within the jazz community itself. Before Buster Williams embarked on his first professional tour—with Gene Ammons and Sonny Stitt's band—his father took him aside and taught him how to smoke marijuana "without inhaling" so as neither to offend other musicians nor pick up their bad habits. He also warned him always to stuff a few dollars in his Bible, in case dishonest managers left him "stranded on the road." And everyone has advice about problems with love relationships, their wisdom the product of the profession's transiency and the economic instability inherent in it.

With respect to the technical aspects of jazz, mentors typically create a congenial atmosphere for learning by conveying the view that student and teacher alike are involved in an ongoing process of artistic development and that the exchange of knowledge is a mutual affair. Barry Harris jokes warmly with students in his workshops, insisting that he is simply "the oldest member of the class"; he takes obvious pride when he learns "something new" from another's musical discovery. He delights in quipping, "I try to steal as much as I can from my students. After I steal enough, I will refuse to be the teacher any longer." This is received as a great compliment by learners, who know Harris's own knowledge to be inexhaustible.

Wynton Marsalis reveals comparable humility on his mentor's part, whether at the New Orleans Center for Creative Arts where he used to teach or at home:

> My father's so much hipper than me and knows so much more, but I can tell him, "I don't like what you played on that," and he'll just stop and say, "Well, damn, what do you want?" Then I'll say, "Why don't you do this?" and he'll try it. That's my father, man. . . . If I said that I didn't like it, he'd change it and at least look for something else, because he's a sensitive musician. The more I get away from him, man, the more I know how much I learned from him just by looking and watching. I grew up with one of the greatest examples.

Learners grappling with the hardships of mastering jazz often derive as much inspiration from their personal interaction with idols as from the information they acquire. "More than anything specific, it was a matter of Jackie McLean being a model for me," a saxophonist remembers. "It had to do with his personality, too, his sense of humor about life. He was always so positive that just to have a word from him was enough to send me home to practice for hours. It was enough to keep me going until the next time I saw him again." Such relationships are especially significant when they are the first adult friendships of youngsters outside their families, friendships earned as members of a professional community.

## Jam Sessions

As essential to students as technical information and counsel is the understanding of jazz acquired directly through performance. In part, they gain experience by participating in one of the most venerable of the community's institutions, the jam session.³ At these informal musical get-togethers, improvisers are free of the constraints that commercial engagements place upon repertory, length of performance, and the freedom to take artistic risks. Ronald Shannon Jackson's grade school band leader allowed students to conduct daily lunchhour jam sessions in the band room. "During those years, I never saw the inside of the school's official lunch room."

Ultimately, sessions bring together artists from different bands to play with a diverse cross section of the jazz community. "New Yorkers had a way of learning from each other just as we did in Detroit," Tommy Flanagan says. "From what I heard from Arthur Taylor, Jackie McLean, and Sonny Rollins, they all used to learn from just jamming together with Bud Powell and Monk and Bird. Even though Bird wasn't a New Yorker, he lived here a long time and got an awful lot from it."

Some sessions arise spontaneously when musicians informally drop in on one another and perform together at professional practice studios. Improvisers also arrange invitational practice sessions at one another's homes. Extended events at private house parties in Seattle "lasted a few days at a time," Patti Bown remembers, and they held such popularity that club owners temporarily closed their own establishments to avoid competing for the same audience. Guests at the parties "cooked food and ate, [then] sat down and played," Bown continues. Musicians "could really develop there. Sometimes they would really get a thing going, and they would keep on exploring an idea. You would go home and come back later, and it was still going on. . . . [Improvisers] sometimes played a single tune for hours." Other sessions were similarly very relaxed: "Everybody was in the process of learning. Some guys were better than others, but it was always swinging, and the guys went on and on playing. We played maybe one number for an hour, but nobody ever got bored with it" (BB).

Jazz organizations such as the Bebop Society in Indianapolis and the New Music Society at the World Stage in Detroit, where Kenny Burrell served as president and concert manager, promoted more formally organized sessions. Others took place in nightclubs, especially during weekend afternoons or in the early hours of the morning after the clientele had gone. In Los Angeles, according to Art Farmer, opportunities abounded for young people. "During the day you would go to somebody's house and play. At night there were afterhours clubs where they would hire maybe one horn and a rhythm section, and then anybody who wanted to play was free to come up and play. Then these clubs would have a Sunday matinee session. We used to just walk the streets at night and go from one place to another."

Musicians distinguish some sessions in terms of the skills of participants. The New Music Society would have a group "the caliber of Elvin Jones, Barry Harris, Tommy Flanagan, and Kenny Burrell," and then they would have "the next crew of guys" like Lonnie Hillyer and his schoolmates, who rehearsed a couple of weeks in advance to prepare for their own session. The youngsters "wouldn't interfere" with those involving "the guys of high caliber." At times, the arrival of musicians from out of town intensified session activities—artists like Hampton Hawes and John Coltrane "who'd be working in some band and had that night off. It was a hell of a playing atmosphere going on there" (LH).

Likewise in Chicago, musicians knew that the session "at a certain club down the corner was for the very heavy cats and would not dare to participate until they knew that they were ready," Rufus Reid recalls. As a matter of respect, "you didn't even think about playing unless you knew that you could cut the mustard. You didn't even take your horn out of your case unless you knew the repertoire." At the same time, naive learners did periodically perform with artists who were a league apart from them. David Baker used to go to sessions including Dexter Gordon and Wardell Gray "when they came to Indianapolis." He adds with amusement, "I didn't have the sense not to play with them."

Although initially performing at sessions in their hometowns, musicians from different parts of the country eventually participate in an extensive network of events in New York City, "mixing in with players from everywhere." In the late forties and fifties, they made their way each day through a variety of apartments, lofts, and nightclubs, where they sampled performances by impromptu groups and joined them as guests during particular pieces, a practice known as sitting in. In addition to having pedagogical value, the sessions served as essential showcases.[4] As Kenny Barron points out, "That's how your name got around." Count Basie's club in particular "was like a meeting ground" during Monday evening sessions, as was the renowned club Birdland, although the latter was difficult "to break into without knowing somebody" (GB). There were also well-documented sessions at Minton's Playhouse and Monroe's Uptown House in Harlem.[5]

Tommy Turrentine's fondest memories of the mid-forties concern Small's Paradise Club "in Harlem. . . . Everybody used to come there." Spanning four musical generations, the artists included trumpeters Red Allen, Hot Lips Page, Idres Sulieman, Dizzy Gillespie, Miles Davis, and Clifford Brown; saxophonists Charlie Parker, Sonny Rollins, Jackie McLean, and Stan Getz; pianists Bud Powell, Walter Bishop Jr., Walter Davis, and Mal Waldron. The house band was led by Big Nick Nicholas, who knew "every tune that's ever been written." Nicholas was, in fact, an important teacher of the community for his role in challenging players to expand their repertories by constantly choosing unfamiliar compositions on the bandstand (LD). Within the context of such a rich and varied repertory, the improvised interplay, night after night, served as inspiring learning sessions for Turrentine and his friends. "That was Paradise University. You would hear so much good music each night that, when you went to lay down, your head would be swimming!"

Rivalry among the participants added spark to an already charged atmosphere. "During that time, there was somewhat of a mutual respect among the musicians, and they had cutting sessions. They would say, 'I am going to blow so and so out.' It wasn't with malice. It was no put-down; it was just friendly competition." Turrentine goes on to describe actual events. "Maybe two tenor players would get up; maybe there would be about seven horn players on the bandstand. Everybody had the sense to know that saxophones was going to hang up there tonight—they was going to be blowing at each other—so we all got off the bandstand and let them have it. Maybe the next night, two trumpet players would be getting up there at each other; then there would be drummers. I have seen it many times. It was healthy really, just keeping everybody on their toes."

Interaction with an increasing number of musicians in these settings provided aspiring artists with stimulus for their own growth as improvisers. Don Sickler speculates that one renowned trumpeter "became so great" because he was aware of the competition around him: "Booker Little was born just a few months before him, and Lee Morgan was just a little younger. He really had to work hard to keep up with that level of competition."

### Sitting In at Concerts

The custom of sitting in also extends to professional engagements, or gigs, where guests display their skills before paying audiences. Louis Armstrong spoke fondly of coincidental meetings with other performers in towns throughout the country where their respective bands toured. They routinely visited each other's clubs during performance intermissions and on their free nights, listening to one another, socializing, and performing together.[6] Keith Copeland vividly recollects the thrill of performing drums with Thelonious Monk's band on occasions in which his father, band member and trumpeter Ray Copeland, had arranged for him to sit in. Young Copeland, who on this occasion was barely in his teens, could "already play pretty good time."

From the newcomers' perspective, the respect that veterans offer them as artists, simply by consenting to perform with them in public, provides invaluable encouragement. "Don't be apologizing for yourself," a band leader once advised Leroy Williams when he began his request to sit in with a self-deprecating remark about his abilities. "Anytime you have heart enough to come on this bandstand, it's okay for you to be here. You have to believe you can play in order to play." On other occasions, saxophonist Gene Ammons complimented him with "little remarks like 'Hey, stick with it,'" encouragements that were enough to inspire Williams during what was to him a particularly "questionable period" in his life. "When someone like Gene Ammons said those things, you knew you were okay."

Art Farmer also tells touching stories about his encounters during a period in which he "didn't know from A to B." When renowned swing bands performed in Phoenix, Farmer and his peers sought out the musicians and invited them to Farmer's house to "play some." If the visitors could afford the time, they would sit in with Farmer's teenaged band and perform their "little stock arrangements." A few even created original musical arrangements for the band. Farmer did not hesitate to approach the artists because he "always had it in my mind that these people loved music, and the only thing we were trying to do was learn how to play from them. And that's the way they were. No one ever said, 'Ah, get away, kid!' "

One unforgettable night, Farmer was performing at "some little club" when Roy Eldridge, who was in town with the Artie Shaw Band, walked through the door.

> First of all, he sat down and played the drums with us. And then, since he was on his night off, he went back to his hotel and got his trumpet and brought that back and played it with us. It was just wonderful because he was at one of his peaks of popularity. For him just to spend his night off with some dumb kids was really marvelous. The next night there was a dance at the club where we played. The Artie Shaw Band played the first part of the dance from nine to one. Then we played from one to five, and they just stood around and listened to us. So we thought that we were pretty hot [he laughs]. We were very flattered by their attention.

Opportunities to sit in with bands ultimately vary with the personalities and policies of the leaders. When musicians approached Charlie Parker for such privileges, Parker received them with gracious enthusiasm. He was interested in what he could learn from others and overlooked their weaknesses to praise positive aspects of their performances. In contrast, some of the other younger band members resented musicians who failed to uphold the band's standards (WB); they viewed such musicians as parasites who sought to raise their own standing through the claim of having performed with Parker. Poor musicianship is not the only cause for resentment in these situations. Performers might not know a band's unique arrangements and spoil a performance. Occasionally, an unknown guest, if extraordinarily gifted, can be a liability, potentially catching the ear of the band leader or club owner, thereby threatening the positions of other band members.

Because attitudes surrounding guest appearances are unpredictable, musicians have to learn the etiquette appropriate to each situation. George Johnson Jr.'s initial experience was very encouraging. After a year of following Eddie Jefferson around, Jefferson surprised him once by calling him up on the stage to sing duets. His mentor had faith that, despite his nervousness, Johnson would know the material well. Somewhat later, however, he received a devastatingly negative reaction from a well-known pianist when he inadvertently interrupted his performance with a request to sit in. Johnson resolved never to ask another musician directly for this favor. Instead, he seated himself in the front row of clubs, night after night, listening attentively and conspicuously to the featured performers until they recognized his interest. Some evenings his strategy succeeded. As often as not, it failed. Over time, however, Johnson sang with Lou Donaldson, George Coleman, Frank Foster, Slide Hampton, "Philly" Joe Jones, and James Moody—"just about everybody in New York." Such experience bolstered Johnson's self-confidence and developed his skill, ultimately leading to his first recording contract with Pharaoh Sanders.

### Professional Affiliations with Bands

Musicians also cultivate their skills through extended tenures in successive bands, sometimes developing their first affiliations shortly after obtaining an instrument and learning a few scales. "From the beginning," Josh Schneider "performed with other musicians who were all at the same level trying to learn to play." Working also became "something regular" for Tommy Flanagan's teenaged band, which performed for weekend dances at community centers. "The older" the band members became, the more invitations they received. Melba Liston and her peers gained initial training in an extracurricular junior high band. They joined the musicians' union when they were about sixteen, gaining access first to membership in a vaudeville theater band and later to community swing bands. In these organizations, they interacted with veterans twice their age who had left the road bands of Chick Webb, Benny Carter, and other famous leaders to settle down in Los Angeles.

Reflecting the multilevel learning method in the jazz community, formal engagements also serve as important opportunities for youngsters to observe other players. After Barry Harris acquired a few chords and boogie-woogie patterns from neighborhood children, he gained additional material at dances by looking over the shoulders of players he admired, such as Tommy Flanagan and Will Davis. Additionally, just as study groups sometimes develop within the context of bands, bands sometimes evolve from study groups organized by charismatic teachers. Initially in Chicago, and later in New York City, Lennie Tristano drew Lee Konitz and a cadre of other talented students around him, serving as their mentor and band leader.[7] In Detroit, Barry Harris's own bands included such advanced students as Paul Chambers, Curtis Fuller, Lonnie Hillyer, and Charles McPherson. It was in the context of interacting with fellow band members in a group that Harris had formed with trombonist Kiane Zawadi, Yusef Lateef, and others that Harris actually "came up with the rules" on which he based his important improvisation system and teaching method.

After increasing their competence, first within neighborhood bands, then within the most established groups in their regions, aspiring performers seek to further their experience by joining renowned bands. Lee Konitz gained increased national exposure within Miles Davis's nonet. Curtis Fuller eventually accepted positions within such prominent bands as Art Blakey's Jazz Messengers and the Benny Golson–Art Farmer Jazztet. Lonnie Hillyer and Charles McPherson became featured members of Charles Mingus's bands. "Barry and his contemporaries prepared us for guys like Mingus," Hillyer explains.

Opportunities for promotion arise when new groups form and when musicians who hold chairs in major bands quit or require a temporary substitute. Usually, leaders would ask for recommendations from the remaining group members, who, in turn, would pass news of the vacancy among their friends. For a generation of learners during the late thirties and early forties, World War II created unexpected opportunities in this regard. Stan Getz maintains that "the reason I got the job [with the Jack Teagarden band] after playing horn for two years was because it was wartime and all the good musicians were drafted."[8]

Because of the jazz community's surplus of talent, performers must compete for the attention of band leaders to be considered for desirable appointments as supporting players or sidemen. Those whose relatives are musicians commonly have the edge. When Buster Williams developed facility as a bass player, his father recommended him as his replacement for engagements that he himself was unable to accept. Regional contacts are equally important. Leroy Williams initially worked in Chicago with bassist Wilbur Ware, who preceded him to New York and developed "lots of connections" that were ultimately "instrumental" in Williams's career. Ware would call up Williams and say, "Sonny Rollins needs a drummer. Can you handle that?" Ware had also worked with Thelonious Monk's band earlier and recommended Williams as Ben Riley's replacement.

Newcomers without contacts often struggle to establish a reputation. Having worked steadily before coming to New York, John McNeil was surprised at the difficulty he encountered. Nine months of unemployment depressed him. According to Gary Bartz, "Longevity plays a large role in letting people know you're around. You have to go around to sessions and sit in with different people, letting them hear you." Art Farmer's experience also bears this out. When Lionel Hampton came to town, Farmer met Quincy Jones and some other members of the band at a jam session. They were the ones who told him that Hampton was looking for a trumpet player. "I went around to the next gig, and we had a little session. That's the way you got the gig. You didn't just sit down and play the parts, you know." Hampton would suggest difficult compositions like "All God's Children" and require the hopeful young artists to improvise on them. "If you did well, he'd say, 'All right. You got the gig.'"

Other leaders conduct auditions of a more formal nature. Around the time that James Moody was about to be discharged from the service in 1946, Dizzy Gillespie's big band performed for his camp. Afterwards Gillespie invited musicians in the audience to try out for a new group he intended to form in New York. Moody appeared for the audition but was "so nervous with Dizzy and all these great players around" that he could hardly project his sound. Moody remembers one of the adjudicators "yelling, 'Can't you play any louder than that?'"

Of course, performers themselves can also seize the initiative for employment. When he was a graduate student at Northwestern University, Rufus Reid called Eddie Harris at home and introduced himself over the phone. Harris, who had already heard Reid perform in Chicago with the house band at Joe Segal's Jazz Showcase, offered to consider him for a position after he completed his studies and could work full time. George Duvivier was equally direct on one occasion:

> In the winter of 1939, I wrote Coleman Hawkins a letter after hearing his record, *Body and Soul.* I had heard of him before that, but I was knocked out by his record; that's what everybody was talking about. He lived eight blocks from me, and I felt I had nothing to lose. The letter was the usual "I heard about you and I liked your record" kind of thing. And I also told him the truth, that I had been classically trained and only played jazz a few years, but I would appreciate it if I was given the opportunity to work with him. And I included my phone number and address. That was a lot of nerve, let's face it.
>
> Two days later, the phone rang and there was this deep voice, "This is Coleman Hawkins." I almost dropped the phone. "Are you free this afternoon? I'd like to hear your playing; bring your bass by." When I got to his place, I found out he was also a pianist. He played the piano while I played the bass; he never touched his saxophone. We went through a couple of tunes, all in different keys that you wouldn't expect them to be in. I played and he seemed to be satisfied. He said, "Do you have a tuxedo?" I said, "Yes." He said, "Fine. We open Monday night, nine o'clock at Kelly's Stable."

Within these general social patterns of interaction among musicians are ongoing, on-scene opportunities for evaluating potential professionalism that avoid the awkwardness of auditions. Band leaders may invite prospective band members to informal social evenings at their homes. Dizzy Gillespie once called Art Davis "over to his house," where the two "just listened to music together and played through a couple of his tunes." A few days later, Gillespie invited Davis to go on the road with his band. Leaders also scout for new talent by slipping in and out of nightclub audiences to evaluate players and performances.

In some instances, leaders take extreme measures to recruit musicians for whom they have strong preferences. One morning Milt Jackson "crashed" into the classroom where Keith Copeland was teaching at the Berklee College of

Music, outraged that Copeland had not received Ray Brown's message from California to join them at the Jazz Workshop the previous night. "Anytime something like this happens, it's time for you to leave Boston!" Jackson shouted, oblivious of the class. "I'm telling you right now that this is April eighth, and I'm giving you a gig at the Village Vanguard on May twenty-third. I've got Harold Mabern and Sam Jones. Now, write it down and make sure you have your bags with you when you come. I don't care whether your wife divorces you and your family breaks up, you bring your bags. I'm not giving you this gig to come to New York for the week and then run on back to Boston. I'm expecting you to stay. It's time for you to come back home now." Copeland resigned his teaching post shortly after the confrontation.

The status of young musicians within their community rises dramatically upon their first performance with a renowned band. Months after his audition for Dizzy Gillespie's big band, James Moody returned home at the end of the day and found his mother waiting at the door, smiling and holding a telegram from Gillespie that read simply, "You'll be with us at the Spotlite tonight!" Moody scrambled to put his things together, and when he arrived at the famous New York club on Fifty-second Street, "everybody was there: Ray Brown, Thelonious Monk, Kenny Clarke, Howard Johnson, and out in the audience was Coleman Hawkins and Lester Young. I said 'Oh, my goodness.' It was something, man."

Visibility in such positions often leads to tenure with other major groups as well, initiating an ever-expanding chain of professional affiliations. When Walter Bishop Jr. left the military, Art Blakey was the first to hire him. Then, during the band's ten-week stint at Minton's Playhouse, Max Roach and Miles David heard him on a night when they were off from work, and Davis asked Bishop to join their group. Subsequently, Charlie Parker heard Bishop perform with Davis's quartet at "Three Deuces and hired [him] from there."

Finally, when players in leadership positions leave established bands to form their own, they sometimes hire constellations of musicians who have already established rapport in another band. "Gerald Wilson was a trumpet player and a fine arranger," Melba Liston says. "When Gerald left Lunceford's band and started a big band, he came over to the theater where I was working and took many of us from that band into his own. During that time, he introduced me to Dizzy and Basie and Parker and everybody who came to Los Angeles and got me music copying dates. Later, I joined Dizzy's big band in New York City. Then when that band broke up, I went with Billie Holiday. Gerald was the director, and he pulled many people from Dizzy's old band over to Holiday."

Performing with renowned bands, newcomers hone their skills and expand their initial store of information about jazz. Generations of jazz musicians have described their training in bands by using metaphors of formal education. Just as Zutty Singleton likened his early engagements in New Orleans riverboat bands to conservatory training,[9] for Lonnie Hillyer, "working with Charles Mingus on and off for those twelve years was like school." George Duvivier describes Coleman Hawkins's band as "the University," and Red Rodney compares his experience in Charlie Parker's band to being in graduate school. What band members learned from one another "depended on what they wanted to know," Duvivier explains. "Sometimes, it was a simple thing like 'How do you play this figure?' or 'What was the chord that this was based on?' Whatever it was, they always ended up learning more than they asked because the fellows were so enthusiastic about helping people." Miles Davis recalls his professional affiliation, when he was fifteen, with Eddie Randle's band in which older members of the trumpet section constantly monitored his efforts, correcting even the subtle problems that arose in his breathing technique and warning him about the potential physical harm in performing with air pockets in his cheeks.[10]

In similar spirit, experts guide younger members in applying their technical knowledge by constantly rehearsing and performing with them, thereby transmitting their deep sense of responsibility for the music. When Kenny Washington joined Betty Carter's band, she informed him that "all" she could do was to teach him what she knew and let him go. Carter could "be hard" on young musicians because "she really cared about the tradition and wanted people to carry it on. 'I won't be here forever,' she used to say."

With time and experience, newcomers gradually accept greater responsibilities within bands, not only serving as soloists, but contributing original ideas for repertory and musical arrangements. As they become more confident, many form bands of their own. Over the course of such developments, changes in the ways others regard emerging musicians reinforce their growing confidence in their own abilities. It can be a dramatic turning point for the musicians when younger aspirants approach them with questions, placing them, for the first time, in the position of adviser. Subsequently, whether visiting their hometowns or touring from site to site, they routinely share their expertise through the very institutions that contributed to their own early growth. They hang out with peers and youngsters who come to hear them at nightclubs, form loose bonds of apprenticeship with especially promising students, and sit in with various bands during formal engagements and at jam sessions.

As a consequence of the interaction of musicians, information acquired in any part of the country concerning the latest jazz compositions, innovative improvisation methods, alternative techniques of instrument performance, and outstanding new talent spreads quickly through the jazz community's national network. In San Francisco, a local trumpeter learns special technical exercises from his counterpart in a visiting band from Boston, exercise that the musician, in turn, had learned from a player who had received them from his trumpet teacher in Rochester. In Chicago, young musicians listen spellbound as an instrument repairer regales them with stories about the touring artists from New York who visit his shop—John Coltrane and Eric Dolphy—chronicling their aesthetic preferences for saxophone reeds and recounting the lightning speed with which they traded improvised phrases back and forth while testing their instruments.[11]

Affectionate, often colorful, personal accounts from the jazz scene frequently accompany the exchange of technical information among players. Some of the more revered of these accounts—a veritable repertory of cautionary tales and exempla—concern the sharing of hard-earned professional wisdom among jazz greats. For instance, advice that Miles Davis gave to John Coltrane and other band members in various backstage incidents, recounted frequently among acquaintances, guides many improvisers facing artistic dilemmas comparable to those of their renowned counterparts.

## Paying Dues as Learners

Although the jazz community's largely supportive atmosphere is a prominent theme in personal narratives by improvisers, this is not the complete story. Students face enormous challenges in mastering both their respective instruments and the complex musical language for which, until recently, there have been few written aids. Moreover, the driving passion of the experts, even those who assume the role of teacher, is, of course, their own music. None assume exclusive control over the training of their students, nor do they typically provide a program of instruction comprehensive enough to form the complete basis for the education of students. Even the young musician in a lengthy apprenticeship with a master artist-teacher supplements this training with various other learning opportunities. The jazz community's traditional educational system places its emphasis on learning rather than on teaching, shifting to students the responsibility for determining what they need to learn, how they will go about learning, and from whom.[12] Consequently, aspiring jazz musicians whose educational background has fostered a fundamental dependence on teachers must adopt new approaches to learning. Veterans describe the trials and tribulations that accompany the learner's efforts to absorb and sort out musical knowledge as examples of "paying dues."

Amid the jazz community's kaleidoscopic array of information, students glimpse varied elements as they appear and reappear in different settings and are interpreted by the performers whom the students encounter. Learners synthesize disparate facts in an effort to understand the larger tradition. Gary Bartz "basically learned one thing" from each of the musicians who assisted him— "saxophone technique" from one, "dynamics and articulation" from another, "chords" from a third. Similarly, an aspiring pianist learned the general principles of jazz theory from Barry Harris, discovered "how to achieve the independence of both hands and how to create effective left hand bass lines" under pianist Jaki Byard's tutelage, and expanded his repertory with someone else. Greg Langdon "worked on a lot of things all at the same time" by playing in different bands, attending jam sessions, and taking private saxophone and solfeggio lessons. He would "get a snatch of information from a workshop," and he would later play duets with a musician he met in the practice studios "who'd turn me on to something else. Things I learned in one situation would be amplified in another."

If certain encounters with artists deepen the insights of learners, other encounters may seem to contradict their impressions, temporarily baffling and discouraging them. In one setting they are urged to adopt practices or to conceptualize the music in ways that in another are criticized sharply. Furthermore, the willingness of experts to share their knowledge can itself depend on youngsters proving themselves to be "sincere, capable," and generally "worthy of attention because there are so many people trying to play jazz" (TT; FH). Some veterans favor rather aggressive methods of testing the mettle of newcomers that, however disconcerting initially, ultimately serve as competitive bonding routines that establish close ties of friendship.[13]

Students may also find their learning programs hampered by competitive aspects of professional life that arise from the insecurity and self-interest of those whom they encounter. One singer gives an insightful appraisal of such situations:

> Competitiveness, jealousy, and resentment are inherent in the jazz world. The economic success that any jazz performer can have is limited by the fact that they play jazz, so like any minority group, jazz musicians sometimes turn on their own members. Sometimes, this is manifested when you meet people for the second time; there is this little drama of "I don't know you; have I met you before?" Or people will come into a club and act as if you're not there. It hurts, you know. Also, a lot of musicians could have been a lot more helpful and supportive. You hire musicians when you have a gig, but when you're out of work and they're working, they don't hire you. Sometimes they have contacts with record companies and won't put in a good word for you. Or they won't share information about their contacts for tours or festivals.

In the face of hostility or indifference, young musicians may require of themselves considerable gumption to make their talents known to band leaders. Charles Mingus "used to push" Ronald Shannon Jackson "rudely out of his way" whenever he asked to be considered for the group. Jackson eventually forced the issue strategically by sitting in at the Village Gate with Toshiko Akiyoshi when she performed as "the opening act" before Mingus's band. At one point, says Jackson, "I heard this loud clapping right behind me. 'Yeah, I like your playing,'" Mingus declared. It was then that Mingus invited Jackson to perform with his band.

Once within renowned bands, new members must sometimes establish credibility before gaining full acceptance from fellow players. Booker Little and Art Davis became good friends eventually, but in the beginning Davis thought that Little seemed not to accept him.

> I had to prove myself. It was like paying your dues. Who was I to be coming into the band at that time? I hadn't worked with anybody else of note before joining Max Roach's band. Anyway, we were living in the same hotel, and after practicing with the band, Booker and George Coleman and myself would stay behind and practice together. After Coleman left, it would just be me and Booker. He had incredible endurance as a trumpet player and always wanted to keep rehearsing after everyone else had quit. At the same time, he continued to be standoffish. But one day, after we finished playing, he asked me if I wanted to go to dinner with him. I knew then that I had been accepted.

The practice of paying dues also enters into the dynamics of jam sessions.[14] In New York City in 1957, "many well-known musicians were cold and critical," and when a newcomer approached the bandstand, they would play "some very difficult song or take a fast tempo that they thought you would sound bad on, so that they could laugh at you or show you up" (HO). Similarly, the house band at a nightclub in San Francisco developed a reputation for capriciously changing the key of a piece during performances; whenever a soloist failed to follow them, they would stop playing and leave the stage in contempt.

Such behavior set the general tone for the interaction of the other participants. One evening a newcomer, attempting to establish rapport with a saxophonist and elicit his sympathy, described his difficulty mastering a Charlie Parker composition replete with awkward fingerings. The performer listened patiently until he finished speaking, then said, "Well, brother, I guess that some of us have it and others just don't." In another instance, a young player who had mustered his courage to sit in with the house band politely inquired of another musician in the audience about the piece's harmony. "Use your ear!" the veteran snapped. The novice quickly retook his seat, both to recover from this slight and to listen more closely before proceeding to the bandstand. The young player's solo, insecure from its outset, faltered to the progression's close, at which point the soloist up next placed a foot on the small of his back and sent him sliding into the wings.

In the heat of embarrassment, a rebuff seems to indicate sentiment little more noble than meanness; of course, in some cases, there may be no more to it than that. In other cases, such slights simply reflect the tradition's high performance standards, revealing the prevailing view that students learn best when they figure out things for themselves. Indeed, there is little inclination to coddle beginners, for they must be discouraged from taking a passive stance in their education. "If you got in there and started goofing like a lot of cats do," Lou Donaldson explains, "they'd say, 'You go in the woodshed a little bit.' You'd hear what they were playing and say, 'Well, man, if I don't know that song, I'd better go check it out.'"

By testing the resilience of emerging musicians, veterans also determine those who warrant direct assistance. Barry Harris and his peers "could be pretty hard on musicians in those days by chasing them away from sessions, but we never refused them when they came back and wanted to try again." Correspondingly, students attempting to regain the respect of the performers who challenged them eventually learn to turn failure and humiliation into the resolve to overcome weaknesses in their musicianship.

Maturity comes with experience, however, and the dues exacted from young musicians in the meantime cause confusion and pain to those trying to gain realistic appraisal of their own abilities. "In New York, I'd sit in with some great players I had known from records, and the music would sound bad and feel bad," a pianist remembers. "I'd think they didn't like my playing and I'd blame myself. Sometimes, the heavy players themselves would mess up because they weren't as capable of playing as their reputations had it, and they'd blame their problems on you. Or they would deliberately mess with you, and you'd go home and cry or feel like you couldn't play. It was only later that I realized that the problem wasn't me; it was somebody else. You have to learn everything the hard way."

Acceptance in the jazz community depends not only on how well newcomers weather their encounters with established performers, but on how aggressively they pursue them. Harold Ousely was "sort of timid" when he first moved to New York from Chicago. "I didn't feel relaxed enough to approach musicians I didn't already know." Formerly, in Chicago, most of Ousley's "music time" had been spent practicing with other musicians who "were all trying to get their craft together," but in New York, most of his "music time" was spent actually performing. In retrospect, Ousely considers this to have been his mistake. If he had gone to the homes of the musicians "where the cats were practicing and hanging out," then he "could have gotten into what was happening downtown in New York. You could get to know players like Coltrane and get a certain camaraderie going, practicing and performing together."

The experiences of learners also reflect the distinctive atmospheres that characterize particular communities and regions over time. When Jimmy Robinson came to New York City from Los Angeles, the scene seemed "strange" to him. He had become used to the "closeness among musicians in Los Angeles, but everybody in New York was doing their own thing. Everybody was a star here." From Curtis Fuller's perspective, the camaraderie among performers in New York was itself "much deeper" in the early sixties than in the eighties because everyone "likes to play it safe now. People don't want you to know that they don't know this or that. They get uptight and don't want to expose themselves to criticism, so they won't get together. You've got a lot of individualism today."

Finally, the ordeals of students are all unique, depending on personality, ethnicity, age, gender, and myriad other factors that affect the chemistry of relationships between students and teachers. Of equal importance is the predisposition of experts. Some, like Barry Harris, are dedicated teachers with boundless generosity.[15] This is not always the case, however. Doc Cheatham recalls that Freddie Keppard "performed the trumpet with a handkerchief over his right hand and another player performed with his back to the audience," each preventing onlookers from learning his finger patterns. In his youth, Cheatham approached renowned performers cautiously "because you never knew who was willing to show you something and who was not."

### Formal Educational Institutions

Besides the jazz community's own institutions for learning, improvisers have benefited in varying degrees from colleges, universities, and conservatories. Formerly, the role of such institutions was indirect. They extended the rudimentary music education that students received in public schools by providing intermediate or advanced training in the interpretation of Western classical music literature, instrument performance, and, occasionally, theory and composition. From the earliest days of jazz, influential artists have studied classical music at private conservatories or acquired technical performance skills from teachers with conservatory and academic backgrounds. In New Orleans, Jelly Roll Morton and other musicians frequently attended concerts at the French Opera House and immersed themselves in compositions by Verdi, Massenet, Donizetti, and other masters. Ultimately, associations between jazz artists trained by ear in African American music and those with additional academic training blend differing worlds of musical knowledge, thus contributing to a mutual artistic exchange that continually enriches jazz tradition.[16]

Musicians have also benefited—increasingly since the fifties—from jazz training at formal educational institutions. Some, patterned upon the conservatory model, have roots in the pedagogical efforts of William Handy, James Reese Europe, and Len Bowden in the late teens and early twenties.[17] The concern with formalizing jazz education initially arose as a response to the Eurocentric values of the American academic music establishment, ill equipped and indisposed to teach jazz at the time. In later years, the commercial dominance of rock provided additional impetus, threatening the economic base of the jazz community's own educational system. Pioneering programs establishing jazz education on an equal footing with classical music education include Schillinger House in Boston in 1945 (later the Berklee School of Music) founded by Lawrence Berk, and the Lenox School of Jazz in Massachusetts in 1957, with summer clinics directed by pianist John Lewis.[18] The intention in establishing these programs and institutions was to ensure the continuing transmission of jazz and, in a sense, legitimize its study.

The American civil rights movement of the 1960s helped draw attention to the important cultural components of the African American community nationwide, dramatizing the timeliness of the programs mentioned above and galvanizing support for similar ventures elsewhere in the public and private sector. In 1968, the formation of the National Jazz Educators Association, an affiliate of the Music Educators National Conference, reflected a growing awareness of the role that secondary schools might play in supporting the jazz tradition. The civil rights movement also served as a spearhead for change within the nation's institutions of higher education, prompting the design of new courses on African American culture. Several conservatories, colleges, and universities hired jazz performers to assist in developing relevant music curricula, this within a larger trend to establish departments of African American studies. African American music courses and specialized jazz programs multiplied across the country by the mid-eighties.

College students majoring in jazz typically participate in jazz ensembles and take courses devoted to jazz history, theoretical aspects of improvisation, and composition and arranging in the styles of great masters like Count Basie and Duke Ellington. Students also enroll in a basic core of Western classical music courses that commonly include music history, education, and theory and composition. Beyond their jazz ensemble experience, collegians perform Western classical music in bands, choirs, and orchestras. There have been pedagogical developments in American colleges, such as jazz correspondence courses, that have influence abroad. Scholarships enabling international students to study at American institutions likewise strengthen the jazz community's global ties. So, too, do jazz programs at institutions abroad and organizations like the International Association of Schools of Jazz, founded by David Liebman in 1989.

Musicians describe their classes as useful forums for reinforcing or supplementing the knowledge about jazz that many had acquired as youngsters. At the same time, most stress the importance of jazz performance in college. In the face of the jam session's decline and of decreasing employment opportunities with road bands, colleges provide an environment where students can interact with peers who share their concerns. At Lincoln University, Ronald Shannon Jackson occupied a dormitory room with John Hicks, and he formed close friendships with other serious jazz musicians in the student body, students like Oliver Lake. Throughout their undergraduate days, the friends "spent as much time performing together as studying."

Universities also serve as a base for exploring neighboring jazz communities. Jackson initially chose to attend Lincoln because he would have access in St. Louis to great musicians who toured through the Midwest. Similarly, while Don Pate was a graduate student, first at the Berklee College of Music and afterwards at the New England Conservatory of Music, he performed jazz "nonstop" in the greater Boston area, establishing many important professional contacts for his career. Such features of college life are particularly compelling for students who have already benefited from the jazz community's traditional training and attained fluency as improvisers before leaving high school.

Also reflecting the trend toward more formal jazz education since the sixties are private organizations such as the Association for the Advancement of Creative Musicians in Chicago (1961), whose first president was Muhal Richard Abrams; Jazzmobile in New York City (1965), whose first president was Billy Taylor; Karl Berger's Creative Music Studio in Woodstock (1972), founded by Berger together with Ornette Coleman; and Barry Harris's former program at the Jazz Cultural Theatre (1982–87), all providing master classes in jazz for their surrounding populations.[19] Traveling jazz workshops by Jamey Aebersold, also have found national and international followings. Within regional jazz communities, musicians increasingly offer private improvisation lessons, formalizing the dissemination of information acquired themselves through traditional learning practices.

### Developing Extraordinary Skill

To account for the remarkable skills that many develop as youngsters within the jazz community's educational system, improvisers acknowledge the early onset of a sense of professional identity.[20] "We started young when our minds were open, and we had no obligations—no wives, no babies, no rent to pay" (LH). Unencumbered by adult responsibilities and enjoying support at home for their disciplined study, teenagers pursue jazz with the single-mindedness and unbounded energy that typify their impassioned involvement with other interests. When Bobby Rogovin first discovered baseball, he "would go to the library and get all the statistics of all the guys and memorize anything that could be memorized." In like manner, he later became a "storehouse of information about jazz" by reading all the *Down Beat* magazines he could get hold of and "memorizing all the liner notes of records." If anyone asked him, "Who was in the trumpet section on such and such Woody Herman album?" he knew the answer immediately. It was not so much a matter of design that he "developed total recall for the lineage of trumpet players. I just ended up knowing all those things because I loved to read about them so much."

Unwavering devotion to music listening also characterizes the learning programs of students. Many recall years in which turning on the radio or the record player was their first act in the morning and turning it off their last at night. Lee Konitz often lay awake far beyond his official bedtime with a radio hidden beneath his pillow excitedly awaiting jazz broadcasts from different parts of the country. Time did not weaken these attachments. Don Pate maintained so constant an environment of recorded jazz around him as an undergraduate at Central State College that his roommate moved out and the college administration offered him the only single room in the dormitory.

Beyond the pleasure that they derive from listening, students also treat recordings as formal educational tools. Since 1917, this fixed representation of the historical literature of jazz on commercial recordings has, in effect, served as the aural musical score, well suited to scrutiny and analysis.[21] In part, recordings enable young musicians to apprentice unilaterally with artists they may never actually meet. As Lonnie Hillyer puts it, "All the great jazz musicians have also been great teachers. Their lessons are preserved for students on every recording they made."

During their formative years, musicians display similar fervor toward live performance, at times exercising great ingenuity in overcoming obstacles posed by their youthful ages in relation to the music's adult nightlife. Melba Liston's aunts "sneaked off" to jam sessions at neighborhood rent parties when Liston's grandparents were not present to stop them. Leroy Williams and his young friends falsified their identification cards to gain entry to Chicago's nightclubs and soon became "hooked on going out and watching musicians." Club owners saw through their ploys but tolerated the presence of the youngsters as long as they were quiet and occupied a table not needed for paying customers. Other owners gained permission from licensing authorities to maintain special galleries for underage audiences, including, of course, aspiring musicians.

Typically, young learners cultivate their own performance skills with dedication and determination. Wynton Marsalis was "a really intense practicer around school and at home at night, constantly trying to get better. That was all I could think about." Pursuing "every musical challenge" that presented itself, Marsalis played in jazz bands and in the civic orchestra, and occasionally substituted for various New Orleans Philharmonic Orchestra trumpeters. He adds: "If a cat called me for a gig to play kazoo, I'd do it too." Similarly, everyone in Max Roach's early circle worked hard; music was a "twenty-four-hour situation for us. We practiced all day, and if we were fortunate enough to be working, we'd gig all night." Afterwards, perhaps at three o'clock in the morning, "we went looking for jam sessions." Employees at nightclubs sometimes helped to facilitate these arrangements. Before Barry Harris was of legal age, he made friends with a club's pianist who allowed him once each night "to run in from the street, play one number at the piano, and run back out again." Harris celebrated his twenty-first birthday at the club "to make sure they knew I was twenty-one!"

As discussed earlier, budding artists take control of their own music education with what must seem to them to be daring assertiveness. Equally impressive is the self-possession that characterizes their behavior. "When I was learning, you heard people play things that sounded nice and you thought about what you were playing," Art Farmer recalls. "You thought about how you sounded and how you would like to sound, and you went home, and you worked on it. If you couldn't learn by what you heard, well then, it was your own fault." Marsalis is equally adamant. "There is so much information out there for you to get access to, if somebody has to tell you how to get it, you don't deserve it. You know what it is; you've got to get it. If you hear somebody say, 'Man, I think so and so is really great,' then you listen to that person and decide for yourself. You don't take anything for granted."

The value that the jazz community places on personal responsibility is especially appropriate for the artistic growth of initiates. Self-reliance requires them to select their own models for excellence and to measure their abilities against them. It enhances their powers of critical evaluation, cultivates their tastes, and provides them with an early sense of their own individuality. Overall, the jazz community's educational system sets the students on paths of development directly related to their goal: the creation of a unique improvisational voice within the jazz tradition.

These aspects of the young artists' self-awareness illuminate fundamental areas of the jazz community's musical life and artistry. Emerging improvisers, in coming to terms with jazz's varied conventions, do not simply absorb them. Rather, they interpret and select them according to personal abilities and values, formative musical experience and training, and dynamic interaction with other artists. Ultimately, each player cultivates a unique vision that accommodates change from within and without. It is clear, then, that from the outset an artist's ongoing personal performance history entwines with jazz's artistic tradition, allowing for a mutual absorption and exchange of ideas. These processes—and the complementary themes of shared community values and idiosyncratic musical perspectives—are already evident in the lives of learners soon after they begin to acquire knowledge of those formal structures of jazz on which their own performances will depend.

# PART

## II

### Cultivating the Soloist's Skills

# THREE

## A Very Structured Thing

### Jazz Compositions as Vehicles for Improvisation

*Jazz is not just, "Well, man, this is what I feel like playing." It's a very structured thing that comes down from a tradition and requires a lot of thought and study.*—Wynton Marsalis

*Jazz tunes are great vehicles. They are forms that can be used and reused. Their implications are infinite.*—Lee Konitz

Composed pieces or tunes, consisting of a melody and an accompanying harmonic progression, have provided the structure for improvisations throughout most of the history of jazz. Enjoying favor to varying degrees from one period to the next, spirituals, marches, rags, and popular songs have all contributed to the artists' repertory of established compositions or standards.[1] Performers commonly refer to the melody or theme as the head, and to the progression as chord changes or simply changes. It has become the convention for musicians to perform the melody and its accompaniment at the opening and closing of a piece's performance. In between, they take turns improvising solos within the piece's cyclical rhythmic form.[2] A solo can comprise a single pass through the cycle, known as a chorus, or it can be extended to include multiple choruses. Just as the progression's varied timbral colors provide a rich setting for the head, they also highlight the features of solos. Moreover, the chords' pattern of change and its undulating scheme of harmonic tension and release create constant rhythmic motion, adding momentum to the performance.

The artist's repertory of jazz standards includes many "popular tunes that were originally used in musical theater," Lee Konitz explains. "For example, there are jazz standards from the thirties and the forties that have great melodies and harmonic sequences. Even the lyrics are great.[3] There are also other good vehicles. More and more, musicians have been getting away from the standards and writing their own songs." Konitz's emphasis on form is appropriate within the discipline of jazz, for learners must, as he concludes, "become familiar with these tunes and their frameworks before taking any liberties in playing variations or in improvising."

### Building Up a Jazz Repertory

Novices develop a storehouse of music from recordings and from demonstrations. When Tommy Flanagan and his high school peers got together at one another's homes, "one guy would try to play a tune from a new Bird record, and someone else would say, 'No, that's not right,' and we'd hash it out together. Then we'd all go home and work on it and come back and see who had advanced the most." As the house bass player at the Jazz Showcase, Rufus Reid routinely borrowed or purchased records made by the featured artists so that he could learn their compositions before engagements. The repertories that students acquire from recordings enable them to perform jazz at a fundamental level and to prove themselves worthy of the assistance of experienced musicians who teach them through painstaking demonstrations.

Although youngsters rely heavily on aural means of learning, most eventually learn to read music in order to gain access to additional material. Written sources of repertory include printed renditions, or lead sheets, that provide a piece's notated melody and accompanying chord symbols; fake books, roughly drawn compilations of lead sheets—in many instances, technically illegal; and written musical arrangements or orchestrated versions of pieces providing specialized parts for each band member through representations of melody and accompaniment.[4]

The degree to which performers can succeed in their community without reading skills depends both on their aural abilities and the specific demands that bands make upon them. Groups tend to strike different balances between the proportion of material that they compose and arrange in rehearsals and that which they improvise during performances. Moreover, some expect band members to read elaborate, written scores, or charts, while others rely upon relatively spare aural scores, or head arrangements, whose parts are transmitted through demonstration and memorized on the spot.

A band leader once fired young Charli Persip in front of the other musicians upon discovering that he could not read the drum parts. The incident ranks among the most terrible in Persip's childhood; he compares it to being disciplined by his father "thumping" him painfully on the head. Persip decided then and there that he would learn to read music so that no one could ever humiliate him like that again. Similarly, it was a "big breakthrough" for Walter Bishop Jr. when he "decided to take private lessons and learn seriously how to read and write music." Despite twenty-eight years of professional experience before he became a proficient reader, he "still felt like just half a musician."[5]

Bringing different tools to the task, young musicians develop their repertories largely by performing in various bands. Seasoned members of John Hicks's early groups urged him to "learn some new tunes" so that they could play "something else together besides the blues." A leader recognized similar limitations on Rufus Reid's part and taught him how to compile his own fake book that included all the pieces for their duo. Newcomers also feel the pressure to increase their knowledge so that they are not left behind in other settings. At some jam sessions "the guys didn't even call the tunes' names. They just counted off the tempos and played. They expected you to recognize the tunes and to play along" (CH).

Musicians faced with the prospect of enlarging their repertories proceed by tackling representative examples of forms that present unique challenges. In the late forties, "the older guys" advised, "if you could play a blues, 'I Got Rhythm' changes, and a ballad, you were well on your way" (LH). Youngsters also study specific genres and pieces by certain composers fashionable within the intersecting worlds of jazz and popular music. "For a while Latin things were in," so Keith Copeland and his peers learned "Tito Puente's, Machito's, and Cal Tjader's tunes." He also discovered Horace Silver and "tried to do his songs." Later, when Barry Harris came to New York, Copeland studied "all those Charlie Parker heads," practicing along with records so that "I could go out and sit in with Barry."

Kenny Barron also noticed the particular pieces "being played on the scene by different groups" and shifted his own focus accordingly, absorbing compositions by Benny Golson, Dizzy Gillespie, Lee Morgan, and Donald Byrd. Because some of the bands he played with performed for dances, he "also had to know 'Night Train,' 'You Go to My Head,' and standard rhythm and blues tunes."

Other groups exposed learners to a stock of pieces reflecting the personal tastes and compositional skills of their band leaders and members. "Betty Carter always picked tunes that nobody else did; she never wanted to be like anybody else" (KW). As a member of Art Blakey's Jazz Messengers, John Hicks "had to learn the old tunes like Wayne Shorter's tunes and the Messengers' standards like 'Moanin'.' Some went back two, three, four generations of Messengers" and created a sense of tradition in the band which Hicks "really loved."

### Rendering Composed Melodies

As youngsters study repertory from disparate sources, they find considerable variation among versions of the same compositions. Lonnie Hillyer would "learn a tune from records and then go out and play it with different people, and they'd have their own little ways of doing it." Artists may make decisions about particular features of their renditions outside of performance, but they reserve other decisions for the actual performance. Composers like Thelonious Monk vary their own pieces "each time they play them." Ironically, artistic creativity sometimes seeds new inventions as a result of the monotony of repeated performance routines. "After you have sung a song one hundred and fifty times," Carmen Lundy observes wryly, "the chances are that you are going to begin doing little, different things with it." Finally, the initial learning process itself may contribute variants to the pool. Tommy Flanagan and his friends found some pieces on records to be "really tricky, like 'Ko Ko.' You can still listen to the intro and wonder exactly what Bird played there—both the notes and the phrasing. We might have three or four different versions of a tune among the players." Flanagan remembers that they would write them all out periodically and compare them.

Among the characteristics of a composition that can distinguish one artist's version from another is the choice of tonic. Awareness of this characteristic can itself come as a "shocking revelation" to beginners who assume that all music is composed in the key of the first scale they learn or that pieces are played only in the key of the first printed version they encounter. John McNeil went into a panic during an early jam session in which saxophonist John Handy "called the tunes in different keys." Afterwards, McNeil says, he "hid from other musicians for months," until he had made up his deficiency by relearning his repertory "in all twelve keys."

To meet the challenges of key transposition, students must train themselves to hear a piece's intervals, that is, to imagine their precise sounds, at differing pitch levels. Many experts advise learners to practice singing tunes initially with nonverbal or scat syllables—to master the melodies aurally without relying on physical impressions such as fingering patterns or the visualization of an instrument's layout. Learning to sing the letter names of the pitches or words of a piece is another method. To introduce students to rudimentary music theory, some players like Julius Ellerby vary these approaches by numbering each pitch in relation to the piece's tonic and suggesting that pupils sing the numbers instead of scat syllables in every key (ex. 3.1). After thoroughly absorbing a tune through these exercises, students work on reproducing it on their instruments to develop control over each version's unique fingering patterns—including their distinguishing points of ease or awkwardness.

The relative hardships associated with this practice vary, of course, with the complexity of each melody and the nature of its form. Some blues pieces comprise a single repeating figure (ex. 3.2a) or simple phrases based on AA'B melodic prototype—sometimes at multiple structural levels (ex. 3.2b)—and present little difficulty. More elaborate pieces rely on ABAC or AABA melodic prototypes. The interval patterns of intricate ballads extending over thirty-two-bar progressions (ex. 3.2c) can be demanding, as can ornate, highly syncopated melodies of pieces that require seemingly endless repetition to master. Rapid, intricate bebop pieces such as "Donna Lee" and "Anthropology" (ex. 3.2d) are formidable "musical etudes" and keep improvisers in top form technically by providing challenges as great as any presented in "method books for classical musicians" (LH).

Beyond its variable key, a piece's precise melodic features can differ from version to version. Within an arrangement, singers or instrumentalists who carry the melody can transform it to varying degrees, engaging in compositional activities of increasing "levels of intensity" that Lee Konitz distinguishes along a continuum from interpretation to improvisation.[6] Success at one level provides the conceptual grounding and "license" musicians need to graduate to successive levels, each increasing its demands upon imagination and concentration.

At the outset of a performance, players commonly restrict themselves to interpretation. They reenter the piece's circumscribed musical world along the rising and falling path of a particular model of the melody, focusing firmly on its elements and reacquainting themselves with the subject of their artistic ventures. Musicians take minor liberties when orienting themselves to a piece at this level of intensity, coloring it in numerous ways. They vary such subtleties as accentuation, vibrato, dynamics, rhythmic phrasing, and articulation or tonguing, "striving to interpret the melody freshly, as if performing it for the first time" (LK).

With masterful control, players maintain uniform tonal quality and even articulation at times. At other times, they create interest along a melody's contour by coloring it with myriad tonal effects (ex. I.1). They may forcefully exaggerate or repress the use of vibrato and dramatically change articulation patterns. At one moment, they may emphasize slurring, at another, tonguing. Moreover, they employ different tonguing syllables to create varied mixtures of light and heavy accents, sometimes swallowing or "ghosting" pitches so that they are, by gradations, more felt than heard. Wind players can vary the tonguing positions associated with such syllables as tu, ta, to, go, ku, or vu to produce different tone colors. Miles Davis appears to emphasize vu articulation if seeking to give his sound a soft, airy diffuseness, and to produce a ghosting effect on a grace note by using lah-dah syllables.[7] Alternatively, to increase the complexity of tone, improvisers can sing or growl through instruments, tinting and thickening their sounds.[8] Other techniques include scooping into a pitch, bending within a pitch or between pitches, and falling off, or concluding a pitch with a short, downward glissando. Yet others are the shake, a rapid lip trill between pitches a whole step or larger interval apart; the flare or rip-up, a rough, rapid gliss that lightly touches all the harmonics between the initial pitch and target pitch; and the doit, an extended rip whose sound trails off toward an indefinite pitch.[9]

Artists describe subtle bends and other microtonal melodic inflections—pitches sharpened or flattened for expressive effect—as blue notes. Charles Mingus once underscored this technique at a workshop by drawing a vertical column of overlapping notes on a large staff, indicating that each note had potential for stretching into the domain of the others just above or below it (CI). Lou Donaldson, too, emphasizes the importance of learning to play "quarter-tones . . . to bend a note . . . to make a horn talk, to make it cry. Johnny Hodges would actually make it cry," pulling pitches "ever so slowly in and out of tune with the band," so that other band members were "on the edge of their seats hoping he'd get back in there." And, of course, "he always did." As a model for such practices, Donaldson recommends that aspiring jazz musicians "concentrate on the blues," absorbing its special "feeling" so they can project it into their improvisations. Without cultivating "that type of sound," he cautions, "you never can play jazz."

Along similar lines, early New Orleans jazz clarinetist Louis deLisle Nelson insists that "you must handle your tone. . . . You can put some *whining* in the blowing of your instrument. There are a whole lot of different sounds you can shove in—such as *crying*—everywhere you get the chance. But . . . with a certain measurement and not opposed to the harmony." [10] When pitch inflections are combined with speechlike rhythmic cadences, soloists sometimes actually "sound like they're speaking words. It's like you're talking when you play. That's what it's about" (DC).

In part, the aesthetic values and procedures described above (ex. 3.3a) reflect the African side of the dual heritage of African American music.[11] In many parts of Africa, tuning systems use pitches outside the Western system of equal temperament; human voice and instruments assume a kind of musical parity. Voices and instruments are at times so close in timbre and so inextricably interwoven within the music's fabric as to be nearly indistinguishable. Furthermore, some drums, marimbas, horns, and flutes can actually function as surrogate speech by impeccably reproducing the melodic-rhythmic patterns of the tonal language of their respective culture.[12]

As early African American composers forged their musics from the diverse African and European musical elements around them, they preserved different African elements to varying degrees, adapting them to their own evolving social and musical tradition, much of which centered on the African American church. Sacred genres like the ring shout embodied many of the fundamental values that defined later black musical forms.[13] Carrying sacred musical practices over into the jazz tradition, early improvisers included spirituals within their repertories and created instrumental arrangements from the different parts that they sang at religious services. Joe Oliver and other New Orleans musicians were renowned for their ability to use mutes to imitate the timbre and cadence of the stylized speech of sermonizing preachers and to re-create the spirit and sounds of holy-roller meetings.[14]

Within the jazz tradition, instrumentalists and vocalists continue to influence one another. A reflection of this is instrumentalists' predilection for copying the pitch colorations and inflections of blues and jazz singers, and their phrasing of song texts. To this day, Barry Harris reminds instrumentalists at his workshops to "play legato" and to allow their vibratos greater prominence "like singers do." He elaborates: "Vibrato is what gives your sound individuality, because everyone's got a different natural vibrato."

Besides their use of such interpretative devices, jazz musicians can individualize the piece further, moving along Konitz's scale to embellishment. Even at the level of subtle embellishment, unique patterns of imagination lend a distinctive character to each artist's practices. A player can append grace notes to the melody's important pitches, articulating both pitches clearly, or, for variety, draw them out to produce a smear or dwa-oo effect.[15] Some routinely favor the use of a single ascending chromatic grace note at the beginnings of phrases, but others use the same embellishment only sparingly or favor descending grace notes. As a matter of taste or due to idiosyncratic, physical features of performance, individual artists may consistently embellish particular pitches. Many players use an eighth-note upper mordent between a pitch and the adjacent scale degree; some tend to phrase this as a triplet, and others as an eighth note and two sixteenths. Inventive pitch substitutions, and occasional chromatic fills added between consecutive melody pitches, are also common. Additionally, soloists can rephrase the melody subtly by anticipating or delaying the entrances of phrases or by lengthening or shortening particular pitches within them.

Lonnie Hillyer once commented on the combined effect of these practices after hearing a recorded rendition of the ballad "Alone Together" by his late friend, trumpeter Kenny Dorham.[16] Rendering the piece with his warm, intimate tone, Dorham embellished the melody with spare grace notes and varied its phrasing with subtle anticipations and delays. He articulated sustained pitches with soft unaccented attacks before bending them down and drawing them quickly back again, then allowing them to sing with an increasingly wide vibrato. Only once did he interject into the performance a phrase of his own by filling a rest with melodic motion. Seated beside the speakers, Hillyer responded immediately to Dorham. He leaned forward, covered his eyes with his hands, and remained perfectly still until the performance's close. Then, sighing, he shook his head, as if waking from a dream, and softly marveled, "K. D.! To think he could say *all that,* just by playing the melody."

When rendering ballads or slow expressive blues, musicians sometimes confine performances to the subtleties described above. Alternatively, they may venture into the arena of variation, transfiguring the melody more substantially by creating shapes that have greater personality but whose relationship to the original model remains clear. The liberal application of some of the techniques associated with embellishment can accomplish this goal. Lee Konitz "displaces certain pitches in the melody" with pitches of his own, and saxophonist Lou Donaldson inserts "different clusters of notes at different places" along its contour. Joe Giudice creates "extensions of the melody by reaching out and grabbing neighboring pitches or by leaping to important chord tones and painting a picture of the harmonic segment of the piece," procedures he describes as "natural ornamentation." Common practices also include prefacing a phrase from the melody with a short introductory figure or extending it with a short cadential figure.

Finally, musicians periodically raise performances to improvisation, the highest level of intensity, transforming the melody into patterns bearing little or no resemblance to the original model or using models altogether alternative to the melody as the basis for inventing new phrases. These artistic episodes can occur at various points in a performance, as when players add short melodic figures in such static areas of tunes as rests or sustained pitches at the ends of phrases. Additionally, if the player carrying the melody is the first soloist in the group, he or she may depart from the melody before its completion to improvise a musical segue to the solo. In other instances, an individual improvises an introduction to the piece before the group's entrance, or a cadenza at the piece's conclusion, or a short "break" passage, during which the other players suspend their performance. Jazz compositions like "Oleo," having chord progressions with only partial melodies, provide space for the player to improvise passages for either a couple of measures or a major harmonic segment of the piece during the melody's presentation. Moreover, some compositions consist of chord progressions alone at the time they are recorded. Pieces like Lester Young's "Jumpin' with Symphony Sid" and Charlie Parker's "Meandering" and "Bird Gets the Worm" required the extemporaneous invention of an entire melody in performance. Typically, however, players restrain themselves during the melody's formal presentation, reserving their most extensive compositional activity for improvised solos.[17]

At the same time, the combined operations from interpretation to improvisation have the potential to "carry musicians more than halfway to creating a new song" within the framework of another melody (LK). Such situations underscore the extent to which pieces serve jazz musicians not simply as ends in themselves but as vehicles for invention.[18] Just as these procedures, taken in sequence, provide artists with a routine for practicing pieces, their sequential mastery corresponds, for some artists, to the progressive stages of their development. As a youngster, trumpeter Warren Kime first learned the "melodies of a lot of tunes" from his father, a professional musician. "After I had been play-ing the melodies straight for awhile," Kime recalls, "I started making little embellishments around them. Gradually, my embellishments became more ex-tensive, and eventually I learned how to improvise." Excerpts from transcribed performances of jazz compositions illustrate the differing emphases that artists place on these practices, accounting for the distinguishing features of rendi-tions and, in turn, providing students with alternative models for their own versions (exx. 3.3b–d). Gary Bartz would routinely purchase records "of the same song by many different artists" and analyze their different approaches.[19]

## Learning the Harmonic Basis for Tunes

Learners must also master the chord progression of each piece as a funda-mental guideline because of its roles in suggesting tonal material for the mel-ody's treatment and in shaping invention to its harmonic-rhythmic scheme.[20] Players liken a progression to a road map for charting the precise melodic course of a rendition. The importance of such a consideration, however, is not always clear to beginners who have yet to confront their naive notions about improvisation. When Lonnie Hillyer was a young teenager, he imagined that if he could only muster the courage to join a renowned musician on the band-stand, inspiration would carry him through the event. Pursuing his family's acquaintanceship with Miles Davis, Hillyer obtained an invitation to sit in with Davis's band. He laughs ruefully as he recalls losing his place after the first eight bars and how brutally thereafter each pitch of his impassioned perfor-mance clashed with the band. When the dismal solo finally aborted, Davis pulled him off the stage and grumbled hoarsely, "You don't know your chords, do you?" When Hillyer confessed to this, Davis told him not to return to the club until he had mastered harmony.

Students with natural gifts and special musical backgrounds have a great advantage in learning the harmonic basis of pieces. By the age of three or four, prodigies with perfect pitch can already comprehend the precise mixture of elements that make up the distinct structures of chords, and they can anticipate their place within a piece's larger repeating progression. Roberta Baum used to "wait excitedly for the key changes in music performances"; the alternating chords thrilled her. In part, she remembered the piece's events through visual and emotional imagery so lively that they entered her mind's eye as cartoon dancers stretching and spinning in space, "doing incredible things." Long be-fore Patti Bown acquired a technical knowledge of music she amazed family members, friends, and local band leaders by her ability to remember the com-posite sounds of chords on jazz and classical music recordings and reproduce their movements at the piano.

Carmen Lundy cultivated her harmonic sensibilities at rehearsals of her mother's gospel choir. Immersed in exuberant performances of hymns, she assimilated the music's inner and outer voices, learning to appreciate their vertical blends as well as their independent horizontal attributes as lines. Eventually, singing the harmonizing alto lines held more appeal for her than did singing the soprano melodies, "which seemed so obvious." Later, Lundy found jazz equally intriguing. Its melodies and harmonies seemed to her to be extensions of the church music she had already learned. Lundy also recalls the revelation that certain jazz pieces were "the same structurally" as blues pieces by artists like Leadbelly, Big Mama Thornton, and Lightnin' Hopkins, artists whom her mother "always listened to at home."

Pianists and guitarists commonly learn about chords as part of their early instruction. They become well practiced in apprehending harmony because even the simplest repertory exploits the capacity of their respective instruments to combine melody and accompaniment. Youngsters whose melody instruments lack the capacity to perform multiple pitches simultaneously sometimes lag behind their friends in harmonic development. Those who have difficulty hearing chords commonly adopt piano as a second instrument, providing them with the key to harmonic understanding.[21]

The accompanying role that some single-note instruments play in jazz groups, of outlining the forms of compositions with linear arrangements of pitches derived from the underlying chords, compensates students for their early deficiencies. "All the time I was playing the trumpet in high school, I could never really relate my knowledge about chords to improvising a melody line," says Rufus Reid. "The association never clicked for me until I learned the string bass and had to deal directly with playing chord progressions." Curtis Fuller adds that because the trombone was a "tailgate instrument that played a moving bass line in groups, I had to deal with chord progressions from the start."

Although distinguishing their more gradual development from that of prodigies, many other players also describe learning chords and the structures of compositions by ear, before receiving formal musical training. Doc Cheatham absorbed structural elements in a piece "step by step" as he "went along, playing in carnival bands and other groups." Under his high school band leader's guidance, David Baker gained experience singing the root movements of chord progressions and imitating the sounds of chord patterns with his instrument. As discussed earlier, learning by ear commonly entails more complex impressions. Students conceptualize the successive sound clusters of harmonic forms as mapped out in particular positions on instruments, and as visual images of abstract designs whose colors and tints may represent different shadings of harmonic tension. These kinetic and visual conceptualizations serve as mnemonics for harmony for musicians at whatever level of knowledge (ex. 3.4).

Although some artists remain ear and hand players, many others eventually supplement their knowledge with a theoretical understanding of harmony. After Kenny Barron had been "playing tunes by ear for a while," his older brother Bill "worked through them" with him methodically, going over all the chord changes and teaching him their symbols and names. Melba Liston learned theory in her junior high school music youth group, whereas Arthur Rhames studied harmony directly with jazz musician Gigi Gryce, who worked periodically as a substitute teacher at Rhames's high school. Benny Bailey recalls pianist John Lewis's daily theory seminars for members of Dizzy Gillespie's big band aboard a ship bound for their European tour in 1947.

Improvisers also grasp basic harmonic principles from college textbooks about Western classical music theory and commercial manuals recommended by jazz community members. When Lonnie Hillyer failed in his early efforts to sit in with Miles Davis's band, Davis directed him to "a chord book." Tommy Turrentine remembers that in the forties a textbook by Percy Goetschius was known among some jazz musicians as the "Bible of Harmony." Turrentine adds the important caveat that "the rules of harmony are meant to be broken, and these guys did it. They learned the theory of Western harmony, and then they went for themselves!" Musicians accomplished this by adapting the language and symbols of Western harmony to the harmonic conventions of the tradition of jazz and to their own musical styles. Over the years Western music theory books such as those by Paul Hindemith and Walter Piston have also served as learning aids, supplemented by theory texts specifically devoted to jazz.[22]

One of the benefits of theory is the shorthand it provides musicians for talking about harmony and for representing the structure of compositions in written form. J. J. Johnson used to "write out a couple of new chord progressions" for Curtis Fuller whenever Johnson performed in Fuller's locale and they could "hang out together." Lou Donaldson routinely "pulled the coat of the pianists" with whom he performed at nightclubs to obtain the chords to the complicated sections of particular compositions. "There were some jam sessions with Eddie 'Lockjaw' Davis, in which he played so much stuff, it was terrible," he recalls with mock horror. "If Lockjaw was playing tunes I wasn't familiar with, there was no way in the world you could get me up on the bandstand with him. I wouldn't ask him anything because, at the time, I didn't want him to know that I didn't know the tune. But when the gig was over, I would catch the piano players like Walter Bishop and Red Garland, and they would tell me. It was a great learning experience."

One system of theory classification and terminology commonly used in Western music provides a language for naming the constituent elements that give different types of chords (major triads, minor triads, major seventh chords, seventh chords, etc.) their particular qualities. Musicians commonly identify each chord with a capital letter describing the pitch that serves as its root. In addition, roman numerals serve as a form of chord identification and analysis, describing a chord's relationship to the tonic; upper case signifies a major quality, and lower case a minor quality. Finally, beside the letter of each chord or its roman numeral are arabic numbers describing additional elements or tensions that supplement the basic triad. Artists name them in terms of their numerical positions in a stack of thirds build up from the chord's root, either diatonically (in the initial key) or with chromatic alterations. Reflecting the conventions of the past several decades, chords typically include selective mixtures of the pitches of a major or minor triad (the first, third, and fifth degrees of its related scale), the triad's diatonic upper extensions or tensions (its seventh, ninth, eleventh and thirteenth degrees), and the triad's altered extensions (its flatted-ninth, raised-ninth,[23] raised-eleventh, and flatted-thirteenth degrees).

Familiarizing themselves with theory, students also learn to distinguish the functions of different chords and their harmonic activity within progressions. In their most fundamental function, chords create tension or provide release. Artists commonly view the tonic chord (I) as being the most stable, and the dominant (V7) as the most unstable. Every kind of movement between and among chords creates its own effect and contributes to the music's flow. Radical departures from the progression's initial key dramatically increase harmonic tension; direct returns unequivocally resolve the tension. Other patterns created by diminished and augmented chords are more ambiguous in their temporary suspension of harmonic motion.

Yet other movements are indirect, delaying resolution with a fleeting scheme of passage through different tonal centers before returning to the piece's tonic key. When dominant chords built on scale degrees other than the fifth resolve up by a fourth to major or minor chords, for example, they create new areas of relative stability away from the tonic and perform a "tonic or resolution function." When dominant chords move to other dominant chords, they perform a "dominant or tension function" and sustain or redirect harmonic tension to further points of resolution. In fact, transient tonalities at times may lead far away from the fundamental key without ever actually establishing a new one. They are simply elaborations upon basic diatonic progressions.[24] The unique character of a composition's overall progression derives from its length and arrangement of successive harmonic areas, each defined, in turn, by its tonal center, its relative duration, and the qualities and precise root movement of its chords.

Whereas theory simply reinforces aural understanding of such features for some performers, it assists others to enter the world of musical forms. At one of his workshops, saxophonist Billy Mitchell distributed copies of a lead sheet and suggested that students tap to the beat of his band's performance to follow the chords from measure to measure over the progression. With each pass through the piece's cycle, the class endeavored to memorize the individual sounds of the chords together with their symbols. Eventually, they could follow the progression's features, as interpreted by the band, without referring to the lead sheet. "In the beginning I couldn't hear the chords," a participant recalled. "I couldn't feel where the chords changed in a piece. Today, I might not be able to identify all the chords in the tunes I hear, but I can hear it when they do change, and that's a big step from where I started" (GL).

Once students develop the capability of distinguishing and naming chords, they can more readily augment their understanding of compositional form on their own. When listening to a live performance, they strive to apprehend the piano and bass accompaniment in relation to the melody, creating a mental picture or representational map of the structure of each piece from its combined parts. Similarly, when learning a composition from records, John Hicks initially memorizes its melody and reproduces it at the piano; then he copies the bass line's "counterpoint to the melody." After learning to play the two outer voices together, he works on the pitches in between them in an effort to match the music's precise blend. For many, the process is largely "a matter of trial and error, trying out different pitches until you get as close as you can to the quality of the chords" (KB).

Over the years, various methods have prevailed. Just as Bix Beiderbecke slowed the speed of his record player, "a wind-up Columbia graphophone," to learn compositions by the Original Dixieland Jazz Band, Duke Ellington slowed the play of piano rolls so that he could copy renditions like those James P. Johnson made of "Carolina Shout." [25] So painstaking is the nature of this practice that Lou Donaldson and his band members once "scuffled around for about six months" learning pieces like "Sepian Bounce" and "Jumpin' the Blues" from Jay McShann recordings. They played them repeatedly and "wore them right down to their aluminum bases." A few generations later, Wynton Marsalis participated in comparable sessions with his brother, saxophonist Branford Marsalis, to analyze the structure of recorded compositions of Miles Davis and Wayne Shorter. Within Tommy Flanagan's early study groups, when he and his friends encountered complex compositions that eluded their powers of aural analysis, "whoever had enough money to buy the sheet music" would do so and share it with the others.

Musicians who cannot afford sheet music or record players adopt methods even more taxing, striving to memorize compositions as others performed them. During the twenties, some artists routinely requested performances of popular pieces from the pianists who worked as sheet music demonstrators at music stores. Pops Foster "used to pick up ideas from everybody. Sometimes I would find an alley guitar player, playing only blues, and give him a quarter to play all those pretty chords they used to go through." [26]

In the forties, Jimmy Robinson sat by the household radio with trumpet in hand waiting to catch a few additional pitches from the periodic replay of new pieces on jazz programs. Kenny Barron learned several Horace Silver compositions during school recesses by running back and forth between his family's piano and a local diner's jukebox. With each excursion, Barron extended the previous portion of a melody or altered a chord, eventually figuring out an entire composition. Beyond the immediate rewards of repertory expansion, it is hard to imagine a more rigorous training for cultivating the skills of musical apprehension and musical memory.

### Differing Harmonic Prototypes

The succession of forms that students learn commonly begins with the blues, one of the most venerable vehicles in the jazz repertory. Buster Williams and Don Pate learned about the blues from their fathers, bassists Charlie Williams and Johnny Pate. One of the simplest blues forms is a twelve-bar progression in which three triads are arranged in three four-bar phrases or harmonic chunks (fig. 3.1). In its general scheme, the stable tonic or I chord of the blues alternates first with its related subdominant or IV chord, whose root is an interval of a fourth above the tonic, and then with its related dominant or V chord, whose root is an interval of a fifth above the tonic. This highest point of harmonic tension is finally resolved by a return to the tonic at the progression's close. As discussed further in this chapter, more elaborate jazz blues follows the same basic pattern. Having learned the blues, young musicians study more expansive pieces like "I Got Rhythm," in which two eight-bar chord sequences—an A section and a B section—are arranged to produce a thirty-two bar progression in the AABA format typical of many American popular songs. Students also discover that other pieces comprise thirty-two-bar progressions whose eight-bar components form such common arrangements as ABAB' or ABAC (figs. 3.2–3.4).

Some youngsters are initially mystified by the concept of a B section, known as the bridge, channel, release, or inside. Its harmonic design differs markedly from that of the A section and commonly involves fleeting movements through a succession of different tonalities. David Baker remembers how "ecstatic" he and Slide Hampton were, as youngsters, the day they "found

Figure 3.1   Simple blues progression

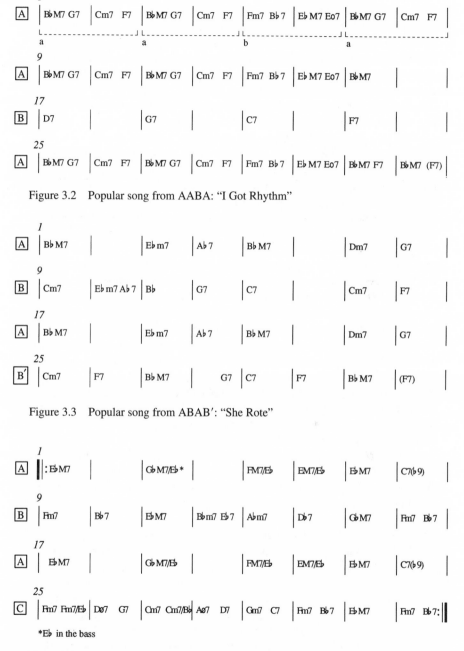

Figure 3.2   Popular song from AABA: "I Got Rhythm"

Figure 3.3   Popular song from ABAB′: "She Rote"

Figure 3.4   Popular song from ABAC: "On Green Dolphin Street"

77

out that a tune could have a bridge. For the next month or so, we played thinking they all had the same bridge." Art Farmer retrospectively imagines Roy
Eldridge's incredulity upon hearing Farmer's teenage band play a unique version of "Rhythm" before they "knew that it had a [specific] bridge" and performed "any old thing" in its place. A veteran once scolded the young Barry
Harris on the opposite count. Although Harris understood the B section of
"Rhythm," he was oblivious to the A section and simply substituted a twelve-
bar "chorus of blues changes in its place"—creating an expansive forty-four-
bar rendition overall. John Hicks's first version of "A Night in Tunisia" unwittingly deleted the bridge altogether. He also "couldn't understand the bridge of
some compositions like Bud Powell's 'Parisian Thoroughfare,' so," he recollects, "I never attempted any solos on it until later. It was a simple thing, a
I–vi–ii–V in A major, but I just wasn't into it at the time."

As students become more familiar with jazz repertory, they develop a
comparative perspective on its forms. In Chuck Israels's experience, an "essential ingredient in learning to be a musician is the ability to recognize a parallel
case when you're confronted with one. If things remind you of other pieces
when you approach a new piece," he states, "you generally catalogue them very
quickly so that you can draw upon your accumulated knowledge." Israels's high
school peers cultivated their skills by playing "musical games" with recordings
in which they tested one another's abilities to identify pieces from their progressions alone and "relate them" to other pieces. Such activities teach students
that, despite the unique melodies of compositions, some pieces share their entire underlying structure in common. Sonny Rollins's "Oleo" and Charlie Parker's "Anthropology" are based on "I Got Rhythm." Parker's "Donna Lee" is
based on "Indiana"; his "Bird Gets the Worm" is based on "Lover Come Back
to Me"; "Warming Up a Riff" on "Cherokee"; "Marmaduke" on "Honeysuckle
Rose." There are countless examples.[27]

The progressions of other compositions differ overall, although they share
many of the same harmonic chunks or structural building blocks. "The first
four bars of 'Can't Get Started' are the same as the first four bars of 'I Love
You, Porgy,'" Walter Bishop Jr. explains, "and the first eight bars of 'Body and
Soul' are the same as those of 'Nancy (with the Laughing Face).'" Recognizing comparable relationships between and among compositions commonly
suggests directions for the expansion of repertories. John Hicks initially gravi-
tated toward Horace Silver compositions based on the blues and on popular
pieces like "I Got Rhythm" and "There Will Never Be Another You," whose
"moving patterns of seventh chords" he had little difficulty recognizing. Hicks
found Fats Domino's boogie-woogie compositions to be especially accessible
because their prominent bass lines outlined the blues progression. The oscillat-
ing E♭ and B♭ chords of Thelonious Monk's "Bye-ya" reminded him of the
blues as well, although the song was not in a strict blues format. Similarly, Josh

Schneider first learned "simple blues changes," then "jazz blues changes" that he describes as "the same as the basic blues, but with a few additional chords thrown in. I now think of everything as a blues pretty much. Every tune is just made up of different turnarounds [harmonic cadences] that resolve to different places."

For many youngsters, newly acquired theoretical concepts constitute "exciting breakthroughs," which assist them in generalizing about such features of pieces. Not only do they learn to recognize chords of the same quality as they recur in different parts of the composition, but they begin to appreciate their relationships to adjacent chords, apprehending them as discrete groupings or movements—the component chunks of the composition's larger A, B, and C sections. Among the most common movements found in compositions are short diatonic patterns like the ii7–V7–I7 progression (in the key of C: Dm7–G7–CM7) and its components ii7–V7 and V7–I7, whose root motion descends partly around the circle of fifths. Larger recurring harmonic gestures embodying comparable elements include the "I Got Rhythm" turnaround, I7–VI7–ii7–V7, and such progressions as III7–VI7–II7–V7, v7–I7–IV–IV (altered), and many others.[28]

Further probing reveals that harmonic gestures like ii–V movements may repeat at the same pitch level in different parts of a piece's structure, or they may repeat at different pitch levels, forming sequences that venture briefly outside the tonic key of the piece to tonicize other keys temporarily. Within the larger progressions of many standards, sequences of this nature are commonly linked by movements of descending fifths or seconds and ascending thirds. Unusual compositions like John Coltrane's "Giant Steps" are comprised entirely of ii–V–I patterns arranged in an unusual scheme of ascending and descending movements of major thirds and augmented fifths (fig. 3.5).

Through analysis, students also come to grasp the building blocks of form on different hierarchical levels. In "I Got Rhythm," for example, the ii–V pattern, Cm7–F7, comprises a component of the tune's initial two-bar progression: B♭M7–G7–Cm7–F7. The recurring motion of this progression surrounds the two-bar Fm7–B♭7–E♭M7–E°7 movement in measures 5 and 6, creating an eight-bar harmonic phrase whose components are arranged as aaba (fig. 3.2). This internal design represents a microcosm of the piece's larger structure in which the opening eight-bar phrase becomes the A component of the thirty-two-bar AABA progression.

Students familiarizing themselves with the common harmonic building blocks, their root motion, and their organization into larger schemes can reconcile the initially perplexing relationship between various blues progressions and more complex popular song forms by interpreting their different features as variants of one another. Fred Hersch eventually concluded that "there were as few as ten or so different harmonic patterns" whose combinations and varia-

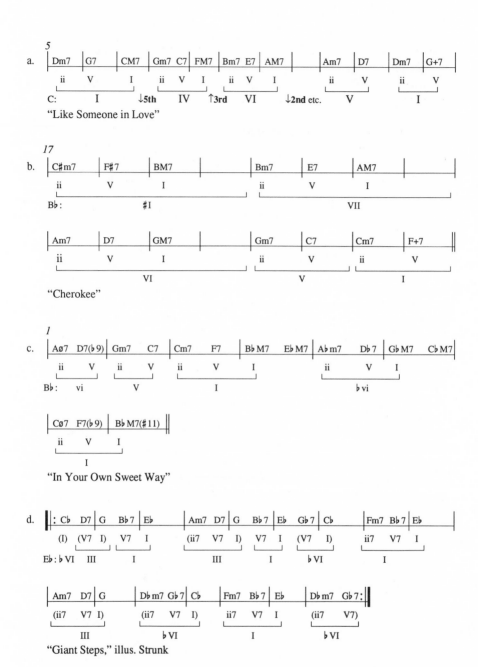

Figure 3.5  ii–V–I progression within different compositions

tions formed the basis for much of the repertory of jazz standards.[29] Graphic representations portraying the harmonic structure of different compositions illustrate the creation of unique progressions, in part, through various arrangements of common harmonic components (ex. 3.5). From piece to piece, subtle chord alterations add distinctiveness to the components, as does stretching or compressing their harmonic rhythm. Over the course of each progression, movement from the tonic through the circle of fifths creates increasing tension that peaks at the dominant chord and resolves with a return to the tonic.

While students grapple with these matters and develop repertories on their own, they also amplify their understanding of harmony and compositions through interacting with other musicians on the bandstand. Many even have the courage to sit in with bands during unfamiliar numbers, learning new pieces, in effect, by performing them. This involves the potentially dizzying activity of analyzing the surrounding parts to formulate a map of the progression's fundamental features at the very time they are inventing an appropriate part for themselves.

Toward such ends, Rufus Reid strove to improvise a bass line to complement the pianist's chord movements, which he anticipated on the basis of his "general knowledge of harmony." Whenever Reid's pitch choices clashed with the piano part, or whenever he lost his place within the progression, he would "[lay] out for a moment," put the bass to his ear, and softly experiment with different pitches, looking perhaps for the elusive key of the bridge. Reid then continued his bass line until stumped by another "questionable part of the progression." Each time through the piece, he would figure out additional details that had eluded him and fix their positions within his evolving map. After initially roughing out the placement of major and minor triads, "the main pivot points of things," Reid eventually filled in the piece's complete form. In this regard, the first challenge he encountered in his early development was learning to distinguish aurally major and minor triads, the "big letters," he called them at the time. Having mastered them, Reid could turn his attention to more complex structures. "I even think it took a long time before I could really understand a major-seven function [as distinct] from a dominant-seven function," he admits.

Some musicians infer the structure during performances from the bass pitches in the pianist's own bass lines or chord voicings—either identifying the pitches aurally or reading the keys depressed by the fingers of the pianist's left hand. Reid recalls a remarkably adroit mentor who, whenever the harmonic rhythm of a piece allowed, would sustain the sound of his chord with the pedal so that he could raise his little finger from the keyboard and point toward the next bass pitch, thus guiding Reid's anticipation of the chord change. In other instances, newcomers receive direct verbal coaching. Upon hearing Kenny Barron's harmonic errors at a jam session, for example, a kindly veteran once approached him from the audience, stood discreetly beside the piano, and whispered the piece's correct chords.

In the final analysis, it is performance that reinforces the musician's grasp on a new piece. George Duvivier learned chord changes "through sheer repetition, doing it so often, it became like breathing." Many ultimately develop the ability to imagine progressions outside of performance with the same assurance as recalling melodies. "You start with a simple blues and keep doing it over, memorizing the basic chords, getting them into your psyche. Eventually, you get into the habit of hearing the chords inside your head, in the inner ear" (PB). Certain jazz compositions are "so ingrained" in Gary Bartz's memory, he says, that even after a lapse of ten years, "I only need to hear a tune once and its harmonic structure comes back to me."

## The Malleability of Form

The learner's first version of a piece is commonly a discrete chord progression based on a particular oral or written model. With exposure to different renditions, however, students soon discover that experts transform the harmonic structures of a piece as routinely as they do their melodies. Artists make decisions about certain harmonic features during private sessions and rehearsals, fixing them as part of their formal musical arrangements. They determine other features immediately before music events or while actually performing.

Because the operations of seasoned musicians include the melodic transposition of compositions, youngsters embark on the correspondingly arduous course of learning to reproduce the relative movements of a composition's progression in every key. Many grapple with these challenges early in their professional lives as they encounter bands that avoid comparatively standard versions of pieces to exploit their varied moods and distinct qualities in alternative tonic keys. Additionally, because of the effects of transposition on a melody's range, singers select keys that are most comfortable for their vocal range. "Some sing 'Star Dust' in E," George Duvivier notes humorously, "when everyone else on the planet plays it in D♭." At sessions, moreover, musicians commonly test one another's skills by performing pieces "through all the keys," modulating by descending half steps or by ascending fourths with each chorus. "Every day, I would get hung up on something else," says Walter Bishop Jr., recounting the anguish of such computations, "but I always left those sessions resolving that I wouldn't return until I really knew the tune so that I would never be embarrassed like that again. That's how I built up my repertory."

Youngsters also find out that actual chords are subject to variation—a considerable surprise to those who initially learn the most basic forms of chords as immutable structures. One pianist remembers her early puzzlement when a musician presented her with a tune's lead sheet at a session and told her "to do something interesting" with the chords. "At the time, I just played them the way I learned them, but for days afterwards, I kept wondering what he meant by that." It was also a "great discovery" for Carmen Lundy when "real jazz buffs taught me about such things as seventh and ninth chords or altered chords. Up till then, I had only been playing triads."

Advanced performers draw upon numerous pitch collections in creating their own personal versions or voicings of chords, leaving unchanged their fundamental character or their function within a progression. For the composer and learner respectively, constructing and interpreting voicings involve consideration of endless combinations and permutations of related pitches. The exploration of each chord's inversions, for example, alters the interval arrangements created from chord elements, changing their placement and spacing in the upper and middle parts of chord structures as well as their prominent positions in the bass. Pitch reinforcement in different octaves through the use of doubling also creates different effects.

As a matter of personal taste and other factors discussed later in this work, artists may, at times, emphasize voicings that are spare, utilizing perhaps only two elements of the chord such as its third and seventh or its root and third. Alternatively, they may emphasize voicings that are rich, combining many chord elements and chromatically altered pitches. Some may prefer to create airy structures, leaving open space between chord elements and spreading them over two or more octaves; others may favor dense, thickly textured voicings using pitch doubling. Adding further distinctiveness are such features as emphasis on right-hand (treble clef) or left-hand (bass clef) formulations or their combination; emphasis on wide or close intervals (for example, clusters including seconds) or various mixtures; and emphasis on rootless or root-oriented voicings, the latter presenting the root in the bass or, more subtly, in another voice. Grace note embellishment also gives voicings a special character, in some instances, creating blues effects by moving between the flat third and the natural third (ex. 3.6a). Even in the realization of a single chord type, the possibilities seem endless (exx. 3.6b–c). "Probably the most frustrating thing was trying to figure out the hipper voicings from records," Kenny Barron says. "It was no problem for me to get the basic character of the chords, to figure out what chords were minor or major, but you can drive yourself crazy trying to figure out the notes in between the bass notes and the treble notes."

Rootless voicings compound such challenges, requiring players to infer the character of a chord from the pianist's elusive mix of other chord tones and color tones, or from the bass player's part which commonly includes the root. In fact, difficulties in apprehending chords and learning a composition's structure from a recording or a performance can produce inadvertent variants among players. Demonstration frequently compensates for these differences. According to Kenny Barron, "At sessions, people would sometimes sit down at the piano and say, 'Why don't you try putting a flat nine in that chord and voicing it like this?' " Tommy Turrentine "copped voicings" by watching Barry Harris when he played, and sometimes he simply asked him directly, "What was that thing you did on such and such a chord?"

Besides representing a particular version or model of a composition's progression with different voicings, players may decorate its structure with embellishing chords, enlivening the piece's harmonically static segments. Such practices are reminiscent of those within the realm of melodic treatment by which soloists embellish and vary pieces. Typical embellishing techniques described by pianist Bill Dobbins include stepwise motion created by the addition of diatonic or chromatic neighbor chords (exx. 3.7a–b) and passing chords between the structural chords. Neighbor chords move away from and back to the structural chord; passing chords connect different inversions of the structural chord. When alternating a diminished seventh chord and a chromatic embellishing chord, improvisers can also create dramatic appoggiatura-like motion between them by approaching the embellishing chord from an interval of a third or larger and resolving the dissonance through chromatic movement in the opposite direction.[30] For novices, apprehending the sounds of structural chords amid the surrounding motion of embellishing chords can itself require intense training.

This is by no means the extent of the youngster's dilemma, moreover, for seasoned improvisers also commonly transform features of their model of a piece's actual harmonic plan. While retaining its conventional rhythmic cycle, players ornament core movements with different types of chord substitutions, drawing, in part, on an elaborate rule system, only sampled here, whose structures and procedures have been passed from generation to generation among jazz artists.[31] Curtis Fuller considers options for substitute chords to be harmonic family members with ties of varying degrees of closeness from "first cousins . . . to fifth or sixth cousins." Dobbins describes as "harmonic alteration" one type of substitution that keeps the original root but adds diatonic extensions or chromatic alterations or changes the quality of the chord. Examples of the latter practice would be changing a dominant seventh to a minor seventh or a major seventh to a dominant seventh (exx. 3.8a–b).

The artist also has the option of substituting a new chord with a different root for the original chord (exx. 3.9a–b). Chords can usually serve as effective replacements for one another when they are closely enough related through common tones to perform the same function within the piece's structure, preserving "essential lines of the original progression."[32] At times, substitute chords can have the effect of modifying a distinctive portion of the conventional progression, as when minor chords substitute for diminished chords.

A third approach to substitution is "harmonic insertion," adding connecting chords between those in the original progression. As for embellishing chords, harmonic insertion chords are commonly used to break up the static harmony of a piece's form, but they accomplish this through more radical movements away from the structural chords. Insertion chords can be a basic ii–V movement anticipating a structural chord or an elaborate sequence between structural chords (exx. 3.10a–b). At times, players introduce distinctive features to the progression by inserting a diminished chord for color or producing blues effects by alternating a structural chord containing a natural third with an insertion chord containing the flatted third (ex. 3.11). Artists commonly use the terms *turnarounds* or *turnbacks* when referring to insertion chords found at the end of either a major harmonic phrase or a complete chorus. Typically, they are excursions of four chords that lead back to the initial chord, providing a smooth transition to the next harmonic phrase or returning to the start of the progression (fig. 3.6).

Chord insertions, changes of chord quality, and chord extensions create effects easily observable by comparing a common jazz blues to a basic model (ex. 3.5). The jazz version enriches the basic root progression by replacing some triads with seventh chords and inserting new chords into previously static harmonic segments. In measures 11 through 12, this creates an "I Got Rhythm" turnaround and provides greater harmonic motion throughout. Similarly, a comparison of the same bars of compositions as represented in different lead sheet versions illustrates principles of harmonic transformation (fig. 3.7). This

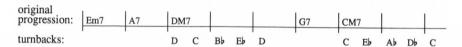

| original progression: | Em7 | A7 | DM7 | | | | G7 | CM7 | | |
|---|---|---|---|---|---|---|---|---|---|---|
| turnbacks: | | | D | C | Bb | Eb | D | C | Eb Ab Db C |

Figure 3.6   Harmonic turnbacks (illus. Baker)

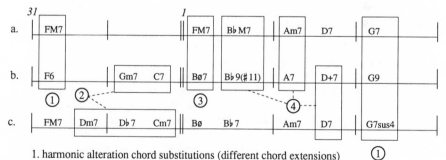

1. harmonic alteration chord substitutions (different chord extensions)   ①
2. harmonic insertion chord substitutions
3. chord substitutions with different roots
4. harmonic alteration chord substitutions (change of chord quality)

Figure 3.7   Lead sheet samples of alternative harmony ("I Thought about You")

is also true of scanning the alternative courses adopted by accompanists on different groups' recordings of the same piece (ex. 3.3c).

Selecting from their varied options, artists pursue the goal of designing an imaginative, graceful version of the progression that clearly delineates the piece. Enumerable conventions within the jazz tradition guide players. Pianists endeavor to formulate successive structures that involve minimal movement in the left hand and create a sense of melodic shape and flow in the upper voice of the changing chords. They commonly resolve chord extensions and chromatic alterations, and the like, by leading them through descending steps to the triadic pitches of subsequent chords.[33] As is implicit in the discussion of harmonic practice above, the jazz community also values the formulation of a strong, smooth root movement. Moreover, the appropriateness of the bass line "as a counterpoint to the original melody" is of special importance to artists like Bill Evans, inspiring them to create unique harmonic designs for compositions, even those sharing the same basic progression (CI). Joe Giudice, too, considers "the melody and the bass line to be the most important features of my arrangements of pieces. After putting the melody note on top of a chord, I'll spend months working on a small harmonic section of the progression— trying out different chord substitutions until I've found the ones that produce the most beautiful bass lines and the most intricate inner voices."

To achieve this through chord insertions, players may choose to precede a major, minor, dominant, or half-diminished chord in a progression by a dominant chord whose root is either a fifth or a half step above that of the structural chord or by a diminished chord whose root is a half step below it. Connecting chords generally create such desirable root motion as descending fifths or major thirds or ascending diatonic scale steps or minor thirds. Other popular movements feature a series of descending half steps or whole steps, or alternating half steps and whole steps.[34]

George Duvivier learned about these and comparable matters from Clyde Hart, the pianist in Coleman Hawkins's band. Hart was a "wonderful arranger" and a "kind, gentle, human being," he says.

> And whenever I did anything wrong on the bandstand, he'd look at me and wink. And when the gig was over, he'd say, "Come by the house tomorrow afternoon." . . . He'd sit down and play the piano and explain this and that . . . [and] would say, "Tomorrow night, let's do this here [in the progression]. . . . For example, say you're going from an Ab[m]7 to a Db. Assuming that he had time, he would run cycles like Bbm [to] Eb[7], A[m] to D[7], Ab[m] to Db. And no one was doing that then. They'd say Ab[m] for four beats: ding, ding, ding, ding; Db[7] for four beats. . . . [In three months with Hawkins's band] I learned to play jazz in all keys. I learned all the tempos and a lot of harmonic things I'd never come across before.

    If artists sometimes restrict their application of chord substitutions to lo-
calized portions of progressions, at other times they freshen their renditions by
replacing larger harmonic segments such as bridges. Doc Cheatham recalls
how bored he became with hearing seemingly endless repetitions of stereotyped bridges on some popular standards and show tunes. "But," he adds,
"Dizzy really straightened out jazz," by inventing new bridges for pieces like
"I Got Rhythm." In yet other instances, elaborate substitutions permeate an
entire progression, imbuing it with a continuous sense of harmonic motion.[35]
Harold Ousley and Barry Harris describe an exemplary one having many chord
sequences in which artists change chords nearly every bar (fig. 3.8). Beyond
their initial design of a particular version of a progression, over the course of
performance improvisers continually select from among the options at their
disposal. As they reinterpret the form, they can give it a very different complexion. Through combined or selected operations of embellishing the principal
chords and engaging in chord substitution, including changing chords' harmonic qualities, they can either accentuate or elaborate selected features of the
progression. Alternatively, they could remain close to the basic structure or
simplify its features (exx. 3.12a–b).
    Extensive transformations can require major readjustment on the young
musician's part. Once, to assist me in learning "Oleo," a pianist recorded two
takes of his own performance of the piece and encouraged me to study them.
Listening repeatedly to the first, I gradually absorbed the spare, relatively consistent chord changes that made up the version's contrasting A and B sections
and mapped out their larger arrangement within the piece's form. Feeling secure in my understanding of the piece, I proceeded to track the harmonic
course of the second version. But there I received a rude shock: I began to feel
as if I had entered an awesome and alien musical forest, a dense harmonic
environment whose features changed more quickly than I could grasp them,
presenting alternative routes consisting of root movements and successive
qualities of chords that I could neither anticipate nor follow.
    With repeated listening, fragmentary harmonic movements embedded
within the new version gradually became familiar. I could also recognize that,
at various pivotal points of harmony, the alternate progression momentarily

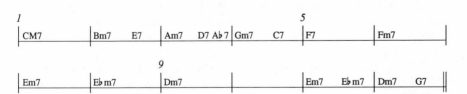

Figure 3.8    Elaborate blues progression

incorporated a chord from the first version, then departed from it. As my ear grasped these familiar aural landmarks and fixed their positions within my original map of the piece, I began to appreciate the chord substitutions as embellishing, rather than obscuring, the basic structure. Only after weeks of concentrated study did the second take of "Oleo" become as familiar to me as the first, and both assumed clearly related identities as two versions of the same piece.

### Deepening Knowledge of Repertory and Original Composition

With a growing appreciation for the malleability of melody and form in the jazz tradition, learners become less bewildered in the face of a piece's disparate written and oral/aural renditions. Collectively, the versions are models for realizing the piece's infinite possibilities surrounding the core of features that comprise its essence. Just as musicians infer the core from the patterns shared by many performances, they also note the varying subtleties of melodic embellishment, rhythmic phrasing, and chord movement that distinguish each rendition. Artists acquire options for their own performances by cataloguing the variants at corresponding positions within their flexible conceptual maps of pieces.

In part, new versions represent a unique fusion of attractive traits borrowed from other versions. For a period of time when John Hicks played with Pharoah Sanders, the band "used Benny Carter's bridge for the composition 'When Lights Are Low.'" Subsequently, they "cornered" Tommy Flanagan in Stockholm one summer and "ran the changes down, and we all messed around and played it in a few different keys and whatnot and got comfortable with it." Another well-known example is "'Round Midnight," composed by Thelonious Monk in 1944 and first recorded by Cootie Williams. According to some accounts, Williams added embellishments to the melody during the recording session. Consequently, his embellishments were incorporated as formal features of the melody when sheet music renditions were produced based on the recorded version. Subsequently, when Dizzy Gillespie recorded the piece in 1946, he added to its form an eight-measure introduction and coda that he had originally used as the coda of his version of "I Can't Get Started." By 1955, after the "imported introduction" had itself become a standard feature among renditions by various artists—including Monk himself—Miles Davis personalized the composition further by adding a three-measure interlude to the end of the first chorus, which other artists subsequently adopted as a formal part of the composition.[36]

As implied above, cross-fertilization within the larger jazz repertory contributes additional features to new renditions. Musicians can alter a piece by applying the general principles learned from analyzing a variety of pieces or substituting the precise features of another. One version of "Honeysuckle Rose" has replaced its standard bridge with the bridge to "I Got Rhythm."

Finally, aspiring musicians replenish their models by experimenting, sometimes at the urging of mentors. Although veterans can be generous initially, they expect their demonstrations to be but a point of departure for learners' independent initiatives in pursuit of a personal style. One novice was rebuffed when he resisted such work and pressed an expert for more material. "My voicings are my voicings," his friend replied roughly, "and I've already shown you enough to get you started. Go off and find your own voicings the same way I did, just by sitting at the piano and trying them all kinds of ways until you find the ones you like" (HL). Similarly, when a youngster once attempted to please an early teacher by patterning faithfully upon his interpretation of a ballad's melody, taped at the preceding lesson, his teacher responded with annoyance: "That's my way of playing it. You were supposed to find *your* way of playing it."

Once students experience the excitement and satisfaction that accompanies their own discoveries, they are less willing to depend on other oral or written sources or to be bound strictly by the conventional rules that had assisted them initially. The more Fred Hersch "learned tunes from sheet music," the more compelled he felt to make up his own voicings. "You have to be able to hear chords your own way," he insists. "It's better than someone else telling you what to do and just formulaically filling in the chord symbols when reading charts." Benny Bailey also remembers his satisfaction in discovering the "secrets of how to add or take away chords from a standard tune and put in your own to make the thing flow. Once you'd learn the principle of it, you could apply it to any other tune, actually."

Performers also develop increased confidence in judging alternative versions of progressions. During the forties, musicians who regarded the progressions of sheet music publications and big band stock arrangements as "too sparse" or "awkward" designed "more musical, more sophisticated" personal versions (BB). As Howard Levy explains, contemporary written sources can be problematic for other reasons. "Some modern fake books have really raw or incorrect changes which aren't in the spirit of the music. Also, they will put in their own idea of the substitutions instead of the basic changes, which distracts you from the main thing that's going on, taking you one step away from where the tune is and getting you away from the root from which you should be able to substitute."

Over the life of a composition, as a musician tries out various renditions, integrates their elements with his or her own inventions, and evaluates the results, the composition's model enjoys periods of relative flux and relative stability. In the latter instance, musicians sometimes consolidate their favorite features into a formally arranged rendition. John Hicks performs a ballad in different meters and keys; he also alters its harmony in conjunction with the melody melody until he finds his "own interpretation." Fred Hersch similarly works on a new composition "by playing it and playing it and playing it." Initially, he adds his "own chord changes to the original sheet music, looking for nice chords which are strong without being obtuse, which are fun to play and make the melody sound good, and which pay attention to the lyrics, preserving the character of the piece. After I've played a tune in public once or twice," Hersch explains, "a way to do it usually comes to me, and then I'll do it that way. The tune kind of arranges itself."

As indicated earlier, artists designing an arrangement's progression consider not only the vertical blends of successive chords, but the nature of their resultant lines as well. To ensure the continuity of the individual inner voices, they may create predominantly stepwise motion and keep registral placement constant throughout.[37]

A musician's ongoing experimentation with the jazz repertory ultimately provides the basis for original pieces. As already mentioned, many fashion new melodies according to conventional harmonic structures. Some creations emerge as countermelodies to the original compositions.[38] Tommy Flanagan's peers routinely "composed new songs based on Bird's progressions and played them for one another." Other pieces contain original harmonic forms. Improvisers of different eras have challenged themselves by designing compositions with dense chord movements and performing them at extremely fast tempos. In the sixties and seventies, musicians considered John Coltrane's "Giant Steps" to be "the tour de force." In its harmonic setting, they would have to negotiate through tonalities with unusual relationships at a tempo of approximately 285 quarter-note beats per minute and a rate of harmonic change exceeding one hundred chords per minute.[39] During the forties and fifties, the jazz community's adoption of the show tune "Cherokee" served the same function at jam sessions.

Additional trends include modal or vamp tunes that are harmonically static—that is, comprised of a repeating single chord or pair of chords—and accompanied by a short repeating bass melody. Eddie Harris's "Jazz Freedom Dance" is based solely on a B♭7 chord.[40] Other examples of modal pieces are Miles Davis's "So What" and "Flamenco Sketches." "So What" has an AABA structure that minimizes harmonic movement by alternating between tonalities suggestive of the D Dorian mode (for sixteen bars) and the E♭ Dorian mode (for eight bars), then returning again to the D Dorian mode (for eight bars); in "Flamenco Sketches," artists proceed through a series of different tonalities in ABCDE format, but have the option of remaining within each section for either four or eight bars before moving on to the next. Horace Silver's "The Outlaw" deviates from standard structures by providing a fifty-four-bar progression divided into phrases of thirteen bars, thirteen bars, ten bars, and eighteen bars. In Ornette Coleman's "Bird's Food," within an overall AABA format, "each A is a blues variant. After an introduction of two measures, the first A uses the first nine and a half measures of a blues chorus; the second A uses eleven measures; and the last uses ten." Jaki Byard's ballad "Ode to Charlie Parker" gradually unfolds a twenty-four-bar progression with harmonic components bearing little similarity to one another.[41]

Complementing experimentation with harmonic rhythm are experiments with unconventional meters for jazz pieces. With some precedent in Benny Carter's innovative "Waltzing the Blues" in 1936 and Bobby Hackett's recording of "Jammin' the Waltz" in 1938, Sonny Rollins and Max Roach, in 1956, devoted an entire album to improvising on pieces in 3/4. Additional experiments since the bebop era include Thelonious Monk's 1952 version of "Carolina Moon," in 6/4 time, and compositions in 5/4 by Dave Brubeck, Booker Little, and others. In some cases, composers alternated these meters with 2/4, 3/4, and 4/4. The wealth of possibilities seems endless, encompassing compositions with extended forms and experiments in free jazz, the structure of which is to be described later.[42]

Pieces with unconventional forms can be "really challenging," requiring exceptional concentration. Such was Rufus Reid's experience with the music of Bobby Hutcherson and Harold Land. Instead of constructing progressions with symmetrical four- and eight-bar phrases, they "might have a five-bar phrase going to a seven-bar phrase and then to a three-bar phrase," Reid explains. "The music was also more advanced harmonically than what I was used to. They didn't necessarily use tertian harmony, voicing chords in thirds. Instead, they often voiced the chords in fourths. The harmony of Joe Henderson's music was even harsher," he asserts. "There were lots of major seventh augmented chords, plus augmented ninths and elevenths."

Whether composing new pieces or adding original detail to standards, jazz artists are guided not only by purely musical concepts but by wide-ranging experiences that shape the artists' need for self-expression and infuse their creations with distinctive attributes. Booker Little's wonder at the abruptly changing moods of children inspired his unusual use of tempo changes and alternating meters in the piece "Quiet Please"; the falling, staggered melody and scat syllables of a Jabbo Smith piece recapture the delighted laughter of Smith's granddaughter the day she accompanied him on her first trip to the zoo.[43] In Thelonious Monk's "Ruby, My Dear," the cadence of the title's affectionate address serves a melodic-rhythmic theme, empowering subsequent phrases with the import of love poetry, its aural effect as much speech as music.

The rhapsodic melodies and harmonies of Jaki Byard's "Ode to Charlie Parker" and Benny Golson's "I Remember Clifford" reflect tender feelings of nostalgia for their renowned friends who died tragically and too young.[44] Max

Roach's intense rhythmic interplay with Nigerian drummer Michael Olitunji and Abbey Lincoln's heartrending cries on their "Freedom Now Suite," composed by Roach and singer-writer Oscar Brown Jr., present the symbolic portrayal of hardships endured by early African Americans and the struggle for independence by African nations under the grip of colonialism.[45] The project, revealing the artists' strong concern with cultural identity, represents a union of their musical and political preoccupations. From the most basic to the most complex human dimensions, such varied practices demonstrate the dynamic interplay between tradition and innovation within the jazz community as improvisers transform its musical conventions and imbue them with deep personal meaning.

### Jazz as Ear Music

As indicated throughout this chapter, the improviser's knowledge includes not only differing ways of rendering pieces but differing ways of thinking about and conceptualizing them. These are central issues for jazz musicians, who, despite their varying use of arrangements, often perform without written scores, creating much of the detail of their music in performance. Some musicians conceptualize the structure of a piece primarily in aural and physical terms—as a winding melodic course through successive fields of distinctive harmonic color and as a corresponding sweep of movement over an instrument's terrain. Others find it useful to reinforce such images with notational and theoretical symbols. Before Carmen Lundy learned theory, she "always had to wait for the pianist to play the chords" so she could react to them. Now, however, visualizing the structure of a piece helps her "know where the tune is going," and she no longer has to depend on the pianist.

Still others find theoretical representations helpful initially when studying a piece's form, but unnecessary afterwards. They quickly reach the point where, as George Duvivier put it, "my fingers can pick out the chords without my always thinking of them." Improvisers liken this transition to learning a new route in the physical world—for walking between home and work, for example. Initially, the walker gives full attention to reading street signs, memorizing turns of direction, and gaining a sense of characteristic pacing between identifiable landmarks. Eventually, taking in such features becomes so routine that it happens instantaneously, almost unconsciously, as the legs alone seem to take over the walk's direction. Subsequently, the walker can concentrate on other things—noticing obscure details in the surroundings or thinking of unrelated matters—without becoming lost along the way. Similarly, once improvisers fix in their memories the features of a piece's road map, they need no longer mark their changing positions within its piece's form by consciously imaging chord symbols. Rather, they can instantaneously gauge their progress by the band's collage of sounds and the relative positions of the sounds on their instruments. This frees their full attention for the precise details of their own parts as they move confidently, creatively, and in tempo through the piece's harmonic course.

The experience of negotiating through the ever-changing patterns around them from the perspective of their personal structural maps is a rich and dynamic one for improvisers. It potentially involves the imaginative play of sounds, physical gestures, colorful shapes, and abstract symbols, whose gestalt creates the impression of perpetual movement through a multidimensional musical realm. Although the emphasis upon distinct imagery can differ from individual to individual and vary within performances, artists commonly describe aural musical representations in their thoughts and perceptions as preeminent. Not surprisingly, then, the jazz tradition generally elevates aural musical knowledge, with its associated powers of apprehension and recall, to the paramount position.

Such learning practices as requiring students to sing tunes in every key before performing them reflect this priority. Acting upon a related expectation, a band leader once inquired casually from a newcomer whether she had heard "the head" to a particular piece before. When she answered that she had, he turned directly to the band and counted off a tempo for its performance. In immediate protest, she explained that she had only heard the tune once and had never performed it. "If you heard it," he replied crisply, "you ought to be able to play it."

Recommendations about learning the structures of a piece reflect similar values. "Fake books can really stultify your development if you have the wrong attitude toward them," Howard Levy says. "Really, the best way to learn," he continues,

> is to take tunes off records, because you're utilizing your ear. It takes a lot of knowledge and experience to be able to do this, but it becomes so easy to hear pieces in their component parts if you actually do the work yourself. Then you start trying to write the changes out by ear. In the beginning, you're going to write out things wrong. You're not going to know what's right for the first few years that you do this. But in the end, you see your mistakes and you really learn it.

The ideals and discipline embodied by these methods prepare students directly for the challenges that they face as artists. Improvisers must depend greatly upon their ears for repertory because there is frequently a lag between the introduction of new pieces to the jazz scene and their availability in printed form. In fact, much of the jazz repertory remains part of the community's oral tradition and is not published as single sheet music items or in fake books. Moreover, musicians must be able to apprehend the unique features of each rendition as they unfold during a performance, instantly adapting their parts to those of other players. If the band takes exceptional liberties, individual players must continually alter their formal models of the piece as well. In the final analysis, a jazz piece is not a single model appearing in a fake book or on a recording. Rather, it is the precise version of a piece created by musicians at each performance event.[46]

Ultimately, veterans develop such exquisite skill that many can negotiate even new pieces successfully upon a single hearing. At a recording session, Ricardo Ray once asked Doc Cheatham to add his own solos to a tape of several fast mambos that the band had already recorded, and to "play behind a beautiful ballad that the singer had sung. So there I was," Cheatham recalls, "sitting out there with earphones on and a microphone before me, and I was supposed to overdub solos on these tunes I hadn't even heard before. But I could hear the changes. They came to me just like the air that I'm breathing, and I just went through it, and the people were very happy. I couldn't have done that if I hadn't had the training I'd had, learning all the chords and harmonic things I learned playing over the years."

Cheatham's account underscores how comprehensive is the artist's understanding of the vehicles that inspire and mold jazz creations.[47] As the following chapter delineates, the agile performances of soloists depend not merely on mastery of composed melodies and their forms, but equally on being proficient in the conventional improvisational language of jazz tradition.

# FOUR

**Getting Your Vocabulary Straight**

Learning Models for Solo Formulation

*When you're very young, you don't have the harmonic knowledge to create solos yourself, so you begin by copying things that sound good in other people's solos.*—Benny Bailey

*I decided the best I could do would be to write the solos down, note for note, and line them up with the harmony of the song, analyzing the notes according to the chords that were being played. Then I would learn, "Well, you can do this at this time. You can do that at that time." It was like getting your vocabulary straight.*—Art Farmer

Just as children learn to speak their native language by imitating older competent speakers, so young musicians learn to speak jazz by imitating seasoned improvisers. In part, this involves acquiring a complex vocabulary of conventional phrases and phrase components, which improvisers draw upon in formulating the melody of a jazz solo. Complete recorded improvisations also provide models. Saxophonist Jerry Coker absorbed a storehouse of solos during his grade school years, simply because his parents played their favorite recordings so frequently at home.[1]

George Johnson Jr. developed the early habit of singing with his father's prized Eddie Jefferson recordings. By his teens, he had memorized Jefferson's unique interpretations of instrumental improvisations. Wynton Marsalis once warned me good-humoredly, "Look out for my young brother. He's only three, but when I call home from the road, he can already sing some of Miles's solos over the phone!"

Once youngsters develop a serious interest in jazz, they complement haphazardly gained knowledge with deliberate effort to master the performance styles of great improvisers. Applying their earlier method, many initially continue to memorize solos by singing or whistling them. For Tommy Flanagan,

95

whose family piano and record player were in different rooms, this was a necessity. For Bud Freeman and his friends, it was largely a social activity.[2] Similarly, years later, Melba Liston and her companions hung out at one another's homes "listening to records together, humming the solos till we learned them." This is a beneficial approach from a number of different standpoints. Cultivating an aural grasp of a solo before its reproduction with musical instruments avoids unnecessary guesswork when playing an instrument that might frustrate technique or exhaust endurance. It also trains the voices of students and gives them a grounding in what are for improvisers essential linkages among voice, ear, and instruments.

Some musicians, when learning new solos from recordings, can imitate consecutive patterns with the ease of "catching a ball and throwing it back" (CP). More typically, they commit endless hours to the task.[3] With each replay, they reinforce the memory of previous musical fragments, and they work on matching the next several pitches by singing or playing them. Tommy Flanagan recalls sudden displays of virtuosity by musicians like Art Tatum. "I'd say, 'Wow, what was that?' and I'd put the needle back to that spot." To master technically advanced passages, many divide them into "smaller parts," just as they might learn "long words by studying their syllables separately and recombining them" (HO). Others copy "the principal pitches in a long melodic run," then try repeatedly to match those blurred intermediate pitches that had eluded them (KB)—until a weary voice from another part of the house protests, "Haven't you learned it yet?"

Early record players had controls enabling listeners to slow a record's speed by gradations until they could catch a particularly fast passage, albeit at a lower pitch, transposing the retarded phrase into its original pitch immediately thereafter. Those lacking such equipment slowed the turntable by applying slight finger pressure to the record (HO). Tape recorders with half-speed controls, which drop the pitch a complete octave, are an additional help, as are recent compact disc players, which allow for the repeated play of isolated passages. Adopting an alternative method, Gary Bartz acquired a stock of Parker solos simply by playing along with the recordings at normal speed "all day long, day after day," circumventing the role of vocalization as mediator.

Once absorbed from recordings, solos sometimes pass from one aspiring artist to another. The dynamics of the exchanges are themselves instructive, as in the teasing interplay between trumpeters Dizzy Gillespie and Charlie Shavers. "Why don't you go steal your own shit, instead of getting Roy [Eldridge] secondhand?" complained Shavers before indulgently teaching Gillespie the solos that Shavers himself had memorized from recordings.[4]

Once musicians have learned a solo's discrete phrases, they seek to reconstruct the whole solo, performing it along with the recording from memory. Initially, youngsters are satisfied to anticipate the proper sequence of figures and approximate their phrasing, but as they gain greater confidence, they listen more intently to the recording artist, playing and regulating their parts accordingly. With practice, musicians come to penetrate more deeply into the solo, hearing the music as if their ears had developed greater powers. An illusory transformation occurs: the solo seems to ensue more slowly, presenting, paradoxically, ever finer yet enlarged details. Within a phrase, each pitch reveals its individual character, its own articulation, inflection, timbre, dynamics, and rhythmic feeling. Eventually, students anticipate and re-create the solo's every nuance, blending their performance of the solo inextricably with all the other parts emanating from the recording. Breathing together, following the same line of musical thought, and experiencing the same sense of urgency and shades of feeling that motivated the soloist's initial expression, young performers become engaged in an intimate union with their idols. This thrilling experience assured one student that, because he had acquired "the understanding and the technique to perform some of the greatest musicians' ideas," it would not be "too long" before he would be able to improvise his own solos.

Ultimately, many strive to duplicate the subtle features of the improvisation without the recording, a feat that some pursue even further by transposing and practicing particular solos in every key. The improvised solo is so integral to the jazz tradition that mastering respected examples can be almost a rite of passage for a youngster. Communities that appreciate jazz afford youngsters considerable status when they demonstrate their prowess. Fellow students at Harold Ousley's high school treated him "like a superstar" when he performed Lester Young's solo on "D.B. Blues." Other musicians report similar experiences.

### Transcribing Solos and Re-creating Them in Public

Whereas many musicians learn solos essentially by ear, others find it useful to transcribe solos, rendering them as closely as possible in conventional Western music notation. For this task, musicians typically use their instruments as tools. After learning to perform a recorded solo, they translate each phrase's finger patterns into the letter names of notes; they then write them on the staves of music manuscript paper. While in junior high school, Melba Liston transcribed the classic Coleman Hawkins solo on "Body and Soul" and copied it "so many times" for young saxophonists that she could eventually "write it out by memory." David Baker's high school band leader also "wrote out" and taught students to sing classic jazz solos.[5]

Published solos have been available at least since the twenties. Melrose Brothers of Chicago established an early prototype with its two 1927 collections of Louis Armstrong improvisations, *50 Hot Choruses for Cornet* and *125 Jazz Breaks for Cornet*.[6] Similar publications of performances by Charlie Parker, Miles Davis, Dizzy Gillespie, John Coltrane, and other masters have increased over the past few decades, as have those appearing along with analysis in scholarly articles and theses. Since the mid-thirties, specialized trade magazines such as *Metronome* and *Down Beat* have also featured transcribed solos, accompanied in some instances by brief discussions of their merits. Enthusiastic learners spread the influence of these publications among their circles. Baker brought an early book of Gillespie solos to his band leader, who selected material from its contents for the band and featured it during halftime performances at football games.

Commercial arrangements of compositions played by swing bands provide yet other sources for solo transcriptions. Sheet music versions of Duke Ellington's "The Creeper" and "Birmingham Breakdown" published by Gotham Music Service in 1927 are important examples.[7] Benny Bailey recalls others:

> They were just like the records, and whole solos were written out. They had all of Basie's tunes, and they were very big in those days. You could get almost all of the things that Woody Herman's band was playing. I think they still sell them to rehearsal bands. There was one popular thing, "Tuxedo Junction"—the biggest thing that Erskine Hawkins ever did, really—and Dud Bascomb's solo is an important part of it. There were other classics like Roy Eldridge's solo on "Rocking Chair," Bobby Hackett's solo on "String of Pearls," and the solos that Thad Jones played with the Basie band on "April in Paris" or "Pop Goes the Weasel."

Although experienced improvisers regard the published materials as valuable learning aids, they caution youngsters about becoming too dependent upon them. Without comparing transcriptions to the original recordings, students cannot determine the accuracy of the transcription work or its reproduction. Moreover, however useful they may be for accomplished musicians who can interpret them, all transcriptions are reductive or skeletal representations of performances and provide learners with little information about fundamental stylistic features of jazz. Finally, if students rely upon publications rather than recordings as sources, they deprive themselves of the rigorous ear training that traditionally has been integral to the improviser's development.

Typically, musicians learn a repertory of complete recorded solos that they practice as musical etudes and perform periodically for friends during informal sessions. Among the various improvisations that Wynton Marsalis learned was John Coltrane's famous solo on "Giant Steps," which he "practiced every morning" at a particular stage in his development.[8] A few conventions encourage the public re-creation of recorded improvisations. When bands play stock arrangements, they may play the solos written off the recordings. "If a band had an arrangement of 'String of Pearls,'" Benny Bailey says, "you almost had to play Bobby Hackett's solo. It's a beautifully constructed solo which fits the tune. It helps the tune somehow, and it's part of the whole picture. If you played any other solo, it would take away from the tune."

Whether transmitting solos through written or oral means, such practices have considerable precedent in the jazz tradition. Just as early admirers of Joe Oliver re-created his recorded solos (ex. 4.1), Wynton Marsalis, in a 1984 appearance with Sarah Vaughan and the Boston Pops Orchestra, played the tasteful solo in "September Song" that Clifford Brown had recorded with Sarah Vaughan in 1954. The transmission and performance of solos associated with particular pieces sometimes become part of a band's performance tradition. At times, successful solos even find their way into the arranged parts for entire instrumental sections.[9]

Beyond the practice of re-creating outstanding solos as an integral feature of compositions, artists in the tradition of jazz vocalese often treat the melodies of their favorite improvisations as new tunes and compose lyrics to them. George Johnson Jr.'s experience casts light on both dimensions of the practice. Years after copying Eddie Jefferson's recorded renditions of famous solos, Johnson received training from Jefferson on the bandstand, where the two sang his material as duets, "the same lyrics, note for note." Eventually, Johnson learned to create vocalese texts himself.

Once I've learned a solo, I put my words to it. It's like telling a story. It's like talking, carrying on a conversation. I love to talk about things.
  When I wrote the words to Bird's solo [in "Chi Chi"], I didn't know much about him, but everyone talked about Fifty-second Street, and I knew it was unique, so I wrote:

  Remember 52nd Street,
  the sounds were unique.
  Yes,
  the music had a message,
  you see.

And I knew what it was like when Bird hit the scene, so I wrote:

  Bird hit the scene,
  he was so melodic,
  his music swept the nation,
  in fact;
  Everybody started boppin'
  when he came along.
  Just listen
  to the rhythm.
  He took
  the people
  by surprise.

He opened
their eyes
in some
other type of
musical things.

Bird loved to play
and his music
will live
forever and forever,
in fact;

Charlie Parker
is the reason
I am singing
this song;
Just listen
to the
rhythm
flow.

So, all I actually did was to tell the story of what I heard through other people and what I read about Bird.

Praising the great soloists is a common subject for lyrics. Vocalese composers derive others from their personal lives, such as encounters with love, and yet others from the abstract moods and themes that improvisations suggest to their creative imaginations. In discussing the context for some of his composing, Johnson states:

After I recorded Pharaoh Sanders one night on my little tape recorder, I took the tape home and played it for a week and wrote the words to Pharaoh's and John Hicks's solos. Pharaoh's music is peaceful and very spiritual. It's always talking about love. That's just what I felt; that's the story I felt him saying. As I listened to the tape, I also kept hearing the word *freedom* in the solos, so I wrote:

You got to have happiness,
you got to have freedom.
We got to spread love and joy.
We got to have freedom.
Confusion is everywhere
because no one gives a care.

Pure freedom, freedom.
Tell the world:
freedom.
So, go tell the world.

> You got to go
> and tell the world.
>
> So, hurry,
> spread the news;
> You've got to have happiness.
> You've got to have freedom.

In shaping words to a soloist's intricate melodic-rhythmic patterns, vocalists like Johnson and his mentor bring to full circle the influence of language upon music suggested earlier, underscoring the constant cross-fertilization of ideas between jazz singers and instrumentalists.

Like vocalese performers, instrumentalists may occasionally pay tribute to the composers by playing or even recording personal interpretations of famous solos, treating them as the heads of tunes and the basis for their own improvisations. For the most part, the jazz community contains public re-creations of solos through its tacit assumption that improvisations belong to the creators. Generally, a performer "couldn't play someone else's solo note for note; that just wasn't considered cricket" (RR).[10] This attitude limits the practical value of developing a large reserve of complete solos as the basis for an initial vocabulary.

## Learning Discrete Patterns from Recordings

There is no objection to musicians borrowing discrete patterns or phrase fragments from other improvisers, however; indeed, it is expected. Many students begin acquiring an expansive collection of improvisational building blocks by extracting those shapes they perceive as discrete components from the larger solos they have already mastered and practicing them as independent figures. They acquire others selectively by studying numerous performances of their idols. For some musicians, this is the entire focus of their early learning programs.[11]

Securing a repertory of discrete patterns offers a clear advantage to young performers whose mastery over their instruments is insufficient for copying solos in their entirety. Correspondingly, "a whole solo can be just too much to take in at once. Little sections or melodic fragments" are more easily absorbed (ER). As youngsters cultivate their tastes and become more discriminating, they also find that the phrases of solos differ in quality, some not warranting the time and effort involved in acquiring them. Finally, whereas analysis of complete solos teaches students about matters of musical development and design, analysis of discrete patterns and melodic cells elucidates the building blocks of improvisations and reveals commonalities among improvisations that are not necessarily apparent in the context of larger performances.

At the same time, this approach involves its own distinct challenges, some akin to learning a second language. Just as the beginning foreign language student finds that the cadences of fluent native speakers frequently blur the audible boundaries between and among words, phrases, and sentences—confounding the student's ability to understand them—rapid, dazzling jazz improvisations may also initially sound seamless to beginners. As elaborated later, the fact that improvisers subject the components of their improvisations to different interpretations and transformations in performance compounds the already challenging task of identifying the components and their precise distinguishing boundaries. Only immersion in the music's oral literature and the assistance of fluent speakers of jazz enable learners to grasp the actual components and their variants that improvisers use to construct complex musical statements.[12]

Veterans refer to the discrete patterns in their repertory storehouses as vocabulary, ideas, licks, tricks, pet patterns, crips, clichés, and, in the most functional language, things you can do. As a basic musical utterance, a thing you can do commonly involves a one-measure to four-measure phrase.[13] Depending on the artist's treatment of material, however, an idea or crip can range from such simple formulations as a sustained or repeated pitch, or a short rhythmic figure reminiscent of those of early jazz solos (exx. 4.2a–b), to an elaborate melodic phrase characteristic of later performance styles (exx. 4.2c–d). Tommy Turrentine points out that, in fact, "you can play a crip for thirty-two bars if you want to. Some do it." Ultimately, as Harold Ousley says, the "set phrases that musicians practice and perfect" provide readily accessible material that meets the demands of composing music in performance. "The old guys used to call those things crips. That's from crippled," Turrentine elaborates with characteristic wit. "In other words, when you're playing a solo and your mind is crippled and you can't think of anything different to play, you go back into one of your old bags and play one of your crips. You better have something to play when you can't think of nothing new or you'll feel funny laying out there all the time [he laughs]. That's all I play is crips [laughs again]."

The vocabulary that students acquire from the improvisations of their mentors varies in origin and in character. Some derive from the common language of jazz.[14] As the "kinds of things that everybody plays," they include short melodic figures like traditional blues licks (exx. 4.3a1–a2) and repeated riffs known as shout patterns (ex. 4.3b). Such figures were once associated with particular soloists or repertory genres like the blues but have since been passed anonymously from generation to generation and put to more general use. From the earliest days of jazz, artists absorbed these and other patterns in the context of performance. Although many originated in solos, others originated in a band's musical arrangements—their introductory figures, musical interludes, and background lines that accompany singers and instrumental so-loists.[15] Artists sometimes identify anonymous patterns with their respective jazz idioms; for example, they characterize them as swing figures, bebop licks (ex. 4.3c), and free jazz gestures.

Primary materials for the jazz artist's vocabulary also include excerpts of jazz pieces, popular songs, Western classical compositions, and compositions from other musical traditions that appeal to a soloist (exx. 4.3d1–d3). "There's a little improvisation technique in which you learn to pull things from other songs and insert them into what you're singing at the moment," Carmen Lundy says. "Someone like Ella Fitzgerald will often use quotes from other songs in the middle of a song. She'll sing a few lyrics and then she'll scat sing, taking you into another song."

Unique patterns or signature licks from mentors constitute additional pri-mary materials in a learner's storehouse (exx. 4.3e1–e2).[16] Charlie Parker "in-tentionally played many of the same phrases over and over in his solos. They had become part of his vocabulary, the medium that he was speaking through" (LH). Such is also the case for other improvisers, those who, as Tommy Tur-rentine describes them, will

> always play some kind of recognizable lick and right away you can say, "Oh, that's so and so." Everybody uses them in jazz. Like Charlie Rouse. He's a very unique tenor player. I have heard him play some licks that nobody else plays, and he's been playing them for years. They sound good and they fit. It's the same with Eddie "Lockjaw" Davis or Sonny Rollins or anybody. They all have their things that they play. I can tell by the fourth bar of a solo who it is that's playing.

Students absorb yet other patterns that their teachers themselves have bor-rowed from leading artists.[17] Benny Bailey recalls Miles Davis performing an extensive quotation from a Dud Bascomb solo on the classic recording of "Tuxedo Junction" by Erskine Hawkins's band. In the recorded performance, Bascomb had displayed a "highly original way" of playing over the tune's "I Got Rhythm" changes by improvising a "beautifully constructed solo," Bailey states. "Miles played the quotation in his own way at a faster tempo," but "if you knew the solo previously, you would know where he got it." In a similar light, "Brownie [Clifford Brown] used some of Dizzy's phrases. All the tenor players were influenced by Coltrane and Charlie Parker. You can hear them use their phrases all the time" (JR).

Beyond their functional and pedagogical value, quotations from the histor-ical literature of jazz establish the relationships of improvisers to their larger tradition. Arthur Rhames speaks eloquently of this: "The great players always give homage to their predecessors by recalling certain things that they did. They give it in appreciation and in understanding of the validity of their predecessors. Being able to quote from songs and solos is always part of a mature artist because he's aware of the contribution of others and its impact, how valid it is. Something that is really valid is timeless." [18]

Of course, learners must cultivate the ability to grasp precise gestures within the contours of fluent improvisations, and they must, Carmen Lundy says, be "well versed in the music" in order to appreciate these distinctions. Over years of study, Lundy found that she could "discriminate increasingly finer things" in her listening. Initially all she could identify were "jazz licks." Later she learned to distinguish "bebop licks," and finally "Charlie Parker licks and Sonny Rollins licks." Correspondingly, before students can grasp the intricacies of complex phrases, they absorb into their vocabularies relatively simple and unambiguous phrase components bounded by brief rests or delineated by dramatic changes in melodic direction. At the same time, they learn such complete musical ideas from the language of jazz as short solo figures, call and response patterns, horn riffs, the phrases of familiar tunes, and the like.

As they develop a storehouse of vocabulary patterns, students strive to understand the relationships of the patterns to the larger musical settings from which they come. This, in turn, reveals the construction and application of phrases. "When you listen to a record," James Moody says, "you listen to all of the surrounding harmonies and rhythms that go with whatever the melody is, and you hear it. Suppose somebody were to sing 'Body and Soul,' but they put the chord changes to 'Star Dust' behind it. Your ear would just reject that. It's the same with licks. It's a matter of ear training." Experienced improvisers respond negatively to sounds that are harmonically "out of context," just as they would "to a scream in the middle of a peaceful street scene," Moody concludes.

Within their tradition's larger context, associations among vocabulary patterns, compositional forms, and particular chords remain strongly tied to the imaginations of exemplary improvisers, providing ongoing models for other players. When Harold Ousley performs the composition "Tune-Up," for example, he knows that at the opening Em7 chord he can pursue various options, including "certain things that Bud played, or it might be a phrase that Sonny Rollins played, or it might even be something Trane played."

Many complement their aural understanding of the relationship between harmony and melody by theoretical analysis of patterns, a practice whose value for improvisers is implicit in their criticism of standard publications of solos. "It may be helpful just to see what someone like Miles played, but the books don't really teach you anything about why Miles did what he did, what his thinking was. That's what's needed" (BB). Art Tatum assessed one of his imitators accordingly. "Well, he knows *what* I did on record, but he doesn't know *why* I did it." [19] Artists are on a continuous search for illuminating the what and why of great improvisations. A case in point is Doc Cheatham's response to

Bobby Hackett's recorded solo on "Jada." Cheatham asked himself, "How can a man play like that on that melody? . . . What is he thinking about? How could he think of something like that?" Ultimately, Cheatham's transcription and analysis revealed to him the concept of "alternate chords." He recalls that "how to build one chord off from another" was a novelty to him at the time.

Two music generations later, Art Farmer transcribed "the fantastic things" his idols improvised in the bebop idiom so that he could learn "where their choice of notes came from. There's value in learning the licks just to see what people did, how a solo was constructed, and to see what you could do with chords." Tommy Flanagan also comments on his personal experience:

> Sometimes, you would try to duplicate something the soloists did. It was almost like they put it down there for you, like they were showing you something. So, you might try to duplicate a run or buy a transcription book to see how it looked on paper and then apply it, use it yourself from there. Mostly, they showed you a general way of thinking about playing a song or a phrase. Or they showed you another way of looking at a chord, how it related to other things—like the way you can make one little phrase cover three or four chords. It was very interesting and a good study for the ear.

In such fundamental applications, music analysis explains the complementary relationships between jazz phrases and chords, in which the former can be viewed as the horizontal counterpart of the latter.

### Learning by Observing Performances and Demonstrations

Despite the value of recordings as an important source of musical vocabulary—especially during major periods of innovation in jazz—they are not equivalent to live performances. Because many artists have but infrequent opportunities to record, their music is usually available to learners only at concerts or jam sessions. Moreover, some performers hold back their best material during recording sessions, keeping their ideas less accessible to imitators. Some, like Freddie Keppard, have been reluctant to record at all. In other cases, the limitations individual improvisers place on taking risks during recording sessions, the conservative policies of record companies catering to a commercial market, which constrains artists' adventurous productions, and the common lag of six months or more between recording sessions and the subsequent release of the recording can render albums unrepresentative of the improvisers' current performance practices.[20]

Recordings also have various technical drawbacks. Twenties recording equipment could not always adequately process the dynamic range and complexity of the drum set's patterns, forcing some drummers to simplify their performances and even to restrict their use of the drum set's components.

Changing fashions in sound transparency and taste can also complicate the efforts of learners. During the fifties, when record companies boosted the string bass within the overall sound mix of recordings, Ronald Shannon Jackson and his peers could not hear the complete drum parts; the bass drum patterns or the ride cymbal patterns were annoyingly obscured at times. Moreover, malfunctioning recording or remastering equipment has, in some instances, transformed an original performance, substantially changing the tempo, and correspondingly lowering or raising the pitch as much as a half step and distorting the music's tone quality.[21]

Inability to see performers and their instruments poses numerous other problems for aspiring musicians trying to reconstruct the playing techniques of recording artists. Shortly after Kenny Washington's father invested in a new drum set for him, Washington, then ten years old, became enthralled with Max Roach recordings in which the drums sounded "very high pitched" and tuned precisely in large intervals "like fourths or fifths." To match Roach's equipment, Washington tightened the tuning pegs of his own tom-tom drums, stretching their skins. Although he was initially ecstatic when the adjustments enabled him to imitate Roach's "melodic" drum solos, his excitement was short-lived. After three days, the tension on the drum heads collapsed their shells. Washington still vividly remembers the great trepidation he felt in bringing this news to his father—a strict disciplinarian who conducted weekly inspections of the drums—and his ultimate relief when his father merely burst into laughter at the well-intentioned experiment. Without seeing Roach's instruments, Washington did not consider size as the factor principally responsible for their pitch.

Keith Copeland likewise acknowledges that "it's hard for drummers to learn from records because you can't see what the drummer's doing with his hands and his feet, what sticks he's using and exactly what part of the drum he's hitting." Encountering comparable difficulties, one young trumpeter, fascinated by the microtonal effects of blue notes on some favored recordings, sought to master them. Unable to see his idols making slight depressions of valves, he achieved the same effects by distorting his embouchure and varying the pressure of his air stream. A further complication for many beginners is that studio and audio equipment often artificially enhance a performance in ways impossible for them to recognize. The student just mentioned also acquired an unconscious habit of forcing his air through the trumpet, in a naive effort to match the extraordinarily large sound of his models as amplified by the stereo system. Without the correct and constant air support required for performance, the trumpeter eventually lost his endurance and had to relearn with a teacher the very fundamentals of trumpet playing.

On the other hand, learning from recordings sometimes has serendipitous effects. In George Duvivier's endeavor to master a recorded bass solo distinguished by its extraordinary rhythmic complexity, he developed a special complex fingering technique that allowed him to play most of it. Later, Duvivier attended the band's performance of the piece, "The Big Noise from Winnetka," and discovered that the solo was actually a duet: drummer Raymond Bauduc performed rhythmically with drumsticks upon the bass strings near the instrument's bridge, while bassist Bob Haggart fingered different pitches on the neck of the bass. With great amusement, Duvivier recalls how his own misunderstanding led to his unique version of the solo. It also gave him a new technique, involving light finger action across the strings, that increased his facility on his instrument.

To avoid potential difficulties, aspiring musicians make a point of observing their idols in performance. "When you see people you admire doing what is so difficult for you, it's a whole new experience," Buster Williams says.

> You can not only hear it on records, but you can see it happening and you understand. When I saw Ray Brown for the first time, I was totally floored. In fact, I had a dream as a result of seeing him. In the dream, Ray Brown was actually Percy Heath. The bass was like ten feet tall, and Percy was like twenty feet tall, and his fingers were about a yard long. It seemed like he just stood there and laid his hands on the fingerboard. His fingers just crept all over the fingerboard and played all the notes. That was the effect that seeing Ray Brown had on me.

From such studied observation, horn players learn alternate fingerings and valve or key combinations that, however unconventional by the norms of classical music performance practice, enable improvisers to execute intricate jazz figures that are otherwise awkward or impossible to perform. They may have further use as well, making it possible for students to assimilate idiomatic improvised passages by performers of other instruments that are not easily translated onto their own. Moreover, alternate fingerings can serve as rhythmic articulation devices for repeated pitches or tremolos, and produce diverse timbral and microtonal effects, some with speechlike inflections.[22]

Figuring out other features of the performance of their idols can be critical for students if they are to duplicate precise sounds. Some musicians go so far as to purchase the artist's brand of equipment. When Harold Ousley discovered that Gene Ammons played a Conn saxophone, he obtained one of the "same make," as well as "the same kind of mouthpiece that Ammons used, a white one, real hard." Another musician chose a Martin trumpet so that he could reproduce Miles Davis's "especially dark, moody sound during those days when he played that kind of instrument."

Through observation students can also surmise whether horn players stylize their personal vibrato with subtle movements of the instrument, or whether they depend exclusively on the manipulation of air flow and subtle movements of the tongue and lips. John McNeil learned to imitate Miles Davis's effect of "putting a lot of air in his sound," by sticking out his lower jaw when he played. To color the instrument's sound more radically, Doc Cheatham copied the hand positions Joe Smith used for manipulating a rubber plunger mute to create such vocalized tonal qualities and effects as a singer's rasp, nasality, and pitch inflection. He also perfected the growling and flutter tongue techniques used by Paul Whiteman's trumpeters.

Investigating comparable matters for his own instrument, Kenny Washington "watched drummers like 'Philly' Joe Jones. My brain would take pictures of the ways they were playing, like the different brush strokes they used, and I would rush home and work on that." A young bass player copied "certain glissandos and double stops and triple stops," pitch clusters characteristic of the styles of Buster Williams and Richard Davis (GD). Young Barry Harris also routinely lodged himself next to pianists at jam sessions and dances, "trying to see something, trying to learn a few runs" or a chord that he could "take home" with him. Harris initially memorized the finger movements of pianists over the keyboard because "I was not yet that good with sound." [23]

Such practices are of long standing within the jazz tradition. Early ragtime pianists who could not read music learned their art partially by observing the patterns made by the depressed keys of scroll-driver player pianos, then re-creating the patterns on standard pianos. Some musicians gleaned information from record jacket photographs showing the posture of an artist's hand or precise finger positions on a musical instrument, or studied the early film clips or three-minute soundies of swing bands, which could be seen at bars and clubs in the forties. [24] At one time, aspiring artists could observe performance techniques of musicians at local music shops where their performances promoted the sale of sheet music. Extended viewings of jazz performances, historical as well as contemporary, are now readily available on video cassettes.

Beyond building vocabulary, such close observation of detail leads self-educated musicians to an increased understanding of performance technique, whose rudiments they had acquired earlier from method books and personal experimentation. Sometimes, learners fortify their new understanding by re-hearsing it silently during presentations by other musicians. At one Count Basie concert I attended in New York, two young teenagers seated themselves strategically in the front row of the balcony, where throughout the program they rocked back and forth to the music's beat while miming their idols. One swept the air before him and imitated the broad circular movements of the drummer's brush strokes; the other plucked up and down the strings of an imaginary bass.

Copying choreography integral to a performance also facilitates the assimilation of an artist's precise style. Only after imitating his teacher's posture and movement at the piano could David Sudnow re-create such salient elements of his improvisations as their breathing and singing qualities.[25] Similarly, a young saxophonist "started watching Von Freeman play and tried to imitate his dance, the way he moved and swayed, the way he moved his horn up and down when his phrases went up and down." By doing this, the student felt, he could play "much more" in Freeman's manner and style, and he felt more like a "real jazz player" himself. "I was surprised at how much easier playing became when I began to move more correctly. Now, I try to image great jazz saxophone players before I take a solo. That's one thing that's made a big difference in my playing."[26]

Many expand their knowledge by learning directly from experts outside of performances. Leora Henderson recalls Louis Armstrong teaching her "how to make riffs," a prelude to her learning to play "hot trumpet" in her own right. Just as Red Nichols showed Armstrong the alternate fingering patterns he had worked out for jazz trumpet figures in the twenties, two music generations later Freddie Hubbard learned Dizzy Gillespie's system of "auxiliary fingerings" from his demonstration. Similarly, after joining Gillespie's big band in New York in 1949, Melba Liston asked a friend in the trumpet section to sing slowly the characteristic phrases of the new and bewildering idiom of bebop so that she could transcribe and study them. "I didn't understand their language," she recalls, "because bebop hadn't come to California yet, really." Kenny Washington expanded his repertory with rhythmic patterns that Gillespie's drummer Rudy Collins demonstrated for him during private sessions.[27]

Others absorb new material by attending formal master classes or by hanging out with peers and mentors in informal settings. Returning from a concert, a drummer and his disciple once responded with great animation to a renowned percussionist's solos they were listening to on a cassette player in the back of the car. When an interesting pattern appeared, the expert smiled and nudged his student, then vocalized the figure with scat syllables and mimed its drum strokes until the younger musician began to copy them. Turning to the tape again, the musicians repeated their interplay in response to every inspired phrase. Occasionally, the expert performed minor variations on a phrase after seizing it. Grinning with delight, the student attempted his own variations, raising affectionate laughter from his mentor. Throughout the ride home, the drummers continued their lively discourse, evaluating, absorbing, and sharing musical ideas from the recording and exploring their implications for invention. Not so much as a word passed between them.

Barry Harris adopts a similarly varied pedagogical approach in workshops. One of his techniques for teaching improvisation is to compose exemplary phrases and solos for participants. Standing away from the piano, Harris initially dictates examples in a theoretical language that he has suited to jazz. Typically, he creates a phrase through the elision of a few discrete gestures. "The chord is C7," he would alert the class. "Triplet chord up from the second with a half step below and run [a scale] down to the third with a half step between the 1 and the 7. Diminish up from the third, skip a note, and chromatic back to the tonic" (fig. 4.1). In response, students scramble to transpose the numbers into letters in their respective instrument's key, then translate the letters into sounds. Musicians who have learned Barry Harris's theoretical system become so adept at interpreting the streams of numbers Harris dictates to them for model phrases that they can perform the phrases in unison almost immediately.

Harris also directs musicians to master vocabulary in physical terms. He suggests that horn players finger each phrase repeatedly without blowing into their instruments, encoding it in muscular and visual memory as sequential movement among discrete places on an instrument's terrain and as an accompanying patter of valves. This isolates the rhythmic features of the phrase for practice, as well. "Your fingers should articulate phrases like tap dancers," Harris asserts. Likewise, Harris requires his class to master figures "on sound alone," and, like many improvisers, he suggests that students cultivate this knowledge by singing or whistling the figures at various pitch levels.

Another teacher, Alan Swain, stresses visual and spatial impressions derived from the physical layout of an instrument, instructing pianists to learn phrases as patterned configurations of white and black keys. Swain formalizes this practice by printing a pictorial keyboard on index cards, labeling each with a chord symbol, and having pupils ink in the appropriate arrangements of keys. Students drill with the cards until they can visualize precise key clusters for every chord symbol. Such varied forms of representation provide artists with alternative, complementary ways of apprehending and remembering musical figures.

### Increasing Apprehension and Recall of Vocabulary Phrases

Over time, musicians strengthen their abilities to learn new vocabulary. Concentrating on recorded solos with increased understanding, they can apprehend faster, more intricate patterns from fewer replays and without slowing the recordings. Many can absorb new material under circumstances in which little or no replay is possible. Eventually, live performance itself serves as a vehicle

Figure 4.1    Barry Harris's dictation of common bebop figure

for the absorption and transmission of music. "Some things just seeped into my system and style when I sat in with guys like Jonah Jones, Rex Stewart, and Joe Smith," Doc Cheatham recalls. Similarly, Red Nichols would sit in with Pops Foster's bands "all night . . . picking up ideas. You'd hear him later doing the same thing you did."[28]

Moreover, various conventions guiding group interplay depend upon the artist's skill to assimilate patterns immediately after their performance. Bass players sometimes learn pieces by copying a pianist's bass lines. Horn players, when alternating four-bar improvisations—trading fours—may pattern their melodies upon one another with impeccable precision. Similarly, horn players may improvise the melody for a new tune with one player echoing the short phrases of the other in call and response fashion throughout.[29] Epitomizing such extraordinary abilities of near-simultaneous copying is the practice of shadowing, in which one performer can nearly cover another's solo as it is being improvised (BH). "My teacher would have you improvise over a song," a student reports, "and when you tried, he'd sit at another piano and play *your* improvised lines a fraction of a second behind you. It could drive you nuts."

If one of the developmental issues for learners cultivating a vocabulary is grasping ornate phrases, a related challenge is simply remembering them. In general, the development of ability in jazz depends upon honing the memory. Some veterans with phenomenal long-term memories can remember their favorite solos after twenty, even thirty, years. When listening to recordings, they can sing along not only with featured tunes but with every pitch of the improvisations. Additionally, when entertaining their friends, they routinely place the record needle in the precise groove of cleverly improvised phrases, illustrating the virtues of particular soloists with the infallibility of poets turning to a favored line of verse in an anthology or music theorists to an exemplary passage in a printed musical score. Without even needing to consult the original recording, a friend once corrected pitches and added subtle embellishments to my transcription of a Miles Davis solo that he himself had learned in childhood.

For young players, a common method of memory training is the simple but rigorous repetitive act of checking the accuracy of learned solos against their original models, constantly reinforcing the proper interpretation. Over time, learning and retaining solos in this fashion creates the strong and flexible aurality that the jazz world expects of its accomplished artists. One older jazz student, upon recognizing the importance of this skill, realized that his early training in Western classical music had emphasized the supremacy of reading skills. It had never occurred to him, and certainly had never been pointed out, that a recording could serve as a viable alternative to a written score. It was not until he was immersed in his jazz training that he discovered that his exclusive dependence on written music had, in fact, undermined the development of his aural skills. As a result, his retention of material learned from recordings greatly lagged behind that of musicians who had grown up in the jazz tradition. It required years of experience with the jazz community's methods for him to close the gap.

This also proved a point of frustration for those of Harris's workshop participants with poor short-term memories. Harris expects students to add successive patterns to their mental stockpile as he demonstrates them. "If you've played a phrase once correctly, there is no reason for you ever to play it incorrectly," he insists. For many, however, the concentration required to transpose each new phrase for their own instruments and to memorize its finger patterns drives all preceding phrases away. Some compensate by notating and reading sketches of phrases in class or by tape recording the demonstrations for later study. Although Harris does not disallow such practices, he frowns upon them because they appear to weaken the session's rigor and prevent students from developing retentive powers. Harris's own abilities are exemplary. After grueling evening meetings that leave his followers mentally exhausted, he commonly invites them to work again on an entire solo learned four or five hours earlier or even on one from a previous workshop.

As Harris's students begin to cope with the pressure of memorization, and as they become more familiar with jazz conventions generally, many experience considerable improvement in their retentive powers. After a year of attendance, a saxophonist suddenly realized that she could later remember new phrases learned in the workshop and could practice them without having to refer to her notation. Another student reported an increased absorption of patterns from recordings. He found that whenever his job required less than his full concentration, especially effective passages that hung perpetually on the fringe of his consciousness intruded as musical daydreams and consumed his imagination. The same thing happened at social gatherings, where the patterns periodically overtook him, insulating him from the surrounding conversation. When thus preoccupied, he could maintain but a semblance of social grace as he withdrew into the repeating images, retracing their melodic contours and subtle inflections, envisioning their finger movements, and allowing his emotions to be infused with their evocative moods.

Listeners with the capacity to assimilate phrases so thoroughly can eventually treat live performances themselves as musical scores, gleaning vocabulary patterns that they can subsequently review outside of their performance contexts. Musicians describe returning home after exciting late-night jam sessions to lie in bed, their heads virtually "swimming" with sounds. Like flickering flames, tantalizing musical ideas remain suspended in their thoughts, seeming at one moment to fade away with the incursion of sleep, at the next to intensify their luminescence, driving sleep away. "Oh, it's getting to you now!" playfully joked a veteran when an exhausted novice complained of the tenacious passages that occupied his mind through the entire night. "The next thing you know, you won't think of anything else during the day either, and you'll find yourself forgetting about eating too."

A dramatic breakthrough in the retention of musical ideas occurred for another young musician when a repeating fragment of a solo he had studied several weeks earlier actually entered his dreams, dancing as fleeting note heads and as sounds, finally rousing him in the early hours of the morning. The impressions of the patterns, in which Wayne Shorter's variations on a blues riff acquired tremendous rhythmic momentum, were so clear that he could sing them aloud. Never before had the student experienced anything like it.

As implied by similar accounts of jazz dreams, improvisers gradually increase their conscious command over vocabulary and become fluent in converting images from one form of representation to another. In this regard, although improvisers caution students about becoming too reliant upon written notation—"anything you have to read in order to play will not help you in this tradition"—they acknowledge the usefulness of the musical symbols for fortifying ideas, and ultimately for interpreting or reading ideas in their own imaginations. In a related application, experienced artists can analyze other players' patterns without having to transcribe them. After copying a soloist's phrase with their instruments, they translate its finger patterns into notes that they hold in memory while envisioning the phrase's position within its progression and determining the tonic pitch of the underlying chord. This enables them to convert the notes into numbers, identifying the phrase's harmonic elements.

Eventually, many develop such facility that they can interpret phrases in theoretical terms at the very moment of their performance. "You learn that jazz is composed of certain kinds of phrases, for example, minor sevenths, flatted fifths, ninths, thirteenths, and each has its individuality. Then, when you listen to someone play, you begin to know when they are playing a major or minor chord and you say, 'I hear a thirteenth in there or a seventh.' Or you'll hear a musician play a phrase and you'll say to yourself, 'That's just a G7 chord with the notes run up a particular way. That's one way you can play a G7 chord'" (HO). With increasing skill at apprehending and remembering music, listeners who once may have depended on transcription and formal analysis to reveal the commonalities among solos suddenly find that they can simply pick out an interesting figure in a solo and bear it in mind as they scrutinize other performances, live or recorded, for related figures. As a result of their training, many artists develop such a fine sense of relative pitch that they greatly reduce the gap between their own abilities and those of other artists with perfect pitch who could take musical dictation with ease from the start.[30]

Seasoned players can also instantly construe phrases as physical movements. When listening to solos, Rufus Reid sometimes visualizes corresponding finger patterns on the neck of the bass, and pianists commonly imagine their hands assuming idiomatic movements on the keyboard. At other times, players move from physical representations to their corresponding sounds. Jerry Coker reported a dream that portrayed his hands at a piano slowly and methodically working through a complex solo that, in fact, had frustrated his earlier efforts at transcription. Waking excitedly, Coker discovered that he could reconstruct the problematic passages by recalling the finger patterns from his dream.[31]

In many instances, different forms of imaging interact fluidly over the course of an idea's realization. A musician may initiate an ascending phrase by envisioning its first two notes and playing them, but as their interval sounds, the musician may continue the phrase on sound and feel alone without the necessity for further visualization. Barry Harris's method trains students in the versatile handling of different forms of music conceptualization. When teaching an extended phrase, he may sing the first component, dictate the second in numerical scale degrees or in the letter names of pitches, and demonstrate the third through sound and finger movement at the piano. Ultimately, control over alternative forms of imaging leads improvisers to master the language of jazz, providing options that facilitate fluid thinking under the pressures of performance. It does not seem an exaggeration to say that jazz musicians achieve this mastery from every conceivable standpoint, including sounds, shapes, musical symbols, and physicality.[32]

### Early Limitations and Physical Mastery over Instruments

As learners endeavor to internalize the language of jazz, matters of physical constitution, relative mastery over instruments, and hearing acuity begin to dictate choices of material. Young pianists are literally able to grasp only those voicings of a mentor that lie within reach on the keyboard, just as young trumpeters are restricted to those patterns of an idol that require only moderate flexibility and strength to execute. When John McNeil discovered that he "didn't have the technique to copy Miles Davis's performance on *E.S.P.*," he pursued an alternative course, "copping a lot from guys like Nat Adderley who were easier to hear—the stuff he played based on a blues scale especially. Also Chet Baker, when he wasn't moving fast, since he played real simple."

Another youngster, who yearned to improvise like John Coltrane, described months of concentrated study before he could perform "just a few phrases" from a Coltrane solo. At the peak of his frustration, the student was calmed by a dream in which Coltrane appeared to him and offered gentle encouragement: "You're doing fine; just keep it up." The student adds that Coltrane "made the phrases sound so easy on the record." It was not until he tried to learn them that he realized "how difficult they were to play, let alone to have thought up in the first place." Naivete occasionally proves to be an asset in negotiating the gulf between student and master. No one had explained to Gary Bartz how difficult Charlie Parker solos were, so he simply copied them along with those of lesser masters.

Faced with an idol's inaccessible vocabulary patterns, learners may adopt various tacks, for example, transposing the patterns into keys less difficult for them to perform. In Miles Davis's case, he played Dizzy Gillespie's figures in the middle and lower register of the trumpet because initially he could not perform or "hear music"—that is, imagine it precisely—in the trumpet's highest register as could Gillespie.[33] Grappling with these limitations drives home to youngsters that they must gain such physical control over their instruments that their musical knowledge literally lies beneath their fingertips. As J. J. Johnson pointedly advised David Baker in his youth, "Any idea that you can't get out the other end of your horn is of absolutely no value in this music."

The most fundamental use of jazz vocabulary, then, requires the ability to perform patterns in time and at various tempos. This in turn requires learners to cultivate various technical performance skills tied to physical strength and agility. After George Duvivier trained himself to use two and three fingers for playing bass in his "solo work," his increased flexibility to reach across wide intervals on the same string and adjacent strings enabled him "to play ridiculous tempos without getting tired" and to play "groups of notes you can't possibly play with one [finger] because you can't move the finger back [to the next position] in time."

Emily Remler recalls going "through just such a frustration. I'd go to a session, not be able to express myself on guitar, and cry afterwards—I was so miserable. My technique was lousy, and my time was bad. My time was bad basically because I couldn't get to the phrases in time." Remler's frustration led to an intensive practicing binge known among musicians as woodshedding. She withdrew temporarily from the jazz community and subjected herself to a musical discipline that necessarily carried over into other aspects of her lifestyle. "I played and practiced the guitar constantly, five hours a day. At one point, I went down to the Jersey shore and locked myself in a room for a month. I lost twenty pounds, stopped smoking, and became a serious guitar player. It took a lot of muscle building to reach the point where I got a really strong and full sound on the guitar. I practiced my tail off trying to play octaves and different things to build up my muscles." After months of practice, Remler began to overcome her problems. Eventually, she developed a "reservoir of technique" that she was able to "tap" for many years.

Beyond developing the control to use vocabulary patterns instantly and "in time," artists typically pursue the goal of mastering them in all keys. "Maybe you would work on a phrase to fit one chord, or maybe you would work on something to fit the whole bridge," James Moody says, "but to use something in playing chorus after chorus, you must learn it in all keys." Per-

formers like Art Farmer and Kenny Barron possessed early musical gifts that
enabled them to transpose phrases without great effort. Fred Hersch similarly
"never had to work at it specifically." He states that, from years of piano study,
"I just had the kind of ear and the kind of facility [to] play what I heard around
the cycle of keys if I wanted to."

On the other hand, John McNeil initially "couldn't even play 'Happy Birthday' in all the keys to save my life. [I decided] to really work at this, [practicing
the] licks I'd learned from records in every key for two or three months or so."
The period was a very discouraging one for McNeil. "I just couldn't seem to
get on top of it; every time I took a phrase in a new key, I'd make different
mistakes." Although this learning process involves "a very gradual process of
getting better for some," in McNeil's case, it was just the opposite: "One day,
after all the struggling, I suddenly found that the phrases just seemed to fall
into place in every key, and I no longer had to work on those things anymore."
The dramatic transformation of McNeil's abilities was like being in "a fairy
tale" to him and remains "very vivid" in his memory.

Through the rigors of transposition exercises, artists develop intimate
knowledge of the characteristics of their vocabulary: each phrase's precise
length, its particular on- and off-beat character, its harmonic complexion, its
contour profile, its intervallic structure, and its span. Accessible at every pitch
level, in each key, and in any octave, a figure not only acquires different timbral
qualities with distinct effect and meaning, but it can be readily appended to
the beginning or ending of other figures to create longer formulations. In motor
terms, control over each version's unique fingering patterns increases its compatibility with those of prospective adjoining figures and, through physical
ease of movement, encourages particular couplings. Complete fluency represents an ideal for musicians, however. Many eventually find that the fingerings
associated with particular phrases remain easier for them in some keys than in
others, and they tend to favor the performance of the figures accordingly.

As their abilities develop, the field of approachable models continues to
open up before youngsters. Arthur Rhames led off his early training by copying B. B. King's blues solos. This experience, followed by six years developing
proficiency as a guitarist, enabled him to absorb John McLaughlin's more technically demanding, intricate jazz improvisations. When Tommy Flanagan's
hands grew large enough to cover the span of a "tenth" on the piano, he could
copy, at last, the special chord voicings of his favorite pianists. Earl Hines
experienced comparable breakthroughs.[34] John McNeil eventually assimilated
rapid chromatic figures within Miles Davis's performances that had baffled
him initially.

Meaningful improvements in the expressive use of the language of jazz
follow a musician's increasing physical comfort and dexterity in negotiating a
musical instrument. After Walter Bishop Jr. adapted the fingerings of classical

music technique to the lines he "wanted to play in jazz," he gained the freedom to play particular "melodic runs" ascending, runs that his previous technique had restricted him to play as descending patterns. Specifically, learning to move the thumb of the right hand under the extended fingers as they climb higher to the right on the keyboard enables the pianist to achieve "a longer ascending hand position" with increased possibilities "for melodic range and contour."[35] For many instrumentalists, the mastery over new, alternate fingerings can suggest new combinations of vocabulary patterns that were previously too awkward to adjoin in a single flow of movement. Improved control also enables horn players to extend former patterns into higher parts of an instrument's range, allowing them to conceive new melodies there.

When Fred Hersch assimilated one teacher's "choreographic concept" of piano performance, learning to "play up off the keys with loose hands and caressing the keys rather than bearing down on them," his touch imbued solos with new subtleties of dynamic contrast. For saxophonist Jeff Morgan, it was not until he adopted a routine of practicing six hours a day that he began to feel that the instrument was truly a part of him and that he could improvise with great freedom. For the first time, he was able to experience what he had often heard Barry Harris describe in his workshops as the expressive feeling of actually "talking" with the patterns he played.

Mastery over particular technical features of performance increases both the nuances of musical sound and the artist's ability to express emotion. Over a four-year recording history, Booker Little mastered infinitesimal valve depressions for ornamenting pitches with refined microtonal scoops that added pathos and distinction to his language use. In Harold Ousley's case, the goal has been to cultivate qualities of sound characterized by their "sheer beauty." He uses the "essence of Gene Ammons's sound" as a source of inspiration and is "still striving to reach the level of beauty" he discerns in Ammons's playing. "Due to the law of infinity, sound can be improved and improved and improved. So, I'm constantly striving to improve my sound to get to the point where the sound is so beautiful that when people hear it they're caressed; their souls are inspired and nourished just by the sound itself. I'm working toward a style that would leave people on a plane with a feeling of complete elation."

Because of the constraints that improvisers' abilities as instrumentalists place upon the realization of musical ideas, many advocate formal study with classical musicians who can share with them the most advanced academic methods of musical training. Barry Harris attributes his facility as an improviser in part to his early study of classical music and, in more recent years, to his study of a remarkable technical method for piano developed by master teacher Abby Whiteside. Harris continues to hone his skills as a private student with Sophia Rosoff, another disciple of Whiteside's. He also satisfies his varied musical interests by participating in a classical music recital class conducted by Rosoff, assuring it a regular place within his own demanding schedule of jazz teaching and performance.

Just as technical training received outside the jazz community affects the dialogue between improvisers in their own language, it exposes them to various features of other music systems. If absorbed, the features assume a distinctive place within the vocabulary of improvisers and enter the stream of the larger jazz tradition. One trumpeter periodically incorporates melodic patterns from Bach into his storehouse, and pianist Cedar Walton once told John Hicks that he had derived some ideas for chord voicings from his analysis of Beethoven sonatas.

Some artists cannot initially afford the technical training associated with classical music. Or, as described earlier, they simply choose to teach themselves musical instruments. Many augment their efforts with information gleaned from friends and from teachers of varying quality at neighborhood music centers. Learning without skilled instruction can lead potentially to idiosyncratic performance techniques and unique stylistic traits, both highly valued in the jazz tradition.[36] Or it can produce poor performance habits that eventually demand correction. Art Farmer was initially a self-taught trumpeter who did not receive instruction in even such fundamental practices as warming up before playing. After Farmer graduated from high school, his prodigious talent initially compensated for his deficient foundation, but the physical demands of an engagement at the Apollo Theatre exhausted his endurance. Playing six- to seven-hour shows seven days a week, he was performing with insufficient air support and excessive pressure on his lips. This eventually caused a tooth "to drop down" and lacerate his lip, bringing his professional life temporarily to a standstill. Refusing to be defeated by the experience, Farmer worked as a janitor in a theater, where he earned barely enough to support himself, and, at the recommendation of legendary trumpeter Freddie Webster, studied with a private trumpet teacher to acquire the "proper technique." It required two years of training before he could resume his musical career.

The physiological requirements of jazz performance occasionally lead improvisers to consult various experts on the fringes of the jazz community. Among them are the "chop doctors," who, in the years before there was a performance medicine specialty, attended to what is known as the chops, the combination of physiological structures integrally linked to playing technique, which can be strained in musical performance. The chop doctors had "their own different approaches—certain exercises and practice routines to help musicians get their chops back."[37]

To address more general issues bearing on the body's performance, some improvisers study with dance teachers, physical therapists employing relaxation techniques such as the Alexander method, advocates of meditative practices associated with yoga, or proponents of various Eastern religions. Others

seek similar ends by regulating their diets or using drugs for relaxation or stimulation. One trumpeter who had noticed the teeth formation of his idol went
so far as to have a dentist file down and slightly separate his own front teeth in
the hope that this would "free up" his air stream. (The results were inconclu-
sive.) Another player's performance was immeasurably improved when, after
years of difficulty, a skilled dentist replaced the player's poorly fashioned den-
tures with a set that fit properly. Such problems are not uncommon among
musicians whose incomes, often but at subsistence level, render standard medical care and health insurance beyond their means, or among those who neglect
their health while traveling the road band circuit.

Regardless of the complexity of maintaining their physical well-being,
many improvisers remain preoccupied with improving their technical proficiency because they are greatly dependent on instrumental performance for the
assimilation of jazz vocabulary and its expressive use.

# FIVE

**Seeing Out a Bit**

**Expanding upon Early Influences**

*It all goes from imitation to assimilation to innovation. You move from the imitation stage to the assimilation stage when you take little bits of things from different people and weld them into an identifiable style—creating your own style. Once you've created your own sound and you have a good sense of the history of the music, then you think of where the music hasn't gone and where it can go— and that's innovation.* —Walter Bishop Jr.

Many beginners select as their exclusive idol one major figure in jazz. They copy that idol's precise vocabulary, vocabulary usage, and tune treatment, striving to improvise in the idol's precise style. Progress toward such a goal is necessarily gradual; at times, it is barely evident to the aspiring performer. In many cases, it is through encounters with veterans that they notice signs of significant advancement. Bobby Rogovin remembers his astonishment and pride the day a friend of trumpeter Donald Byrd burst into Rogovin's practice studio and called out Byrd's name, having mistaken Rogovin's performance for that of his mentor. A saxophonist once received unexpected praise when musicians, having heard his improvisations filter through the walls of a neighboring apartment, inquired about the title of the Charlie Parker recording they thought they had just overheard. One anecdote that epitomizes a student's awareness of his own success concerns a young artist—a skilled "copier"—who once approached his idol on the bandstand during the latter's uninspired performance and declared with irony, "Man, you ain't you. *I'm* you." [1]

Although encouraging students initially to follow a particular musical master and acknowledging the discipline required of faithful understudies, seasoned improvisers ultimately view such achievements as limited. Curtis Fuller feels that it is "great for a musician to walk in the shoes of the fisherman" because imitation is a great compliment, but, he cautions, "I wouldn't want to lose my personality or shut down my development that way." Otherwise, he says, "I wouldn't have enhanced what's been done before. I would rather be an extension than a retention."

Direct counsel reinforces this view within the jazz community. It helped to be in an environment with "Bud Powell, Charlie Parker, Oscar Pettiford, and others who were so creative and like-minded," Max Roach admits. "We had all been instructed that to make an imprint of your own, you had to discover yourself. . . . We fed off of each other, but encouraged each other to do things that were individual." Everyone studied "the classics, like Bud studied Art Tatum," but they were aware of the "danger of concentrating so much on someone else's style that it was becoming predominant" in their own playing.

Some view too close an imitation of a master as an ethical issue. Arthur Rhames stopped trying to duplicate "exactly what other artists played" because he realized that "they were all playing out of their experiences, their lives— the things that happened to them." Even though he could "relate in a general way to most of it," he decided that jazz performance is "too personal" to try to duplicate exactly what other artists "were saying." There was, moreover, the spectre of imitators deliberately or inadvertently taking credit for musical ideas not original with them, or exhausting the professional jobs their mentors might otherwise have acquired.[2] "He's living on Eddie Jefferson," George Johnson Jr. heard people say of him after he had absorbed his mentor's style. This did not really "hurt" Johnson's feelings at the time, because he was glad that others could relate him to "somebody." At the same time, he knew that he could not keep singing Jefferson's material because people would conclude that he was merely a "mimic."

Ultimately, Max Roach recalls, it was only after aspiring players had devoted years to developing their "own musical personality" that experts began "to look at you, to single you out and select you for their bands." Lester Young and others in Roach's early circle advised artists with cleverly rhymed aphorisms like "You can't join the throng 'til you write your own song."

One of the ways in which learners modify an initial mentor's influence is by studying the styles of other artists, a practice that is a natural outgrowth of their growing appreciation for the larger tradition of jazz. Barry Harris and his peers each had a particular idol, but as they grew they began "to see out a little bit." Suddenly, they stopped "idolizing" and listened "to all the giants." They realized that their tradition was "bigger than Bird, bigger than Bud Powell, much bigger than any of them." Even the greatest artists "hadn't done it all." Some youngsters, not intent upon exclusive apprenticeships, adopt this perspective from the start, absorbing features from different mentors through saturated listening, aural analysis, and transcription.

### Discovering the Larger Jazz Tradition

As their understanding expands, students learn that during particular periods in the history of jazz the innovative practices of outstanding soloists and bands drew a strong following, eventually influencing artists across the jazz community's national network. There arose distinct but interrelated performance schools, known also as idioms or style periods. Labels include *New Orleans jazz,* a reference to the turn-of-the-century style named for the locale of its originators; *swing,* a description of the practices of the big bands and small ensembles during the thirties;[3] *bebop,* a possibly onomatopoetic term from the forties based on a characteristic rhythmic pattern of the idiom; *hard bop,* a fifties development of bebop; *free jazz,* a phrase of the late fifties and early sixties reflecting the ideological rejection of former jazz conventions; and *fusion,* a particular blend of rock and jazz. Each movement "had its particular giants. In the bop thing, Bird and Dizzy were the originators, and the hard bop school has its certain giants. They all have stylistic differences" (AR).

As new personal and regional performance styles spawned rapid changes in the language of jazz, successive generations of learners considered an ever increasing range of models. In Doc Cheatham's view, "up until Dizzy" there were really only two basic jazz styles: the New Orleans style and the Western style. If a player "could get one style, they would be happy." Joe Oliver was one of the chief proponents of New Orleans jazz and "everybody was copying after him." In St. Louis, he adds, "there were also great trumpet players" like Charlie Creath, whose Western style differed from the New Orleans style; "everybody tried to copy off Charlie Creath." Since Dizzy Gillespie and others in the bebop movement, however, there has been a perpetual blossoming of styles. Clark Terry, Fats Navarro, and many others have been innovative "'cause everybody's thinking differently now," Cheatham explains. "Everybody's trying to think of something that the other guy hasn't done." He considers the new styles to be for "the young kids" who find them "easier to keep up with" than he does. "Because they're born in these different styles, they can pick them up right away, one after another. And it's going to continue like that," he emphasizes.

Of course, even among members of the same generation, students form different views of their tradition. Some, in especially diverse jazz communities, are exposed to a wide range of styles at sessions attended sometimes by artists of four music generations. But the experience of others is more limited. Growing up in Nashville with minimal exposure to jazz musicians, Doc Cheatham first learned about jazz through Paul Whiteman and Ted Lewis recordings. He expanded his horizon through hearing such traveling artists as Johnny Dunn and Louis Smith, but it was with his move to Chicago in the mid-twenties that the greatest revelation came to him. There, he heard all the important musicians from New Orleans and understood "how corny" some of his own early influences—like Whiteman—had been. Cheatham subsequently adopted Louis Armstrong as his principal mentor.

Similarly, Melba Liston only became aware of bebop after she joined Dizzy Gillespie's band in New York City in 1949. The first inkling Fred Hersch had that there were, in fact, different jazz idioms was during his college years when, at another musician's recommendation, he "read LeRoi Jones's [Amiri Baraka's] *Black Music*." The book introduced him to "free jazz and the spirituality aspect of the music" and led him to performers such as Pharaoh Sanders, John Coltrane, Archie Shepp, Albert Ayler, and Cecil Taylor.

Artists grounded in the jazz mainstream can find new styles to be bewildering at first. Raised in a little town in California, the very young John McNeil stumbled upon jazz through a chance viewing of a televised performance by Louis Armstrong. The program so inspired him that he decided to become a jazz trumpeter and began learning to play by listening to Armstrong recordings. At sixteen, McNeil joined a territory band in northern California, where he was immediately confronted by a trumpet player in his twenties who urged him to consider "Miles Davis or someone more hip."

Although McNeil had never heard of Davis, he followed the trumpeter's advice and sought out Davis recordings. It was by chance that he bought the album *E.S.P.,* featuring especially adventurous performances by Davis. With Louis Armstrong as his chief point of reference, McNeil judged *E.S.P.* to be "Martian music!" Because the older player had said it would be good for him, and despite the little sense he could make of it, he listened to the record "once or twice every day after school." One thing led to another. McNeil asked for other suggestions and "borrowed somebody's *Down Beat*." After reading about different trumpet players, he bought albums he found to be more accessible—those by such players as Clark Terry, Freddie Hubbard, Lee Morgan, Chet Baker, and Nat Adderley. McNeil recollects that he expanded his "knowledge of jazz three thousand percent" in the space of a single year.

Other students find that the reorientation required by encountering new idioms is as "natural" as it is exciting. Tommy Flanagan had been listening to Teddy Wilson and Art Tatum when he first heard Coleman Hawkins records with such pianists as Hank Jones and Thelonious Monk and started building his interest in "more modern things." In a sense, Tatum had prepared Flanagan for the "big difference" that distinguished one style from another. "It was good to hear someone else like Bud [Powell] playing logically but on another scale. Bud had his own kind of energy going that matched Bird and Diz." Under the influence of peers like Tommy Flanagan, Barry Harris similarly copied boogie-woogie and swing masters until he discovered bebop innovators Parker, Powell, and Monk and turned his attention to their styles.

As in cases cited above, many learners complete a successful apprenticeship with a proponent of an established idiom, then become enticed by the performance practices introduced by emerging personalities. "Young kids are usually anxious to learn whatever is happening now, whatever the latest thing is," and to spread the word within their early circles (AF). Conversely, students who cultivate their skills during a new performance movement eventually become interested in earlier styles. Years after Art Farmer learned the language of bebop from Gillespie and Parker, whose "ideas seemed more interesting and fantastic than any I had heard up to that time," Farmer realized that he "had not given the older players the respect that was due them" and began seriously studying Louis Armstrong's records. He came to appreciate that "Louis was the master. In all the years since Armstrong," Farmer maintains, "there has not been anybody who has played any more or any better than him."

Kenny Washington's study of drummers was also "backwards historically." He began by imitating Max Roach, "Philly" Joe Jones, and Arthur Taylor, artists who were in the public eye when he was learning. Later, he methodically perused recordings by early drummers like Shadow Wilson and Big Sid Catlett. "I learned something new from everybody," Washington says. The quest to understand their successive heroes commonly leads learners through a series of formal study binges. Keith Copeland remembers an "Art Blakey period" when he focused on Blakey's albums with the Jazz Messengers, a "Max Roach period" when he collected every album by Roach's groups, and an "Elvin Jones period" when he reviewed all the albums on which Jones had performed as a member of John Coltrane's historic quartet. Implementing comparable programs, youngsters not only sample the precise vocabulary patterns of each idol, but they isolate and analyze the wide-ranging performance traits and musical concepts that make up an idol's improvisational style.

As their level of sophistication advances, students grasp the multitude of attributes comprising each artist's "musical personality," from the most specific features of timbre and melody construction to the most general issues concerning musical texture and tune treatment. They learn, moreover, to interpret such matters within the changing stream of their music's historical conventions and come to value the processes by which individuals establish their own identities through interacting with peers and predecessors alike. "It helps your playing to have some tradition behind you," Washington states. "To understand Tony Williams, you ought to know 'Philly' Joe Jones and Sid Catlett. It's the same with drummers as with other instrumentalists. Unless you understand James P. Johnson and Fats Waller, you don't really understand Ahmad Jamal, or Bud Powell, or Herbie Hancock."

### Features of Musical Personality as Models

An idol's personal sound is commonly the precise object of imitation for learners. It is a clearly discernible, all-encompassing marker of an individual artist's identity. Tommy Turrentine considers it to be the "one way you can tell an instrumentalist right away when he solos." Chuck Israels and his high school friends tested each other's sensitivity to these matters through musical games. Although Steve Kuhn had a more "highly developed ear for recognizing different jazz tunes from records, I had a good ear for timbre and inflection and the personal marks of the player," Israels observes, "and I could always recognize the soloists."

Various elements contribute to an artist's sound profile, timbre being the most obvious. Charlie Parker's tone quality had a "hard, brittle edge, rich in upper partials," which was very different from the "sweetness produced by older alto saxophone players like Johnny Hodges or Benny Carter." Vibrato is another essential characteristic of style. Parker's vibrato was "narrow and slow" compared to that of Lester Young.[4] Representing similar distinctions, Coleman Hawkins performed tenor saxophone with a "rich, guttural tone" and a "wide, fast vibrato," whereas Young performed the same instrument with "a light tone and a slower vibrato."[5] Musical texture comprises an integral part of the timbre of players whose instruments have the capacity for multipart performance, a subject discussed later in this section.

An artist's articulation of pitches with various qualities of hardness or softness to produce alternately focused or diffused sounds similarly personalizes timbre. Clifford Brown periodically compresses the air stream behind his tongue, bottling up his sound to create dramatic tension and unique timbral effects, before releasing the air into the mouthpiece with a "slap-tongue" attack of varied intensity.[6] For some instrumentalists, the development of what musicians call touch is a pertinent issue. The "very personal sound that drummers produce" rests not only in the "choice of sticks and choice of tips, but also in the hands, in the execution, and in the amount of force used" (KC). Pianists like Thelonious Monk express their "immediately recognizable sound [and] their whole attitude about their music just through the way they touch the keyboard" (JH).

Concern for comparable issues leads aspiring singers to copy the individual diction and the "shaping" of words they notice in their idols. "Some people sing *love* so differently—*luuv* or *lahv*," Carmen Lundy observes. "There are different ways of saying words like *cry*. You can say *cryie* or *crahy*. Also, singers may place their emphasis on different words in the same song," shaping them, at times, to their own improvised melodies. Lundy has noticed that individuals exploit their vocal range differently in this respect. Virtuosos like Sarah Vaughan can create phrases that leap over their entire range "in only two bars." Freeing themselves from the constraints of delivering song texts, singers turn to scat performance to create abstract improvisations as complex as those of instrumentalists. Choice of scat syllables is yet "another thing you can get from singers," Lundy points out. Scat vocables serve as devices for manipulating the voice as an instrument and molding sounds, allowing singers to explore diverse features of pitch articulation, coloration, and resonance. Some syllables enable them to imitate singular qualities of different instruments, whereas other syllables bring out the unique sounds that the individual vocalist develops as signature traits. "Everybody has their little things," Lundy continues.

> Certain scat singers use the syllable dwee a lot. Ella Fitzgerald doesn't really use a lot of dwee. She uses a little more bee-bop-bop-bah-ooo-bee-doo-bee. She uses more of the bee and dee sounds. But then I came to listen to Betty Carter, and she would use more of the louie-ooie-la-la-la, like it was more of a tongue thing with her. Sarah Vaughan would be shoo-bee-oo-bee shoo-doo-shoo-bee-ooo-bee. She had more of this shoo-eee-bee-eee sound. Al Jarreau had another thing; he was more rhythmic with his. Also, it would be more a sound than it was a note coming out at times. It was like ooo-ah-ah-ah.

Mastering the subtle qualities of sound associated with different syllables allows singers to perform with new shades of expression just as mastering the subtleties of personal timbre develops the instrumentalist's sound.

Pitch inflections like scoops and more extensive, embellishing microtonal shapes can be equally distinct. Booker Little tended to scoop up to pitches for nuance, whereas Lee Morgan liked to articulate pitches at their normal level, then flatten their sound slightly as if he were sighing. Miles Davis transformed the character of his instrument with such a variety of inflections that "at times he didn't even sound like he was playing a trumpet. It was just the sound of his voice" (LH). Musicians ultimately imbue their phrases with varying amounts of vocalized expression. Since the free jazz movement especially, some combine traditional vocabulary with a personalized repertory of extended instrumental techniques such as multiphonics, in which improvisers perform cries made up of complex pitch clusters.

The many components of sound serve both as primary vehicles for affective performance and as signature traits. "Sound itself has a power we're turned on or off by," Harold Ousley says, expressing what he learned in the course of emulating Gene Ammons's ballad style. "A screech like scraping a skillet turns us off; it can get on your nerves. But a fantastic sound, a beautiful sound, so mellow and pleasant, like Gene Ammons's sound, is something wonderful."

Finding words to describe musical subtleties like tone color and affect is a challenge that the verbally agile and creative jazz musician meets with the descriptive language of personality and emotion found in poetry. Ella Fitzgerald "sounds so young, having that coquettish, little-girlish quality," whereas Billie Holiday has "that soulful, worldly quality" (RB). Within the hard bop school, trumpeter Clifford Brown's "sheer exuberance" distinguishes his performances; Lee Morgan has "sassiness," and Booker Little a "bittersweet" quality. Clark Terry varies "fiery" passages with others that are as often "playful, witty, and humorous." Miles Davis's "tone quality and moods changed constantly—on one note and from note to note—and he sounded almost like a different guy at times" (JMc).

John Coltrane solos, on the other hand, are consistently intense, if not melancholy. To Lonnie Hillyer, Coltrane "sounded a lot like he was crying when he played, and it took some getting used to at first." Youngsters model their own sounds not only upon those they find attractive but on those whose moods they, too, wish to evoke in performance. "In the beginning," Arthur Rhames "copied B. B. King" when Rhames's own music was "simply an expression of my introvertedness and pathetic feelings. I wanted to make people sad, to make them cry from hearing that twangy blues guitar."

## Personal Sound in Relation to Other Traits

In addition to developing a palette of skills that enhance the musician's sound, artists can develop a myriad of other stylistic traits to reflect their individual visions as interpreters and creators of music. For example, improvisers treat fundamental musical elements of phrase formulation in personal ways. Even if two drummers perform the same time-keeping pattern, experts can identify them by the subtle differences in their "placement of quarter notes in relation to the main beat," that is, in their rhythmic phrasing (MR). Rhythmic values also matter. Horn players like Sonny Stitt invent relatively uniform phrases, whereas Sonny Rollins favors greater variety. "He likes to play with the time." Over a fast beat, he may begin by improvising "slow, elongated phrases or [by] sustain[ing] a note over two or three bars before getting into faster playing" (HO).

Soloists also differ in their predispositions toward symmetrical or asymmetrical divisions of the beat. Despite the fact that Fats Navarro and Dizzy Gillespie "were working in the same direction," their approaches to rhythm remained distinct in certain respects (BH). According to Lonnie Hillyer, Navarro "played so cleanly and evenly, with a lot of eighth notes and sixteenth notes, that you can write his things down easily. He was like a painter who proceeds carefully, one stroke at a time." On the other hand, Hillyer continues, Gillespie is "like a painter who takes a can of paint and just throws the whole thing at a canvas and tries to make something out of it, playing with great daring in between the spaces of time and sound." Barry Harris adds a humorous twist to his description of a "crammer." He explains, "Dizzy can take a phrase that you never thought could be played in a certain space, and he'll just cram it in there and make it work beautifully" (ex. 5.1).

Accentuation and articulation are equally important to phrasing. Charlie Parker had a penchant for accenting the highest pitch within any stream of pitches, creating "a lively, unpredictable syncopated rhythm." He also was known for grouping "notes into subphrases that move from the weak to strong part of the beat." His practices during slow pieces were especially varied, ranging from long slurred passages to phrases in which articulation is varied with distinctive finesse.[7] Some performers display a predilection for slurring or tonguing pitches. Clifford Brown often tongued pitches individually, at times applying the technique to create complex rhythmic patterns with a single pitch, as if drumming with the trumpet. Lee Morgan absorbed and personalized this tonguing technique, but Booker Little tended to avoid it, preferring to articulate pitches lightly or to tie them together by slurring them. Don Sickler's observation that the great players with whom he has collaborated as a publisher do not always recognize his transcriptions of their solos until articulation and phrasing marks have been added underscores the importance of these elements of musical style.

Characteristic phrase lengths also distinguish performers. Benny Carter's innovative melodies reveal a "different way of phrasing stuff" in comparison to the melodic phrasing of other swing players. "He was more like the guys who eventually ended up playing bebop. He flowed. He kept moving all the time" (LD). Since the free jazz period especially, the cultivation of circular breathing techniques has enabled some horn players to perform extraordinarily long phrases without breaking their flow. Singers periodically make use of comparable techniques. It was a gratifying moment for one puzzled student when he finally figured out Al Jarreau's unusual method "of alternately inhaling and exhaling as he sings" to produce continuous call and response patterns.

Also integral to artists' personal traits or concepts is their handling of melody and harmony. Although soloists commonly mix vertical and horizontal musical elements in their conceptions, some may favor a vertical concept, emphasizing chord arpeggiations and interpreting a progression's individual chords faithfully, "articulat[ing] each chord that comes up" with selected pitches.[8] Particular features in the solos from the early performances of Coleman Hawkins and John Coltrane epitomize such practices within the swing and hard bop idioms respectively (exx. 5.2a1–a2). Other performers may favor a horizontal concept, which they view as providing greater "freedom of movement . . . rhythmically and in the line."[9] Their creations display a high degree of scale patterning or "especially lyrical" melodies (HO).

Horizontal playing is less concerned with describing each chord and incorporating the features of chord changes in the formulation of melodies, although it does rely on progression as a general guide. Its particular mix of chord and non-chord tones is often harmonically ambiguous or neutral, neither confirming nor opposing the underlying structure.[10] Passages from Lester Young's performances demonstrate the concept. His style "wasn't a vertical style with a lot of runs, but was more like taking a phrase and laying it across the changes. His phrases just seemed to float on top of the chords, and he might use the same chord for two bars and not even double up on it—maybe just play sustained notes" (HO) (exx. 5.2b1–b2). As part of their trademarks, some performers favor inside or outside playing, designating the degree to which improvised melodies emphasize chord tones or non-chord tones.

George Russell likens the approaches described above to taking different kinds of trips along a river where every small town represents a chord and larger towns represent "tonic stations," points at which two or more chords resolve—as in the case of ii–V chords resolving to I. In terms of emphasis, to continue this metaphor, Hawkins solos are like the trips of a local steamer with stops at each town along the way, whereas Young solos are like the trips of an express steamer that stops primarily at the larger towns. Like Hawkins solos, Coltrane solos follow the local steamer's route, but between each town Coltrane jets off to visit neighboring towns; his side excursions ascend into the "chromatic sphere of each chord, [whereas] Hawkins stays on the ground close to the sound of" the chords on the primary route.[11]

Additionally, artists discriminate among players on the basis of the emphasis each places on common elemental figures for solo construction. Drummers, for example, make different uses of the "rudiments: twenty-six elemental rhythmic patterns," including different kinds of drum rolls and paradiddles derived from eighteenth- and nineteenth-century "European military percussion techniques," which have become a standard feature of drum pedagogy.[12] Many jazz drummers like "Philly" Joe Jones and Alan Dawson draw their fundamental phrase components from the rudimental figures they feature in their teaching methods (KC). Others have "studied drum rolls and things," but are not "paradiddle persons" to the same degree (LW). In fact, some "didn't have the same kind of technical training" as their counterparts, who, in turn, regard them as never having "played anything that sounded like it came out of a book" (AT). Players have mixed rudiments with patterns of their own invention, and those specific to African American musical traditions, since the early days of New Orleans jazz.[13]

Their application of other melodic and rhythmic components of their vocabulary stores also distinguishes players.[14] Gestures such as common chromatic blues figures in Kenny Dorham solos (ex. 5.3a), rhythmic tremolo patterns in Lee Morgan solos (ex. 5.3b), and recurring cadential figures in Dorham and Parker solos (exx. 5.3c–d) are almost entirely absent from Booker Little solos. On the other hand, many of Little's patterns are distinctive (exx. 5.3e1–e2); and one in particular, although used by various improvisers, assumes a signature function in Little solos because he performs it so frequently (ex. 5.3f). Improvisers also differ in their pointed references to the signature patterns and compositions of other artists. Some exploit the practice minimally, others routinely. Charlie Parker is renowned for his quotations from a vast musical literature.[15] Similarly, during a single performance of "Take the 'A' Train," Betty Roché devotes different segments of her vocal improvisation to the scat styles of Dizzy Gillespie, Sarah Vaughan, and Ella Fitzgerald, and whimsically quotes such tunes as "Pop Goes the Weasel."[16]

These and the other features of language use described above pertain to improvisers generally. Dramatically shaping their precise application in some instances, however, are the particular characteristics of instruments and the instruments' changing performance conventions. Developments within string bass solos in jazz provide a case in point. The late twenties trend toward larger groups coincided with replacing the tuba with the bass as the focal point of the rhythm section, causing many tuba players to switch instruments.[17] As George Duvivier conjectures, however, few early tuba players "made a successful transition to the bass, because they had nothing to guide them from a wind instrument to a string instrument." Consequently,

> they made up for their deficiencies by slapping the bass, twirling it, and being active. Also, in the old days, the [bridge and therefore the] playing action of the strings on those basses was high, and the strings were a heavier gauge, so you worked harder when you played. This meant you also had less facility. If the action was high, you couldn't play a lot of notes easily. You had to allow for the strings' reactions after you played them. So, in the late thirties, you could almost count all the bass players on one hand that could influence anybody: [Jimmy] Blanton, [Milt] Hinton, Billy Taylor Sr., Wellman Braud. Bob Haggart was interesting.

As implied above, these developments reflect the musical background and training of early bass players and the design or set-up of the instrument itself. Musicians like John Lindsay used bowing techniques at times, but typically they plucked bass strings with the right index finger, cultivating a percussive style that was generally suited to the rhythmic aspects of jazz.[18] Among the methods they favored were slap-bass techniques, whose combined percussive and tonal effects increased their instrument's volume and complexity of sound. The slow playing action of the basses of that period meant also that bass solos were relatively spare. Contemporary bass players, when reflecting on the style of their New Orleans and early swing predecessors, characterize their articulation of pitches as "short, frumpy, and tuba-like" and their musical conceptions as "more rhythmic than melodic."

Few bass players during the swing era were featured often as soloists, not even the noted artist Walter Page of Count Basie's band. The first jazz bass virtuoso soloist was Jimmy Blanton of Duke Ellington's band; he had cultivated a remarkable facility both with bowed (arco) and plucked (pizzicato) playing techniques, and his prowess overcame the difficulties of playing an instrument with high string action.[19] George Duvivier recalls especially Blanton's 1940 solo on "Jack the Bear."[20] At a time when many bass solos consisted largely of regular stepwise walking bass lines, Blanton agilely manipulated "bass note exercise-type figures" so that they "came out melodically." The solo had a great impact on jazz bass players because no one had ever done anything comparable on the bass before. Duvivier, who had formerly patterned his improvisations after Slam Stewart, learned Blanton's solo and performed it periodically as a "bass feature."

Subsequently, bebop bass players like Oscar Pettiford cultivated this approach further by occasionally infusing the walking bass lines with more complex melodic phrases, akin to the approach of horn players (AD). In the forties, the technology of amplification and the replacement of the bass's gut strings with steel strings reinforced the trend by allowing the production of instruments with lower bridges and faster action. This enabled Ray Brown and other great artists to improvise with ease and facility.

Over the past few decades, an increasing number of bass players have studied with classically trained teachers, developing great technical mastery over the bass and learning conventional bowing techniques. Moreover, in order to meet the considerable demands that jazz performance places upon endurance and flexibility, many have adopted the multiple-finger techniques of classical guitarists. Not surprisingly, they also invent their own.

Chance encounters among bass players produce revelations in this regard. At the recording session where they first met, George Duvivier and Scott LaFaro, who was "more or less the pioneer of facility on the bass," expressed surprise at each other's playing technique. LaFaro had thought that Duvivier played with two fingers, as did LaFaro himself. In fact, Duvivier was using one finger like Ray Brown, who managed "a lot of speed with it." Never having observed two-finger playing before, Duvivier was equally fascinated by LaFaro. Over the years, players like Scott LaFaro, Charles Mingus, Paul Chambers, Eddie Gomez, Niels-Henning Ørsted Pedersen, Richard Davis, and many others ultimately attained a level of virtuosity as improvisers comparable to that of other exemplary jazz instrumentalists.

Moreover, since the sixties, free jazz players like Charlie Haden, Jimmy Garrison, and Dave Holland have extended the expressive capacity of the bass by improvising simultaneous independent lines, making use of unconventional parts of the instrument's body and strings to create new sounds, and exploring the possibilities of playing both high harmonics and double stops.[21] "The technique of bass players today is one hundred times what it was when I started out playing," Art Farmer says. "Instead of playing walking bass, they can play all kinds of pitch clusters—millions of notes. It's called the guitar style on bass."

For soloists whose instruments have the capacity for multipart invention, such as pianists, the relative activity produced at different levels of their performance's general musical texture is an important trait of personal style. As mentioned earlier, in creating personal chord voicings, pianists combine decisions about pitch selection with decisions about such matters as utilizing the keyboard's range, emphasizing right- or left-hand playing, and determining the relative lightness or heaviness of their parts. Individual considerations reflect alternative concepts associated with the lineage of the artist's instrument. Early pianists like Jelly Roll Morton and Fats Waller "exploited the piano's full potential" by utilizing the whole keyboard and giving equal weight to patterns played by both hands. Their improvisations invite descriptions like "dense, lush, polyphonic, and orchestral" (FH).

In much the same way, one can discern a variety of concepts within the general orchestral approach. In the early twentieth century, Scott Joplin and other individuals influenced by ragtime—and later, great stride pianists like James P. Johnson—maintained strict time with the left hand by "alternating pedal notes with chords in the 'oompah' manner of the marching band" and, with the right hand, overlaid this pattern with "syncopated 'raggy' figures, often derived from chordal hand positions, in the treble." [22] In the style of boogie-woogie, which developed in the twenties and enjoyed subsequent periods of resurgence, pianists like Pete Johnson commonly played eighth-note rhythmic ostinatos in the left hand, outlining a simple blues progression. The right hand improvised high repeating riffs, "single-line melodies and punctuated chords" performed tremolos or played adjacent pitches, creating dissonances and simulating blue notes. [23]

With the innovations of New Orleans jazz pianists like Jelly Roll Morton, the right-hand part took greater liberties in improvising around the piece's theme and changing its phrasing in relation to the left hand's beat, playing rhythms slightly ahead of or behind it. Of special importance was the increase in the music's rhythmic swing achieved by subtly varying the long-short relationships among successive eighth notes. At the same time, the left-hand part became ever more linear, producing "walking tenths and octaves, and melodic runs." During the transition from ragtime to early jazz piano, the trend toward a less heavy and more independent right-hand voice reflected in part the influence of the horn player's formulation of solos and gradually provided the basis for an alternative concept to that of orchestral piano. Earl Hines developed a trumpet style of performance "in which he played octaves instead of full chords in the right hand," employing crisp hornlike attacks and using "tremolos on long notes to simulate vibrato and/or a breath crescendo." [24]

Continuing along this course, players like Teddy Wilson and Count Basie strove for a lighter sound in the right hand and commonly improvised single-note melodic runs. In response to the faster tempos of the swing period, many also adopted "single bass notes and simple chords" to lighten the left-hand part. Sometimes they would perform "broken tenths or seventh chords" in the earlier ragtime manner; at other times, they would use "walking tenths" as a technique "for connecting chord progressions." Basie varied his accompaniment to include four-beat time-keeping patterns, as well as "quietly jabbed . . . left-hand chords," whose unpredictable rhythmic patterns anticipated later developments by bebop pianists. His spare improvised right hand and minimal use of his left hand also allowed a more prominent accompaniment to his solos by bassist Walter Page and drummer Jo Jones.

During the bebop period, pianists like Al Haig and Bud Powell freed the left hand from its conventional function of keeping time. Bud Powell improvised complex right-hand melodies in the fashion of Charlie Parker. With his left hand he varied his part with "ostinato octave leaps . . . spare intervals such as tenths and sevenths; and occasional single notes in the bass moving in half notes." Bebop pianists made use of other approaches carried over from the big band era as well. One, associated with Phil Moore and Milt Buckner, is the "'locked hands' block-chord style," imitative of the chord voicings of saxophone sections. The pianists produced a thick musical texture by harmonizing each melody note "with a four-note chord in the right hand" and doubling the melody note an octave lower in the left hand. This procedure generates "nonharmonic tones in every voice [producing the effect of] 'passing chords' and 'neighbor chords' within the basic progression." Another approach associated with virtuosos like Phineous Newborn consists of playing intricate single-note melodies in both hands simultaneously, one or more octaves apart.[25]

Jazz pianists of the sixties added a wealth of other techniques to those they inherited. Modal players like McCoy Tyner commonly featured rootless left-hand seventh-chord voicings, as they improvised melodies derived from pentatonic scales in the right hand.[26] Free jazz pianists like Cecil Taylor availed themselves of more radical devices, at times creating music without reference to a steady beat. Their solos featured the use of "tone clusters, atonal motivic development, and unusual attacks (with the palm or fist, etc.)," plucking the strings inside the piano and exploiting figures "originating through . . . physical gesture[s]" on the instrument.[27]

The general prototypes of hornlike or orchestral concepts of performance, along with the block chord approach, continue to distinguish the styles of some piano soloists even today (exx. 5.4a–c). Players like Duke Ellington, Art Tatum, and Cecil Taylor carried orchestral characteristics across the idioms from swing to free jazz. As bass and drum accompaniment within groups increased in complexity during the fifties and sixties, soloists like Bill Evans and Herbie Hancock sometimes favored right-hand improvisations and entirely eliminated the role of the left hand. Of course, many pianists have mixed different concepts to create dynamic contrast. Kenny Kersey of Cootie Williams's big band mixed elements of stride and swing: sometimes maintaining a steady beat in his left hand; at other times varying his performance with low pedal pitches, block chords, "unison playing with a single note in each hand," and his own "angular" rhythms.[28]

Comparable distinctions that have evolved among drummers over time concern the difference between linear and vertical concepts. Drummers employ a linear concept when they play a figure one stroke at a time on the surface of a single drum component, or orchestrate a figure among the various voices of different components, weaving the voices into a linear wash of sound (ex. 5.5a). They favor a vertical concept when they strike various components simultaneously to articulate a complete rhythm figure or to emphasize and color particular portions of the figure, blending selected qualities of cymbals and drums as chording instruments blend pitches (ex. 5.5b).

The application of such concepts in relation to the larger formal considerations of solo construction and the timbral and melodic subtleties of drum set performance is also germane. Learners have had diverse models, from Sid Catlett to Gene Krupa to Max Roach to Elvin Jones to Tony Williams, upon which to pattern their own styles.[29] Although some drummers primarily showcase their technical abilities during solos, many, inspired by early players like Sid Catlett, construct solos around the harmonic forms of pieces, creating a "rhythmic analogue to the harmonic progression" by employing different instruments and patterns.[30] Or they concentrate on the motivic development of precise melodic or rhythmic figures, quoted, in some cases, from the tune.[31]

Max Roach elaborates on the skill that enables a drummer "to play the song" with the drum set. "I knew the harmony to 'How High the Moon,'" he says, "so I would play a solo that had a certain design, using drum techniques such as rolls—single stick, double stick, closed, open, press. I would phrase so it sounded like I was dealing with the piece. If it was a four-bar sequence, I would play within the sequence, pause, then play again. Or, if it was an AABA tune," he adds, "I would change timbres, dealing with the drum set a different way when I went to the B section so it almost sounded like I was playing the bridge." This approach was so effective that other band members could follow Roach's solos without having to count measures to keep track of the form, and Roach did not have to cue the band at the close of his solos.

Paul Wertico is insightful concerning melodic aspects of drum solos that complement formal considerations. He explains that, although drummers deal with limited tonal possibilities compared with other instrumentalists, they may have at their disposal "four different tuned drums," whose tonal palette can be expanded by the hardness of the drum stroke (the harder the strike, the higher the pitch) and the placement of the stroke (the closer to the rim, the brighter the sound). Additionally, cymbals can produce different pitches and timbres depending on whether the strike is on the tip or the shoulder, that is, the raised portion, of the instrument. A drummer's manipulation of such subtleties produces varied emotional effects, which Wertico views as analogous to those produced by the horn player's manipulation of blue notes. "Like if you hit a higher note and it goes whang! it's different than if you go boo! Just that whang! has a different cry to it," Wertico emphasizes. Ultimately, the exploitation of the melodic capacity of the drum set depends on a player's special control over the instruments and on the equipment itself. The sounds of contemporary drums are "dead" by comparison to the older masters' instruments, which were, in Wertico's opinion, "more ringing and tuned higher." Their cymbals also had a rich, ringing quality. The instruments' special qualities are discernible on such "masterpieces of melodicism" as Max Roach's solos on the album *Drums Unlimited.*

Additional differentiations among drummers concern their individual approaches to time-keeping and emphasis on different drum set components. Drummers in the thirties commonly centered their action on the snare or tom-tom drums, accompanying themselves with a steady four-beat bass drum pattern and with punctuations of cymbal crashes. In the fifties and sixties, players like Elvin Jones and Tony Williams established the trend toward a more implicit than explicit representation of meter, the exploitation of diverse timbral colors, and greater activity involving different drum components in complex polyrhythms and asymmetrical phrases. Since the free jazz period, drummers Andrew Cyrille, Sunny Murray, and others have tended to minimize the use of conventional cymbal patterns and ostinatos, instead exploiting their instruments for wide-ranging "percussive textures and dynamic shadings."[32]

## Constellations of Traits and Concepts

Eventually, students learn to identify the musical personalities of great improvisers through comprehending the various constellations of traits and concepts described above. For example, matters of diction for singers are commonly tied to other issues bearing on the formulation of melodies. Singers with a dramatic concept are primarily concerned with the literal meanings of songs, and they deliver texts precisely. Others, whose approach some view as more personal, may sacrifice the clarity of song texts for increased musical inventiveness, taking great liberties with a song's rhythm and melody.

Sound, melodic range, and performance technique may be inextricably linked for wind players, representing a unique trade-off of artistic possibilities. Trumpeters like Cat Anderson distinguish themselves as high-note virtuosos, capable of improvising in the range of double high C, a pitch once considered well above the range of a B♭ trumpet. Typically, they achieve this dazzling feat by performing with a tight embouchure and a shallow mouthpiece, which renders an unusually light tone. Trumpeters like Tony Fruscella perform in the middle and lower range of the instrument, with an unusually dark, warm, flugelhorn-like tone. To achieve this, they typically choose a deeper, more conical mouthpiece and perform with a loose embouchure.[33] Between these extreme approaches, players like Clifford Brown and Booker Little perform melodies over a full three-octave range with more conventional bell tone trumpet sounds.

John McNeil describes other combinations characterizing an individual's approach. Louis Armstrong "tongued a lot and played lots of quarter notes and lots of triads, whereas Freddie Hubbard slurred his notes and played a lot of eighth notes and sixteenth notes and scalar things instead of arpeggios."

By comparing the distinct profiles of leading improvisers, learners also gain insight into the formative influences of improvisers upon one another. John McNeil observes that "Freddie Hubbard never messed around with his sound in his early years, but he did in his later career when he began copping Miles's stuff—putting air into his sound like Miles did on 'My Funny Valentine.' " Another young musician, initially under the impression that the phrases he had copied from Lee Morgan were unique, realized, after learning several Kenny Dorham and Dizzy Gillespie solos, that Lee Morgan "had taken phrases from both of them." Young artists continue to flesh out and revise their musical genealogies as they study increasing numbers of artists. Eventually, they learn to discern, for example, elements of style and practices of improvisation passed directly from Joe Oliver to Louis Armstrong to Roy Eldridge to Dizzy Gillespie to Fats Navarro and Miles Davis, in addition to Gillespie's subsequent disciples, Lonnie Hillyer and John Faddis, and through Davis to Wynton Marsalis, Terence Blanchard, Wallace Roney, and on to the youngest generations of trumpeters (fig. 5.1).[34]

Just as their early idols had learned from numerous mentors, aspiring musicians learn to re-create faithfully discrete bundles of traits and concepts from a succession of idols. Veteran artists reflecting on this aspect of learning recognize a few resulting constraints on early improvisations. When Roberta Baum reviews tapes of her own early performances, she says, "I can hear very distinctly which song is Ella Fitzgerald and which song is Betty Carter." A promising saxophonist's recording reveals Dexter Gordon's predominant influence on one track and Sonny Rollins's influence on another. "He's still a young man," Red Rodney comments. "All of us go through that."

In the long run, however, the habit is more valuable than restrictive. Sometimes, a mature musician has reason to assume the musical personality of another artist. Rahsaan Roland Kirk once guided his improvisations during a deeply moving memorial concert for John Coltrane with the precise concepts that Coltrane had explored on his final album, *Expression*. Similarly, as recalled by Lonnie Hillyer, in a Charles Mingus composition built around "parodies on different musicians," Jaki Byard once depicted the entire chronological development of jazz on the piano "from Scott Joplin and ragtime through free jazz." During the appropriate historical segments, drummer "Dannie Rich-

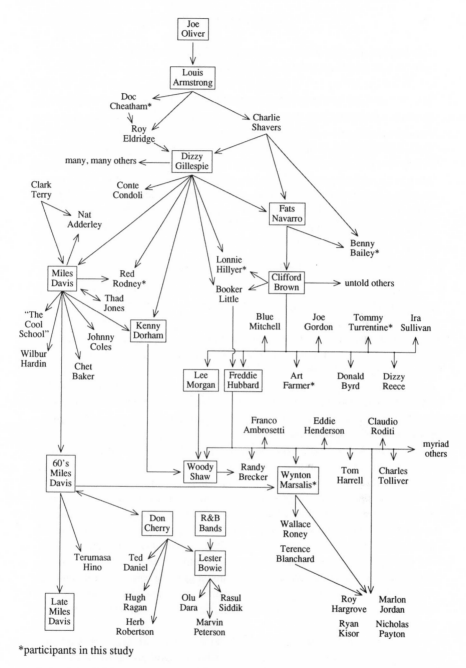

*participants in this study

Figure 5.1   John McNeil's genealogy of representative trumpet players, with focus on the years 1945–93

mond would play like Max Roach or 'Philly' Joe Jones," and other band members "would mimic some of the old horn players."

When the piece "progressed to Miles Davis," Lonnie Hillyer took the spotlight. He not only imitated Davis's performance but, he adds, "behaved like him too. I'd put the music in the end of the horn like a mute and play 'Bye Bye, Blackbird' and turn my back to the audience. One night I was doing this," Hillyer recalls, "and Miles walked into the club. I didn't know it, but the audience went wild. Miles just walked onto the stage, and I gave him my horn. It was beautiful! Spontaneous things would always happen like that. One night [a saxophone player] had been imitating Sonny Rollins, but when Sonny Rollins walked into the club, he stopped. He wouldn't do it [Hillyer laughs]. But it's like they say, imitation is the greatest form of compliment, and I had known Miles from the time I was a kid."

### Creativity as the Act of Fusion and Transformation

Although successful imitation requires the invention of new solos within the distinct bounds of an artist's style, conventional wisdom ultimately encourages musicians to cross over these boundaries by exploring the relationships between and among the ideas of different improvisers. "When you're playing, play by all of them. Play by all of them because you learn from them all," a sax player once advised Hillyer. Arthur Rhames similarly views great jazz players as those who have "the ability to take different musical perspectives and to integrate them into their own. They symbolize the potential that everyone has to draw on many sources and bring different understandings together in the perspective of their own lives."

In light of this, many youngsters redefine their early artistic goals to include an amalgam of the features of their favorite improvisers within their instrument's lineage. As implied earlier, this approach enables students to move in the direction of forging personal styles, while at the same time operating confidently within the bounds of the jazz tradition. Students faced with an ongoing array of models find themselves carefully weighing the value of each influence. When reviewing the recorded literature of jazz, for example, aspiring players are drawn to some artists over others. Moreover, from the recordings of an individual artist, they are drawn to some solos over others. Even when the same solo appeals to several young musicians, each commonly derives unique lessons from it, perhaps selecting different phrases for their vocabularies.

Ideally, Bobby Rogovin wants to be "a reflection of all the world's greatest trumpet players: a little of Dizzy, a little of Kenny Dorham, a little of Freddie Hubbard, all sort of combined into Bobby." Tommy Turrentine's approach has been much the same. "Fats Navarro, I loved him; Art Farmer, I listened to him. Miles, Dizzy, Woody [Shaw], Donald Byrd, Blue Mitchell; a lot of cats, man.

I listened to them all. I'd take anything that pleased me, anything that sounded beautiful. It might be a phrase. It might be a scale. It might be anything. I guess if it hadn't been for them, I wouldn't be sounding the way I'd be sounding."

Leroy Williams similarly absorbed Max Roach's "melodic approach to the drums," Kenny Clarke's "sense of swing," and Elvin Jones's "concept of polyrhythms," striving to "make one drummer out of them all." Vea Williams imitated Sarah Vaughan's "tonal quality and vibrato" and Carmen McCrae's diction. "In the case of a pianist," Walter Bishop Jr. says, "you take this person's rhythms, that person's harmonic structures, and another person's lines, and you put it all together yourself."

Personal taste evolves along with the styles of aspiring players, with different layers of their features revealing the influence of successive mentors. Kenny Barron initially acquired Horace Silver's "hard touch and strong rhythmic feeling," subsequently imitating Wynton Kelly's "sense of swing." Later, Barron copied Tommy Flanagan's "smooth, fluid, lyrical" melodic concept and his "light touch," developing the ability to articulate pitches "softly, but with great intensity." More recently, he has learned McCoy Tyner's "unique ways of voicing chords and concept of playing with power." Producing ever more subtle mixtures, one bass player patterned his upper register upon Scott LaFaro's sound, but imitated Ron Carter's sound in the lowest register, particularly the unique resonance of his low C. In similar fashion, a young tenor saxophonist copied Billy Mitchell's sound in the subtone register but John Coltrane's sound in the altissimo range.

As their search for ways to express their ideas advances, students begin to imitate jazz's most imaginative artists, regardless of the instruments they "happen to have adopted" (LH). This practice pays homage to performers as music thinkers and different instruments as inspirers of invention. Because the trumpet "lends itself most naturally to scalar patterns" and the saxophone is especially well suited to the performance of "wide intervals," Tommy Turrentine studies saxophone solos for "intervallic ideas" that he might not otherwise conceive in his own performances. Guitarist Emily Remler has imitated "Bill Evans's acoustic piano sound and his chord voicings," and she performs other material learned from drummers. "They can really expand your usual repertory of patterns, showing you millions of different ways to approach rhythm, because we melodic players are babies rhythmically," she explains. In an ongoing cycle of influence, drummers like Max Roach have acquired unique patterns from the footwork of tap dancers they accompanied, and Baby Lawrence absorbed into his "jazz tap percussion" routines the influence of pianist Art Tatum's remarkable sense of rhythmic phrasing.[35]

Indeed, some improvisers periodically avoid listening to performers of their own instruments in order to absorb varied influences. Lester Young found the model for his light tenor saxophone timbre in the C melody saxophone's characteristic sound as interpreted by Frankie Trumbauer, and he absorbed Trumbauer's way of slurring pitches as well. He also adapted alto saxophonist Jimmy Dorsey's technique of producing "honks."[36] Those who switch instruments during their careers commonly transfer practices from one instrument to another. According to one interpretation, Young favored the use of alternate saxophone fingerings to create rhythmic and timbral changes on the same pitch, performing rhythmic patterns that he had absorbed from his early experience playing the drums.[37] John Coltrane's performances on soprano saxophone led, as he put it, to his "pulling up my conception" on tenor saxophone, prompting him to develop the technique of performing ideas in the soprano range.[38]

Earl Hines's development of the trumpet style of piano performance, described earlier, grew out of his own early training as a cornetist and his admiration for other great players like Louis Smith and Louis Armstrong.[39] In another instance, when the leader of an early band lacking clarinetists required trumpeter Jabbo Smith to play the clarinet parts on his instrument, Smith acquired, in effect, special training in hearing and conceiving dexterously fingered, intricate patterns in the trumpet's high register. This ultimately established the ground for his high, fluent trumpet style, rare for trumpeters of his generation.[40] Subconscious visions may inspire such transferences on occasion. An instrumentalist once dreamed that Dizzy Gillespie was performing the trumpet, but instead of the trumpet's sound, scat syllables poured out of his horn. At the end of the dream, Dizzy Gillespie's image merged into that of the dreamer. The experience encouraged the musician to pursue his interest in vocal improvisation.

Not all musical ideas translate well from one instrument to another, however. One player who copied several spare figures improvised by Yusef Lateef during a flute solo found, to his disappointment, that they sounded "simplistic and silly" when he tried them on the trumpet. Their original vitality and effectiveness had depended on the flute's full-bodied, pulsating sound. Additionally, technical problems can cause a lag in the transmission of ideas among instrumentalists. Just as string bass players faced challenges adapting Charlie Parker's fluent melodic lines to their instrument, many trombonists initially found learning bebop patterns discouraging. When artists like J. J. Johnson and Urbie Green, through the use of such techniques as alternate slide positions, demonstrated the possibility of performing pitches rapidly with minimal movement of the right arm and wrist, trombonists began to feel at home with the new idiom (CF).

Ultimately, the early musical capabilities and personalities of students influence their interpretation and selection of an idol's solo features, producing, in the course of borrowing them, sometimes subtle and sometimes bold transformations of musical materials. When copying vocabulary patterns, students can absorb the model's timbre, or they can infuse it to varying degrees with their own. Eddie Jefferson was "thrilled" to hear George Johnson Jr. perform his vocalese texts because, as Jefferson had told Johnson, he felt self-conscious about his own vocal quality and "always wanted to know what his things would sound like if they were sung by a young cat with a smooth, silky voice." In other cases, youngsters initially absorb a particular idol's sound before altering it. Harold Ousley, for example, after successfully imitating Gene Ammons and seeking to cultivate his own personal sound, experimented with different brands of saxophones, mouthpieces, and reeds.

Musical training also affects the student's reproduction of model phrases. Akira Tana points out that "Jimmy Cobb took 'Philly' Joe Jones's rudimental approach and cleaned it up." Cobb's rudiments "sounded clearer" than those of Jones, whose technique was "rougher, more natural," he explains. In a comparable instance, a trumpeter imbued borrowed lines with distinct articulations of double and triple tonguing techniques, which he had learned in the classical music tradition, and a classically trained bassist adapted to bowing some patterns that his mentor performed by plucking.

Representing more substantial changes, learners who transpose the vocabulary patterns of an idol into keys in which they can easily perform them also vary the pitch levels and timbres of the patterns. Such changes, when combined with the artist's individual sound and personal approach to phrasing and embellishment, are sometimes great enough to mask the identities of the original models. Discovering that certain, apparently different phrases gleaned from disparate solos share a similar basis is a familiar revelation for students and encourages subsequent efforts to identify and catalogue common jazz components and their variants (exx. 5.6a–k).

Even more radical transmutations result when, in the course of learning entire solos, students encounter passages that exceed their abilities to imitate them or that are obscured by the volume of the band's accompaniment or the soloist's imprecise articulation. Some youngsters delete the inaccessible passages, substituting rests for their performance. Others copy the discernible pitches and complete the passages with pitches of their own. Unconscious changes occasionally occur as students unknowingly alter the rhythmic phrasing or pitch configuration of recorded passages and add them to their storehouses as inadvertent variants. Sometimes it is only after years have passed that, upon reviewing earlier transcriptions with the perspective of "older ears," they discover these alterations. Musicians may decide, of course, that they prefer their own variations to the original phrases.

Sooner or later, personal affinity for particular musical elements can also modify patterns. When Chuck Israels was a youngster, he could "always" recall the rhythms of other artists' phrases, but he had difficulty remembering their melodies. As a precise contour faded in memory, Israels compensated by adding new pitches to the phrase's rhythm. Such transfiguration sometimes operates on models offered up by the subconscious. After John Coltrane's death, a musician was once awakened by a vivid dream in which Coltrane's group presented a sensational and extraordinarily vibrant performance, one that the musician could not recall ever having heard before. He struggled to recall fragments of its sounds as they receded from his memory. Although the experience left him but a small legacy of actual music, the psychological and emotional impressions were lasting ones.

The most elaborate changes commonly occur when students deliberately vary phrases learned from their mentors by adding personal marks to them, in a sense legitimating their use. Because the jazz artist "was given credit for being innovative as a soloist," Max Roach and his peers "grew up wanting to do something a little different from everybody else. It was the crowning achievement if you could invent an idea, and everybody would say, 'That's Max!—even if it was the simplest thing." Roach refers here to such details as taking a common pattern and orchestrating it differently among the drum set's instruments. He also recounts an incident from his very young performing years. Roach was only fifteen when Cecil Payne came running up to him at one jam session, calling out, "'I heard the music from the street, but I knew it was you who was playing!' That was a great compliment at the time."

Reinforcing such values, veterans who teach jazz vocabulary directly to students never suggest that phrases be ends in themselves. Instead, they represent their demonstrations as examples of the kinds of things you can do. Learners eventually recognize this as well. "If you hear something intriguing in somebody else's solo, the main thing is to find out how it works, to find out what's intriguing about it, and then to apply it differently in your own way" (BB).

## Applying Knowledge toward Original Invention

To discover their own applications for model phrases, musicians commonly analyze a phrase for its central elements, focusing on one derived principle as the basis for creating new analogous patterns. Sometimes a phrase's melodic contour is its salient feature. "You can copy Wes Montgomery—just one little thing that he uttered, just one bar or a four-bar phrase—and it's such a well-developed melody, such a well-developed composition, that you could base ten million of your own licks, or a whole solo, on that one thing. By using thematic development, you could write forty tunes from that one bar" (ER).

Rhythmic ingredients can also constitute the fundamental idea for original figures. Walter Bishop Jr. says that after absorbing Bud Powell's phrasing he "began to think like Bud" so he could abandon Powell's precise lines and create his own "in the same idiom, playing with the same kind of feeling and intensity." Arthur Rhames views the process as analogous to emulating personal

styles of speech. Because all artists speak with "their own natural rhythm and
sequential order," it is possible to "emulate a person whose speaking you like,
using his same effect—how he comes into a sentence or the way he constructs
his things"—but without saying the "exact same thing." That is how Rhames
learned from John Coltrane.

> Without directly copying his melodic line, I tried to get the feeling of
> the line, the phrasing, which allowed me to understand how Trane
> was talking when he played. What I wanted was the form, the basket
> that he was using, but the contents I wanted to fill myself. I knew that
> I had something to say, and I wanted to deal with that. So what I
> copied was the way John constructed his phrases and their rhythmical
> base, the stems without the notes, and I put my own notes and har-
> mony—the things I thought about—on top of it.

In other instances, it is a pattern's harmonic content that inspires. When
transcribing an exceptional phrase by Charlie Parker, for example, and discovering its "use of a fourth over a minor seventh chord," Benny Bailey composed numerous figures in which the fourth remained the predominant component.

Experimentation also teaches students to create new figures by applying
to model phrases the same techniques they had learned for embellishing jazz
tunes and by combining fragments of different phrases, both those of other
artists and those of their own design. From the beginning, Jimmy Robinson
"put my things together with the technical—the real intricate, hard-to-do—
things I liked in different players' solos." Don Friedman invented his "own
melodies" to complement the voicings he copied from Bill Evans. Fred Hersch
has combined musical traits from his principal jazz mentor, Herbie Hancock,
with the "contrapuntal practices" of classical music composers like Mozart.

If original sparks of musical imagination and unique technical abilities
are ever-present ingredients within the earliest improvisational blends of some
students, prolonged apprenticeships initially content others, who succumb to
more inventive practices only after they become bored with mere imitation of
their idols. "Even if I didn't sound as good as the people I copied when I made
up my own things," one musician says of the first turning point in his development, "at least I was starting to express myself, and that was the most satisfying
thing for me at that point."

Others find the impetus for personal development in the realization that
attractive idiosyncratic features of a mentor's style are impossible for anyone
but the mentor to re-create. This can be a function of unique physical aspects
of the elder's control over an instrument, the characteristics of a particular instrument itself, or hidden techniques underlying musical effects that baffle students.[41] "A lot of Bud Powell's playing may sound simple when you hear it,"

Tommy Flanagan says, "but then trying to play it yourself is another matter." This itself is something that "helps people create their own styles." When learning great artists' recorded solos, Flanagan sometimes composed original phrases to replace those he "couldn't figure out," a practice that encouraged his development as an improviser. "So after a while," he concludes, "you're just playing your own lines." With self-effacing humor, Lee Konitz maintains that he developed an overall style that was relatively independent of Charlie Parker, not only because he was already under the influence of Lennie Tristano, but also because he lacked the virtuosity required to imitate Parker as closely as he might have liked. In a comparable instance, when limited endurance prevented one trumpeter from fashioning solos after a model's long melodic lines, a more experienced musician advised him to devise an approach that took advantage of what he could do—building solos around shorter, simpler phrases and exploiting the use of space; this strategy provided more frequent rests when he played.

Eubie Blake describes the trials and tribulations by which young artists sometimes learn to appreciate their own uniqueness.

> You hear another guy play and say to yourself, "Man, listen to that! I wish I could play that good." Then you hear somebody else and you say the same thing. Then comes a time when you realize that the first guy can't do what the second guy can and the second guy can't do what the first guy can. That makes you feel a little better when you know that. Well, then, when you come to find out *you* can do things *both* them other guys can't do, you discover that ain't got anything to do with who's good and who isn't. It's just that everybody puts his own personal *style* to the music. Of course, if he *doesn't*, then he just ain't a musician.[42]

As youngsters follow the jazz community's traditional learning methods, they cultivate skills outside of performance that prepare them effectively for the demands of individual and collective improvisation. Absorbing features from a large selection of virtuoso artists, emerging musicians learn the musical conventions associated with different performance schools. At the same time, students, already familiar with the characteristics of their own instruments, acquire specialized skills to hear and interpret across instrumental lines patterns of sound distinctive by virtue of their diverse timbres, unique playing techniques, and different ranges.

The actual benefits of such training sometimes catch learners by surprise. One young saxophonist who had transcribed numerous piano solos at his teacher's insistence was excited to find that, for the first time at sessions, he could hear details within the piano accompaniment to his own solos. Similarly, one aspiring trumpeter striving to master his idol's solos slowed them to half speed, thereby lowering their pitch an octave. The practice of transferring the passages from an octave below the instrument's range to their original pitch inadvertently left him with such a proficiency in apprehending pitches in the lower octave that, from then on, he could discern the precise patterns of trombone parts and bass lines that had formerly eluded him in performance.

Through other exercises, such as replacing the inaccessible passages of recorded solos, young artists train themselves in matters of musical logic and stylistic continuity, learning to compose smooth melodic transitions between the preceding and following passages and to shape their creations to appropriate harmonic forms. Finally, when experimenting with an idol's phrases as models for invention, students are, in effect, practicing those fundamental techniques of variation soloists need in order to develop their own ideas in performance and respond appropriately to the ideas of other musicians. This combined training eventually enables students to interact appropriately with various kinds of jazz bands.

## SIX

**The More
Ways You
Have of
Thinking**

Conventional
Rhythmic and
Theoretical
Improvisation
Approaches

*The more ways you have of thinking about
music, the more things you have to play in
your solos.* —Barry Harris

*Thinking of rhythm can be very effective; you
can just play a few notes and with the right
rhythm, it makes them very interesting. Other
times, you're thinking in intervals, or you're
thinking in scales. Actually, the first thing cats
did was to play vertically, running chords.
They really learned chords from top to
bottom. That was the way I learned; I didn't
know about scales until later. Lately,
musicians have been playing intervals. It's a
way of getting out of running chords really,
because if you play a lot of intervals, you can
play them anywhere against the most difficult
chords.* —Benny Bailey

The improviser's evolving storehouse of knowledge includes musical elements
and forms varied in detail and design: jazz tunes, progressions, vocabulary
patterns, and myriad features of style. Performers can draw faithfully on their
assorted materials, as when they treat a formerly mastered phrase as a discrete
idea and play it intact. Soon, they realize the infinite implications of their
knowledge, for virtually all aspects can serve as compositional models. Pursuing subtle courses, musicians carry over the inflections and ornaments of particular phrases to embellish other phrases. Venturing further, they may extract
a figure's salient characteristic, such as melodic shape or rhythmic configuration, and treat it as the rudiment for new figures.

Gradually, artists come to generalize about the underlying tonal and rhythmic properties of their materials. This is essential if improvisers are to develop
the conceptual grounding on which their operations depend. "In improvisation
you've got to have a melodic concept and a harmonic concept," Tommy Turrentine maintains, "and a rhythmic concept especially."

The principles that artists derive from their studies ultimately provide
them with the basis for diverse approaches to musical thinking, encouraging
flexible invention in the styles of jazz that are more independent of the individ-

ual's precise repertory of patterns. Perhaps the most fundamental approach to improvisation emphasizes rhythm, commonly known in the jazz community as time or time-feel.

## Playing off of Time

Ken McIntyre once commented that a great improviser could play an entire solo based on one pitch alone. Coincidentally, during an interview with a young drummer, a soft background recording featured flugelhornist Wilbur Hardin, who was generating tremendous excitement with a stream of single-pitched rhythmic patterns at his solo's opening.[1] Carrying on the tradition of soloists like Louis Armstrong who could also create great variety in this manner (ex. 6.1a), Hardin manipulated timbre and articulation subtleties to cause his pitches to form different rhythmic groupings, in effect superimposing varied metric schemes upon that of the piece (ex. 6.1b). The drummer suddenly burst out laughing and, with an apology for his distraction, added: "Did you hear that? That's what our music's about. Listen to all that brother can say with one note!"

The performer's rhythmic conception can produce phrases whose melodic content is secondary, but it also forms the underpinning of successful melodic excursions. Praised for their swing, effective improvisations are "natural, flowing, uncontrived, and spontaneous"; they display strong rhythmic momentum, "rhythmic elasticity, bounce, and vitality." These essential aesthetic qualities are the product of a combination of the rhythmic elements that make up improvised figures, the manner in which the figures are articulated, their placement within the piece's metric scheme, and their relationships to the surrounding figures of other band members.

Such critical aspects of performance may be rooted in the appreciation for rhythmic complexity and drive evident in many parts of Africa.[2] In Ghana, for example, traditional compositions for singers, dancers, and percussion orchestras commonly include multilayered cyclical parts performed by several drums that support the master drum part. Based on duple or triple meters or carrying connotations of both, the drum parts are unified through their relationship to a repeating bell part or time line, itself supported by an interwoven shaker pattern and by polyrhythmic handclapping patterns. The liveliness of compositions derives not only from the sheer variety of their rhythms, orchestrated at distinct pitch levels and voiced in the colorful timbres of different instruments, but also the rhythms' dynamic relationships.

Individual parts produce different schemes of counterpoint with each of their neighbors as their patterns alternately reinforce or cross over one another within the larger musical texture. Additionally, like multidimensional sound sculptures, the compositions exhibit new features as listeners adopt different rhythmic viewpoints or frames of reference for apprehending and organizing them. When listeners shift perspectives from the triple to the duple handclapping accompaniment—framing the music in terms of the slower delineation of time—the bell, shaker, and drum parts alter in stress, phrasing, and shape. They seem to begin and end at different points along their cycles and to bear different relationships to the surrounding parts, displaying a playful ambiguity.

Within this kaleidophonic array, melodic-rhythmic elements of comparable pitch, timbre, or hardness of attack appear at times to break away from their original configurations to form new parts. This phenomenon compounds the effects of the changes that musicians occasionally create through variation and improvisation. Together with dancers' dramatic interpretations of the music and vocalists' overlay of successive song texts, the performance comprises a constantly changing musical environment around the orbit of the time line and its underlying polymetric foundation. Ultimately, the compelling interplay of each composition's dance, vocal, and instrumental patterns—in which different groupings coincide at one moment to relax rhythmic tension, then pull away from one another to increase rhythmic tension—keeps the music in a perpetual state of excited motion.[3]

In the New World, early African American composers strove to preserve a semblence of the rhythmic life of their musical heritage within the comparatively simple framework of European music composed in single meters. Underscored by the motion of the conductor's baton, the stress patterns of melody and accompaniment in hymns, marches, and dance tunes characteristically reinforce the downbeat and other strong beats of the meter, such as the third beat in a four-beat measure. This orientation reflects the value that Europeans and their American counterparts generally attach to rhythmic congruity and uniformity in the organization of musical parts, while allowing for periodic contrast by creating polyrhythms and stressing weak beats to create syncopation.

When African Americans interpreted European pieces in light of their own values and performance practices and adopted their structures as vehicles for original composition, they commonly increased the music's rhythmic complexity by accenting the weaker upbeats or backbeats, that is, the second and fourth beats in a four-beat measure. As James Reese Europe explained in 1919, "We play the music as it is written, only that we accent strongly in this manner the notes which originally would be without accent."[4] By imposing a contrasting rhythmic frame of reference upon that implicit in the music, listeners and musicians create a dual accentuation scheme that exerts an alternating pull upon the music from one beat to the next and imbues performances with a rocking, swinging quality like the dynamic motion of a pendulum.[5]

In many African American musical genres, the accents of the drummer's hi-hat cymbal, together with the audience's complementary handclapping and finger snapping, reinforce patterns that fall on the backbeats and intensify the backbeat's pull away from the strong beats. This, in turn, maximizes the force of the subsequent swing back toward the strong beats. For this reason, the backbeat provides an important rhythmic target point for improvisers. In this sense, from the viewpoint of African American music, the backbeat itself can be viewed as the strong beat. John Coltrane explains that he "thought in groups of notes . . . [and] tried to place these groups on the accents and emphasize the strong beats—maybe on 2 here and on 4 over at the end. I would set up the line and drop groups of notes—a long line with accents dropped as I moved along."[6]

Carmen Lundy provides a comparative perspective on her preferences, explaining that they are the product of her upbringing.

> Certain cultures feel the rhythm on the downbeat more so than the backbeat. I have been brought up in a culture where I feel the backbeat of the rhythm as opposed to the downbeat. Not to say that I don't feel that too, but the stress is on the backbeat for me, and all the other things that I hear in the music are intertwined with the backbeat. In this way, there was something about the rhythm of jazz that I equated exactly with the gospel. I mean, the way we used to sing and clap our hands in church was just like the jazz drummer playing cymbals. It was the same swing feeling—the gospel swing and the jazz swing.

Similarly, for early jazz players like Buddy Bolden through bebop innovators like Dizzy Gillespie, and for prospective jazz musicians from outside the black community as well, the sanctified church was commonly the training ground for absorbing essential rhythmic features of African American music.[7] In its vibrant musical setting, congregants learned to keep their bearings with respect to meter and "stress" amid a complex, ever changing scheme of rhythmic counterpoint. The "sanctified church had a deep significance for me, musically," Gillespie reports. "I first learned the meaning of rhythm there and all about how music could transport people spiritually. . . . They used to keep at least four different rhythms going, and as the congregation joined in, the number of rhythms would increase with foot stomping, hand clapping, and people catching the spirit and jumping up and down on the wooden floor, which also resounded like a drum. . . . The sanctified church's rhythm got to me as it did to any one else who came near the place."[8]

Young artists build upon their early experiences by engaging in formal time studies. Under the tutelage of a former vaudeville performer, Melba Liston's junior high school music group learned various song and dance routines and the handclapping and dance exercises of "eurhythmics." Competing in "counting contests," they pitted their skills against one another to grasp and imitate increasingly complex rhythms. David Baker's high school band leader required members to tap and sing syncopated passages from a swing method book. Aspiring drummers commonly practiced and shared exercises from "syncopation" or "modern drumming" method books by Jim Chapin, Ted

Reed, and others. In Barry Harris's workshops, students learn a store of patterns with short figures of eighth notes and sixteenth notes occasionally embellished with eighth-note triplets and sixteenth-note triplets, as well as figures including sustained rhythmic values with alternating on-beat and off-beat characters. From these cells, learners could create longer phrases. Moreover, those youngsters who recognize the necessity of acquiring a "rhythmic vocabulary" discover that they can derive a complementary repertory of rhythmic patterns from their repertory of melodic phrases by extracting "the stems" of the phrases from their "note heads" (AR).

Meanwhile, learners strive to develop an unwavering sense of the beat to serve as a conceptual anchor for the flexible use of their vocabulary. Many cultivate this basic skill during years of handclapping in rhythmic accompaniment to pieces at both religious and secular music events. As suggested above, this experience also results in an aesthetic appreciation for rhythmic complexity, a sensitivity to rhythmic counterpoint, and a flexible orientation toward the interpretation and treatment of meter.

Children lacking special rhythmic gifts or comparable training sometimes find the beat to be a hazy concept initially. It belongs, after all, to that category of intangibles made comprehensible by being properly envisaged or accurately inferred from their effects upon other things. Sailors cannot see the wind, but they feel its pressure and observe whether a ship's sails are taut or luffing. Swimmers cannot see the ocean's current, but they feel its pull upon them and gauge its character from patterns of undulating waves. Similarly, musicians cannot see a beat, but they learn to discern it within the band's collage of patterns when a particular musician's part expresses it explicitly, or otherwise, to infer it as the common underlying pulse of the band's collage. In the latter case, and when performing alone, improvisers imagine the beat as a series of evenly spaced points or regularly generated hits along a continuum of time.

Various factors can complicate the perceptions of learners, however. Even when some group members perform the beat directly, playing a regular four-beat time-keeping pattern, the actual points of the beats acquire slightly different definitions from instrument to instrument, the acoustical properties of which display differing patterns of attack and decay. Its definition also varies with individual styles of articulation, as for a horn player's selection of tonguing syllables or for a pianist's particular touch. Moreover, veterans can assert their interpretation of the beat with minute shifts in emphasis, creating variations in time-feeling. Pianists, for example, can widen the beat by "playing the left hand slightly ahead of the right hand in unison or chordal passages."[9]

Charles Mingus once underscored the flexibility of such practices at a workshop by drawing an overlapping sequence of quarter notes at the same pitch level, indicating that, theoretically, each note's rhythmic value could be

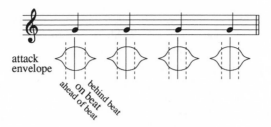

Figure 6.1    The beat as an elliptical figure

pulled slightly forward or backward into the domain of the adjacent note (CI). In fact, most musicians "talk about playing on three different parts of the beat without making any difference in the overall tempo" (AT). Imagining the beat as an "elliptical figure," the drummer or bass player can play either "ahead of the beat" (that is, on the front part of the elliptical figure), "behind the beat" (that is, on the very end of the elliptical figure or in varying degrees toward the center of the figure), or "on the beat" (that is, the center of the figure) (fig. 6.1).

Fred Hersch similarly maintains that in the course of a performance

> there should be ten, fifteen different kinds of time. There's a kind of time that has an edge on it for a while and then lays back for a while. Sometimes it rolls over the bar, and sometimes it sits more on the beats. That's what makes it interesting. You can set a metronome here and, by playing with an edge or playing behind it or right in the center, you can get all kinds of different feelings. That's what makes it come alive. People are human, and rhythmic energy has an ebb and flow.

To experiment with these subtleties and strengthen the ability to supply a steady beat in the imagination, some artists follow the advice of experts to practice faithfully with a metronome, leaving it on even when carrying out other chores to absorb its regular delineation of time (CH). Paul Wertico made his own "time much more secure" by listening to a metronome setting of 200 at the beginning and end of each day. Once having memorized its precise tempo, he acquired the ability to gauge other tempos in relation to it.

Beyond imaging the beat as a pulsating sound, performers commonly adopt physical means for its representation. The great New Orleans–style trumpeter Tommy Ladnier required Doc Cheatham to imitate him by "patting" his foot when they performed together. Ladnier insisted that it would teach Cheatham "how to play good jazz" and enable him "to really feel what he was doing." Jelly Roll Morton gave Cheatham the same advice during their collaborative performances. In subsequent eras as jazz tempos increased, some musicians found that tired ankles caused tempos to slow down or become erratic, and they chose to omit every other beat, tapping on the music's backbeats or, alternatively, on "one" and "three." Others kept time with a slight nod of the head to avoid potential problems of foot tapping.[10]

Not only does the physical embodiment of the beat provide concrete reference points during performances, but it informs artists' ideas by infusing them with appropriate rhythmic vitality. "In order to swing, not just to approximate swing, the rhythm has to come from your body," Fred Hersch maintains. He knows that when his playing is "really swinging, I'm unconsciously moving from side to side or back and forth on the piano bench." For Cheatham, as well, "it's like dancing; it's the movement of the body that inspires you to play. You have to pat your foot; you get a different feeling altogether than when you play not patting your foot." In a continuing cycle, the physical representation of the beat inspires soloists' rhythmic conceptions, which in turn provides renewed physical stimulus that finds immediate expression in improvisations. "You need rhythm for the real life of this music, for the real dance," Hersch acknowledges.

In addition to metaphorizing swing in terms of dance, many performers also emphasize the importance in their upbringing of black social dance, which sensitized them to the subtleties of rhythmic expression, training them to interpret time and to absorb varied rhythms through corresponding dance steps and other patterns of physical motion. Practices mentioned earlier in which drummers actually reproduce and play off of patterns emanating from the intricate footwork of tap dancers, and vice versa, epitomize the influence of body movement upon rhythmic conception in jazz.[11]

Once performers can envisage the regular passage of time at different tempos, they acquire in effect an internalized "metronome sense."[12] The beat takes on a tangible quality and serves as a referent for understanding the mathematical relationships among the elemental components of jazz phrases. Typically, artists interpret the components as subdivisions and multiples of the beat, an interpretation that aids artists in creating and applying their patterns whether envisioned in sound alone or in the diagrammatic representations of rhythmic values familiar to them from theory manuals. Lennie Tristano directed students to formulate new phrases by dividing the beat symmetrically into patterns of eighth notes, sixteenth notes and thirty-second notes, and asymmetrically in any number of ways (LK). These were common practices for John Coltrane, who at times favored "uneven groups like fives and sevens."[13] Louis Armstrong's foot-tapping practice provided reference for the beat's subdivision and for the intricate off-beat phrasing that became one of his trademarks.[14] Within the realm of beat subdivision, myriad nuances of phrasing in between an even eighth-note subdivision feel, a dotted-eighth and sixteenth-note feel, and a triplet eighth-note feel are associated with the dynamism of swing.

Triplet subdivisions have special significance. Carmen Lundy finds that triplets are "unlike straight eighth notes or any other kind of rhythms," possessing something that's "hypnotic," especially once the patterns begin "piling up on one another. Those interrhythmic things really create a special feeling," she remarks. "They joggle one another, and that's what makes a person want to dance. When you hear that, it moves the body. It's a natural thing to want to do that. Oh, it can really take you!" The feeling triplets create in both gospel and jazz served as an initial bridge between the two musical fields for Lundy, enabling her "to identify with jazz rhythmically."

Students also learn "polymetric or polyrhythmic" invention, such as "playing five notes in the space normally left for four" (CI). Emily Remler finds that she has "gotten much stronger rhythmically just from doing little tapping exercises that drummers have shown me, playing polyrhythms like two against three or three against four." Lester Young was especially "fond of three-against-four cross-rhythms, which he would repeat two to four times consecutively." [15] Instrumentalists restricted to single-part performance can mentally superimpose a second meter upon that of the piece maintained by other band members, but performers of instruments with multipart capabilities can perform patterns derived from different meters simultaneously. "See, the triplet feeling in rhythm, 'dah-dah-dah, dah-dah-dah,' makes you relax," Charli Persip points out. "It makes you hold back; you can't rush triplets. But the duple part of the rhythm is like marches, 'one and two and' or 'one and two and three and four and.' That kind of division of time makes you move ahead, forge ahead, march—'boom, boom, boom, boom.' That's the push of the rhythm. And that's why it is so nice when you combine those two feelings. Then you get a complete rhythm that marches and still relaxes."

For Persip, performances by "Brother Elvin Jones," an artist who "has dug very deeply into his roots from the Motherland, Africa, for his message for the drum," epitomize these practices. "Elvin gets into all kinds of triplet feelings against the rhythms that he plays that may be in four. Amazing, man! And that's what makes his music sound so complex. At the same time, it's like a whole mass of rhythm coming at you, but because it's so triplety, it is always relaxing. The first time I heard Elvin play was one of the most unique thrills that I have had in my life."

In its most basic form, polymetric invention creates a recurring cycle of rhythmic counterpoint. Within the same time span, the basic beats of different meters cross over one another, creating syncopation and temporarily increasing the music's rhythmic instability and tension. They then coincide with one another, resolving the tension. This relationship is simply a springboard to further exploration on the part of improvisers who grasp its implications. "Just learning rhythmic figures like two against three can lead you to do hundreds of other things" (ER). By adopting the conceptual framework of a superimposed meter, musicians gain a set of theoretical reference points, which they can continue to subdivide in different ways, then subdivide again, creating an ever-expanding "rhythm tree." Pitches added to alternative sets of points derived from the tree produce new and complex patterns in relation to the underlying meter.

While applying these and other fundamental principles to compose varied rhythmic components, improvisers also join the components together to create phrases of different lengths.[16] As a young player, one trumpeter initially practiced "making up two-bar phrases in all kinds of different ways," an exercise he "had to work at methodically" because he neither "came from a music background" nor had "an intuitive feeling for phrasing like some players do."[17] Similarly, students in Barry Harris's classes practice singing short rhythmic patterns (fig. 6.2) and combining them in varied arrangements to create phrases of roughly two, four, and eight measures that correspond to the common harmonic segments of jazz pieces. Arthur Rhames explains the value of such training in his own development. "I understood that there was a legacy and a tradition in the phrasing, in the bringing together of the ideas, that the great jazz musicians were playing. I knew I needed this too, in order to be able to speak the language of jazz." He gives credit to his study of John Coltrane's phrasing because, he says, it "allowed me to develop an order—a way—to sequence my own thoughts." Learners eventually absorb the features of particular models for phrasing by fashioning innumerable patterns after them, developing the ability to feel and think in terms of the time spans and rhythmic configurations of the models.

Equally important is the ability to inset phrases based on particular models within different sections of progressions. Artists can reinforce a piece's harmonic rhythm by improvising two- or four-measure phrases that are congruent with the underlying progression, or they can begin patterns in the middle of harmonic segments and carry them over into the next, "dovetailing the obvious lines of demarcation" and bringing the solo line into cross-rhythmic relationship with the progression's structure (ex. 6.2).[18] In this regard, selected points on an artist's superimposed polymetric frame also provide targets for the introduction of larger chunks of formerly mastered vocabulary, allowing for their placement in abstract and varied rhythmic positions in relation to the meter. This may explain, in part, the effective character of passages of even eighth notes within many solos that initially appear to be on the beat but turn out, on close examination, to position themselves with assurance almost imperceptibly behind or ahead of the beat, thereby acquiring a subtle, floating quality.

By exploiting these practices, artists can imbue solo lines with dramatic, constantly alternating patterns of on-beat and off-beat accentuation, an essential feature of swing. The leader of Tommy Turrentine's teenaged band once explained this general principle on the way home from a rehearsal by instructing Turrentine to walk with a steady pace and observe where the phrases he was carrying in his "head" fell in relation to his footsteps, noticing espe-

a. One-measure patterns emphasizing beat subdivision

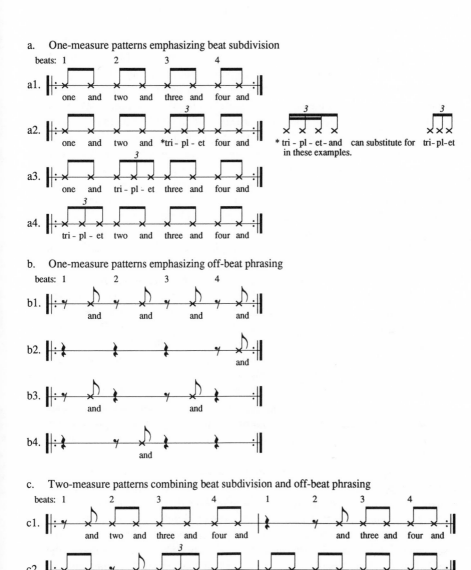

b. One-measure patterns emphasizing off-beat phrasing

c. Two-measure patterns combining beat subdivision and off-beat phrasing

Figure 6.2   Barry Harris's rhythmic chanting exercises

cially where they "came out on 'one.'" Stepping on the horizontal lines, which divided the sidewalk into successive units, and on the invisible lines, which halved them, Turrentine interpreted each pair of units as a measure.

Subsequently, he discovered that the beginnings and endings of some phrases coincided with the sidewalk's lines, falling on the strong beats, while others fell on the invisible lines or backbeats, and in between them on the off-beats. Along with clarifying the concept of syncopation, this graphic demonstration sensitized Turrentine to each tune's unique rhythmic counterpoint in relation both to the meter's regular grouping of beats and to the rocking motion of its dual accentuation scheme. Turrentine found the same principles of syncopation and off-beat phrasing embodied by the background riffs that he and his peers learned in order to accompany singers and other soloists.

As in the momentum of effective tunes and riffs, improvisers propel solos forward partly by beginning and ending phrases on different beats within measures. Moreover, they animate the internal features of phrases with comparable procedures. Over the span of a phrase, they produce subtle shifts of accentuation between backbeats two and four—temporarily challenging the metric structure and generating rhythmic tension—and beats one and three, reinforcing the metric structure and resolving rhythmic tension. The alternation between off-beat and on-beat emphasis creates similar schemes of tension and release (exx. 6.3a1–a2). Various techniques accomplish the same goals, each with distinctive qualities of expression. Artists may produce diverse accentuation schemes simply by varying the selection of beats or parts of the beat on which they change dynamic levels or melodic direction. They may throw different accents on the contour of a recurring gesture through rhythmic displacement, that is, by performing the gesture at different metric positions (ex. 6.3b).

Articulation is another important device. Ghosting on-beat pitches in an eighth-note sequence creates de facto accents on every off-beat, increasing rhythmic tension. Reversing the procedure relieves rhythmic tension. Ken McIntyre once suggested that I practice patterns of eighth notes by slurring and tonguing them in different groupings so that their accents fell in unpredictable sequences on and off the strong and weak portions of beats. Similarly, the varied application of hard, soft, and ghosted attacks can shift accents within a repeated eighth-note triplet, changing its perceived rhythmic configuration and its relative syncopated quality. Moreover, when articulated as alternating pairs of slurred pitches, the triplet figure assumes a polymetric relationship to the underlying meter (ex. 6.3c). Other essential devices include timbral change and pitch inflection, each contributing to the rhythmic complexion of phrases (exx. 6.3d1–d2).

For variety, musicians can also lightly segment a melodic line into different groupings by weighting selected pitches with embellishments or, in more substantial terms, altering breathing patterns in the unpredictable, playful production of short rests (ex. 6.4). "Bebop is like the music of Mozart or Bach," Fred Hersch says. "Bach will have these unbroken sixteenth-note phrases, but there are little things that talk in the music, and you have to bring them out in your performance. With bebop, you've also got to articulate the phrases and shape them, making variety and music out of the notes." In a similar light, Miles Davis once advised Tommy Turrentine that players could "play simple and sound good," if they understood how to "phrase." Turrentine elaborates, explaining that improvising "linear or melodic" ideas is like "writing a sentence. The commas, the periods, and the exclamation points have to be very pronounced."

Equally important is musical space, accomplished through the use of substantive rests, the unvoiced rhythmic trailers whose irregular time spans offset those of the phrases that precede and follow them. In effect, rests introduce soft accents into the solo line as its sound subsides and the rhythm section temporarily moves to the foreground of the music. Suspended over the passing beats, a rest also invites listeners to reflect upon the soloist's most recent figure, challenging them to anticipate the entrances of subsequent figures. Musicians commonly cite Miles Davis as an inspired model for the effective use of space, which increases the potency of his phrases and heightens their dramatic quality.

Once aspiring performers have cultivated a rhythmic conception and gained the ground for playing off of time, they can generate an ongoing succession of rhythmic patterns around an unfailing sense of the beat and imbue them with the attributes of swing. Ronald Shannon Jackson sometimes "sets up" for practice sessions by imagining an increasingly intense flow of rhythms until he "hears" their heavy patter "raining down all around" him. From this deluge, Jackson selects the most interesting patterns and plays them, varying their orchestration among the components of his drum set.

During actual performances, seasoned soloists can similarly enter a piece's progression at a designated tempo and keep track of their metered progress through the form while taking great rhythmic liberties. Playing inside the time, they double up or triple up on the tempo—improvising patterns precisely twice or three times as fast as the beat. In other instances, mathematical calculation guides excursions outside the time. Superimposed metric frames aid in placing pitches with great rhythmic accuracy at finely distinguished, abstract points in relation to the underlying meter, thereby creating subtle patterns of syncopation and polymetric activity.

In other instances, speech rhythm provides the means for soloists to create interesting cross-rhythms in relation to the rest of the band. When singers shape phrases according to natural cadences of song texts, and when players imitate the models of language by uttering speechlike patterns with their instruments, they pull their phrases momentarily outside of the time. The physical constitutions of improvisers sometimes dictate comparable changes. In the execution of a long technical phrase, the fingers may perform some maneuvers evenly and others unevenly, causing pitches to lag slightly during particular key sequences and to edge ahead during others.

Moreover, artists attain great freedom in their rhythmic dance when they deliberately superimpose different tempos upon that of the piece, rushing ahead or falling behind, applying different degrees of pressure to the beat before resubmitting to its regulation.[19] At other times, the group abandons tempo as a constraint upon performance altogether. "Tempos are very important," Carmen Lundy says, "and there's also taking a tune out of tempo—*rubato*. There are so many ways of dealing with a tune, and I like the freedom to take a song anywhere when I'm performing." Performances unbounded by a strict metric frame are not free in the sense of being unrhythmic. Rather, they are driven by rhythmic goals that are elastic. Musicians create constant motion in their parts by mentally supplying and pursuing a movable model of the beat, which they stretch or compress as they improvise. Ultimately, seasoned artists develop the control, within metered performances, to place virtually any number of pitches within any portion of the piece's underlying structure (ex. 6.5).

The rich and varied effects of these practices elude precise description and graphic representation in staff notation, which, of course, was not designed to portray them. This is one reason why published solo transcriptions are skeletal representations typically, and efforts to perform them as written sound stilted and lifeless unless performers can interpret them in light of the rhythmic conventions of jazz. Alternatively, efforts to capture the complexity of jazz despite the limitations of notation often result in dense representations—double-dotted noteheads tied together in odd configurations, stems connected with multiple layers of beams, and the like—that are difficult for performers to interpret. Consequently, students absorb and store the rhythmic features of jazz aurally by patterning their playing upon that of mature artists through participating in live performances and practicing along with recordings.

Once improvisers can conceive rhythms clearly and manage them agilely, they can use the figures as rhythmic templates for the underpinning of melodic and harmonic ideas by combining them with pitches derived from various sources. "I hear rhythms, mostly," Dizzy Gillespie reports, "and then I put notes to them."[20] Ultimately, the learner's storehouse of melodic phrases, which yields a repertory divisible into discrete rhythmic models, also yields a repertory divisible into discrete tonal models, "the note heads of the phrases without their stems." The discovery that, for leading artists, recurring combinations of pitches form the basis for different phrases encourages students to experiment with the abstract pitch collections. They mull over the effectiveness of each collection's permutations—their resulting interval configurations and melodic contours—when set to different rhythms.

Many performers also learn other approaches to improvisation in which they apply their rhythmic templates to pitches derived from theoretical constructs. Just as music theory initially provides an analytical tool for classifying vocabulary patterns in relation to complementary chords, it ultimately serves as a useful generative or prescriptive tool. Among the jazz community's cumulative options, the earliest appear to have emphasized the invention of melodies from chord tones.

### Improvising from Chords

Before soloists learn music theory, they formulate melodies by ear, kinetically (by hand), and through abstract visualizations in relation to the sounds of each piece's underlying harmony. Their early efforts are commonly "hit and miss," as Melba Liston says. She and her friends "knew what notes didn't fit the chords and didn't sound good," so they "just tiptoed around them" when they played, "trying to avoid them." The increasing complexity of jazz during the forties compounded the challenges faced by the young teenagers. In contrast to pieces based on simple blues forms in which artists "could just about play in one key the whole time," the bebop repertory featured compositions like "Lover" whose chords "went through a lot of keys" (AF). Youngsters who had yet to learn about harmonic modulation did not necessarily appreciate this distinction, and some improvised stubbornly within the initial key of pieces, producing harmonic clashes that were as distressing to them as they were puzzling (DB).

Exclusive dependence on ear knowledge eventually limits many performers, even those who acquire great skill in negotiating tunes aurally.[21] After unsuccessful efforts at jam sessions playing "on complex tunes like 'You Stepped out of a Dream,'" Gary Bartz turned for assistance to trombonist Grachan Moncur, who subsequently taught him the theoretical principles of harmony and their application to jazz. The theory was "a great revelation" to Bartz, who had relied heavily on a piece's melody when formulating solos. At the time, he says, he "had no idea that you could solo from sheet music chords without even knowing the melody of the tune." Benny Bailey also remembers his surprise at an early session when the guitarist informed him bluntly that he was playing the "wrong harmony." That day, Bailey "bought a guitar chord book" and stayed up the entire night practicing, "getting fluid connecting chord to chord. It was like a whole new world opening up." Subsequently, Bailey would not play a composition with other musicians until he "knew the chords."

Following the changing conventions of jazz, particular generations of improvisers have formulated solos from various harmonic models. Early soloists commonly played inside the chords by emphasizing their most basic elements.

"When I began," Doc Cheatham says, "we wouldn't know anything about the sixth or the seventh or the ninth, because jazz was played on the one-three-five chord. . . . Once in a while, [the other pitches] seeped in around there where Louis and Bix started coming in." He remembers a rehearsal of Eubie Blake's band in which "at the end of the tune, [saxophonist] Joe Hyman hit the seventh and Blake jumped up and hit the ceiling, [yelling] 'Don't play those seventh chords in there!' [Cheatham laughs.] It was beautiful."

Since the twenties, musicians have increasingly shaded progressions with diatonic upper extensions and altered tones of chords, and incorporated them into their improvisations. Art Farmer initially invented "very basic solos, riding on notes inside the chords like the tonics and dominants [that sounded] consonant" with a piece's background, then later experimented with other chord tones. Eventually, however, he decided that "spelling chords in performance was nothing by itself," he explains. "It didn't give you a melody. Playing C–E–G–B♭ on a C7 chord might be nice occasionally, but it still leaves a lot of space to be filled up. You had to find out what notes you could add to it to make some kind of musical idea, some kind of phrase." In part, aspiring players found the answer by analyzing the pitch choices of great soloists. Subsequently, many visualized their own options as mixtures of individual elements of chord and non-chord tones.

As the music's harmonic tension increased during the fifties and sixties, improvisers dealt, at times, even "more in the upper partials of chords than with the main chord tones." Some conceived of pitch selections as chords superimposed one upon the another—"two triads or the polychord type of things," as Rufus Reid describes Eddie Harris's playing. According to Reid, instead of picturing one chord with six or seven individual elements in it, as, for instance, an eleventh or a thirteenth on top of an F minor triad, Harris pictures an "E-flat triad on top of the F minor triad which," he says, "automatically gives [him] the seventh, the ninth, and the eleventh." He could "think real fast that way and superimpose different kinds of harmonic things on the chord," Reid explains, because the materials of triads were already second nature to Harris and readily at hand.

Performers also experiment with the use of polychords or compound chords to mix triads with altered pitches, in some instances emphasizing elements outside of the tonality of the key. John Hicks experienced a "new freedom" in his performances when he first began thinking of "two chords a tritone apart" as a way to mix a triad with its raised-eleventh, flatted-seventh, and flatted-ninth degrees. At these operations, as Reid describes it, Eddie Harris's facility "was so enormous that he could go in and out of key so fast that you wouldn't even know that he had put a whole other sound on the chord. That is also what Harold Land and Bobby Hutcherson were doing." Many liken such controlled harmonic mixtures to the subtle blending of colors by visual art-ists.[22] "Everybody's approach to chords is different. Some people move in and out of harmony so quickly that you would hardly recognize the difference, but that adds beauty to the music. It's just like someone's making a picture. You can take the same chord, but add different colors to it. You can make a little red streak, then you add a little pink to it and a little streak of black, and it makes it more beautiful" (DC).

Beyond imaging inventive mixtures of chord tones and color tones, solo-ists can stimulate their melodic ideas by envisioning various chord insertions as they perform. Lee Konitz finds constant challenges in devising new substitu-tions that "add enrichment to the basic harmonic progressions" of sophisticated compositions like "All the Things You Are." Similarly, Harold Ousley puts substitute chords like those designed by Charlie Parker in "different places" within a progression to prevent his own playing "from sounding too monoto-nous." He also regards John Coltrane's improvisations as exemplary in this regard. Instead of playing the same chord for two bars, "Trane might move through two, three, or four chords, just giving a beat or two to each," imbuing that portion of the progression with "a different sound" (exx. 6.6a-c).[23] Substi-tutions are equally helpful in the face of awkward progressions that are inhospitable to improvisers, however suitable for the tune's accompaniment, making it difficult for soloists to weave melodies through them that do not sound "contrived" (HO).

### Improvising from Scales and Intervals

The theoretical construct of scales, like that of chords, provides an alterna-tive way of thinking about pitch relationships. An awareness of scales has not always been a part of the young musician's perspective on music, however. As youngsters, Barry Harris and his peers "just thought about chords. We didn't know about scales until later." Many musicians became aware of the value of scales through the practices of Dizzy Gillespie and Charlie Parker, whose inter-est in creating phrases of longer lengths and greater rhythmic density than their predecessors' led the innovators to combine chord tones with additional material, emphasizing at times a linear concept in their improvisations.

Previously, soloists "had been playing a more riffing style, playing little licks," Tommy Turrentine recalls. He also regards early artists like Dud Bas-comb, Ray Nance, Buck Clayton, and Harry Edison as being "more melodic," or tuneful in a conventional sense, than were Gillespie and his collaborators, who "came along playing all kinds of new scales. They'd hit those flatted ninths, flatted fifths, and those whole-tone progressions, turning the music all around."[24] David Baker adds, "You had Don Redman and Duke Ellington ex-perimenting with chromaticism in the swing period; but only with bebop do you get the breakthrough of adding extra chromatic notes to the various scales to make them . . . symmetrically correct [rhythmically]." From Baker's standpoint, the styles of Harry Carney, Ben Webster, Johnny Hodges, Coleman Hawkins, and even Lester Young are more emphatically "diatonic." The players of their generation did not emphasize, to the same extent, "those extra half steps that you hear when you listen to Dizzy or Bird."

For learners, the discovery of scales and their theoretical relationship to chords constitutes a major conceptual breakthrough with immediate application. They can construct a scale or mode that is compatible with each chord by filling in the diatonic pitches between its tones, increasing the chord's associated pitch collection from four to seven, and grouping optional tonal materials together as a string of neighboring notes. Images of scales or scale fragments provide ready combinations of pitches inside and outside the chord for creating smooth linear phrases. Furthermore, rather than addressing the chords individually, improvisers can use the scale as a compositional model over the span of a diatonic progression. In the bebop era, these models provided soloists with efficient ways of conceptualizing melodic options as tempos increased substantially and the harmonic structures of pieces became denser, changing every two beats in some instances.

Besides parent diatonic scales, jazz performers use a wealth of additional materials. Soloists can produce a common pentatonic scale from a major scale by eliminating its fourth and seventh degrees. There are, of course, also blues scales mixing harmonically ambiguous chord tones and altered tones.[25] Such theoretical abstractions for melodic patterns, inherited from the earliest days of jazz, utilize the tonic, third, fifth, and sixth degrees of the major scale in variable combinations, as well as such blue notes as the flatted-third, flatted-seventh, and flatted-fifth degrees. "Listening to different cats" taught Wynton Marsalis that the "blues is the key to playing jazz."

Art Farmer and Benny Bailey, as members of George Russell's band, experimented with his improvisation method based on the "Lydian chromatic scale."[26] Popular among students at the Berklee College of Music was the melodic or "jazz" minor scale. "When a dominant seventh chord moves, resolves down a fifth, like it should properly," Emily Remler explains, "you can use the jazz minor scale up a half step from the root of the dominant seventh." A case in point is the movement from G7 to C major, which invites the use of the A♭ jazz minor scale. "That gives you all the best tensions to use upon it—sharp eleven, flat nine." Providing further contrast are such symmetrical scales as the chromatic scale; the diminished or double-diminished scale, comprising alternations of half steps and whole steps; and the whole-tone scale—a signature pattern of Thelonious Monk. The peculiar pitch collections and varied interval configurations of different scales distinguish the harmonic color and shape of the melodies created from them.

Overlapping to some degree with the use of chords and scales is another theoretical approach to improvisation emphasizing intervals as compositional models. Musicians sometimes use particular interval arrangements derived from chords as threads in their performances, transposing them to complement the piece's progression. At other times, they favor interval sequences that weave in and out of diatonic harmony. "Today, you can use one interval like a fourth and play it anywhere," Benny Bailey says. "Even if all the notes don't fit the chords, the ear accepts them because they're a complete pattern of fourths. Like on a C7 chord, you can play E♭, A♭, D♭, and G♭, and it won't sound too far out, even though the notes are not in the chord. There are so many different kinds of things you can play like this that there are books full of fourth studies. That's all a lot of young players are studying and playing these days."

As Bailey indicates, thinking in terms of interval patterns enables musicians to call up alternative sets of pitches having different harmonic relationships to the underlying chords. By pursuing Bailey's example, the soloist formulates a melody from the flatted-third, flatted-fifth, raised-fifth, and flatted-ninth degrees, deliberately avoiding the chord tones and producing relatively high harmonic tension. If the same interval sequence were built on the chord's tonic, the resulting phrase would include two chord tones—the tonic and the flatted seventh—and produce comparatively less harmonic tension. During the sixties, artists who popularized intervallic improvisation approaches included McCoy Tyner, Oliver Nelson, Eddie Harris, and Woody Shaw.

Emphasizing sequences of larger intervals, like fourths, distinguishes melodies from those based on thirds, which more readily derive from chords, and from those based on seconds, which more readily derive from scales. At the same time, aspiring performers experimenting with different theoretical approaches discover that their materials sometimes overlap. Greg Langdon had a "revelation" when he played a "G harmonic minor scale up from the fifth degree" and found that it produced the "same pattern" that he had learned from another musician as an "E♭ major arpeggio with half steps" added below each degree. Similarly, the double-diminished scale that Langdon learned from a performer at one session turned out to be the "same as the diminished chord with chromatics added beneath each note" that Barry Harris had taught him at a workshop. Another student found that the pattern he had learned as a pentatonic scale was simply a particular ordering of an interval pattern of fourths. For example, the scale B♭–C–D–F–G is simply a reordered compression of the arpeggio D–G–C–F–B♭.

Although such discrepancies sometimes initially confuse students trying to understand jazz in consistent theoretical terms, many apparent conflicts simply reflect the complementary relationships among chords, scales, and intervals in which each can be defined in terms of the other. Learning jazz is like circling a large "globe," Josh Schneider proposes. Players constantly strive to understand it from different perspectives, different angles. Ultimately, performers make choices among constructs on the basis of their effectiveness as memory devices. Greg Langdon decided that it was more efficient to think of one of the patterns described above as a "diminished chord with chromatics" because he could recall its pitches "much faster" by picturing stacks of minor thirds and embellishing them with routine chromatic gestures than by "trying to remember all the notes of different double-diminished scales."

Artists typically design and perform intensive musical exercises based on theoretical models, initially striving to master them outside of the contexts of compositions. Wynton Marsalis rehearsed the blues for an hour each day when he was in school. "Sometimes, I'd skip lunch and I'd just be playing up and down that blues scale in the stairwell every day." Similarly, Bill Evans practiced scales in "as many different ways as he could," exploring their varied versions in every key (CI).

Through such procedures, jazz musicians emphasize equally the development of technical control over the materials' elements and their methodical exploration. Scales, for example, are mastered not only through practicing their inversions, but through practicing discrete exercises that probe endless arrangements of diatonic intervals (alternating seconds, alternating thirds, and so on), triads, chords, and their various extensions. From one drill to the next, musicians strive to "exhaust all the possibilities" through the "law of permutations," as a student of Jimmy Cheatham's recalls him saying in his workshops. How else can improvisers discover what patterns they especially like?[27]

Eventually, the sheer persistence with which learners study theoretical models—absorbing their elements through various mnemonic devices—concretizes the models for learners and embeds them deeply in memory. Within teenaged bands, recommended exercises strengthen recall of musical materials and teach students to appreciate their cross-relationships. One pianist used to sustain a B♭ on the keyboard just before he and Tommy Turrentine left rehearsals, instructing Turrentine to remember it. As they walked home, the pianist hit different iron poles with a hard object to set them ringing, then quizzed Turrentine about their pitches. Turrentine would figure this out by recalling the sound of B♭ and calculating the number of scale degrees that separated it from the pitch of each pole.

Whereas numerical and lettered imagery remains an integral part of the musical conceptions of some performers, for others it is but a useful learning tool that eventually metamorphizes into firm aural and physical impressions. Miles Davis recalls his early rigorous training in the language of bebop, which included the exploitation of tritone pitch relationships. "We really studied. . . . If a door squeaked, we would call out the exact pitch. And every time I heard the chord of G, for example, my fingers automatically took the position for C♯ on the horn—the flatted fifth—whether I was playing or not." [28]

The amount of time and practice required to reach such goals is itself a surprise for some learners. Benny Bailey reflects on disciplinary demands of jazz, citing the case of Joe Farrell, "a traditional-type tenor player," who once reported that it "took him a year of studying those fourth patterns before he could work them into his solos." Bailey explains, "It's one thing studying something every day, and it's another really using it. That's difficult. You just have to keep on doing it over and over and over again until it comes automatically. Woody Shaw is an extreme example of that; every note he plays is a pentatonic, and he really makes it work. He says he thinks like that automatically now. He hears things in fourths." One surprised beginner recalls his mentor's counsel: "I can show you the basic theory you need to play jazz in a few hours, but you will spend the next five to seven years studying it before you can make much use of it in your playing."

### Integrating Different Theoretical Models

Besides mastering individual theoretical models, artists doggedly explore their relationships. Barry Harris's integrated theory of improvisation and teaching method, derived from his analysis of solos by bebop masters, well illustrates the practice of combining models from different approaches to improvisation. [29] In Harris's method, major scales and mixolydian or dominant seventh scales (often simply called "seventh" scales) serve as focal points for the mixture of other compositional elements. Altogether, they can be performed over related major seventh and dominant seventh chords. Harris begins by teaching a basic set of rules governing the scales' chromatic embellishment and the embellishment of arpeggios, chords, and intervals found diatonically "on scale." Within an initial framework of two-measure phrases, students practice performing simple scale patterns in descending streams of eighth notes, occasionally ornamenting them with spare embellishments. One common embellishment, described earlier in connection with tune renditions, is an triplet eighth-note inverted mordent. Another is a sixteenth-note inverted mordent on triplet rhythm, incorporating the motion from a pitch to the scale degree above it, a return to the first pitch, and then the scale degree below it (exx. 6.7a–c).

As students increase their proficiency, the class designs increasingly varied patterns based on the material. Students "run" from any pitch in a scale to any other pitch. They repeat pitches, skip pitches, "double back" over scale fragments, and combine them with chords and intervals on scale and their inversions. Harris further stylizes the inventions of students with practices that dictate precise melodic shape. One practice is "pivoting," using one pitch as a launching point for leaps to any other chord tones, then arpeggiating the chord in the opposite direction (exx. 6.8a–b). He also suggests sophisticated harmonic mixtures of pitches derived from different types of chords, intervals, and scales. Combining fragments of diatonic scales with diminished chords or with augmented triads, or alternating the elements of minor chords and diminished chords, can produce melodies with diverse colors. There is no end to the possibilities. One common effect of Harris's system is to weight the use of chord tones. Even when surrounded by neighboring or altered pitches, chord tones commonly emerge as the prominent pitches of melodic shapes and as the target pitches of phrase endings, occurring, in many instances, on the beat.

While sharing basic theoretical elements with other methods, Harris's is unique in both its emphasis and detail, for it teaches students precisely how to transform the elements into credible phrases and focuses as much upon the creative processes of improvisation as upon its products, effectively clarifying the relationship between theory and performance practice in the jazz tradition. Before one class member studied with Harris, he had received advice from many other musicians that he needed to know chords to play jazz. The student, however, could never really see the connection. Whenever he played "patterns out of chord books," as he put it, "they just sounded like patterns out of chord books." Similarly, another pupil used to "hate" scales because his teachers insisted that he play them "like technical exercises—straight up and down the octave." That, he thought, was "all" scales were. Having learned from Harris what improvisers "can do with scales," however, he now finds them to be "really interesting," and he asserts, "I never get tired of practicing them."

The explicitness of Harris's method in describing the elements of great solos provides students with a language and an analytical key that enables them to "unlock the mysteries of jazz" for themselves. When analyzing recorded improvisations, they begin not only to grasp formerly impenetrable patterns, whose components had eluded them aurally, but to name them in theoretical terms. "I've heard that before; that's just a descending seventh scale with a half step between the one and the seventh, run down to the third, and diminished up from the third." Each revelation carries students over another threshold toward understanding the common language of jazz and its personalized vocabulary as coined by the great improvisers. For instance, although many artists periodically superimpose the sound of a diminished chord over a seventh chord, students find that each may favor different pivot notes, melodic shapes, and articulation schemes.[30]

Learners take heart in their own developing skills as they come to recognize the intimate details that characterize stylized treatments. Initially overwhelmed by the complexity of jazz and the gulf that separates their abilities from those of their idols, they eventually gain confidence. Having lived with the familiar impression "Oh, no. I could never do that!" they begin gradually to indulge a new sense that encroaches upon their awe until they can assert with some cockiness, "I know what that is; I can do that!" Sometimes, this expression of confidence is followed by a slight tinge of disappointment. The sense of lost innocence that accompanies the demystification of their elusive art diminishes quickly, however, in the face of new challenges to the learner's understanding and development.

In this regard, Harris's theory is an expansive generative method. It encourages musicians to create original phrases based, in part, on the cross-fertilization of rhythmic, melodic, and harmonic models embodied in the rules Harris promulgates. These activities gripped Lonnie Hillyer and Charles McPherson as youngsters. They would get together unfailingly after school and practice making up lines, "playing two-bar phrases back and forth all night long." One of "the great things about Barry's system," Hillyer observes, "is that everyone who studied it came out sounding different." Similarly, another learner who had just come to appreciate the method's "infinite possibilities" once animatedly shared his vision with me after class: "Now that Barry's laid it out for us, I know what I need to work on for the rest of my life." This is a fine testimonial, indeed, to the method's effectiveness and comprehensiveness, a grand tribute to a master teacher.

### The Ongoing Interplay of Theoretical and Aural Ideas

Over the careers of improvisers, their theoretical and aural knowledge constantly inform one another. Sometimes, artists design phrases from theoretical calculation and, as was true for some in their early training, derive stimulation from theoretical expositions in such other musical fields as classical music. Musicians at Boston's Schillinger House (later the Berklee College of Music) studied the *Schillinger System of Musical Composition* during the forties.[31] Doc Cheatham also studied for a couple of years with a musician "who had his own ideas" about the Schillinger system. Cheatham could relate his aural knowledge of various facets of jazz harmony to the system and, subsequently, found it useful in his own experience teaching jazz to younger musicians. Two decades later, in the course of pursuing graduate studies in music, Donald Byrd discovered Nicolas Slonimsky's *Thesaurus of Scales and Melodic Patterns,* a reference book that is "systematized in a manner convenient for composers in search of new materials." Byrd brought the book to the attention of John Coltrane, who, having absorbed some of the principles of Barry Harris's method years earlier in Detroit, now found Slonimsky's material useful for his own music. As word spread within the jazz community that Coltrane was practicing from the book, performers from San Francisco to New York City experimented with its use.[32]

It is also possible for theory to bridge different realms of musical knowledge for students, facilitating their appreciation for the common foundational materials used by improvisers and classical music composers. George Duvivier recalls that within the jazz community "Dizzy Gillespie made people aware of the flatted fifth and the flatted ninth—which actually goes back to Bach fugues." Similarly, when Barry Harris once discovered that a group of classical music students who attended his master class had difficulty assimilating even the rudiments of his theoretical approach to improvisation, he shook his head incredulously, then seated himself at the piano for a demonstration. To the surprise of listeners expecting to hear jazz, he began by performing an exquisite melody with a diminished quality from a Chopin composition. With the passage's completion, Harris admonished the students: "Now, if Chopin hadn't known his diminished chords, he never could have thought of this." Then Harris quoted a compelling Charlie Parker solo, interjecting: "And if Bird hadn't known his diminished chords, he never could have thought of that."

At the same time, artists' aural understanding and appreciation of music guide interpretation of theoretical material and drive its applications. Attraction to the sounds of their own successful constructions and to the inventions of others commonly enlightens students to the relevance of theory. Josh Schneider has "often had the experience of working on things" and realizing he has "just rediscovered" a principle that "someone told me about years ago, but I wasn't ready for it at the time. It may be a certain way to go through a certain chord, a different way to play a dominant chord, or a way of using the notes on the top of the minor chord going to a dominant chord, or applying a certain pattern like a diminished pattern to a dominant chord. After you've done it, you say, 'So that's why that worked on this particular thing!'" Comparable revelations in his analysis of solos by Charlie Parker and other great artists provided the basis for Barry Harris's improvisation theory and method (ex. 6.9).

For many, the ability to interpret an appealing idea in theoretical terms facilitates exploration of the idea's implications, generating new phrases in the process of experimentation. Barry Harris's pupils learn that every detail noticed or discovered in an effective improvisation opens the door for further invention. If one thing is true, they reason, inspired by Harris's tutelage, then what follows from it? Suppose an artist's beautiful gesture contains a descending seventh scale from the second with a half step between the tonic and the seventh, run down to the third, diminished up to the flat ninth, and resolved to the tonic. What would it sound like if the descending scale were run up a chord on scale from the third degree instead of run up a diminished chord? What would it sound like if the pattern were run past the third to the seventh below the tonic and then up a chord on scale? What would it sound like run up an augmented chord? What would it sound like if the half step were put in a different place within the descending scale? What would it sound like if a major scale were substituted for the seventh scale? And so on. Students answer these self-construed questions by performing the different possibilities and selecting for practice those patterns that most appeal to them.

In a continuing cycle, analysis of exciting, aurally conceived phrases can reveal new relationships among their elements, leading to the formulation of yet other theoretical constructs, which, in turn, stimulate further composition. In this sense, artists constantly "make up their own rules in jazz" (WB). "Dizzy's got a very complicated brain, and he comes up with some funny lines that are really a knockout," Benny Bailey says. "He's got a whole lot of things that he's figured out for himself—funny oriental-type scales and things. He's always happy to discover new ones, and he uses them in his solos. His mind is always working on those things." In recent years, Art Farmer, too, "mainly make[s] up different scales and practice[s] making melodies from them." Representing a particularly imaginative strategy, Jimmy Cheatham sometimes advocates inventing a unique scale from the pitches of each composition and using the scale as the basis for the composition's respective solos.[33]

Like their vocabulary stores, performers' individual theoretical methods typically synthesize their personal discoveries with the most useful ideas gleaned from other players. The ease with which artists can negotiate patterns derived from theory when actually mapped out on an instrument, in part a function of their idiosyncratic physical characteristics, further delineates individual methods and contributes to the basis for personal styles or systems of improvisation.

Improvisers have increasingly formalized the fruits of their studies by producing method books, teaching tapes, and, most recently, videorecordings, which are available to peers and learners within the jazz community.[34] Altogether, the varied music models associated with theoretical and rhythmic approaches to improvisation complement the artists' models of jazz tunes and fully formed vocabulary patterns, diversifying options during performances and guiding the conception of solos.

## SEVEN

**Conversing with the Piece**

Initial Routines Applying Improvisation Approaches to Form

*Soloists elaborate upon what the structure of the piece has to say; what it tells them to do.*—Tommy Flanagan

*Keeping the melody in mind, you always know where you are, even when you play intricate things.*—Lou Donaldson

The routines by which artists absorb different approaches to improvisation and learn to create phrases based on their materials are but preliminary exercises during practice sessions. Performers go on to consider the applications of their materials within such formal musical contexts as tune and solo renditions. Pianists and guitarists have the instrumental capacity to reproduce harmony while simultaneously performing tunes or inventing melodic lines. Others practice along with records. As they sense the progression from the rhythm section's accompaniment of soloists, they superimpose their own improvisations over those of the recording artists, "weaving in and out of what they're doing" (RB). In fact, artists like Henry "Red" Allen learned to improvise "in all keys in New Orleans by playing along with records set at every different speed. Each speed would put the music in a new key."[1] For Billie Holiday, singing publicly with Bessie Smith and Louis Armstrong recordings formed part of her early teenage apprenticeship.[2]

Performing with music on the radio provides supplementary practice opportunities, introducing the increased challenge of grasping the forms of new compositions during a single hearing or over the course of unpredictable replays.[3] Adopting alternative methods, some artists use playalong records, in which the rhythm section performs in a spare supportive mode. Performers of

170

chording instruments may record their own versions of progressions and drill with them. As often as not, improvisers also practice formulating solos without accompaniment by reading lead sheets or envisioning their personalized representational maps of pieces.

As a prelude to extensive melodic invention, some artists routinely warm up by practicing a piece's melody. Its rendition, typically the first event in a formal jazz presentation, assists musicians in making a transition from their normal world of verbal thought and visual imagery to the precomposed world of sounds, effectively stimulating thought in the language of jazz and awakening the musical imagination. Before their performance, artists also commonly consider the meanings of compositions. Song texts often provide a key to a piece's meaning. "The oldtimers always used to tell horn players to learn the lyrics just like a singer does, so that they know the meaning of the piece," Max Roach recalls. This enabled them "to get underneath the piece, to really sing with their instruments and play with more feeling."

In practicing the melody, artists experiment with the various transformational activities discussed earlier, along a scale from interpretation to improvisation. In negotiating a song's features, for example, they need not leap directly over a wide interval. Rather, they might travel its distance via sonic paths selected from their tonal models—ascending chords, scale fragments, or vocabulary patterns of appropriate dimension—arriving at the same place through routes of distinctive interest.[4]

Having worked on the rendition of a piece's melody, students prepare for creating original solos.[5] Toward such ends, preliminary exercises emphasize technical mastery over the application of various musical models within each composition's progression. The point is to perform unfalteringly and without harmonic error. To accomplish this, musicians sometimes alter the formal constraints they place upon themselves. Initially, to lessen the pressures associated with thinking in time, they perform in free rhythm. More confident, they perform to a steady beat. Artists also begin and end their drills at whim, isolating discrete portions of a progression for practice, methodically addressing its features.

Eventually, they advance through the piece's form. "I'd set the chords in front of me and play the melody, watching where the chords fall in relation to the melody," Gary Bartz remembers. "Then I'd start to solo on it, playing through it one section at a time, the first eight bars, the first ten bars, the first twelve bars, the first half a chorus, and so on, up to the bridge. Then I'd just play the bridge. Once I could do that, I'd play through the whole chorus." Performers do not necessarily make an effort to remember the products of their early drills. Successes simply assure them that each section will present minimal difficulty during formal solos. When problems arise in the course of their trials, however, musicians stop to study the piece's structure again.

Of the many conventions for creating solos, learners commonly begin with an approach known as "playing off the melody." That is, after performing a piece's melody at the opening of an arrangement, artists can continue to bear the tune in mind as a constant reference for the solo improvisation. Percussionist Alan Dawson cultivates this orientation in students by having them sing jazz tunes while practicing intricate technical exercises and, ultimately, while practicing the formulation of drum solos. They soon become used to hearing the exercises and improvisations in relation to the piece, and vice versa (AT).[6] In performances, pianists, bass players, and guitarists sometimes vocalize the tune softly to themselves as they improvise, thereby supplying a subtle counterpoint to their instrumentalization.

Through this approach, the melody can also provide the conceptual basis for solos, prompting artists to pursue various options described earlier for its treatment. During some renditions of ballads and blues, soloists preserve the melody's characteristic shape throughout by limiting themselves to minor embellishments and periodic improvised commentaries. Such performances blur the distinction between the melody's presentation and the improvised solo.

On the other hand, soloists may treat the melody of a composition allusively. In Art Farmer's early efforts to improvise, he avoided strict imitation of the melody, striving instead to fashion phrases in each piece's "general style" so that solos were "like an extension of the melody." As Curtis Fuller observes, others make only slight reference to the composition by "flirting" intermittently with its specific tonal, harmonic, or rhythmic features, creating variations on them. Deriving more substantial guidelines from the composition, improvisers may adopt its rhythmic phrasing as the entire underpinning of a solo's design. "Pres could really feel a song," Lou Donaldson says. "He could make you hear the song just from his phrasing."[7] Common examples are found in blues choruses in which players improvise three four-bar phrases modeled upon the classic AA'B structure of many blues melodies and song texts: introducing a phrase, repeating it (perhaps with slight variation), then following it with a contrasting phrase or punch line. This procedure typically occurs in initial solo choruses (ex. 7.1) that serve as a transition to more adventurous improvisations.[8]

Soloists can also quote partial or complete passages from the piece, combining them with their own in different ways (exx. 7.2a–d). "Sometimes, the performer plays part of the melody and then he improvises something," Lonnie Hillyer says; "then he plays something else from the melody and then improvises some more. . .[as if] answering or accompanying himself." Hillyer views such excursions as commentaries inspired by the play of the music upon the mind. They represent a kind of conversation between the improviser and the composition. References to the melody provide a useful connective tissue between a solo and its respective vehicle, reaffirming the identity of the latter and imbuing the former with special characteristics. This approach contributes significantly to "what makes your improvisations on different tunes different," Lee Konitz offers, especially when pieces share comparable harmonic structures. Of course, artists may decide to pursue a radical course and ignore the melody of the piece altogether, in effect, says Konitz, "composing their own songs from wholly new melodies."

Besides using the melody as the conceptual basis of solos, practicers adopt another fundamental approach in which they conceive ideas largely in terms of the component shapes of formerly mastered vocabulary patterns. When musicians abandon the melody as a model for invention—whether temporarily in the context of its rendition or during their solos—they depend on the progression's salient features as signposts for the improvisation's "progress." Moreover, the syntactic implications of harmonic structures assist artists in their endeavor. Once they cultivate a "feeling for form, the form will guide you; it will almost play itself" (FH). For many students, the early effort to speak jazz, that is, to use the vocabulary, begins with imitating the precise placement of phrases within the structure of a piece where an idol originally performed them. Listening to "the way guys like Bird played" taught Lonnie Hillyer about appropriate usage, about "where a phrase fit and where it wouldn't."

Jimmy Robinson similarly took "the best things" from different solos and "worked it out" so that he could put each phrase into "a certain part of the tune" each time he played it. Harold Ousley elaborates upon the process: "You practice using a phrase when you play along with records and when you go to sessions. After a while, you begin to hear and feel where a phrase goes, and, suddenly, you are able to play the phrase in the right place. Eventually, it becomes ingrained in you because you practice it so much. It becomes a natural habit when you improvise."

In the meantime, learners observe that their mentors use vocabulary flexibly, maximizing its potential for creating different solos. Analyses of jazz masters' performances reveal important information to aspiring artists, leading the way for their own trials. After hearing "Bird take things he used at one particular point in a tune and play them in other places," Lonnie Hillyer "figured that he must have been trying to make them come out differently. That's all it's about, just trying to make things come out differently every time you play them." Probing more deeply, Hillyer and his friends gradually discovered the principles that ensured that Parker's phrases would "come out" correctly as well as "differently" in each instance.

One essential "secret" is that performers can potentially introduce a particular phrase in their solos wherever its complementary chords occur. This realization immediately creates new possibilities for vocabulary usage within the structures of compositions that had served as initial vehicles for students. Once Bobby Rogovin and his peers had, as he says, "taken a certain amount of licks off records, we would take two that were about the same and switch them around in different parts of the solo." The same principle applies throughout the jazz repertory. "There may be a certain set of chord progressions that you find in different places in different tunes. If you know a crip that fits that chord progression, you can use it on different tunes. You can prove that if you listen to any record by Bird. He'd play crips all the time. He'd play a crip to a set of progressions on 'Night and Day' and then use it again on another tune like 'Embraceable You'"(TT). Practicers expand their options further by transposing phrases to fit different chords of the same quality arising in different progressions.

Moreover, many phrases are compatible with different kinds of chords. Combined with various harmonic settings, the figures produce diverse timbral colors, differing degrees of harmonic tension, and differing schemes of tension and release (exx. 7.3a–b).[9] Thus, although they apply figures consistently in many instances, artists like James Moody also "practice trying to play something that you like and being able to put it anywhere you want in a tune." Harold Ousley's experience is similar: "The same phrase will sound different in different places in a progression; it works on different chords. It's like having a red shirt on or having a blue shirt on—the same style made by the same company, but each with a different hue. Or, if you play the phrase on a certain chord, it will sound more flavored. It's like using Accent [a spice product] to flavor food, bringing out the taste more." As Josh Schneider learned from Barry Harris, this process entails not only exploring "how far on top of [compatible] chords or away from their roots" a player can perform a pattern, but how effectively a player can resolve the pattern within the context of the progression to different adjacent chords or key centers.

Adding further interest to their creations, improvisers cull the skills of rhythmic displacement, which enables them to vary the positions of their phrases within compatible harmonic territory (exx. 7.4a–e). "Bird had an uncanny sense of rhythm, and he was always unique with the way he would play the same passage," Tommy Turrentine says. "In one tune, he might take that passage and bring it on the first beat of the measure of a progression. Then, on another tune, he might take the same crip and start it on the 'and' of the third beat of the measure so that it would come out in a different place." Through comparable practice routines, artists gain technical mastery over their vocabulary's flexible applications.

Improvisation drills emphasizing tunes and vocabulary patterns provide fully formed shapes, that is, detailed melodies, long or short, for the artist's consideration. Furthermore, within formal musical contexts, musicians methodically practice applying rhythmic and theoretical approaches whose emphasis is on models not yet formed into phrases. One, in particular, cultivates "rhythmic inventiveness." Ken McIntyre encourages aspiring players to begin by restricting themselves to the roots of a piece's successive chords or even to the piece's tonic pitch alone. By severely limiting tonal options, students focus their efforts on creating rhythmic phrases varied in substance and length and spanning different portions of the progression. Similarly, at times, Barry Harris encourages students to improvise rhythmic patterns by chanting them in a monotone within the framework of compositions.

Alternatively, artists practice performing a composition's chords, initially "spelling out" their elements and eventually going on to explore their varied permutations. Benny Bailey typically sees "the changes in front of me when I play and try to image what to do with them—different kinds of ways to approach them." For James Moody as well, "what's hip about it is that you can take a set of chords and play different inversions of them." He continues:

> Maybe, one time through the tune, you play all the first inversions of the chords, just for their sound; then you play all the second inversions for a different sound. Starting on a certain note and going to another note within the same chords gives a different texture to the solo. You listen to what it sounds like one way, and then you say, "I wonder what it would sound like if I switch it around." There are so many different ways to switch chords around.

Some musicians routinely alternate approaches to acquaint themselves with a composition, formulating their first solo chorus around the piece's melody, their second around its chords, and their third around its related chord-scales. In addition to practicing these approaches with their principal instruments, horn players commonly experiment with them vocally or at the keyboard, where they can invent patterns in relation to an audible harmonic accompaniment. Subsequently, they learn them on their other instruments.

As artists explore different approaches to improvisation—whether vocally or instrumentally, or conceptually improvising away from an instrument without vocalizing their creations—their ideas can assume different forms of representation.[10] Improvisers sometimes emphasize aural thinking. At other times, they emphasize theoretical thinking. Additionally, their rich field of imagination can feature abstract visual displays. Curtis Fuller "tries to paint little pictures" when he improvises. Fred Hersch, too, "sees things very graphically that way." He visualizes what he plays as "a kind of big playground with things jumping around on it, usually in terms of melodic movement: things going up this way, balanced by something going down that way." Or he will see "large masses of things moving along: one string of notes jumping up and down, stopping, twitching around. Music has a feeling of space around it; it exists in space, these little mobiles of things. I like to think of music visually like that," Hersch explains.

Numerous other impressions can come into play as well. At times, Emily

Remler visualizes the music's beat as a regular sine wave in relation to which she varies the phrasing of her melodies. One saxophonist speaks of visualizing precise linear figures in staff notation the instant before performing them. Several pianists mention that, having learned versions of a piece's structure and distinct melodic routes through them as alternative configurations of black and white keys, they can subsequently envision the designs as a matrix of superimposed patterns on their keyboards—a composite tablature-like image whose reading can suggest different pathways for invention.

Additionally, as elaborated in this work, an artist's intermittent internal verbalizations cut across these varied aural and visual designs to evaluate and direct performances. Depending on the nature and demands of a particular improvisation, the soloist might also move mentally between musical and extramusical matters, dwelling on memories or engaging in free association to the music's impulses. The images soloists receive during performances influence the improvisation in various ways. Beyond simply reinforcing its current musical content, they can generate a spontaneous elaboration of mood or melody. Sometimes, this involves experiences that artists associate with the titles or the key lyrics of songs, prompting the use of musical quotations. Roy Haynes fondly recalls an occasion when Charlie Parker improvised a "burning" solo in which he quoted "The Last Time I Saw Paris" repeatedly "in different keys." Unable to contain his curiosity afterwards, Haynes asked Parker what actually had happened "the last time" Parker saw Paris.[11]

### Early Efforts and Tribulations

Armed with a basic reserve of musical models, young musicians, once they take the plunge and apply their knowledge, encounter the varied challenges that accompany the task. In Curtis Fuller's terms, the "road" is indeed "a long and rocky one" over which learners must travel to acquire a jazz vocabulary, grasp the aesthetic issues that surround its rudimentary use, and work toward fluency. Initially, for many, it is a revelation itself that their solos must "complement the chords, the progression, the meter and the melody—the whole composition." When Tommy Turrentine was learning to play, people would say to him, "Man, why don't you slow down and think about what you're doing? Why don't you think about that chord? Why don't you think about how you're going to come out of that phrase and go into another one?" He continues:

> For all them cats, it was a matter of conception. Lamont Young was the first person to make me aware of that word. One day, when we was walking home from a rehearsal, he said, "Hey, Tom, you have to start thinking about conception, man." I said, "What do you mean?" He said, "Because you sounded sadder'n seven thousand muthafuckahs on that tune. You didn't know where you were going." About

which he was right. In improvisation, you've got to have a basic conception of whatever you're playing just to know when to start and stop. If you don't, something funny's going to jump off.

As Turrentine suggests, musicians require a fundamental understanding of melody and form before they can know, literally, when "to start and stop" their solos.[12] Before Lonnie Hillyer had developed an extensive repertory and learned about progressions, the precise boundaries between individual interpretations of composed melodies and improvised solos sometimes eluded him. At one instructive rehearsal in which he tried to re-create Miles Davis's recorded rendition of a piece, Hillyer played "right through the tune and halfway into Miles's solo" before the laughter of the older band members stopped him.

Kenny Washington's early difficulty was equally basic. Having not yet grasped intellectually the cyclical harmonic basis for jazz, he followed solos by other musicians in strictly linear terms, perplexed by their widely varied lengths. Likewise, when he improvised with a Music Minus One playalong record that provided gaps for drum solos within each arrangement, Washington had difficulty fitting in his part. The band invariably dropped out before Washington began his solos and started up again before he completed them. However, over time, as the record accumulated scratches, he was able to turn this experience to his advantage, solving his problem with the ingenuity appropriate to a percussionist. He learned to anticipate one arrangement's events by measuring off the popping patterns that the record's scratches produced: two prominent pops effectively cued the entrance and conclusion to his solos.

Even after students learn to follow other musicians' solos in formal terms and to interpret them as successive ventures through the piece, many still experience difficulty in their own performances. One fundamental problem for the learner involves conceiving and performing patterns in time. In this regard, Barry Harris once dictated a harmonic progression to a group of classical music students at a university workshop and directed them to perform an ascending diminished figure at designated points within the form. The task involved the mental gymnastics of following the progression while quickly transposing the figure to suit the progression's changing chords.

Although the students had a good enough understanding of the concept of diminished structures and chords and would have had little trouble recognizing them in a written score, this was their first experience with interpreting and performing them off the page. As a result, their trails produced one failure after another, each fiasco followed by a spate of embarrassed laughter. Having been defeated by exercises in musical thinking that for seasoned jazz musicians simply constituted preliminary routines—far down the scale of difficulty from transforming chords into viable melodies—the workshop participants came to appreciate, for the first time, both the intellectual rigor of improvisation and the agility required to translate ideas into sounds instantaneously.

Similarly, serious jazz learners soon discover that to think in terms of rudimentary jazz models, conceiving different possibilities for their application, is one thing; to speak in terms of the models by expressing the possibilities with their instruments is quite another. Even the experts themselves "really have to practice the coordination between the mind and the fingers, the ideas and the body," Art Farmer affirms. "You have to practice finding the ideas on your horn, getting there at the same time the idea comes into your head. It's a matter of developing instant touch." Musicians commonly practice this synchronization even when away from an instrument by making up figures and miming their finger patterns simultaneously. The goal is to achieve such close coordination between the body and the conceptualizing mind as to articulate musical patterns with the ease and directness of speech or any expressive gesture.[13]

Additionally, as revealed by the incident in Harris's workshop described above, students must learn to maintain different musical perspectives simultaneously, conceiving patterns for their own evolving part while, in the expert's terms, engaging in a "conversation" with the piece, regulating their ideas in relation to its formal elements.[14] Managing each task is a trial in itself; managing them together is the focus of the learner's struggles. Greg Langdon worked with more advanced players, but many could not help him to "hear better." He would play a piece with them and they would "sound great," he recounts, "but I'd get completely lost." In similar fashion, disoriented novices commonly fail to anticipate the chord changes, instead clashing with the underlying harmony. In other instances, they manage to complement successive chords but lose sight of the larger form.

Repeated trials and arduous practice routines eventually correct such deficiencies as students gradually memorize a progression's chords, learn to predict the chords' rate of change, and gain greater technical mastery over jazz vocabulary and other materials. In Harold Ousley's development as a young musician, there was "an inner awareness" that gradually began "to do all these things" for him, making connections between the various requisite skills. He likens the process to a child's mastering different operations when learning to ride a bicycle. At first, it "wobbles dangerously from side to side," but after hours of practice, "you find your center of balance, and suddenly you have the power to control it so it won't fall either way. It's the same with music," he suggests. In developmental "breakthroughs," aspiring musicians may suddenly discover that they have acquired the control to manipulate phrases accurately in tempo in relation to a progression's changing features.

Ousley's analogy, with its salient features of balance, coordination, and forward motion, is an apt one for jazz veterans, who commonly liken improvising to a mental journey. When tracking the chords of a progression, veterans commonly experience the basic structure itself as stationary, and themselves as moving through it. The form's successive harmonic chambers seem distinctly multidimensional. Passage through them has about it a feeling of time and space, as artists absorb and negotiate the aural features of their changing surroundings.

To clarify these issues, trumpeter Dick Whitsell once broke into a little dance in the doorway of his living room. Bobbing up and down and snapping his fingers to the pulse of an imaginary rhythm section, he announced: "We're going into a blues. The first chord is B♭," and he stepped in perfect time onto the floorboards. Propelling himself forward with the passing beats, Whitsell delineated each chord as a discrete space in the room. Dancing within the perimeters of the prescribed chord for its duration before moving on to the next, eventually he advanced through the piece's entire structure. Going through the choreography a second time, following the same floor plan, he added scat improvisation to his performance, interrupting his vocal lines only long enough to announce each impending chord.

Whitsell's clever kinetic dramatization illustrates how translatable into concrete analogies are harmonic-rhythmic places, once soloists develop a deep understanding of structure. For Whitsell, it is clearly an obvious transition from body language and scat vocals to the trumpet improvisation that follows. His scat phrases translate easily into trumpet patterns. The harmonic places he explores are not designated spatial areas within the living room, but conceptual coordinates encompassing successive tonal centers and related compositional elements, which change according to the progression's dictates. When he solos, Whitsell's swaying to the music's beat and fingering of his instrument as he pursues particular melodic routes through the form are themselves subtle dance movements creating an integrated performance.

Youngsters develop comparable ease as soloists only after they have assimilated the conventional harmonic movements of jazz and have become adept at determining the tonal models that provide effective pathways through them. As with every operation in jazz requiring choice, it is each artist's "musical intelligence"—an "inner essence"—that directs the decision-making process (HO). Eventually, artists learn to conceptualize the structure of a piece so they can include appropriate selections of vocabulary. At various points within their structural designs of a composition, artists begin to envision cumulative patterns associated with particular chords beside related variants of the composition's melody. Together with the player's rhythmic and theoretical materials, these conceptualized tonal models provide numerous options for improvisation.

Depending on their backgrounds, artists may encounter different challenges in achieving versatility in the use of these options. When learners whose understanding is primarily aural take up theory, they commonly require a period of readjustment before assimilating their newly acquired knowledge into their storehouses and maps of compositions, so that thinking in terms of chord symbols calls up the sounds of melodic patterns, and vice versa. The ability to translate rapidly between aural and theoretical realms can be useful to artists as they face musical dilemmas. Many periodically interpose thoughts of a theoretical nature on the flow of an improvisation when problems threaten their aural grasp on a composition's form. "If the rhythm is right and the band is really jumping," Lou Donaldson "doesn't even think about the changes. But if the rhythm is dragging or something," he says, "I really do visualize the changes to make sure I'm playing correctly."

Toward the same goal, testing the form with particular vocabulary patterns can be effective. If, while playing a piece like "I've Got You under My Skin," Harold Ousley is unsure about the portion of the progression he is approaching, whether, for example, an anticipated chord is to be, in his words, "a Gm7 or a G♭ chord, I can play certain phrases when I get there that will enable me to figure it out." His understanding of how the phrases sound in relation to different chords clarifies the issue for him. Reaffirming or revising his mental chart of the progression accordingly, Ousley then applies vocabulary patterns with greater assurance throughout the performance, combining them with other suitable options in the solo's ongoing invention. Ultimately, a soloist strives for such mastery over form as to improvise without external support. This became apparent to Patience Higgins during his early study with Barry Harris. "You should be able to outline a song without a rhythm section," Higgins maintains, "and be able to tell when you're at the bridge or the last eight bars of the tune."

### The Singing Mind's Conception: From Technical Exercises to Ideas

Once musicians achieve technical control over their materials, methodically plotting out their course and correctly applying selected options within the settings of compositions, they build upon their success by changing the emphasis of their practice routines. Increasingly, they strive to apply their materials "musically." For many, this means stressing aural conceptualization over other forms of music representation when interpreting and negotiating the constructive elements in their store—even those elements initially derived from theoretical models. Kenny Barron does not "think in terms of scales and chords" when he improvises, but he does "think in terms of their sounds." Similarly, Josh Schneider's goal is to improve his ear so that he can "hear millions of different intervals" in his imagination "before he plays them" and then "play them instantly."

Experts use the metaphor of singing to elucidate their own experiences with this mode of conception. According to Lee Konitz, "Improvising is a singing, whistling phenomenon when it's really happening. It's the expression of the sound that you can conceptualize on your own steam. It's a matter of getting intricately and sophisticatedly involved with a melodic line so that it is one with the performer." New Orleans trumpeter Mutt Carey elaborates, "When

I'm improvising, I'm singing in my mind. I sing what I feel and then try to reproduce it on the horn."[15] In his own case, Fred Hersch is not really sure which "comes first, the singing or the playing, but it's the same thing really." He teaches his students that "any jazz player should be able to scat sing his solo." This wisdom is long standing. Indeed, early New Orleans musicians cautioned, "If you can't sing it, you can't play it."[16] It may be possible to perform phrases on an instrument mechanically, the argument goes, by translating representations like chord symbols directly into finger patterns without prehearing the sounds for which they stand, but singing requires that artists both grasp ideas firmly in their imaginations and invest them with expressive qualities.

As suggested earlier, many artists practice conceiving patterns through singing before transferring them to instruments. It is said that Clifford Brown devoted as much time to singing as to instrument practice. Moreover, Louis Armstrong and many other outstanding soloists developed the skill to double as vocalists. Not only could they render unique interpretations of song texts, but they could expertly alternate instrumental and scat improvisations. Others, like bassist Slam Stewart, sing or hum simultaneously with their instrumental solos, creating special timbral effects and reinforcing their conceptualization.

One saxophonist cultivated comparable abilities through another stringent routine that won the admiration of the musicians who were his housemates. While the other players improvised constantly in their practice sessions, apparently performing all the material that occurred to them in order to hear and evaluate it, the saxophonist restricted his own performance to his most effective conceptions. Practicing while seated cross-legged on the floor, he combined melodic rumination with meditation, sounding his discrete phrases only sparingly, separating them, at times, by silences of fifteen minutes or more.

Under the aegis of the singing mind, players continue to practice small-scale invention within the forms of compositions but concern themselves with a higher level of expression by training themselves to produce viable jazz phrases. Improvisers, in Kenny Barron's words, "primarily think in terms of musical ideas. An idea would be a melodic phrase." Or as Art Farmer puts it, the idea could be "one bar long, two bars long or as much as eight bars long." The reference to musical patterns as ideas is prevalent among veterans. Such language metaphors complement that of singing to distinguish initial practice routines aimed at mastering musical materials from the artists' subsequent goals and achievements.

Although the use of theoretical models serves learners by isolating "correct" tonal options from the vast possibilities available, eliminating some of the guesswork and harmonic error inherent in the soloists' early inventions, the models themselves comprise only raw compositional materials.[17] Transforming them into ideas involves exploiting these materials from different vantage points and treating their elements creatively. Each artist's rhythmic conception provides an important key. Improvisers breathe life into pitch collections by applying their rhythmic templates to them, imbuing them with swing. A cornerstone of Barry Harris's improvisation method extends those practices already described by involving students in composing attractive, new rhythmic patterns, then adding pitches to them.

Rhythmic procedures also assist players in altering materials from other music systems, adapting them to the jazz tradition. Drummers alter the rudimental figures from conventional drum pedagogy by "accenting them in unique ways and making them swing in the jazz style" (KC). John McNeil tailored "certain scalar patterns" from Herbert Clarke's *Technical Studies* to his own use by "adding chromatic eighth-note pick-ups" because "phrases usually begin before the downbeat in jazz." He also changed "the tonguing marks around so that the accents would come on the off-beats." Clifford Brown's rhythmic transfiguration of what appears to be an excerpt from a technical exercise in Arban's *The Complete Conservatory Method for Trumpet* is also instructive on this point (exx. 7.5a–b).

As artists methodically experiment with transforming different pitch collections into ideas, each soloist's "melodic conception" is also a guide. Included in a performer's melodic conception is the essential sense of contour shaping and phrasing learned from studying such models as jazz compositions and vocabulary patterns. It encompasses, as well, the timbral subtleties embedded within the models—the endless shades of color and microtonal inflection reminiscent of the human voice. Characteristically, when Emily Remler "uses arpeggios and scales in a solo," she strives "to make valid melodies out of them, melodies which would be so good that you could make a tune out of each four-bar phrase." Buster Williams received an especially "good foundation for melodic playing" from his father, who used a bass method by Bob Haggart that provides "different types of patterns to play within scales and teaches you to play scales in many different ways." The senior Williams, who used the approach himself, "had a way of incorporating those patterns in his solos so that they didn't sound like those patterns." Similarly, Benny Bailey may "think about a scale" during his solos, but he strives to "play it so that it's a little different—so it won't sound like a cliché and you won't recognize it."

Soloists commonly combine the elements of different musical models to mask their respective characters and to increase the interest of phrases fashioned from them.[18] "It's the same if I played fourths," Bailey continues. "I'd try to play them so that they didn't sound like fourths. No one wants to run things so that they sound so academic because it's boring after a while. We try to mix it up with other things so that it's not so obvious that we're using fourths." More specifically, as Doc Cheatham learned in his youth,

If you could jump out of a chord, you could always jump back in. That was a trick I learned from listening to Louis Armstrong and many of the New Orleans musicians like Joe Oliver and Jimmie Noone. You hear the same thing if you listen to trumpet players like Clifford Brown play melodies.[19] They call what they use grace notes. Theoretically, they call them neighboring tones, and they're beautiful. So, if you play a solo and you're smart, you can jump out of those chords and jump back in by using those. You've got your half neighbors and your whole neighbors, so you can get three notes out of the way and still come back in there. All those things come to me when I'm playing.

Bass players typically embellish this basic approach when improvising walking bass lines within the rhythm section's accompaniment, "using the roots and fifths to outline chords, adding occasional passing notes or higher or lower neighbors and adapting such harmonically correct pitches to idiomatically acceptable rhythmic patterns" (CI).

Harmonic colors and tensions produced by combining chord tones and altered tones derived, say, from diminished structures are equally intriguing to players. When they lead an improvised line with a clear sense of melodic direction and harmonic grounding into a diminished pattern, they temporarily suspend the line's tonality and experience the excitement that accompanies the expansion of possibilities for melodic exploration. Subsequently, when they exit from the diminished pattern, moving from an altered tone to chord tone, they resolve the ambiguity of the line and continue its progress. At a certain point, someone said to Chuck Israels: " 'Here's a double-diminished scale that fits certain harmonic situations.' I could see it as a beautiful, ambiguous piece of music which was marvelously pivotal and wonderful, like running down the street and all of a sudden jumping on a lazy-susan turntable and being able to come out facing in another direction. It was a great turning device."

Similarly, when Al Olivier learned how to use diminished chords from Barry Harris, he gained the control, he says, "to color my playing with chord changes in and out of the melody line, sliding in and out of the harmonic structure of the piece without getting the feeling of being lost." As in the case of other structures like augmented chords and pentatonic scales, the unvarying and ambiguous character of diminished figures can restrict their application. Barry Harris recommends that learners tastefully introduce, as Charlie Parker often did, a diminished or augmented sound into their performances by periodically applying it to major seventh or seventh chords at prominent harmonic pivot points within progressions such as the movement between the eighth and ninth measures of a blues. The mixture of different kinds of musical models vastly expands their applications for creative invention.

### The Implications of Ideas

The language metaphors adopted by jazz artists to describe their conceptions convey more than the notion that, within the bounds of their unique language system, "musical ideas" should have substance. They also suggest that, for improvisers, the patterns are not ends in themselves, but have ongoing implications for thought. In this light, the interest in exploring the relationships among ideas is fundamental to both musical and verbal thinking. As implied earlier, improvisers experiment with the vertical relationships of their ideas by applying vocabulary patterns within different parts of a piece's harmonic-rhythmic form where their blend assumes distinctive attributes. At the same time, improvisers pursue the linear relationships of their ideas by combining vocabulary patterns in different ways to create new phrases.

Students first glimpse these aspects of improvisation when studying their mentors' solos; direct discussion amplifies their understanding. In listening to Charlie Parker, Lonnie Hillyer learned that he "could intermingle and interchange the same phrases in different combinations." Similarly, when a famous saxophonist once asked Walter Bishop Jr. how he played "those long, long lines that just keep going," Bishop replied that it was "easy really; you just string together lots of smaller melodies." The component parts of pieces also function this way for him. He regards them as being like "toy structures," which he can easily rearrange. "If I want to, I can improvise on the blues all day long, just by quoting from my colleagues' compositions, paying tribute to Thelonious Monk or Bud Powell or any of those people who have written tunes based on that same structure," Bishop says.

In Curtis Fuller's experience with this process, rumination over musical options is itself reminiscent of moments of self-conscious language use. "So many words," Fuller explains, "convey the same basic meaning. I'll stop sometimes when I'm talking and ask myself, 'What is the best word to use here?'" When creating musical phrases as an improviser, Fuller sometimes hears different melodies that fit the same chord "superimposed," one upon another, and strives to select the best ones. He regards the alternative patterns as musical synonyms for their shared harmonic elements.[20] At other moments, however, players are less self-consciously aware of the subtle processes by which the brain constructs and transforms ideas; their full attention is on the musical ideas themselves. Their consciousness is fully occupied by the musical lines of thought they are developing. Josh Schneider makes the analogy to acquiring skill with a second language; he "first learned the words" of jazz, then, after having "mastered them," found himself recombining them "naturally" when improvising.

At the same time that improvisers draw upon a common language, manipulating it as the basis for formulating ideas, their activity entails coining new musical words as much as inventively applying conventional ones. To a greater degree than for verbal expression, the two are integrally related processes for jazz musicians.

Artists gain experience with these operations when, characteristically, they experiment with their vocabulary patterns in practice sessions. Many initially practice them in a simple key such as C, perhaps visualizing them in relation to a C7 chord independent of a particular composition's setting. Simple keys serve as convenient meeting grounds for improvisers to introduce the patterns within their vast storehouse to each other, preparing them for their role in the construction of solo lines.

The same harmonic concepts that initially guided students in their theoretical analysis of figures can also provide principles for systematizing and efficiently retrieving them for integration into other patterns. At one level of organization, musicians can call up discrete families of harmonic synonyms. At another level of organization, they can divide each family into subgroups whose patterns begin on the same chord tones and chord extensions. The association of individual patterns with different pitch levels facilitates the artist's effort to join synonyms into composite shapes. In the course of experimenting with different combinations, musicians memorize the distinctive sounds of the patterns' opening pitches and their special qualities of consonance and dissonance in relation to the tonic, ultimately reinforcing and finely honing fundamental aspects of their harmonic understanding.

To describe the methodical nature of these preliminary routines, however, is only to begin to penetrate the complexities of musical thinking for improvisers, only to hint at the potency of their vocabulary store. Because of the rich associations that vocabulary patterns have as musical ideas and their capacity to form dynamic relationships with their counterparts, the patterns function, in a sense, as living entities, capable of stimulating the player's creative powers. This becomes apparent when, in the natural course of artists' musings in the practice room, they focus on exploring the potential of particular figures. They might hold one of them in mind, perhaps, or perform it repeatedly, while trying out its combination with other vocabulary patterns within a discrete community of ideas.

As individual figures encounter one another in thought, they can produce various types of imaginative unions whose precise features may have unexpected implications for artists, suggesting a wealth of derivative ideas for consideration and pursuit. In the absence of a commonly held terminology, one kind of union might be called direct coupling.[21] This results when the last pitch of the leading pattern is contiguous to the first pitch of the following pattern, enabling them to adjoin in stepwise motion, or when a larger interval formed by the pitches provides a smooth, seamless link between the two figures. In such instances, figures unite relatively easily, without actually necessitating changes in either, but the process produces a unique shape whose components may be recognizable no longer.

An alternative process, which might be called fusion, results when the last pitch of the leading pattern is the same as the first pitch of the following pattern. On the one hand, should the pitches merge or elide in their union, with the former swallowing up a portion of the rhythmic value of the latter, the latter figure can become displaced. On the other hand, if the rhythmic values of the adjoining figures' redundant pitches are merely tied together, displacement does not occur. Players may also modify the last pitch of a leading pattern to conform to a chord change at the juncture of two adjoining patterns.

Fusion, pitch modification, and direct coupling often act as partners in formulating chains of ideas. In addition, related processes, contour crossover and overlap, occur when two discrete envisioned shapes intersect one another. The overlapping component serves as a segue from the initial portion of one to the remaining portion of the other, suggesting the creation of new phrases from uniquely combining the segments.

It is partly by methodically practicing the formulation of phrases over discrete sets of chord changes that artists discover new cross-routes through the chords' associated vocabulary patterns, creating new models for larger chains of ideas (ex. 7.6). Such models provide an unlimited field for exploration. Artists can practice generating phrases of differing lengths by beginning and ending their performance at different points in the chain. Or they can experiment by holding a particular figure within the chain constant while trying out new melodic routes for entering and leaving that figure, discovering effective schemes of pattern substitution. Substituting variant components slightly longer or shorter than an original component subtly expands or contracts the chain. Each generative experiment contributes new melodic possibilities to the ever-expanding network of ideas that comprises the artist's personal system of improvisation.[22]

Still other inventions arise through the process of interpretive extraction. That is, as players reflect on the dynamic quality of a phrase, they may subject it to different interpretations, perceiving new emergent shapes within its contour and performing them as discrete ideas (exx. 7.7a–b). These experiments can lead players to discover, in turn, the value of two other related practices, truncation and contraction (exx. 7.8a–b). Truncation occurs when the deletion of the last chunk of the original phrase leaves a remaining chunk that can stand on its own as a viable pattern. Contraction occurs when the deletion of the midsection of the original phrase produces two remaining segments that couple comfortably. These can be joint operations, as when, for example, a player truncates the first component of a two-component model phrase and leads it into a variant of the second component or a substitute for it (ex. 7.8c). Whether used jointly or independently, the procedures of extraction, truncation, and contraction provide ready options for generating jazz figures from phrases.

As musicians become fluent at thinking in terms of particular figures, they treat the ideas with increasing flexibility each time they perform them. With virtuoso control, they eventually manage the dramatic operations of joining vocabulary patterns into larger phrases, as they self-consciously apply the diverse processes of interpretation, embellishment, and variation to their models of patterns, processes they had cultivated earlier for transfiguring compositions.

Traveling along the contour of an evolving phrase, improvisers may envision the uninflected model of an upcoming pattern, but add interest to its performance by bending its tones or varying its timbral qualities. When instrumentalists growl through their horns and inflect pitches, or when singers feature different scat syllables with marked changes in head or chest resonance, they can alter the mood of the original figure and even create the impression that its contour has changed. During my experiments improvising vocal phrases and endeavoring to calculate the interval between the phrase's first and last pitch, I was surprised to discover that changes in syllables sometimes initially disguised the fact that I had ended on the same pitch on which I had begun.

Additionally, players may create changes by retaining the pitches of the envisioned model but altering its rhythm.[23] Conversely, they may preserve its rhythm but change its pitches. Within such general approaches, operations can be subtle, as when artists substitute individual pitches for one another within a pattern's contour (exx. 7.9a–b). As mentioned above, substitution can also be applied to larger musical units. Artists may replace a component of a phrase, such as its midsection, with distinctive vocabulary patterns that occupy their predecessor's precise space and intervallic span so as to hook up successfully with the adjacent components and play the same role, creating, perhaps, melodic motion between the chord's third and seventh pitches that describes the harmony clearly.

Further along the evolving phrase, players may conservatively rephrase, through rhythmic substitution, the internal features of any of the model's components (exx. 7.10a–b). Periodically, they substitute two eighth notes for a quarter note, or an eighth-note triplet for two eighth notes, or vice versa—adding or deleting pitches that do not dramatically disturb the component's overall shape and character. Should they feel more adventurous, however, they can adopt radical rephrasing procedures, which extend beyond the rhythmic boundaries of the phrase component to vary its form (exx. 7.11a–b). Changing the distribution of quarter notes and eighth notes along the same line of pitches can create different melodic groupings with altered on-beat and off-beat characteristics. Comparable alterations occur as a consequence of fusion operating among adjoining patterns when the latter figure shifts metrically to the preceding beat or displaces by half a beat, reversing its particular on-beat or off-beat character and producing a transformation in its melodic shape as well.

An alternative technique is rest fragmentation, which also can result in radical rephrasing (ex. 7.12). Artists can substitute short rests for pitches or insert rests at different points within the contour of a phrase, cleverly causing it to break up into consecutive shapes whose relationship to the original model may, at times, be barely discernible. Similarly, through Barry Harris's technique of "outlining," students learn to generate new material by preserving the overall span of a favorite phrase, and, perhaps, its opening and closing rhythmic fragments, while selectively altering the phrase's internal rhythmic features, deleting particular elements or creating variations on them.

Varied articulation and accentuation methods can accomplish comparable results, not only invigorating old ideas, but suggesting new patterns contained within the larger phrases for interpretive extraction, and, possibly, for linkage with other associated patterns. Substantial rests that shift the figure's placement within a measure can also cause the figure to become transfigured in unexpected ways. A single-bar pattern initiated on a downbeat is perceived as a unified shape, framed by the entire measure. Initiated on the fourth beat, however, the barline intersects its shape, causing, in some instances, three-quarters of the pattern to emerge as a discrete idea within the next measure.

Trial bouts with performance teach that the complexity of musical ideas can derive as much from their rhythmic relationship to form as from their actual content. Here is an account of one player's revelation. Trading phrases with his teacher over the accompaniment of a playalong record, the student botched an intricately embellished figure. In response, the teacher stopped the record and stripped the pattern down to a mere succession of eighth notes, which the student copied without great difficulty. It was only two beats long, and he thought of it as beginning on the measure's first beat. When the student tried to repeat the musician's subsequent example along with the record, however, the same disorientation overcame him, forcing him to stop again. In the context of the piece, the pattern actually spanned the last beat of one measure and the downbeat of the next. This displacement caused the pattern to assume a complexion radically different from his expectation, producing the feeling of "turning the beat around." That is, it reversed his perception of the meter's delineation of weak and strong beats and called into question the plot he constructed for the boundaries of measures.

The veteran did not immediately understand the student's difficulty. Because his own flexible orientation enabled him to initiate phrases with equanimity on every beat of the measure, and because, for him, the life of the phrases lay in their placement over the barlines, it had not occurred to him to simplify this aspect of his demonstration when the student had faltered initially. Only after considerable practice could the student introduce the phrase into the music's flow with assurance. Eventually, he learned to maintain his conceptual framework for the meter while taking pleasure in the phrase's rhythmic pull and temporary challenge to the piece's order.

Such flexibility is a requisite for improvisers. "Music is [rhythmic] feeling," says Harold Ousley, "and you have to learn how to feel the phrase you want to play in relation to the chords. You have to know how to get into the chord with your phrase because, depending on what you're playing and what you hear, the phrase may not start on the first beat of a new chord. It may start on the 'and of one' or on the 'two,' or the phrase may start in the middle of one measure and go to the middle of the next and you've got to feel that."

Equally radical options include phrase expansion through interpolation—the opposite of phrase contraction—inserting chromatic pitches or short patterns into the model (exs. 7.13a–b).[24] Moreover, artists can reorder a model's tonal elements, applying techniques learned earlier for personalizing a mentor's vocabulary. John McNeil mainly practices phrases so that he "can absorb what makes the phrase work—the principle of it—and discover why it appeals to me. Not so that I can play it exactly like that," he maintains. "I might practice a particular phrase going from a D minor to an A♭ minor to C, then practice another one that used the same kind of thing, getting that sound." Subsequently, when he is "improvising along," he will sometimes "just go to the notes those phrases use at the right spot in the progression and try to make a new phrase out of them." It might turn out to be something he "practiced before, but it might not." Specifically, Harold Ousley sometimes performs a variation on an envisioned pattern by "playing it backwards."

Finally, adopting another technique when approaching the end of a phrase, artists can vary their model of its last component with short cadential extensions or more substantial melodic excursions (exs. 7.14a–g)—the opposite process of phrase truncation. After Bobby Rogovin began to associate "particular lines with chords," he started "building other lines like the ones I played and extending them in different directions." Ousley sometimes performs the first "half" of a phrase and then "adds something else to it."

## The Physical Realization and Exploration of Ideas

As improvisers practice these maneuvers, simultaneously grappling with the tests on their imaginations and the demands of negotiating their instruments, they contend with different relationships between the singing mind and the body. Under the aegis of the singing mind, there are moments in which musicians see no further into their evolving line than a few pitches, their body and mind so tightly joined as to be fully absorbed into the performance's immediate progress. One artist colorfully likens the intense experience of prehearing an idea, then grabbing onto and following it, to "chasing after a piece of paper that's being blown across the street."[25] At other moments, however, the ideas that soloists realize during performances depend as much on the body's own actions as on the body's synchronous response to the mind. The body can take momentary control over particular activities—such as articulating a well-worn vocabulary pattern or a lengthy new phrase transmitted to it—while the mind shifts its focus to the next idea.

When Henry Allen improvises, he says, "I concentrate a couple of bars ahead at all times. You have to have an idea where you are going."[26] Chuck Israels's "mind sometimes jumps ahead" to think of a pattern for his own solo's initiation as he concludes his accompaniment to another musician's solo with a conventional bass line. Benny Bailey periodically resorts to "automatic patterns of fourths and repeated high-note riffs requiring little thought." Both enable him to maintain the momentum of his performance while he "rests," considering other ideas and preparing to perform them. In fact, the improviser sometimes prolongs the repetition of a phrase as a deliberate tactic to awaken a sluggish imagination, forcing it to respond creatively to the material's increasing momentum or, alternatively, to its impending monotony.

The body plays an even more active role when, through its motor sensory apparatus, it interprets and responds to sounds as physical impressions, subtly informing or reshaping mental concepts. The dance of agile fingers on the keyboard can infuse melodic patterns with swing. Furthermore, as students learn early, the body can engage itself directly in the composition of new phrases, revealing its own capacity for creative thinking.[27] "Sometimes, the ideas come from my mind, and I have to find them quickly on my horn," Harold Ousley says. "But other times, I find that I am playing from finger patterns; the fingers give it to you. As I play, my fingers are walking through the yellow pages [in the phone book], so to speak. They roam around and they come up with ideas that I like."

When leading, the body pursues physical courses shaped not only by the musical language of jazz, but by idiomatic patterns of movement associated with the playing techniques of an instrument. These, in turn, reflect the instrument's particular acoustical properties, physical layout, and performance demands. Ultimately, all of these factors define the body's world of imagination, inviting it to explore their relationships. Emily Remler, as a case in point, "sometimes falls into going up the neck in a guitar sense, finding a certain riff, repeating it, and doing different things with the rhythm."

Whereas the piano's regular arrangement of keys and the mechanical nature of its sound production enable competent improvisers to sustain musical invention in any register, Chuck Israels considers that "it's hardest to achieve a keyboard kind of freedom in the low register of the bass or trombone." If the intention is to "improvise in subtle and quickly changing ways," the performer must "move into the highest register of the instruments, because that's where the notes are physically closest together." In contrast, the demands of high-note playing for trumpeters may temporarily erode endurance. Unless they possess exceptional strength, these artists typically venture into their highest register only for short excursions, for instance, to provide peaks to melodic phrases or to create musical climaxes. Other distinctions also come into play. Wide leaps with the trumpet involve demanding embouchure changes, whereas saxophonists can exploit an octave key and bass players can play such large intervals as fourths with the ease of movement over their instrument's open strings. There are, however, efficient trumpet patterns requiring only slight embouchure change that can be produced with the simple, repetitive motion of a single finger (ex. 7.15).[28]

Within each instrument's general constraints, the pleasure that individuals derive from particular motions can also influence performances. "I like to play swing," a drummer once explained while demonstrating a swing pattern for snare drum and brushes with wide, circular arm motions. "I like the way my body feels when I'm moving like this. But there are other ways I like to move too, other ways my body likes to feel." In Paul Wertico's experience, drummers commonly "feel [that their] legs are dancing" when maintaining the regular hi-hat or bass drum beat, in relation to which their "arms" can take greater expressive liberties through movement, "doing whatever they want."

Finally, incidental factors can enter into the bodily negotiation of musical instruments. Pianists sometimes discover interesting melodic patterns when working around such literal obstacles as broken keys on a nightclub's unfamiliar instrument. Art Davis recalls the dramatic incident that occurred on a tour with the Max Roach quintet in which fellow band member Booker Little accidentally closed a car door on Davis's hand. During the quintet's subsequent performances, Davis's broken finger forced him to explore alternative techniques involving multiple fingers that resulted in ways new to him of moving around the bass. He has continued to develop this approach over the years, evolving a technique that involves four left-hand fingers as well as those of the right hand to achieve maximum speed and agility in bass playing.

With experience, students become increasingly sensitive to varied nuances of the body's interplay with the singing mind. Adjusting to the role played by the body is a requisite to handling vocabulary patterns, as learners proceed to the next creative level of expression through the language of jazz.

# EIGHT

**Composing in the Moment:**

**The Inner Dialogue and the Tale**

*After you initiate the solo, one phrase determines what the next is going to be. From the first note that you hear, you are responding to what you've just played: you just said this on your instrument, and now that's a constant. What follows from that? And then the next phrase is a constant. What follows from that? And so on and so forth. And finally, let's wrap it up so that everybody understands that that's what you're doing. It's like language: you're talking, you're speaking, you're responding to yourself. When I play, it's like having a conversation with myself.*—Max Roach

As practicers discover the challenges and rewards of formulating musical ideas, they devote less time to applying fixed tonal materials within harmonic forms and more time to interpreting the materials in different ways. As described earlier, the natural tendency toward transformation displayed at times by the body and the singing mind aids students in their efforts, as does their growing appreciation for the value the jazz community attaches to invention. At the same time, aspiring players must learn to manage artfully the impulse for change.

Experts drive home the point once again by invoking language metaphors. Whereas previously these images of verbal expression crystallized such general processes as constructing musical sentences from vocabulary patterns, this time, in elucidating these other features of their music system, their purpose is to emphasize fundamental principles of musical logic and development that guide expression in jazz.[1] For Lonnie Hillyer, as for Max Roach, improvising "is really like a guy having a conversation with himself." Hillyer sometimes thinks of himself as "making statements and answering them" when he performs. His objective is to "expand on" musical patterns, "trying to get the notes to grow into something, shaping them into different ideas. It's like taking a couple of words and expounding with them." Others agree. "The phrases you play . . . are your message while you're playing. [They] should relate to one another," Tommy Flanagan states, "and they should be logical." The "vital part" for Lee Konitz, too, "is thinking while you're moving, and once the momentum has been started, I don't like to break it. I'm concerned with the continuity in motion. . . . If you're not affected and influenced by your own notes when you improvise, then you're missing the whole essential point."

One conventional approach for achieving such qualities focuses on what players describe as motivic or thematic development, in which they subject an idea to recurrent use and variation while preserving its fundamental identity.[2] For learners, there are plentiful examples of this approach within the developmental sections of jazz compositions and recorded solos, as well as in the works of other musical traditions.[3] Also exemplary are performances in which jazz veterans alternate quotations from tunes with their own related commentaries and interject imitative fills between the phrases of singers when accompanying them.

Analysis of other artists' performances reinforces the knowledge of motivic development students acquire from direct experience, as, for example, when they perform a vocabulary pattern in the course of their practice, then use their recollection of it as a model, transforming it to produce consecutive variants. This involves procedures similar to those already discussed, in which artists use envisioned but unvoiced models to produce variant figures that do not function as motives, such as when they appear as isolated events in separate performances or as seamless components of larger phrases. When practicing motivic development, artists may initially apply it to vocabulary patterns in free rhythm, but they subsequently increase the challenges by creating variants in time. Eventually, they acquire the ability to treat new ideas motivically, holding onto them the instant they conceive them, manipulating them, and exploring their implications within the framework of a passing beat.[4]

Although the process of establishing thematic relationships between musical ideas can be daunting initially, aspiring improvisers eventually discover that the method actually facilitates the ability to think on their feet by providing them with well-defined materials for composing their ongoing parts. This, in turn, reduces the infinite field of elements for consideration, relieving the pressure of conceiving new figures unrelated to the current stream of events. Within the constraints performers set for themselves, the possibilities for developing ideas, which constantly present themselves, still seem vast.[5] So, too, are the challenges associated with realizing their ideas, for, with split-second responses, they must project before them, and pursue in musical time and space, images and goals derived from the sounding model or the one immediately preceding it.

As soloists immerse themselves in their internal dialogue, the most obvious way for them to advance their conversation—responding to their "own notes"—is by pausing briefly after an initial statement, then repeating it, perhaps with minor changes such as rhythmic rephrasing. This also allows time for the player to conceive options for the subsequent phrase's formulation (ex. 8.1). Taking a slightly different tack, artists may "run" the figure directly "into itself," perhaps through a slight extension or short connecting pattern, treating the figure as a component within a longer phrase (ex. 8.2). Or they may answer the idea by rephrasing it an octave lower (ex. 8.3), or re-create its shape at multiple pitch levels, creating sequences (exx. 8.4a–c). Harold Ousley might begin a solo with "two phrases a flatted fifth apart," an effective approach he learned from Kenny Dorham. He then adapts it to the upcoming chords during a chorus "all the way down the line." In a similar vein, to prepare students for such musical discourse, Barry Harris has them practice transposing effective figures compatible with seventh chords and applying the figures to a progression like the "Rhythm" bridge.

Beyond strict imitation, a more subtle way for improvisers to imbue successive phrases with a sense of logic is by varying the initial contour of the pattern when they first repeat it. They may re-create its general shape but change its intervals. Or, they may append to the pattern a short cadential extension (exx. 8.5a–b), or a short introductory figure (ex. 8.6a), or both (ex. 8.6b). Taking another tack, they can create rhythmically balanced imitative phrases whose respective endings rise or fall in relation to one another, as if asking, then answering, a question (ex. 8.7). Alternatively, through interpretive extraction, soloists select particular features of a figure they have just improvised— whether a single prominent pitch or a melodic-rhythmic fragment—as central ideas for the figures that follow (exx. 8.8a–c). It is common for players to focus on the rhythm of an invention, devoting entire developmental sections to its treatment as a rhythmic ostinato.[6] Throughout, they vary its pitches to produce imitative shapes and, in some instances, varied accentuation schemes (exx. 8.9a–c). The opposite procedure is as common. They may introduce a simple tonal idea like spelling a triad and develop it through rhythmic variation (ex. 8.10).[7]

The longer and more complex the musical idea artists initially conceive, the greater the powers of musical memory and mental agility required to transform it. Experienced improvisers can create variations on each feature of extensive melodic-rhythmic material within the framework of lengthy antiphonal phrases (ex. 8.11). Or, given a complex call of three components, soloists could subsequently formulate a response by repeating any of the three for its motivic value, while radically altering the others. Or they can drop two of the components and select, perhaps, the last component for continued use, either beginning the response with it, or approaching it through another figure so that it becomes the second component of the new pattern.

Phrase length and range can themselves serve as models for evolving ideas. Lonnie Hillyer illustrates this by improvising pairs of short call and response patterns that alternate between the trumpet's upper and lower registers. "One approach is for me to think of myself as being two players. See, the upper player was one guy and the lower player was another guy. I was telling the story as if there was a dialogue going on between the two players. I've heard Trane and Bird and other players do that kind of thing on records, like they were accompanying themselves." Lester Young and Miles Davis sometimes constructed ideas for the larger part of blues choruses and major sections of thirty-two-bar pieces by performing variations on short call and response patterns (exx. 8.12a–b).[8]

Within a performance's normal stream of events, improvisers typically allow their adequate inventions to pass by without necessarily treating their elements motivically. Rather, they await the appearance of figures that especially interest them, then explore their implications. The identification of such patterns and the treatment of their features vary with the soloists' changing sensitivities. They may hear different possibilities in, and derive new value from, the same vocabulary pattern as they perform it on different occasions. For immediate use, they may adopt the shape of a selected component, an appealing feature of harmonic color, or, perhaps, a particular rhythmic configuration highlighted by a slight hesitation in phrasing that throws a new accent on its form. Moreover, within the artist's personal store of knowledge, these differing elements can each carry associations that influence the performance of subsequent ideas: harmonic qualities suggesting linkages with particular harmonic synonyms, rhythmic elements evoking other patterns with similar configurations, and yet other features invoking figures with comparable contours, phrase lengths, compatible moods, or finger patterns.

The interdependence of a soloist's ideas and the oral literature of jazz can also prove stimulating. Once, after an improviser's solo led directly into one of Kenny Dorham's characteristic cadential phrases, the player found himself coloring subsequent phrases with Dorham's pitch inflections before the associations weakened for him. Doc Cheatham sometimes performs "a few little bars from players like Clifford Brown, Clark Terry, and Dizzy that come to me all of a sudden in my solo work." In another instance, when Harold Ousley improvised a melody that reminded him of "Old Man River," he worked other patterns from the tune into his performance and "played off them for a while." Connections between the extramusical meanings of compositions can also come into play. George Coleman once concluded his improvisation on "You Don't Know What Love Is" by quoting the musical chant from John Coltrane's "A Love Supreme."[9]

The chains of ideas that guide the soloist also reflect unself-conscious absorption of material. From time to time, Ousley plays a pattern that sounds new to him, but he "realizes afterwards" that it is actually something he had previously heard "someone else play on a record."

Just as a figure's embedded associations may involve the ideas that surround it in different musical contexts, at times leading a player to quote subsequent material from the original performance, it may also include a range of actions for the treatment of ideas. That is, each figure has a particular history of usage and transformation—its own track record of applications—both within an artist's own performing experience and within the larger musical tradition.[10] One short pattern that occasionally occurs as an isolated idea in the improvisations of Kenny Dorham and others forms the basis for many short developmental episodes in Clifford Brown solos, where it functions as a signature pattern. A version of the same pattern arises as the theme for a Rahsaan Roland Kirk composition dedicated to Clifford Brown, the motive for an entire blues chorus by Booker Little, the introductory figure for his original composition "Memo: To Maurice" (exx. 8.13a–c).[11] Associations of this nature abound within the oral texts of jazz, bringing the features of improvisations, compositions, and arrangements into cross-relationships.[12] Forty-six years in the life of a lick, as it reappears across performances by different instruments in bands representing different jazz idioms, epitomize such relationships (exx. 8.14a–o).

Alternatively, artists may adopt yet another thematic approach that is distinguishable from the motivic treatment of successive patterns. Max Roach, for example, sometimes finds it useful to emphasize a discrete phrase by periodically "coming back to it or going away from it" during a solo (ex. 8.15).[13] In the context of a single ongoing melodic line, a related maneuver is "double backing," occasionally leading the evolving line "back over" an earlier phrase component at its former pitch level or in a different octave (exx. 8.16a–b). Through diverse practices of repetition and variation of discrete elements from phrase to phrase, soloists convey a sense of both continuity and closure in their development of particular musical ideas before going on to others.

At the same time, improvisers are concerned with striking an appropriate balance between repetition and variation, and they find a fundamental paradigm in the melodies, texts, and horn riffs of the blues. "Ideally, the phrase would go something like this," Chuck Israels says. " 'Going to Chicago; can't take you. Going to Chicago; can't take you. Nothing in Chicago a girl like you could do.' It's as basic as that. The first time you make a statement, whatever it is, its importance is not known [to the audience]. The second time you make that statement, its importance is clear because you repeated it. . . . As soon as you start it the third time, they're asleep if you don't finish it differently."

Israels argues that, typically, repeating a figure twice is enough unless the artist changes one or more of its elements the third time. On the other hand, artists may repeat an improvised four-bar phrase three times within such structures as the blues, because "at least the changing tension of the phrase against the harmony gives it some variety." Musicians can guide invention with comparable principles within the framework of multiple choruses and extended harmonic forms by moving through a series of different motivic sections. One phrase introduces a new idea, the next phrase imitates it, the next varies it, "then the next one is a wrap-up of that. Then there's something else." [14]

Other designs can be equally effective. In contrast to using vocabulary patterns motivically, soloists use them as construction units of new extended ideas in which the identity of the original patterns is fleeting or obscure. The interest and logic of the constantly changing melodic-rhythmic shapes of such creations lie in their "continuity, smoothness, contours, note choices, and placement of rhythmic accents" and, generally, in their imaginative interpretations of, and complementary relationships to, the underlying chords. [15] In negotiating a blues progression, for example, soloists could lead an evolving line at the end of the fourth bar from the third of the C7 chord to the flatted seventh of the F7 chord. This follows the logic of the changing chords with smooth chromatic movement, granting them "permission" to enter the second chord (HO).

Once within the second chord's tonality, players create different contours, drawing upon various conventions to convey an impression of their ideas' completeness. Familiarity with the most basic techniques lends a bit of assurance to the soloist's performance. Artists may, for example, end phrases with the pitch on which they began or on its octave equivalent. A phrase's initial pitch provides an easily remembered goal or target for the phrase's formulation. Similarly, an artist can establish relationships between consecutive phrases by using the preceding phrase's closing pitch or its octave equivalent as the opening pitch of the following phrase (exx. 8.17a–b). "Working off of" a single pitch, constantly leaving it and returning to it, is another common maneuver, which one player describes as a "melodic pedal" (LG). [16]

An improviser may also provide a sense of continuity and closure to sections of long twisting melodies by delineating a particular interval for exploration, creating varied kinds of melodic motion within its boundaries before proceeding to another interval and working it (exx. 8.18a–b). Different melodic concepts commonly underly an artist's ventures. When Josh Schneider thinks "vertically," he conceives of "each chord as a separate tonality for the duration that it's happening in a song and play[s] different kinds of intervals within it." Sometimes, he says, "I work on certain ways of getting through the chord changes with particular intervals I want to incorporate in my playing." At other times, he conceives music "horizontally, [thinking of] going, say, from the third of a minor chord to the third of the dominant chord and making a line that passes through them." In a similar vein, a satisfyingly effective procedure involves weaving in and out of the guiding model of a short step progression, so that the melodic accents of a phrase create the strong motion of an ascending or descending scale pattern (ex. 8.18b).[17]

As in the case of short call and response formats described earlier, artists may create a sense of balance and continuity within the larger designs of long consecutive phrases by remembering and using phrase length itself as a model (ex. 8.19). Alternatively, players develop ideas by inventing consecutive phrases, each slightly longer than the one before, as if an outgrowth from it (ex. 8.20). Such practices also produce the effect of varying the phrasing of melodies in relation to the progression, which, as described earlier, can alter the selection of pitches from the underlying chords and suggest grouping alternative vocabulary patterns into composite phrases. In other instances, soloists convey a sense of development by gradually expanding the range of consecutive phrases (ex. 8.21).

Artists exploit other schemes as well, derived generally from jazz language use and embodying fundamental principles of tension and release. One involves producing such "essential" qualities of African American music as swing by manipulating a line's rhythmic feeling, for example, playing just behind or just ahead of the beat before returning to on-beat performance and resolving the phrase's rhythmic tension.[18] Alternatively, they create interest and suspense by improvising melodic phrases that cross over barlines and assume abstract rhythmic relationships to the meter. Concerning the application of such techniques to solo development, Grachan Moncur once told Gary Bartz that "one way to improvise was to think as if your instrument was a bass. You follow chords and connect them, add a few non-chord tones, play a little more rhythmically, and then you start to solo" (exx. 8.22a–b). Performers also engage periodically in "harmonic syncopation" by subtly offsetting pitch selection from the piece's structure, drawing on pitches that either anticipate the following chord or delay the preceding chord's resolution.[19]

Similar to the dynamism created by general movements between off-beat and on-beat figures, and outside and inside harmonies, are the general effects of movements creating other contrasts: for example, between increased and decreased rhythmic activity, inflected and uninflected pitches, and registral ascents and descents. Each produces schemes of tension and release, ultimately imbuing inventions with a sense of flow. So, too, does the progression among such different musical events as lyrical phrases; driving, finger-generated patterns; intricate chromatically embellished lines; swinging bebop gestures; and diminished chord patterns that depart from a prevailing meter (exx. 8.23a–b).

Initially, the qualities of logic that define nonthematic formulations can be more difficult to grasp for learners than those presented by motivic treatments.[20] While imitating their idols, students gradually absorb models for these elusive attributes, experiencing periodic breakthroughs of self-awareness that provide encouragement. When, as a young player, I first copied Clifford Brown solos, learning their every pitch was taxing. After many months of study, however, not only could I generally grasp new phrases more quickly, but, after hearing their opening fragments, I could envision logical—that is, effective— possibilities for their extension or amplification. Guessing where the next several pitches might go and trying them out, I listened further to the recording and found that I had anticipated Brown's maneuver correctly in some instances. In others, I was incorrect for the passage at hand, but a phrase comprising the precise alternative occurred at another point in the solo or in another solo altogether. This newly acquired ability to predict the direction of improvised melodies reflects increasing familiarity with an idol's pattern of vocabulary usage and a more general sense of the musical logic of the jazz idiom gained through intensive studies of many artists.

Barry Harris's exercises also prepare students to appreciate comparable aspects of improvisation. At workshops, after teaching students several discrete patterns compatible with seventh chords and drilling them in the sequential application of each over the eight-bar "Rhythm" bridge, Harris places additional demands upon them. They must construct "new bridges" by selecting four of the phrases and performing them each time in a different order. Within the compositional bounds Harris provides, students cull the precise skill of making selections rapidly from a limited store of optional patterns and placing them appropriately within a progression, one musical statement to a chord. "That's how the music works," Harris advises them. Because Harris has cleverly selected patterns for the drill that work well in every combination, with each trial, students absorb their complementary qualities.

Other aspects of the requirements of musical logic, whether created through motivic or through nonmotivic approaches, likewise harken back to the wisdom of the rigorous training of emerging artists. Disciplined practice to master the instant absorption and reproduction of phrases from recorded solos also cultivates the ability to precisely imagine ideas and immediately re-create them.[21] In a sense, this call and response interaction with idols on recordings represents a general model for the very process of improvising in which soloists must constantly respond to their own phrases, whether repeating or transforming them. Additional exercises that extract elements from a mentor's phrases for the invention of new patterns by analogy teach novices the most basic skill required for developing ideas, the ability to carry over selected material in the formulation of successive phrases.

These procedures depend on the agile handling of multiple activities: conceiving, articulating, and remembering ideas. These are no mean feats for beginners. In one class, a teacher arbitrarily stopped the solos of students and requested that they perform their last phrase again. When they could not manage this, he chastized them for being "like people who don't listen to themselves while they speak." Aspiring improvisers must cultivate impressive musical recall in both aural and physical terms if they are to incorporate within their ongoing conversation new ideas conceived in performance.

Furthermore, while they are performing their ideas, artists must learn to juggle short- and intermediate-range goals simultaneously. To lead an improvised melodic line back to its initial pitch requires the ability to hold a layered image of the pitch in mind and hand while, at the same time, selecting and performing other pitches. The requirements of this combined mental and physical feat become all the more taxing if, after improvising an extended phrase, soloists decide to manipulate more complex material, developing, perhaps, its middle segment as a theme. In all such cases, they must not only rely on their memory of its contour, but their muscular memory must be flexible enough to locate the segment's precise finger pattern instantly within their motor model of the phrase.

Taking good advantage of the latitude that the practice room affords them, performers devote much of their time there to experimenting with these options. Improvising by starts and stops, they develop the ability to formulate credible ideas in jazz and to develop them—carrying their part of the conversation forward—over increasing stretches of time. With growing skill and assurance, their goal is to control evolving lines of thought over an entire solo, minimally one chorus in length.[22]

Toward such ends, students practice applying themselves to longer progressions, using the same operations Harris recommends for fashioning new "Rhythm" bridges. Lonnie Hillyer, a former protégé of Harris's, once taught me a number of discrete phrases that fit different parts of a blues. He subsequently asked me to improvise complete solo choruses by making different selections from them. As Hillyer intended, this exercise led me to practice further options. Students soon realize that they can create comparable exercises for themselves within different structures by extracting from favorite solos different patterns that "work well together," creating unique formulations from them (ex. 8.24). Of course, from Harris's and Hillyer's standpoint, these are but preliminary exercises preparing students to create viable constructions from complementary phrases of their own. Such drills enable students to absorb the larger dimensions of harmonic form at the same time as they gain experience conceptualizing and manipulating ideas in relation to them.

Ultimately, however, youngsters must also learn various skills associated with the overriding aesthetic principles that guide the activities of advanced artists. These involve mastery over expressivity, over the shaping and pacing of ideas, and over any referential meanings that musical patterns have acquired in the jazz tradition.[23] Improvisers illuminate these principles with perhaps the richest of their language metaphors, storytelling, whose multilayered meanings have been passed from generation to generation within the jazz community since its earliest days.

## Storytelling

In part, the metaphor of storytelling suggests the dramatic molding of creations to include movement through successive events "transcending" particular repetitive, formal aspects of the composition and featuring distinct types of musical material.[24] For early jazz players like Louis Armstrong and Sidney Bechet, and for swing players like Lester Young, storytelling commonly involved such designs for multiple choruses as devoting an initial chorus to interpreting a piece's melody, devoting the next to expressive liberties varying it, and then returning to the melody or proceeding on to other events such as single-note riffing patterns.[25]

For contemporary players, who may place less emphasis on the melody, the considerations of shaping remain just as essential. Typically, when it comes time for Buster Williams to solo, he "wants to tell a story, and the best way to tell a story is to set it up." If someone who is "very excited about something that just happened" comes running to Williams "saying, 'Buster, blah-blah-blah-blah,' the first thing I'm going to say is, 'Look, wait a minute. Calm down and start from the beginning.'" Williams's plan is the same for solo work. "Start from the beginning," he advises. "It's also like playing a game of chess. There's the beginning game, the middle game, and then there's the end game. Miles is a champion at doing that. So is Trane. To accomplish this, the use of space is very important—sparseness and simplicity—maybe playing just short, meaningful phrases at first and building up the solo from there."

Similarly, Kenny Barron tries "to start the solo in a way that's sparse or low key" so that he has "somewhere to go, so that the solo can build." From listening to Dizzy Gillespie when he performed in Gillespie's band, Barron learned how to "save" himself in his playing. "You don't have to play everything you know every minute," Barron says.

You can leave some spaces in the music. You're not going to start off a solo double-timing. You start off just playing very simply and, as much as possible, with lyrical ideas. And as the intensity builds, if it does, your ideas can become a little more complicated. They can become longer. The way I look at it is that you're going to start down so that you have somewhere to go. It can build to different points in different parts of the solo. It's hills and valleys. That's what it is anywhere. There are certain sections of the tune which build harmonically and suggest that the intensity should also build at that particular point. That's a very natural thing to happen, and what you play will always build there. Other times, it's a matter of wherever it occurs, wherever you feel it coming. It could happen in different spots within the tune at different times.

A related feature of storytelling involves matters of continuity and cohesion. Paul Wertico advises his students that in initiating a solo they should think in terms of developing specific "characters and a plot. . . . You introduce these little different [musical] things that can be brought back out later on; and the way you put them together makes a little story. That can be [on the scale of] a sentence or a paragraph. . . . The real great cats can write novels." Wertico expresses admiration for the intellectual prowess of these players. Throughout a performance, they creatively juxtapose ideas that they introduced in their initial "character line," and at just "the right time" in their story, they can "pull out" and develop ideas that they "only hinted at" earlier in the performance but have borne in mind all along. "That's what's really fantastic about a solo," Wertico maintains.

To develop the skills of expert storytellers, artists find it essential to devote some practice time to improvising under conditions that simulate formal music events, thereby imposing maximum constraints upon performances. Negotiating a composition's structure as "one cohesive string," with each chord leading to the next in strict rhythm, they formulate complete solos, pausing but momentarily to reflect on their inventions. "To learn to play a song better," Art Farmer would "work on its chords, chorus after chorus, trying to play whatever came to mind. Even if it didn't come out right, I'd keep playing," he says. "At certain times, it's not good to stop."

Musicians commit themselves to the rigors of developing the ideas that occur to them at the moment, cultivating powers of concentration upon which larger-scale invention depends. "After a lot of practice, you find that the phrases just begin to fall in the right place," Harold Ousley recalls. "You are able to play a whole chorus of phrases together, and you are ready for the next chorus. The more you do it, the smoother and the easier it gets. When you begin to feel proficient at this, you feel a certain sense of freedom, and you get the inspiration to really get into your horn and to try out different things. There's a great excitement about that."

As Ousley's remarks imply, the improviser's world of imagination considers more than musical abstractions. Emotion serves as a partner to intellect in the conception and expansion of ideas. Beyond emotional responses to their evolving creations, artists speak generally of "tapping an emotional reservoir," whose "energy" represents a distillation of their experiences with life (ER). Roberta Baum considers emotion to be "the biggest part of singing. It has become an extension of how it is to be alive," she says. In this sense, performances can reflect the individual's characteristic scope of expression, including extreme fluctuations of feeling.

As alluded to earlier, artists can also draw upon the extramusical associations of the compositions that serve as vehicles. They sometimes set up for performances by dwelling momentarily on a piece's moods and meanings, recalling, perhaps, the sense of personal identification with the theme of a standard piece that prompted its incorporation into their repertory, or envisioning the characters and incidents depicted in their own original compositions. At times, Dexter Gordon actually sang a few lines of a ballad's lyrics to invoke its meaning, before switching to saxophone improvisations.[26] With song texts, or in their absence, the emotional sentiment and the imagery suggested by titles and musical features also offer direction.[27]

Overall, a piece's precise mood has a powerful tempering effect on improvisers, guiding their personal feelings to blend with those appropriate for the performance. For Arthur Rhames, " 'God Bless the Child' [evokes] one set of moods about the remorse of not being on your own or having to depend on others, while a tune like 'Giant Steps' may be about advancing yourself"; each provides "different perspectives, different feelings, different moods. And those moods govern a lot of what's going to come out in your interpretation of the chord changes in your improvising." Chuck Israels also routinely takes the mood of the piece into account when he prepares to solo. Over the course of an evening, "I'll play a tune like 'The Preacher' that has a certain gospel flavor; then a tune like Bill Evans's 'Peri's Scope,' which is an outgoing, dancing, lighthearted tune. [Next, I will] play something melancholy, like 'Nardis.' "

There is a constant spending and replenishment of a player's emotional reserves. Israels performs "tunes that have different emotional states" in order to give himself "different things to think about, different things to feel and to play" when he improvises. Each tune has "its own feelings, its own shapes and patterns that occupy me when I play it," he explains. "You just jump from one emotional mood to another because the moods change with each piece." Sometimes, Emily Remler says, "when I play a ballad like 'I'm in a Sentimental Mood,' I feel almost sick to my stomach because it is so heartrending and takes so much from me." A piece's emotional associations commonly influence an artist's rhythmic approach or selection of tonal materials, in the latter instance suggesting, perhaps, an emphasis upon blues-inflected melodies rather than brighter, uninflected melodies or upon tense rather than relaxed harmonies.

Throughout the piece, artists may prepare themselves to respond to each of its varied nuances, beyond its most general tenor. Emily Remler, looking forward to "a gig tonight," knows "that there are sections where I'll feel a lot of different emotions. The [composition] breaks into a real happy part, and it makes me feel really happy. Then there are other parts where I'll just feel determined." In some instances, the elements of a piece combine to reinforce a particular emotional shape overall, suggesting that improvisers structure their own creations accordingly. In a blues, an artist may build toward peaks of intensity at the same point as the harmony and poetic text reach a dramatic climax.

Various aspects of the meanings of compositions are also tied to their performance histories, especially the ways in which earlier improvisers have handled their original compositions (BH). When Jimmy Robinson prepares to solo, he "thinks about the things that have been done on the tune in the past" and what he would "like to do on it." Of course, he says, if he has "never heard the tune before" or is performing his own pieces, he "just strikes out" on his own. If it is a recent piece by someone like Dizzy Gillespie, however, he wants "to know what Dizzy did on it just to give me an idea to start with, so I won't be too far off with it." Robinson's intention is to be respectful to "the idea" of the composer. "That also shows that I've been influenced by Dizzy," he says, "since he did some very intricate things on it that I wish I had come up with [he laughs]. You try to play in relationship to that to learn what he's doing, and then you try to build and improve on it."

Renowned artists have sometimes improvised so effectively within the framework of other composers' works, bringing fresh interpretations to them, that they leave an indelible mark upon the works' performance traditions and on those of pieces with comparable styles. Walter Bishop Jr. learned the general principles for formulating solos within modal compositions by analyzing Miles Davis's solos. Another trumpeter admitted that after "Miles's playing on 'Sketches of Spain,' it is impossible to improvise on any Spanish-type piece without using some of Miles's inflections." A composition "like 'Nardis' also has a lot of connotation because Bill Evans played it so much," Fred Hersch observes. Along similar lines, even if Roberta Baum "were to give my own interpretation of a song by Cole Porter, there is no way that I could forget how Ella Fitzgerald had phrased something." A commemorative piece lends itself particularly to an interpretation imbued with the stylistic traits of the honored namesake. In rendering the ballad "I Remember Clifford," Lee Morgan integrates his own personal blues-oriented commentaries into the ballad's theme, at times adopting Clifford Brown's wide, singing vibrato, unique articulation devices, and characteristic embellishments.[28] Sometimes, it is in the very act of improvising that players discover and pursue the deep connections that compositions and the individual styles of soloists reveal to them.[29]

For improvisers, the meaning of a piece incorporates layers of nuance derived from intimacy with its imagery, its rhythmic and tonal associations, its performance history, and its relatives within the wider repertory of pieces. Among the myriad resources that soloists filter through their imaginations, one of the most striking is the vibrancy of the human connections that inhabit the piece—myriad inflections, personalities, voices, fingerings, and stances, coursing through the mind and into the musical performance. Such varied imagery informs and deepens every story in the telling. In a sense, each solo is like a tale within a tale, a personal account with ties of varying strength to the formal composition.

While absorbing the conventions associated with idea formulation and storytelling in the jazz tradition, artists place different emphases upon the conventions. They apply them uniquely according to each individual's temperament, personal style of jazz oratory, emotional response to compositions, and specific goals for the solo under formulation. As expected, the differing emphases result in correspondingly varied transformations of jazz vocabulary and in different formal characteristics among the solos produced by improvisation (exx. 8.25a–d).[30]

Underlying their efforts to achieve such diversity of expression is rigorous practice on the part of jazz learners, as they develop flexibility in the use of initially limited stores of vocabulary, devise a systematic way of relating vocabulary patterns one to another, and absorb the aesthetic principles that guide vocabulary usage. Students with such comprehensive training are in a far better position as improvisers than are those among their counterparts who may have acquired a large store of vocabulary patterns, chords, scales, and the like, but yet fail to appreciate these other critical aspects of jazz knowledge. Ultimately, learning the tools and techniques of the art provides only the ground for the student's development. To build the foundation, aspiring musicians must commit endless hours to practicing improvisation—mentally simulating the conditions of live performance events—if they are to acquire the cumulative experience upon which effective storytelling rests. Among the challenges practicers confront in their earliest efforts are improvisation's capricious aspects, which can operate as powerful forces to influence a work's musical outcome.

### The Teller's Trials

Under the pressures of thinking in motion and amid the rapid-fire interplay and continually shifting frames of their conceptions, improvisers routinely contend with a variety of challenging, potentially daunting, experiences. One concerns the unpredictable relationship between the musical materials they have mastered for their large store and the actual ideas that occur to them during solos. Things are always happening "spontaneously," according to Harold Ousley. He "practices certain phrases" but finds at times that "none of those phrases will come out in my solos, and I'm playing something altogether different." Or, to his surprise, patterns "come out that I've only practiced a few times and didn't think I knew well enough to play."

Even an artist's own allusions to the jazz literature can catch the artist by surprise, as when Cheatham "jumped right into playing two choruses" of a Charlie Parker solo. "I didn't realize that I was going to do it till afterward," he recalls. "I just automatically fell into it." Years earlier, Cheatham had learned the solo when working with Lionel Hampton's band "from the younger fellows in the trumpet section." They used to perform it together as part of an arrangement of "I Got Rhythm."

If at some moments soloists must respond artistically to unexpected phrases arising from their vocabulary store or from their improvisations' associations, at other moments they must contend with the occasional repetitive or hackneyed use of vocabulary. "Sometimes, when you get ready to play, you say to yourself, 'I don't want to play the same stuff I always play,' so you deliberately try not to play it, but you end up playing the same old stuff anyway," Bobby Rogovin says ruefully. Lonnie Hillyer's experience is much the same. "Just trying to make phrases come out differently is hard at times, very hard," he says, "because we're programmed. It's almost like working against the grain at times because you want things to come out differently, and they just don't." Improvisers may push themselves off one well-known melodic course as soon as they realize that they have started down it, only to find themselves proceeding along another familiar path.

In one of the great ironies associated with improvisation, as soon as artists complete the rigorous practice required to place a vocabulary pattern into their larger store, they must guard against its habituated and uninspired use. The demands of improvisation make this challenge unavoidable. "Everything is passing by very fast when you're playing, and you've got to play something," Harold Ousley says. "I remember a time when I wouldn't want to play anything that I had heard before. I always wanted to play new and different things. But that attitude used to hang me up because I would refuse to play certain familiar phrases that came to me, and it would make me late in playing something else. When I'm practicing or performing a piece now," he continues, "I'll play whatever comes to me." Typically, soloists must be prepared to manage ideas arising in various transformations without the artist's preconception or volition. "When it's time for a particular phrase to come out," John McNeil observes, "it'll come out, but it's usually not the way you practiced it. It's usually altered somewhat. Maybe, it comes out a half beat to the right or left of where you practiced it, with a few extra notes thrown in. Or it might be connected to a different phrase," he reports.

These capricious occurrences can be explained partly in terms of the pressures under which improvisers operate and the inevitable discrepancies that occur at times between intended and realized ideas. Beneath the surface of such discrepancies is the potentially complex nature of musical conception in the face of myriad subtleties that define improvisation as an activity. Like the improviser's store of musical knowledge, the ideas that occur during a solo assume different forms of representation: sounds, physical gestures, visual displays, and verbalizations. Each potentially involves distinctive thought processes and distinctive qualities of mediation with the body.

Amid the interplay of a performer's shifting modes of thought, different mental images sometimes occur simultaneously to reinforce the same musical pattern; other times, one kind of image predominates, favoring ideas peculiar to its own world of representation and imagination, and temporarily altering the nature of the solo. As different modes of thought wield varying degrees of influence within their separate or overlapping spheres of activity and periodically prevail over one another, their ever-changing balance constantly affects an improvisation's progressive musical events. The balance is, in turn, constantly affected by them. Ultimately, the dynamic interplay among different modes of musical thinking forms the heart of improvisation as a compositional process.

In response to a problematic musical gesture, the verbalizing aspects of the player's mind might come to the fore, assuming an evaluative role and reminding the player of aesthetic issues integral to jazz language use.[31] Emily Remler is "constantly reacting" to what she plays, giving herself "little congratulations and little condemnations." In Fred Hersch's experience, "it's like you've got this third ear that oversees the whole business—the craft part—and that's what tells you what to do when you solo." He explains, "If you're going to repeat a phrase, repeat it in a different way, change it a little bit; make it say something; make it speak differently. Make the phrase I'm now playing shed light on the phrase I just played or the one I'm about to play. Do something to give the music contrast. Don't keep beating a dead horse this way. Try something else. Be resourceful. Use your left hand more."

If Hersch "plays the whole keyboard or just one part of it, it's a conscious decision. If I switch," he says, "it means, I was bored with whatever else I was doing, and this presents a contrast. I'm really just trying to keep it all interesting for myself." The nature of this dialogue can affect the overall length and shaping of the solo. John Coltrane also speaks to this. If in the middle of a solo "I feel like I'm just playing notes . . . maybe I don't feel the rhythm or I'm not in the best shape . . . I'll try to build things to the point where this inspiration is happening again, where things are spontaneous and not contrived. If it reaches that point again, I feel it can continue—it's alive again. But if it doesn't happen, I'll just quit, bow out."[32] The third ear's various concerns include blending emotional energy with the logic of musical ideas and keeping them in balance. When improvisers reach "ecstatic states" during solos, they must eventually "pull back and ask, 'Where can it go from here?'"[33]

In response to the question—or, otherwise, in response to waning inspiration or to performance problems described earlier—theorizing aspects of the improviser's mind might invoke the image of a theoretical model, and successfully urge that the next few pitches be drawn from its collection. If Melba Liston has "got the feeling going," she says, "then I'll go by ear. If not, I'll pay attention to the chords and go by the changes. I know my chord scales and all that business, so I can pick out the notes whether I'm inspired or not." Liston is generally "more deliberate" when she solos "nowadays," and she does not always rely on her ears alone. Similarly, Benny Bailey says he tries "to open up my mind a bit so that I can play something a little different, because I'm boring myself sometimes by playing the same things over and over again." Bailey laughs and elaborates:

> So, I'm trying to work on things outside the chord, to approach the chord indirectly—like from a half tone above it or below it, the outside notes—and to mix those with the inside notes. If you think of something outside, it's going to make you play different things. It will give you a bigger overall picture of music and stimulate the fantasy. Or I'll think of playing certain intervals. If I think of an interval like an augmented fifth, it's going to change the way I play. I'll surprise myself and play things I'm not expecting to play.

As immediately as the artist responds to such a theoretical concept and performs the interval, however, the singing mind might assume control and choose the next several tones aurally, extending and binding the entire succession of pitches into an effective phrase. Then the singing and verbalizing mind, approving of the action, prepares to repeat the phrase, when suddenly the player's body unilaterally pursues another option. A trumpet player, for example, transposing the figure for sequential development, might begin it at a miscalculated pitch level that requires the figure's instantaneous transformation at the outer limit of the player's range, cutting off the figure prematurely or reversing its melodic direction.

Under other circumstances, the fingers substitute pitches within the intended phrase's contour to make its execution more comfortable. During one performance in which an arranged bass ostinato "cramped" Don Pate's fingers, he invented variations on the ostinato for physical relief. Idiomatic figures that lie readily at hand on an instrument and are easily negotiated over its physical terrain commonly fulfill this role. Alternatively, the fingers may dance an inventive rhythmic variation upon an intended figure in response to an emotional impulse, or proceed as a matter of reflex to an altogether different phrase, one associated with the piece's sounding chords.

Additionally, the fingers can alter the singing mind's conceptions by exploring their physical relationships to other patterns. On one occasion, I had no sooner begun a phrase designated for my solo's eighth measure than I found myself playing another phrase altogether, one that I had practiced rigorously months earlier and then abandoned. What was interesting about the maneuver was that the intended phrase and its inadvertent replacement, although comprising different melodies, began with the same finger pattern sequence. It was as if my fingers considered the two phrases to be logical equivalents on this basis and switched me from one to the other with the ease of a signalman switching a train to an adjacent track.

In another instance, when I was practicing a long Lee Morgan solo from memory, my fingers leaped smoothly and directly from the first half of a phrase in one solo chorus to the second half of another phrase in another chorus. Only then did I realize that the two phrases contained a fragment in common that, serving as a bridge in performance, led me instantly across all the intervening material and created a new phrase in the process. These incidents illustrate the body's capacity to dictate with great assurance during improvisations by giving momentary primacy to the physical logic of patterned movement over the strictly aural logic of melodic form.

The changing character of the body during performances can also amplify or modify the improviser's conceptions. Betty Carter contrasts classical music, wherein the performer's body is asked to reproduce the musical gestures of another composer, with the self-expression of jazz performance. By constantly monitoring her own instrument's responsiveness as she scats and by shaping her inventions accordingly, Carter not only "spares" her voice but provides each solo with unique musical features.[34]

Particular issues can differ from instrument to instrument. As the fingers of pianists warm up and become more dextrous, they have access to a greater variety of rhythmic patterns and tempos. As the facial, lip, and tongue muscles of brass players become more limber, they can extend the range of their solos. Conversely, as players tire, they can lead melodic lines into a lower, less taxing register, perform shorter phrases, interject more frequent rests into the performance, or limit the lengths of their solos overall.

Moreover, the body influences events simply by faltering in its efforts to accommodate the singing mind. "If you're playing an instrument like the trumpet, which is based on the overtone series, sometimes you go for one note, and another one comes out. You might have a certain phrase in mind that you intended to begin on an A, but instead of A, some other note like G or B might come out. God knows why," Art Farmer laughs, "but it does." Such discrepancies are sometimes incidental to the ongoing realization of an idea, as when one rapid pitch inadvertently substitutes for another within the intended pattern. At other times, the spontaneous soundings produce results that performers regard as significant and desirable. If bass players "reach for a note physically and miss it," Chuck Israels observes, the accident can produce "a nice effect. For example, in certain situations, the chord might be G7(#9). If you are up in the high register of the bass and go for the sharp ninth, you might hit the natural ninth instead and still find that it's a nice, juicy thing to do."

From time to time, problems with equipment can play a substantial role. At one Village Gate performance I attended, a valve on Miles Davis's trumpet became stuck in the midst of an improvisation. Davis simply accepted the loss of its associated pitches as a compositional constraint and formulated the rest of his solo without them.

The unpredictability of musical events produces results along the full spectrum of satisfaction from serendipitous to undesirable. Harold Ousley comments on the problems that can arise when a player prepares to initiate a phrase "and it doesn't come off, either because a saxophone pad is sticking, or, for a trumpet player, a valve might stick or the embouchure might not be set right." Sometimes problems arise concerning the actual value of ideas and the relative precision with which artists conceive them. As with language use, it is sometimes not until individuals actually express ideas borne in mind that they discover how firm a grasp they have upon them and whether they are generally to their liking. Art Farmer is enlightening on this matter:

> Here and there you have unrealized ideas. Either you have an idea and it doesn't come off the way you conceive it, or else you might have a stupid idea to begin with—and you have to try them all. Like if you have an idea that comes to your head, and you don't know whether it's going to work or not, well then, you have to try it. That's the only way you're going to find out. By a certain idea, I'm talking about a particular choice of notes, some kind of melodic idea that would come into your head. Like you hear something in the music and would like to play something against that. Like if you're playing in the key of C and the chord is C, but instead of playing the notes that are in the chord, you play some notes that are completely outside of it. Sometimes it comes off and sometimes it doesn't. Or you might start out an idea okay and you want to develop it, but then you go as far as you can with it. It gets to the point where you can't handle it anymore because you don't have the technique and coordination between the head and the body.

Such commentaries underscore one of the special conditions of composing music in performance. Improvisers cannot retrieve their unintended phrases or unsuccessful "accidents." Rather, they react to them immediately, endeavoring to integrate them smoothly into their performances. Mistakes, in particular, they treat as spontaneous compositional problems requiring immediate musical solutions. The solutions result in what may properly be described as musical saves.

## Musical Saves

Experienced improvisers raise the musical save to the level of high art. According to Kenny Barron, "part of the act of performing jazz is taking chances, and sometimes the chances you take don't work. But the craft is taking an idea that doesn't work and turning it into something that does work." Art Farmer elaborates:

Whether the chances you take come off or not, either way, you have to preserve the continuity of the ideas that you're playing. If an idea comes to you and you don't make it, you have to experience making something else out of it. That happens all the time when you're improvising. Or if a wrong note comes out, you have to make something out of that note. You can't just let the solo fall apart. As instantly as a note comes out which is not the one I intended, some other alternative comes to me. Of course, years ago, when I didn't have the technique I have now, a lot of times an idea would come to my mind and then doubt would follow it: no, you can't play that; you have to think of something else that you can get to.

To address specific musical problems and to stabilize solos, there exist, within the jazz community, conventions for effecting musical saves. "I'll go for one note and hit another that has the same fingering, and say to myself, 'Damn, how am I going to get out of this one?'" Tommy Turrentine says, laughing. For him, the answer sometimes lies in the advice a veteran player "gave me long ago: 'Your chromatics will get you out of anything. Man, you hit a wrong note and just go to your chromatic. You ain't got but two ways to go—up or down or wrong—so your chromatic will bail you out.'"

In another instance, Turrentine says, he might "think of another interval that's complementary to the chord or to the phrase I just played and slide out of the mistake that way. Cannonball [Adderley] was a master at that. He'd be going fast, man, and a chord would sneak up on him and bam, hit him upside the head. He'd just go 'Oh, oh!' and get right out of it. Yes, sir. That's just knowing your horn and knowing your scales, being in command of your instrument."

Comparable strategies can address even the most "horrible accident" successfully. Suppose the basic harmony was a C minor chord, and a player "dives for an E♭, but overshoots and hits an E♮," Chuck Israels posits. "He had better use that note as an appoggiatura to an F or it's going to sound awful. There are few notes that sound as awful as a major third on a minor chord or that would be any more difficult to resolve," he asserts. In addition to saving the situation with a chromatic movement, a really gifted artist could "pick a bunch of intervallic relationships and, say, move away from the E♮ quickly, in fourths, like E, A, D, G, C, F, or something like that, so it would feel like you had deliberately started out with a tension away from the harmony of the chord and then deliberately moved back toward it."

In some instances, surprises in the conversation between soloist and the piece, such as encounters with unintentional rhythmic displacement, may suggest the use of particular options. One way of responding to the deviation is to subject the displaced figure to further displacement for a couple of measures until it arrives at its intended metric position. To manage such changes successfully, however, soloists must remain undeterred by the different rhythmic feeling figures acquire with each entrance. Another resource for offsetting the effects of displacement anticipated during the fusion of vocabulary patterns is for improvisers to enlist techniques of embellishment, inserting chromatic pitches between the patterns, perhaps, to adjust their rhythmic relationships to the beat.

Or suppose a player, after beginning a long phrase several beats later than intended, finds its last fragment threatening to spill over into incompatible harmonic territory. Several options present themselves. One is to head off the problem by altering the fragment to fit the new position's requirements, transposing it into another key or raising or lowering one of its elements to suit a chord of a different quality. Deleting the problematic fragment altogether and truncating the original phrase also serves the player well, as does substituting a more suitable fragment for it. Compressing the original figure by speeding its performance is another common method. If artists begin an intended phrase too soon, so that it threatens to fall short of filling its portion of the progression, they can compensate for this by expanding the phrase through various means. They can sporadically insert chromatic pitches, rests, or short melodic figures along its contour, replace a particular component with longer substitute patterns, either formerly mastered or invented at the moment, or improvise a cadential extension.

Other saves combine short corrective patterns with the deliberately reproduced mistake, as when soloists conform to their initial misinterpretation of a piece's form. Curtis Fuller has a copy of a Coltrane album in which, he notices, "on one track, he got to the bridge too soon every chorus. He did it every time, and now when you listen to it, it sounds like it's intentional. People listen to that and say: 'Man, he sure was slick when he played there' [Fuller laughs]. Those are the treasures of my craft."

Kenny Barron gives similar counsel: "One of the tricks is that if you play something that you didn't really mean to play, play it again. If you repeat it, it sounds like that's what you meant to play." Barron recalls Dizzy Gillespie's advice to him: "When you make a mistake, make a loud one, because if you're timid about it, then it really sounds like a mistake. It really sounds like you messed up." Sometimes, Barron says, when he begins an idea he can "tell that it's going to come out wrong." He continues:

> You can tell before your fingers land on the final note that it isn't going to work, but rather than backing off, you just keep going—whatever happens. The important thing is that you're not lost. You can repeat that same wrong idea and make it work. That's part of the craft of it. For example, suppose you're ending a phrase on a note that is really out in left field. We have a tendency to end phrases or to end lines almost without fail on the first, third, fifth, seventh, or ninth degrees of a chord. So, if you're ending on an E♭M7 chord and your phrase

ends on an E♮, that's going to sound wrong no matter how you look at it. And you can tell a split second before you land there that that's where the line's headed. If I did that, I might repeat the line and then find a way of moving the E♮ to a note that's in the chord.

A performer also periodically reworks a problematic phrase whose flaw lies in its articulation rather than in its design so that it can serve a predetermined musical function. If Harold Ousley tries for a particular "starting phrase that doesn't come out properly—there aren't enough notes and it doesn't fit within the context of the space—I'll repeat it in the second bar because it's something that I want to lead me to other things. I've even heard Bird and Clifford Brown do this."

As in Ousley's case, personal experience with comparable operations informs the artist's interpretations of performances by other players and increases appreciation for their adroit responses. At one concert, a soloist's drumsticks slipped through his fingers and rebounded on the drum head with a unique syncopated figure. As soon as the drummer reclaimed his sticks, he deftly repeated the syncopated figure, treating it as a motive. In another instance, when a trumpeter overshot a target pitch and hit a painful wrong note, he instantly pulled his finger off the offending key—inadvertently raising the pitch a step—then produced a rapid descent to the original target pitch. At that point, he deliberately proceeded to ornament each pitch of the chord in the same manner, creating a new phrase from the maneuver.

Other features of mistakes in improvisations contribute an endless variety of effects. The involuntary reversal of two fingers in a patterned sequence of movement imbues a phrase with a new melodic twist for the artist's consideration; a grace note inadvertently appended to the initial pitch of a phrase by sluggish fingers might suggest ornamenting other pitches accordingly. "When my fingers come up with an idea, I'll hear it and say, 'Oh, I like this!' and I'll consciously play it again," Harold Ousley says. "Later, I'll practice the phrase, re-recording it in my mind so that I'll know it and be able to get a playback on it when I need it." If the consequence of weighting subsequent pitches with grace notes was to segment the line into different groupings, the pattern created by the segmentation can provide the model for the next idea. Similarly, if the tongue does not move quickly enough for a clear attack on all the pitches in the phrase, the melodic shape of the partially ghosted and fully articulated pitches can catch the soloist's ear and serve as a design for other phrases.

Suppose that, in the context of executing a larger phrase, the soloist's fingers inadvertently strike a tone above an intended pitch, then overcompensate by striking a tone an interval below it. In such a case, the artist can use an ascending scale fragment to return to the original target pitch, continuing the original phrase as planned, although with a slightly expanded midsection. If the player loses the grip on the initial idea in deviating from it, or if the deviant maneuver appeals, the player can use its melodic shape and rhythmic motion as the improvisation's next statement. An alternative would be to rest after departing from the phrase, then start it over again from the beginning.

If a piece's successive chords will not accommodate the immediate revision of a passage, a performer can reserve it for the next compatible part of the progression. This requires the mental agility both to imagine and perform new short-range ideas while planning and managing longer-range strategies. Curtis Fuller occasionally conceives an idea during a solo that takes him longer to work out than he has anticipated. "If it doesn't come out right," he says, "I'll go back and try the thing again the next chorus to see if I can resolve it." Artists face comparable challenges when, as increasingly sophisticated musical thinkers, they derive stimulation from performance. "Sometimes, when you go through a channel, you figure, 'Well, what I really should have done is something else.' So, the next time I get to that spot again," Lou Donaldson reveals, "I'll use some other phrase I wanted to play, but didn't get to before." Under such circumstances, soloists typically strive to lead an evolving line through the remainder of the form, then directly into the intended figure, or they can provide the line with a logical conclusion just before the figure's entrance and use the figure to begin the next phrase.

A story familiar within the jazz community, as recounted by Fuller, brings to light the dilemmas that these challenges can hold for artists:

> Sometimes, I won't approach a part of the tune right. It's like a pilot coming in for a landing and not approaching the runway right. "Oh, wait a minute, I've got to go back and do it again." That's why some guys can't stop their solos. Like Trane was playing a record date one time, and he must have played ninety choruses. Afterwards, he got a big frown from Miles. Trane said, "I'm sorry, Miles. I just couldn't stop." Miles said, "Just take the horn out of your mouth" [Fuller laughs]. I think of little things like that when I get caught up with an idea that is not resolving right. I can try to make it work out over two choruses or so, but I put a limit on that. It's like the old saying goes, "If it don't fit, don't force it."

Should artists be successful in such maneuvers and strive to repeat them in subsequent choruses as planned events, they face continued risks of handling multiple ideas, performing some while plotting others. "I might play magnificently on the outside of a tune [the A section]," Fuller reports, "but get to the bridge and go, 'Oh, my God!' and mess it up. Then I'd figure out the bridge, but when I'd go to play again, I'd get so involved thinking about the bridge that's coming up, I'd blow the part that I was playing [at the time]. That's natural." Fuller remembers being in the recording studio one time with a friend "who wanted to do forty-one takes of a song. Every time we did it, there was something he wasn't happy with in his solos. Sometimes it's like that," he says ruefully.

As suggested above, individual interpretations of unexpected events, changing impressions of the original ideas, and the choice of alternative saves have different consequences for the solo's development at each turn. Through the skillful negotiation of problems associated with particular phrases, artists commonly change their intended emphasis upon them. Nevertheless, in the process, they accomplish the same developmental goals for which they strive during the normal course of performance. Reworking a troublesome phrase at separate harmonic positions within the piece's form can provide the solo with a unifying theme. Alternatively, immediate repetition can serve such a phrase as a satisfying tension-building device, with its successful resolution retroactively imbuing the sequence with the character of a planned motive variation.[35]

With increased experience and skill, improvisers respond to accidents with composure and ingenuity, performing saves with such speed and assurance that listeners are unaware that any element of the performance is unintentional. Beyond the immediacy of these occurrences, artists sometimes "remember their successful solutions to past accidents." The musical saves become part of their "musical knowledge, and they can draw on them when they come across other musical circumstances involving similar elements" (CI).

Ultimately, musical saves require that a soloist have the imagination to conceive an instant solution in the face of error and the technical control to implement it. To repeat a problematic pattern, musicians must initially grasp and remember its precise variation on the intended model. One teacher expressed exasperation when his students could not remember, for repetition, their "good mistakes," those inadvertent but acceptable variations on the model phrases he dictated to them. "They're supposed to be your discoveries," he implored. Moreover, to resolve unfortunate accidents, the artist must be deft enough to treat pitches outside the piece's structure as grace notes, passing tones, appoggiatura, or other figures leading into chord tones. To transform the troublesome portion of a phrase to suit unexpected formal circumstances requires experience with the full complement of improvisation techniques rehearsed endlessly in the practice room.

The methods underlying musical saves are the payoff of the musician's intensive, rigorous preparation. Mastery over scales, intervals, and arpeggios allows the student to change melodic direction via any of their tonal paths at a moment's notice, stepping or leaping to optional points within each piece's chord progression and resolving dissonant pitches. Similarly, the sense of rhythmic phrasing that Barry Harris's students absorb from drills embellishing two- and four-bar scalar patterns with chromatics prepares students to expand ill-conceived melodies instantly with extra pitches so that the phrases "come out right," ending, perhaps, with an intended target pitch such as a chord tone

on a particular beat of a measure. It is logical here to draw a connection between these techniques and those described earlier as conventional procedures
for ornamenting and varying jazz tunes, vocabulary patterns, and theoretical
materials. Such conventions themselves may have initially grown out of, or
been reinforced by, the special challenges improvisers face as composers, resolving the disparity between musical intention and realization in performance.

Accidents and saves may have contributed additional stylistic traits to jazz,
in some instances cultivated by originators who appreciated the effects of their
saves, or in other instances unwittingly perpetuated by students and by the
recording industry before the development of sophisticated editing techniques.
Jim Maxwell observes that some effects, "like the fall-off," are closely tied to
the idiomatic characteristics and difficulties of an instrument. "Instead of holding a note way out there on the trumpet when your chops start to hurt you,"
Maxwell says, "you let it drop in pitch. Also, the rip-up. It's hard to make large
interval leaps on the trumpet, so if you just start ripping up, hitting all the notes
in the overtone series, eventually you're going to hit the note you're striving
for an octave above where you began." Maxwell adds that he first heard the
doit in a Harry "Sweets" Edison solo. "It sounded like an overshot at that note
to me, but other people picked it up off the record as an intentional effect, and
it became standardized. Another is the shake. The first time I heard that effect
was on an early Louis Armstrong record. It sounded like a wide vibrato that
had gone temporarily out of control, and again, people imitated it from the
record as a distinct effect." [36]

### The Improviser's World of Consciousness

As the multiple associations of their ideas wash over improvisers, they put
into operation their well-practiced skills at negotiating the many possibilities.
They select some for development and tightly manage their interrelationships.
Besides those unexpected transformations that periodically arise from the discrepancy between conception and execution, improvisers constantly strive to
put their thoughts together in different ways, going over old ground in search
of new. The activity is much like creative thinking in language, in which the
routine process is largely devoted to rethinking. By ruminating over formerly
held ideas, isolating particular aspects, examining their relationships to the
features of other ideas, and, perhaps, struggling to extend ideas in modest steps
and refine them, thinkers typically have the sense of delving more deeply into
the possibilities of their ideas. There are, of course, also the rarer moments
when they experience discoveries as unexpected flashes of insight and revelation.

Similarly, a soloist's most salient experiences in the heat of performance
involve poetic leaps of imagination to phrases that are unrelated, or only mini-

mally related, to the storehouse, as when the identities of formerly mastered patterns melt away entirely within new recombinant shapes. "There are times when you don't even try to do anything new, and all of a sudden it will happen; you avoid all the clichés," says Bobby Rogovin. "Something fresh will come up which you didn't even know you could play. That's what playing is really all about, the magic that happens when you least expect it." An improviser sometimes initiates the first few pitches of a familiar phrase, then conceives a new melodic shape for the pitches' extension and abandons the initial model altogether. Amid the ongoing bends and twists in the contour of an evolving solo line, players commonly have the impression of a constant alternation between known figures and new figures. Soloists "always have crips that they can play when they improvise, but in the course of playing them, other things would come to them," Tommy Turrentine explains. "A crip is like a crutch. It's like a brace or a bridge from one idea to another. Bird might rip off something real mean and then play a crip. And after that, he'd come out of the crip, and he'd rip off something real mean again—melodically or harmonically or rhythmically."

It is in dramatic movements from formerly mastered phrases to unrehearsed patterns, from commonly transacted physical maneuvers to those outside the body's normal reach or hold, and from familiar frames of reference within compositional forms to uncalculated structural positions, that improvisers typically push the limits of their artistry. Kenny Barron surprises himself in his playing "in a lot of different ways." He may play "a chord or a particular voicing or chord substitution" that had not occurred to him before and say, "Oh, wow!" Or, he reports, it may be "a technical thing, a particularly difficult run that I had never played before, but executed perfectly the first time." Fred Hersch has experienced this as well: "I was playing this week, and I played all this technical stuff that I couldn't sit down and play now—even if I could practice it for eight hours. At that moment, the music was happening. Everything just fell into place in my hands and in my head. I felt I was expressing something with everything I played. When I'm playing well, there's a certain freedom of just being able to do anything, really."

Under the soloist's extraordinary powers of concentration, the singing and visualizing aspects of the mind attain a perfect unity of conception with the body. The artist becomes intensely focused on thoughts in the language of jazz, and as they come—one upon the other—they are articulated as instantly as conceived. No lead time separates conception from expression, and the gap between intention and realization disappears. Some illuminate this experience with the metaphor of dance in its broadest sense. When Curtis Fuller gets "caught up" in the music, he says, "I dance with it. That's my emotional state when I play. That's my feeling of expressing my total self in the music." At such moments, a soloist is propelled through the structure of a piece by the logic and flow of the performance, with each phrase opening the door to others. Figures that normally complete an idea turn spontaneously into transitional bridges to other figures. Preplanned events are either integrated smoothly into the solo or simply evaporate in the face of more pressing thoughts.

As exciting ideas flood their imaginations, continually presenting new melodic options, improvisers articulate them so effortlessly that they feel at times like recipients and conveyers, rather than inventors, of ideas. John McNeil describes himself as "a spectator in a way, and I'm usually surprised by what I play," he admits. Similarly, although Art Farmer sometimes "thinks about form in the long range of things," his improvisations "seem to have a life of their own. From the first note I play," he says, "one note leads to the next. It just goes from one place to another, developing by itself."

Carried during each improvised tale by the momentum of invention, artists are as eager as their audiences to discover precisely where the story will lead. There are constant revelations over their narrative's unfolding course. So that's how you can get from here to there! exclaims the third ear as the artist improvises effective musical segues among new combinations of vocabulary or transforms larger phrases with uniquely fashioned substitute patterns. Moreover, there are the gratifying feelings associated with long-range achievements. "The natural progression of the melody is set from the first phrase you play," Buster Williams explains, "and it becomes exciting by itself as you move forward toward the punch line. The excitement is shared by everybody. When I start off, I don't know what the punch line is going to be. It's all formed as it goes." The intense joy that accompanies successful musical journeys causes some soloists to "break up laughing" in mid-performance (BB).

Throughout, the artistic poise that improvisation requires is evident in the soloist's instant response to the musical turn of events and agile handling of vocabulary. It also underscores the musician's tolerance for ambiguity and courage in the face of risk. The attitude Roberta Baum carries within her when she sings is, she reports, "throw all caution to the wind!" Each performance is "an adventure," and from moment to moment "I don't necessarily know what I'm going to do next." For players, the adventure of jazz can be both exhilarating and awe-inspiring. Abdullah Ibrahim likens the improvising musician to "a samurai warrior," implying that it is the "fearless" confrontation of almost limitless challenges under tremendous pressure that leads to artful mastery and the ultimate achievement of "bliss." [37]

At times, the soloist pursues musical conceptions aggressively, undaunted by the complications that arise from unforeseen technical or aesthetic problems. In fact, a veteran in pursuit of a challenge often deliberately introduces problems into a solo and then proceeds to solve them. Following an impulse to reach for a pitch of indefinite determination, performing a melodic shape on which there is only a tenuous hold, experimenting with especially dissonant

sounds in relation to the harmony, or inventing complex rhythmic figures outside the meter and tempo, the improviser strives to work out the ramifications
of ideas by reconciling them within the piece's form. In the process, the player
commonly transforms the ideas in unusual ways, leading to discoveries that
provide further stimulation for the performance. Players may proceed rapidly
along the model of a familiar chain of ideas, then suddenly deviate from it,
bringing about a change, perhaps, by altering the rhythmic value of a prominent pitch or rephrasing a component, then taking up the new rhythmic features
motivically (ex. 9.8).

At other times, artists feel that realizing their goals depends on having the
self-assurance and flexibility to back off from intentional pursuits—to relin-
quish control. A conga drummer in Chicago once followed this course as he
periodically dropped his hands limply onto the drum head from different
heights, allowing them to rebound freely, then immediately imitated their complex aleophonic patterns and played off of them. "There is such a thing as
letting the music take you, if you are willing, or if you are open enough" (DP).
"Instead of trying to play the music all the time," a musician advised Leroy
Williams years ago, "you sometimes have to let it play you, and you have to be
relaxed enough to let that happen." Developing the confidence to do this can
be an important turning point in the maturation of improvisers.[38]

This paradoxical relationship between musical actions calling for a
passive performance posture and others calling for precise artistic control contributes to the mystique that surrounds improvisation.[39] Typically, Walter
Bishop Jr. is sometimes "leading" and sometimes "being led through" his performances. "I'll plan quotes from different tunes or solos and use them, but
spontaneous things also happen in my playing. Or I'll let something else in the
music take me somewhere. I'll deliberately pick up on the last soloist's phrase
and build my solo from there." Barry Harris characterizes the soloist's optimum
state as "calm but alert, ready to go with any possibility."

Artists in many fields experience a creative tension when they explore new
lines of thought and interact in unpredictable ways with materials and ideas. A
sculptor chipping at a marble block mediates between the initial vision for the
sculpture and its evolving shape. Each chisel stroke potentially alters its form
in unintended ways or reveals new features in the grain's internal flow that
suggests modification of the artwork's design. Similarly, for novelists, writing
is not simply an exercise in recording formerly held thoughts, but one for pursuing their unexplored implications. No sooner do authors create characters
than they struggle to control them in the face of ever-expanding possibilities
for their development and interaction. In the heat of writing, novelists are at
times spellbound by their own characters, who, much like the melodies of improvisers, appear to assume lives and voices of their own, revealing new insights that can shift a work's emphasis in unanticipated ways.

The sense of exhilaration that characterizes the artist's experiences under such circumstances is heightened for jazz musicians as storytellers by the activity's physical, intellectual, and emotional exertion and by the intensity of struggling with creative processes under the pressure of a steady beat. From the outset of each performance, improvisers enter an artificial world of time in which reactions to the unfolding events of their tales must be immediate. Furthermore, the consequences of their actions are irreversible. Amid the dynamic display of imagined fleeting images and impulses—entrancing sounds and vibrant feelings, dancing shapes and kinetic gestures, theoretical symbols and perceptive commentaries—improvisers extend the logic of previous phrases, as ever-emerging figures on the periphery of their vision encroach upon and supplant those in performance. Soloists reflect on past events with breathtaking speed, while constantly pushing forward to explore the implications of new outgrowths of ideas that demand their attention. Ultimately, to journey over musical avenues of one's own design, thinking in motion and creating art on the edge of certainty and surprise, is to be "very alive, absolutely caught up in the moment" (GL). Few experiences are more deeply fulfilling for improvisers than the compelling, all-absorbing nature of composing music in performance.

# NINE

## Improvisation and Precomposition

### The Eternal Cycle

*If you listen to many jazz compositions, a lot of times the melodies were actually once solos. I know because a lot of songs which I've written have come from just my plain practicing of certain solo phrases. When I'm soloing, I'll hear a certain phrase, and I'll say, "Hey, I like this; I think I'll write a song with this phrase in it."* —Harold Ousley

In creating solo after solo, jazz improvisers continually explore the relationships of musical ideas, negotiating among a mixture of fixed elements, which derive from their storehouses, and fresh, variable elements, which present unique challenges and surprises. Reflecting this dichotomy are the different uses to which artists put the very term *improvisation* as they apply it in different contexts, thereby illuminating various facets of their creative activities.

When players use *improvisation* as a noun, referring to improvisations as artistic products, they typically focus on the products' precise relationship to the original models that inspired them. In describing tune renditions, Lee Konitz distinguishes improvisations, by which he means the most radical transfigurations of the melody and "altogether new" ideas, from progressively subtler alterations falling within the realm of variation, embellishment, and interpretation. Similarly, in terms of this full range of transformations, artists can describe the relationship of their formulations to such musical models in their storehouses as theoretical materials and vocabulary patterns.

When artists use *improvisation* as a verb, however, they focus not only on the degree to which old models are transformed and new ideas created, but on the dynamic conditions and precise processes underlying their transformation and creation. Typically, they reserve the term for real-time composing—instantaneous decision making in applying and altering musical materials and conceiving new ideas. Players distinguish such operations during solos from the recall and performance of precomposed ideas, those formulated outside the current event in the practice room or in a previous performance. From this standpoint, unique features of interpretation, embellishment, and variation, when conceived in performance, can also be regarded theoretically as improvised.

Over a solo's course, players typically deal with the entire spectrum of possibilities embodied by these separable but related applications of improvisation. At one moment, soloists may play radical, precomposed variations on a composition's melody as rehearsed and memorized before the event. The very next moment, they may spontaneously be embellishing the melody's shape, or inventing a new melodic phrase. There is a perpetual cycle between improvised and precomposed components of the artists' knowledge as it pertains to the entire body of construction materials on any and every level of solo invention. The improvised exploration of individual pitch combinations produces new vocabulary patterns that, once entered into the improviser's store, take on the nature of relatively fixed, precomposed materials. When the soloist retrieves them in performance, however, they serve as improvisational elements that recombine in unique ways in the construction of phrases. During this process, invention can turn back toward precomposition when the exploration of relationships among vocabulary patterns produces increasingly fixed vocabulary chains, capable of being retrieved as elaborate construction materials for that or other solos. The proportion of precomposition to improvising is likewise subject to continual change throughout a performance.

The dynamic interplay that characterizes the artists' manipulation of the linear arrangement of their musical ideas in relation to one another in the solo line is comparable to their manipulation of these components in relation to the formal structures of pieces, whose elements are also subject to variability. In infinite permutations, improvisers alter particular features of compositions as they explore their maneuverability with fixed features of their vocabulary, and vice versa.

### The Creative Interplay between Vehicles and Ideas

Just as the value of the ideas in the artist's storehouse lies both in their intrinsic interest and in the ongoing models they provide for invention, so, too, the value of pieces' distinct musical environments lies in the continuing stimulation they provide. Improvisers commonly find the impetus for musical discovery in the creative interplay between the two. For instance, although a recurrent block of chords in several pieces can invite the use of the same complementary figure, musicians can uniquely transform the figure by joining it with quoted material from each piece's melody in that part of the progression where the block occurs. Moreover, from one progression to the next, features of the block's surrounding harmony may suggest entering and leaving the figure through distinct pitch collections or particular vocabulary patterns, in the process creating different phrases.

If at times soloists agilely adapt their vocabulary to the precise features of compositions, at other times they transform the compositions' features in order to suit their evolving melodic ideas. Even with all of his experience, James Moody says he still "looks at a chord progression sometimes and sees a new pattern that goes with it or sees somewhere else it can go, like some chord substitutions in place of it, that I never saw before." In like manner, Charlie Parker describes an eventful December evening in 1939 during a period in which he had "been getting bored with the stereotyped changes that were being used all the time . . . and I kept thinking there's bound to be something else. I could hear it sometimes but I couldn't play it. Well, that night, I was working over 'Cherokee,' and, as I did, I found that by using the higher intervals of a chord as a melody line and backing them with appropriately related changes, I could play the thing I'd been hearing. I came alive." [1]

In a comparable light, performers interpret their music's historical developments as a function of the interplay between ideas and vehicles. Some musicians hold the view that after Parker and others perfected the vocabulary of bebop and mastered its application within blues and show tunes, the artists and their disciples challenged themselves further by using their language within the novel settings of original pieces.

The harmonic motion of new compositions has been especially varied since the forties. According to Howard Levy, "Trane wrote 'Giant Steps' after he had mastered all of the common progressions in the bebop repertory and had tired of them. I heard that 'Giant Steps' just grew out of the exercises he had been practicing at the time, exploring different kinds of harmonic movements and trying to make his lines resolve to different places." Don Friedman praises the subtlety of Booker Little's varied resolutions of a two-bar chord pattern within one of his compositions: initially the pattern, Fm–E♭–A♭–G♭, resolves to a D♭ chord; in another part of the progression, it resolves to an F minor chord. Such formal variations challenge soloists to think differently in each instance, thereby avoiding the possible repetition of composite vocabulary patterns when negotiating the same chord sequences. Pieces whose progressions consist of nonrepeating components or whose harmonic chunks display minimal similarity are, for the same reason, uncommonly demanding.

Still another procedure involves the radical transformation of one composition's structure by superimposing structures of other compositions upon its frame. Larry Gray sometimes performs the kinds of motion associated with Coltrane's "Countdown" within the simple framework of a blues, "alternating minor third and perfect fourth movements in different cycles." Spanning the tonic and subdominant chords in the first and fifth measures, he creates progressions like B♭ to D♭, G♭ to A, D to F, A♭ to E, E♭; or B♭ to A♭, B to E, G to B♭, D♭ to E, E♭; or, at a slower rate of change, B♭, D♭, G♭, B to E, E♭. Gray likens such improvised movement to the chess player's calculation of alternative moves on a chessboard: two squares forward and one to the side carries the knight to the same place as one square to the side and two forward. Creating unique harmonic routes between the pivotal chords of a composition is effective "as long as you're moving in a logical, sequential manner so that the listener can hear a progression."

The use of unconventional meters as frameworks for jazz improvisation also creates special opportunities for invention. Teachers like Lennie Tristano have directed students to practice composing melodic patterns in 3/4, 5/8, and 7/8 to prepare themselves to handle comparable forms as improvisers. Kenny Washington, for instance, learned a variety of "Latin rhythms in 6/8" from one of Dizzy Gillespie's drummers.

Unusual harmonic-rhythmic schemes present additional stimulation within the respective meters of pieces. Wynton Marsalis once told me of his satisfaction at mastering the asymmetrical form of an original composition that required him to phrase his lines and color them harmonically in relation to "odd-numbered" groupings of measures rather than to the standard symmetrical groupings of two, four, and eight bars.

During the sixties, modal pieces accommodated other aspects of improvisers' evolving concepts. One interpretation holds that John Coltrane began working with modal pieces because he had become so fluent within the rapid movements of standard chord changes that they no longer "gave him enough room to express all the ideas which came to him with each chord." The newer forms allowed him to "stretch out the harmonic rhythm of each chord to give himself more time to explore each tonality before moving on to the next" (HL). Harold Ousley discusses comparable procedures:

> What Freddie Hubbard and other guys usually do today is to make a scale out of certain intervals, like alternating seconds and minor thirds, and make up a tune on that scale. Then they work out lots of phrases on that scale—their own licks—that they can run all together when they play. They will basically play that way through the whole tune. They also structure the chords so that they lend themselves to playing those kinds of patterns. The chords probably aren't any more minor than they are major. When players like McCoy Tyner use this approach, the whole song basically has the sound of that scale. There is a modal kind of sameness because they are working within the context of one or maybe two chords. Things have moved in that direction since Miles Davis and others moved it that way.

Alternatively, artists "work and rework a mode" by superimposing different theoretical models upon its simple frame and by embellishing it with elements outside its tonality, applying, in a sense, the same concepts of inside and outside playing that characterize the improviser's formulation of melodies from chords.[2] James Moody considers that

> the challenge with the modal thing is to make your playing sound complex and intricate when you're staying in one key. The way you achieve that is that when you're in the key of C, you have different chords that you can use in the same mode—C major, D minor, E minor, F major, G major, A minor, B diminished, and C major again. You've got to use all of them, rather than just playing C major all the time. Also, while you're working off all of those, you must remember that if you've got a C, you've also got a C♯; if you've got a D, you can also use a D♯. What you're really doing is working toward a kind of chromaticism.

Representing even more radical developments, the free jazz movement gave soloists the license to apply conventional jazz vocabulary and other materials to improvisation outside the constraints of harmonic form. Kenny Barron first encountered "the challenge of learning how to play free things" when he joined Freddie Hubbard's band. At the time, Hubbard "was flirting with the avant-garde," performing music that was quite different from that which Barron had previously played with Dizzy Gillespie. "I learned how to play melodic lines that were very free atonally, without any kind of harmonic reference," Barron recalls. "The only reference was the tune's melody." In some such cases, artists adopt the melody's rhythmic span as a formal guideline for their improvisations.

In other situations, musicians perform a composed melody at the opening and closing of their renditions, but do not draw upon its formal properties when improvising. The lack of harmonic and rhythmic reference allows players to create their parts without concern for moving from one predetermined harmonic goal to another or remaining within particular tonal centers for designated periods. Accordingly, Gary Bartz creates

> a chord pattern that is my own when I play free—still playing chords in the sense that if you play three or four notes, you've played a chord. It's just that it's not part of a chord pattern that's the same each time you play it. So, that's free. I'm making up the chord pattern as I go along. You just keep going on and on; it's one long melody. I don't think it's that different from how I ordinarily play because it's the same music, just another type of song, really, where you don't have the structure set up before you play. So, you work out your own structure as you play, really taking improvisation to the epitome.

Some musicians who are influenced by free jazz avoid using formal compositions altogether. Others maximize the harmonic tension of their solos by superimposing atonal melodies on the frameworks of conventional pieces, playing vocabulary patterns and pitch collections that are only loosely related to the underlying chords. Still others vary their performances by combining or alternating different methods. Ornette Coleman's improvisations sometimes take extensive liberties with a piece's tempo, meter, and chord progression, momentarily departing from the latter, or, perhaps, relating only to a segment of it. The harmony implied by Coleman's solo on "Congeniality" remains largely in B♭ but oscillates at times between B♭ and C minor, and occasionally ventures into extended sequences such as D♭–B♮–Cm–B♭, or even F♯–Cm–E♭–D♭–A♭–D♭–B♮–Cm–B♭.[3]

Similarly, Joe Henderson improvised "more freely with the structure of the tunes" than many other players Rufus Reid worked with. If Henderson played a piece like "'Round Midnight," he would "play for a while harmonically, and then he'd play freely, just on sound. At that point, you couldn't relate what he played to the harmony of the piece." Sometimes Henderson would play the melody of the song "real pretty," but at other times he would "take all kinds of liberties in his solo. He'd take things outside, playing notes from chords superimposed on the original chords of the piece." Throughout, however, Reid "could always hear the phraseology of the song underneath it all. That was a great experience." Reid explains that after a master like Henderson has performed the same composition for thirty years or more, it becomes "like Silly Putty in his hands." No matter the direction in which he stretches it, nor how far, Henderson never allows it to break, but returns it always to form.

Like different improvisation methods, an artist's choice of repertory is itself a highly personal matter requiring considerable experimentation. It is sometimes only after years of experience that soloists determine which are the compositions, traditional or original, that serve as the most sympathetic vehicles for their improvisations. While continuing to try out new pieces, they retain favored selections within the core of their repertory. To this day, Benny Bailey "tries to find different ways of playing" the pieces in his repertory by experimenting "over and over again, soloing on a standard tune for hours and hours" until he creates "something that's interesting and sounds good." For Kenny Barron as well, "musical knowledge is an ongoing thing. I'm continuously learning things about chords and voicings," he observes, "and the different kinds of melodic lines that you can play."

Lee Konitz has performed standard compositions "like 'All the Things You Are' for over forty years now" because of their unlimited substance as frameworks for invention, inspiring him to probe ever more deeply into their "possibilities." And Charlie Parker explained to Red Rodney that he routinely practiced formulating solos "on the blues, 'Rhythm' and 'Cherokee' in every

key." Over artists' lives, mastery of form resulting from the repeated performance of favorite compositions obviously contributes to their extraordinary
fluency as soloists. Konitz adds that improvising on familiar repertory also
serves players "as a measuring device" for assessing their creative powers "at
that moment" in relation to their recollection of their past improvisations on
the composition.

### Figures, Patterns, Phrases: The Lives of Licks

When musicians conceive satisfying patterns in their practice sessions,
coining new words for their improvisational language, many stop their performances and work on absorbing the patterns outside the formal context of
pieces, adding them to their storehouses. Some players notate their inventions
so that they will remember them. Lennie Tristano, in fact, required Lee Konitz
and other students to bring written versions of complete solos to lessons for
evaluation. Others tape-record portions of their practice sessions for later evaluation, studying their best phrases and disregarding less successful phrases.
Most typically, musicians etch patterns in memory through repeated performance. When Harold Ousley "comes up with new things that I can do on a
song, I'll keep going over them," he says, "so that I can approach my solo from
that particular angle."

Once thoroughly absorbed into a storehouse, new patterns take their place
beside the multitude of other set patterns—the precise shapes from which musical thoughts are fashioned. There, within the artist's imagination, they lead a
rich existence, continuously transformed in relation to other vocabulary patterns. As soloists call the figures repeatedly into action and redefine their relationships, however, they sometimes find that the figures occur to them more
frequently in some settings than others, interact more comfortably with certain
other individual patterns, and even evolve increasingly consistent forms of usage with specialized syntactic functions.[4]

Artists appreciate some figures for their special catalytic powers at the
beginning of phrases. Their strong rhythmic qualities inspire the soloist to extend the patterns imaginatively, or their striking melodic contours and intervals
suggest endless possibilities for motivic development. According to individual
taste, musicians consider other patterns to have cadential qualities suited to
concluding musical lines of thought. Once when Barry Harris composed "a
perfect answering phrase" for students, they generated numerous possibilities
for antecedent patterns and discovered that each worked well with it. Yet other
figures, intricate and fast, serve to display the technical prowess and virtuosity
of the soloist, as well as adding contrast and excitement to the performance. In
Dizzy Gillespie's big band, "the guys always were working on tricky rhythmic
phrases that were like an optical illusion on the ears. You could never figure
out how they played them unless they showed you" (BB).

Patterns with low melodic content, such as untransformed scales, commonly assume a traveling function, providing the musical means for moving from one register to another where more substantive melodic material is introduced. They may also serve as efficient routes between and among discrete sections of an instrument's terrain where the player can manipulate tonal material most agilely. When interpreting tunes, artists use comparable gestures as fills. At one workshop, Barry Harris recommended the use of an ascending major scale to approach a particular phrase within a ballad. Students practiced the run repeatedly until they could articulate it with a precise crescendo and accelerando, leading smoothly into the phrase's performance. Some patterns carry out holding operations. They may repeat a pitch rhythmically or alternate it with different neighbors, reinforcing the same tonality until the music proceeds to a different key or until the artist thinks of another idea to play. Yet other patterns are negotiators, guiding the player through difficult waters within a progression.

Episodic figures also lie readily at hand within the player's store. These include pairs of call and response patterns, sequences, or other short chains of ideas that work especially well in succession, conveying a sense of flow and logical development. Also maintaining a significant presence within the improviser's vocabulary are little turns and short musical maneuvers that may never stand alone as discrete ideas in solos, but routinely serve as embellishments and connections, enhancing and joining together other patterns in the creation of longer phrases. Simple idiomatic gestures for wind instruments—like a gliss or a rip—used to join discrete vocabulary patterns favored at different pitch levels are also effective in this capacity, as are fragments of theoretical models like chords, scales, and short chromatic movements.

The performance histories and associated meanings of figures can also influence their applications. Players feature traditional patterns that have special emotional intensity—like repeated riffs in an instrument's highest register or expressive blues cries—to evoke dramatic power. Correspondingly, learners must master figures and specialized performance techniques that re-create the associative shapes of verbal language and abstract vocalizations, which in some instances convey specific meaning to listeners.[5] At the same time as these allusions inspire new ideas, they may pay homage to the soloist's predecessors and contemporaries. Other, less dramatically expressive patterns can also assume this role for soloists. Harold Ousley has "recently been using the ideas of Freddie Hubbard and Woody Shaw, playing off modal scales, like a pentatonic sort of scale. I wasn't familiar with Woody Shaw's sound when I first heard him," Ousley recalls, "so I bought his first two albums and started listening and finding out what notes he used, what intervals his phrases were composed of. I took those phrases and played them in different keys and began to get the essence of it. I try to use that now to a certain degree. I try to incorporate it into my style."

As improvisers manipulate either traditional or original figures as a constant thread in performances, they accord them the additional status of signature patterns. "We all have our little bag of tricks, our special riffs that are identified with us," Red Rodney says. "You may gain some new ones and drop some of the old ones. You get different personality traits as you get older. But you never lose your bag of tricks completely. That's just our personalities."

Ultimately, while some vocabulary patterns may play consistent roles in the improvisational language of individual artists—used only to begin phrases, perhaps—other patterns play multiple, variable roles from improvisation to improvisation.[6] Catalytic figures in some settings serve just as well as cadential figures in others, and vice versa, taking on a different character in each context. A distinctive diminished pattern that is treated motivically in some improvisations—appearing in short sequential treatments, or as the basis for an extended developmental section within a chorus or a cadenza—may appear in others as a fleeting harmonic coloration device.

As this implies, the player's concern with varying the roles of vocabulary patterns is tied, at times, to the concern with varying their prominence within a solo. Artists emphasize some patterns over others by repeating them, by isolating them with rests, and by featuring them at the beginnings or endings of longer phrases or at the outermost curvatures of their contours. Performers can avoid particular patterns altogether, however, or significantly reduce their presence when treating them as construction components by relegating them to transitional bridges between more prominent figures. They may even go so far as to bury them within composite phrases where they blend into adjacent figures, compromising or sacrificing their original identities in service to the larger musical gesture (exs. 9.1a–b).

Similar practices occur at the level of phrase embellishment. A single triplet mordent that occurs as an incidental embellishment in one phrase may be applied to every pitch in another phrase, where, densely embedded within its contour, it comprises an integral part of the idea (exs. 9.2a–b). In other instances, the mordent's appearance as an ornament among consecutive nonmotivic passages can serve as a subtle unifying element, tying the passages together. A grupetto-like gesture that merely ornaments a composition in some settings can serve, in others, as the catalytic component of an improvised phrase or the phrase's principal feature (exs. 9.3a–d). Comparing sample appearances of a lick during a year and a half in its life makes evident its unceasing creative potential for the formulation of unique musical ideas (exs. 9.4a–i).

Gradually, the shifting emphasis that improvisers place on particular patterns changes the accessibility and standing of others within their vocabulary storehouses. This became apparent with Max Roach's quartet in trumpeter Cecil Bridgewater's performances, two years apart. At the first concert, Bridgewater introduced an effective device that teased the audience's perceptions during each solo. Subjecting rapidly repeating pitches to subtle dynamic changes, he created the impression that the source of the pitches was moving alternately closer or farther away from the listener. Ultimately, they trailed off, but in a distant echo. After the concert, Bridgewater explained that he had just "discovered" the technique while "practicing the other day" and thought he would try it out that night. It represented a successful simulation of his personal experience manipulating the sounds of echoes when practicing outside in the city at night. Two years later, however, the figure was absent from his performances. When I shared my recollections with Bridgewater after the concert, he indicated that the figure had simply slipped from memory as his interests turned to other things. "But I liked that," he added. "I'll have to think about using it again."

If some vocabulary patterns play a lesser role in performances and eventually disappear altogether, they can also reappear again, at times to the player's surprise. Patterns that Walter Bishop Jr. "worked on three years ago will suddenly occur" in his solos. There are other changes in vocabulary that may result from unconscious transmutations. In the transition between the artist's short-term and long-term memory, the pitches and rhythms of some phrases metamorphize into particular variants. Others transform into more general ideas, which take hold in the artist's storehouse and serve as compositional models. These include patterns of harmonic motion, impressions of timbral change, and traces of melodic shapes or time spans, whose precise pitches and rhythms artists fill in when improvising. The latter procedures constantly generate additional, fully detailed figures, which replenish the soloist's vocabulary. As discussed earlier in this study, the interplay between the general and the specific features of their musical ideas is a common theme in artists' accounts of creativity.[7]

### Preparing Strategies for Individual Pieces

Amid their drills at solo formulation, performers sometimes find that specific approaches to improvisation work most effectively within the contexts of particular compositions. Subsequently, they may adopt the approaches as guidelines for different solos based on the same composition.[8] From a practical standpoint, aspiring players discover that it can be helpful to narrow their options for individual improvisations to a manageable size. Additionally, as students become more discriminating and attune themselves to each piece's subtleties, they strive to interact with its features in ways that preserve the piece's integrity.

With increasing sophistication in such matters, students adopt a more

studied approach to solos, assessing each composition's character before performance, adapting their "thinking [to] whatever the type of tune calls for."
Patti Bown likens this practice to "an actress doing research before she's on
stage, preparing for the great role that she's going to play."

Some pieces suggest the approach of creating solos around the melody.
"Songs based on the blues and more elementary progressions often have a very
strong, lyrical, positive melody," Curtis Fuller says. Exemplary are those "by
writers like Benny Golson, Quincy Jones, J. J. Johnson, and Miles Davis, and
classics from the twenties and thirties, like 'September Song,' [whose melo-
dies] just walk around whistling the song." The time elapsing between the beats
of a relaxed blues or a ballad like "September Song" invites players to personalize renditions with subtle pitch inflections, timbral changes, and flurries of
melodic ornaments, most practical and effective at slow tempos. They also
provide the greatest opportunity for "phrasing a beautiful song" with rhythmic
nuance, exerting different degrees of pressure on the beat and subdividing it
cleverly during improvised flights of fancy.

Up-tempo pieces with "strong melodies" can also offer themes. "If it's a
tune worth playing, it should teach you something," Fred Hersch insists. "A
Charlie Parker tune like 'Confirmation' should give you information; that's
what a theme does. If we're going to play theme and variations, let's pull it
apart and play it in twenty different ways, not just one. So, improvising on
'Confirmation' is like breaking up the little motives, redefining certain aspects
of the melody." Moreover, a composition's specific "built-in" rhythmic features
that distinguish it from other pieces can inspire artists to "do certain things,"
to play with a particular rhythmic concept. Hersch elaborates:

> A tune like "Confirmation" is jubilant, and it should be articulated the
> way you articulate a theme from a Mozart sonata. In contrast, those
> really lush Ellington or Strayhorn ballads like "Star-Crossed Lovers"
> or "Mood Indigo" give a feeling of much more space than some of
> the bebop tunes. Or, comparing bebop tunes to a mysterious piece
> like "Nardis," even if I played them at the same tempo, improvising
> patterns of eighth notes, I wouldn't play the notes with the same edge
> or as cleanly articulated on "Nardis." I would play more shapes and
> rolling time. With "Confirmation," there's a time going on that's more
> precise. "Nardis" is more evocative; it's more moods. I wouldn't swing
> it. I might imply swing for a second or two, or maybe half a chorus,
> but even if I did, it wouldn't be a rollicking swing like "Confirmation."
> It's not that kind of piece.

Besides features of melody and rhythm, soloists examine the harmonic
features of pieces to determine an appropriate approach. "Some songs' melodies are not strong enough for the musician to play them over and over again.
If a guy writes a tune without a strong melody for the player to lean on, then the

development is all in the chord progression" (CF). A piece's chords sometimes suggest precise guidelines. When Benny Bailey plays on "a normal, basic blues," he would not "think much in terms of chord substitutions unless the tune were written with a harmonic background that would support" them. Otherwise, he would "clash with it." Similarly, he might try "to play a little of the fourth things that cats are playing nowadays, but not too much." In general, Bailey says that he would "try not to get too far away from the basic structure, or," he continues, "I'd keep coming back to it. Some tunes are very strict, and you have to follow them very closely."

In rendering an expressive blues performance, soloists may consider conventional blues licks and various theoretical materials, whose relationship to the underlying chords and whose relative harmonic flexibility influence the extent of their use. Improvisers can create phrases within the successive harmonic areas of a simple blues by drawing on three corresponding seventh scales that each unambiguously describes its respective area's tonality. Alternatively, players can formulate an entire solo from a single blues scale that embodies the combined tonality of the blues chords, or they can play different blues scales built on the tonic of each seventh chord to add greater variety to the performance. In more general terms, Clark Terry teaches his students "the concept that the old-timers used. They knew," he explains, "that they could play a series of notes that they called the blue notes, which was the tonic, the minor third, and the flatted fifth. . . . If you can find those blue notes from any given note on your horn, you can play with the greatest rhythm section in the world. You'd be surprised what you can do with those three notes."[9] Another choice is to base an entire solo on a pentatonic scale that increases its ambiguity over many other scales by eliminating half-step intervals.[10]

The density of a piece's progression, as well as the nature of its movement, also influences the choice of the approach to improvisation. Compositions based on the changes of "I Got Rhythm" introduce soloists to a more extended harmonic form than the blues, whereas others test the technical skill and ability of soloists to "think on their feet" at extremely fast tempos under maximum pressure. In "Cherokee," for example, artists must negotiate a hazardous bridge that extends the circle of fifths through the most difficult sharp keys; for "Giant Steps," they must invent melodies through an unconventional chord progression. "Songs like 'Giant Steps' are difficult for a guy," Curtis Fuller points out, "because you have to learn little phrases and figures that fit the progression and follow it. You have to have a strong sense of harmony to deal with a song like 'Giant Steps,' because that is what the song is." Some artists develop a "special language for the tune," unless they "use the changes to hang some pentatonic patterns on or use substitute changes that are far removed from the original changes." Although compositions "like 'Giant Steps' are far more difficult than others technically, they have their own built-in interest. If you just make the changes and the tempo, it's going to be pretty amazing" (JMc).

As implied earlier, modal or vamp tunes based on one or a few alternating keys pose the opposite challenge. Walter Bishop Jr. recalls his initial puzzlement. "What do you do with a piece like 'So What'? You can't think in terms of the piece's chords, because there aren't a lot of chords." John McNeil makes a similar observation. "'Little Sunflower' has a very slow harmonic motion and an easy Latin tempo. It's got like three chords in it and is about eighty bars long. . . . Nothing happens harmonically, so you have to be conscious of other things when you improvise, like changing registers for contrast. Also," McNeil continues, "when you play on that, you're going to leave a lot of space. If you tried to leave that much space on 'Giant Steps,' half the tune would have gone by." Artists who hold that "modal playing involves using more space than does bebop" recommend staggering solos with substantive rests and breaking up "fast runs" with sustained pitches.

Beyond technical considerations, artists may also consider the emotional character of solos associated with particular vehicles, planning rich accompanying visual imagery to guide them in achieving a particular mood when telling their own tale with the narrative of the piece. Duke Ellington explains, "*Call* was very important in that kind of music. . . . People send messages in what they play, calling somebody, or making facts and emotions known. Painting a picture, or having a story to go with what you were going to play, was of vital importance in those days. The audience didn't know anything about it, but the cats in the band did." [11]

### The Combined Use of Improvisation Approaches

Although a vehicle's character sometimes warrants the use of one approach over another, in many cases the piece lends itself to the greater variety of combined approaches. Fred Hersch draws an analogy between this type of improvisation and a poem by Wallace Stevens that consists of "thirteen little haikus describing different ways of looking at a blackbird." Sometimes, Hersch "feels that way" as an improviser, wanting "to look at a tune from a whole bunch of different perspectives—from a textural point of view, from a melodic point of view, or from a rhythmic point of view." In some instances, the general characteristics of a progression's differing segments compel improvisers to conceive distinctive melodies for each. On a recording of one Booker Little composition, the progression alternates between the A section comprising "quickly-moving chords" and the B section comprising "more open spaces where one chord repeats." Each time Little came to the first part of the progression, he improvised intricate nonmotivic melodic lines, but when he came to the bridge, he deliberately changed his approach to "show the form of the tune," as improvisers sometimes "like to do" (DF).[12] There, he played "lyrical melodies" with sustained pitches, "left more space between his figures," and occasionally performed single-note riffing figures or developed simple patterns as sequences.

Beyond ensuring their performances a degree of diversity, soloists commonly prepare different approaches to address problematic features of a piece, just as "chess masters study different moves and plan strategies before a match" (AD). Lou Donaldson sometimes "runs into a different type of song like 'It Was Just One of Those Things,' which won't fit the common categories" and requires intensive practice. There are "a couple of spots that are really hard to play" because few conventional patterns fit them. Artists have "got to know what's to be played there." It is not enough for them to rely on their ears. Donaldson "used to work out little patterns" to make sure he could "get through" the difficult spots.

These kinds of considerations are often on players' minds. At a rehearsal in New York, Benny Bailey and Charlie Rouse stopped during a new composition by John Hicks to work out their own strategic models for use within a difficult part of the progression. Whereas Hicks conceived of the harmony as compound chords, which he visualized as "triads imposed over the basic chords," Rouse invented a scale that embodied the chords' tones and altered pitches, and Bailey composed a few melodic phrases that suited the harmonic segment. When Bailey and I got together on a later occasion, he discussed additional approaches he calls on when preparing to play a piece, in this case "Aquarian Moods." Scanning the lead sheet, he skipped over the chords "whose logic" he could "see right away" and located the "tricky" harmonic sections. Coming upon a D7 chord with a flatted thirteenth and a raised ninth, Bailey decided to think in terms of a B♭ triad or B♭9 chord in that section to exploit the compound tonality implied by the original chord. "This way I would only play the top notes of the D7 chord," he said. "You get a very effective sound like that, just playing a few notes; the fewer notes the better, as long as they are the important ones in the chords."

In considering the harmony further, Bailey said that

> this tune lends itself to different ways of playing because the chords are so big. This chord is about three or four chords in one. It's very intriguing, and it's very challenging. Each time through it, I would try to play it a different way. For example, the way it's written, the chord goes beautifully into the next one, the G minor. When a cat writes chords like that, you can apply all these new fourth techniques, and it works beautifully because you've got the F and the B♭ in the first chord carried over into the G minor. Or, instead of playing that, I'd just play the ninth of the G minor. This tune has a lot of possibilities. What I always like to do is to find a common factor between the dif-

ferent chords so that what I play sounds simple. Instead of trying to play all the notes in the chords, I try to find the common tones so that the solo flows and doesn't sound like I'm running a lot of changes.

Continuing his scan of the piece, Bailey stopped at a symbol written A/B♭. "Here are some of the weird, tricky chords," he remarks. "See the B♭ in the bass and the A triad on top of it? I'd have to hear that on the piano to know what the composer meant. Sometimes, you can look at the melody and that gives you a clue; sometimes the notes of the melody adhere to the tune's chords, and sometimes they deviate." Discovering that the composer used the third of the A triad as the melody's focal point in this section, Bailey elected a similar approach for his solo. "One thing that you can do when you get to this part of your solo," he explained,

> is just play the C♯ there. I would like to do other things there too, but it sounds good just playing around the C♯ like the composer did in the melody. But I'd play it with a different rhythm; sometimes, it helps to just play the melody and then mess around and deviate from it. Further over here, see the chords E7(♯11), B♭13, E♭M⁶₉ and D7(♯9, ♭13)? The composer is also sticking around those predominant notes in the melody there, B♭ and F, and the whole four bars has the flavor of B♭. Thinking around those notes, you can actually improvise the whole four bars with them. You can play around with other notes to connect them, but if you just think of those notes, you'll come out okay.

Completing his analysis of the piece's last four bars—"a wild chord sequence"—Bailey commented that they produce a very "open sound [in which] you can play most anything." To develop a consistent approach to the section, however, he invented a scale from the important tones and altered pitches of the chord, and added it to the other performance models he had mapped out for his solos.

Such possibilities for planning are endless. When expert players work from the most general kinds of designs, they may simply restrict a portion of a solo chorus to one register or another, emphasize an off-beat rather than on-beat feeling, or create shapes that are more melodic than rhythmic. During his rehearsal, Benny Bailey mapped out such models for use as chords superimposed on those of the progression, common tones within particular chord sequences to serve as focal points for his inventions, discrete pitches from the tune intended for rhythmic and tonal variation, and pitch collections of particular scales and interval configurations.

Physical considerations may enter into these general theoretical strategies. A soloist might routinely minimize the difficulty of improvising over a segment of a progression whose chords involve awkward fingerings by playing common tone tremolo patterns, by quoting a phrase from the piece, or by resting for the duration of the segment each time through the chorus. Curtis Fuller favors particular chord substitutions to bypass keys involving awkward movements of the trombone slide. Other individuals use substitutions to facilitate the conception and execution of particular kinds of melodic patterns. For Kenny Barron, playing in "different keys brings out different things" in solos. Because of the "different fingerings and because of the physical structure of the keyboard, certain ideas that I might play in the key of B won't suggest themselves in the key of B♭. It's very different playing in E major or in A♭ major or in C major, because the fingering is so different."

Regarding large-scale strategies for structuring improvisations, artists sometimes apply, over an entire solo, the operations described earlier for developing ideas from phrase to phrase. For example, they may develop each new pattern as an organic outgrowth of the preceding one. Within the framework of a short form, they may introduce a new idea in each final turnaround section and treat the idea as a motive for the chorus that follows.[13] The exploitation of range can be especially effective. Starting "in the middle register, gradually bringing in the registral extremes," John Coltrane often "construct[ed] successive waves, each one reaching for a higher note then rapidly falling off." In this manner, he "[built] methodically toward the highest note of the piece, which may [have reached] far into the altissimo range," the climax of a solo commonly occurring about "two-thirds of the way through."[14]

Other plans create a three-part ABA shape in which soloists work initially within certain bounds, then expand the possibilities for invention through a contrasting approach, and return, finally, to the original approach. Sonny Rollins commonly begins improvisations by varying short rhythmic patterns of restricted range; then he gradually explores longer phrases of increased range; and finally he returns to simpler patterns, varying them as in the initial part of the solo.[15] An alternative design involves an ABC structure in which the performer gives each section successively greater intensity. For instruments capable of multipart invention, textural strategies can play a role. Wes Montgomery often structured his guitar solos by improvising initial choruses of unaccompanied melodic lines, following them with choruses of phrases doubled in octaves, then bringing the solo to a climax with thickly textured melodies in which each note is harmonized by a chord.[16]

The character of individual pieces or particular harmonic forms sometimes influences an artist's use of materials with distinct functions to mark off discrete parts of a solo. With respect to AABA compositions, for example, Lester Young would sometimes adopt a three-part "rhetorical plan" over a two-chorus solo. In the initial part, he emerged from the band with a relatively simple idea, generally a four-bar phrase. Subsequently, he demonstrated his technical mastery of the instrument or his mastery of the idiom; in the latter case, for instance, he might resort to "polymetric or otherwise unbalanced phrasing rather than rapid playing." Finally, he "return[ed] to the band" and wrapped things up with "an expressive peak reached by using common property, a riff, or a well-known lick."[17] In contrast, when improvising on a blues structure, Young would often begin each chorus with "a very distinctive idea," which developed "organically for the rest of the chorus," at times concluding the solo with repeated riffs that built up great "rhythmic intensity."[18]

As indicated above, the improviser's precompositional activities can range from designing the most general strategies of rhythm, harmony, texture, and mood to plotting specific figures, either for liberal use wherever complementary chords occur in a progression, or, more sparingly, for a particular harmonic segment such as an especially challenging bridge within each solo chorus (LD). In practice, such plans guide the artist's musical formulations and assist in achieving goals for solos.

## Inferring Soloists' Models

If in some instances advanced players discuss these matters with learners—providing insight from a personal operational standpoint—in other instances learners discern in the performances of other artists the elements they can interpret as improvised and precomposed. To the extent that artists remain faithful to particular plans when improvising, students may be able to infer them by comparing different recorded versions of solos and, within each version, comparing successive solo choruses, scrutinizing them for resemblances. Precise correspondences at different levels of invention suggest the operation of precomposed models, whereas looser similarities, such as patterns displaying a mixed bag of shared and individual features, lend themselves to wider interpretation. The figures may be variants of one another, or both may be variants of one common unstated model in the mind of the improviser.[19]

The circumstances under which artists compose musical ideas and the time frame within which they retain or transmit them are also matters for conjecture. Recurring features in an improvisation may reflect either that players prepared ideas before the performance, or that they conceived them while performing, subsequently retaining them from chorus to chorus, or even from take to take (that is, over successive recorded performances of the piece). The learner's own powers of musical apprehension and recall also bear on the analysis. The subtler or less detailed soloists' models are to begin with, or the more soloists transform model patterns in performance, the greater are the skills students need to detect the presence of the models and to appreciate the commonalities models represent across different choruses or solos. As learners grapple in their own performances with the imaginative union of figures and other transformational processes described earlier, they are better able to discern comparable processes at work producing variants in great solos.

Repeated figures, only thinly veiled, are obviously the simplest for students to identify. Individual strategies for quoting from the melody of a familiar composition can be especially accessible. In Booker Little's extended improvisation on "Old Folks," he quotes and varies a particular phrase from the A section of the melody during nearly every solo chorus. Kenny Dorham adopts another approach in his performance of "I Love You," quoting his own initial rendition of the composition's melody throughout the bridge of each solo chorus.[20]

An improviser's own recurring vocabulary patterns are most apparent when they are isolated by rests or otherwise exposed within the context of surrounding material. Examples abound. In Miles Davis's solo on "Miles Ahead," he performs minor variations on a discrete figure, in the same part of the progression, four times during consecutive choruses, and over the course of his solo on "Freddie Freeloader," he varies the model of a distinctive call and response pattern (exx. 9.5a–b). In the A section of Dorham's performance of "I Love You," he uses an ascending minor arpeggio as a catalyst for his improvised phrases three times and repeatedly features a descending melodic pattern as a cadential figure. Performances like John Coltrane's solo on "Giant Steps" make constant reference to the same figure.[21]

Other models can require greater skill to discern. In improvisations based on "Mohawk," Charlie Parker performs many phrases that, although different overall, conform to the same general profile. Each is relatively short, two to three bars in length, and comprises a rhythmically active pattern that comes to rest on the same target pitch—the sustained third of the tonic chord, approached, typically, from below with a leap of a third or fifth. The target pitch sometimes forms a cadential pattern with a subsequent pitch a fifth above it and may be extended slightly further.[22]

As implied above, improvisers differ both in the proportion of material they fix in relation to the larger solo's design and in the liberties they take with the material. In some instances, performers adopt the entire melody of a tune as a solo's underpinning, preserving the tune's shape throughout. Similarly, they may depend on extensive chains of their own preplanned vocabulary patterns. By narrowing vocabulary options from chord to chord over a piece's progression or a major segment of it, artists can produce a relatively consistent model to play off of during solos. Unless listeners have exceptional abilities to grasp and retain musical ideas, they may initially be oblivious to the role of such models, especially when they are long and complex and soloists perform them at fast speeds. It often requires transcription to bring them to light.

Examples of this type of model are found in improvisations based on Booker Little's original composition "Minor Sweet," in which he guides successive choruses with strategically placed patterns that form a melodic line running through the better part of the progression's A section.[23] From chorus to chorus, Little sometimes interprets the line faithfully, while at other times he contracts, expands, embellishes, and displaces its features with the techniques for small-scale invention described earlier. Moreover, he cleverly disguises the model by performing only selective excerpts from it. Starting and ending at various positions in the model has the effect of varying the lengths of phrases and highlighting different idea components at the opening and close of phrases, contributing to the fresh impression each makes upon the listener (exx. 9.6, 9.7a–e). Moreover, Little periodically interlaces the model with patterns unrelated or only loosely related to it, at times developing them sequentially (ex. 9.8).

A comparable range of models and operations arises in double and triple versions of solos by Clifford Brown, Miles Davis, Lee Morgan, Fats Navarro, and Charlie Parker, as well as early players like Joe Oliver. These performances reveal the transmission of musical ideas over a longer time frame, that is, from one take to another during a studio recording session and, in other instances, from performances executed a month or even years apart.[24] As for the successive choruses described above, resemblances among solo versions involve models that differ in character, occur in different parts of the form, and represent different proportions of the overall performance.

The takes of solos also reveal that artists may assign individual phrases a specialized role, not simply within a progression's scheme, but within the scheme of the larger performance. Players also describe this. Harold Ousley sometimes specifically "begins a solo with a certain phrase because," as he says, "it gives me a head start, a starting point to work with. It's like shoving off from go. . . . Getting into that phrase could also lead me to something else." Other figures are particularly effective for closing solos, for they leave a lasting impression on audiences. "Miles always seems to save something special for the last part of his solos," Benny Bailey notices. Soloists would favor particular ideas for elaboration in some instances, be it in improvised introductions to pieces, in improvised cadenzas, or in improvised breaks.

As such practices are borne out by the multiple versions of solos mentioned above, small-scale correspondences include Navarro's intricate five-bar catalytic phrase to open two solo takes on "Lady Bird," Davis's opening to three takes of "Barbados," and Brown's distinct, virtuosic motivic figure developed in the middle of three takes of "I Can Dream, Can't I?" In Charlie Parker's work, large-scale correspondence appears in two versions of his solo on "Red Cross," including an entire precomposed bridge and surrounding material, amounting to eighteen bars in all, and in three takes of "Tiny's Tempo," in which there are several recurrences of a four- to six-bar phrase, featured, in particular, at the conclusion of his solos.[25]

Displaying another profile are triple performances of solos by Navarro and Morgan that are framed by planned events: five- to eight-bar phrases repeat at the openings of the first, and in some instances successive, solo choruses, and additional models of two- to five-bar phrases conclude the same solos. Some alternate takes by Davis reveal the repeated use of a plan for the better part of an entire blues chorus, and, in one instance, Davis applies the model outside the boundaries of the piece, treating it as a long crip for improvisations within other blues.[26]

Finally, representing the extreme end of the spectrum are two-chorus performances of a Navarro solo on "Jahbero" that involves a nearly through-composed model.[27] From take to take, as with the successive choruses by Booker Little discussed earlier, Navarro treats the model's phrases with varying degrees of liberty (ex. 9.9). Different versions of solo performances by Joe Oliver in the twenties, and by Rex Stewart and Louis Armstrong in the thirties, demonstrate the continuity of the improviser's practices of precomposition.[28] So do "different out-takes of the Ellington Band playing the same pieces," in which as Don Sickler observes, "some of the solos by the same players sound almost exactly alike."

Continuous perusal of the artworks of improvisation increases learners' insight into the underlying processes of their production. Eventually, they discover that fundamental principles govern many different aspects of musical invention. Precomposed materials from the most modest to the most expansive can be manipulated as construction components: pitches combine into vocabulary patterns as patterns combine into phrases and phrases combine into solo choruses. Even complete bridges or choruses can be reused in the formulation of larger solos.[29] Players can apply other procedures across these diverse models to transform them: pitches substitute for one another within a pattern as patterns substitute for each other within a phrase.

Learners' observations also provide insight into the assignment of musical functions to components and the creation of designs for solos. Just as particular precomposed patterns may play a cadential role within the setting of longer phrases, particular phrases may play a cadential role within the setting of different choruses or within the overall scheme of improvisations. Every musical feature that students notice in expert solos—every procedure that they infer from analyzing them—expands knowledge acquired from personal experience with improvisation and contributes to their ongoing development as jazz orators.

The diversified approaches that artists adopt for solo formulation, and the particular blend of improvised and precomposed features of performances that they achieve, can reflect the musicians' whims and, as enumerated later in this work, the variable conditions surrounding performances. Additionally, the use and treatment of preplanned material can also reflect the different value that individuals generally attach to spontaneity of invention relative to other issues such as the cogency or coherence of musical ideas and originality.

Minimizing spontaneity, some musicians view improvisation as a process with the goal of creating an original but relatively fixed solo particular to the piece that has served as its vehicle, and they deliberately consolidate their most successful patterns from previous performances into a fully arranged model. "One older player explained to me," Don Sickler says, "that he was a melody player. After he came up with a basic melody for a solo on a certain tune, then he'd vary other things during his performances—like the dynamics, the phrasing, the embellishments, and so on. He still felt he was improvising when he approached the solo that way, but improvising within a different parameter."

The technology of recording has facilitated and even encouraged the use of through-composed solos. Musicians who initially conceived them during recording sessions sometimes relearned them later from recordings to satisfy audiences who grew fond of the solos and regarded them as integral parts of the compositions' performance tradition.[30] As described earlier, members of other bands followed suit, making substantial references to the solos or performing them in their entirety in specific performance settings.

Once solos evolve to a fixed state in which they consist of minor embellishments or slight revisions of completely arranged models, they function for improvisers like the melodies of compositions. In fact, they sometimes acquire independent lives as compositions.[31] "Well, it's the same thing really," Harold Ousley says. "In jazz compositions, most of the time the melodies are solos, the difference being that in a solo, it's more or less a spontaneous kind of situation. But when you have some solo phrases that you lock in together and play over and over the same way, then you have the melody for a song. What makes it a melody is that it has taken on a consistent, finalized identity." In between the extremes represented by complete model solos with "finalized" identities and those created "spontaneously"—that is, without any specific blueprint beyond the progression—jazz musicians typically apply different kinds of consideration to their musical parts and plan different amounts of material for use in each.[32]

Moreover, the fact that artists map out particular patterns does not necessarily mean that they will actually rely heavily on them. Knowing that should better ideas fail to occur to them they have ready ideas at hand simply gives artists confidence going into a formal musical event. From performance to performance—and during the performance itself—soloists can alter their guidelines or, as they tire of them, formulate new ones. Furthermore, it is one thing to prepare materials and strategies for solos, but another to implement them. As discussed earlier, improvisation involves reworking precomposed material and designs in relation to unanticipated ideas conceived, shaped, and transformed under the special conditions of performance, thereby adding unique features to every creation.[33]

The process does not end here, however. Successful features of improvised conceptions commonly join the artist's store of precomposed materials where, in forms ranging from the most general strategies to freshly coined vocabulary patterns and skeletal models for solos or new tunes, they await yet further use and transformation in performance. As soloists are perpetually engaged in creative processes of generation, application, and renewal, the eternal cycle of improvisation and precomposition plays itself out at virtually every level of musical conception.

# TEN

**The Never-ending State of Getting There**

Soloing Ability, Ideals, and Evaluations

*My development was a gradual thing. I didn't wake up one day and have it. As you grow older, you realize that you've got tomorrow. When I was younger, I used to hear Blakey and Monk say that: "Well, we've got tomorrow. We can try it again." If you mess up a song, you can try it tomorrow. Learning those things, you begin to understand that you don't have to play all those notes right then and there.*

*I don't think my playing style has really changed over the years; it's just gotten better. I can hear the improvement in comparing older records and later records. I'm referring to soloing ability, to having a better sound, to knowing chords better, and getting rhythmically stronger. It also has to do with ideas—learning how to edit your ideas and being better able to follow ideas out to a logical conclusion.*—Gary Bartz

The notion of the ubiquitous third ear is as helpful as it is appealing. As discussed earlier, this ultimate critic of the artist in action guides and evaluates the improvisation in the making. The third ear also assists musicians in aural analysis of other artists' solos, whether in live or recorded performances. As audience members, artists routinely evaluate each other's inventions, sharing opinions within the social network of the jazz community. Newcomers soon discover that the discussion of aesthetic issues comprises an essential component of their community's intellectual life. Some discussions throw light on the interrelated web of values that are integral to jazz, whereas others concern features associated with particular idioms or with the musical styles of individuals, the latter an outgrowth of the intensely personal nature of improvisation. Evaluations address all aspects of the improvisation from a particular solo's content to a player's overall contribution to jazz.

Venturing into the arena of music criticism in the presence of knowledgeable improvisers may be as intimidating to the vulnerable student as venturing onto the performance stage itself. As expected, opinions that find general agreement among musicians, for whom art is characteristically a passionate

243

business, promote a feeling of solidarity and reaffirm common musical values. When they are not shared, however, they can cause contention and even embarrassment, calling into question the student's own knowledge, powers of perception, or taste. Ultimately, by observing critical discussions and participating in them, learners become sensitive to wide-ranging criteria appropriate for the evaluation of jazz that occupy community members, and they gain a deep respect for the refined listening abilities that attune seasoned artists to every nuance and detail of improvised performances.

### Swing: Judging Rhythmic Substance

Within the musician's scale of values, rhythmic aspects of performance are fundamental. "One of the most obvious aspects of the music to people who know jazz," observes Chuck Israels, "is: How does it feel in the swing? These are things that are very subtle and that jazz musicians appreciate in a particular way. I appreciate the way that Tommy Flanagan swings, the way that Barry Harris swings, the great pulse that Hank Jones and Bill Evans have—and every one of them is different."

Criticism distinguishes such salient features from the melodic and harmonic content of ideas. A veteran of Charles Mingus's band once abruptly stopped his rehearsal of Boston's all-city high school jazz band after two talented saxophonists, the most cocky in the group, had completed their solos, and he insisted on hearing the rest of the band's opinions of the performances. When the intimidated youngsters failed to volunteer a response, the director continued: "Well, let me give you a hint. What both saxophonists played was garbage. But there is an important difference between them." Then he smiled and added, "The second player's garbage swung!" The first soloist reddened, and the rest of the band chuckled as they exchanged knowing glances. Evaluations highlighting Charlie Parker's ability to swing drive home a similar point. "The rhythms of Bird's solos were so strong," a musician once remarked in conversation, "you could almost add any notes to them, and they would still be great."

The achievement of swing ultimately depends on the interplay of numerous factors described earlier, ranging from the sheer variety of the artists' rhythmic conceptions to the stylistic manner in which they articulate and phrase them, imbuing them with qualities of syncopation and forward motion.[1] Such subtleties depend in part on the player's sense of time or tempo. Whether Billie Holiday performed "the fastest tune in the world or . . . a dirge," her time was impeccable.[2] In the absence of the appropriate rhythmic quality, performances "feel like they never get off the ground," a pianist contends. "It's like reciting poetry with the wrong rhythm." More specifically, he claims that they lack "rhythmic flow," that their feeling is "too calculated." One artist dubbed a former commercial dance band musician as "corny," or aesthetically naive, because his pitches were "too short and staccato, not legato enough. They sounded rinky-dink, like Lawrence Welk."

In the opinion of Paul Wertico, "there are some drummers who are great technically and can play the most complicated polyrhythmic exercises, but they can't make them swing. Their figures are mathematically precise, but they're stiff and mechanical." Fred Hersch expresses a general view when he says, "There's a certain kind of time that's metronomic, that's correct, but doesn't make you want to dance. It doesn't make you want to move, and it doesn't make you want to play."

At the other extreme, however, phrases fail to swing when they lack the requisite "rhythmic punch and definition," sounding "wishy-washy," weak, flaccid. One bass player complained that a musician who auditioned for his band "didn't place things firmly enough; there was no strength or subtlety to his rhythmic placement of notes." A former soloist with Horace Silver's band recalled the pianist's constantly exhorting him to "dig in! Dig in more!" As implied above, improvisers differ in the assurance with which they define the beat or groove; some perform with greater rhythmic conviction than others. The great players enrich performances with minute, controlled fluctuations in their interpretation of the beat. "A lot of guys in New York will only play with an edge. They find their groove and that's their groove," Hersch says. "To me, once I do that, there's no point in playing anymore because it should always be a mystery. Depending on who you're playing with, there are hundreds of ways of playing. I think that a master can play all those different kinds of time."

In part, players create subtle schemes of tension and release through changing accentuation patterns and altering the placement of rests within their lines. The trials and tribulations of students bring to light the importance of such features that demonstrate mastery over timing. When a Clifford Brown solo that I had practiced by memory eventually lost its excitement, I checked the original recorded version and discovered that I had inadvertently altered the solo's intricate off-beat accentuation scheme, causing phrase accents to coincide with the music's beats and depriving the music of its rhythmic vitality. Similarly, early in pianist Howard Becker's career, he performed for a jazz veteran the phrases of an idol's re-created solo, playing the phrases in their proper sequence but leaving pauses of arbitrary lengths between them. The veteran nodded politely, then, exploding with laughter, reprimanded him, "Now go back and learn all the rests!" From the veteran's viewpoint, the logic of the solo depended as much on its use of space and the rhythmic relationship of its phrases to form as on their contours and harmonic implications.

Because the foundational harmonic blocks of many pieces are square, made up of regular repeating two-, four-, and eight-bar phrases, improvisers evaluate solos as being square, in a pejorative sense, when their patterns consistently coincide with the composition's harmonic blocks. By altering the design of phrases within a progression, varying their spans, and, at times, superimposing secondary meters on those of the piece, mature artists can obscure the formal elements that guide their inventions in much the same way as the architect, in designing an impressive structure, obscures its underpinnings.[3] "Great jazz players start and end in different places as they go from chorus to chorus," Chuck Israels explains.

> It's often beautiful to start a phrase just before the end of one chorus and carry it over into the beginning of the next. Because that's such an obvious line of demarcation in the form, you want to dovetail that joint together. These are the formal issues, and some people have an instinct for them and some don't. Charles Mingus once said, "How come all these modern players play 'I Got Rhythm' with the same eight-bar phrases? How come they don't play from the end of the second eight bars into the bridge or from the end of the bridge into the last eight bars? Why do they always breathe after every eight bars?" With great players like Louis Armstrong and Charlie Parker, you could never predict the places where they were going to breathe.

Barry Harris similarly appraises solos of uniform phrase length to be as "monotonous as the drone of a dull speaker."

Another sensitive issue is the variety of rhythmic values that improvisers incorporate within phrases. One performer considers even extraordinarily fluent solos to be "boring" when they involve regular streams of unaccentuated and uninflected pitches without diverse articulations and dynamic nuances, that is, without "rhythmic shape." A related problem concerns the predisposition of youngsters to "fast, flashy" patterns, which, for their lack of substance, seasoned artists regard as "filler" material. Lee Konitz remembers Lennie Tristano trying to keep him "away from mechanical playing, the tendency to play double time—that sixteenth-note kind of facility that doesn't necessarily come from anyplace." Ellis Marsalis similarly cautioned his son Wynton, "'You're playing too many notes. Look, man, calm down.' That was because of my technique," Wynton recalls. Having heard Clifford Brown "play all those fast runs, I used to really practice Clarke trumpet exercises all day long so that I could play fast. That's all I wanted to do. I was like a child with a toy," he recalls with laughter.

For some novices, the performance of unvaried patterns serves as a crutch for marking each passing beat in its progress through a piece's structure. It is only after developing command over the forms of compositions and the diverse rhythmic models of jazz that they can engage in creative rhythmic thinking without losing their bearings. At a workshop, Alan Swain once forced this issue by insisting that young musicians follow his cues to begin and stop playing during the course of solos, in effect directing the insertion of rests into performances. By breaking up the students' constant stream of pitches, even in the most arbitrary manner, Swain immediately and markedly improved their improvisations. Filler material eventually becomes less attractive to students as they awaken to the deeper values of jazz. One of Barry Harris's students "went through a stage in which," he says, "I just played the right notes real fast through the changes; but that just doesn't do it for me anymore." Another says he "used to admire players who could play fast, but since then, I've learned to listen for other things in solos. I've become disappointed with some of the same players I used to enjoy," he rues, "and I don't listen to them anymore."

## The Melodic Substance of Ideas

Closely tied to the musical component of rhythm is melodic substance. As John Lewis puts it, this involves fashioning notes into "independent recognizable idea[s]," finding "a graceful way to get from one place to another, one note to another, one phrase group to another."[4] One goal is to create lyrical or tuneful phrases, "pretty" phrases, "the ones you can sing, the ones you can remember" (JS). Sometimes musicians draw out the word with a slight pitch ascent in obvious pleasure—"purrrrr-iiii-ty"—indicating that they are not offering faint praise. Rather, they are recognizing qualities they deem exceptionally beautiful. Sometimes an artist specifies the pleasing melodic contours at issue by singing them or naming their theoretical pitch collections. It is common for artists to observe that analysis of the "hippest" figures in a favorite solo reveals "some kind of diminished or augmented thing happening" (HL).

An important aspect of the improviser's maturation as a melodic thinker involves learning to imagine, manipulate, and edit ideas derived from various musical models in performance. Dizzy Gillespie tries to "play the bare essence, to let everything be just what it's supposed to be in that particular spot. . . . You have many things to pick from while you're playing," he explains, "so you try to train yourself to pick out the best things that you know."[5] Lee Morgan used "to stand behind me," Gary Bartz says, "when I was playing a ballad and he'd be hollering, 'Play the pretty notes, man, play the pretty notes.' I thought I was playing the pretty notes," Bartz laughs. "But you know, things like that help you to reach a little further." Other improvisers are "constantly trying to think of some other way of doing things like playing a four-bar phrase, eliminating things that just don't fit well" (MR). In this light, Wynton Marsalis still does, in his words, "play too many notes at times, but," he explains, "it takes all your life to learn how to choose the best notes. That's the difference between the good players and the great." Playing with Lester Young taught Art Farmer about "economy: that what you played had to have meaning, not just a bunch of sixteenth notes." Farmer sometimes finds patterns that he has played on earlier recordings that he "wouldn't be interested in doing anymore," he admits. "You learn to make better choices of notes as you get older."

The related standards of economy of expression and lyricism, described earlier, are underscored by the traditional maxims of the jazz community that forewarn newcomers of improvisation's potential pitfalls. New Orleans musicians advised, "If you can't sing it, you can't play it," exhorting soloists to perform melodies that they can conceptualize clearly in their singing minds, rather than allowing the physical aspects of performance to dominate a solo. Lee Konitz observes that "there's a line built into an instrument, and when people play that, the music becomes mechanical and technical." Konitz's ideal is a "note to note kind of playing," with corresponding control over the selection of pitches and shaping of melody.[6] When the physical drive to perform an instrument becomes a nervous tick creating problems for soloists comparable to those of compulsive talkers, seasoned players criticize them for "not saying anything; not making a real statement" (MR). Solos "should talk," a veteran once advised a novice, "and when you don't have anything to say, you should stop playing."

In addition to potential problems with the role of physicality in melodic invention, improvisers may face difficulties arising from the interplay between theoretical and aural musical thinking. Artists concerned with disguising compositional technique, for example, object to the unsubtle use of theoretical improvisation approaches and criticize some players as being "chord connectors" rather than actual improvisers. "I don't need to have people spell the chords for me," Curtis Fuller argues. "This isn't a spelling bee. It's all in the book. I like to hear chord progressions when they've been altered lyrically." Here, the process of transformation is again tied to editing. Miles Davis "used to play fast, but the older he got, he started just taking out the pretty notes of the scale and just playing them. That's what you call mellowing" (TT). Similarly, as Emily Remler puts it, "If I take a lick from [some players], I'm not going to get that many variations from it, because their phrases are just based on a scale. That's why I say Wes Montgomery has more substance than others. I find myself listening to the older players. You see one bar of theirs and you can get one hundred more licks out of it."

Remler's observations suggest that older soloists, who initially learned jazz by ear, absorbing models for melodic shape, phrasing, and inflection from their idols' performances, developed a comprehensive base of aural musical knowledge that enables them to transform theoretical models effectively. Contemporary jazz students, however, whose learning methods emphasize theory over the arduous discipline of aural learning, risk confusing theory with performance practice, thereby developing naive notions about theory as a compositional tool.

An incident in one of Barry Harris's workshop sessions illustrates this problem. When he requested that, for additional color, the class invent phrases based on his "rule" mixing a scale's pitch collection with those of a contrasting chord, four students demonstrated their phrases. After each, Harris smiled warmly and nodded in approval. At a fifth student's performance, however, he shook his head and remarked, "No, you wouldn't do that in this music." Stung by the rebuke, the student defended himself: "But you said to follow the rule you gave us, and this phrase follows the rule." "Yes," Harris admitted, "but you still wouldn't play a phrase like that." "But give me one good reason why you wouldn't," the student protested. "The only reason I can give you," Harris replied, "is that I have been listening to this music for over forty years now, and my ears tell me that that phrase would be wrong to play. You just wouldn't do it in this tradition. Art is not science, my son." The student left the workshop early that evening, not to return for months.

Harris's admonition stems from his understanding that the same theoretical rules that account for the multitude of aesthetically pleasing possibilities for invention within the jazz tradition can also generate phrases that fall outside the field's idiomatic bounds and its dictates of good taste. Therefore, the learner must devote years to studying the breadth of jazz literature and to participating in the music's performance practices before it is possible to develop an appropriate, informed perspective for evaluating personal musical creations. Improvised melodies that fail to display the basic stylistic conventions of jazz commonly stand accused of "lacking roots or lacking history." In one instance, an advanced performer criticized the solos of a former classical musician as "corny" because he articulated pitches uniformly, failing to imbue them with the nuances of attack, inflection, and color associated with jazz. In another instance, an elderly musician advised a young soloist: "I like your feeling, but you need to listen more and learn more of this music's vocabulary."

Beyond providing models for melodic shape and phrasing, the absorption of conventional vocabulary patterns establishes the basis for the relationship between aspiring performers and their tradition. If Arthur Rhames "uses a particular motive the way that Bird would use it, it's only," he insists, "to let the listeners know of my awareness of what Bird did with this. That's the mark of a novice going into the intermediate stage of music, where he's actually aware of what he's saying. He's aware of his place in the music and his predecessors." According to Jimmy Robinson,

> Whenever those licks really fit in with the story you were telling, you'd stick them in your solo. Then, other people could tell by listening to you that you were influenced by Diz or Fats or whoever. Most players held Diz and Fats and those fellows in high esteem, and you could tell whether other musicians were also working on those things. There wasn't anybody else coming along with anything as good or anything better, so you had to listen to them. And if players weren't working on those things, well then, they weren't trying to be artists in a true sense.

The evidence of respect for the melodic substance of musical ideas found in pretty notes and exemplary phrases, knowledgeably rendered, is reflective of jazz's great stylists. Clearly, it is a significant mark of being a jazz artist in the "true sense."

## Judging Harmonic Content

Performers are also sensitive to the relationship between the constituent elements of phrases and their harmonic backgrounds. On the one hand, Benny Bailey praises Miles Davis for emphasizing chord tones in his melodies, making "beautiful choices so deeply into the harmony. It's much harder to play that way," he explains, "than to play a lot of notes." On the other hand, Herbie Hancock remembers an evening in which his performance "had gotten into a rut," and Davis advised him to avoid the "butter notes" in this instance. Hancock interpreted the butter notes as being the "fat notes, the obvious notes that tell tale what you're doing," notes such as the third and the seventh. Reasoning that leaving them out might lead him "in another direction," Hancock implemented the strategy and enjoyed renewed success in his solos, eliciting the most enthusiastic response of the week from the audience.[7]

For the most part, it is the relative mixture of pitches inside and outside of the harmony that creates interesting melodies. "Playing inside the changes means playing enough of the important notes of the chord progression at important times," Chuck Israels says. "A good solo might be very free, but every once in a while it loops or hooks into an essential note that describes the harmonic change . . . [playing a chord tone in] one of the two or three basic lines of the harmony. Artistically successful jazz players go in and out of that in their solos." Kenny Barron extends this point. "The more your level of hearing gets better, the more you can hear complicated kinds of ideas, and assuming that you are technically proficient enough, you can execute those ideas. By more complicated ideas, I mean ideas that would be both longer in length and make use of notes that might be considered outside the chord. Being able to play complicated ideas means being able to position those notes in such a way that they flow back and forth between the notes that are in the chord."

To be critically appreciative of such features of solos and to manage them in performance, students must develop an ear for the vertical aspects of music and "for the tone center of every chord" (LD). One learner recalls an early lesson in which he finally improvised a solo with credible melodic shape, only to have his teacher, Charlie Mariano, simply inform him that he had played "too many wrong notes." That he had not even perceived the clashes between harmony and melody that troubled Mariano was a sobering revelation for the student.

At issue here are the precise harmonic relationships defined as dissonant and the judgments applied to an artist's treatment of them.[8] Experienced improvisers can "play anything in relation to chords as long as you resolve it right," Josh Schneider asserts. This means developing the control to return to "the key center at the time you want to," resolving the mounting tension of "the curve" of a solo line by ending it inside the chord, that is, on a chord tone. "Unresolved dissonances are the true mark of an amateur," Alan Swain says. One musician expressed his irritation that a younger player did not, in particular, "resolve major seventh pitches over seventh chords." Another artist faced criticism for not resolving flatted ninths and using them indiscriminately. After the player perfected the use of flatted ninths in his own improvisations, he noticed comparable problems in solos of other performers and found them objectionable himself.

Non-chord tones, as implied above, present different liabilities, depending on their placement within melodies and their relationship to underlying chords. Within a vocabulary pattern that spans chord tones, the passing motion of intermittent dissonant pitches can add interesting harmonic color to the solo. Even a stretch of dissonant pitches can serve as a dramatic tension-building device before resolving to a chord tone. If the same pitches are redistributed within a figure, however—with non-chord tones assuming prominent positions of emphasis without resolution—they can create the displeasing effect of wrong notes. In this regard, theoretical models of scales can be problematic for improvisers unless they learn to weight their pitches variably in melodic invention, treating non-chord tones with special sensitivity. To free students from such concerns, some teachers initially restrict student solos on simple blues progressions to limited pitch collections they regard as "working harmonically" with underlying chords, either matching the tones or displaying a harmonic neutrality that avoids or minimizes conflicts (JMc).

Comparable challenges arise when soloists experiment with applying a vocabulary pattern within the settings of different chords in which the pattern's pitches assume new relationships to the root, exchanging identities as chord and non-chord tones. One of Barry Harris's theoretical drills addresses this issue by cultivating in students a relative sense of the role of individual pitches in relation to a piece's quickly changing harmony. In increasingly rapid exchanges with the class, Harris calls out the name of a pitch and a succession of chords, to which students respond by instantly calling back the pitch's recalculated position with respect to each chord change. (The pitch C, for example, is "the second" of a B♭7 chord, "the sixth" of an E♭7 chord, "the seventh" of a D♭M7 chord, and so on.) Such drills prepare students for the challenges of applying their models flexibly in performance.

With experience, students become increasingly sensitive to the effects produced by their patterns' applications. "Using a phrase with a certain chord in a certain part of a tune gives it greater meaning and allows it to make a stronger statement than it would in another part of the tune," Harold Ousley

states, "where it would be kind of lost." Because of the interdependence between the effectiveness of patterns and their larger musical settings, learners
are sometimes surprised when an exciting figure copied from an album turns
out to be "only a basic construction material like a chord or a scale fragment"
(RuR). Such figures commonly lose their luster when removed from their musical surroundings. It is when a great player like Ron Carter performs a simple
scale fragment in relation, perhaps, to an imaginative, tastefully dissonant
chord of Herbie Hancock's, Rufus Reid explains, "that it sounds really slick!"
Similarly, without their original timbral colorations and inflections, quoted material from expert soloists may become bland and lifeless to disappointed
novices.

In working out the most effective applications of their phrases, artists'
theoretical positions on issues like dissonance can, at times, run counter to
their own aural imaginations. One renowned pianist indignantly rejected another person's transcription of one of his solos because it contained pitches that
the pianist insisted were, from the standpoint of theory, "wrong notes" that he
"couldn't have played." In point of fact, the transcription was accurate. Patterns
that had been acceptable to the pianist's ear in performance deviated from his
theoretical concept of correct practice. To the improviser concerned as much
with the consistency of theoretical method as with the validity of aural imagination, these distressing discrepancies require the accommodation of one to
the other. Such dilemmas are sometimes compounded by the conflicting perspectives of different music cultures. Doc Cheatham cites the case of a great
clarinetist in Fletcher Henderson's band who allegedly lost his improvising
abilities after studying music theory at college. In part, he could never overcome his confusion regarding incompatible features of the harmonic principles
of Western art music and those of jazz.

Within the jazz community's intellectual life, the relationship between theoretical notions and practice remains a source of lively debate. Miles Davis
recalls his argument with Charlie Parker, who maintained that players could
"do anything with chords. I disagreed, told him that you couldn't play D♮ in the
fifth bar of a B♭ blues. He said you could. One night later at Birdland, I heard
Lester Young do it, but he bent the note. Bird . . . just looked over at me with
that 'I told you so' look."[9]

Because of the potentially daunting nature of the dilemmas described
above, some improvisers are ambivalent toward theoretical approaches to improvisation. Their concern is that the approaches might inhibit them, leaving
them preoccupied with following rules, undermining their ability to think creatively. Whatever the forms of representation, jazz players appreciate the vertical aspects of music, and, whatever the pitch relationships players choose to
define as dissonant within the bounds of their jazz idiom or personal style, they
regard the artful handling of dissonance as an indication of mature artistry.

## Originality and Taste

In constructing phrases, considerations of originality and taste intersect judgments about proper practice. Benny Bailey still laughs with appreciation when he considers the sheer innovative qualities of Dizzy Gillespie's forties solos with their unpredictable phrasing, intricate chromaticism, and fresh harmonic concepts. "If you speak to Dizzy, ask him something for me that I wanted to ask him all those years I played in his band. How in the world did he ever think up ideas like that?" Such questions apply to the most subtle gestures of improvisers. Paul Wertico praises older master drummers like Jo Jones for the "insightful little details" in their playing, such as the ways in which Jones "would draw little rim shots out in the middle of a phrase. They're clever. He's like a sly fox, and it makes you laugh. You can feel the mind and the soul behind what he's doing."

Don Pate similarly appreciates innovation. "What's intense about a solo is when somebody does something and it makes one think, 'What's THAT he's playing?' or 'WHERE is that coming from?' or 'HOW did he ever do that?'" With playful language, Pate coins the term *otherwhere* to describe the destination of soloists' explorations—conceptual operations that David Sudnow illumines with his neologism *melodying*.[10] Taken together, the terms are as succinct a definition of the goals and activities of improvisation as any: improvisation is "melodying" to "otherwhere."

Artists' undertakings are not uniformly successful, however. Their travels do not always take them very far. "Someone may play something very obvious and predictable, and you know right away what he's doing," Pate says. Indeed, another improviser describes one bass player's solos colorfully as being "so simple-minded, they're embarrassing to listen to. They find all the common tones and one blue note and drive that into the ground." He continues:

> If you played one of his solos on the trombone, people would say, "Jesus, who is this corny trombone player?" It's like listening to someone read a Dick and Jane book rather than poetry. His phrases sound like "See Spot run." Not everybody has to play the same way or have the same degree of complexity. There are things that Miles and Lester Young did which had classic simplicity and were pristinely beautiful. But this player pitches his solos to the lowest common denominator.

A famous pianist once expressed surprise at the variable quality of ideas in the performance of another highly regarded artist, attributing the discrepancies, in part, to the capricious nature of improvisation. When he followed his friend's performances from phrase to phrase, he was at some moments "bowled over, thinking, 'That's incredible! I could never come up with anything like that,'" whereas at other moments he thought, "Oh, no! What he's doing now is so corny."

One common basis for such criticism is the overuse of conventional jazz vocabulary, the very opposite condition to lacking roots. In rehearsal, a band leader once stopped a newcomer's solo at its outset, scolding, "Everyone plays phrases like that on a Spanish tune. If you can't think of anything else to play, let's play a different tune." Some patterns, however, reveal a soloist's comprehensive knowledge of jazz literature. "You can always tell cats who have the whole body of the music down by the licks that they play, because there are certain licks that are phrased a certain way that you just won't know unless you've listened to a lot of music" (BR).

At the same time, musicians sometimes differ strongly over the precise influences others absorb from the literature. To infuse pitches with a high content of air like Miles Davis may be "fun to do and nice to do for about eight bars or every once in a while," says John McNeil, "but it stamps you as not being very original." Wynton Marsalis questions not only the propriety of borrowing material but also the taste governing its selection when he observes that "some people copy the worst licks of second-rate players." Illustrating yet another consideration, Keith Copeland maintains that there are "certain things that are sacred—that you don't copy—like Art Blakey's press roll." Asserting this value backstage one night after graciously receiving a young singer and listening to a recording that she had brought for appraisal, Betty Carter remarked, "Why are you using scat syllables like 'shoo-bee-doo-bee?' Those belong to Sarah [Vaughan], and they belong to the fifties. What you have to do is to find your own syllables."[11] Other performers raise practical rather than ethical considerations. "You don't try to duplicate certain things that other cats do," Marsalis asserts, "because you could never do it as well as they do. Nobody can get on that tenor saxophone and play like Trane, because he's the only one who can spell out chords and sound good when he does it."

Sensitivity to conventions associated with repertory is as important as the soloist's prudent application of material learned from idols. One renowned pianist objected to a trumpet player's superimposition of a complex chord substitution over a simple blues progression because it created harmonic tension "inappropriate for that kind of tune."[12] In a similar spirit, Barry Harris criticizes performers who constantly pepper improvisations within the framework of "pretty ballads" with blue notes. "It's like the old people used to tell us when we were growing up, 'People who curse the most are generally people who have the fewest words at their command.'" Older musicians also complain about younger performers who routinely "double time" their renditions of ballads, "playing all their licks fast like they do on every other tune," thereby avoiding the challenges of phrasing a beautiful melody at a slow tempo.

From this perspective, improvised performances that fail to preserve the style of their vehicles are "shallow," not bringing out the individuality or depth of pieces, or making understandable "how much there really is to them." As a band leader, Max Roach periodically calls these things to the attention of a musician after a concert, cautioning, "Every piece has its own character. You went outside the character of the piece tonight." Roach does not tell artists exactly what they should play, but allows them to figure out "how to improve their performances along these lines." Similarly, when improvisations by a well-known trumpeter once strayed too far from the appropriate feeling of a ballad, Art Blakey shouted across on the bandstand, "Think of the lyrics; think of the lyrics."[13] These experiences exemplify the balance between discretion and originality that jazz musicians demand from themselves—and from each other.

### Emotional Substance

In the preschool classroom where Harold Ousley is music director, a large tapestry looms with the message "I Feel Therefore I Am." The words might well be an anthem for emotional substance, another important component of the improviser's art. Part and parcel of originality and taste is a performance's "soul," its "spirituality," its "integrity of expression." Musicians refer to the emotional content of improvisations in part by alluding yet again to the metaphor of storytelling. "When you solo, you attack the tune, shading the notes, creating the expression, and getting the idea of how you feel about that tune across to the person who's listening. If they can feel that, then you've told your story" (JR). Similarly, Chuck Israels describes the emotion in Miles Davis's performance (with Cannonball Adderley) of "Autumn Leaves" as "extraordinary; what concentration—what commitment to the feeling of that piece! That's my idea of how to be a performer. When you give it all to the piece."

Ousley describes, as well, the "power of concentration" and analysis required on the part of listeners if they are to interpret a great artist's performances accurately and derive "some kind of feeling or meaning from it." He generally distinguishes "visual listening," with its rich accompanying imagery, from "verbal listening, . . . the ability to hear conversations" in jazz as if a player "were talking to someone." Correspondingly, the skill to incorporate verbal language patterns within improvisations is well recognized in many players, including Lester Young, Charlie Parker and John Coltrane.[14] In the latter regard, Doc Cheatham informs us that "if a guy plays a beautiful solo and he's playing from the heart or he's talking with his horn, we say, 'He's telling a story.' If he's playing bad, we say, 'He plays like he's got rocks in his blood.'" In more general terms, the ability of an instrumentalist to perform with all the nuance of the voice also matters. Trumpeter Joe Louis's "tone had soul and packed so much emotion that it could easily have been mistaken for a woman singing."[15]

Soulful performances embody such affective qualities as pathos, intensity, urgency, fire, and energy—each solo expressively rendered as if it were "the last one you were going to play in your life."[16] Musicians use the term *energy* both literally and figuratively. Just as it requires energy to produce and project sounds on musical instruments, it requires energy for performers to draw upon feelings as they infuse sounds with emotion. Moreover, the sound waves themselves comprise a form of energy that touches listeners physically, potentially also touching them emotionally. Miles Davis remembers distinguishing, at an early age, perfunctory radio performances by white swing bands that "wouldn't go in my body" from the visceral impact of substantive performances by the black bands that inspired his career in jazz.[17] Benny Golson describes the "mystical charm" of Clifford Brown's style, in particular, which "radiated emotional impulses," making listeners "react physically . . . twitch, move your feet . . . as though something tangible was reaching out and shaking [your] body."[18] Because of the close association between music and dance in black music traditions, one indication of successful performances is their effectiveness in inspiring listeners to respond by expressing themselves in varied and subtle ways through myriad forms of dance, as they feel "dispose[d] . . . to bump and bounce, to slow-drag and steady shuffle, to grind, hop, jump, kick, rock, roll, shout, stomp."[19]

Along similar lines, "jazz is not," for Lonnie Hillyer, "about a particular instrument." Rather, in more general terms, it is about "a player's sense of love—love of music and love of life." It involves the "human soul" and the ability to express "the whole span of human emotions from jealousy and love to hate and all of those different things. How some people express this through their music is unbelievable. That's what separates Charlie Parker from many of his imitators." Hillyer also regards Miles Davis as "one of the most gifted people, who knows well how to work with moods when he plays." Once when Hillyer was a "kid back in Detroit," Davis took him along to a dance where he was playing.

> At one point, people were dancing, and he started to play a ballad. The people just stopped dancing and crowded all around him, listening to this cat play this ballad. You know? Miles STOPPED people from dancing, and I'll never forget that as long as I live. That's mood. And of course, Miles can also make people dance when he wants to. Another is Gene Ammons. I was working with Gene Ammons in one of Mingus's big bands when this cat played one note and hushed the whole room. The emotion behind one note, it was fantastic!

The sounds that artists manipulate are sometimes earthy and sensual, other times "gritty," reflecting the rough side of life. Especially evocative are the muted, growling "gutbucket" techniques of horn players, which, for Doc Cheatham, still carry associations of the "gutbuckets" in which plantation slaves carried the entrails of animals. "Bubber [Miley] used to say, 'If it ain't got swing, it ain't worth playin'; if it ain't got gutbucket, it ain't worth doin'."[20] Like the sounds of spirituals, sounds that embody the moods and inflections of the blues signify various facets of African American culture. For W. C. Handy, they reflect "our history, where we came from, and what we experienced"; they harken "back to slavery, back to longing."[21] Duke Ellington recounts that when "[Artie] Whetsol . . . played the funeral march in *Black and Tan Fantasy,* I used to see great, big ole tears running down people's faces," adding, "I like great big ole tears."[22]

Within the broad emotional spectrum of performances, humor, too, assumes its rightful place, as when improvisers display their mastery over the language and tradition of jazz by flaunting its conventions in the creation of musical jokes. Such practices can also be interpreted as a kind of musical signifying, analogous to the practices of certain African American vernacular "rhetorical games."[23] Typically, humor involves deliberately distorting particular musical elements and stretching the limits of form. Humor often allows the artist to operate temporarily outside of formal constraints before successfully returning to them—in the process, teasing listener expectations. One evening Bill Evans concluded a piece by improvising what seemed a limitless series of endings. "You couldn't help but crack up when you heard it. It was amazing that Bill could keep generating cadence after cadence like that" (CI).

Calvin Hill describes the rambunctiousness of Jaki Byard's band during one of their performances as deliberate "rhythmic anarchy." Byard eventually resolved the group's energetic activity with a rhythmic signal, bringing his players back into alignment just moments before the composition's conclusion. In another instance, a trumpeter brought peals of laughter from the audience when he led an intricate melodic line into a simple rhythmic phrase of restricted range, distorting the timbre of its pitches and pulling them increasingly out of tune before resolving the idea.[24] At a concert in Connecticut, Rahsaan Roland Kirk once exploited a similar device to deride a competitor, as the two players traded fours, by imitating and exaggerating the trumpeter's improvisation style to the point of caricature.

Self-conscious verbal parodies periodically woven into performances represent another side of these practices. In response to an abusive audience member who "got up to walk out" on a performance of Charles Mingus's band, Clark Terry once manipulated his trumpet and plunger mute so skillfully that he clearly pronounced the retort, "Go on home! Go on home!" causing the audience to burst into laughter (LH). Mingus and Eric Dolphy carry on a musical dialogue in their classic recording of "What Love" that mockingly depicts a former disagreement between them so faithfully that the listener can almost follow their arguments literally.[25] Conversely, in a popular comedic pantomine routine, drummer Frankie Dunlop used to play recordings by Eddie "Lockjaw"

Davis and Fats Navarro on stage, while he and a female companion interpreted the rapid musical exchanges between saxophone and trumpet as lively banter between husband and wife (HO).

In other instances, performers create jokes by deliberately juxtaposing patterns that are incongruous, quoting a trite popular tune within a sophisticated solo, for example, or shifting a solo's mood unexpectedly.[26] Incongruous elements sometimes permeate a piece's performance. One saxophonist produced hilarity by weaving a medley of nursery rhymes into his improvisations, "swinging them so hard it didn't matter what he played" (TT). Chuck Israels remembers that

> Bill Evans had a way of playing "Take Me Out to the Ball Game" in which the melody was displaced rhythmically, and it, too, was terribly funny. He also did a version of "Tenderly" in which each individual note in the melody was harmonized with a chord which fit it but which didn't fit with the chord that either preceded it or followed it. If you just froze each beat and listened to the melody with its chord, it was just beautiful. But the progression that the chords created together was absolute gibberish and wonderfully funny.

Youngsters commonly begin to respond to such nuances as humor when they absorb enough of the conventions guiding musical logic in jazz to begin anticipating soloists' ideas during performances. One learner remembers a solo in which Kenny Dorham played "this whimsical little chromatic pattern which seemed to be going somewhere, but, in the end, it led right back to the place where it started. It really cracked me up," she recalls. "It was the first time anything I ever heard in music actually made me laugh." As young performers mature, they become increasingly adept at following solos in terms of their subtle shifts in mood. This type of musical apprehension, an alternative to focusing on its technical elements, allows jazz initiates that additional layer of shared meaning—and at times a complementary kind of charged meaning—to tighten their hold on the tradition.

Of his mental involvement as a listener to jazz, Bobby Rogovin recalls, "I thought of the soloist's lines like the way we talk sentences, and I heard all the emotion in them." Rogovin appealingly recapitulates one of his internal commentaries on a performance event as follows: "He's saying this now; he's saying that next. He's sad there. He's getting a little cocky here. He gets a little happy there. He builds up here. He relaxes there. Things phrased in a certain way have a certain meaning. Like if you bend a note, it's almost like trying to be cute. Miles is really good at this. It's not so much the notes he plays as the way he plays the notes." Mentally annotating a performance is common practice among interested, knowledgeable listeners.

As learners develop their skills at listening, they make efforts to deepen feeling in their own performances. This involves control, not only to imbue phrases with particular moods but to sustain and manipulate them over a performance's course—playing off of emotion, in a sense. Harold Ousley emphasizes that an integral feature of the "maturity of musical ideas" is their "emotional content," their "depth of feeling." Life experience is a teacher in this matter. Tommy Turrentine recalls two instances, one during a tour with Max Roach's band and another with Dizzy Gillespie's, in which the leaders, angered by offensive treatment (in the first instance by a rude radio interviewer, and in the second by management), infused their solos with such intensity that the two experiences remain among the "high points" of Turrentine's memories. For Percy Heath, too, the way he plays has "to do with the way you feel that night. You hear that your kid was hit in the face three thousand miles away or you're lonesome and haven't found anybody to talk to or you're tired of the town and sick of each other; it all comes out in the music. . . . You have to know how it feels to be miserable, how it feels to be sad, how it feels to be in the dumps before you can project it. When that slave cried out in the field, he wasn't just making music, he *felt* that way." [27]

For students, responses by a veteran to their own efforts sometimes signal major breakthroughs in development. One student used to take lessons from a great artist who had the reputation of being extremely critical. The teacher listened to him month after month without expressing encouragement. One day, soon after the student's devastating "break-up" with his girlfriend, he "played a blues during my lesson and, somehow, all the welled-up feelings inside me came out. The whole time I played, they filled my sound and just hung in the air around me." At the solo's completion, the teacher stared at him curiously for a long time. "You can have a future in this music if you want it," he suddenly remarked and walked out of the room, leaving behind a student "in shock."

While improvisers strive to project feelings with great conviction, like actors, they must also learn to control them, relating them to other elements of performance. One soloist describes the danger of "too much emotion" potentially hampering a performance and the occasional need to restrain expression rather than "overplay a piece for its intended feeling." [28] Fostered early in such special environments as the preschool classroom whose decorations exhort children "To Feel and Therefore Be," and, more typically, in the musical life of sanctified churches discussed earlier, the fundamental value of expressivity in performance continues to find nourishment at every stage of the artist's education in improvisation.

## Instrumental Virtuosity and the Technical Features of Ideas

Because of the constraints that musical instruments potentially place upon the expression of feelings and ideas, technical command over instruments—

commonly described as chops—is a matter much discussed by artists. "Sometimes, it's exciting just to hear a trumpet played high and fast and clean" (BR). Discerning listeners may "admire the difficult technical aspects" of the ideas of players, Harold Ousley explains, "because it shows they've spent a lot of time developing their technique. Some ideas are built around that." It is a tribute to the skills of great improvisers that performance techniques requiring years of rigorous practice sound effortless in their solos. "There was a time when Miles played a lot of notes too. Those scales would just run in his plate" (TT).

The prowess of some artists is legendary in this regard. Their dexterity and physical adaptability permit them to manipulate instruments as if they were "toys." Many create innovative approaches to performance inspiring the awe of others who play the same instruments, in some instances developing techniques for performing outside the conventional range of the instrument. "One day, if they ever dredge the East River in New York," a swing trumpeter wryly remarks, "they're going to find a whole layer of trumpets on the bottom, because that's what every trumpet player felt like doing with their instruments when Roy Eldridge came to town. No one else could play with that range or that fluently." [29]

Similarly, problems related to the uneven quality of material and manufacture of an instrument or its idiosyncratic characteristics present challenges that great virtuosos have the capacity to overcome. Bass players routinely confront such challenges when sitting in at various sessions, borrowing the instrument of each house bass player rather than "lugging" their own around. This requires them to adapt to instruments of different sizes and to strings of varied tension and gauge arranged at distances different from those on the soundboards of their own instruments. "Many musicians used to complain about that, and they'd blame the instruments when they didn't play in tune or made a puny sound," a drummer says. "But when Wilbur Ware took over the instruments, no matter whose they were, those basses always played in tune, and they filled the whole room with sound. And that was without amplification."

Another account epitomizes the virtuosity of renowned players. Charlie Parker once visited a pawnshop in a European village where a "beaten-up old saxophone" was displayed in the window for the equivalent of twenty-five dollars. Despite its unplayable condition, Parker tried out the instrument and performed a solo with such incredible facility that the astonished shopkeeper immediately raised the instrument's price three hundred dollars when Parker left the shop. [30]

Beyond the issue of natural talent, musicians account for the capabilities of players according to their discipline. "He never was that much of a practicer," a friend explained after hearing a trumpeter's "shaky" intonation and muffled execution of a few pitches on a recording. "Other players, like Woody Shaw, never stop practicing."

While praising individuals for their technical mastery, musicians rarely appreciate such accomplishment as an end in itself. Many distinguish the physical strength and technical dexterity that performers sometimes exploit in "empty displays of virtuosity" from the ability to play with sensitivity, to create meaningful music with an instrument. Artists are alert to these distinctions in their own musical development. "I can't say that I've become a better player technically, but I have become a more expressive player," Tommy Flanagan remarks. "I can feel better about what I play because I have been playing so long that I can express it better than I did twenty or thirty years ago, although I may have played better technically then. I play with more feeling now than I did then. I played what I knew I could play then, and now I play what I feel I can play, which is the way I've grown musically."

Similarly, Lonnie Hillyer was "another kind of player when he was nineteen." He does not try to use the trumpet "as technically" as in the past. Twenty years ago, he might have been "a little better—played stronger, higher, and with more endurance." He regards that as "a physical thing" he could master again if he wanted to. "I don't look for that in the trumpet anymore," he insists. "All I'm looking for is to get what I feel through the horn. When I was younger it was like I was trying to get what Dizzy felt through the horn, but, eventually, it's got to come to be about you. Emotions are what it's all about."

In evaluating other artists, Hillyer also distinguishes between "feeling players" and "sound players," the latter referring specifically to musicians whose sounds are beautiful by conventional standards of Western classical music. Trumpeter Freddie Webster's sound was "so pretty, so big and forceful," Hillyer says, that "he had to stand far back from the microphone in order to blend with the rest of the band." Similarly, Clifford Brown, whose style was strongly influenced by Fats Navarro, "had one of the purest sounds you ever heard. His notes used to reach out and just shake. It was almost like what he played was really secondary."

Hillyer contrasts sound players to such feeling players as Miles Davis, Kenny Dorham, and Blue Mitchell. "Blue was a cat who felt what he played, and he was the most intricate kind of player." Mitchell, however, because problematic trumpet technique limited his ability to project his sound, just "whispered" his ideas and feelings through his horn rather than singing them vibrantly as did Clifford Brown. Similarly, Billie Holiday epitomizes feeling singers: "Her voice had little to do with technique; it was the sound of her soul" (RB). Such performances embody traditional African American musical values that feature a varied timbral palette and encourage soloists to develop their own personal sound. In fact, artists like Miles Davis are often praised as "sound innovators," players who redefine the possibilities of their instruments and even put to rest the notion that an instrument itself has a limited capacity for expression.[31]

Hillyer's general distinction between sound and feeling players does not imply that individuals who produce "beautiful sounds" are necessarily less expressive or less unique than their counterparts or that musicians without "beautiful sounds" are simply, by nature of that fact, expressive. Rather, the special affection that musicians have for feeling players merely underscores the value that the jazz community attaches to expressiveness, irrespective of whether the sounds conform to conventional notions of beauty in the Western classical music tradition. In fact, the values that are associated with Western classical music sometimes provide a basis for contention among jazz players. A bass player once announced that he no longer planned to perform with a renowned saxophonist because the latter had "screwed up his sound" by studying technique with a classical music teacher, thereby losing the rich personal marks that had formerly distinguished his style.

## Storytelling Ability

Once again employing the metaphor of storytelling, the jazz community praises such attributes as the suspenseful development of ideas and the dramatic shaping of sound. These represent values related to those described earlier: the artist's ability to tell personal stories and to convey emotion through music. Trumpeter Thad Jones likens the experience of listening to Roy Eldridge's solos to "being caught up in a thrilling mystery novel that you can't put down."[32] Eldridge himself found a comparable model for performance in the playing of Louis Armstrong, who "built his solos like a book—first, an introduction, then chapters, each one coming out of the one before and building to a climax."[33] Similarly, for Dizzy Gillespie, "superior organization" is what makes a great solo: "This leads into that, this leads into that."[34]

When great artists explore ideas with the force of conviction, they mesmerize the audience by moving toward goals with such determination and logic that their direction seems inevitable, their final creations compelling. Among the "hippest thing[s]" Wynton Marsalis's father showed him was a Coltrane solo in which the whole solo formed a beautiful melodic curve, "and the key points in the phrases he was playing all went in a line."[35] Greg Langdon compares the gradual acquisition of dramatic precision and skill in executing ideas to the experience of an aspiring baseball player who initially must learn "to meet the ball with the bat," but ultimately strives to learn "how to place the ball."

In musical terms, the first challenge is to "make the changes" by correctly negotiating the structure of a piece and complementing the logic of its underlying progression. Failed improvisations, whether of melodists or drummers, tend to be "disconnected demonstrations of technique removed from the piece's form. After a minute, you wouldn't know where a guy was in the solo" (AT). One distraught pupil described his frustration at "getting stuck" within particular key centers, "playing up and down" their related scales but unable to figure out how "to get out of" the tonality of one and into that of another. Only after analyzing vocabulary phrases whose movements described key changes and absorbing their general characteristics could he begin to invent new patterns that met the minimal requirements of logical harmonic practice, improvising through progressions with steady streams of harmonically correct pitches. The second challenge, akin to "placing the ball," is to achieve the expressive treatment of pitches by "breaking up" their streams into interesting ideas "thematically and rhythmically."

An additional aspect of a musical story's logic is the motivic development of material. The insistent intrusion of physical reflexes sometimes complicates this objective. One student remembers, for example, the laughter of players at his improvisatory slip when, at the conclusion of a solo, he inadvertently departed from the bebop figure he had been developing by playing a cadential Dixieland figure. Directives of the verbalized or singing mind that suggest a rigid use of vocabulary can also be a problem. Very early, John McNeil discovered that "if you try to force something that you've learned into your solos, say a phrase that is real hip, it will sound really contrived, like it doesn't have anything to do with what you just played before it." To avoid the artificial ring of musical non sequiturs, Miles Davis cautions soloists to develop the ideas that enter their imaginations as they improvise rather than being overly dependent on preplanned patterns: "Play what you hear, not what you know," he advises.[36]

While negotiating the practical challenges inherent in thematic maneuvers, improvisers consider various aesthetic issues. One thing Chuck Israels notices in a player is "whether he hangs onto a motive long enough to follow his investigation of it, or whether he is just rambling from one thing to another." Naive notions about the search for new ideas sometimes obscure such considerations for novices and lead them to strive for radically different patterns from phrase to phrase. When this tendency deprived my early solos of coherence, Ken McIntyre taught me about melodic sequences. His direction subjected me, for the first time, to the discipline of using discrete melodic ideas as a solo's conceptual basis. Also, I was unaware of how effective subtle embellishments and slight variations on particular musical models could be in transforming them. Thus, I continued being concerned about sounding repetitious. As I was absorbing McIntyre's teaching, however, I realized that I had begun to create solos that were not static but unified and distinct. Not long afterward, at a jam session, a young musician familiar with my considerable limitations as an improviser expressed astonishment. "I never heard you sound so together. I'm not sure what it was, but your solo sounded like something you might even hear on a record."

Too strong a reliance on repetitive devices can, nevertheless, render solos too predictable, bogging down a story. "You need repetition as a basic part of musical form, but what you want is both repetition and development," Israels says. "It's a matter of how much change you want and when you want the change in a solo. Artists are always juggling such things, either instinctively or analytically." In Lee Konitz's view, contemporary learning practices that "overemphasize" sequences cause improvisers to err on the side of repetition, "sounding like they're playing out of exercise books. Two-five-one patterns are essential material certainly, but by itself, it doesn't lead to an organic kind of playing. It's a contrivance."

Similarly, after once composing a solo for students, Barry Harris reconsidered its opening phrases, in which the second imitated the first in a different key. "No, let's change that," he remarked, as a prelude to performing a variation on the transposed phrase. "Sequences should not be so obvious." There are times, however, when mature soloists abandon their reservations about repetition in order to create specific dramatic effects. They may perform a short phrase continuously for several measures to create momentum and suspense within a solo, heightening the listener's expectation for change.

Whereas some features of a musical story's logic derive from the motivic relationships of successive phrases and from their complementary relationships to chords, other features derive from the general flow of successfully improvised lines, lines with a continuity of rhythmic feeling and "smoothness" in their contours. They convey an ongoing sense of melodic coherence produced by the adjoinment of especially complementary shapes. In contrast, the early efforts of youngsters to improvise produce characteristically "jagged" lines. They "still sound young" to the experienced artist. In the beginning, "I didn't have the incredible flow of ideas that the players I admired did. You mature into that," Tommy Flanagan remarks. Eventually, learners increase their control over the precise shaping of melodies, "rounding off their edges." In part, this entails figuring out how to extend vocabulary patterns effectively. "If you're putting two phrases together when the chords change, one thing has to flow into the other," Harold Ousley says. Curtis Fuller gratefully acknowledges Barry Harris's crucial role in teaching him and his young friends how to achieve this essential quality in their playing, "how to flow . . . the hardest thing to learn." Ultimately, learners distinguish aesthetically pleasing possibilities for expanding melodic shapes that convey a sense of forward motion and momentum, rejecting other possibilities that by comparison would be awkward or illogical—"a fragmented series of things, a bunch of isolated fragments," as Lonnie Hillyer puts it. Hillyer sometimes keeps "one simple thing" in mind with a solo, "playing it from beginning to end as one complete thing."

Jazz is "real linear music in terms of the way it goes forward," Akira Tana says. "You're developing linearly whether you play a saxophone or the drums. I understand more about this conceptually than I did three or four years ago." In the beginning, Tana could "embellish phrases rhythmically, but had no control over where they would end up." Similarly, a young trumpeter routinely "began his solos well, but they always seemed to fall apart very quickly." He could conceive interesting patterns before he began playing, but quickly lost their thread in performance. Some artists compare the efforts of young soloists to those of children learning to speak. Although periodically producing actual words, correct word groupings, and even credible short sentences within stretches of garbled sound, they cannot yet consistently convey meaning.[37] Even for experienced jazz artists, control over such features remains a variable of improvisations. Tommy Flanagan "can't say when it became easy because it's still not easy. Sometimes, you still have days when you just don't feel right, like there's some kind of congestion, and the flow isn't there. You're just not playing clearly."

In evaluating the stories that improvisers tell, musicians also consider the overall range of compositional materials in use and their imaginative treatment. "In a good solo, there should be variety in rhythm, melody, form, texture, color, development, contrast and balance, and so on," Fred Hersch maintains. "Either that, or one aspect should be worked at so intensely that it transcends the need for all the others." Artists are vulnerable in the latter case, however, when they fall short of their goals. The musician quoted earlier criticizing a bass player for "finding all the common tones" in his solos and "driving them into the ground" adds: "I do it too, sometimes. I run out of steam, sometimes. Okay? I can play the sharp nine on a dominant chord and just sit there playing that and the flatted third degree of a blues for a chorus or two. But I don't do it forever, and at least I look for some rhythmic invention."

Concerned with comparable pitfalls, Barry Harris constantly critiques student solos when their emphasis on particular elements causes the neglect of others. At times, he reminds them to "break up the running of scales" with varied intervals, chords, and arpeggios. "Different intervals are what's pretty!" When student inventions lack harmonic nuance, Harris playfully exhorts them: "Remember to use your diminishes and your augmenteds." Harris, as often, emphasizes rhythmic variety: "Don't forget different rhythms. Rhythm is what's pretty!"

From moment to moment, changes as basic as those produced by introducing sustained pitches and rests within a solo's busier rhythmic activity can provide welcome contrast. Alterations as subtle as periodic repetitions of pitches within a scalar pattern can also be very effective, standing out from neighboring musical shapes. The same principle of variety is likewise found in broader gestures. A case in point is the style of Booker Little, whose solos characteristically include high sustained vocal cries, short interjections of phrases with speechlike cadences and rhythms, long, rapid passages mixing complex scalar and chordal elements, and melodies with simple singable qualities often treated as sequences.

There are limitless aspects of performance to satisfy the music's insatiable demand for variety, and improvisers are open to them all. Carmen Lundy's accompanist offered invaluable advice about dynamics, reminding her that singing in a "whisper" could be as effective as "screaming to get your message across." Wynton Marsalis recalls, "A cat once came up to me after a solo, and said, 'Well, man, play low.' I said, 'Damn, that's valid. I really don't play enough in the lower register.'" Such feedback keeps improvisation's infinite considerations before musicians, enhancing the dramatic qualities of their stories.

With criticism received or overheard, learners gradually become more discriminating themselves in their evaluations of players, able to distinguish those individuals whose handling of the language of jazz is sophisticated and varied, replete with clever turns of phrase. "When Tommy Flanagan plays, every note of his is saying something," Fred Hersch remarks. "He doesn't throw a note away. He has his own little language, and you listen for the subtleties in his playing as you would listen to the subtleties in a Mozart piece. Like the way Tommy might make a change of voicing here, a little change of quality, the way a melodic line will kind of halt at a certain moment and turn back on itself, the way he'll extend a little motive. Anybody who has a sense of musicality will hear what he's doing. He's just communicating."

A related concern is the pacing of ideas over an improvisation's larger course. "Does the solo's feeling sustain, mount, diminish, and change from chorus to chorus and within a chorus?" Chuck Israels asks. Reflecting a similar understanding, Emily Remler usually "does the old climb-up-and-come-down action—build and release, tension and resolve. That's a great thing," she asserts. In part, the acquisition of the ability to create increasingly sophisticated and longer musical patterns facilitates this process, thinking "in terms of whole choruses instead of two-bar and four-bar phrases," she continues. "Building the tension over a whole chorus and ending on the 'one' of the next chorus for the release are very typical things to do, but it takes a certain sense of maturity."

Mature soloists constantly balance such factors as predictability and surprise, repetition and variation, continuity and change, displaying the discipline to make choices among different possibilities and to work with them methodically throughout a performance. In one instance, Miles Davis confines one chorus of his solo on "Blues by Five" to the trumpet's middle register, featuring a short, repeated off-beat rhythmic figure and varying the timbres and inflections of its restricted pitches. In another chorus, he shifts the emphasis from rhythm and timbre to melody, improvising longer, artfully shaped phrases and climbing slightly higher in range. In yet another, he provides contrast and excitement by leading his melody with an arpeggiated leap into the instrument's high register, gradually descending with intricate chromatic movements (ex. 8.25d). Improvisers also create climactic events in solos by gradually increasing the rhythmic density of their creations.

Before cultivating the mental rigor to handle varied musical elements within a solo successfully, measuring their application, young musicians meet frequent criticism for "trying to play everything they know all the time on every tune." Tommy Turrentine refers to "cats who jump out there like it's the last tune they'll ever play. They blow their load even before they're out of the second chorus. That's pitiful." Similarly, Barry Harris criticizes a young player for failing to allow his ideas to develop "organically," instead "forcing" the conclusions of solos with "screaming," contrived intensity. "Endings must come naturally," Harris insists. "You're supposed to let it happen, not just to make it happen like that."

Ultimately, just as jazz musicians differ in their abilities to imbue musical patterns with the subtleties of wit and emotion, they differ in their abilities to control and develop their ideas overall. Some are simply better storytellers than others. Carrying listeners with them through each stage, their solos begin with patterns having the character of "real beginnings," build to a climax, perhaps through a series of peaks, and close with patterns having the character of formal endings.[38]

"Timeless masterpieces," exemplary solos are regarded as works of art equal to the compositions that serve as their vehicles (AF). Some solos even surpass them. Barry Harris praises the young Miles Davis for "improvising his own song over the song he was playing," that is, for "playing beautifully, lyrically, not just playing lines." Similarly, many improvisers strive to create solos that, whether in theory or practice, lend themselves to repeated listening and performance. "You can create new melodies in your solo that can become the melody of a new song," Buster Williams says. "I want my playing to have that kind of cohesiveness, that connection, that kind of syntax."[39]

As described earlier, compositions sometimes actually do evolve from the player's own improvisation of solos, and occasionally instrumentalists adopt another player's recorded solo as the basis for a composition. Finally, the vocalese composer's creation of lyrics for improvisations reinforces the narrative features of invention, giving literal translation to the metaphor of storytelling for improvisation, showcasing the dramatic musical content of outstanding solos.

### The Spontaneity, in Relation to the Uniqueness, of Invention

Spontaneity of conception also figures into the jazz community's evaluation of improvisation. To his description, given earlier, of his excitement in formulating a solo "as it goes," progressing "naturally" toward an undetermined "punch line," Buster Williams adds, "If it was all thought out before it was done, there would be no need to do it, you know?" As Williams implies, many musicians go into improvisations with a minimal plan of events and with the intention of limiting the predictable use of formerly mastered vocabulary. The intention is, rather, to apply general principles of solo formulation to ideas as they come to the player's mind. This attitude both maximizes the challenges associated with composing music in performance and optimizes the possibilities for conceiving imaginative ideas.

"I try not to be a repeater pencil" is Lester Young's clever encapsulation of the nature of spontaneity.[40] If "I were to try to play mechanically, playing things that I've worked out before," John McNeil explains, "it might make me sound real good, but it would also make me feel guilty—as if I haven't really done anything good. I'd prefer to make things up as I go along. You never make everything up," he concedes, "but I'd like to make it up as much as I can with the smallest amount of prefiguring possible." Red Rodney also has "licks that identify me, but I try to create all the time. I may not succeed all the time," he admits, "but when I do, and I surprise myself, that's when I'm the happiest. I get the most rewarding feelings when, instead of playing what I'm comfortable with and know is going to sound good, I try something different and it works."

Doc Cheatham adopted comparable goals after analyzing his idol's performances.

> That's the trick that I learned in Chicago. If you went to hear trumpet players like Louis Armstrong, for instance, they would play any tune like "Chinatown," and they'd play fifteen or thirty different choruses, and they would never repeat the same thing. They had so much talent. Every time they'd play a tune, the solo would be different, unless there was some little gimmick that they would want to do. Like on "King Porter Stomp," they would always jump back to play little breaks [patterns played without accompaniment] and things like that.

As discussed earlier, however, the absolute equation of spontaneity and unique invention with solo formulation belies the varied music-making practices favored by jazz players. Artists bring different individual attitudes to improvisation as a compositional process and engage in different degrees of preparation for particular performances. Where precisely along this spectrum musicians are located is something that fellow band members can freely observe as, night after night, they hear artists' solos on the same compositions.

One of his associates describes Lester Young's response to a trumpeter with Count Basie who "took the same solo on a certain tune every night, and when he'd start Lester would look at me and say, 'Damn, Lady Kay, there he goes again,' and we'd sing the whole solo note for note right along with the trumpet player." At the other end of the spectrum, Jimmy Heath recalls his and John Coltrane's reactions when listening to Dizzy Gillespie's introduction to "I Can't Get Started," which Gillespie's big band performed regularly: "He'd play it differently each time, and we'd look at each other in amazement."[41]

Some improvisers are not as concerned with spontaneity as an issue in its own right. Relying more heavily on well-liked prefigured material, they strive instead to enliven its use during each performance with nuances of interpretation and embellishment. From improvisation to improvisation, they infuse features that are similar with fresh conviction and emotion, whether negotiating stretches of planned vocabulary or an entire through-composed solo.

In some instances, the issue of spontaneous invention is tied to personal limitations. "I'll teach students different chord voicings for a tune each week," a pianist complains, "but some always come back playing the tune the last way I showed them. They can't seem to remember earlier voicings or to figure out how to mix them in new combinations when they play." More often, as their need to rely strictly on preplanned models for improvisation gradually diminishes, students develop their skills and abilities over time. Years ago, Lou Donaldson would "work out little patterns" for solos, but generally he does not "have to now."

Similarly, Warren Kime used to perform entire Harry James solos in public when learning how to play jazz. "Many people thought I could improvise at the time, but I really couldn't yet." Don Sickler took a similar tack in his own youth, aurally composing original solos outside of performance, but "switching them around" from event to event to create the impression that he had improvised them. Another musician "wrote out" and memorized solos for his first few recording dates in an effort to avoid making "mistakes" that might jeopardize the performances of his "more spontaneous" band members. With experience, Kime, Sickler, and countless others acquired skill and confidence, relying less and less on such practices.

The artist's response to wide-ranging performance variables influences the spontaneous aspect of invention. Having to perform under the pressure of a slightly faster tempo than customary for an artist can provide a useful psychological edge and inspire creative thinking, but very fast tempos may cause the artist to rely heavily on preplanned and repetitive material.[42] "There is one player I heard recently," Lee Konitz says,

> who can be very razzle-dazzle, and this is very impressive to me. I give him credit for the dues he had to pay to be able to do that, but his playing always feels worked out. He must play pretty much simi-

larly all the time, because he plays at a certain tempo where you can't improvise too much. That's a sock-it-to-me kind of energy and the whole philosophy behind it is to make an effect. He's like a lot of players who are always preparing and calculating for the home run when they solo. They can deliver that kind of a blow with the music and it's very effective. But for someone who demands more, the effect is suddenly over and done with and you're not going to get any more.

When Konitz's own performances develop comparable difficulties, becoming "technical and mechanical," he tries to slow the tempo down so that he can be affected by his "own notes."

The length of an improvisation is also germane. When solos are long, improvisers may "run out of ideas" and fall back on an uninspired use of their vocabulary. "Sometimes, if I really extend myself and play more than two or three choruses," Harold Ousley says, "I find it hard to keep creating." Indeed, for their general limitations, some improvisers are characterized as "two-chorus players."[43] Others, like Art Tatum and Coleman Hawkins, amaze their admirers by creating improvisations that remain "interesting chorus after chorus," displaying an "ability that comes with years of playing and study" (TF).

A piece's formal properties also potentially influence the player's approach, with "rapidly changing harmonies" allowing less time for the flexible treatment of vocabulary patterns and motivic development, perhaps, than for modal structures.[44] A musician may work out a complete model solo for a piece based on complex harmonic movements to ensure a competent performance, yet, in the case of another piece, rely upon planned licks to negotiate only particular features of the progression. Barry Harris recalls such moments even in solos by the most creative musicians, punning, "When they reached the bridge of 'Cherokee,' they'd be lickin' like dogs." Stories abound concerning keen critical powers sometimes applied specifically to the inspired use of ideas. Charlie Mariano describes jam sessions in Boston, for example, which were packed with musicians who socialized boisterously while others performed for them. Whenever musical events progressed to the most difficult sections of choruses, however, it would "suddenly become so quiet in there, you could hear a pin drop." Once the listeners had discerned whether soloists had discovered new ways to play particular chord changes or whether they had simply repeated the same phrases used during previous choruses, the audience instantly resumed its animated interaction.

The advice Miles Davis once gave Curtis Fuller after having heard him perform a solo also speaks to the importance of spontaneity in creative invention. Davis "said in his hoarse whisper, 'Hey, man, every time you get to that part of the tune, you keep playing the same thing. You keep playing that B♭ minor against that D♭ sound. Sounds too dark every time you get there. Get with a piano player and work on something new." Fuller recalls that "it sounded cruel and harsh at the time, but I realized he was right, and it enhanced my growth." In another instance, Charles Mingus once actually reduced a promising young saxophonist to tears, before an audience, with his running commentary of "Play something different, man; play something different. This is jazz, man. You played that last night and the night before."

Artists can avoid such problems by treating planned phrases flexibly—creatively displacing, varying, and recombining them as underpinnings for new ideas. Additionally, repeating phrases in relation to particular segments of a lengthy progression separated by stretches of contrasting material presents risks different from those an artist faces if repeating phrases within short forms, where similar phrases are more likely to be noticed.[45]

Many describe their performance histories as ongoing cycles of creativity during which the proportion of old to new musical ideas conceived during a particular composition's solos constantly changes. At early stages of the cycle, as when initially learning a new piece, improvisers may plan particular patterns that, from performance to performance, result in a high degree of fixity in the display of their ideas. Arriving at the cycle's later stages, a player, having become comfortable with a piece's structure, may take greater liberty with patterns, varying or departing from them frequently in the conception of new phrases. This is observable, for example, in Booker Little's solo on "Bee Vamp," alternate takes of which reveal a high concentration of planned and repeated phrases. At the same time, Little's actual treatment of the phrases distinguishes each take.[46] In the first, the shorter of the two, he appears to interpret the material rigidly, as if he had designed its underlying model as a composer's sketch or warm-up routine, a prelude to the second performance's more radical departures.

The same cycle may be reinitiated as an artist adds the latest inventions created within the piece's form to the vocabulary store, and they recur with increasing frequency in subsequent improvisations. Should the patterns gradually coalesce into longer chains of ideas that comprise another relatively fixed model for the solo, the artist once again strives to use them judiciously. "Oh, God, I've played this a million times before," John McNeil sometimes says to himself during a performance. "'What am I doing standing up here playing?' I feel like this when it gets to the point where I can almost write my solo down before I play it."

Similar changes in the relative fixity of ideas can cut across the solos associated with different pieces. Even without planning specific patterns, improvisers commonly develop habits of musical thought. These habits evolve out of the general use of their language or the focus of their latest practice routines, both of which lead them to favor particular current patterns and composite phrases among their otherwise unique features of solos. Artists accept the ebb and flow of inspiration as an inevitable condition of the creative process, but many endure considerable frustration at the bottom of their creative cycles when, as is characteristic, they cannot anticipate their next breakthroughs. McNeil articulates how the cycle itself can inform an artist over time. He knows that he is "just about to make some progress when everything sounds so boring that I hate what I play. Then, right about that time, for some reason, I get a whole lot better. I improve a lot and I improve real fast. But then I reach another point where I don't improve, and I'll just stay the same for a while. It's always worked that way for me."

The constitution of players and their physical command of material affects the larger concern of spontaneous and unspontaneous musical conception. "I haven't been touching my guitar at all since my last recording date," Emily Remler admits at one point. "I guess I just got sick of my playing. Now, I'm struggling to get back to where I was because I lose the vocabulary so quickly. So lately, I haven't been surprising myself when I play. You have to stay in good physical shape for that." From Jimmy Robinson's perspective, the fact that improvisers "have bad nights is understandable because that's the way your body is. It doesn't respond the same way every night, and you can't be as consistent as you would like. Some nights are real good, and others you just can't do a thing." He adds that lack of the proper rest can prevent the body from responding as it should. Once Robinson returns to a regular practice schedule and, as he says, "my chops get right, then I'll get the freedom to play like I know I can, and I'll be able to surprise myself in my playing again."

Relaxation, mental and physical, is an essential ingredient in the dynamics of performing. Extreme conditions reveal the extent of its importance and may override that of other aspects of performance described earlier. As a case in point, years ago at a jam session, Warren James improvised a solo in the early hours of the morning when, he says, "I was so tired that I could hardly stand up." He was sure he did not have the energy needed for the task. When he got to the bandstand, however, his mind and body were so relaxed that, for the first time, "I really let go and played by far the best solo I had ever played in my life." Conversely, tension can severely compromise a performance, causing rigid muscles and inhibiting a soloist's breath control, ultimately undermining flexibility and, at times, endurance, range, and phrasing. Moreover, tension can block powers of concentration and imagination. "The main problem is to free your mind when you play," says Art Farmer. "I find that in my own playing, whenever I feel any kind of tension, I'm restricted to playing the most fundamental kinds of things."

Predisposition toward risk on the part of an artist's personality, to whatever degree, is an influence on improvisation, already widely perceived to heighten the vulnerability of the artist. "I have seen great musicians have a horrible time with their playing some evenings," Joe Giudice says. "Any fertile mind will have difficulty at times. When someone is trying to discard some things he has already mastered and tries to put something else in its place, he's going to cut some hogs." Not all artists are willing to tolerate risk in equal measure. One musician expressed his reluctance to learn new improvisation approaches, which would require him to "live with sounding bad for six months or more" as he gradually mastered fresh materials and learned to integrate them successfully into more familiar vocabulary. Red Rodney has observed a dwindling of spontaneity in the work of some artists as time takes its toll. "Now, as some people get older, they just play all their tricks. I can hear that in great, great names in jazz. Those are players who are no longer interested in creating all the time."

When evaluating a performance, the improviser typically favors inconsistency in the service of spontaneous, creative exploration over consistency in less extemporaneous invention. "If you're closed, then the music can't take you anywhere. It's just back to 'Well, now I'm going to play this, and then I'm going to play that' " (DP). Most admired among players are the controlled risk takers, those who are neither complacent in performance nor overconfident, routinely overreaching their abilities. Within the bounds they set for themselves, consummate artists expertly turn musical miscalculations into "musical gems."[47]

## Evolving a Unique Voice within the Jazz Tradition

On the grand scale of judging the overall contribution of the artist to jazz, a fundamental criterion for evaluation is originality, also a highly valued component within an individual solo. The categories against which improvisers evaluate originality correspond roughly to the definitive stages of artistic development described earlier by Walter Bishop Jr.: imitation, assimilation, and innovation. It is to be expected that only some individuals within the jazz community complete the succession of developmental stages and realize success within them.

Musicians who remain at the imitative end of the spectrum enjoy the least prestige. Some, having undergone the years of intensive training required to develop fundamental improvisation skills, succeed only in absorbing the most general performance conventions of a particular jazz idiom. Although at times receiving praise for "competence," they are often characterized as "generic improvisers." One unsympathetic artist views their solos as comprising "the same phrases you hear from everyone else, a string of acceptable, idiomatically correct pieces of jazz vocabulary, riffs, and motives—little figurations, all strung together in a trite and uninspired way."

Displaying greater ability, but equally vulnerable to criticism, are "clones," musicians whose keen ears enable them to absorb an idol's precise style, but who improvise exclusively within its bounds. One famous musician, in responding to a question on this issue, referred to the disciple of another renowned artist as a "clone" but added, "You have to give him credit just for being able to play that well. Still, it's odd to hear someone sounding so much like somebody else all the time." Commonly, the predominant influence on clones changes over their careers.

Related to clones, but a step removed, are "eclectic improvisers." Their solos reflect diverse apprenticeships, presenting a hodgepodge of the traits of different idols, but fail to personalize them or to integrate them into a unified style.

As an observer of jazz for over thirty years, Art Farmer comments:

> I have seen a lot of things come and go. Basically, ninety-nine and nine-tenths percent of everybody out there is just copying somebody else. Here in New York, I remember every piano player was trying to play like Horace Silver at one time, and then later on, everybody was trying to play like Bill Evans. Some of the guys who were playing like Horace a couple of years later were trying to play like Bill. And then everybody was trying to play like McCoy Tyner. It's just something that comes and goes. Horace was dominant at one time and everyone dug that, and then along came Bill with a different style.

Although imitation is a mode that all players go through in their formative years, the direction they take from there marks varying levels of achievement along the continuum from imitation to innovation. Soloists who have reached the assimilative stage command greater attention and respect than those who have not. For an individual "fully to play himself, rather than to sound like someone else, is possibly the hardest thing to do," Gary Bartz says candidly. The difficulties are widely recognized within the jazz community. "To actually come up with that sound," identifiably expressing a musician's individuality, "is something that everybody dreams about, but not a whole lot of people have actually achieved" (JH).

In fact, the emergent voices of most artists include varied mixtures of their own stylistic features and those of an idol or idols. One trumpeter "was essentially playing Dizzy Gillespie," whereas another was playing himself, "which had Gillespie in it, as well as some other trumpet players."[48] Bobby Rogovin recalls Lee Morgan saying in a *Down Beat* interview that although he did not create a new performance idiom, he had a "certain identity." Rogovin elaborates, "He means he played a lot of the same things other people played, but it came out Lee Morgan. Most of the great players are all coming from the same tradition, but they're just putting their own identity on it."

Artists in the assimilation stage typically develop a unique voice within the bounds of a particular performance school. Once having established their personal identities, many are not concerned with larger gestures of change. "Some people are supposed to sustain certain areas of this music, and they don't look for anything new. That's their thing," Walter Bishop Jr. states, "and I appreciate them for what they do." Improvisers who "play earlier styles are like musical monuments" to Arthur Rhames. "They represent particular schools of jazz and provide excellent examples for younger players who pass through those schools." Tommy Flanagan muses, "It's really interesting the way different people arrive at something that they're comfortable with, a way of playing and being. . . . Even if Clifford Brown had lived longer, I think he still would have sounded just like Clifford."

Moving along the continuum of artistic achievement are improvisers whose development moves through the stages of successful assimilation and fashioning of identities to innovation. They create personal approaches to improvisation that influence large numbers of followers across different instruments, in some instances forming the basis for a new performance school. Commonly, these artists devote the remainder of their careers to exploring the possibilities for invention within the framework of their new concepts. "Coleman Hawkins always sounded the same to me," Flanagan continues. "Charlie Parker also sounded about the same from the first time I heard him till the last time I heard him. It seemed to me that he had gone as far as he could go on the saxophone." At the same time, myriad subtleties within the improvisation styles of unique artists like Lester Young continue to change over an artist's career.[49]

Presenting yet another profile as innovators are artists whose musical explorations lead them beyond the bounds of the idiom in which they establish their initial identity. "McCoy Tyner is one of those people whose style evolved from when I first heard him," Flanagan recalls.

> When I first heard him, I thought that his style was going to change, although I don't know many pianists like that. It's just like five or six years made the difference in some people's playing. Like Herbie Hancock and Chick Corea also basically played the way I was playing at one time. But they were still moving; they were in a period of transition. They moved along compositionally, and their keyboard technique moved right along with it. I also remember hearing Cecil Taylor when he was playing standards with Steve Lacy's group. He was on his way then, developing to where he is now.

In the rarest instances, leading innovators pass through a succession of influential stages during their careers. Retaining their personal identities by carrying over characteristic elements of tone color, phrasing, and vocabulary from one stage to another, they cultivate different approaches to music making that excite the imaginations of other performers and provide the foundation for successful musical movements.

With his roots in bebop, Miles Davis helped form the basis for particular schools of hard bop, cool jazz, modal jazz, and free forms of improvisation, and, most recently, jazz-rock fusion.[50] "Miles Davis was always a big sense of direction for us in the fifties and sixties," Buster Williams recalls. "Each time a record came out with Miles and the band, it created a new dimension for me. It was like a new awakening." Calvin Hill similarly remembers that "in the old days when I used to buy records, I was always into Miles, whatever Miles came up with. Like, you could hardly wait for the newest Miles Davis record to come out because you knew he was going to come out with something different. You just couldn't wait. You'd go and buy the record and rush home and put it on and see what was new."

John Coltrane's personal style also evolved through different innovative stages in which he contributed to schools of hard bop, modal improvisation, and free jazz.[51] "You can always let people know that you're still evolving. You can show people signs of what you're working on. Trane always did that. He always had periods of where you say, 'Wow, where is he going next?' He kept moving" (TF). Arthur Rhames credits Coltrane with being "able to see what should be done after he had passed through the hard bop school in order to expand the music. From listening to Trane's early albums to the last, you can hear a steady progression, a continuous, sequential order that goes from one album to the next. He was constantly plotting each course, each step he was taking to be an expansion of the last step. That's the highest type of mature artist in the music."

It is only a minority of individuals whose passage from imitation to innovation produces compelling visions with major ramifications for other players and for their field. "We all take more from them than we do from one another" (RR).

### Accommodating Musical Change

As the larger tradition of jazz constantly changes, certain junctures in its evolution generate turbulence in which artists reappraise their personal values, musical practices, and styles in light of innovations then current. Individuals may find themselves closed to new ideas at one time and open to them at another, adaptable in one case and rigid in another. Between such poles, deep ambivalence can confound the musician. Tommy Turrentine "wasn't very experienced playing before the transition from swing to bebop came along. When I first heard Dizzy Gillespie, I got confused and I said, 'Wait a minute! I gotta stop playing and decide if I want to play like Dizzy!' It sounded funny at first: right but wrong, wrong but right." A generation later, a bebop performer described comparable skittishness in the face of the free jazz movement. "I'd get up to solo and wouldn't know what to do: to play the chord changes or to ignore them—just play colors, textures. Sometimes, I'd let a whole chorus go by without playing, turn around, and walk off the stage. I had to drop out of the scene for a while and figure out what direction I wanted to go in."

New ways of improvising raise the passions of advocates and adversaries alike, causing a realignment of loyalties within the jazz community. Some members change in response to peer pressure. Turrentine followed his friends "into bebop to keep up with them. I really had to practice hard to play in that style." When Harold Ousley came to New York from Chicago bearing the influence of Lester Young's horizontal improvisation approach, he was initially snubbed by local performers who favored John Coltrane's vertical approach and considered Young "dated, not hip." Subsequently, Ousley "started changing, playing the types of phrases Trane played that were doubled up and used chord inversions." He also absorbed elements of style from Sonny Rollins and other contemporary saxophonists, gradually gaining acceptance in New York.

Others remain largely faithful to their former style, continuing to deepen their knowledge and skill within the artistic parameters they had already defined for themselves. "What Herbie and Chick did was just beyond me," Tommy Flanagan says. "It was something that passed me by. I never bothered to learn it, but I love listening to it." There are also those artists who resist modifying their current way of playing because they "don't think that going any further is progress" (RR).

Among individuals who summarily dismiss new movements, some never question their decisions, whereas others are gradually seduced by the same ideas that formerly had seemed inappropriate, even ridiculous. One musician, whose tastes were rooted in New Orleans "hot jazz," as epitomized by Louis Armstrong's brilliant, brassy sound and wide vibrato, initially "hated Miles Davis's cool jazz playing," with its dark sound and minimal use of vibrato. Whenever a Davis record came on the radio, he turned it off immediately. Despite his protestations, however, the player found that the few snatches he heard were deeply affective. "They kept coming back into my head—something about the sound and the feeling." The musician grew to appreciate Davis eventually, actually emulating him in his own playing.

In contrast to gradual converts are artists who immediately embrace new movements, finding their particular qualities intriguing. The attraction to new styles may also reflect the fact that an artist's current interests are on the wane or that the artist's creativity has become stymied within another performance school. Moreover, change itself is of value to many performers. "Some people can have a house, and they will stay in that house for fifty years," James Moody observes, "and another person will want to change houses every five years. They're not satisfied staying in one thing." Similarly, Moody must have "some kind of change in my life, and musically I think that way too."

At the same time, artists who value change may draw different implications from a new performance movement. Some display a singularity of vision and devote themselves to its improvisational approach with messianic zeal, minimizing or abandoning that of a former school. Others seek simply to diversify their experiences. "There are musicians like Clifford Jordan who play different styles very well," Art Davis observes. "He can play bebop, and he usually does when he plays with Barry Harris. But then he goes and plays free jazz with other people. He can do that very well too. I also like the way George Adams plays. He plays free, but he can also play conventionally. It all depends on who the music is coming from," Davis continues. "There are people who are well versed in both and can do both, and there are other people who just can't. There are some free jazz players who can't play the other way and vice versa."

Besides compartmentalizing their knowledge of different idioms and keeping their approaches separate in performance, musicians commonly combine them experimentally. In the late sixties, Rahsaan Roland Kirk's extended solos sometimes began with clarinet improvisations in the New Orleans style and culminated in free jazz creations encompassing fantastic simultaneous performances of three reed instruments.[52] His medley of styles in these solos spanned the history of jazz at the time.

Some pursue a middle ground between the core conventions of distinctive performance movements. From listening to and performing with players in more contemporary bands, "different things just seeped into my system," Doc Cheatham says. "When I went to play in the New Orleans style, I would play some other styles too, mixing them up all together." In this regard, improvisers like Art Tatum, whose personal styles successfully amalgamate elements from different performance schools, elude precise categorization.

Personal taste dictates the precise mix of elements such fusions of materials contain. One bebop player periodically introduces figures based on the theoretical approach of fourths within the flow of his lines, but shuns any greater emphasis upon that material. Influenced by the avant-garde in the sixties, another soloist pursues new melodic courses unconstrained by bebop's harmonic conventions, but avoids the increased vocalizations and multiphonic techniques associated with "screamers," a radical faction within the free jazz school. Musicians who share this soloist's values and admire the fine line he toes praise his improvisations as "free, but not freaky."

Sometimes, the musicians' decisions reflect their sense of propriety about musical style as a generational emblem. Red Rodney adapts his bebop vocabulary to suit the "modal structures of contemporary pieces because it helps me stay young." Doc Cheatham occasionally "throws some bebop phrases" into his solos to show that he has been listening to younger players and to keep him "from getting corny in the music business." As a member of his generation, however, he feels he would "look like a fool" performing primarily in the bebop style. Yet another factor is the extensive conceptual and technical retooling required by different emphases or major changes in approaches to improvisation. In learning the language of bebop some swing trumpeters encountered great difficulty modifying the earlier style's wider, more constant vibrato, which had become a habit for them, and developing the flexibility in their lips and fingers necessary for the tempos of bebop (RR). A generation later, Warren James reflects ambivalently on his own efforts to "make the transition" to free jazz by excising the conventional harmonic patterns of bebop from his improvisations. "Sometimes, I'm not sure it's worth all the dues you have to pay in order to learn to play bebop; it's so hard to unlearn afterwards."

The initial controversies surrounding stylistic changes in jazz have to some extent been carried down to the present jazz community by discrete camps of musicians with specialized loyalties to one or another of the tradition's idioms. Regardless of how creatively bebop players improvise, their solos are sometimes deemed, on the one hand, old and unoriginal by free jazz musicians whose notion of "new" minimizes or precludes the use of conventional jazz vocabulary and traditional jazz pieces as frameworks for improvisation. On the other hand, when free jazz musicians depart from older conventions, bebop players commonly object that their improvisations lack discipline and roots.

The camps also differ in the predilection to harmonic tension, the treatment of dissonance, and the interest in such qualities as lyricism. A free jazz player praises Eric Dolphy for his experiments with "polytonality," whereas a bebop player puts down the same performance for containing "too many wrong notes." Similarly, a free jazz musician praised for his vocalizing timbral qualities and emotional intensity as "screaming beautifully" by one school is ridiculed by another for his "noise." Improvisers sometimes temper such judgments about the styles of individuals by considering the relative values of different schools and the era in which individuals learned jazz. One artist accepts specific performance practices as appropriate for older drummers, while maintaining that young drummers who play that way are "corny."

Controversies of a smaller order concern specific features of repertory treatment or approaches to improvisation or, at times, both. The constraints of improvising within hard bop compositions of dense chord progressions may frustrate even the most skilled of artists. "When the chords change every two beats, all you can do is spell chords to get through tunes like that" (CF). In another situation, a renowned singer objects to harmonically static modal pieces, which allow soloists to avoid the rigors of improvising within harmonic progressions. "Anybody can improvise in one key," she says contemptuously. Other artists take issue with various contemporary improvisation approaches. "A lot of players today are playing different cycles of interval patterns like fourths. I like to study them to open up my ears, but to play like that," a musician complains, "you could be anybody. Everybody sounds the same, playing that stuff. A lot of guys I know are going in that direction, and they're going to get trapped if they're not careful. They're going to find out that once they get into that, they're not going to be able to get out of it," he warns. "After learning to play that way, they go on a record date and have to play on more conventional tunes, and they don't know where to begin. They can't play that way as well anymore."

Lou Donaldson similarly feels that "all players are sounding alike today. They're all working out of Oliver Nelson's book. They play mechanical sequences of changes that will fit anything. When they get to a chord change, they skate through it. They work out clusters of notes, whole-tone patterns and things, to get through it. In the old days," he recalls, "we played the exact chord that was supposed to be played. They don't have a feeling for tonal centers in the music anymore, or they just improvise on the harmony in ways that have nothing to do with the song."

As new practices draw enough of a following to ensure their survival within the jazz community and acquire greater legitimacy, former detractors sometimes soften their positions. Reinterpreting the relationships of new to older practices, they may stress the continuity of particular values. Innovations initially regarded as radical departures from convention, for example, can begin appearing to be unique syntheses and subtle transformations of traditional musical elements drawn from the jazz community's cumulative pool of ideas.

"Parker was just a little more evolved than the music before him," Lou Donaldson explains, speaking of the development of bebop. "He was really like Eddie Vinson soundwise—and the way he phrased the blues. He was just a lot faster and more involved." Jay McShann likens Parker's early playing to that of "Prof" Buster Smith, in whose band Parker worked, and describes once having mistaken the former for the latter when Parker replaced Smith on a radio broadcast.[53] A bebop saxophonist commenting on the transition between bebop and free jazz "didn't understand Eric Dolphy at first, but after a while I realized the rhythm of his playing was a lot like Bird, but his harmonic concept was different." Similarly, a swing trumpeter recalls, "Ornette Coleman's playing seemed very different when I began listening to him, but I finally figured out that what he was doing was playing a lot of old swing patterns and putting them in different places than we did, phrasing them differently within the beat."

While indicating the predominance of different core conventions during particular historical periods, many performers ultimately eschew simplistic generalities about jazz idioms or schools.[54] They express concern that categorical views of music history misrepresent the complex nature of musical style, at times even obscuring either the diverse improvisation approaches favored by some contemporaries or the overlapping concepts shared by members of different generations. David Baker comments that the "reason why so many of the avant-garde players sound like the earlier players is that they rejected the excesses of chromaticism which you had in bebop and their playing is basically diatonic like the playing of the swing period."

It has always been the case that, just as the conservative features of some artists recall earlier performance practices, the progressive elements of other artists distinguish them from their peers and anticipate subsequent practices. One pianist in Barry Harris's workshops reports that, as early as the thirties, he heard Art Tatum use in his improvised bass lines contemporary intervallic approaches based on fourths, and Mary Lou Williams describes Tatum's harmonic concept as anticipating that of bebop.[55] Lee Konitz describes participating in Lennie Tristano's first recorded experiments in free improvisation in the late forties.[56] Tommy Turrentine recalls one of his career's illuminating moments when Ray Nance called him over to his apartment and said he had a record he wanted Turrentine to hear. Nance said, "You ain't going to believe it, man." When Turrentine arrived and listened to the album, he could tell by its "fidelity" that it was recorded during the twenties. Also, "you know how the rhythm section was playing then—that style. [But] this trumpet player was so clean and playing changes, and weaving in and out of these changes." When Turrentine was unable to identify the trumpeter, Nance said, "Jabbo Smith!" Smith "was making runs like Dizzy, man, back in twenty-three." After that, "Ray said, 'See, man, there ain't nothing new under the sun!'"

## Negotiating the World of Critical Judgment

Within the jazz community's social network, students take notice of the critical issues that consume the artists around them, and they learn to interpret the varied ways in which artists express their views. Musicians require, on the one hand, no more than the momentary meeting of eyes or a brief smile or nod, to confirm the shared judgment about a soloist's exceptional phrase. A blank look at the wrong moment, on the other hand, can be self-incriminating, indicating that a musician has failed to apprehend or appreciate a soloist's tasteful chord substitution or a momentary excursion into a radically different improvisation approach.

Offering overt judgment, one pianist listened impassively to the greater part of his own recording. Whenever he improvised an asymmetrical pattern that created an interesting counterpoint to the band's accompaniment, he muttered almost imperceptibly under his breath, "Not bad." In another case, a great artist whom I had invited to listen to selected numbers from my record collection warned me that he had a habit of falling asleep to music that bored him. We laughed together at his remark as I placed the needle on one of my favorite solos by a well-known trumpeter. Moments after the solo concluded and another began, this one by a pianist, my guest slumped in his chair. With some embarrassment, after several minutes, I stopped the record and shook him gently awake. Milt Hinton remembers direct feedback on the bandstand from Dizzy Gillespie, who sought to coach his development in the new bebop style.

After completing each solo, Hinton would look back at the trumpet section, and if Gillespie "liked what I was doing he would nod his head. Or if he didn't, he would pinch his nose as if to say, 'That stunk.'"[57]

In other instances, students develop their understanding from observing open critical discussions, discovering that evaluations reflect not only the different values of critics, but also their predispositions toward collegiality. Musicians who are generous in their praise sometimes describe their counterparts as "monsters" or "muthafuckahs" or as "hip" or "bad" for their formidable skills, drawing out "bad" with a descent, "baaaad," to signify *great*. Others, having attested to a player's basic talent, are not inclined to elaborate. They simply appreciate the musical statements of artists on their own terms. Lonnie Hillyer and his peers "used to listen to guys and say, 'Well, that's what it means to him.'" Or, as a common maxim in the jazz community expresses, people play the way they are.

At times, artists' views can be very harsh. They indicate with classic understatement that an acknowledged master, simply, "can play," or they comment tersely that a player whose taste differs from their own "can't play." Equally damning are overriding judgments that individuals "can't swing," "are corny," or are "saaad," the last referring not to emotion but to incompetence.

Performers can be equally unsparing in their self-criticism.[58] A trumpeter recalls Miles Davis once remarking that if he improvised four good measures a year, he considered that it was a good year. Art Farmer remembers in his early career always

> feeling my own playing was awful. I never thought that it was great. I felt the same thing for years, even when I was working with really great players like Lester Young and Oscar Pettiford. I would go to work with a very enthused feeling, like "Now's the time to play!" But by the end of the evening I always had the feeling that I was slinking home with my tail between my legs. I always felt like that character in the old ad for Ben Gay. There's a character with a little tail who's supposed to be pain. And somebody rubs the Ben Gay on this cat and it would disappear and the caption would read, "Curses, foiled again!" And that's the way I felt.

Musicians grappling with their critical standards sometimes develop a modesty and shyness that they constantly struggle to overcome in performance. When Melba Liston toured with Dizzy Gillespie's big band in the forties, she "played some lead parts which were written—musical interludes and things—but wouldn't stand up and take off. I don't do that with Dizzy's band, even now. A month ago when we played together, he looked at me and he asked, 'Well, are you ready to take another solo?' I said, 'No,' and he said, 'Oh, yes you will' and I said, 'Oh, no I won't.' We went back and forth like that [laughter], but in the end I did take some choruses on 'Manteca.'"

The critical reflection improvisers express toward their own abilities and those of other players underscores the comprehensive artistic demands of the jazz community. It reflects the general view that most soloists have specialized sensitivities and talents. In fact, creativity and intelligence display themselves in endlessly varied and subtle ways within the intimate realm of improvisation. Charlie Parker's appraisal of artists was especially "positive" in this respect. He found reason to praise others if only for such unique features as tone color or technique (WB). Art Farmer also focuses on the strengths of artists, as when he compliments Freddie Hubbard for "playing the horn so well" or Miles Davis for the "depth of his feeling," indicating that "those two things are what it's all about." He also admires Don Cherry solos for their "sheer spontaneity."

Just as often, performers juxtapose strengths and weaknesses. Artists who are great interpreters of ballads and slow pieces are not necessarily great players on fast pieces with complex harmonies, or vice versa. Among pianists who are fluent chord-change players, some improvise "elegant, thoughtful melodic lines, but are not resourceful in terms of the colors you can get from different voicings." Another player, a guitarist, "has an incredible harmonic ear and a rhythmic concept full of surprises, but lacks a melodic ear." Other performers who are "harmonically or melodically sophisticated lack rhythmic strength and sensitivity." Yet another's solos are appealing "intellectually" because of their interesting intervallic patterns, but are ultimately "cold," missing emotion. Two trumpeters are "great power players," but are not "touch players" who can perform with nuances of mood. A saxophonist improvises with "great personality, energy, and aggression—and with wonderful feeling," but stands in need of harmonic development. He "plays things out of thin air with no harmonic basis."

For some artists, what is a specialized capacity for either improvisation or written composition can generate other dichotomies. One musician is a "great [jazz] composer in the written medium," but incapable of composing music satisfactorily as an improviser, unable to limit and control his ideas under the pressures of performance. Another player, however, is an exceptional improviser within the framework of the compositions of other musicians, yet lacks the interest or the skill to compose formal pieces with song-like characteristics: his "compositions are unmemorable throwaways." Representing further distinctions, some artists have limited training and experience interpreting written arrangements in big bands, but possess an extraordinary aural memory for repertory, "knowing every tune that's ever been played." To the amusement of friends, some singers display such mental prowess by breaking into a different song whenever a conversation's turn of subject or key word reminds them of a corresponding lyric. Musicians with a limited recall for repertory may be skilled "music readers" and "lead section players," interpreting written music with great conviction.

Finally, there are special individuals, musicians whose excellence is far-reaching, encompassing many or most of the features discussed above. Roy Haynes recalls that Fats Navarro was

> a spectacular musician because, in a time when some cats arrived on the scene with nothing, he came on with everything: he could read, he could play high and hold anybody's first trumpet chair, he could play those singing, melodic solos with a big, beautiful sound nobody could believe at the time, and he could fly on fast tempos with staccato, biting notes and execute whatever he wanted, with apparently no strain, everything clear. And every note meant something. You know there are those kinds of guys who just play a lot of notes, some good, some bad. Fats wasn't one of those: he made his music be about each note having a place and reason. And he had so much warmth, so much feeling. That's why I say he had everything.[59]

Young improvisers struggle to develop competency in the fundamental language of jazz and to assert their individuality within a world of criticism preoccupied with comprehensive artistry, impassioned by allegiances to different performance schools, and responsive to personal taste. Because musical development can be so gradual as to be imperceptible to students, they take heart in praise received from experienced players and reflect on weaknesses revealed through criticism. Youngsters must also learn when and when not to take advice, a principle often confusing in practice. Complaints that a vocalist uses too much vibrato, countered by complaints of too little vibrato, remind Vea Williams of Sarah Vaughan's general advice, "Don't let anyone change your style." Rufus Reid confronted just such a basic challenge after an early performance with a famous group when he learned "through the grapevine" that the leader "didn't like my playing. The news just destroyed me," he recalls. "It was just like another growing pain. I said to myself, 'Well, you don't expect everybody to like what you play, do you?' I realized that I could play one of the greatest solos there is, and there might be one person who would agree with that and three who'd say, 'Oh, man. That's nothing.' So, I've grown to accept that you can't please everyone."

Students inevitably weather such rebuffs, gaining, in the process, firmer footing as critics themselves. Ultimately, a young artist clarifies personal objectives and assumes responsibility for an independent musical direction. Moreover, time and experience provide emergent musicians with a more realistic perspective on the nature of artistic growth and creativity. "When I was younger, I never felt that I really put it all together in my solos," Art Farmer remembers.

> And of course, I learned much later that you never do. You have good nights and you have bad nights. And some nights are exceptionally

good. But no night is ever just fantastic from the beginning to the end. You never put it all together the way you would like to. You can always find something wrong with it. Nothing is ever fully realized, and you never say, "Well, this is it." You're always on your way somewhere. To me, playing is generally a never-ending state of getting there.

Sometimes, I feel like a breakthrough is happening in my playing, and then I go back and listen to records I made years and years ago, and I can see the basis there of what I'm doing now. I might go to work and play something and think, "Well, that's new. I never played that before," and then I might hear that I played something very close to it ten or twelve years ago. There hadn't been any real break-off that you could put your finger on and say, "Well, I went from here to there."

I hear some players who make big changes in their styles, but that's not that important to me. The only goal is to play better. And I feel my playing has gotten better over the years. I have better control of the horn, greater freedom to venture out more on the horn and to be more expressive. Basically, my ambition is just to be more expressive.

As improvisers continue to strengthen their expressive and conceptual abilities through self-criticism and peer discussion, they also benefit from direct interaction with others on the bandstand. There, the intricacies of musical discourse remind learners that, within the characteristically collective art form of jazz, the solo is simply one part amid a complex texture of accompanying patterns that are themselves commonly improvised as the whole group interprets a composition's elements. Correspondingly, as the next section discusses, jazz performance depends as much on each player's knowledge of the practices governing all aspects of group interplay as on any player's soloing ability.

# PART

# III

Collective Aspects of Improvisation

# ELEVEN

**Arranging Pieces**

Decisions in Rehearsal

*People never understood how arranged Bill Evans's music really was. Sure, it was free and improvised. But the reason we could be so free is that we already knew the beginning, the middle, and the ending.* —Chuck Israels

Performers' attention to the artful regulation of their interaction expresses itself most formally in the creation of musical arrangements, details of presentation worked out for each piece in advance of music events. Arrangements represent varied degrees of planning and impose different compositional constraints upon improvisers. They introduce stable precomposed elements to group interplay, providing overall shape to performances and reducing some of the risks associated with collective improvisation.

Learners begin grappling with the challenges of arranging music through their early experience with groups. Needing separate parts for each group member, young players strive to formulate multiple components from the sparse, often skeletal, versions of tunes available to them. Toward such ends, they draw upon principles learned in much the same way that they mastered other aspects of jazz, by gleaning and synthesizing bits of technical information from various sources.

Once again, as complete aural scores of favored renditions, recordings provide invaluable models. "If you could only afford a few records," recalls one performer, "you learned them so thoroughly. You played them over and over and over, studying them for every musical detail, every bit of information you could get about the heads, the solos, and the arrangements before you wore them out completely." Jimmy McPartland and fellow band members in the Austin High School Gang copied their individual parts from records by the New Orleans Rhythm Kings and the Wolverines.[1] Similarly, Lonnie Hillyer and Charles McPherson spent "endless hours" together, learning musical parts from recordings by Count Basie's band and other popular swing bands. Occasionally, fledgling bands included musicians who could transcribe recorded arrangements for fellow members. Printed arrangements of some popular swing compositions were also available to those performers with the means to purchase them.

Eventually, many try their own hands at creating new arrangements, drawing not only on versions by other artists but, in some instances, on knowledge gained from method books and private study with composers in the classical music community.[2] George Duvivier's early training in four-part harmony provided him with a useful "starting point," but he still needed to learn more about each instrument's capacity. "I wrote one early arrangement in which there was something completely out of the range of the poor trombone player [laughter]. I didn't know what the problems were, so I got a book about all the instruments, what they could do and what they couldn't." Tommy Flanagan recalls the bewilderment of his friends when they attempted to perform his first arrangement, an introduction to an Oscar Pettiford piece in which he had written all the parts in the same key. Flanagan had yet to learn about transposition.

Veterans within bands help remedy such deficiencies. When Tommy Turrentine toured with the Snookum Russell band in his mid-teens, he had the good fortune to share a room with bassist Ray Brown, who taught him about orchestration, "how the pitches and ranges of different instruments related to the keyboard." Other formal opportunities for study arose when, as the size of bands expanded during the late twenties and thirties, many leaders hired specialized arrangers or music directors to help regulate aspects of group interaction and to shape the styles of their bands. In many instances, bands rely upon oral or head arrangements. In other instances, musical scores or books of the band's repertory preserve the details of arrangements and served as texts for learners. Tommy Turrentine partially learned "to write music" by looking over the shoulders of fellow musicians who wrote out arrangements of Ellington compositions for their early group. Moreover, the task of copying individual parts from master scores creates jobs for younger members, enabling them to serve as apprentices to arrangers. "Gerald Wilson was a trumpet player and a fine arranger," Melba Liston remembers. "I started copying for him in the [Jimmie] Lunceford band and studied his scores so that I could write just like him. He didn't like that too much, and he finally let me go—everybody was saying he wasn't writing any of his music [she laughs]. But he was good to me and taught me a lot. I reached the point where I was writing about half his book."

Saturated listening night after night further amplifies the skills of learners. George Duvivier found it "pretty easy" to write arrangements for the Lunceford band because he already knew the voicings just from "being around the band so long." He wrote "half the book" for the band, for eight brass, five reed, and four rhythm section instruments. Ultimately, each tenure with a different group provides an artist the opportunity for enriched understanding of arranging and developing a repertory. So important are these patterns of development that they become the subject of anecdotal conversation within the community. Tommy Turrentine, for example, relates a typical profile of the development of jazz arrangers. "J. J. Johnson had previously been in the Snookum Russell band, and Russell also got him on his P's and Q's about writing. Later, J. J. went on to work with Benny Carter, who opened him up to Carter's writing style."

## What Goes into Arrangements

Significantly, the initial decision a leader makes about a band's instrumentation, thereby determining the collective palette of sounds, is the first step toward defining the nature of arrangements overall. Models for these and other decisive group features commonly originate with historic bands whose sheer excellence of musicianship, forceful musical personalities, and innovative concepts exert a disproportionate influence on their contemporaries. As an increasing number of groups emulate these bands, their arrangements and collective performance practices gradually acquire the status of conventions, contributing, in some instances, to the definition of different style periods or jazz idioms. Joe Oliver's Creole Jazz Band in the twenties, Fletcher Henderson's orchestra featuring Don Redman's arrangements in the thirties, Charlie Parker and Dizzy Gillespie's quintet in the forties, and Ornette Coleman's pianoless quartet in the sixties each became the prototype for many bands performing, respectively, in their New Orleans, swing, bebop, and free jazz styles.

Small groups predominated during the early jazz or New Orleans period, featuring standard "front line" instruments—cornet, clarinet, and trombone—with variable accompaniment. During the swing period, larger ensembles with fifteen or more members enriched the possibilities for orchestration and musical interaction. Entire sections of brass or reed instruments engaged in contrapuntal interplay. They also provided thickened presentations of melodies and harmonic textures, as well as a great variety of contrasting sonorities.

Arrangements returned to a simpler format during the bebop period, placing a renewed emphasis upon small groups. Typically, they would feature the voice of a single horn or a pair of horns playing the tune with accompaniment.

In the aftermath of the bop period, some groups involved with the cool jazz and third stream movements experimented with combining conventional jazz and orchestral instruments, including flute, oboe, bassoon, french horn, and strings. Additionally, they increased the size of ensembles and the amount of ensemble performance in relation to that of their soloists. Within the early free jazz movement, bands also experimented with different instrumentation. To diversify their colors, some incorporated into their arrangements traditional instruments from around the world—Indian and African percussion and melodic instruments, for example—as well as a myriad of "little instruments" ranging from slide whistles to kazoos.[3] In recent years, jazz fusion arrangements have combined acoustic instruments with synthesizers, sequencers, drum machines, and, in some instances, the sounds of prerecorded tape tracks. Moreover, affordable studio technology such as "digital delay and reverb" units and "multi-effects" processers (which typically include such devices as a harmonizer, a pitch transposer, and various types of noise gates) has allowed artists to manipulate their instruments' sounds to produce a vast array of special musical effects.

Although influenced by the prevailing conventions for instrumentation and other features of arrangements associated with particular style periods, jazz musicians are not bound by them. Many engage in idiosyncratic practices, carrying earlier conventions across idiomatic and generational lines to place them in different group contexts and rework them to their tastes. In the twenties, Louis Armstrong recorded unusual duo renditions of pieces with pianist Earl Hines on which Roy Eldridge later patterned his own arrangements with Claude Bolling in the early fifties.[4] Similarly, Coleman Hawkins's experimental solo for unaccompanied saxophone on "Picasso" in 1948 and that by Sonny Rollins in 1958 on "Body and Soul"—a tribute to Hawkins—anticipated practices of extended solo improvisations and solo concerts by free jazz horn players that were to become common in the sixties.[5] Although small groups were the norm during the bebop period, Dizzy Gillespie presented bebop soloists successfully within the framework of his big band. Furthermore, he added an African Cuban rhythmic flavor to the music's accompaniment by collaborating with Chano Pozo, the renowned hand drummer.

Beyond the issue of group instrumentation, arrangements can differ markedly. They range from the "strict, unadorned rendering of a tune" to the most imaginative "reworking . . . [or] recomposing of such material," unique transformation equivalent to the composition of original works.[6] In between these extremes, arrangers typically design a particular treatment for every piece's melody and harmony, and decide upon the larger performance's sequence of events. Within this framework, they designate each part's opportunity for improvisation in relation to the performance of precomposed material. In addition, by determining which instruments play together, and when, they establish a balance between events featuring soloists and events featuring the ensemble.

The regulation of these matters offers artists musical guidelines with differing degrees of specification. The conventional arrangement allowing individual horn players their own interpretation of a piece's melody at the opening and close of the performance, with various group members alternating solos in between, is, perhaps, the most general. Meanwhile, the rhythm section— bass, drums, and piano (or another chording instrument like banjo, guitar, or vibraphone)—provides accompaniment, interpreting the harmony and generating a constant beat. Easily incorporated within the design are such conventions as short improvised introductions, "trading fours" among individual group members, and concluding performances with a repeated unison riff or with an intense chorus of improvised polyphony.

For variety, artists can specify a multitude of precise details. "We'd work on a tune like you would paint a portrait," Jimmy Robinson remembers. "You want something special to come from it. We'd work on all the possible shadings, the softness, the loudness, balancing the way the tune sounded. We'd work on phrasing the tune. There are so many things you can do to make each tune say something so that you wouldn't forget it and its effect would be lasting. Working this way is a matter of sensitivity. It's what I call being a true artist." Similarly, encouraging expressive interpretation, Max Roach once coached musicians at a rehearsal, "Play every phrase as if it were the whole song." Performers also consider articulation and accentuation. "On one particular tune," Horace Silver asked John McNeil "to tongue a little harder on specific patterns that had the character of drum patterns."

Arrangements differ in the keys and progressions they assign to particular pieces, altering their mood and providing new challenges for improvisers. "Even when Joe Henderson and Bobby Hutcherson played something standard, like a blues, they wouldn't do it in a standard key like B♭. They did it in A♭ or D♭" (RuR). Tommy Turrentine recalls the imaginative arrangements that trios in his hometown of Philadelphia, like Ahmad Jamal's, would work out. Jamal "wouldn't play 'I Got Rhythm' changes the standard way." He would devise his own version of the progression, or "he might do it like Monk did it."

Musicians sometimes alter larger harmonic plans to give their arrangements individuality. Kenny Washington remembers Betty Carter advising her band, "If you're going to do a standard tune that's been done a lot, don't do it like everybody else does it. Change it. Do it your own way." Another alumnus of her bands, John Hicks, elaborates, "First of all, we'd work out the form of the tune. Betty would usually alter the standard form." For example, many "old standards" originally had verses composed for them, "introductions with lyrics," and although most singers and instrumentalists cut them out today, Carter would sometimes sing them as "extensions" of the songs. Kenny Washington recalls that "in one version of 'But Beautiful,' she sang the verse as the bridge of the song instead of putting it at the beginning." He laughs: it was "such a hip extension of the tune, you'd swear it was part of the tune." Along similar lines, a group may add variety to its production by designing a progression for soloists to use as a vehicle that differs from the progression used for the melody's accompaniment.

Bands also commonly arrange rhythmic features. "People have given me specific advice about tempos," Fred Hersch says, "like really taking a couple of seconds to find out exactly what tempo you want before you count it off— not being casual with tempos because every tempo is different. Certain tunes will really feel strange if they're a hair too fast or a hair too slow." If the challenges associated with some arrangements involve recalling and maintaining one precise tempo, other arrangements challenge improvisers to recreate "tricky" changes. "The hardest thing" for Ronald Shannon Jackson to do in Betty Carter's group "was to learn her arrangements, because you could be going along at a fast tempo and instantly change into a ballad." Moreover, within the same piece, "you might have to change from sticks to brushes or switch from playing bebop to a march-type thing."

Choice of meters can further distinguish a tune's treatment. "As you know, 'My Favorite Things' was originally done in 3/4, and then Trane went on to do his version of it in 6/8. Betty didn't want to do it either of those ways, so she came up with playing it in straight-ahead 4/4 time" (KW). Similarly, when Rufus Reid "was working with Bobby Hutcherson and Harold Land, their music might switch back and forth between six bars of 3/4 and six bars of 4/4. I had never seen anything like it before."

Artists also regulate such aspects of improvised interplay as the order of soloists and the lengths of performances, limiting players to one or two choruses, perhaps. In the absence of specified guidelines, etiquette commonly dictates solos to be roughly the same length. In this respect, players take their cue from the first soloist.[7] Other planned events designate that particular individuals trade improvised statements of two, four, or eight measures over the progression's course for a number of choruses, or that they improvise introductions and endings. When fulfilling the latter responsibilities, performers typically incorporate musical elements from the melody within their inventions so that they bear "a logical relationship to it" (TF).

Arrangements may also sanction different degrees of improvisation and varied intensities of performance at various times within ensemble parts. In conventional polyphonic settings of New Orleans–style jazz groups, cornet typically plays each piece's melody with minor variations while clarinet plays a contrasting part in a higher register and trombone or tuba creates a bass part, which outlines the chord progression. These restrictions to specified roles for the greater part of each piece's performance are sometimes suspended in the last chorus, or out chorus, of a piece, where the front-line players may take the liberty of creating spectacular parts with the character of simultaneous solos, carrying the music to full intensity and bringing about its final climax (DC). An example from the bebop era would be a rendition of "Mean to Me," in which Dizzy Gillespie initially performs the first half of the tune with minor variations while Sonny Stitt improvises a counterpart that weaves in and out of Gillespie's line. In the second half of the tune, the horn players switch roles. Similarly, within the rhythm section, one accompanist may play variations on a composed part while another improvises a complementary part.

Within the largest frame of presentation, some leaders organize entire repertory programs in advance of an event. They imagine alternative sequences of pieces, balancing the need for continuity in mood and style at one point against the need for contrast at another. Each piece should "set up the audience for the next" (CF). Medleys of related pieces formalize this consideration. "Betty [Carter] was also great at putting medleys of tunes together," Kenny Washington recalls.

> We used to do a Charlie Parker medley and medleys of old ballads. The way she'd hook all these tunes up was so beautiful. We would do a breakneck tune like "My Favorite Things," and after that, she'd say to the audience, "Thank you. This next tune is about a couple that's living together, but they're not speaking and somebody's got to break the ice." Then she'd pause and ask, "Can't we talk it over?" and the band would come in with the tune, "Can't We Talk It Over?" Then, at the end of the song, she'd say to the audience, "Because it's love or it isn't," and the band would go right into another ballad, "It's Love or It Isn't."

Other band leaders provide more extensive introductions to compositions, in the form of dramatic commentary or praise for the artists who inspired the renditions. In effect, they create narrative segues or interludes between numbers.[8] "There comes a time in every tenor saxophonist's life," a renowned player on the instrument announced at one event, "in which he must attempt to solo on the tune that Coleman Hawkins made famous, 'Body and Soul'. The arrangement I'd like to do for you," he added, "is the one that Dexter Gordon recorded." In words familiar on the bandstand, he concluded self-effacingly, "Although I can't guarantee the performance will be up to Dexter's, I'll give it all that I can." Groups may also compose musical segues that continue the performance's momentum from piece to piece, carrying listeners through formal transitions in key, meter, or mood. John Hicks describes Betty Carter's use of key changes to further personalize a tune like "But Beautiful," which inventively uses the original verse as the bridge. After singing the verse, "she modulates," Hicks says. "She'll have a note . . . and a particular range that she's going [for], say, from a G to an E♭. Now, when she hits the E♭, she may want to go to an A♭ major, coming from the C, like say, the G is the dominant of C major. So, she'll hit the E♭, like the minor sixth, and we'll go to A♭ major." Carter uses the same design for her rendition's ending or tag section. Moreover, after modulating there, she sometimes extends the performance by going "into a slow blues in A♭." With minimal theoretical discussion, Carter composes and transmits such ideas, according to Hicks, "on sounds alone," constantly creating unique forms for her band to interpret.

Finally, it is not uncommon for groups to plan the use of a particular break tune at the end of a performance set to signal periodic intermissions in the evening's program.

### Specifying Parts within the Larger Designs of Arrangements

Within the larger formal design of renditions, musicians exploit their group's sound palette by varying the use and roles of instruments from one musical episode to another. Early jazz arrangements often designated only piano to provide the accompaniment for a soloist during one segment of the performance, then used the larger ensemble in contrasting accompaniment to another soloist. Another practice allowed the string bass occasionally to double "the trombone or cello part during melodic interludes or bridge passages in multithematic compositions."[9]

Arrangements, then and now, highlight particular instruments, or groupings of like instruments, such as the brass section, in the performance of repeated melodic riffs during designated parts of the music's structure. Jelly Roll Morton, one of the most influential of early jazz arrangers, maintained that "a riff is something that gives an orchestra a great background and is the main idea in playing jazz."[10] Additionally, bands often feature alternating brass or reed sections in call and response routines, or involve members of one section or the other in unison performance of elaborate lines with the character of solos, or combine the sections in complex schemes of polyphony. "Personally, I love the undercurrent created by the third or fourth horn parts in big ensembles," Tommy Turrentine says. "The way the voices move and cross each other. At times, that can be more interesting than the melody. I listen to how those parts are constructed in any arranged composition."

The harmonic qualities of parts can be as varied as their linear qualities. Arrangers cleverly combine the sounds of instruments to create new timbres, just as painters mix primary colors to invent new colors and endless variations of hues. "Some of Ellington's voicings and orchestrations were so unique that you couldn't tell which instruments were playing together on the records," a musician recalls. "You had to see the band in person to figure it out." Ellington's works epitomize the elaborate, inventive design of jazz arrangements, as do those by Gil Evans.[11]

Mixtures of the precise timbres associated with the musical personalities of individual artists create interest for discerning listeners by revealing sounds within sounds at the microlevel of an arrangement's orchestration. This is so even within renditions by smaller groups, such as bop or hard bop quintets, in which the horns perform the melody in unison or parallel intervals. The blend of personal sounds contributing uniqueness to renditions of compositions is distinguishable from band to band (MR).

When Jazz Messengers trumpeter Lee Morgan and tenor saxophonist Benny Golson perform the melody of "Moanin'" in octaves, Golson's warm, reedy, diffuse sound enfolds Morgan's bright, finely articulated melodic line. Equally unique unison effects are achieved when Dizzy Gillespie's cup-muted horn blends with Charlie Parker's alto saxophone or Miles Davis's harmon-muted horn blends with John Coltrane's tenor saxophone. Within such closely fashioned unison parts, subtle differences in phrasing and vibrato stand out, and slight pitch movements sometimes forcefully emerge in relief. In Eric Dolphy's and Booker Little's band, trumpet and alto saxophone meld in perfect unison for the greater part of their arrangement of "The Prophet," then separate into a brilliant, searing, sustained minor second.[12]

As horn players perform their specified parts, arrangements guide the rhythm section parts to varying degrees. Some prescriptions are general. "There may be a certain way of playing, a certain routine, that band leaders want you to adopt," Don Pate explains. "It may be a matter of creating a particular feeling or a particular kind of swing. Or they may want you to leave out certain things that you do." Other prescriptions require designated patterns at particular points in the music's presentation or throughout. New Orleans drummer Baby Dodds reports that certain jazz pieces require "particular beats or rhythmic patterns," much as forms of Latin American music like the samba and rumba require specific accompanying patterns.[13]

In George Duvivier's experience as well, players make specific "suggestions like, 'Let's play this on the introduction. Let's do this on the ending.' With Diz's music, there are many things for the bass that happen with particular tunes' arrangements," Duvivier says, "like the bass patterns on 'Manteca.' If you don't play them, you're not playing the tune." Rufus Reid adds:

> In Hutcherson's and Land's band, they were very explicit about the concept they wanted for the bass. They'd say, "After we do this, we're going to put a vamp in the middle of this part" [an ostinato over one or two repeating chords]. In another part, they'd say, "Now, in this section, don't walk [avoid stepwise bass lines, four beats to the measure]. Play in two or you can float [suspend the regular sense of the beat]. When we get here, then you can walk. On this other section, it's all rubato. Use your bow, if you like. When I nod, you can play whatever you want."

Betty Carter's arrangements likewise specified details for the bass. Kenny Washington recounts that she liked to hear "low notes," especially notes on the "E string." Also, at the end of pieces, Carter "never wanted the bassist to play the same note she was going to sing. . . . She would always tell the bassist to find another note in the chord," Washington recalls. "She'd say, 'Don't play the root.'" At rehearsals, she told Calvin Hill "things like, 'In this part of the tune I don't want you to play in 4/4.' Or, 'I want you to walk here.' Or, 'In this section, I want you to play Latin. Here, I want you to play in the lower register.' She didn't ask for particular notes."

With respect to drummers, arrangements may not only designate particular patterns, but may provide an outline of events that includes the orchestration of the patterns among the drum set's instruments and the appropriate technique applied to each. "Sometimes, people will require you to do specific things that they feel are sensitive to a particular part of the piece you're playing that you might not otherwise hear," Max Roach says. "They may say, 'Here, I want you to go to the mallets or brushes'; or, 'There, I want you to play a broken rhythm, but don't use the bass drum.' Or, 'Here, I want you to only accent the first and third beats of the measure for so many bars and then do something else.' In another section, they may ask you just to use the snare drum alone."

Kenny Washington details his experience: "Betty Carter had a lot of ideas about what she wanted a drummer to do behind her," he says. Washington had previously worked with many singers who liked him to play brushes on the snare drum when they sang a ballad. But when "I first joined Betty and I started doing this ballad, she stopped the tune right there and said, 'Listen to me. I don't want to hear no brushes on the snare drum on ballads. I can't stand that.' She wanted to hear just cymbals [the first and third beat on the ride cymbal, and the second and fourth beat on the hi-hat]. She didn't want to hear any swishing with the left hand." Consequently, meeting Carter's demands was initially "harder to do" for Washington.

In addition, such directions sometimes include precise approaches to accompanying the melody and to representing its harmonic form. When Keith Copeland "played Bird's tunes [while sitting in] with Barry Harris, you didn't have to play along with all the melody notes. You could just play part of the figures at the key rhythmic points to enhance what the horns were playing. Those heads went by very fast. So, if you really wanted to accent them—whether it was to play the whole head with your left hand and still keep the ride cymbal time going or just accent parts of it—you had to know the tune just like the horn players did." Along related lines, Betty Carter used to tell Kenny Washington, "Watch your 'ones,'" when he joined her band. This reminded him of advice he had received earlier from other musicians about using the bass drum to perform off-beat accents delineating the piece's harmonic-rhythmic structure, typically just before the downbeat of the A section and that of the bridge. From Carter's perspective, not only did such practices assure her that the rhythm section kept its place within the form of the piece, but "the music hooked up better that way," making it easier for listeners to follow. "She felt very strongly about those anticipated 'ones' especially at the end of the last beat of the A section of the tune, showing that the group was closing that and opening up the bridge. It was like punctuating different sections of a letter."

Arrangements can also delineate the precise mix of figures that provide the background for different soloists. According to Dicky Wells, Sid Catlett would ask newcomers in the Snowden band what they wanted him to play behind them, whether brushes or sticks or Chinese cymbal. "And he'd do whatever it was until you told him to change it." [14] Leroy Williams has played with horn players "who like to hear more sock cymbal [hi-hat] because they feel that they can play off of that better. Booker Ervin always wanted me to play a lot of sock cymbal," Williams recalls. "He needed more than most people. Others might want more bass drum or less bass drum." Soloists have also given instructions to pianists. Tommy Flanagan mentions that "horn players sometimes taught me things, too. They'd hear things differently from the way I heard them, and they'd share them. They'd sit at the piano and say, 'I voice that chord like this.' I worked with Miles for a short time," Flanagan continues. "He told me the kinds of things he likes to hear and then showed them to me at the piano. He had a specific way he likes the piano to play for him." [15] At times, Miles Davis prefers to improvise with the bass and drum accompaniment alone and asks pianists to lay out, that is, temporarily refrain from performance.

Convention commonly dictates that drummers and bass players receive proportionately fewer solos than other musicians, in part to avoid adding undue burden to the demands of constant performance in their roles as accompanists. Bass players and drummers typically take solos without musical support, so they must track the composition's form unerringly as they improvise. "With McCoy [Tyner], the situation was basically, 'It's the bass's solo, so you've got it.' The rest of the band would drop out," Calvin Hill says. At the same time, bands may experiment with alternatives. Pharoah Sanders would "sometimes have a percussionist as well as a hand drummer, so a lot of bass solos involved playing with percussion instruments" (CH). Departing further from convention, Max Roach routinely likes to have "some kind of accompaniment" when he takes an extended drum solo, just as if he were performing any other instrument. "Sometimes, I just have bass play behind me, and I'll embellish around the bass figure. Other times, I like to have a horn accompaniment, which adds another dimension to the whole solo. Sometimes, you have to write that in order to get what you want. Other times, musicians can deal with that improvisationally."

Rhythmic features of each solo's accompaniment are sometimes specified by arrangements. Arranged tempo changes may require the rhythm section to double up for a chorus or more, performing twice as fast as the original tempo while the piece's harmonic rhythm remains the same. Other devices, with roots in early jazz practices, include arranged breaks, in which the entire rhythm section suspends its performance for a few measures—commonly at the beginning or ending of a chorus—leaving the soloist temporarily without an external rhythmic point of reference. Jelly Roll Morton regarded the break, with its "musical surprise," as being essential to the special quality of jazz, providing a foil to the continuity and momentum established by the band's background riffs, which provided the music's "foundation."[16]

Adding distinctiveness to their music, groups introduce breaks at different points in a composition's form, featuring different individuals and combinations of players.[17] Breaks can extend over different durations, even over the larger part of a chorus, at the extreme. Another arranged device is stoptime, in which the rhythm section collectively suspends its normal routine, restricting its performance to the articulation of each measure's downbeat. Dramatic changes in rhythmic accompaniment, like changes occurring in arranged horn riffs, elaborate background lines, and harmonies, build variation into each performance's larger structure and provide different impulses to stimulate the imaginations of soloists.

A sampling of aspects of four different renditions of "Like Someone in Love" illustrates the constellation of features that distinguish small group arrangements. Chet Baker delivers his group's vocal version in a slow ballad style, whereas versions by Art Blakey's Jazz Messengers and by a recording session band featuring John Coltrane move at a medium bounce tempo. The rhythm sections of Baker's group and Coltrane's group maintain a regular beat and improvise complementary parts throughout, but Blakey's rhythm section has worked out syncopated figures that they perform in unison at particular points in the progression. Individual artists clearly state the melody in each of these versions, taking liberties primarily in embellishment.

Providing a greater contrast is Eric Dolphy's and Booker Little's distinctive version, in which, after a brief introduction, Little's trumpet, Dolphy's flute, and Richard Davis's bowed bass interpret the piece allusively, without accompaniment. They improvise a tightly interwoven three-part polyphony that proceeds through the piece with an elastic sense of rhythm at an almost dirgelike tempo. At the head's conclusion, Davis switches to an active pizzicato style, joining the rhythm section to provide solo accompaniments that alternate between a medium tempo and double time. After the solos, Little and Dolphy resume their reflective discourse on the melody, accompanied by the rhythm section's steady beat. Then, the entire ensemble, with Davis again on bowed bass, creates a free-rhythmic section that culminates the performance. In these four renditions of "Like Someone in Love," each band's arrangement is unique, allowing for differing interpretations of the piece and representing different qualities of amorous experience.[18]

### Transmitting Arrangements

Bands usually arrange and teach their material during formal rehearsals. Consequently, the amount of time they allow for rehearsing, usually a function of the particular circumstances surrounding performances, strongly influences the nature of arrangements. When touring headliners or featured soloists meet local rhythm sections for the first time just before performances, or when pick-up groups hastily form for particular engagements, their interplay commonly assumes the character of a jam session and includes little planned activity. In such situations, leaders dictate minimal directions at each number's outset or simply assume the adoption of the simplest conventional format for arrangements described earlier.

Groups that work as stable units, on the other hand, have the opportunity to rehearse regularly and arrange their repertory formally. "We used to rehearse all the time when we were together with Harold Land," Jimmy Robinson declares. "We'd get together maybe two or three times a week if we weren't busy with other gigs. We'd play every night, and then, later in the day, we'd go back to the club and rehearse." As mentioned earlier, some bands develop books of arrangements, which provide continuity to performances even as band membership changes. "Most of the tunes we did with Blakey were from the Jazz Messenger's *Mosaic* album and other albums that they did when Freddie Hubbard and Wayne Shorter were in the band," John Hicks recalls. "Those arrangements were already set."

Some groups rely exclusively on the oral transmission of head arrangements. Lou Donaldson recalls his surprise when an old musician who played "the fourth sax part" in a New Orleans band informed him that he had learned the band's entire repertory—complex counterparts, interludes, breaks, and all—through patient demonstration and memorization. Similarly, for years, Charles Mingus required that musicians "learn everything by ear. It wasn't until he formed his big band in the late sixties and seventies that we read any music," Lonnie Hillyer recalls. "For the most part, it was very difficult music. Mingus heard all these strange intervals. His compositions were very intricate, with a lot of chords. He also had a hell of a knack for range," Hillyer continues. "He had this very high-pitched voice, and he heard things that way. He'd sing some things and then play them at the piano, and we'd learn them from there."

Tommy Turrentine elaborates on performing with Mingus:

> Once everybody had gotten the melody, Mingus would play the rhythm. Once you had the two together, he would work out the harmony. He'd say, "Alright, Tommy, I want you to play such and such."

Once I could play it back, he'd say, "Okay. Now, tenor player, I want you to play this." Then he'd say, "Let me hear you play it together." He'd do that through each tune, section by section, and then we would work on the background lines. That's how we'd rehearse. The ways we did Mingus's music was so complex, the only way to be able to play it was to live with it. I remember one suite we did called "Tours of Manhattan." The ensemble part alone was thirty minutes long. With solos, it was about forty-five or fifty minutes.

Other groups use a combination of written and oral methods. Sometimes, Bobby Hutcherson's and Harold Land's group used written arrangements; at other times, they "would just hand me a blank piece of paper," Rufus Reid recalls, "and dictate the things they wanted me to remember to do at different points in the pieces." At Miles Davis's rehearsals, he "would have some of the music written down, and other things he'd just play for you and you'd learn directly from him" (GB). Yet other groups rely upon scores. In Horace Silver's band, John McNeil and cohorts "never played anything that we didn't rehearse. We even had rehearsals on the road. If Horace wanted to add a new tune or do one of the old ones, he'd just hand out the music and tell us to memorize it. We played so many different kinds of pieces, including one that was through-composed. There was no improvisation in it at all. It had some repeated sections, which made it easier to memorize, but it was quite long."

Given the difficulty of notating idiomatic nuances of jazz, and, in some instances, of reading idiosyncratic manuscript styles, credible interpretation of written parts depends on general understanding of jazz performance practices and knowledge of specific conventions developed within each band. Despite the fact that the through-composed piece mentioned above "was so detailed," John McNeil recollects, "Horace [Silver] spent a lot of time getting the bass and drums to play the right patterns, accents and everything." Benny Bailey describes similar practices:

When Dizzy taught us in his big band, he would show us the way to think when we were playing. Every pattern was a different challenge. Accents had a lot to do with it. You can take triplet figures and, by accenting them a certain way, you can create an optical illusion on the ears. The figure sounds like it's turned around; a lot of it has to do with false fingering also. Those figures get very tricky, and nobody would ever find out how to play them unless someone showed them how to do it.

The interpretation of a piece's melody may depend on comparable subtleties. As a trumpeter eager to learn about jazz, I once was invited to try out for the lead trumpet chair of a swing band. At the first rehearsal, I interpreted the written music according to the Western classical performance practices with which I was most familiar and blended somewhat inconspicuously with the rest of the brass section. The leader hid his disappointment but, at the next rehearsal, invited an experienced trumpeter from another band to share my position. Seated beside him, I was amazed by the music's transformation. The trumpet assumed the most prominent voice within the band, and he filled the room with his sound. He phrased his part with great conviction together with the drummer, not only breathing new life into it, but pulling the entire band along with him in shaping its performance.

In between pieces, the trumpeter leaned over and counseled me concerning aspects of the performance that were nowhere indicated on the written music. The eighth-note patterns, which I had articulated distinctly and with equal value, should instead be slurred together in longer phrase groupings and performed with a triplet swing feeling. "Remember," he added, "since we're playing in a section now, no constant vibrato when the parts are unison. Begin phrases softly. On a sustained note at the end of a phrase, attack it hard, then back off, then let it get loud again, putting a big vibrato on the end." Subsequently, when I doubled his part, I strove to memorize its sound and to match its exciting qualities. By repeatedly recalling his powerful performance, I gradually came to interpret the music properly on my own.

In such situations, group members other than the leader, and in some instances former members, commonly help newcomers. John Hicks initially learned the Jazz Messengers' compositions on his own, but then he "got a fine-tuning from cats like Lee Morgan, Curtis Fuller, and John Gilmore who were in the band. Most of my rehearsing was done on the bandstand," he reveals, "because, with just one or two new guys coming into the band, there wouldn't be special rehearsals unless something special came up—like a television program. I got my experience right there on the bandstand listening to some of the vets with the band who already knew the arrangements." Art Davis recalls that "in Max Roach's band, we did some of Kenny Dorham's arrangements, because he was in the group before Booker Little. So, Kenny would come over sometimes and rehearse his pieces with us. He'd make certain suggestions like, 'This isn't right; phrase that this way.' We'd just play the arrangements down, getting the phrasing of the melody right for the horns and getting the bass notes right. There were certain lines written for the bass."

As indicated above, there is not always a correlation between the forms of music representation that arrangements use and their complexity. Band leaders sometimes teach elaborate arrangements orally or expect members to learn them from records. Even when bands use written arrangements, many restrict their use to that of learning aids. "With Blakey, you had to memorize the music since you couldn't have it on the bandstand" (JH). Similarly, in Horace Silver's band, "there were never any music stands, so we read [new music] off the floor half the time, or off the piano. Basically, you memorized it as soon as you could so you didn't have to mess with it" (JMc).

Some leaders consider it unprofessional for their members to read music during performances, particularly in small groups. They view the dependence upon written scores as an indication that musicians do not yet know the music. In this regard, performers who collaborate with veterans with primarily aural knowledge express awe at the clarity of vision and strength of memory that the older artists embody. Rufus Reid remembers that "Nancy Wilson hadn't studied music formally, but her ears were as big as this house. She always knew what she wanted to hear. If I might play some funny lines behind her, she'd say, 'No, don't do that.' Or she'd say, 'Something's wrong with that,' and invariably it would be a note that was written wrong in the arrangement."

## Collaborating on Arrangements

The processes underlying the creation of arrangements vary according to the skills of band members and the social structure of individual bands. Some leaders create groups in order to perform original pieces that they have conceived in great detail. When leaders appreciate the peculiarities of instruments and share a technical musical language with band members, they can communicate their ideas easily and directly.

As often as not, however, leaders have flexible views on repertory and arrangements, and they invite other members to contribute favored standards or their own works to the band's repertory, and assist in arranging them. In such instances, arrangements represent the sum of the talents of group members. One musician with a gift for melody may collaborate with another to fashion an appropriate chord progression, and, perhaps, with a singer to create lyrics. Yet another player is an especially imaginative orchestrator, who, once provided a strong melody and progression, can envision complementary parts for the full ensemble. The strengths of other band members may lie primarily in composing parts for their own instruments.

When the ideas of those leading the collaborative process are incomplete or imprecise, musicians assist one another in clarifying or refining proposed concepts. In some instances, composers whose knowledge of music is largely aural enlist the aid of specialists within their group, and occasionally outside the group, to set their arrangements into written form, thus speeding the transmission process among music readers.[19] When individuals lack a technical language for discussing music, or when their goals lie outside the descriptive limitations of technical language, they sometimes suggest extramusical associations such as mood, story lines, or abstract, poetic, or graphic images to guide the group effort.[20]

In general, however, the principal dialogue of artists remains the language of music itself. One performer proposes a piece's basic idea by performing a melody, and, in response, other musicians compose alternative complementary patterns. The continuity of such practices reaches back to the earliest days of jazz. In 1919, Lieutenant James Reese Europe described his band members' proclivity for "embroider[ing] their parts in order to produce new, peculiar sounds. Some of these effects are excellent."[21] Of his collaborations with Jelly Roll Morton, Johnny St. Cyr reported, "The solos—they were ad lib. We played according to how we felt. Of course, Jelly had his ideas and sometimes we'd listen to them and sometimes, together with our own, we'd make something better. . . . Reason his records are so full of tricks and changes is the liberty he gave his men. Sometimes . . . *we* get an idea . . . and we ask *him* to let us play a certain break, and he was always open for suggestions."[22]

Years later, Billie Holiday recalled her experiences.[23] While Benny Goodman

> always had big arrangements[,] . . . with Basie, we had something no expensive arrangements could touch. The cats would come in, somebody would hum a tune. Then someone else would play it over on the piano once or twice. Then someone would set up a riff, a ba-deep, a ba-dop. Then Daddy Basie would two-finger it a little. And then things would start to happen.
>
> Half the cats couldn't have read music if they'd had it. They didn't want to be bothered anyway. Maybe sometimes one cat would bring in a written arrangement and the other would run over it. By the time Jack Wadlin, Skeet Henderson, Buck Clayton, Freddie Green, and Basie were through running over it, taking off, changing it, the arrangement wouldn't be recognizable anyway.
>
> Everything that happened, happened by ear. For the two years I was with the band we had a book of a hundred songs, and every one of us carried every last damn note of them in our heads.

Duke Ellington detailed his orchestra's varied approach to arrangements:

> You've got to write with certain men in mind. You write just for their abilities and natural tendencies and give them places where they do their best—certain entrances and exits and background stuff. . . . My band is my instrument.[24]
>
> The music's mostly written down, because it saves time. It's written down if it's only a basis for a change. There's no set system. Most times I write it and arrange it. Sometimes I write it and the band and I collaborate on the arrangement. Sometimes Billy Strayhorn, my staff arranger, does the arrangement. When we're all working together, a guy may have an idea and he plays it on his horn. Another guy may add to it and make something out of it. Someone may play a riff and ask, "How do you like this?" The trumpets may try something to-

gether and say, "Listen to this." There may be a difference of opinion on what kind of mute to use. Someone may advocate extending a note or cutting it off. The sax section may want to put an additional smear on it.[25]

In contemporary jazz groups, as well, musicians explore various ways of rendering pieces throughout rehearsals, starting and stopping their performances at whim, and evaluating the outcomes. Eventually, in a give-and-take process, they settle on those that are mutually satisfactory and incorporate the most successful elements into the evolving designs of arrangements. Sometimes, Lou Donaldson asks a piano player to play "certain chords" before trying out a piece, "but usually," he says, "I'll just start playing the melody and let the pianist catch up." When the performance is over, "I'll ask him what would be the best sequence of chords to use in certain spots. Naturally, he'll have two or three sets of chords that he wants to play. Whatever he suggests, we'll try out."

The possibilities for consideration are endless. On one occasion, a leader proposed that his band perform a 4/4 piece in 6/8, but when he reformulated the melody in the latter meter, it sounded contrived. Faced with the skeptical expressions of fellow band members, he immediately withdrew the idea. Another leader once raised the question of a piece's ending, and the group's saxophonist suggested that the horns repeat a short phrase from the melody as a tag, slowly fading out together. After rehearsing the figure several times, the band approved it unanimously. John Hicks recounts his experience with Betty Carter, who

> had a concept of the different kinds of sounds she wanted, especially on her original music, and we would discuss it together. There's one tune where she wanted something different from a straight diatonic sound. We played this particular line that was going stepwise. It started on the A♭ and went to the B♭ and then to a C, etc. With each one of these chords, we played a different triad to give it a sort of augmented sound. With the A♭, we played a C triad, with the B♭, we played a D triad, and so on. Betty had a lot of ideas like that; she had a real fertile imagination as far as the things she wanted us to do harmonically. She might say, "John, can you dress that chord up and play it in a different way?" I'd play it in a different way, and she'd say, "Yes, that's what I want." She might not have the exact name of the chord, but she would have the sound in her head, and from the note she was singing, she could figure it out. Sometimes, we'd play a couple of different chords and see which one actually fit. These are the kinds of things we'd work out.

Because of the interdependence of ensemble members, decisions concerning each part's details commonly affect others, involving members in an ongoing process of mutual accommodation. At a rehearsal of Benny Bailey's and saxophonist Charlie Rouse's quintet, a lead sheet designated that the pianist improvise an introduction of a prescribed length. John Hicks considered the part and remarked that he would like "to extend it a bit" so that he could "really get into it." Bailey agreed, and Hicks experimented with an expanded intro. At its close, however, when the horn players endeavored to play the melody, their parts lacked synchronization. Bailey stopped the music and suggested that Hicks incorporate a "more rhythmic figure" into his performance that would indicate the tempo clearly, "setting up" the rest of the players. After trying several versions on his own, each failing to meet his satisfaction, Hicks settled upon a likely solution to the problem and signaled the others for another trial. He began the introduction in free rhythm, gradually evolved a more regular feeling of the beat, and ended with a repeated riff in the bass that delineated the meter precisely. This approach effectively cued the horn players, and Hicks announced that he would make a mental note to preserve his performance's "rhythmic shape" as a feature of the introduction.

Turning next to a bossa nova by Hicks, the group performed the melody once, then alternated solos. Bailey improvised a lively solo chorus with an open trumpet, then a contrasting chorus with a cup mute, playing simply and softly. Afterwards, Hicks praised Bailey and explained that, although the arrangement had not specified it, the muted timbre of Bailey's solo and its relaxed performance style had captured his piece's feeling perfectly. Responding appreciatively, Bailey made the decision to adopt this approach for future performances. He also discussed with Keith Copeland softening the drum accompaniment whenever he muted his horn. Copeland decided to switch from sticks to brushes to complement Bailey's dynamic levels.

In some instances, the possibilities players hear in each another's ideas and encouragement from other players within the group inspire the originators to expand upon their ideas, leading sometimes to exceptional creations. Such was the genesis of Bobby Timmons's classic composition, "Moanin'," in a "funky" eight-bar phrase that Timmons played for amusement in between numbers at rehearsals, self-effacingly dismissing it as "nothing, not really a tune." The phrase was so infectious to Benny Golson that he urged Timmons to compose a bridge for it, and, as the saying goes, "the rest is history." [26]

## Changing Arrangements

Many musicians, although benefiting from the guidance of arrangements, alter them over time. As the frameworks of compositions serve as inspiring vehicles for improvisation, new arrangements provide comparable inspiration, challenging group members to negotiate fresh musical models in performance and stimulating the conception of ideas in the process. Performing a piece "thousands of times over a career, you're always going deeper and deeper into its possibilities, discovering new ways of doing things," Chuck Israels explains. Alternative arrangements by Bill Evans sometimes treated "serious pieces with humor" or, conversely, "viewed silly pieces with serious thought." On different occasions, Israels has performed pieces like "I'll Remember April" in ways that "related directly to their lyrics" or in ways that ignored their associations and treated the melodies as musical abstractions. Thelonious Monk epitomizes the artist's intensive attention to revising arrangements, commonly practicing a single composition for two hours at a sitting: experimenting with chord voicings and substitutions, subtly altering the melody's contour and phrasing (BH). His plans remained in a constant state of evolution. He "always played his own tunes in different ways" (LH).

Although arrangers work out fundamental ideas on their own, they depend on rehearsals with other artists and live performances to test and evaluate ideas, especially for elaborate arrangements. "There's nothing like hearing your music played night after night," George Duvivier says. "You can always hear things you can improve upon, like the voicings. The ways some things move may look fine on paper, but they may not actually work when the musicians play them. With Chick Webb's band, sometimes I'd try to get a heavier effect in a certain section and I'd weight the parts too much. They'd play through the parts and someone would say, 'It's a little too heavy in bars 4 and 5.'"

Art Davis recollects that

> Booker Little did a lot of the writing in Max Roach's band. Sometimes, he would write things on the spot for us to play. Other times, he'd have things already written. Also, Booker would modify the arrangements at times. He'd tell George Coleman to play something else here or there, or he would pick up his horn and try something out himself, playing something different from what he had written. This would add a little bit of flavor to the arrangements; just one note might make a difference. Sometimes, he would change whole sections just to get it in there.

Flexibility is also the rule in Betty Carter's bands. "We were constantly changing the songs around," John Hicks remembers. "None of them stayed the same for very long. I didn't write much of this down with Betty. Writing wouldn't have helped that much. My own memory just developed over a period of time." Kenny Washington appreciates Carter's ingenuity, as well. "Take 'My Favorite Things' from *The Sound of Music*," he suggests:

> Betty had been doing it in 4/4 for some time . . . and had recorded it on her record called *Inside*. By the time I joined the band, she was doing the tune at twice the tempo it was on the album. Then, a few months later when we're playing it in a rehearsal, she says, "No, wait a minute. I don't want to do it like this anymore. Listen, here's what I

want you to do. I want you to play in 3/4 time in the beginning, and then when you get to the bridge, play real fast in 4/4 time, and then when you get to the beginning of the chorus, switch back to 3/4 time." That's the way she conducted things. She would sit there at the rehearsals, and on a whim, she would say, "Let's change it this way or let's change it like that."

She had a big drawer full of music, and sometimes she'd pull out an arrangement of a song she had done maybe fifteen years before. We'd start playing the arrangement, and she would say, "No, I don't want to do it like that. Kenny, I want you to switch to brushes and come in on the second chorus." Sometimes she would do tunes and rehearse them, and you'd figure they would be on the next gig. But they weren't. Then several weeks would go by, and suddenly she'd pull out one of those tunes, and you had better be able to play it. So Betty was hip for me. She kept my mind sharp. She'd change the music around so much, you really had to be on the ball.

Challenges of this nature can become points of contention or humor among performers. During Benny Bailey's and Charlie Rouse's rehearsal, momentary confusion arose over several versions of a piece that John Hicks had written. After determining the final version and performing it, Bailey expressed his admiration to Hicks with the teasing plea, "Now that you got it, don't work on it anymore. Don't change it!" Then he recalled how Duke Ellington "used to have all those different versions of his pieces floating around the band. All the cats had five or six arrangements of the same piece. And when you joined the band, no one would tell you which one was the current one. They'd let you find out too late that you were playing the wrong one, and you'd scramble for another," Bailey laughs. "Ellington was always rewriting the parts."

When bands alter their plans during rehearsals, members have the time to absorb new directions before performances. The challenges increase, however, when leaders extemporaneously introduce changes at formal music events. Leaders may vary repertory programs at whim as the evening progresses. As implied above, a related area of change is tempo. Billie Holiday never performed the same piece at the same tempo twice. She constantly varied its mood to suit her own.[27] Within the group such decisions by leaders may have implications that differ from player to player. In Lee Konitz's experience, for example, improvisers may function better at different tempos from day to day, whether in reference to music thinking, emotional temperament, or physicality.

Precise patterns within individual parts or within the larger scheme of arrangements are also subject to spontaneous revisions. At one recording session, pianist Red Garland began an introduction to "You Are My Everything" with free-rhythmic arpeggiations. Miles Davis called out, "Block chords, block chords!" Garland immediately stopped playing and, for the second take, altered his introduction.[28] On another occasion, when saxophonist George

Adams and John Hicks approached the bandstand, Adams asked Hicks whether he could play a piece in 3/4 that they usually performed in 4/4. When Hicks concurred, they featured the new version as the set's opening number. Later, Hicks cited other examples of the agile responses required of players.

> In Blakey's band, some of the older tunes from a few generations ago would be updated, and we would make new arrangements for them. The way that this would come about was that Art would tell Lee Morgan that there was a particular thing that he wanted you to do, and Lee would tell the rest of the guys, and we'd put it into the form of the tune. He'd break the tune down into sections and say, "At letter A, I want such and such to happen." It might be a different meter or break time or stoptime. That would usually be done right on the bandstand.

Rank and file band members may also introduce changes. At one engagement, a conga player spoke to the group's trap-set drummer as they prepared for the second set. "I'm feeling wasted tonight," he lamented. "Can you support me on my solo? Keep a strong thing going on your hi-hat and watch me. If I tire, we can trade fours like we did the other night." The drummer nodded in agreement.

The flexibility of an arrangement depends in part on the band's size and on the form the arrangement takes, whether it be oral or written. The quartet Art Farmer organized with Jim Hall "was very free. We had arrangements, but if someone wanted to change, you didn't feel you had to do it the same every night," he recalls.

> If you have six people in the group and you want to do something different, you have to go around whispering to everyone on the bandstand. It's like the more people you have on the stand, the more restricted you are. If you try to do something different without telling everybody else what you're going to do in advance, then they're thrown and they don't know how to react. If you've had a rehearsal and told people you're going to do one thing and then go on the job and do something else, it's disruptive. Especially if the arrangements are written up.

The practices associated with arrangements can also differ, even under the same leader, as a function of the band's changing membership, the ability of players, their sympathetic understanding of the music, their familiarity with one another's styles, and various circumstantial factors surrounding specific engagements.[29] As is clear from musicians' comments, however, many features that jazz's dynamic tradition values would stultify if players could not apply their myriad skills to revising arrangements to some degree. Successful alterations themselves heighten the creative excitement of improvisation.

## Conducting Arrangements

With the exception of big bands, jazz groups typically perform in public without a conventional conductor or conductor's baton to coordinate different parts or direct transitions between events. Band leaders or members acting as music directors periodically assume particular responsibilities for guiding the group. Sometimes, they announce each piece before its performance and count off the tempo. If the order of soloists has not been established beforehand, they may signal each soloist's entrance.

For cohesion, groups most commonly regulate performances through a variety of subtle cues. In the absence of specified directions, performers may infer the appropriate tempo from a soloist's initiation of the melody, or a rhythm section introduction. "Betty Carter had different ways she'd want you to play in terms of the tempo," Kenny Washington remembers. "You had to watch her on the bandstand, her hands and her movements. She would bring her arm down a certain way to establish the beat. There would be no counting off, like 'one, two, three, four.' The secret was being able to figure out the tempo from the way she brought her hand down." Barry Harris recalls Lester Young dictating the tempo with subtle movements of his shoulder, and Max Roach describes Dizzy Gillespie directing the band through his inventive dance movements.[30]

Similarly, if arrangements do not designate a solo's length, the soloist, perhaps by raising the instrument slightly, can indicate that the chorus in process is the last and its ideas are near completion. This allows the next soloist to get ready for performance. Within the free jazz context, artists sometimes give musical signals for such additional operations as "changing modes by holding tones related to the modal level toward which the music is moving."[31] Other cues relate to dynamics. "I might tell the drummer, 'When I pick up the bow to play, I want you to play stronger,'" Rufus Reid explains. Without such planning, he finds that when he begins bowing, "drummers stop playing or play timidly. I would rather they play with a little more gusto because that gives me a little more to play off." Kenny Washington learned about comparable cues in Betty Carter's band. "Betty also taught me a lot about dynamics," he asserts. "She would have a certain arm movement which meant play soft and another one which would mean to stroll or lay out altogether. Not only that, she'd also cue you in for certain accents while you're playing. Like she wanted you to play what she called 'anticipated ones,' that is, the 'and of fours.' You'd be playing a tune at one of her fast tempos, and she'd make this body movement on the 'and of four' just at the same time you played it, and it was so hip for the audience."

When an instrument restricts physical gesture, musicians commonly signal with slight movements of the head or eyes. As mentioned earlier, Bobby Hutcherson and Harold Land sometimes direct transitions from one section of an arrangement to another by nodding. Such nonverbal gestures serve equally well to regulate performance in the face of error. "There was a lot of pressure from within the bands," Lou Donaldson says. "You just missed one note in the arrangements or blew the dynamics, and every head in the band turned toward you. Nobody would have to say anything. You'd never do that again." In a lighter vein, Dicky Wells remembers Lester Young reprimanding fellow band members with "his little bell. If somebody missed a note, or you were a new guy and goofed, you'd hear this bell going—'Ding-dong!' . . . Jo Jones had another way of saying the same thing. *Bing-bing-bing,* he'd go on his cymbal rod. . . . And if Pres [Young] saw someone getting angry, he'd blow the first bar of 'Runnin' Wild.' "[32]

Some leaders take more dramatic measures to ensure their music's faithful rendition. At a Charles Mingus concert in which the pianist forgot a portion of his part, Mingus rested the bass on his shoulder and mimed the performance of broad, sweeping arpeggios until the pianist took his meaning, switching from block chords to arpeggiated figures. Mingus also directed the performance verbally at times.[33] So did Jaki Byard in his own bands. Byard would periodically call out for drummer Alan Dawson to "walk it," that is, change the music's rhythmic feeling by improvising with emphatic backbeats. At times, Byard also would orient the band to the composition's form by shouting "one" at the beginning of the chorus or "four" to signal the remaining measures before the beginning of the next chorus.[34]

Tommy Turrentine recollects his experience with Mingus's band:

One night at Birdland, we were playing Mingus's suite "Tours of Manhattan," and I forgot a little interlude that we were supposed to play about Chinatown. Do you know what he did? He stopped the whole band in front of the audience. The place was packed, and he walked up to the microphone and said, "Ladies and gentlemen, as you know this is called the Charles Mingus Workshop. We had just left the Village on our way to Chinatown, but it seems like our trumpet player got lost. So, if he can remember his way now, I'll give him a car check and we can go back to the West Village and resume our journey to Chinatown. Can you remember that, Tom?" I said, "Yes, sir," and we continued playing the suite.

Turrentine concludes the story with a bit of chagrin: "We had just learned the music."

Prototypes for the diverse orchestral designs described here have remained a part of the jazz tradition, cutting across different style periods. From the elaborately arranged events in such early jazz groups as Jelly Roll Morton's Red Hot Peppers and Joe Oliver's Creole Jazz Band to the works of Fletcher

Henderson's orchestra and Jimmie Lunceford's band, in which "everything was written out—chord symbols and sometimes even the bass lines" (GD)—some provide considerable musical detail.[35] Arrangements may even require performers to play a designated part throughout the piece's performance, leaving no room for improvisation.

Other arrangements, however, give minimal detail. Count Basie's arrangements for up-tempo compositions often included only the spare plan of a several-bar introduction, the melody's statement, "brass or saxophone figures" to accompany soloists, and "one or more choruses of climactic riffs by the entire band" as the close.[36] Years later, the arrangements of John Coltrane's *Ascension* band, in addition to occasional reiterations of melodic lines, simply indicated "certain tonalities that particular instruments had to stay within when they improvised" (AD).[37] Kenny Barron remembers that "one of Yusef Lateef's tunes was also very free. We had to improvise using a classical composition technique he had gotten from Stockhausen like a twelve-tone row. Yusef wouldn't tell you specific things to play," Barron recalls, "but he might ask you to project a certain kind of mood."[38] Some free jazz groups perform without using any compositions or formal arrangements as vehicles for improvisation.

In between these extremes, most arrangements entail a general set of guidelines delineating the overall structure of renditions and successive events within them. Whether adopting conventional pieces as vehicles or experimenting with new compositional forms, they allot space for improvisation at selected points and prescribe fully orchestrated patterns at others, ensuring cohesion within the ensemble for the music event.[39]

# TWELVE

**Adding to Arrangements**

Conventions Guiding the Rhythm Section

*The first thing I look for is how well the drummer is propelling the band, because that's his main function. I listen for how creatively he is propelling the band, that is, how he phrases and how well he plays the arrangement: making the proper breaks, punching the melodic figures of the band in the right places. And, of course, I listen to what he adds of his own to the arrangement.* —Charli Persip

With much of the music's detail left to their discretion, jazz musicians improvise their parts around those patterns and events predetermined by arrangements, fleshing out the larger presentation to render each composition anew. An interrelated web of traditional performance practices guides this collective music-making process and contributes to the improvisation of mutually sympathetic musical parts. Some practices are associated with distinct repertory genres, others with different jazz idioms and the personal performance styles of leading rhythm section players. Yet others concern the musical roles of the mainstay rhythm section instruments.

The initial perception that aspiring performers have of these matters sometimes contributes to their early specialization. George Duvivier found the string bass to be an especially compelling instrument because its low resonant sound generally provided the "foundation" of orchestral music, "these big notes pouring out, . . . the powerful descending bottom line." For a similar reason, Keith Copeland decided to become a drummer after his study of records by Art Blakey's Jazz Messengers lead him to conclude that, however subtly, "the drums actually controlled what was going on in the rest of the band." In some instances, musicians deepen their intuitive grasp of these distinctions by learning to perform multiple instruments, gaining direct experience with the ways in which each complements its counterparts within jazz groups. "Art Blakey was a pianist before he became a drummer," Max Roach recalls. "And I also played piano on some dates. Wynton Kelly and Horace Silver were both fine saxophonists when they came to New York, as well as piano players."

In the most general sense, the rhythm section's collective function is to "comp," a term that carries the dual connotations of *accomp*anying and *comp*lementing. To Walter Bishop Jr., this special skill means "to get under the soloist—not over him or on par with him—and to lay down a carpet. One of the reasons why Bird hired me was that he liked the way I comped. Comping has been one of my strong suits." To learn to comp with subtlety and improvise with distinction, young bass players, drummers, and pianists must master the performance conventions associated with their instruments through a long process of disciplined study, trials, and discoveries.

### The String Bass

Since the early days of jazz, the bass has played a central part within rhythm sections by interpreting and delineating the harmonic-rhythmic structures of pieces.[1] Due, in part, to the slow playing action of the early instruments, bass parts were initially spare, in many instances comprising regular two-beat patterns of chord roots and fifths alternated on the first and third beats of measures. At the same time, players like John Lindsay with Jelly Roll Morton's band periodically varied such practices by switching to vigorous four-beat patterns, stoptime rhythm, bowed bass, and slap-bass techniques.[2] The latter involved "slapping the fingerboard with the open palm of the right hand while grasping the string to be plucked" or pulling the string "up away from the fingerboard" and releasing it to produce an especially "forceful slap (or snap) sound." Variations in timbre and dynamics produced by different slap-bass methods were considered the equivalent "hot sound" to growling through a horn.[3]

Pops Foster recalls both the varied procedures of bass players and the changing conventions surrounding bass accompaniment: "In New Orleans we'd have two pick notes in one bar, then you'd go six bars of bowing, and maybe have one note to pick. . . . In New York we started picking four to a bar. Now we pick four or eight beats to a bar."[4] Beyond outlining the chord progression, Foster created "countermelodies" to the horn players' lines in either plucked or bowed bass style and, at times, responded antiphonally to the pianist's creations.[5] During the swing period, Walter Page's largely stepwise walking bass accompaniment in Count Basie's band epitomized the changing emphasis on the four-beat approach to meter described by Foster.

Before amplification and steel strings, the bass commonly receded within the group's overall blend of sounds. Sometimes, its part was reinforced by the bass drum pattern. In the forties, the development of instruments capable of faster playing action and increasingly sophisticated amplification techniques enabled bass players to assume a more dominant role in accompaniment. Amplified, they could stand alone in maintaining the music's lowest voice. Improved playing action also enabled them to perform parts that were more complex. Artists mixed chord arpeggiations with the smooth stepwise motion and four beats to the measure of walking bass lines, occasionally varying such regularity. Bass players in the forties and fifties added to the evolving conventions of bass accompaniment; over the past few decades, the bassist's options have continued to multiply. Players like Charles Mingus departed from their instrument's conventional time-keeping role by constantly changing the rhythmic feel of their performance.[6]

As bass players formulate a part today, they regulate various interrelated features of rhythm, harmonic color, and contour according to basic principles of tension and release, their alternation contributing to the music's swing and momentum. With respect to rhythm, players can structure their improvisations in ways that establish different time-feelings at the level of both pitch-to-pitch movement and metric organization. They commonly reinforce the music's four-beat character by performing steady quarter notes, but enliven it by minutely varying the placement of pitches in relation to the beat.

Artists can enhance the line's syncopation less subtly by emphasizing beats two and four through the performance of double stops, non-chord tones, and, occasionally, ghosted or indeterminate pitches whose effects are predominantly percussive. Moreover, bass players periodically add spice and variety to their more constant patterns by substituting two eighth notes or an eighth-note triplet for individual quarter notes, or by playing syncopated eighth notes tied to quarter notes. The alternative positioning of rhythmically active figures produces varied effects. Triplet subdivisions on beat two or four stabilize the music by drawing the ear to subsequent quarter notes on the third beat or the downbeat. Displacing the triplet by a beat draws the ear to quarter notes on beats two and four, temporarily destabilizing the music, but ultimately increasing its syncopated drive toward subsequent points of resolution on strong beats.

Among the various rhythmic subtleties that players can add to quarter-note playing is "pulsing" or "dead string" playing, a technique integral to the styles of players like Jimmy Garrison. Pulsing consists of adding, underneath the primary figures of a line, "very soft upbeat accents" produced on an open string by an additional finger. Although effective in performance, the technique is not necessarily audible on recordings (LG). Pursuing more radical options, bass players may suspend regular reference to the beat by sustaining pitches or introducing rests into the bass part. Bass players may also perform complex rhythms over the barline.

In addition to such flexible treatments of the underlying meter, bass players may produce a different layer of metric organization within the music's
texture by moving from pitch to pitch at rates consistently slower or faster than
other band members. They can play half-note patterns to create a two-beat
feeling, establishing this, perhaps, as the music's overriding metric framework
while the other parts proceed in 4/4 time. They can also superimpose polymetric patterns over the principal meter, playing ongoing figures of six quarter
notes within the time frame of four.

While managing various time-keeping aspects of their role, bass players
make constant decisions about their part's harmonic and melodic features. The
instrument's function tends to limit their rhythmic activity, but bass players
share many of the soloist's concerns regarding pitch choices, alternative ways
of interpreting harmony, and the like. In the most general harmonic terms, they
have the job of outlining the progression. This is neither a mechanical nor a
static process; rather, it is one of constantly reinterpreting the composition's
chords and their harmonic-rhythmic motion. Bass players commonly lead their
melodies toward such goals as chord tones on beats one and three. Larry Gray
explains, "You're always phrasing into downbeats." In 4/4 time, for example,
players tend not to think in terms of the beat grouping "one, two, three, four"
but in terms of the beat grouping "two, three, four, one." In this sense,
their lines are "always moving ahead," Gray says. "Jazz is over-the-barline
music."

Such general conventions still allow bass players great liberty in formulating their parts. Their options encompass a vast world of possibilities. They can
describe each chord and its rhythmic boundaries unequivocally by playing the
tonic on the downbeat of the change, creating arpeggiated figures throughout
its harmonic area. Adhering to the progression strictly from chord to chord
and emphasizing vertical melodic constructions tend "to divide the music into
different measure groups" one or two bars long and to produce relatively "less
forward motion" than other options. For contrast, bass players can emphasize
horizontal constructions such as diatonic or chromatic scalar passages,
carrying the listener over the barlines of measures toward longer-range goals.
The static harmonic effects of periodic drones or pedals (pedal points), which
typically sustain the tonic or the fifth of the piece's key, further diversify bass
parts.

Within such alternative courses, the precise mixture and placement of
chord tones and non-chord tones reflect musicians' different interests in interpreting chords literally or more allusively—at times, even elusively. They can
portray a new harmonic area allusively with chord tones other than the tonic
and establish the tones' presence at some point other than the downbeat. Moreover, they may emphasize non-chord tones in their formulations, creating harmonic color and suspense. Such operations simply prolong and intensify the

resolutions that typically follow, as artists arrive at harmonic goals within subsequent chord areas.

In this regard, if bass players select some pitches to represent the underlying harmony, they select other pitches with the intention of making smooth and interesting connections between chord tones and bringing about effective resolutions, as they maneuver between adjacent segments of a progression. Neighbor pitches commonly serve this function, as do pitches derived from chord substitutions. According to convention, strong resolutions approach the tonic of a new chord by a chromatic step or by a skip of a fifth. Weaker resolutions result from motion that signals the arrival at a chord less definitively. Every option produces a distinct effect, the appropriateness of which the bass player assesses according to the part's changing requirements, choosing one, or a sequence, that moves to the desired resolution.

The lengths of phrases and their relationship to the progression's harmonic-rhythmic scheme are also variable features of bass lines, creating additional interest. Phrases whose components fit neatly within the boundaries of measures or within the progression's larger harmonic segments reaffirm the composition's form. Phrases whose melodic accents cause distinct components to emerge over the barlines, or phrases that span unusual groupings of measures, provide a rhythmic counterpoint to the form.

The tonal materials featured by bass players within their ongoing lines also have rhythmic ramifications, producing different impressions of the flow of time. If players formulate a phrase by repeating ascending scale degrees, for example, changing pitches every two beats, they place a stress on the first and third beats of measures to produce a certain kind of drive. Pitch change on every beat, achieved, perhaps, through an ascending stream of nonrepeating pitches, creates the impression of greater acceleration and drive toward the downbeat. Producing the sensation of even greater acceleration are movements among the short intervallic steps of chromatic patterns. The "dancy rhythmic feeling" produced when players change melodic direction with especially wide intervallic leaps is also distinctive (LG).

Managing such movements from phrase to phrase and from chorus to chorus, bass players concern themselves throughout with matters of continuity and development. They may devote particular segments of their lines to exploring scalar patterns, and other line segments to creating unique melodic shapes. Like soloists carrying on their internal conversation, bass players sometimes generate ideas through repetition, stressing a particular idea as a theme, or through motivic development, expanding upon the features of previous patterns. After exploiting this approach, they may experiment with wide-ranging dynamic and timbral effects. Alternatively, they concentrate on rhythmic invention, featuring diverse rhythmic subdivisions of the beat or alternating between different metric frames, for example, between four-beat and two-beat playing.

Over the larger performance's course, bass players make comparable determinations about the harmonic features of their lines. They may consistently bring the character of certain chords within the progression into clear profile as structural markers, whereas they take great liberties in the interpretation of other chords. Players may introduce emphatic markers in varying degrees of density in different parts of the form. Some may emphasize root and fifth playing on the first chord of major harmonic segments; others may feature this approach whenever chords change. Still others may favor, generally, a greater emphasis on "outside" harmonic invention than on "inside" playing.

Exploring different registers also adds dynamism to the bass part, casting it in slightly different roles. In the lowest register, it provides the foundation of the group's music, whereas in the highest register, it intertwines with the parts of other instruments or, on occasion, emerges with a soloistic voice. Bass players may change registers in relation to the composition's major formal sections as a way of shaping the performance overall. The precise events taking place within the other parts have a constant influence on the bass line's improvisation throughout the piece. Ultimately, the goal of many players is to create a part that has value in its own right, as well as fulfilling its foundational and interactional roles within the group.

Players describe the art of bass accompaniment and artists' individual styles in historical perspective. "At one time, the bass just provided a thump, thump, thump, thump accompaniment, and you recognized it by its absence," Buster Williams observes. "Now, the bass is a voice to be reckoned with, a voice that helps form the music." This is also Red Rodney's experience as a soloist. "Today, even when the bass player's keeping the basic time going, he's creating different rhythmic patterns behind you." Rufus Reid, interpreting these developments in one historic band, reports that in Bill Evans's trio, it was as if Evans advised LaFaro not simply "to walk," but to become a "voice." Through the innovations of LaFaro and others, "the whole thing evolved," Reid explains, leading bass players to take the same kinds of liberties melodically and rhythmically that a horn player would. The bass continues to develop within the jazz idiom in direct relationship to the skills and creativity of its master artists (exx. 12.1a–b).

## Learning the Musical Role of the Bass

Experienced performers guide younger bass players by instructing them in the subtleties of bass lines. Don Pate's father occasionally brought home written bass parts from recording session arrangements and played through them with his son. He also composed exemplary bass lines for Don and demonstrated their application within the blues progression. Similarly, Buster Williams's father

> would talk about how to keep a bass line moving forward, like the right choice of notes. Certain times, he would indicate which were the best notes to use in certain places. Often, he wouldn't tell me which were the best, and that allowed me to try to find them for myself. Also, other musicians would hear me play, and they'd say, "Better go listen to your father a little more." Or they'd give me specific advice like, "When you go from C7 to F7, try to play the line this way, with this idea." The guys in the band gave me suggestions about different ideas, different melodic shapes to keep the movement of the bass lines interesting. All those things helped to shape my concept.

Bass players develop their understanding on the bandstand, as well. Al Stringer, the organist, was the leader in a duo with Rufus Reid, one of Reid's earliest professional collaborations. Stringer used to play bass lines on the organ for Reid to imitate. At the time, Reid knew generally what was expected of a bass in the situation, but Stringer showed him "many specific kinds of things. Some of the lines he taught me were more jagged rhythmically, like in the rock style. Others were more like walking bass lines with a swing feel. He also showed me how to use scales in certain places, playing different shapes, not just staying in the chords all the time. He didn't give me much slack," Reid says good-humoredly, "but stayed right on me. I just did what I could and tried different things. If they didn't work, Al let me know it right away."

Chuck Israels also acquired some of his musical sophistication from working with groups.

> I picked up a lot by ear on the bandstand, and I learned mainly by osmosis. Steve Kuhn had perfect pitch, and he was sometimes very short with me when I played a wrong note or got lost in a series of progressions. Kuhn might call the tune, and I'd know the melody in a general way and would be able to hear a reasonable facsimile of a correct bass line for the first twelve measures, but then I'd turn right when the music turned left. When that would happen, I was told the correct changes, and I made it a point never to forget them.
>
> Later, when I played with Bill Evans, Bill wrote out his chord progression for his own compositions and for the standard pieces that we would play. Sometimes he'd just write them on the inside of a matchbook cover, and I'd have to read them on the bandstand. He'd write the changes, and I'd play the bass lines. Bill wrote such detailed chord progressions with different chord changes every two beats, there wasn't too much for me to fill in. The bass line was implicit.

While absorbing what musicians offered through peer instruction, Israels found his bandstand experience invaluable in developing broad improvisation skills through an increased understanding of the interrelationship between arranged patterns and those he could amplify from his own imagination. "Of course, I could change melodic directions when I played," he declares.

> Also, I would occasionally take other liberties. If a line of chords were going from D to G, I might play D–E–F–G or D–E–F–F♯–G. Or I would decorate it, sneaking in D–A♭–G or D–A–A♭–G. But actually, most of the decorations, like passing chords, were already in there. One of the things I got from Bill was an appreciation for his enormously detailed set-up and organization of the bass line as a counterpoint to the original melody. Bill's bass lines always felt good to play, because they went so strongly with the melody which you were carrying in your head. The line itself evoked the main melody because the bass line was such a perfect counterpoint.

Students develop their understanding further from recordings, copying appealing bass patterns that complement particular harmonic movements. One of the "little tricks" that Calvin Hill learned was the use of a descending chromatic line over a iii–vi–ii–V progression or turnback as an alternative to playing chord arpeggiations. "If you're in the key of C, you can go E–E♭–D–D♭ and repeat the sequence," he discovered. Ultimately, youngsters' discovery of identical or closely related versions of bass vocabulary in the performances of other players provides models for their own evolving store of patterns (exx. 12.2a–b). For aspiring bass players, as for drummers and pianists, method books providing composed accompaniment models or actual transcriptions of an expert's improvised accompaniments are also instructive.[7]

In the case of some learners, Chuck Israels says, their "non-jazz" musical backgrounds inadvertently prepared them to appreciate the qualities of effective bass parts. He explains in detail:

> When you come right down to it and start analyzing great jazz bass lines, as long as they remain tied to normal tonal harmony, they're like Bach. . . . Except for a few situations, a good bass player will play roots rather than fifths of chords. . . . Some other rules: a scalewise passage can change direction at any time. After a leap, that is, an interval of more than a second, one returns by a step in the opposite direction, except when that leap is followed by another leap, in which case you have an arpeggiated figure, and you're free to continue or change direction. But as soon as you go from a leap back to a stepwise, conjunct motion, you invariably do that in the opposite direction from the last leap you took. Unless, as in Bach, you continue in the same direction only to come back immediately and then turn back in the opposite direction so that the continuation in the same direction becomes an embellishment. If you look at satisfying jazz bass lines, almost all of them follow these rules.

In addition to learning the common musical gestures shared by jazz bass players, performers study the personal concepts of accompaniment and the precise signature patterns that distinguish leading experts. Ray Brown's walking lines impressed Buster Williams for their "sheer strength and happy feeling," as well as for their distinctive melodic contours. When Brown performed, every pitch was "strong, clear, and perfectly in tune," Williams explains. He finds an alternative model in Paul Chambers, who "played a little softer, more gently and maybe more compassionately than Brown. He also had a way of walking and playing chord changes that was different from any other bass player." That is, whereas Brown's lines established a strong sense of melodic direction, Chambers's lines were "a little more subtle" and more difficult to anticipate. "It was as if they'd meet at the same place, but Brown would come in the front door, and Chambers would enter through the back door," Williams concludes.

Characteristic nuances of Chambers's style also include his use of microtones and the liberties he took with pitch inflection, exemplifying the effective ways in which mature artists periodically "break the standard rules" that govern bass lines. "Chambers would sometimes find some notes in between the notes," Chuck Israels explains, "putting four pitches in a line in which there was only room for three. For example, if he had to get from D to F and he had to play four notes in there and he happened to be going chromatically, he would go from a D to a flattened E♭ to a sharpened E♭ to an E to an F. Maybe he played the D on the downbeat of one measure and wanted the F to be the downbeat of the next measure and didn't want to break the chromatic nature of the line, so he made the line even more chromatic, microtonally chromatic. It was a very beautiful thing."

Other subtleties involve articulation. "They nicknamed Milt Hinton 'Frump' because he plays his notes short," Kenny Washington says. "They're not exactly staccato, but they're shorter than players from the younger generation like Ron Carter or Ray Drummond. It was a new experience for me to play with him, because the older bass player's concept is so different. Their time-feel is different." George Duvivier describes other traits imitated by disciples of contemporary bass players and distinguishes the "Stanley Clarke approach" from "the Ron Carter and Buster Williams approach." The former utilizes "glissandos," a "wide vibrato," and "flurries" of pitches, whereas the latter features "low, sustained notes on the E and A strings" and a "certain way" of formulating lines with "doubling up on the stumble," the triplet eighth-note device "Ray Brown introduced" to vary his quarter-note bass patterns.

Finally, students expand their understanding through experimentation, gradually cultivating a large storehouse of phrases that serve as optional components for bass lines. Chuck Israels describes how he

> learned to play by simply building up my vocabulary of musical devices. For example, there are some points in the harmony of a piece

that are very specific in their requirements of the bass notes. One has to be on the root of the dominant chord just before you hit the tonic chord in many situations. Other times, as in the fourth measure of the blues, you'll be on the root of the tonic chord and the chord is going to change to the dominant chord of the key a fourth above.

If you're on an F chord in the key of F, it's going to go to the B♭ chord. So what are you going to play there? F–F–F–F or F–A–C–F are basic possibilities, but what kind of pattern are you going to come up with? I've got to stay on the F chord. How am I going to get away from the root and then get back to it? Or am I going to go from that F to an A and approach B♭ from a half step below? Or am I going to go from the F to the B and approach the B♭ from a half step above? Or am I going to make a progression of minor thirds and end up someplace else? Am I going to go F–A♭–B–D, and then to another F? How am I going to fill the space in such a way that the bass line has integrity against the given melody? . . . There are various patterns that work and various kinds of implied inner voice motions, suspensions, and superimposed chords—all kinds of things which have a greater or lesser satisfaction for me in a given musical situation. It depends, among other things, on what the melody is doing at that point. In working with Bill Evans, I found innumerable examples of extremely satisfying solutions to problems like that . . . and I could use them whenever the problems arose in playing a tune.

From experience fashioning lines in the practice room and during formal events, bass players develop gestures of varying degrees of detail that serve the function of representing particular chords or bridging successive harmonic areas. Like the soloist's vocabulary patterns, some comprise general contours, partial shapes, or, simply, target pitches within a harmonic area—requiring further pitch selection in each performance of the idea (ex. 12.3a). As bass players experiment with different realizations of such ideas, they continually discover new versions that appeal to them, and enter them into their storehouses as fully detailed figures. Subsequently, they may use them with the same chord as it arises in different parts of progressions, and, where compatible, with different chords. At the same time, within the limitations of their role as accompanists, they alter the figures through transposition, pitch substitution, rhythmic rephrasing, displacement, augmentation, and the like (exx. 12.3b–d).

Moreover, as bass players apply the patterns, they find that particular linear combinations work together especially well. They subsequently absorb them into their stores as larger models for invention. Resemblances among the bass lines found in multiple choruses and different takes of blues performances by Paul Chambers and Percy Heath reveal the repeated use of construction pattern models ranging in length from two measures to eight measures, in the latter instance guiding performance over nearly three-quarters of a chorus (exx.

12.4a–b). Heath's performance also illuminates the numerous roles that a bass vocabulary pattern can play over its life: at one time, initiating a chorus accompaniment as a discrete idea; at another, eliding with an adjacent pattern to form a gesture that serves as an accompaniment theme; at still another, interacting with substitute patterns to form a large recurring model (ex. 12.4b). In a continuing cycle of generation, application, and renewal, bass players create new shapes by transforming elaborate models according to personal systems of component substitution and by combining vocabulary patterns with unique conceptions during each performance.

## The Drums

As bass players improvise their parts within the rhythm section, they are typically supported by drummers performing, to use Charli Persip's preferred term, "multiple percussion." The instruments are more commonly known as drum sets, trap sets, or, simply, traps. Persip reports that the modern trap set evolved from a combination of drums and cymbals used in early marching bands and from the various percussive "trappings of circus and commercial drummers." Its nineteenth-century roots lie in "the invention of a bass-drum pedal with an attached cymbal striker" that enables a single theater orchestra drummer to play bass drum, snare drum, and cymbal simultaneously.[8]

Even in its most basic configuration, the trap set is like a small ensemble all its own. Its components provide a colorful array of sound with varied percussive timbres and distinct or elusive pitches, each having unique acoustical characteristics of attack and decay. Typically, the drum set includes a large, deep-voiced bass drum, operated by a right-foot pedal, and a hi-hat or sock cymbal, two cymbals brought together by operating a left-foot pedal. Mounted above the bass drum are any number of additional cymbals used for unique effect: a large ride cymbal often used to keep time; small splash cymbals to create novelty sounds; crash cymbals for accenting the music; and sizzle cymbals, whose loose vibrating rivets produce "a distinctive sustained sound."[9]

To the left of the player is a shallow snare drum, which rests on its own stand; to the right, a variable number of tunable tom-tom drums, either attached to the bass drum or resting on a floor stand. Finally, drummers may extend the drum set's timbral palette with the bright, penetrating sounds of cowbells, washboards, hollow-sounding Chinese woodblocks or temple blocks, or a number of small percussion instruments. Some players also include timpani or African, Latin American, or Indian drums in their assortment.[10] Musicians perform with sticks, mallets, or brushes; sometimes they produce special qualities of sound by striking with their bare hands.

The importance of the drums within jazz groups reflects the general value attached to rhythm in African American musical traditions. Because of the early commercial position of jazz as accompaniment for dancing, the drummer's central function has been to maintain a strong, regular beat within the framework of conventional tempos and meters. The trap set's performance practices have remained integral to the stylistic evolution of jazz as the music moved from dance halls to nightclubs and concert halls where serious listening was the main attraction for audiences, and danceability no longer imposed its constraints upon performance. At the same time, the practices of contemporary drummers reflect the legacy of their early forerunners.

Ragtime drummers performed various operations in a style that "combined simple, march-like figures with syncopation and improvisation."[11] Often, they emphasized the music's formal structure by featuring a particular rhythmic pattern with embellishments throughout each chorus, changing it from chorus to chorus. At times, they increased their written part's density by playing twice as fast as the beat and filling in the rests around their prescribed figures, a practice known as doubling. Reminiscent of playing marches, the drummers also used "suspended cymbal crashes . . . at the end of introductions, . . . at phrase junctures, and at the end of pieces." Additionally, the drummers periodically reinforced the band's accented phrases with strong cymbal accents, or kicks.

In contrast to ragtime, the music of New Orleans jazz was "less sectionalized." Correspondingly, drummers were not tied to marking off choruses with repetitive figures. Instead, they tended to improvise their parts by combining various "one-bar rhythmic patterns" on snare drum or woodblock and by drawing on rhythmic elements borrowed from other band members, including the soloists. They emphasized the suspended cymbal sound less than for ragtime, but continued its style of performance by "choking" or dampening the cymbal sound almost immediately after striking it.

Jazz drummers in Chicago placed renewed emphasis on the suspended cymbal, developed conventions for playing with brushes, and integrated the bass drum within their performance of fills, short one- or two-beat figures interjected into the music "at points of inactivity or stasis (between phrases, choruses, or solos or during a sustained note)."[12] Additionally, when keeping time, they commonly used the bass drum for beats two and four, while the string bass or tuba mark one and three, or sometimes to delineate four beats per measure, "especially during the [final or] out chorus."

During the swing or big band era, drummers like Gene Krupa built upon such practices. Krupa typically emphasized the bass drum on every beat, while performing "repeated rhythmic patterns interspersed with rim shots on the snare drum." Within the context of big bands, an alternative model for drum accompaniment grew out of the contributions of Walter Johnson in Fletcher Henderson's orchestra. One feature of the new approach was Johnson's unique use of the hi-hat, soon after its appearance about 1927. In contrast to the staccato, choked cymbal sound of earlier players, he developed a "smooth, legato hi-hat technique." Playing the hi-hat four beats to the bar, he produced different timbres on every other beat by alternately opening and closing the cymbals as he struck them.[13] Jo Jones used the technique with great success interacting with bassist Walter Page in Count Basie's innovative rhythm section. In fact, Jones sometimes dropped the bass drum from the accompaniment, producing an especially "flowing feeling" of time with his sustained, ringing hi-hat pattern.[14]

During the bebop period, as drums and string bass attained greater musical independence from each other, drummers celebrated new options available to them to express their imaginative concepts. Building upon the lighter time-keeping concepts of their predecessors, Kenny Clarke and Max Roach shifted the emphasis of four-beat time-keeping patterns from the hi-hat and bass drum to the ride cymbal. Before such innovations, Tommy Turrentine recalls, some drummers "came to the gig" with hi-hat, bass drum, and snare drum alone. Typically, in the new style, the ride cymbal played a prominent syncopated pattern that connected regular hi-hat accents on the measure's second and fourth beats—a convention that artists varied to add interest and individuality to their performances (exx. 12.5a–e). Bebop drummers strove to balance their parts in relation to those of the string bass so that both could be heard clearly.

In the meantime, many increased the complexity of their parts overall, displaying the ability to play the drum set as a "cohesive unit" rather than as a collection of individual percussion instruments.[15] The innovators took full advantage of the set's capacity and exploited the independent use of hands and feet, creating intricate multipart inventions—separate but coordinated patterns distinguished at each level of the drum part's musical texture by subtle differences in melodic compass, shape, and color. They also created interest by exploring the possibilities of asymmetrical rhythmic phrasing.

In this regard, once the ride and hi-hat cymbal combination assumed the time-keeping function, drummers used the bass drum for improvising unpredictable rhythmic accents known as bombs, kicks, and punches. Tommy Turrentine regards the bombs in Max Roach's accompaniment as adding punctuation marks like "commas and periods" to the phrases of soloists. Hard bop disciples of the artists preserved and extended these practices during the fifties. "In the original bebop era," Keith Copeland explains,

> the drummers had to play time on the bass drum and drop bombs. The guys laid down the time, and then they made accents around the time, but always went back to the time, so it made for a really solid foundation for other players. But as the music started to become more adventurous, they started stretching out more. In the hard bop era of the amplified bass, the drummers didn't have to play with the bass player in the same way. They created a constant interplay between the snare drum and the bass drum against the ride cymbal and the hi-hat, drop-

ping bombs. Today, especially in big bands, drummers need to be able to play that foundation in the bass drum and to drop bombs, making the accents. They need to be able to function both ways.

As past conventions have been carried down to the present, the drummer's role continues to be a diverse one, including various foundational and interactive aspects. Drummers propel the ensemble rhythmically through driving cymbal patterns that include subtle variations in the interpretation of the beat, syncopation, and corresponding effects of tension and release. Imaginative drum accent patterns of varied rhythmic density also produce forward motion, "punching," or "kicking" different beats within the measure and different portions of beats with expert precision: the second half of the beat at one moment; at another, the last third of a triplet subdivision. At the same time, drummers can imbue figures with distinctive contours, creating high-low or low-high patterns with melodic implications by orchestrating the figures between the snare and bass drum and developing the patterns through repetition and variation (exx. 12.6a–c). These possibilities are expandable through the linear performance of tom-tom drums and additional percussion instruments.

Drummers pursue their diverse options in accord with the music's requirements and their own improvisational system. Like their counterparts, they draw upon a common vocabulary pool, transforming patterns to personalize them. Max Roach recalls his early discovery of the effectiveness of such procedures at a time when the drummer was part of the big band rhythm section and did not "stick out" unless he performed a solo. "On my first record date, Dizzy called me to play with Coleman Hawkins in '43 or '44." Instead of playing two quarter notes on the bass drum, Roach tried out a few "simple" variations, like playing two eighth notes on the snare drum for the first beat and a quarter note on the bass drum for the second beat. "That was very revolutionary, [and] people would say, 'Ahh!'" Receiving this positive response, Roach began to expand on the concept, dealing with different combinations of tom-tom drums, snare drums, hi-hat, and bass drum. "It was good for people like Dizzy and Charlie Parker, 'cause they understood it, you know. The more conventional players who wanted a straight rhythm section [might] raise an eyebrow," he acknowledges.

Similarly, in constructing more complex figures, drummers achieve individual expression by arranging basic rhythmic elements in different schemes of repeating and nonrepeating units to create phrases of differing lengths overall. They add further distinctiveness to the phrases by adding or deleting selected elements and by applying personal approaches to orchestration (exx. 12.7a–c). Redistributing the elements of a conventional figure among drum components in varied sequences can not only change its melodic shape but create the acoustical impression of splitting the figure into different fragments, bringing a variety of rhythmic configurations into relief. Drum or cymbal strokes of like pitch, timbre, or dynamic intensity tend to migrate into new patterns, emerging from the original figures with transformed identities. Ultimately, players can combine ride and hi-hat cymbals or use them independently, alternate the voices of different drums or blend them, integrate the sounds of cymbals as melodic elements within the flow of drum patterns, or treat the cymbals as distinct time-keepers within the larger complex of sound.

Beyond the intrinsic interest variety creates for them within a drum part, the language of rhythmic gesture allows drummers to interact with group members. At times, drum punctuations reinforce fragments of other artists' improvisations. At other times, they provide a rhythmic counterpoint to them. Ronald Shannon Jackson recalls veterans teaching him in particular about the left hand's comping with the snare drum to perform "what they called polyrhythms." Michael Carvin, in differentiating the "solid" or fixed rhythmic patterns within the drum set's performance from the "liquid" or changing patterns, describes giving to the band, for the purpose of maintaining the beat, whichever "limb" he uses for time-keeping on the bass drum, hi-hat, or ride cymbal. Meanwhile, other limbs take greater liberties performing fluid comping patterns, which he likens to the riffs or shout parts of a big band's brass section.[16] Additionally, drummers improvise short fills between the phrases of other players and perform set-up figures that cue solo and ensemble entrances at critical points within arrangements.[17]

Drummers also interpret and represent the music's structure at various levels of organization. To mark the boundaries between four-measure segments of a progression, they can maintain a time-keeping pattern for three measures—embellishing it, perhaps, with spare punctuations—then increase rhythmic density in the fourth measure. They resolve its tension by returning to the time-keeping pattern in the fifth measure, sometimes emphasizing the return with a definitive accent on the downbeat or the second half of the preceding beat. Toward such ends, drummers commonly perform specialized one- or two-bar fills as structural markers.[18] Triplet patterns, or dense, rhythmic patterns with pronounced off-beat accents, or drum press rolls, or other figures providing contrast in dynamics and color commonly serve this purpose (exx. 12.8a–c).

To delineate larger harmonic components, a player can apply the same procedure over the eighth and ninth bars, or the sixteenth and seventeenth bars, or, to signal the close of each chorus, the last few measures of a form. Drummers may reserve the use of particular figures, such as press rolls, for the last turnaround of a solo, marking off the larger performance.[19] Sometimes, players feature particular ostinatos or motivic figures to further highlight the harmonic phrases delineated by turnarounds or to distinguish segments within the phrases.

Applying their vocabulary uniquely, individuals may emphasize time-keeping over conversational interplay in their parts, or vice versa. In the latter instance, they allow the developmental possibilities of their own inventions or those of other players to dictate their part's formulation, at times improvising constantly changing drum patterns. Overall, each drummer individually may favor such differing values as relatively stable, repetitive expression, on the one hand, or dynamic contrast, on the other. Within these aesthetic parameters, they structure their accompaniment according to different designs. One drummer accompanies the soloist with a spare, time-keeping pattern and consistently introduces structural marker figures of greater complexity at the close of eight-bar harmonic segments. Another initiates a performance in this manner, but then deliberately withholds formal markers or introduces figures of comparable complexity where least expected—to add an element of surprise to the music. Varying the length of conventional figures can also produce exciting results. Dizzy Gillespie describes Art Blakey's classic snare drum press roll with great relish, likening its suspension of time to the effect of stretching a huge rubber band. The soloist feels the increasing tension of the mesmerizing press roll, until its eventual release rearticulates the piece's rhythmic structure with so emphatic an accent that "the *world* knows that that's where the beat is."[20]

Similarly, although one individual may maintain the beat unequivocally with a cymbal ostinato and spare drum punctuations, another takes greater liberties in interpreting rhythmic form, obscuring the metric structure to create suspense. Since the innovations of players like Elvin Jones, Eddie Blackwell, and Billy Higgins during the free jazz period, the ride cymbal has come increasingly to imply rather than to delineate the meter. At the same time, drummers have exploited the possibilities of constructing complex polyrhythmic drum phrases across measures. This draws attention away from the beat's maintenance elsewhere within the part and challenges listeners to keep track of the beat. Over the accompaniment's larger course, drummers typically create different designs by alternately increasing and decreasing rhythmic density. They may also shape their part by gradually increasing rhythmic density throughout (exx. 12.9a–b).

### Learning the Drum's Role

Drummers learn many of the conventions they are expected to know by performing in different bands. "I had some experience playing club dates with my father and other musicians older than myself where we had to learn how to play for dancers in that earlier jazz tradition," Keith Copeland recalls. "And I had to learn how to play time in my foot on the bass drum for that. When we played for dances, we weren't playing tempos as fast as they did in the bebop period, and I mastered a little of what drummers refer to as the loud/soft technique. That was the ability to pat the bass drum very softly on all the beats so it's more felt than heard and then to accent louder when you want certain accents to be heard."

The hi-hat has its associated practices, as well. During the bebop period, various groups requested that Ronald Shannon Jackson emphasize the hi-hat cymbal to delineate the music's beat. In response, Jackson added heavier springs to his hi-hat pedal and began rigorous physical exercises to strengthen the muscles of his left leg and ankle. This equipped him to articulate cymbal patterns with greater force within his part's complex of rhythmic patterns, successfully reproducing the bebop drummer's characteristic sound. Later, Jackson expanded his vocabulary of rhythmic structural markers in order to remain abreast of the jazz community's developments. "One of the first things that John Hicks told me when I got to New York was, 'You're going to have to learn some new turnarounds. Turnarounds are the key.' In the bebop style, many people were locked into clichés," he observes.

> The horn players were always listening for a particular phrase for the drummer to play at the end of their solos. All the drummers were playing certain turnarounds that "Philly" Joe Jones had been playing. A lot of turnarounds were basically played on the snare drum, like a steady roll or a triplet figure leading to a crash on the drums. But then, about that time, Tony Williams joined Miles, and he began introducing new turnarounds. The group was still playing bebop, but the turnarounds were different. They made the music move a different way. Then other guys started changing the figures, breaking up the rhythms and playing them on different drums and cymbals. It changed the whole color of the music and freshened it for the other musicians. If they heard the drummers play something different, then they might come up with something different.

Students also develop a storehouse of other patterns appropriate for their instrument's musical roles. From studying records, Akira Tana learned a selection of fills that "Philly" Joe Jones played in between Miles Davis's improvised phrases, and copied specific patterns of other favored drummers "trading fours or eights" with soloists.

Equally important are conventions concerning appropriate schemes of rhythmic density and the shape of an accompaniment overall, which govern the actual application of drum vocabulary. Connie Kay remembers Sid Catlett teaching "little things. He'd stop by where I was working and tell me my left hand was too inactive or my beat on the ride cymbal was too loud, and he'd show me things at his house."[21] Akira Tana was working with Helen Humes down in New Orleans when, at the beginning of one number, he began "playing all these rhythmic figures." Floyd Smith, the guitarist, looked over and said, "What are you doing? If you're going to build a house, you have to build the foundation first, then build on top of that. But if you don't have the foundation, what good is it? . . . Everything is going to collapse." After that, Tana simplified his playing and concentrated on swinging.

Keith Copeland recollects that "the lesson I always learned from my father and from other soloists was to see where the soloist starts off and to build in intensity with the soloist. Don't give him too much in the beginning," he asserts. "If the soloist starts off real busy and burns right from the beginning, then you're going to have to come up to his energy level and build even higher before the solo's over. But other soloists want to start fairly relaxed and build to high intensity as they go along."

Beyond learning such general principles and sampling the vocabulary of a variety of different drummers, many students focus on a particular mentor, absorbing the mentor's precise bundle of musical traits, gaining the ability to improvise new drum parts in the mentor's performance style. As described earlier, one trait associated with "Philly" Joe Jones is his predilection for rudimental drum figures. Personal musical profiles also include signature patterns, such as "Philly" Joe Jones's rim shot—the famous "Philly lick"—and Art Blakey's rim shots and powerful press roll.[22] According to Keith Copeland, just as unique is Blakey's articulation of a ride cymbal beat in relation to his hi-hat pattern "on two and four, which he kept going constantly, even when he soloed."

Roy Haynes's concept, on the other hand, is a "little busier and more complicated rhythmically," Copeland says. "He wouldn't always play the hi-hat on two and four. He broke up the cymbal time, playing all kinds of little fills between his two hands. . . . When I first heard Haynes perform, he didn't seem to play a constant pulse of any kind," Copeland recalls, "yet I could feel a beat coming from all of his broken rhythmic figures. I said to myself, 'Wow, that's another way of playing altogether!'" Charli Persip, too, praises Haynes's unique approach, describing his "very sharp snap, crackle, sassy, shisazz sound in the hi-hat and snare drum. We used to call him 'Snap, Crackle, and Pop' because he had that kind of rhythm."

As in solo performance, the relative melodic and harmonic sensitivity that drummers bring to their accompaniment, and the degree to which they acknowledge the structural elements of a piece, also distinguish personal styles. Many revere Max Roach, not only for his unique signature patterns, but for his "melodic approach to rhythm," as Charli Persip puts it. "Max was so musical," Kenny Washington adds, remembering his own indebtedness to Roach. "Through records, he was the first cat to teach me about melody and form and tuning the drums." When Washington studied Roach's recordings and played with them in practice routines, he noticed that Roach improvised different rhythmic patterns during the contrasting harmonic sections of progressions. Other admirers describe how Roach made periodic references to the melodies of pieces by quoting the rhythmic elements of phrases, at times even simulating their contours. Gary Bartz explains that, from the soloist's viewpoint, Roach's practice of "playing the melody" in the context of an accompaniment "always lets you know where you are" with respect to the composition's form.

Roach's renown as a leader in the "melodic school" of drumming finds a parallel in Elvin Jones's renown as a leader in the "polyrhythmic school." Among other approaches, Jones routinely superimposes patterns derived from triple meters upon those derived from duple meters. "Elvin was breaking up the time on the cymbal," Keith Copeland explains, "and he had a hell of a feeling of six going through all of his playing. He was playing time, but it was like he was dancing with the time, all around these quarter-note triplets and stuff happening against the ride cymbal. It was so laid back. He could do it at fast tempos too. He could still emphasize the time and dance with it, and he'd never miss the 'one.' You always knew where he was." Of course, there is more to the contribution of great mentors among accompanists than the simple identification of prominent characteristics in the styles through which they made extraordinary contributions to the jazz tradition. As long as innovative drummers continue interacting with one another, features of performances they appreciate in others, as well as their own stylistic experimentation, continue to inspire their artistic development.

In the sixties and the seventies, innovators Tony Williams and Jack DeJohnette built upon the practices of their predecessors, taking particular interest in the increased rhythmic activity of Max Roach and Elvin Jones fleshing out their roles as accompanists. The young virtuosos cultivated what has become known as the soloistic concept of drum accompaniment. Musicians adopting this approach within rhythm sections improvise parts that possess the complexity and density of patterns formerly associated with drum solos, providing an intense musical commentary on the featured soloist's performance. "The role of the drummer has changed so much," Akira Tana says, "that today you find a lot of drummers not just keeping the time anymore. I mean, you could take away the rest of the group, and the drummer would be soloing throughout everything. That's the kind of respectability that the drums have now."

**The Piano**

In jazz's early period, the piano was a variable component of jazz groups; since then, it has come to play a fundamental role within the jazz rhythm section.[23] In its unique capacity, the piano typically shares various tasks with the string bass and drums. Like the bass, the piano can suggest harmonic form through the performance of its own bass line, but it can also represent the harmony explicitly through the performance of chords. Like the drums, the piano can punctuate the music rhythmically, yet it has the ability to mix short accentuating punches with long sustained sound. Introducing constantly changing shapes into the accompaniment, the pianist can repeat the same rhythmic pattern while altering chord voicings, or hold particular voicings constant while applying them to different rhythmic patterns. Taking different tacks, the pianist sometimes invents a single-line counterpoint to the soloist's phrases or improvises melodic fills between them as commentaries.

From the many approaches to accompaniment that favor particular musical structures and different aspects of the piano's role, artists commonly distinguish two, in particular, as characteristic: the block chord and the orchestral approaches. In the block chord approach, both hands strike the keys simultaneously, producing vertical harmonic structures in a highly rhythmic comping style. The inventive, ever-changing patterns of accentuation the pianist creates over the course of the chord progression, and their fit with patterns of the rest of the ensemble, are equally important to the pianist's creative harmony.

Learners develop a vocabulary of comping patterns by analyzing recordings, performing with professional groups, and observing the interaction of seasoned improvisers at informal music-making events. "The advantage of jam sessions was that you could learn what a horn player expects or would like to hear from a piano player," Tommy Flanagan remembers. "Such things were often discussed. It was also good to see what other pianists played behind soloists. At close hand, you could see how they really accompanied someone else."

Trial and error follows observation. At a practice session, an expert saxophonist once demonstrated several comping patterns on the piano for a student and requested that he take up their performance so that the teacher could improvise a saxophone solo over them. When the student tried to reproduce and maintain the figures in the face of the contrasting solo part, however, he discovered that his grasp on the patterns was more vague than he had realized; their complex mix of on-beat and off-beat alternations and sustained chords eluded him. Impeding the student's comprehension was the fact that his teacher had not tapped his foot when demonstrating the figure, nor had he given any other direct indication of the beat. "In the beginning, it was very frustrating. I got thrown off right away because I couldn't figure out where 'one' was. It sounded simple when he played them on the piano, but when I tried to imitate him, I couldn't figure out how the patterns fit into the measure and into the progression."

Once students become familiar with jazz's conventional comping figures and what seem like abstract rhythmic relationships to the underlying structure of pieces, they can infer the latter from the former. For many, this skill develops only gradually, as students practice mentally superimposing a model of the piece on comping figures when absorbing them from demonstrations, and subsequently practice retaining the model as a point of reference when performing the figures in their own improvised accompaniments.

Differing from the punctuating, block chord approach to piano accompaniment is another described variously as "orchestral," "pianistic," or "choral." This approach fully exploits the piano and creates wide-ranging textures, in which there is a constant interplay among different voices. Pianists can maximize their instrument's inherent versatility by improvising intricate syncopations and polyrhythms with the independent play of the fingers, exploiting eighty-eight keys and just over seven octaves. They may improvise dramatic intervallic leaps between the two hands or interweave simultaneous melodies, inner lines, and bass parts, producing a dense polyphonic fabric throughout an accompaniment.

Within the bounds of different approaches, pianists juggle possibilities for interpreting harmony in the creation of voicings. The considerations when accompanying other soloists are the same as when formulating a left-hand accompaniment to their own solo lines. At every turn, they make decisions as to the registral placement of chords, the number and nature of chord elements, and their precise arrangement. As described earlier (exx. 3.6 through 3.12), players' individual practices for interpreting chord progressions reflect such harmonic concepts as emphasizing harmony based on intervals of thirds or fourths in the construction of chords. Each approach provides distinctive color.

Pianists like Al Haig emphasize spare voicings with only two elements, at times playing only the root and seventh. Thelonious Monk makes use of dissonant intervals like seconds.[24] Others like Red Garland favor four- to six-voice chords that alternate or combine sevenths and thirds in the left hand. With the developments of modal jazz, many pianists, such as McCoy Tyner—a leader in this movement—would feature voicings in fourths. Representing a related development, contemporary pianists tend to play "less left-hand root music" than their predecessors (DF). Practices like omitting chord roots, building chords around fourths, and increasing color tones result in enlarging the harmonic ambiguity of voicings. In Bill Evans's impressionistic style, rootless left-hand voicings sometimes imply a choice of several chord roots, allowing the right hand to play "contrasting chords, sometimes setting up dual harmonic implications."[25] This was a point of fascination for Emily Remler, who, as a learner, imitated Bill Evans's characteristic "four-note chords, with fourths on the bottom and thirds on the top." Other students emulated Evans's dense, close-voiced chords, including pitch clusters (LG).

Each pianist's musical personality also expresses itself through the relative complexity and density of his or her style of accompaniment. Performances by Count Basie and Monk are relatively spare. Pianists such as Horace Silver, Cecil Taylor, and Jaki Byard are often just the opposite, creating dense or busy musical textures behind soloists. Personal features also emerge in the artist's precise vocabulary of comping patterns and their application within the context of form, as in the balance of on-beat to off-beat accents each favors in rhythmic punctuations. Some emphasize regular time-keeping patterns. Erroll Garner produces, at times, a "continuous strumming in his left hand, articulated by occasional accents in the lower register" as if re-creating the full accompaniment of the "swing rhythm section."[26] Pianists like Thelonious Monk comp with unpredictable, angular rhythms.

Beyond the general characteristics of individual comping styles, pianists make decisions within the boundaries of each composition and from one soloist to the next to lend distinctiveness to a group's music. Pianists constantly determine what emphasis to place on particular rhythmic patterns, where precisely to emphasize repetition and change, when to provide formal markers, and when to withhold them. Like other rhythm section players, they can vary the accompaniment in relation to a piece's harmonic-rhythmic sections, delineating form at different structural levels.

To portray large structural units, pianists can punctuate the music rhythmically with block chords over an A section, then create a contrasting texture by improvising sweeping free-rhythmic arpeggios over the B section, thus floating the time. In subtler terms, they can outline short structural units by repeating a crisply articulated off-beat pattern over the course of four-measure progressions, then resolve the pattern's tension with a chord on the downbeat of the fifth. At the same time, players may use different kinds of voicings to set off a piece's features, for example, shifting the balance between explicit and implicit interpretations of chords from one section of the larger progression to another.

Additionally, they may embellish progressions with personal chord substitutions. According to taste, pianists can increase or decrease the progression's density, and emphasize or ignore distinctive features of the original model in their own interpretations of it. An example of unusually spare density is the practice of an eccentric like Thelonious Monk, who would sometimes strike an occasional chord, then rise from the keyboard to perform an animated dance around the piano before returning to strike another.

Some pianists are generally less concerned with explicit time-keeping aspects of their role and may consequently minimize or abandon the performance of repeating structural markers. They are more concerned, rather, with developing, according to their own internal logic, original ideas that occur to them, or developing ideas that emerge from the collective conversational aspects of improvisation. While situating their overall accompaniments within the larger chorus form, their parts' successive rhythmic figures, phrase structures, and thematic episodes overlap the major harmonic-rhythmic components of the composition. Comparing the comping styles of three influential artists, Red Garland, McCoy Tyner, and Herbie Hancock, demonstrates the varied art of jazz piano accompaniment (exx. 12.10a–b).

Like the styles of the horn players they accompany, the styles of pianists and other rhythm section players ultimately include personal musical traits, vocabulary patterns, and improvisation concepts, fused together with those of various teachers. When drummers fulfill the general role of propelling a band, for example, they may choose between the alternative models of Max Roach's melodic approach or Elvin Jones's polyrhythmic approach. Within such guidelines, they select different possibilities for the orchestration of their patterns, maintaining time with a constant hi-hat cymbal beat or dividing up the time among the drum set's components. Over the course of the performance, they increase or decrease their use of rudimental figures in a particular part of the piece's structure, whereas in another part they rely upon fills learned from their mentors or mix their elements with their own. Similarly, when bass players and pianists improvise their accompaniments, they vary and recombine their precise vocabulary patterns and apply the general principles absorbed from analyzing inventions, those of their mentors and their own. Other times, accompanists depart from patterns or principles familiar to them in order to pursue radical musical ideas that occur to them in performance.

To fulfill their roles effectively, the rhythm section players constantly negotiate between each other's artistic creations, striving to formulate mutually complementary parts. Over the years, pianists, drummers, and bass players have assumed greater independence from one another, facing increased challenges of performance and invention. Not only must they compose interesting individual parts, but they must confidently uphold them amid the group's dynamic and complex musical texture.

### Conventions of Accompaniment Associated with Different Idioms

As implied above, performance practices associated with different instruments intersect other practices associated with different generations of artists and their respective style periods. Consequently, when rhythm section players join bands with an allegiance to a particular idiom, their knowledge of its stylistic conventions shapes their expectations for group interplay and guides their musical accompaniment. "When I was the house bass player at the Jazz Showcase, the concept of many of the musicians I played with was a swinging kind of bebop," Rufus Reid recalls. "Bebop required straight-ahead walking bass lines without much in the way of syncopated rhythmic embellishments or jagged rhythmic lines. Also, no matter who I played with, I knew what was going to go down harmonically. If it's this chord, then you're likely to hear this kind of bebop line played over it. Of course, different people play differently within that, but you can rest assured that it's going to be in a certain fashion."

Practices of the late hard bop idiom diverged considerably from those of its antecedents. "In the 1950s, rhythm sections became much more active in the music than they had ever been before, and the textural variety in the music became tremendous," Chuck Israels relates.

The bass was freed up from playing constant quarter notes. You could play note values that occurred in different places, in very fine subdivisions of the pulse while the actual pulse stayed the same. Bassists like Steve Swallow and I could play with a strong sense of rhythm without having to play every quarter note. Both of us were loose enough to be able to play a variety of note values and still play time. Sometimes, we would skip a quarter note and break up the steady bass pattern. You could come back in on the next quarter note or on an eighth-note subdivision or on a triplet subdivision, if you play it in the right place. Sometimes, if I were playing a piece in 3/4, I would play two dotted quarter notes, or I would play four quarter notes in a 3/4 measure. And if I laid them in there as an obvious polyrhythm, three against four, that was playing time to me. And that was the way that Bill Evans thought about it, too.

Later, things loosened up even more with drummers like Elvin Jones, Pete La Roca, and Donald Bailey. The cymbal pattern was freed from playing a constant ding, ding, ding, ding to varieties of patterns that implied ding, ding, a-ding, ding but were not exactly like that. The drummer's polyrhythms, what they would do with their left hands and left and right feet, also became much more complex. They'd play polyrhythms anywhere in the measure, placing rhythms across the main 4/4 pulse or across the barlines.

During the sixties, the avant-garde advocated even greater liberty for the rhythm section. In some instances, free jazz groups abandoned meter as a compositional constraint and avoided conventional rhythmic vocabulary. "Albert Ayler opened me up so wide, in terms of listening and playing as a drummer," Ronald Shannon Jackson declares.

He'd say, "Fill all that space out. I don't care how you do it, but do it." He didn't want any space or holes in the music. He wanted to hear rhythms all over. The only thing he'd tell me was, "No time, I don't want to hear ching-ka-ching-ka-ding—no bebop." In other words, he didn't want to hear the boom-boom-boom-boom bass drum pattern from the swing period or the syncopated, accented bass drum pattern from bebop. There was a pulse to the music because of the melody being played, but not the kind of pulse you were normally listening for. The time-feeling was more suspended, like waves that moved along with the song. You didn't have to worry about the time. You were either playing before, or after, or in the middle of the notes Albert was playing. He would play three notes, like the first three notes of "Summertime," and each note he played made you hear a pattern of fifteen other notes around them. I was just phrasing on the drums around the notes that he was playing.

Tied to these musical practices are values that relate to the general function of instruments within the rhythm section. "It takes time to learn the proper role of the drums in different groups," Akira Tana says. "There are different ways of playing in which drummers express themselves in mainstream groups, in avant-garde groups, and in groups which came along in that transitional period between the mainstream and the avant-garde. There are different levels at which you can play, different ways and different times in which the drummer expresses himself. It takes time to learn when to play a supportive role, just playing time, or when to take a more aggressive role, introducing a lot of different figures and not concerning yourself with playing time."

Free jazz groups that express concern for democratizing jazz minimize or eliminate the distinctions between soloists and accompanists, at times involving band members in constant simultaneous solos throughout performances. Moreover, some groups reject altogether the use of pieces as formal structures guiding improvisation, depending rather on collective sensitivity to work out, in performance, a consensus concerning the music's formal features of key, harmonic progression, and rhythmic organization. Lennie Tristano's early experiments, unusual at the time, anticipated such practices. "As you may know," Lee Konitz states, "we recorded the first totally free music in 1949 or so. It was just a couple of 78 rpm records. 'Intuition' was the name of one of them. And we were doing that kind of thing where we would just start playing with no plan at all. We knew each other well enough to be able to do that, and it was a lot of fun. . . . It's very difficult to really make a fine art out of, but as a procedure, it's one of the very, very important ones, I think, in playing together."

Other free jazz groups challenged earlier conventions associated with instrumentation and the length and dramatic shape of music presentations. Elvin Jones recalls a performance by John Coltrane's quartet in which the entire three-hour program was devoted to improvising on a single composition.[27] Keith Copeland attended another performance at Birdland where the quartet filled an hour-and-fifteen-minute set "with only two tunes." The music was so intense that, to Copeland's "complete and utter astonishment," pianist McCoy Tyner and bassist Jimmy Garrison dropped out of one of the performances after the first fifteen minutes. This left Coltrane in front of Jones's bass drum "just blowing up and down, an endless flow, [while Jones] remained in back of him just bashing, slashing, and crashing away." Copeland was spellbound by the unconventional duet, having "never seen anything like it before. Trane and Elvin played at such an energy level all the time that it scared you to death the whole time you were listening to them. It was just a constant conversation between them, all the time. They broke all the rules I had learned about starting gradual at the beginning of solos and building from there. Trane would start off at a level that would be way up there, and he'd continue to go from there."

In marked contrast are the more recent conventions of fusion music, which carry familiar features from soul music, rock, and other popular musical genres into the arena of jazz performance, including, in some instances, a clearly delineated, danceable beat. Sometimes, fusion music connects the talents of rock and jazz musicians. At other times, jazz musicians switch to electric instruments and learn what they need from rock to draw upon its elements for use in jazz performance. In fusion groups, bass players called upon to perform rhythmic rock ostinatos commonly take up fender bass to complement the timbre and volume of electric pianos and synthesizers. "Today, rock drummers have a complex rhythmic language of their own, which is different from jazz," maintains trumpeter Donald Byrd, who has contributed to fusion music. "It's also a challenge to work within that." [28]

## Unique Stylistic Fusions

Whereas some band leaders organize groups around the conventions of a particular jazz idiom and strive to preserve its core characteristics, others find artistic stimulation in juxtaposing and integrating diverse idiomatic elements of jazz. As in the case of some jazz-rock fusion groups, leaders may accomplish this by hiring performers whose personal styles embody the aesthetic values of different performance schools. Gary Bartz cites an example of the fusion of swing and bebop: "Coleman Hawkins was the first to hire Thelonious Monk. From Hawkins, I learned that music doesn't have to be dated. Hawk always kept up with the music." In fact, when Hawkins first heard bebop, he expressed it as his intention to "surround" himself with proponents of the new music and make a recording. [29] Years later, Max Roach, who with Dizzy Gillespie was part of Hawkins's fusion record date, recounts that "when Cecil Taylor and I recorded together, people in both bebop and free jazz wondered what we were both up to, and many were skeptical. But we had a great time playing together."

In creating musical fusions, band members sometimes adapt the characteristic improvisational vocabulary of one idiom to another's structural forms and repertory. [30] "Louis Metcalf was somewhere between Louis Armstrong and Roy Eldridge stylistically," Walter Bishop Jr. says. "It was a tremendous experience playing with his band, because I wanted to learn their tunes. They liked the freshness and drive that I brought to the band and were open enough to appreciate bebop. They let me do my thing, so I just played the way I normally played, but in their context." In another instance, Red Rodney claims that "Ira Sullivan and I are still really bebop players, but we've embraced the newer modal-like forms and have molded our individual styles of playing toward them. The young people in our group also help us with this. We're playing original tunes with today's patterns, changes, modes, and feelings."

Alternatively, in performances, groups vary the stylistic constraints upon collective improvisation from one part of a piece to another. Earlier, Lonnie Hillyer described a Charles Mingus composition that depicts the chronological history of jazz, requiring band members to remain faithful to the style of each arranged episode from ragtime to the avant-garde. Representing another approach, groups may combine the performance practices of bebop and free jazz by alternating improvisations inside and outside a piece's structure. Soloists may, for example, periodically perform free or atonal passages against the rhythm section's conventional harmonic accompaniment, a dramatic effect that maximizes the tension between the parts before soloists return to the piece's structure.

Pursuing another approach, the rhythm section may follow the soloist's lead in temporarily abandoning, then returning to, a piece's harmony. In some such cases, an unvoiced and sometimes elastic model of the piece's melody or rhythmic cycle serves as a structural referent. Lee Konitz recalls a period in the forties when Lennie Tristano wanted a strong group capable of playing "firmly together" within the structure of a song and then "letting it go outside, so to speak, from there." The group could "expound upon it, and then come back into the song." Also, as jazz has become "more and more flexible over the years," Konitz explains, there has been that same opportunity, "within the particular discipline" of playing standards like "Stella by Starlight," to improvise within the form, "as well as to take it out and bring it back—in the right place. Miles Davis's groups with Herbie Hancock and Wayne Shorter were able to do that extremely effectively." Such flexibility depends upon the artist's familiarity with the forms of compositions and "newer sophisticated improvisation techniques," which have become part of the jazz tradition since the sixties. Kenny Washington places Joanne Brackeen and some of her peers in this context. Brackeen "played in the tradition, but very free," he explains. "She would slow down the tempo or play straight ahead, and then all of a sudden play free, and then come back in. There is a way to play like that, in and out at the same time. Drummers like Jack DeJohnette, Billy Hart, and Al Foster do that very well."

Such approaches minimize or obscure conventional musical signposts of the structures of pieces, teasing, as a result, the perceptions of listeners and increasing the music's challenges, ultimately testing each player's independent grasp of form and self-assurance as improviser. Buster Williams describes his brief tenure with Miles Davis's quintet. "Playing with Miles, I learned how to keep a structure in mind and play changes so loosely that you can play for some time without people knowing whether the structure is played or not, but then hit on certain points to indicate that you have been playing the structure all the time. When you hear those points being played, you just say, 'Wow! It's like the Invisible Man. You see him here and then you don't. Then all of a sudden you see him over there and then you see him over here.' And it indicates that it's been happening all the time."

As some of these examples indicate, Miles Davis's classic sixties quintet exemplified the cross-fertilization of different idiomatic practices. Striking a middle ground between hard bop groups that retained the aesthetic values of bebop, and avant-garde groups that improvised without formal vehicles, the quintet composed original pieces and arrangements with more ambiguous harmonic structures than bebop pieces and loosened the constraints upon melodic and harmonic invention.[31]

During up-tempo compositions, for example, the quintet's rhythm section often treated the elements of form allusively by producing a steady, unaccented beat that provided little indication of meter or measure. Ron Carter alternated between such regular quarter-note bass lines, fragmentary rhythmic patterns, and sustained pedal points, while Tony Williams provided an equally dynamic performance. In Williams's innovative style, he commonly kept the time with the hi-hat, while producing constantly changing patterns on the ride cymbal, a practice requiring considerable reorientation of listeners accustomed to former bebop conventions.[32] At times, Williams delineated the beat with simple, hard-driving cymbal patterns; at other times, he accompanied the soloist with poly-rhythmic waves of percussion that predominated within the group's sound, encasing it in a brilliant, shimmering atmosphere of cymbal color and suspending the music's feeling of time. Meanwhile, pianist Herbie Hancock punctuated the music with spare comping patterns or dropped out of the performance for extended periods. Altogether, the quintet's conversational interplay was more intense than that of some bebop groups, but more restrained than that of some free jazz groups.

Herbie Hancock elaborates upon the group's artistic vision:

> What I was trying to do and what I feel they were trying to do was to combine—take these influences that were happening to all of us at the time and amalgamate them, personalize them in such a way that when people were hearing us, they were hearing the avant-garde on one hand, and they were hearing the history of jazz that led up to it on the other hand—because Miles was that history. He was that link.
>
> We were sort of walking a tightrope with the kind of experimenting we were doing in music, not total experimentation, but we used to call it "controlled freedom."[33]

Davis's quintet and other musical collaborations described above indeed epitomize the stylistic fusions, each one unique in itself, created by many jazz groups. Bands select and emphasize different features from the jazz community's complex of performance practices, subtly rearranging and transforming their elements, striving to develop original approaches to collective improvisation. These processes highlight, once again, the limitations of applying conventional labels to style periods and idioms when describing the diversity of music making within the jazz tradition.

## Practices Established by the Bands of Renowned Artists

As suggested above, the bands with leading soloists and rhythm section players commonly represent discrete models for collective performance. To Tommy Turrentine, each group displays distinguishable and consistent patterns of group interaction. "The Modern Jazz Quartet sounds altogether different from Erroll Garner's trio," he insists. "Then you've got Miles Davis's rhythm section, Red Garland and Paul Chambers and 'Philly' Joe Jones. They had another way of playing. And then there's Ahmad Jamal's trio with Vernel Fournier and Israel Crosby. They had their own way of playing. Every band should have its own characteristics." Correspondingly, youngsters learning how to function within a rhythm section strive to understand the relationship between the "ways of playing" adopted by their idols and those of fellow players. Don Pate explains that he "always identified with the particular unity that different groups had." For Pate, "it was a trip to hear the different parts within the unity and to focus on who was playing what, to hear what different people were doing."

Appreciation for the aesthetic interdependence of styles of accompaniment associated with individual players has immediate application for students. When joining a band, performers typically assess the musical requirements of a position by recalling an idol's performance in the context of a similar group. Band leaders themselves periodically suggest models to newcomers, proposing particular accompanists whose styles are compositionally compatible with the band.[34] "Within most groups, the leaders would have some drummer in mind that epitomized the drums," Ronald Shannon Jackson says. "You would almost have to play in a certain framework. They wouldn't tell you precisely what to play, but I've had instances where they'd say, 'Give me more of that Elvin Jones type of thing' or 'Give me more of that "Philly" Joe Jones type of thing.'" Such allusions serve as a shorthand for a constellation of musical elements ranging from the artist's original repertory of phrases and performance techniques to such subtle mannerisms as touch, articulation, phrasing, and time-feel. Sometimes leaders are even more specific. Dizzy Gillespie would "make" his drummers play a particular Art Blakey figure because, he claimed, "I must have that in my solos."[35]

In well-established bands, newcomers may also be expected to learn particular musical practices that have become conventionalized over time by players who formerly held their positions. This guarantees stylistic continuity within the group. "Since I was living in New York City, I was often the first drummer to play with certain bands that other drummers from Philadelphia and Boston played with later," Max Roach recalls. "Sometimes, I had the chance to set up a certain kind of feeling in these bands. When some of the others came along, they would be required to do some of the things that I did, along with what they brought of their own." Similarly, pianist Patti Bown remembers band leaders who advised her, "This is the person who played before you. That's the sound I'd like to have."

In fact, despite the jazz community's emphasis on originality, leaders may even fill the vacated chairs of featured soloists with other individuals who have absorbed elements of their predecessors' styles.[36] Just as band leader Teddy Hill replaced virtuoso Roy Eldridge with Dizzy Gillespie, band leader Billy Eckstine later replaced Gillespie with Fats Navarro. Eckstine remembers, "Great as Diz is . . . Fats played the book and you would hardly know that Diz had left the band. 'Fat Girl' played Dizzy's solos, not note for note, but his ideas on Dizzy's parts." He adds that "the feeling was the same and there was just as much swing."[37] Miles Davis similarly replaced John Coltrane with Wayne Shorter because Shorter sounded "so close to Coltrane." Fellow players referred to both saxophonists affectionately as "egg scramblers" for the rapid, intense mixtures of pitch and rhythm that characterized their improvisations.[38] Hiring practices concerned with continuity of style and concept highlight the far-reaching influence of great thinkers within the jazz tradition, whether they contribute new compositional approaches to solo formulation or rhythm section accompaniment.

### Performance Conventions Surrounding Repertory

Accompanists also nurture practices that enlarge their flexibility across a broad repertory with variable demands. "What was great about playing with Eddie Harris was that his repertory covered many different styles," Rufus Reid recalls. "We played many of his tunes, and he wanted you to play each tune in a way that suited its style. If Harris played a ballad, he wanted you to accompany him in a ballad style. What you played had to be pretty, and that was a challenge in itself." Each genre deserves special consideration. "There is a big difference between playing an up-tempo piece and playing a ballad," Akira Tana says. "You have to play with more space in a ballad. Since a ballad is slow and is one of the most expressive kinds of songs, you would probably play with brushes instead of sticks. It requires the development of a special touch, producing a unique texture and a color that differs from playing with sticks or mallets." Ronald Shannon Jackson nicely elaborates the point:

> These are the kinds of things I learned from other musicians by playing in clubs. When you play a ballad, begin the tune with brushes, but when you get to the bridge, switch to mallets. Then switch back to brushes. Build up the singer until the middle or the last part of the song. To give more effect there, switch to sticks, increasing the dynamics. Don't play the cymbals while she's singing—play only softly, with brushes. Don't play louder than anyone else is playing. Shape the dynamics so that you are at your loudest at the end of that person's

solo. At the end of a horn player's solo, play a loud crash, putting a period at the end of his statement.

Other types of jazz pieces require accompanists to perform specific rhythmic patterns. "Albert Dailey listens and he knows what's needed," Gary Bartz remarks. "When you ask for a samba, he knows how to play a samba. If you ask for a bossa nova, he knows how to play a bossa nova. All that's important if you're a piano player or a bass player or a drummer." Similarly, in Eddie Harris's band, "if it was a Latin tune," Rufus Reid says, he and his friends "played Latin rhythms. If it was rock 'n' roll, we played rock 'n' roll. This meant if we were going to play a rock 'n' roll tune, I would listen to the radio to what a lot of rock bass players were doing at the time. We didn't intermix styles like some do. It was very demanding and very challenging." In some instances, particular repertory requires performance practices associated with its related idiom. "If it was a bebop type thing," Reid continues, "Harris only wanted you to play in a bebop fashion, phrasing wise. If he said, 'We're now going to play outside or avant-garde,' he didn't want to hear any triads. He wanted a spacey kind of sound, and he would play freely—contours and colors. He'd alternate playing very fast with playing very slow."

As implied above, the overlapping conventions of idiom and repertory also suggest possibilities for complementary parts within the rhythm section and guide its collective accompaniment. Knowledge of these options is especially useful when arrangements are minimal or incomplete. During a rehearsal of a Latin piece by Walter Bishop Jr., Paul Brown read an arranged bass part that alternated between walking bass lines and a vamp section featuring a repeated rhythmic ostinato. In the absence of a specified drum part, Freddie Waits understood that he should perform variations on a simple swing pattern to reinforce the regular rhythm of Brown's walking bass lines, then switch to improvised patterns with a strong Latin flavor during the vamp sections, providing a rhythmic counterpoint to the bass part. Rufus Reid's experience is similar. "Interaction in a band means responding sensitively to whatever the other people are playing. It's a matter of being complementary," he explains. "If I'm playing with a rhythm section and the drummer is playing with a two-beat feeling, I won't start playing a walking bass line in 4/4 time. Or, if the drummer is playing a swing beat and I play a bossa nova beat, that would be a vivid example of not locking in, stylistically. Or vice versa. If he's playing a bossa nova beat, I wouldn't play a walking bass line unless I was told specifically that that was what was wanted."

In some instances, rhythm section players also heed performance models cultivated by individuals reputed to be successful at interpreting particular genres. "If you're playing modal tunes, you have got long vamps on one chord," Kenny Barron declares. "What works best in that kind of situation is playing your McCoy Tynerish stuff. You have to use different colors and things like that." In part, Barron refers here to Tyner's innovative interpretations of chords voiced in fourths.

Similarly, features of specific pieces and renditions by the composers themselves can suggest guidelines to other musicians, leading, over time, to formalized approaches to interpretation and accompaniment. "A Monk tune is so profound that you have to be thinking about every note that you play," Fred Hersch says. "The whole tune is compositionally tight. Each little inflection—where Monk places an eighth note on one side of the beat or another—means something. Improvising on a Monk tune is like an extension of the composition, because that's the way Monk plays, and that's the way he writes. So, your improvisation grows out of the piece itself."

Leroy Williams agrees:

> Monk's music itself demands a certain kind of accompaniment because the music is so strong. Not many people write that way or think that way. It's so strong that you had to be a strong personality to get your own thing off in it. I used to hear all the drummers that played with Monk, and I thought they sounded alike when they played with him. Now that I've played with Monk, I can understand why. There's a certain feeling, a certain strength, that his music has, the rhythm of it, so that you just had to go with it. There are certain off-beat accents, and the music falls a certain way. At first, I couldn't relax with Monk's music, but eventually I learned to. I started listening to the music more, tuning into the little, finer things.

### Conventions Associated with Instrumentation

Performance practices involving a group's instrumentation figure into strategies for accompaniment and can affect each part's formulation within the rhythm section. Some pianists, for example, tend to improvise comping patterns in the piano's middle register to avoid potential conflicts with the bass player in the lower register or with soloists in the upper register.[39] As a bass player performing "with a horn player," Calvin Hill "might play up in the same range [as the horn], but it might make a [singer's] voice sound weak if I did that. I'd have to really come down to the bottom register of the bass to give a singer support." Playing with Betty Carter brought about a similar challenge. For her, Hill "would play more low notes and be more sensitive to volume than with a horn player."

As different combinations of instruments perform together from one section of an arrangement to another, the rhythm section constantly adapts. Pianists sometimes double their voicings or melodic figures in both hands and move entirely into the treble or the bass register to match the increased volume of other instruments or to complement changes in the music's overall texture.

Drummers similarly vary the dynamics and orchestration of their patterns to provide different soloists with sympathetic accompaniment. "Since the intensity of a piano and a horn is different," Walter Bishop Jr. asserts, "a drummer should not accompany me like he would a horn player. He should play the top part of the cymbal, where it doesn't ring as much, or play with one stick instead of two, or use brushes." Max Roach summarizes the conventions:

> While every different situation presents special problems, there are some cardinal rules. For example, you should try to match the timbres of the particular instrument you're accompanying. If a piano solo is followed by a saxophone solo, you should give each proper consideration, using your imagination to play things that are musically appropriate behind each player and making the multiple percussion set blend with the entrance of each new instrument. To change and keep everything interesting, you might use brushes on the snare drum to accompany the pianist and then switch to sticks on the cymbals when the horn player enters. If there's a soft passage where a trumpeter is playing with a mute, you wouldn't pick up some heavy sticks and start pounding. By the same token, if you are backing an electric guitarist who is blasting away, you wouldn't pick up brushes and tip lightly, or you wouldn't be heard.

Players featured in groups with unconventional instrumentation, or within portions of arrangements that feature unusual combinations of instruments, sometimes experiment with approaches to improvisation that would be inappropriate in other contexts. They may even assume different musical roles, including that of an absent instrument. In such situations, improvisers often have carried over and reinterpreted, within unique musical settings, conventional performance practices associated with other kinds of groups and instruments. With respect to early jazz practices, Jelly Roll Morton advised pianists, "Always have a melody going . . . against a background of perfect harmony and plenty of riffs. . . . No jazz piano player can really play good jazz unless they try to give an imitation of a band, that is, by providing a basis of riffs."[40] Years later, within small hard bop groups, pianists like Jaki Byard incorporated into their accompaniments of soloists specific rhythmic figures and "thick close voicings" derived from riffs and "arranged . . . shout choruses" of big band accompaniments.[41]

This principle of exchange holds true as well for improvisers experimenting with the avant-garde. "When Anthony Braxton and I did our duo album, *Birth and Rebirth*," Max Roach recalls, "Anthony just automatically simulated a bass line on the saxophone, playing half notes and whole notes rhythmically whenever I played a solo. I accompanied him, and he made sure he accompanied me. That was the beauty of the first album we did together." Similarly,

Keith Copeland greatly appreciates the liberty he had to experiment in the atmosphere of jam sessions without pianists and guitarists. He recollects that

> Albert Mangelsdorff didn't use any chord instruments at his jam sessions in Germany—just bass, drums, and horns. It gave me the freedom to really experiment with the way Elvin Jones was playing when he played with other people who didn't have piano players in their groups. It was perfect for me at that time because I was really getting into Elvin, and I was trying to play like him with all those polyrhythms. I was just starting to understand that then, and I was trying to duplicate that feeling. I could really do that with Albert because there was nothing to hold me back like having to make it fit with someone else who was comping. If someone else was comping, I couldn't necessarily take those liberties. Also, when there was no comping instrument like piano and I was just playing off the bass, I had to hear the changes from the bass and the way that the bass was relating to what I was playing. I really had to know the songs and know the changes to play that way.

Rhythm section players draw upon their knowledge of the interrelated performance practices sampled above to improvise compatible accompaniments within arrangements, thereby satisfying the group's expectations for successful interaction. These practices have evolved over the history of jazz as a consequence of technological changes in instrument construction, the advent of amplification, the movement of jazz from the dance floor to the concert stage, reinterpretation of former conventions by great musicians and bands, and artistic innovation. For each generation of improvisers, in effect, the jazz tradition's cumulative performance practices have served as general compositional guidelines, delimiting otherwise infinite possibilities for invention within each instrument's part and contributing cohesion to collective musical invention.

# THIRTEEN

**Give and Take**

**The Collective Conversation and Musical Journey**

*Usually, everyone takes their cue from the soloist, but anyone could initiate something and we would all follow suit. Buster Williams may play something and I'll say, "Oh, yeah?" and try to follow him because it makes the group sound more cohesive. It's a matter of give and take.*—Kenny Barron

Musicians discussing the background and knowledge they bring to performances comment often on how much more complex jazz is than it is possible to verbalize in an interview. Clearly, talking about the preparation for collective improvisation is one thing, the actual experience of improvising quite another.[1] "No matter what you're doing or thinking about beforehand," Chuck Israels explains, "from the very moment the performance begins, you plunge into that world of sounds. It becomes your world instantly, and your whole consciousness changes."

Despite the difficulties of verbalizing about essentially nonverbal aspects of improvisation, artists favor two metaphors in their own discussions about the subject that provide insight into unique features of their experience. One metaphor likens group improvisation to a conversation that players carry on among themselves in the language of jazz. The second likens the experience of improvising to going on a demanding musical journey. From the performance's first beat, improvisers enter a rich, constantly changing musical stream of their own creation, a vibrant mix of shimmering cymbal patterns, fragmentary bass lines, luxuriant chords, and surging melodies, all winding in time through the channels of a composition's general form. Over its course, players are perpetually occupied: they must take in the immediate inventions around them while leading their own performances toward emerging musical images, retaining, for the sake of continuity, the features of a quickly receding trail of sound. They constantly interpret one another's ideas, anticipating them on the basis of the music's predetermined harmonic events.

Without warning, however, anyone in the group can suddenly take the music in a direction that defies expectation, requiring the others to make instant decisions as to the development of their own parts. When pausing to consider an option or take a rest, the musician's impression is of a "great rush of sounds" passing by, and the player must have the presence of mind to track its precise course before adding his or her powers of musical invention to the group's performance. Every maneuver or response by an improviser leaves its momentary trace in the music. By journey's end, the group has fashioned a composition anew, an original product of their interaction.

### Striking a Groove

Among all the challenges a group faces, one that is extremely subtle yet fundamental to its travels is a feature of group interaction that requires the negotiation of a shared sense of the beat, known, in its most successful realization, as striking a groove.[2] Incorporating the connotations of stability, intensity, and swing, the groove provides the basis for "everything to come together in complete accord" (HO). "When you get into that groove," Charli Persip explains, "you ride right on down that groove with no strain and no pain—you can't lay back or go forward. That's why they call it a groove. It's where the beat is, and we're always trying to find that." The notion is shared. "I don't care what kind of style a group plays as long as they settle into a groove where the rhythm keeps building instead of changing around," Lou Donaldson asserts. "It's like the way an African hits a drum. He hits it a certain way, and after a period of time, you feel it more than you did when he first started. He's playing the same thing, but the quality is different—it's settled into a groove. It's like seating tobacco in a pipe. You put some heat on it and make it expand. After a while, it's there. It's tight."

Although potentially involving all band members, the groove depends especially on the rhythm section's precise coordination, the relationship between drummer and the bass player usually being the most critical. "For things to happen beautifully in the ensemble," Charli Persip metaphorizes, "the drummer and the bass player must be married. When I listen to the drummer and the bass player together, I like to hear wedding bells." One basic obligation of this union involves the synchronization between the walking bass line and the cymbals' time-keeping pattern (fig. 13.1). "You play every beat in complete rhythmic unison with the drummer," Chuck Israels explains, "thousands upon thousands of notes together, night after night after night. If it's working, it

Figure 13.1   Synchronization between walking bass and cymbal time-keeping patterns: Paul Chambers and "Philly" Joe Jones accompaniment, "Bye
Bye, Blackbird"

brings you very close. It's a kind of emotional empathy that you develop very
quickly. The relationship is very intimate."

Because the groove depends on the musicians' ability to maintain a constant beat at different tempos, artists concentrate on developing precise timing.
Many prepare for their roles by playing with a metronome. Leroy Williams
and Akira Tana also practiced playing time along with records, getting, as one
drummer put it, as close as possible to performing with a band without actually
joining. Better amplification and the advent of high-quality earphones have
greatly facilitated such methods. With earlier equipment, drummers needed to
exercise great restraint when practicing in order not to drown out the sound.
At times, they simply pressed their ears to a radio speaker, restricting their
movements to brushes on a snare drum, or, as in Charli Persip's case, they
would mime their accompaniment by "playing in the air" along with the music.
Music Minus One records have also served as useful tools for students learning
to coordinate their performances with those of other rhythm section players.[3]

Youngsters would also benefit from the guidance of seasoned rhythm section players. Rufus Reid practiced formulating bass lines with an older drummer who maintained "straight cymbal time" and regulated subtleties in Reid's
performance by periodically calling out, "You're dragging, man," or, "It's not
swinging enough." Buster Williams's father, an expert drummer and bass
player, coached his son's bass playing from the drum set, "giving instructions
from the drummer's standpoint" and coordinating the performance of both
parts. Williams eventually learned to operate the hi-hat cymbal's foot pedal
while performing the bass so that he himself could simulate the interplay of
both instruments during practice routines.

Once the sound of the interaction of two instruments has been absorbed,
many musicians acquire, as a kind of sixth sense, the ability to hear their absent
partner. Ronald Shannon Jackson routinely practices improvisation to an imagined ground of bass lines, and Calvin Hill, a bass player and an amateur mara-

thon runner, when preparing for physically taxing performances with Max Roach's band, used to jog ninety miles a week to the internal resonance of Roach's ride cymbal beat.

As youngsters enter into successive musical relationships, they discover a world of subtle nuances involving the collective maintenance of the beat. At issue are concepts of rhythmic phrasing and differing timbral and acoustical qualities. As Akira Tana knows,

> finding the time is very important. So is how the time feels. A drummer can be very stiff or loose when he plays in terms of the elasticity of the beat. He can play the beat very stiff and staccato, like a European march with a straight eighth-note feel, or he can play more with a swinging triplet feel. I was recently talking to Percy Heath about this. Part of the elasticity of the beat also comes from the way the bass player articulates his notes together with the cymbal beat. It can be made to seem long or short according to whether the bass player plays staccato or whether he sustains his notes between the cymbal beats.

Sensitive to specific timbral characteristics of different instruments and their particular attack envelope, Chuck Israels also listens for "a certain sound" that he and the drummer make together when they play.

> The drummer has such a percussive sound because the beat is carried on the ride cymbal; a wood or Teflon drum stick hitting that metal cymbal makes such a definite sound when it articulates the beginning of each beat. As a bass player, you add your somewhat less defined and fatter bass sound to fill up the space in between those cymbal beats. It feels good when you feel you're right in between those beats. If you feel like your sound is leaking out the front or back of them, you feel a whole lot less comfortable.

Eventually, musicians learn to make distinctions in the interpretation of time that will enable them to articulate a regular four-beat pattern in slightly different positions, before, on top of, and after the beat, without changing the actual tempo. These precise positions, often imperceptible to the untrained ear, assume, for experienced improvisers, such tangible qualities that the beat seems a physical object, a palpable force. "There's an edge I feel when I'm playing walking bass lines on top of the beat. It's like if you are walking into the wind," Rufus Reid observes poetically, "you feel a certain resistance when your body is straight, but you feel a greater resistance if you lean into the wind."

Personal preferences sometimes require minor accommodations among group members. Leroy Williams discovered that saxophonist Johnny Griffin is "the type of player who likes a drummer to play way up on the beat." Although Williams "wasn't what you'd call an on-top-of-the-beat player at the time"—it wasn't "my natural flow," he says—he tried "to play more that way for Griffin." In another instance, a bass player known for playing "way behind on the beat" joined a drummer known for playing "way up on the beat." Despite their opposing tendencies, they adjusted their differences to maintain a "steady, swinging groove" throughout the performance (HL). Tied to individual preferences is the role that the drummer plays in discourse with the soloists. "If you play really ahead of the beat, where you're pushing everybody and telling them where to go," Paul Wertico says, "you're carrying a big responsibility [as to] the direction of a solo . . . [whereas] if you just sit on the beat or on the back of the beat a little bit, you can just kind of cruise and add periods and commas to their statements."

Musicians strive to avoid major changes in tempo, although subtle fluctuations within the groove are tolerable. If one musician shifts positions from behind the beat to just before the beat and others follow suit, the group's overall tempo might edge ahead slightly, then steady itself within a margin of acceptable variation. Rufus Reid refers to this practice when he explains that "some guys can play in tempo together as it swells in and out. As long as everybody is doing it together, they sound like they are perfectly in time." Indeed, when groups desire greater expressive freedom, such controlled flexibility enhances their music. "When you're in the rhythm section and everyone can play in all those places [i.e., on the beat, behind the beat, and on top of the beat]," Don Pate observes, "then you're not limited. . . . There can be a shift in where the beat is. Everyone responds to it . . . as opposed to the predictability of having to stay in one place."

At the same time as musicians introduce subtle variations in the tempo's ebb and flow as a matter of personal taste, the piece's structural features are also influencing them. "When I'm playing walking bass lines, I try to have the line moving somewhere," Reid continues. "This has a lot to do with harmonic phrasing. If I'm playing a ii–V–I progression, I'm not just playing the notes of the chord. I'm moving toward V when I'm playing ii. I'm constantly flowing, pushing toward I. If you think consciously of moving somewhere harmonically when you play, it assimilates this swinging sound, because harmonic sound is motion."

Improvisers sometimes increase the tempo slightly as a piece's harmonic rhythm increases and then relax it during static parts of the progression. They may increase the tempo slightly over the harmonic cadence at the close of a chorus, only to relax it with the beginning of the new cycle. Through the entire performance, group members alternate between asserting their own interpretations of time and adjusting them to those of other players.

## The Rhythm Section's Improvisation within the Groove

Defining the beat is its ongoing responsibility, but the rhythm section must also attend to other demands in order to ensure a truly complementary performance. Toward such ends, the players in the rhythm section delineate the piece's harmonic-rhythmic form, support one another's evolving lines of thought, and fashion individual parts with "inherent interest and change." Musicians often rotate their time-keeping responsibility. "You can play in a way that either states the time or implies it," Walter Bishop Jr. explains. "My preference is to have someone state the time when the others aren't, so that what the others are doing works against the time. Then you have polytime, and it becomes much more exciting, much more creative."

Typically, either the bass player or the drummer provides an anchor or rhythmic ground for the more adventurous performances of the rest of the band. According to Wynton Marsalis, "The bass player is the key. He needs to keep a steady pulse, to provide the bottom and to hold the music together. This frees the drummer up to play." Within this arrangement, it is a challenge for bass players to maintain a steady time-keeping pattern in relation to the tug and pull of their counterpart's complex off-beat figures, even if drummers include a regular reference point within their parts by playing the hi-hat cymbal on beats two and four. "Donald Bailey is an incredible drummer this way," Chuck Israels remembers. "I made a record with him and Hampton Hawes, and his playing was constantly churning and changing rhythmically. It was inventive and interesting all the time so that you never had a moment in which you were not being kept alert" (exx. 13.1a–c).

On the other hand, the bass can also "be free at times," Marsalis observes, "but when the bass player gets free, the drummer has to be restricted somewhat. It's just a trade-off." Calvin Hill shares this view. "Last year when I heard Richard Davis, I was knocked out by the creative energy and natural flow to his bass playing," Hill recalls. "Something was always happening. Rhythmically, he'd walk for a while. Then he'd stop and start playing a broken tempo for a while. Then, maybe, he'd switch to a little bit of arco [bowed bass]. It was very refreshing and very stimulating."

The accompaniment that Roy Haynes and Buster Williams provided Kenny Barron's solo at one New York concert demonstrates a particularly successful and sensitive interchange between bass player and drummer. When Haynes generated complicated rhythmic figures that obscured the beat, Williams stabilized the music with a steady walking bass line, but when Haynes reduced his part to a regular swing pattern, Williams varied his own part's rhythmic tension by repeatedly venturing outside the time, then returning to it. Typically, he entered the performance behind the beat and improvised intricate, gradually accelerating melodic phrases that aligned with the patterns of the other players at major structural points, resolving like successive waves that overtake one another, then break together (exx. 13.2a–b).

Such examples suggest that improvisers are concerned not only with sharing their time-keeping role, but with occupying complementary space within the music's texture and achieving a collective transparency of sound in which each part is discernible. Within horizontal space, musicians seek to create a complementary level of rhythmic activity by improvising patterns whose rhythmic density is appropriate for the room that others leave for them. In vertical space, they try to improvise in a melodic range that does not obscure the performances of others.

Here, the pianist figures prominently within the accompaniment's larger equation. In McCoy Tyner's group, Tyner "played a lot of notes on piano" and the drummer "played a lot of rhythmic things." Because their contributions "seemed to fill up every space" in the music, Calvin Hill confined his bass performance to "Eastern things like drones," playing them in a manner that was "not too rhythmic." Hill improvised parts with greater variety in Pharoah Sanders's band, however, because of the constraints on the pianist. "Pharoah liked to have the piano set up a basslike vamp or ostinato, holding its fixed rhythm in" over the course of a performance. Other approaches that call attention to the piano part, even when it features spare comping rhythms, are "relatively high registral placement" and dissonant voicings.[4] The range and configuration of chord voicings affect, as well, the bassist's inventive course. Larry Gray states that he can pursue greater options in formulating a bass line, without clashing with the pianist, when the pianist omits the chord's root and voices chords above the bass's range.

In other instances, when the rhythmic density of the performances of all three accompanists remains fluid, change in any one is potentially of influence to the others. Ronald Shannon Jackson explains that if pianists switch from sustained chords to "playing driving eighth notes," then he might switch from a regular quarter-note drum pattern to "sixteenth notes, filling in between the spaces of what the piano player plays and increasing its intensity." John Hicks gives another example. "In Arthur Blythe's group, we have this little break tune which sometimes takes the form of a very slow, almost dirgelike tempo. But then, sometimes, Fred will double it up on the bass and Steve will do the same thing on drums. So, what I might do is double it up and stay with the double time for a while, then break it back down. Or, I might just let them play the double time, and I would play something against that like the slower half time."

Besides shifting complementary positions among streams of patterns representing even-numbered subdivisions or multiples of the beat, performers also respond to one another by inventing asymmetrical counterposing patterns and interjecting fills between the discrete phrases of other artists. "Playing with musicians is like a conversation," Chuck Israels observes. "If when I speak, you say, 'Yes,' or you look at me and blink your eyes or interject some comment of your own, that keeps me going. Just listen to Roy Haynes! To say that he's a great rhythmic contrapuntal conversationalist doesn't do justice to what he does. What he does is just magic."

Elaborating upon the drummer's role as musical commentator, Ronald Shannon Jackson recalls early snare drum comping instruction aimed at creating varied "polyrhythms" whose accents occur "either before or with or after the figures of the piano player." Today, if a pianist "plays something that is really driving," Jackson will hold the basic beat on the cymbals or the hi-hat "to provide a foundation," at the same time "comping on the snare drum or the bass drum . . . to inspire the pianist's drive," he says. The two musicians "will work in and out of what each other is doing . . . calling and answering." Similarly, to prevent the music from becoming "stale," Michael Carvin features "short, staccato spurts . . . like a boxer, jabbin', jabbin', always keeping something happening."[5] McCoy Tyner's drummer also conversed with other musicians by performing "lots of polyrhythms," Calvin Hill reports, adding that during breaks the drummer usually superimposed "odd rhythms" derived from such meters as 7/4 over the simpler underlying 4/4.

Within the music's ever-changing texture, new phrases that insinuate themselves above, beside, or below other phrases ultimately provide rich ideas that any of the players can seize and combine within their own. Musicians periodically depart from an independent course to echo fragmentary patterns just heard from another (ex. 13.3a). Alternatively, they can reinforce a recurring phrase or any constant element within another member's performance by repeating it together with the inventor, perhaps with rhythmic embellishments. Common operations include accenting the second half of the fourth beat or briefly developing the combined effect of playing on different parts of the same beat (exx. 13.3b–c). At times, increasing its coordinated punches leads the rhythm section to create intense developmental episodes (ex. 13.4a); other times, sparser routines such as ostinato shout patterns result (ex. 13.4b).

In college, Ronald Shannon Jackson, Julius Hemphill, and other classmates provided John Hicks with invaluable coaching, deepening his understanding of such interplay. In addition to teaching him "how to loosen up rhythmically on piano, listening to the drummer, and locking into a groove," they demonstrated "different rhythmic things done by the drummer on the ride cymbal." This clarified specific figures and "little nuances" that had never been as clear to him from recordings, such as "the drummer's hi-hat cymbal pattern on beats two and four."

Pianist Kenny Barron recalls the relevance of comparable discoveries to his own comping skills. "The drummer has become a very, very important partner for me as my playing has evolved. At one point, I started really listening to the things the drummer would play, and I'd play the same things rhythmically." Barron initially adapted his performances to those of "older drummers" who maintained a regular "almost staccato" four-beat pattern on the bass drum. He subsequently collaborated with younger drummers who performed with a different "time-feel" and with surprising off-beat accents that, he admits, "forced me to play another way. At the time, I loved that."

As Barron's own musical vocabulary grew, he found that "some of the patterns drummers played were standard," and he could periodically anticipate their performance, even within the improvisations of musicians he played with for the first time. "When you just lock up and play rhythmic things together that are not planned," he explains,

> it sounds like you actually rehearsed it all, and it makes a rhythm section sound cohesive. One small example might be to anticipate the "and" of a phrase together with a drummer. Many drummers anticipate the first beat of a measure by playing two eighth notes, accenting the "and of four" and the "and of one" of the next measure. When I do those kinds of things together with drummers, many are surprised and go, "Oh, yeah?" But I can only do that because I listen to drummers so much. The figures we play together are most likely to occur at the end of phrases, like four or eight-bar phrases. That helps to define the form of the tune.

Within their constantly changing scheme of interaction, successive "punches" of pianist and drummer produce different mixes of on-beat and off-beat accents. From beat to beat, elements of their comping figures converge, reinforcing one another, or diverge, creating cross-accentuation schemes or interlocking patterns, one part's components occupying the space left by its counterpart. Throughout, drummer and pianist regulate these features of their interplay, adding momentum to the performance and contributing to its dynamism.

Equally crucial is the relationship between pianists and bass players, because they overlap in their function of representing the piece's harmony. The harmony produced by jazz players is not the uniform representation of a lead sheet model, but a lively composite creation, the product of multiple, ever-changing interpretations of the progression. Enriching the basic structure in endlessly varied ways, players may choose to reinforce or complement each other at one moment, to diverge at another, interrelating different harmonic pathways. The effects of such decisions may require immediate accommodation across the parts. "Buster Williams, or whoever the bass player is, may play a different bass note than I expect or play a chord substitution," Barron comments. "I have to be able to hear that and, at the same time, hear whatever rhythmic pattern is played by the drummer. If the bass player changes the whole chord, then I have to be aware enough of where he's going to go with him, or I may change the chord, and he has to be cool enough to hear where I'm going" (exx. 13.5 through 13.7).[6] As in the interplay between pianist and drummer, the pianist and bass player depend on their knowledge of each other's generation or style period and musical personality to anticipate the ideas their counterparts are likely to perform in particular sections of the composition. Moreover, artists may repeat a pattern periodically or hint at it through variants to set up the idea for simultaneous performance, or for motivic treatment amid complementary counterparts. A bass player may pick up a recurring melodic fragment from one of the voices within a pianist's chord line and incorporate it into a bass part, just as a pianist may pick up a recurring fragment from the bass line and harmonize it as a comping pattern (exx. 13.7c1–c3). Melodic-rhythmic interaction is also common between them (exx. 13.8a–c).

Completing the rhythm section's circle of interaction are exchanges between bass players and drummers (exx. 13.9a–c). "When I'm listening to the other musicians and thinking about the form of a piece," Chuck Israels explains,

> there are little things that arise which I have to negotiate. Suppose I'm coming to a bar in the piece in which I would normally play four notes. The chord progression at that point dictates to me that, in order to keep the four-beat quarter-note rhythm going, I can play either four roots of the chords or I could play two roots and passing notes in between them. But suppose, just before I get to that bar, the drummer plays a pattern that suggests a quarter-note triplet feeling and I would like to latch onto that rhythmic feeling and play the pattern with him. That creates an instant problem, because I had intended to play four notes to the measure and now I need six notes for the two triplets. Where do you find them? Sometimes, you can find them chromatically between the main chord tones or in a chromatic approach from either below or above the chord tones. Sometimes, you find them in an extra secondary dominant chord or in a pattern of thirds. Those are the tricky little problems that arise when you play with other musicians.

While carrying on their discourse, the members of the rhythm section ultimately provide support for the soloist, whose entrance increases the demands upon their attention and musical sensitivity. Rhythm section players commonly require a period of time for their own internal adjustment as a prelude to the discourse. "Years ago you let the rhythm section start playing by themselves at the beginning of the evening," Jimmy Robinson observes. "If they were having any trouble, you just let them play to get the kinks out. After they'd got the feeling for one another and got themselves together, then the horns joined them." When experienced improvisers perform together, such adjustments can occur almost instantly. Just as often, however, musicians need a few pieces or even the better part of a set to lock into meaningful conversation and invite soloists into their lively interplay.

### Soloists and Rhythm Section Players

Although soloists join the performance as featured speakers and tempo-rary leaders of the group's journey, they typically rely upon the rhythm section to provide signposts for the performance's direction. Many horn players listen specifically to the drummer's constant hi-hat cymbal for the beat. Others focus upon the swinging ride cymbal pattern, which enhances their improvisations by providing, as Curtis Fuller puts it, a "smooth carpet" for them to "walk on," or in Paul Wertico's words, a rhythmic "drone to ride on." Representing another approach, veterans in Chicago taught Doc Cheatham "to listen to the bass" because it carries "the time and the harmony." As long as he focuses his atten-tion on the bass during his solos, Cheatham admits, "I can't make too many mistakes." To gain his own bearings, Lou Donaldson also listens to the bass "for the harmonic pivot points" in chord sequences, which, he explains, help him "keep track of the changing tonal centers of pieces." If a piece is "highly rhythmic, I will play mostly off the bass rhythm."

The rhythm section commonly provides more than structural markers amid its multilayered backdrop of musical counterpoint. At times, rhythm sec-tion players interject punctuations and unique melodic figurations between the soloist's phrases in brief antiphonal response to them. As often, players offer simultaneous commentary; their comping patterns overlap or interlock with the soloist's figures, or anticipate their elements precisely, contributing cohesion to the performance. New lines of interpretation can occur to them in ongoing inspiration, as soloists hear and feel features of their ideas reinforced by their counterparts. Moreover, within the reciprocal relationships between soloists and supporting players, interesting ideas that originate in any part can influence others, leading to various kinds of imitative interplay. Lonnie Hillyer "plays well" with Leroy Williams because he can "draw from him." Hearing Williams play a tasteful rhythmic pattern in his drum accompaniment, Hillyer might "play it back to him." Conversely, Williams might hear Hillyer "play a certain rhythm and play it back." Art Farmer notices that to initiate a longer chain of events, a soloist sometimes performs "strong rhythmic patterns just to wake up the drummer" and then "tries to respond to whatever" the partner "does in reaction to that."

Describing this relationship from the drum chair, Williams explains that his role is "to keep the music swinging while embellishing what goes on around me. I'm constantly playing, feeding, and helping everyone, making each soloist sound as good as I can." Ronald Shannon Jackson elaborates from the same perspective:

> The role of the drum in Betty Carter's group was not just a time-keeping device. It was to accent what she was singing. She scatted and phrased the words of the songs with such finesse and style, with

such rhythmic pull, that it was like the drum and her voice were one thing. Betty was very rhythmic, and she loved to play with the drummer with her voice. She used scat syllables to sing the same type of things I could play with my left hand on the drums. She'd sing along with what I was playing or improvise on top of it, and that would be like magic for the audience. We were still calling her "Betty Bebop" at that time, because she could sing the same rudiments with her voice that you could play on the drums.

Michael Carvin once displayed the skillful drummer's ability to play the improvised lines of soloists along with them at a New York performance. Phrasing together with Walter Bishop Jr., Carvin invented drum patterns that not only began and ended with the pianist's melodies but also anticipated their accents.[7] Within these phrases, Carvin sometimes duplicated Bishop's precise rhythmic figures and at other times provided them with a rhythmic counterpoint. For further variation, he would switch to a steady swing pattern, periodically filling the rests between the soloist's phrases with a press roll.

Paul Wertico starting honing such aspects of interaction early, already sensitive, as a drum student, to the harmonic and melodic aspects of music, especially the changing "directions" and patterns of tension and release in a composed melody or in a soloist's improvisation. Wertico learned the essential lesson of responding to such changes by listening to figures played by drummers like Roy Haynes, studying their precise effects on the surrounding parts. There was a difference, for example, between "suddenly striking" the cymbal and bass drum together, which weighs the music down, and striking an open cymbal alone, which creates "a feeling of expanding space." With increasing sophistication in such matters, Wertico would guide his accompaniment by assessing drum set patterns for their likely musical and "emotional effects" on the performance. Accordingly, changes in the musical expression of the other group members also influence the drummer's choice of figures and their orchestration (exx. 13.10a–c).[8]

The soloist's relationship with pianists is equally important. "The piano player might just independently do something as part of the rhythm section that is attention-getting, something he is just directing at me," Lee Konitz points out. "If I hear the piano player play a figure, I'll stop for a moment and then react to that. I'll do something as a result of what he did. Or maybe the piano player does something that is a reaction to something I've just played. That's a surefire way of getting my attention."

Melodic invention is one aspect of this type of exchange. When John Lewis accompanies Milt Jackson's solos, Lewis does what Tommy Turrentine calls "sub-soloing. Instead of just saying ching, ching, ching, ching, he'll do that for a while and then play a little melody in octaves." Although such figures can stand simply as a counterpoint to the soloist's part, at times soloists incorporate them into their performances. Lonnie Hillyer was once performing with pianist Walter Davis when Davis played a pattern behind him that was "really wild, really outside" harmonically—"some Godforsaken interval"—that Hillyer immediately "reached out and grabbed" for his solo. "I like that kind of spontaneity," Hillyer declares. The reverse can be equally exciting. Greg Langdon describes an early band whose phenomenal pianist could "pick up whatever the soloist played, either duplicating it or doing something like it instantly." This was a "great experience" for Langdon, who had "never experienced anything like it before" (exx. 13.11a–d). Once learners have absorbed such conventions for sympathetic interaction, they soon begin to imagine responses of rhythm section players to their own improvisations, even when practicing alone (LH).

The pianist's accompanying figures can also provide a general rhythmic impetus or precise rhythmic ideas. Patti Bown strives to provide a "foundation" for soloists by inventing "some kind of rhythmic pattern that would make it interesting for them to play and to work in and out of." Soloists express admiration for pianists who "have a way of comping that has a strong rhythmic feel. They will anticipate the beat a little, putting a little rhythmic push into it, adding life to the music" (AF). Vea Williams agrees. "I love pianists who enhance or let me feed off what they're doing. Good accompanists like Norman Simmons or Albert Dailey know how to let a singer sing," she explains. "They'll play things that will give you ideas on how to expand a phrase or how to string out a word in a spontaneous and unique way." This requires versatility as well as sensitivity in musical interaction. Freddie Green praises Count Basie, who, as an accompanist, "always seems to know the right thing to play . . . making the rhythm smooth . . . [and] contribut[ing] the missing things" (exx. 13.12a–c).[9]

In addition to setting forth melodic and rhythmic options, pianists stimulate soloists through selected chord voicings. Ultimately, both soloists and pianists need to grasp each other's interpretation of harmony, one through chord voicings and the other through the melodic line. "When you change the harmony a little in your solo and pianists hear it," John McNeil explains, "then they should echo you a bit or play a chord voicing in such a way that it will complement what you've just played and spur you on to something else. Joanne Brackeen is one of my favorite pianists to play with," he asserts. "She doesn't use a lot of space, but she really listens well. She always plays things that go with the things that you play. When I play with her, I'm rarely conscious that she's there, except that everything sounds real good. We're just into the flow of it together."

In Art Farmer's view,

> pianists can be the best musicians in the group. Sometimes, they know far more than anybody else in the band, and they can play things in

many different ways. Fred Hersch is a good example. He's very well trained and knows a lot of things. If I say, "Well, this piece calls for this, Fred," then he can do it. He gives each piece the respect it should have. The thing that really makes the music sound good is the way the pianists voice their chords. Some people leave you space and give you some freedom at the same time they're leading you in a certain way. I'll listen to how the pianist voices a chord, and I'll get an idea of what note would go well with it. I'll get an idea of what starting note to use for my solo.

Curtis Fuller adds that when Bill Evans plays "real pretty chords," their leading tones can be very suggestive, "opening up the soloist's ears." Wynton Marsalis comments along similar lines. Pianists "don't have to put every note in the chord," he suggests. "To find the best possible choice is the thing; four notes can sound like a thousand if they're the right ones."

Finally, there are the mutual reactions of soloists and bass players. The bass player's contributions can be as critical as the pianist's in determining the harmonic complexion of the music. "If Harold Land and Bobby Hutcherson were playing a chord like a major seventh chord, they would voice it in fourths," Rufus Reid recalls. "The harmony was more open that way. If I changed the bass note I was playing, all of a sudden the sound of the whole chord would be different." In equally dramatic terms, a bass player who temporarily switches to a repeating pedal point, suspending a detailed representation of the progression for "a more general articulation of tonality"—perhaps the tonic or dominant of the piece's key—offers "the pianist and soloist considerable harmonic latitude." [10] Similarly, when a bass player "takes the chord progression in a different way" than Tommy Turrentine expects, it can change his thinking and influence the course of his solo (exx. 13.13a–f).

Besides praising bassists' imaginative harmonic concepts, musicians praise their time-feel or swing-feel, their sound, and the shapes of their lines. Kenny Barron describes the experience of performing with inventive bass players like Ron Carter, whose "rhythmic concept is different and . . . choice of notes sometimes can be very unusual. . . . When the chord sequence itself isn't chromatic, he may find a chromatic line that will work and I'll say, 'Oh, yeah?'" Correspondingly, the exchange of melodic-rhythmic elements is common between the bass and solo parts. Patti Bown likes "to have a bass player feed me some energetic ideas to play off of." Conversely, Lonnie Hillyer remembers Charles Mingus imitating things that the soloists played in his band, making "for a conversation" (exx. 13.14a–b). In addition to imitative interplay, soloist and bass player interact through regulating contrapuntal features of their parts. Chuck Israels generally appreciates a bassist's "contrary or oblique motion" in relation to a solo line, but acknowledges musical situations in which "sudden parallel motion becomes the very best thing to do."

Tommy Flanagan and Red Mitchell revealed perfect rapport between solo pianist and bass player in their duo at a New York performance. Their patterns seemed to melt into one another, with only the acoustical peculiarities of their instruments causing their performances to separate periodically, like streams diverging. When Flanagan introduced a radically different rhythmic figure at the opening of a chorus, a look of surprise and good-natured fun spread across Mitchell's face. Seizing a portion of the new figure as a template for his own improvisations, he laid discrete bass patterns onto the piano's evolving melodic-harmonic texture as if matching pieces of a mosaic in progress. In acknowledgment of the successful fit, the musicians exchanged warm smiles of admiration before turning their concentration inward.

Such rewarding interplay depends in the first place upon the improviser's keen aural skills and ability to grasp instantly the other's musical ideas. In a sense, these talents represent the culmination of years of rigorous training begun in students' initial efforts to acquire a jazz vocabulary. In this effort, serious attention goes into copying recorded solos by diverse instrumentalists and practicing translating to their own instrument's idiomatic language, patterns performed outside its range or obscured by alien timbres and techniques. Ultimately, students must learn to exercise these sensibilities proficiently in performance, as they concentrate simultaneously on their own parts. It requires, in effect, "divid[ing] your senses." That is the "real difficulty." [11]

Akira Tana elaborates, "The goal is to mesh your sound with all the other instruments and to create a balanced group sound. I don't just mean this in terms of volume. I'm talking about balancing the figures you play with all the things that you hear coming from other instruments. As a drummer, I'm listening to the rhythm section in relation to what the soloist is doing. I'm still learning to hear the whole group and all the individual instruments in relation to my own." Saxophonist Lee Konitz also "wants to relate to the bass player and the piano player and the drummer, so that I know at any given moment what they are all doing. The goal is always to relate as fully as possible to every sound that everyone is making." Konitz reflects on the task and exclaims, "But whew! It's very difficult for me to achieve. At different points, I will listen to any particular member of the group and relate to them as directly as possible in my solo."

Although hearing everything over a musical journey represents the ideal, listening is typically a dynamic activity and performers continually adopt different perspectives on the surrounding patterns. Their constantly fluctuating powers of concentration, the extraordinary volume of detail requiring them to absorb material selectively, and developments in their own parts that periodically demand full attention together create the kaleidophonic essence of each artist's perception of the collective performance. Moreover, as suggested above, improvisers sometimes deliberately shift focus within the music's dazzling texture to derive stimulation from different players. Walter Bishop Jr. can "zero in on the bass player or the drummer, either one by himself or both together. Or, if the band's a quartet, I can listen in quadruplicate."

Amid the rigorous operations of listening and responding, the overlapping perceptions of all the players potentially compensate for any individual's difficulties or divergent viewpoints and contribute cohesion to the larger performance. The piano player might hear something in what the soloist is playing that the drummer does not hear at the time, but if the drummer hears the pianist's response to the soloist and complements the pianist's idea, then what the drummer plays will also complement "the whole musical thought of the soloist" (LW). Discerning audience members, as well as players, share in the exciting moments of instantaneous conversation across all the parts as performance interaction intensifies, producing such varied effects as a fleeting ripple of accents from player to player or the collective development of motives over an entire chorus (exx. 13.15a–c).

## Interpreting Ideas

Exercising their skills of immediate apprehension, improvisers engage in effective musical discourse by interpreting the various preferences of other players for interaction and conveying their own personal preferences. Sometimes they are familiar with their cohorts on the bandstand, and sometimes they play with artists of whom they know practically nothing. By reputation, some horn players like to "converse rhythmically when they solo; different things played behind them give them ideas. Others don't like any of that. They just want straight time played behind them" (AT). Tommy Flanagan makes similar distinctions. "Sonny Rollins doesn't need very much in the way of you chording for him, because he covers the whole thing in his solos; he plays the chords and the rhythmic part. Miles plays with a lot of spaces, so that leaves more room for the rhythm section to play fills and to do things as a whole." Calvin Hill comments similarly on a couple of his colleagues: "George Coleman is a person who plays a lot of notes, a lot of rhythm and everything," he says,

> so actually, all you have to do is to give him a cushion and just let him go. He'll play right over the top of what you're laying down, so you lay something down that's pretty simple and you keep it straight. It could be a walking line or something else with that feeling. But when you're playing with somebody like Pharoah Sanders who doesn't play as much, you can play a little bit more out front, a little more complex and with more activity, because he uses the rhythm section more than somebody like George Coleman.

Experience over time greatly enhances musical cohesion, of course. Specific knowledge of the concepts or approaches of different musicians—

reflected in their recurring vocabulary patterns, the logic underlying phrase construction and motive development, and long-range storytelling strategies—provides additional clues for fellow band members. Consequently, while attending to their own parts—assessing inventive material and selecting elements for development—performers must constantly exercise musical peripheral vision to make similar assessments about neighboring parts as they endeavor to predict their courses. After a rhythm section becomes accustomed to particular soloists, it can "follow their train of thought and complement it," Akira Tana says. Curtis Fuller elaborates. "In Miles Davis's band, 'Philly' Joe even learned to play little things to set Miles up for his phrases. He'd play things before and after Miles's figures. Little things like that let you know the drummer is listening." In groups that perform together frequently, players sometimes develop a core of common patterns that they periodically reintroduce in performances to stimulate interplay.[12]

Fashioning an internally cohesive accompaniment matters greatly to Miles Davis, who, as Fuller reports, "also spent a lot of time getting the rhythm section to know how each other plays so that they could anticipate one another." Kenny Barron discusses this process. As a pianist who prides himself on being able to "adjust to almost anything that a drummer can do," Barron strives not only to synchronize his comping figures with the conventional accompanying patterns for drums described earlier but to

> do different things with each drummer based on what [each does]. Playing with Ben Riley is playing one way. Playing with Elvin Jones is quite another. Also, Billy Hart does little rhythmic things with his sock cymbal that are different from both Ben and Elvin. Ben and I have been working together for a long time now, and it's almost intuitive between us. Elvin's playing is, in a sense, freer and looser than Ben's playing, so there might not be a chance to do those rhythmic things together in the same way that Ben and I do them. I've only played once or twice with Elvin, so I'd have to listen to him and find out where he places his figures rhythmically—the things he does that he's always going to do. There is something in his playing somewhere that is constant. If we worked long enough together, I would find that thing and key in on it.

Watching a partner can be important in developing such rapport. A musician recalls a concert in which a young drummer "didn't take his eyes off the piano player the whole night," successfully anticipating the pianist's accentuation patterns from the motion of his arms.

As Fred Hersch and Keith Copeland delineate, the constant stylistic features of a bass player can also shape the expectations of other band members and suggest different limitations for improvised interplay. "Sam Jones is a great bassist," Hersch asserts, "but he's fairly conservative. On waltzes, he'll play just one note at the beginning of each bar; on a ballad, he'll end up double timing it usually. If he's playing a walking bass line behind you, the only thing he might do in reaction to what you've played is to introduce a substitute chord change, taking a slightly different harmonic route through the piece." In contrast, other bass players "will stop walking for a while and strum their basses, or play a constant pedal point or play a countermelody, or change the rhythm."

Similarly, Copeland describes Mike Richmond as

> a bass player who can play passages in which he's almost not keeping time, but he's playing around the time. Because I know the way Mike plays and can feel what he's playing, I can follow him during those passages. I can play around the time and play off of his improvisation, and when we return to the form of the piece, we come out in the same place at the same time. He's just one of those cats who's got a beautiful gift for melodic playing, as well as the ability to play with the time rhythmically. When he breaks up the time in different ways, it doesn't make me feel the least bit uncomfortable.

Cumulative experience and longtime association with other artists enhance the ease of negotiating their interplay and musical conversation. After thirty years of performing with bassist Richard Davis, pianist Roland Hanna is familiar enough with the way Davis thinks

> to have an idea of what he *might* play from one note to the next. If he plays a C at a certain strength, then I know he may be looking for an A♭ or an E♭ or whatever direction he may go in. And I know he may be making a certain *kind* of a passage. I've heard him enough to know *how* he makes his lines. So I may not know exactly what note he's going to play, but I know in general the kind of statement he would make, or how he would use his *words,* you know, the order he would put his words in. . . . We train ourselves over a period of years to be able to hear rhythms and anticipate combinations of sounds before they actually happen.[13]

Group members can eventually develop musical signs that reveal one another's intentions. As implied earlier, the soloist's extensive use of rests invites greater activity on the part of the rhythm section. "Pharoah might play something and want the group to react to it," says Calvin Hill. "Like he'll play a little bit and rest, giving the group some time. Then he'll play a little bit more and rest again, giving the group some more time." Although soloists often deliberately leave space to encourage others, at times they may simply tire and require a short rest, or they may have a temporary lapse of imagination after completing an idea. "The give-and-take is ideal," Lee Konitz asserts, "so that if you go down for a second, all you have to do is to keep quiet and let someone else play for a second. In that way, the music continues to grow." Akira Tana agrees: "If a horn player is playing a solo, and in the middle of it he lays out for a moment, the drummer should comp for him and chord for him, trying to inspire him and give him things that will boost him."

Additionally, the repetition of a phrase can suggest a motive for development on the part of other artists or the whole group. "If a piano player hints at a certain rhythmic figure behind the soloist throughout the chorus or during the first half of the tune, the drummer can keep time and comp simultaneously, either playing the same rhythmic figure as the pianist, or playing off of it, or playing against it," Tana explains. "You can do the same thing with the soloist too, answering his phrases, playing along with the things he states rhythmically, or playing variations on those things." As an alternative, rhythm section players can invite intensification of the music by repeating a big band riff and leaving space for their counterparts to fill in with call and response exchanges.[14]

Beyond such overt musical suggestions are myriad subtler ones. An example would be the challenge Don Pate acknowledges when Roy Haynes "signals something to me just through a gesture in his playing." In Miles Davis's quintet with Tony Williams, a dramatic leap to the trumpet's high register on a downbeat was often a signal for the group to switch from a floating rhythmic feeling or a two-beat feeling to a precise four-beat, swing feeling. Similarly, Fred Hersch has a clear sense of a group's expectations when he plays

> a loud rhythmic figure, or a complex cross-rhythm, or certain chords. It's a musical signal that means for the drummer to change what he's doing, to do something that provides some contrast to what has come before. Let's get out of our present format and take the music somewhere else.
>
> When I'm playing with Art Farmer, it's the same kind of thing. Art is very spontaneous. He listens to what you play behind him, and you really play with him. When he plays something that I know I can feel from him, that means for me to do something. For example, when he'll go up to a high note and shake it, that means "Okay. Come on up there with me." Or, when he will choose a series of very remote pitches in a line, that means, "Lay out." It doesn't mean, "Try to find me." It means, "I'm trying to lose you, so just let me play without you for a while."

Kenny Barron also articulates with understanding his sense of collaboration with other musicians as pivotal.

> Knowing when to play inside and when to play outside in Freddie Hubbard's band was really just based on listening to the solos more than anything else. You followed the soloist wherever he wanted to take the music, and many times he wanted to take it out. This was primarily signaled by the soloist's choice of notes and by his line. You

could hear it if he started playing tonally and then suddenly he was doing something else with his line. That was a signal for you to follow suit with your accompaniment.

The vehemence with which a player makes musical suggestions has bearing on the mutuality of the musical exchange. Pianists can make a subtle harmonic offering to soloists by presenting a non-chord tone or color tone in the inner voice of a passing chord. To present the same color tone in the upper voice of a sustained chord is a more pronounced offering, one that can produce dissonance if others ignore it. The particular musical effects that performers strive to produce typically guide such decisions. Similarly, in negotiating over chord substitutions, soloists can follow a pianist's firm lead, but they may decide to continue inventing melodies based on their own versions of the progression, engaging in bitonal invention and producing inventive schemes of harmonic counterpoint by superimposing one pathway upon another.

Amid the group's enveloping mix of patterns—at times dancelike, at times lyrical, at times speechlike—the powerful color of the revealed emotions also demands reaction. Improvisers immediately catch and follow up the feelings of despair or joy or whatever of the endlessly varied shades of meaning conveyed by the evocative timbres of the patterns' mixture. "The amazing thing about playing with Art [Blakey]," says Terence Blanchard, "is that he has a way of tuning into inspiration that can draw an emotion out of you that you may have never experienced before." [15] Jazz veterans have expressed to Bobby Watson their wish that they had performed with Blakey—if only once, to have felt his powerful press roll behind them. [16]

Curtis Fuller comments from the inside as music flows to him from another artist, "When you hear Paul Chambers play some frisky little thing behind your solo, it makes you feel frisky like that and it influences what you play." Kenny Washington makes a similar point: "Sam Jones's feeling is simply unbelievable. It's a down home type of feeling. That's why we call him Homes. Sam plays just like he is—a beautiful, easygoing cat who puts on no airs. If you listen to some of the early recordings he made with Cannonball, there is such a great, great feeling just from the way he plays time. It's like when you're walking down the street and you feel happy and you don't even know why."

Ronald Shannon Jackson compares his experiences with different soloists:

Playing with Kenny Dorham was more like the essence of a dream-type thing. It was a more esoteric, ethereal feeling, and I always felt like I was floating after each set. He was very warm and lyrical. It was like playing with a jazz vocalist. Because of the way he played and the way his tone was, you had to listen a lot to him when you played. Or, more to the point, in order to enhance anything, you had to be right where he was, which would allow him to open the whole thing up, to get the flow going. You couldn't be overbearing in volume. You had to be very, very supportive. He was the type of person who would allow you to lay the foundation first and then would say, "I'll play on top of that," rather than the type of person who says, "I'll lay the foundation, and you play around this."

Playing with Kenny was more like backing a Nancy Wilson–type jazz singer, whereas playing with Stanley Turrentine was like backing an Aretha Franklin–type gospel singer. With Stanley, I could use greater volume. It was like a mixture of blues and funk and bebop, and by the end of each night we would have more of a beat going. Because McCoy Tyner was working in the group, there was more urgency in the music, which meant more drum playing and greater freedom for me as a player. Because the tempos were faster, it was a greater workout musically, and I always felt rejuvenated at the end of the gig.

Finally, the larger framework of a group's common tradition may provide allusions that prompt new ideas and influence the performance's course. When saxophonist Arthur Blythe plays "little phrases" that bring to mind another song for John Hicks, "I might use it," Hicks says, to play off the second song within the framework of the first. Lonnie Hillyer is also the kind of player who likes to quote different compositions in his solos. "A friend of mine says he always hears me quote from 'How Are Things in Glocca Morra?' Now, if I'm playing with a sensitive piano player, he might answer me with something related to "Glocca Morra' in a rhythmic, melodic, or harmonic sense."

As compelling as allusions to popular tunes are improvised patterns reminiscent of the characteristic interplay of renowned artists within historic bands. Tommy Turrentine says, for example, that if, while formulating his solo, he hears the drummer play a figure "ka plum," reminding him of "something Max Roach played behind Fats Navarro," he "would think about the way Fat Girl played" and incorporate that "feeling" within his own performance. If the figure reminded Turrentine of "what Miles played with Max," however, then he might be inspired to perform a phrase by Davis.

Equally important are shared interpretations of the referential meanings of musical patterns. The "exhortative potential" of some phrases, "urging, beseeching, and daring," can inspire "soloists to create ever more exciting improvisations and riffs." [17] The potential of other phrases for humor can be exploited by the playful juxtaposition of materials with different historical and cultural associations. [18]

## Shaping the Larger Performance

In their responses to other players, musicians typically seek to preserve a general continuity of mood. Beginning a solo, John Hicks listens to the "spirit coming from the whole group" to determine "a direction" for expansion that "contributes to the overall feeling." Toward such ends, soloists can draw inspiration from the general approaches or specific ideas of their immediate predecessors. At times, they select a common vocabulary pattern or tune quotation introduced in the solo prior to its final idea (exx. 13.16a–b). As often, they select the solo's final idea. Showing special consideration in this regard, Count Basie was known for "prepar[ing] an entrance for the next man" at the close of his own solos.[19] "If Sonny Stitt plays before me," Harold Ousley says, "I'll listen to the phrases that he plays, and they will give me ideas for related things that I can play. I might take the last phrase that he played and come in on it. Sometimes, musicians do this as a connecting point to their own solos." Soloists may simply treat the "connecting" figure as a fleeting transition, or they may treat it as a motive, transforming it according to the procedures by which they develop their own ideas (exx. 13.17a–f).[20]

When soloists trade eights or fours and other short improvised phrases, they sometimes respond to the most general features of each other's phrases, for example, extending their contours gracefully to create such continuity between the parts that the resultant line sounds as if conceived by one mind. Other times, they adopt comparable practices to those described above, imitating or transforming, to varying degrees, the precise features of the previous player's ideas (exx. 13.18a–b). As often, they combine such operations with developing their own ideas (ex. 13.18c). Tommy Flanagan reflects on the piano duo albums he has made with Hank Jones and Kenny Barron:

> You don't know what the other player is going to play, but on listening to the playback, almost every time, you hear that you related your part very quickly to what the other player played just before you. It's like a message that you relay back and forth. It happens at any tempo, whether it's very fast or whether you're playing a ballad. Or, if we're switching off every eight bars, there will be something in my eight bars that related to the last part of the soloist before me. . . . You want to achieve that kind of communication when you play. When you do, your playing seems to be making sense. It's like a conversation.

Because of the influence that improvisers often exert on those who follow, some band leaders deliberately vary the order of soloists from piece to piece. Featuring different players in the first solo position varies the potential influence each soloist has on the initial direction of the piece's interpretation and, over the course of a set, may vary the overall feeling or concept from piece to piece, as well. A leader may have assertive, self-sufficient soloists perform ahead of those who usually require an inspired model to reach their own potential. Sometimes, musicians unfamiliar with the piece may themselves decide to avoid the first solo to garner ideas for their own approach by studying the ideas of soloists who precede them (HO).

Of course, improvisers can take the opposite musical tack when their cumulative sense of the performance suggests that a strong contrast would enhance its dramatic qualities. "If the music's been really hectic rhythmically, very rhythmic and loud," Calvin Hill says, "I might just be silent for the first four or eight bars" of the solo, "not play anything; or, maybe, play one note every three or four bars." Issues of professional image can also influence such decisions.[21] A musician once advised me that if the previous soloist had "really covered a particular thing well, like playing very high and very technically," the best strategy for avoiding an unfavorable comparison was to adopt a "different approach altogether." Toward such ends, the soloist might draw stimulus from such varied sources as musical ideas unrelated to the performance that "had been going on in my head earlier that day . . . [or even] a sound out in the street" (BW).

As often as not, musicians pursue a middle ground that satisfies their desire for both continuity and change by borrowing material from one another and transforming it.[22] This is as true in the interaction between soloists as in their reciprocal exchanges with the rhythm section. Horn players can create new figures by adding their own notes to rhythmic patterns that they derive from the accompanying parts, perhaps by playing off of the drummer's accents—extracting a simpler pattern from the larger drum phrase—or by seizing a complex rhythmic fragment from the phrase for a template. "You can never know in advance of the situation what you will do at the time," says Leroy Williams when discussing these practices from the rhythm section's side.

> Maybe the soloist will play a phrase, and you will feel like grabbing the phrase and taking it someplace else, doing something else with it. What makes creativity is playing half of this and half of that, interjecting your own thing into it. Or you might let the soloist's phrase go by completely because it would seem too obvious to play it. The unexpected is as cool as the expected, at times. Like Dizzy said, "It's not always what you play that's important. It's what you don't play." Silences can be just as important.

Rufus Reid describes the multiple interpretations that improvisers can put upon one another's statements and the physical aspects of ideas that can affect their discussion within the group. Many times players "will play a certain rhythmic pattern, or melodic motive," he says, "and then I could play a portion of that motive intertwined in my bass line." In a live performance, the listener may not initially hear that "as a separate entity"; it is part of the continuous flow of the music. But if the performance is recorded, a listener who studies the album may "say, 'Wow, did you hear that?'" Reid might have used the pattern in his own playing four bars after it was introduced by the horn player, either imitating it "verbatim" or taking the rhythm of the phrase and adding something different "harmonically." Reid finds it more interesting to take something from someone else and add a little bit to it. Sometimes this is a necessity. For example, a saxophone player might play things Reid never had "thought of playing" because of the different techniques of their instruments. If the entire phrase is too difficult to execute with the bass, Reid typically plays "a portion" of the saxophone player's phrase and develops it in his own way.

Beyond sharing precise melodic and rhythmic material, musicians initiate and respond to change by regulating such general features of their improvisations as range and voicing (exx. 13.19a–b).[23] Contour is also an ongoing feature of interplay, as players anticipate and respond to the nuances within each other's evolving shapes, the distinctive "hills and valleys" of their creations. In contrapuntal schemes with endless possibilities, they formulate lines that, for example, run parallel to one another, or create contrary motion (ex. 13.19c), or provide other kinds of contrast. Dynamic changes also come into play. If the soloist performs something dramatic that goes from soft to loud, Reid explains, it might inspire the rhythm section to do the same thing a few bars later, going from soft to loud and following the soloist's lead. "And then, in turn, the soloist could turn around and play it loud to soft," he adds. Drummers sometimes follow a soloist even more closely. "If I'm playing very loud at a certain point in my solo—really hollering—and then I suddenly come off it and get soft, they will also back off with me," John McNeil remarks.

> You can build and build, and then back off, and then come up again together. I like to do things like that because it's interesting for me to listen to. It's good when drummers stay under me, as opposed to over me, in terms of volume. And yet at some point, they can play right up to my level and just a little beyond to take me a little further. But if he does that and I don't take him up on it by playing any louder, then he should know enough not to push it too far. It's a give-and-take situation that way. I like a drummer to really roar in the back of me sometimes, and it gives me a lot of support; but there has to be a balance.

To avoid excessive imitation, players can respond to the fact of change in another part simply by producing a prominent change with an appropriate original contrasting idea in their own part.

Equally influential for the design of a solo are the relative rhythmic complexity and density of its accompaniment. These features allow the music to breathe and diversify. "Some piano players will let a few bars at a time go by without playing," Lonnie Hillyer explains. "That gives horn players room to establish their ideas." Similarly, Patti Bown "tries to leave space" within the framework of her comping patterns. "It's important to learn to play less," she cautions, "because it's possible to fill up every hole."

As implied earlier, the composition's formal structure dictates, in part, the regulation of rhythmic activity and other interactive features. General collective goals, such as "accenting the endings of harmonic units," assist artists in anticipating and complementing the details in each others' parts.[24] So do shared expectations for events that typically occur at particular "location[s] within the time cycle."[25] Typically, while the soloist extends phrases over principal harmonic section boundaries or highlights them by resting, rhythm section players define structural cadences through various combined operations in the last two bars of sections. They may, for example, increase their parts' rhythmic and harmonic density and tension, or expand their parts' range, then reverse such operations, returning to the tonic on the new section downbeat or just after it. Such events are made all the more dramatic when, at their onset, the pianist drops out of the performance, but rejoins to assist in creating a climactic peak (exx. 13.20a–c). On the other hand, comparable aspects of group interplay can transcend formal units, occurring instead as sympathetic responses to evolving ideas in the various parts, creating unique designs in the process.

Rhythm section members sometimes steadily increase the intensity of their own activity over the course of the solo. "Working with Art Blakey taught me about how to build a solo," Gary Bartz recalls. "Art will build it for you, so you have to go along with him. He starts off nice and soft the first chorus, and he builds the second chorus a little, and by the time you get to the third chorus, he's bashing behind you. You have to build your solo on him, so you learn how to build a solo like that. It isn't necessarily that he plays louder each chorus," Bartz says, "but his playing becomes more intense each chorus, so you learn how to build the intensity of your solo each chorus." Art Farmer also acknowledges the give-and-take between the soloist and the supporting players. "If I would play with Horace Silver, I would learn something about drive," Farmer declares,

> because Horace was so strong on the piano. If I would play with Blakey, I would also have to play something interesting, something with life in it. If you played something dull, then it was just like you were in their way. Horace and Art were supposed to be playing background for you, but at the same time, they were really driving you and pushing you. And if you didn't respond, you might as well stop playing and let them go ahead without you. They didn't let you coast. You had to get into it.

Speaking from the drummer's viewpoint, Akira Tana observes that shaping a solo commonly includes a combination of strategies, "playing straight time, starting with a little interaction, and building from there. You can develop a very nice tension sometimes when you have rhythmic figures going against each other," Tana explains. "You can keep up the tension over eight or sixteen bars and resolve it at the bridge of the piece. Or you can keep it going over the tune's form for a whole chorus, or even beyond that, depending on how much freedom you have in developing your idea. You have to be very conscious of time and the form of the piece when you do this. It has to be in reason."

At one concert in which saxophonist Frank Foster subjected a melodic phrase to motivic variations of increasing rhythmic complexity and volume, drummer Billy Hart increased his part's volume and cross-rhythmic activity accordingly, culminating in a thrashing crescendo just as Foster restated the solo's motive in the saxophone's highest register and brought the performance to a climax. Immediately afterward, Hart created a huge swell of sound with a press roll, leading with a rapid decrescendo to a soft time-keeping pattern that prepared the next soloist's entrance.

Rhythm section players can also vary their instrumentation to effect changes in the overall texture and dynamics of their accompaniment. When violinist Michael Urbaniak began a ballad during a New York club date, Roy Haynes initially restricted his part to cymbals, which he stroked with brushes so lightly that they were as much felt as heard. As the solo developed, however, Haynes began punctuating Urbaniak's lines with bursts of snare drum and bass drum, eventually switching to drumsticks to produce a uniformly hard-driving rhythmic accompaniment.

Later, at the opening of Buster Williams's bass solo, Roy Haynes dropped out of the performance and Kenny Barron lowered the piano's volume. Caressing the keys, Barron embraced the principal pitches of the bass's warm, lyrical phrases with lush chord voicings. As Williams moved in and out of the ballad's metered time, Barron accordingly alternated the percussive articulation of block chords with free-rhythmic arpeggios. At the peak of the duo's momentum, Haynes rejoined the others by playing a surging swing pattern that drew their performances into a strict rhythmic groove and drove the music with increasing volume and intensity to its conclusion.

This ballad rendition exemplifies what Walter Bishop Jr. means when, speaking from the soloist's perspective, he suggests, "Sometimes, the drummer should lay out altogether and let me build my own intensity in my solo before coming back in." Correspondingly, as an accompanist, Bishop "will often lay out on piano for a couple of choruses when the soloist is playing and let him build his own momentum with the bass and drums. Then I'll come in, and it just adds more intensity to the music." Soloist and rhythm section members often work together to accommodate major changes of mood, musical concept, or time-feeling in each other's parts (ex. 13.21).

When soloists create several climaxes over their performance's course, accompanists sometimes choose simply "to hold down the beat," stabilizing the music's foundation in relation to dramatic changes in the soloist's part. This was illustrated at a New York club in which soloist Walter Bishop Jr. suddenly switched from streams of even eighth notes to a repeated asymmetrical pattern, whose accents fell in progressively different places in relation to Michael Carvin's accompanying swing figure, creating varied schemes of rhythmic counterpoint. Instantly aware of the pressure between the two parts, both performers smiled as they sought to steady their components in the face of their growing tension, not knowing when they would find alignment. When after eight measures the patterns finally coincided, the two musicians laughed with enjoyment, and assuredly repeated the same sequence of events before Bishop abandoned the asymmetrical figure and returned to his former groove.[26]

Pursuing yet another course, the rhythm section can follow soloists in structuring diverse musical episodes. At one New York performance, drummer Al Foster phrased together with saxophonist Bob Berg, who was formulating his solo around a clear succession of motives. With the introduction of each motive, Foster reduced the rhythmic complexity and volume of his drum part, then steadily increased them, underscoring with a loud cymbal crash the climax of each thematic section, before dropping to his lowest dynamic level in anticipation of Berg's next motive. Throughout, the soloist's lead and the drummer's response formed an integral part of their successful journey.

### Surprises in Group Interaction

Within the normal compass of their activities, improvisers must respond creatively to surprises that constantly arise during performances. Unexpected turns of events occur everywhere: in the ever-changing details of each part and in the periodic large-scale changes in repertory programs and formal structures that guide improvisations. The latter occur typically when the natural flow of ideas conceived in performance leads a particular improviser outside the group's agreed-upon formats and other players follow along. Ultimately, the flexibility with which musicians treat repertory and musical arrangements, whether subtly ornamenting or substantially altering their features, enhances the improvisatory spirit of performances. "Sonny Rollins might play from one tune to the next," Don Pate remembers,

> without saying anything to the band, and whether the whole band played with him on that particular number depended on who knew the tune and whether or not they could hang [on].[27]
>
> Other band leaders have signals for little interludes they have in the music where different pairs of musicians might solo together, like a saxophone-drum duet. Other times, there are no signals given, and what you play is a matter of having good taste or bad taste and knowing the difference. We played a tune by [one musician/composer], and every time he played the head, there was a discrepancy about where "one" was. He really heard the tune different ways at different times, and you'd sound like you weren't correct if you just stuck to one way.

It meant that you would just have to do it whatever way he did it at the time.

Additionally, the prescribed lengths of solos can be upset by sudden, unusual brilliance on a player's part. At one event, a young soloist so impressed listeners with his fire and imagination that the leader approached him at the end of his solo, saying, "Take another?" The soloist smiled gratefully and performed two additional choruses. At times, soloists spontaneously dictate changes in accompaniment. If Rufus Reid wants to stretch out in his solos, he might signal the pianist and the drummer to stop playing, simply by saying, "I got it," or he might tell the drummer, "I want brushes," or just mouth "brushes." In other instances, the accompanist may decide to alter arrangements. Once during saxophonist Clifford Jordan's solo at a New York club date, Jimmy Robinson turned to Tommy Turrentine and whispered, "Let's catch him at the bridge." Turrentine agreed, and Robinson invented a melodic riff, then sang it softly into his friend's ear until he had learned it. When the performance reached the piece's bridge, the trumpeters performed the riff together in harmony, adding a pleasing background line to the music that stimulated Jordan's playing.

Unexpected occurrences require instant judgment as musicians contemplate alternative courses of musical action. Once when Benny Bailey finished a solo a few measures early at a performance at the Jazz Showcase, pianist Jodie Christian spontaneously filled in the progression with a melodic phrase comprising a series of large, descending intervals, which saxophonist Jackie McLean immediately seized for the opening of his own solo.

On a blues recording by the Jazz Messengers, Art Blakey closed most solo choruses with a cymbal crash or cadential fills, including his powerful press roll.[28] The features coherently outlined the form of the piece and, for each soloist's final chorus, served as periods to their completed statements. Once, however, when soloist Hank Mobley showed signs of continuing at this point, Blakey made a quick decision to hold off his roll, for fear he might cut off the soloist's phrase prematurely. He waited for Mobley to complete his performance before playing the emphatic drum figure between the second and third measure of the following chorus. By accommodating Mobley, Blakey's decision required of the next soloist, Kenny Dorham, the presence of mind to avoid confusion about the displaced rhythmic marker and the skill to begin his own improvisation a few measures into the piece's structure. Flexible practices such as overlapping solos mitigate the musician's strict adherence to form and accommodate the unpredictability of improvised ideas—ideas whose logic may compel soloists to complete their performances just before or after a progression's close.

Other challenges arise when individuals suddenly drop out of the performance or spontaneously vary their musical roles, inviting change within other parts and causing some players to alter their own improvisational approaches. At an event described earlier, Roy Haynes's surprising withdrawal from the performance led pianist Kenny Barron to maintain the music's beat in his accompaniment, normally the bassist's or drummer's province. Walter Bishop Jr. describes the effect of similar changes on his own performance as a soloist. "If nobody is keeping strict time, then I have to keep the time, and it alters the way I think. If someone else is keeping the time, I am much freer to play with the time, floating in and out of time."

When pianists lay out unexpectedly, the music's changing harmonic character can also have major consequences. Benny Bailey says that with a piano background he plays fewer "notes" in his solos, but without the piano he plays "more notes" to make himself "hear the chords of the tune." Art Farmer raises related considerations. "If the piano is not there, then the music is just stripped to its bare bones. What you play has got to sound good by itself. There are certain things that you might play that would only sound good with the piano player, so it is a matter of making an adjustment in your playing." Likewise, if bass players lay out, pianists have the opportunity to pursue different options in their solos. Without having to coordinate their chord patterns with other players, they might take greater liberties within the form of a piece, for example, spontaneously substituting chords of different qualities for one another (DF).

Should more than one band member refrain from performing, changes become especially dramatic. Elvin Jones laughs in enjoyment as he describes the unusual saxophone-drum duets that periodically occurred in John Coltrane's quartet, when, without any signals, both bassist Jimmy Garrison and pianist McCoy Tyner would suddenly drop out of the performance. "After a while I began to understand what it was all about and the reasons for it," Jones says. That "whole vacuum . . . could be filled either rhythmically . . . or with the expanded harmonics of [Coltrane's] horn itself, [with] his own expanded range, and without any preconceived pattern of chord progression. So, he was free of that. It was a tremendous leap into the future, I think."[29] Finally, if the entire rhythm section stops playing, soloists have the freedom to improvise without accommodating anyone else, but must rely entirely on their own resourcefulness.

Unanticipated time changes can also create new challenges, catching off guard musicians who are inexperienced or inattentive. One student confessed to me the confusion he felt on the first occasion a rhythm section shifted into double time during his solo: "I had never heard anything like it before, and I didn't know what to do. I didn't have the technique to play twice as fast as I was playing, but I felt dumb not making any change in my playing, so I just dropped out of the music." Moreover, as Kenny Barron observes, performers might do "something so daring rhythmically that it actually stops the music's tempo all of a sudden."

Even veterans must be alert to complicated and instant shifts in time. "Charles Mingus was one of the first people in jazz I remember who was into freeing up the tempos and meters," says Lonnie Hillyer. "We'd be playing at one tempo, and suddenly he'd slow it way down and change meters. We'd move from 4/4 to 3/4 to 2/4 or whatever. Other times, he'd really speed up the tempos. The changes gave a whole new feeling of freedom of expression to the music." John Hicks recalls like practices:

> Art Blakey would sometimes take the bridge of the tune into this 3/4 waltz time thing and then with a drum roll, take it back into 4/4. Or it might be that he'd play some stoptime pattern in there, or one of the shuffle type things he'd do on "Moanin'," or the kind of thing he played on the "Blues March." He would break up the time and throw these things in different places in different tunes, just to change the whole flavor of the tune around. You would listen to what he was doing and go along with it. You'd have to translate on your instrument what was happening there rhythmically, dealing with the rhythm section, and at the same time, deal harmonically with what the horn players were playing.

Once, at the close of a ballad in a set at New York's Sweet Basil, Lonnie Hillyer slowed his tempo suddenly and began improvising a cadenza in unmetered time. Looking up from the keyboard in surprise, the pianist instantly slowed his comping patterns and exchanged quick glances with the drummer, who switched from sticks to brushes to create free-rhythmic waves of sound with his cymbals. As the music's tempo and texture changed around him, the bass player appeared flustered initially and stopped performing. Soon, however, he began to strum the bass softly like a guitar and phrased in step with his counterparts as Hillyer concluded the ballad. During another concert, Jackie McLean brought his solo to a close with an extended improvisation and was able to conduct changes in the dynamics and tempo of his rhythm section's accompaniment by dramatically raising and lowering his saxophone as a sign.

Finally, musicians sometimes deliberately introduce surprises into their performances, not only to inspire other group members, but to test their abilities. "Mingus demanded so much of a musician that he would bring out stuff in you that you didn't even know was there," Hillyer remembers.

> He'd really put you on the spot, and that helped you to develop your personal strength. One of his devices was to stop the entire band, including the rhythm section, and to leave you soloing out there by yourself, which I thought was beautiful. If you didn't want to look like a fool, you had to play something. One night I overslept for the gig

and came in about forty-five minutes late, and Mingus decided to screw with me. They were playing a ballad when I walked in, and after a couple of choruses, before I had hardly warmed up, he pointed to me and said, "You got it." He just left me out there by myself, and I had to come up with something [laughter]. Actually, it went over very well, and I felt very good about it.

Mingus also had a healthy sense of competition. He would sometimes kick off songs at a breakneck tempo, so fast it would be ridiculous. One night, I was really up and playing well. He was playing something so fast that he tired out and I just kept going. Then I looked at him and said, "What'd you stop for, man?"

In order to work with a guy with such an overbearing personality, you had to shape up and try to toe the line with him.

Calvin Hill also describes a "refreshing performance" by Jaki Byard's band in which bassist "Richard Davis was picking apart the tunes, goofing on everything, and there was a lot of humor." In the middle of one piece,

Richard started changing things all around. At one point, everything was getting very shaky. The tempo was about to fall apart, and the drummer was trying to keep up with Richard, trying to figure out what he was going to do next, which way he was going to go. It got very chaotic for a minute as they were coming to the end of the chorus. It was just like an airplane coming in for a landing that was about to crash. No one knew what was going to happen or how they were going to get out of that. At that point, Jaki was coming to the end of his solo, and he played this really strong rhythmic figure on top of what everyone else was playing, which brought all the different tempos back together and led everyone right into the "one" of the next chorus. Everybody just came right back in together for the beginning of the next chorus.

In that instance, Richard deliberately introduced something rhythmically into the music that made the other players feel uneasy. People will do that sometimes. They might play something that goes against the established tempo, or they might play polyrhythmic things or start playing an odd meter against the established meter, and that makes the music feel unstable. In this case Jaki Byard knew that Richard did what he did deliberately, and he resolved it in the end by bringing it all back in.

To emphasize the value that he places on adventurous experimentation, producing music as "fresh" and "honest as it can possibly be," Miles Davis would periodically encourage his band members to avoid their routine maneuvers. "I pay you to practice on the bandstand," he would exhort them.[30] In a similar spirit, some leaders build extemporaneous interaction into performances—requiring musicians to rely heavily on their ingenuity and their sensitivity to one another—by limiting rehearsals and minimizing discussion about the music. When these conditions conspire with capricious turns of improvisation in a way that defies the expectations of the band altogether, they are what Herbie Hancock likens, within Miles Davis's band, to the unpredictable course of conversations. "How many times have you talked to somebody and you got ready to make a point, and it kind of went off in another direction? Maybe you never ended up making that point," Hancock admits, "but the conversation just went somewhere else and it was fine. There's nothing wrong with it. Maybe you liked where you went. Well, this is the way we were dealing with music."[31]

In yet other situations, musicians pursue musical tangents their counterparts introduce into the conversation, while keeping sight of the original topic as a point of return. Lee Konitz describes such spontaneous interplay in Lennie Tristano's band:

> When we would play "All the Things You Are," we would get to the point where the music was moving so intensely that the music would start to leave the song form, the actual structure of the song. We might get involved with one tonal area and would just stop the progress of the song right there and play freely in that area. That could just stretch out as completely as we would want it to go and then return to the song. This was a note-to-note kind of playing. It was an impressionistic utilization of the song.

## Challenges Presented by Musical Error

To those unforeseen turns of event that form the normal basis for collaboration, errors in performance present additional challenges. "Last week I was playing one song and, during my solo, my mind threw me into another melody altogether," Doc Cheatham reveals. "I realized what I was doing way into the song, and the piano player guided me right back where I should have been. I put my ear right back to the piano because he was playing straight ahead. I realized where he was and I went right on in. Nobody in the audience knew the difference."

During moments when the rhythm section interprets the forms of pieces allusively, however, soloists must rely heavily upon their own internal musical models, and the consequences of any mistake become a problem for the entire group. A miscalculation on the soloist's part can call into question the representations of other musicians and potentially obscure formal landmarks for everyone. If someone is not aware of the problem he or she has created, other members may alert the musician by calling softly on the bandstand or, to avoid distracting the audience, by signaling visually. For Leroy Williams, "watching soloists is as important as listening to them." Similarly, before performances, Roy Haynes used to decide upon the best place for Don Pate to stand, because eye contact between them was crucial. "Sometimes, just a look, just eyes meeting, can tell you what's required of one musically," Pate explains. "That's a very subtle way of signaling without even a spoken word. We didn't need it all the time, but just anytime we wanted it. Between Roy and me, a look might indicate that he wanted to pick up the tempo a little more or that he wanted to play more laid back."

During a Sweet Basil engagement in which Lonnie Hillyer's solo faltered, he temporarily held and played the trumpet with his right hand, while he ran his left through his hair with a single motion, as if to scratch an itch, then lightly brushed his ear before replacing his left hand on the trumpet. Understanding the gesture, the pianist instantly switched from elusive comping patterns to explicit chord voicings, which he continued until Hillyer regained his confidence.

In the event that improvisers are too preoccupied to notice verbal and visual signals, their friends try to reach them through the music itself. One evening at the Jazz Showcase, a pianist fell behind within the form of a piece. Initially, the bass player stared at him and repeatedly formed the word *turnaround* on his lips. When the pianist neglected to look up, the bass player turned up his amplifier and transposed his part into the instrument's highest, most penetrating register, effectively underscoring the disparity between the parts and directing the pianist to the correct position at the close of the chorus.

If the rhythm section loses its harmonic bearings, soloists can assume a temporary place-marking role and alter their own improvisations to stabilize the music. "It can happen if you're playing with inexperienced people, or it can also happen to experienced people," John McNeil states.

> You can be playing along and suddenly there's no bridge where there should be one, say, on an AABA tune. Musicians never seem to put two bridges in there by mistake. They usually add an extra eight bars of an A section. Or, they leave out eight bars of A.[32] That will happen on a tune like "Just Friends," where the two halves are almost identical except for the last major chord. If the guys don't concentrate and their knowledge of the form of the tune isn't really solid, the minor differences between the halves become obscured. At that point, things can really fall apart. If the bass player is playing a pedal then, the piano player can't figure out where he should be from listening to the bass. What I try to do in that situation is to allude to the melody in my improvisation, since the melody's a little different at the end of the tune, and that will direct them back to the form.

Related issues, alluded to earlier in the playful performance by Jaki Byard's band, include the loss of the groove and rhythmic displacement of the measure. When improvisers deliberately stretch the limits of form by placing their patterns in an especially abstract relationship to the underlying meter, they potentially upset their own or others' perceptions of where measures actually begin and end, unintentionally turning the beat around. As Akira Tana explains, there are multiple disorienting possibilities.

> Sometimes, you're trying to play something and all of a sudden the beat gets turned around, and you don't know how to get it back where it should be. Suddenly, you find yourself playing on "one" and "three" where "two" and "four" should be. It might be that you would do a fill or try for some rhythmic figure and you'd come out of it wrong, with an extra beat in there. It also happens to me sometimes when I play with musicians who embellish things rhythmically a lot, or who explore very complex rhythms. All of a sudden their patterns give you the illusion of the beat being turned around, and if your concentration has lapsed, you try to hook up with what you think they're doing, only to find when they come out of it that you're one or two beats behind.

Leroy Williams discusses how unique approaches to time can add an intriguing uncertainty to performances.

> Everybody interprets time differently, but some bass players not only have good time, but creative time. Wilbur Ware was one of my favorite bass players because he had a different sense of time. It was not straight time. He would do unexpected things with it. He had an uncanny way of being there when you thought he wasn't. He might go off rhythmically and you'd say, "How is he going to come back from there?" Some players can stretch the time to that fine line of almost turning the beat around, but they can always come back. For example, with Wilbur Ware in Monk's band, they would play so close to that thin line rhythmically that, if you weren't careful, you'd find yourself playing on "one" and "three," instead of "two" and "four." If you weren't careful, you'd be right off it. It has to do with where you put your accents when you're improvising. It was an amazing experience for me, like walking on a tightrope. Not everybody plays that way, but certain people like Barry Harris do. That's freedom to me. That's what I like.

Soloists are particularly vulnerable to turning the beat around when they improvise without the rhythm section's accompaniment, as during arranged breaks in a piece's performance. "We were playing 'A Night in Tunisia,'" Max Roach remembers, "and we came to a four-bar break in Dizzy's solo. Dizzy was doubling up, and when we came out of the break, there was an uncommon 'one.'" A similar vulnerability carries over to the unaccompanied bass or drum solo. "It's one thing for a soloist to play adventurous things across the barlines when there is a rhythm section behind him, giving him a point of reference; the harmonic progression is holding it together," Chuck Israels asserts. "But when a drummer solos, there is often nothing else going on behind him, and it is harder for him to hold onto the progress of the piece in his own mind and avoid errors. If his adventurousness leads him to make an error," he conjectures, "it's difficult for the rest of us to know exactly where that error has been made and to compensate for this when the whole band comes in."

In the face of this problem, improvisers can pursue various courses. "You can keep playing the way you think it is, or you can just lighten up and forget what you're doing and try to hear what other people are doing," Akira Tana offers. "If you know the song and the chord changes, you can listen to the music harmonically to find out where things fall into place. Or you can just stop and begin again." Max Roach elaborates upon the "Night in Tunisia" incident cited above: "When the beat got turned around at the Festival, it went on for about eight bars. In such a case, someone has to lay out. You can't fight it. Dizzy stopped first because he heard what was happening quicker than the rest of us, and he didn't know where 'one' was. Then it was up to Ray Brown and Bishop and myself. One of us had to stop, so Bishop waved off. Then it was up to Ray Brown and myself to clear it up. Almost immediately, we found a common 'one,' and the others came back in without the public realizing what had happened."

As for the musical saves of soloists discussed earlier, jazz groups simply treat performance errors as compositional problems that require instant, collective solutions, in some cases the skillful mending of one another's performances. In Miles Davis's band, if, despite the rhythm section's effort "to keep the groove happening," it began to fall apart, Herbie Hancock recalls, "Miles with his playing would center it . . . tie it all together—as though he sensed what the link was—and get the thing to grooving so hard that it was like being in the Garden of Eden [laughter]."[33]

When Emily Remler was playing with Eddie Gomez, he gave her such adequate support that if she made a mistake, "he'd do something to make it right," Remler attests. If she played a "wrong chord in a piece," Gomez would "hit the appropriate bass notes to justify the chord" that she had played.[34] Within group interaction, the responses of other artists to unintended events may, in fact, reveal their value to a player. One renowned pianist remembers the relief he felt during a performance when he missed several keys he intended to hit, and Charlie Parker exclaimed, "I hear you," having interpreted the erroneous pitches within the piece's framework as an "interesting chord voicing."

Don Friedman discovered a similar pattern of accommodation when listening to a recording on which he played piano and Booker Little played trumpet.[35] At the time of the session, Friedman guided his performance of a ballad with a structural model that inadvertently deviated from the standard version. In a segment of the progression calling for six beats of D minor, he played one measure of D7 followed by two beats of D minor. It was twenty years later, when Friedman and I were working together to transcribe his piano part, that Friedman recognized the error and how cleverly Booker Little had covered it.

Little apparently realized the discrepancy during his solo's initial chorus, when he arrived at this segment and selected the minor third of the chord for one of the opening pitches of a phrase. Hearing it clash with the pianist's part, Little improvised a rapid save by leaping to another pitch and resting, stopping the progress of his performance. To disguise the error further, he repeated the entire phrase fragment as if he had initially intended it as a motive, before extending it into a graceful, ascending melodic arch (ex. 13.22). From that point on, Little guided his solo according to a revised map of the ballad. "Even when Booker played the melody at the end of the take," observed Friedman with admiration, he varied it in ways "that fit the chord I was playing."

Tactful responses not only mitigate musical errors, but can at times produce unexpected benefits for the entire group. Max Roach observes that "there are chances we all have to take when we're dealing with improvisational music, and sometimes clashes occur between musicians. That's why there's so much skill and sensitivity required to make the music come off well. There are also times when a clash isn't bad," he says. "It can create a tension, and something new can come of it. For example, if two players make a mistake and end up in the wrong place at the wrong time, they may be able to break out of it and get into something else they might not have discovered otherwise."

As Roach indicates, the skills by which performers share ideas during the routine course of improvisation—negotiating the precise details of one another's contributions and unifying the entire group's presentation—are put to great test by error. Like exceptional visions that suggest new paths for exploration, problematic turns can ultimately provide dramatic, even welcome, contrast to the prearranged performance features, their effective solutions contributing uniqueness to the musical journeys of improvisers.[36] Scores sampling different group improvisations illustrate the widely varied musical environments in which improvisers create their artworks and situate within larger contexts the various features of group interplay discussed above (exx. 13.23 through 13.26).

## The Ongoing Interplay between Collective Improvisation and Precomposition

In the final analysis, the spontaneous and arranged elements of jazz presentations continually cross-fertilize and revitalize one another. Precomposed background lines or riffs, which add interest to the performance and, as musical landmarks, help soloists keep their bearings over a progression, also provide material that soloists can incorporate into their extemporaneous inventions. Conversely, supporting players, without external direction, can adopt a soloist's interesting phrase extemporaneously as the basis for a new accompanying riff. As artists absorb and share initially improvised patterns, repeating

them as components of increasingly consistent routines, the patterns shift subtly from the realm of improvised ideas to that of arranged or precomposed
ideas. These are common occurrences over a single performance. In the renowned interplay within the Creole Jazz Band, Joe Oliver would, at times,
introduce a new break figure at the end of one chorus, and Louis Armstrong
would instantly absorb it to perform it subsequently in unison with Oliver at
the break in the middle of the next chorus. Moreover, Oliver's cue to his partner
was sometimes but a silent miming of an intended idea's finger pattern. Before
the targeted break, Armstrong, translating the patterns instantly into sound,
actually composed a second part to the now-anticipated Oliver "lead" in time
to "blend" with his.[37]

From event to event, groups may preserve successful elements of improvisations within an arrangement's ongoing performance tradition. When playing
through a composition together, singer Vea Williams and pianist Franklin Gordon sometimes "get to a place where the chords normally resolve a certain
way," Williams says, and spontaneously "try something different from the way
the tune's written. The other day, we were doing 'Come Rain or Come Shine,'"
she recounts, turning to Gordon for the details of his accompaniment, "and we
came to the place where you go from F7 to B♭7 in the key of F or G minor."
Gordon continues: "Instead of playing the F7, I played B♭∅ going to the B♭. It's
a beautiful sound." Williams nods in agreement, adding, "And it's away from
the melody. It gave me this surge, just this tremendous feeling. We talked about
it afterward and decided that whenever we did that tune, we'd play it straight
the first chorus and add the new chord the second or third time around because
that made the music so fresh."

Larry Gray describes even more radical harmonic alterations during one
performance with James Moody at the Jazz Showcase in Chicago. Feeling adventurous that evening, Gray decided to see what would happen if, in between
the pivotal "signpost" chords of the blues, he pursued in his bass line harmonic
pathways loosely associated with Coltrane's "Giant Steps." Moody instantly
grasped Gray's intention and improvised his own solo along the same lines.
Afterwards, he expressed his appreciation to Gray, and the two decided to
adopt this approach during future blues performances.

Chuck Israels gives a similar interpretation of the way in which rhythmic
features of a group's interplay enter arrangements.[38] "There are cross-rhythms
and other figures that the rhythm section players can catch from each other and
find ways of playing together, like the triplet figures which 'Philly' Joe Jones,
Paul Chambers, and Red Garland play together on Miles Davis recordings.
Things like that are worked out. Some people in the band initially play it and
somebody else says, 'Oh, that's good. Let's do that again'" (ex. 13.4b). In fact,
when Don Friedman once worked with "Philly" Joe Jones in a band with Chet
Baker, Jones taught Friedman some of the "complicated rhythmic figures" he

had performed with Garland, so that they, too, could play the figures together when he initiated them. Friedman recalls, "I used to hear that band with Miles live, and it was fantastic to hear [Jones and Garland] play together, because they had so many things worked out. They'd do all these great [rhythmic] hits," he recalls, that "would suddenly come out of nowhere," breaking up the music's "constant repetitive beat," providing "such a lift." Various features of "Philly" Joe Jones's interaction with Miles Davis also became classic routines, not only re-created by the artists themselves in performance but adopted by other jazz groups as well.[39]

Of course, routines like those within Miles Davis's group can also develop among improvisers without any discussion. "Philly" Joe Jones remembers that, in general, when performing with Davis, "Miles would ask if we knew the tunes, and we did, so we'd play them spontaneously each night. By playing the tunes every night in a certain way, it becomes an arrangement, actually a better arrangement than if it had been written out."[40] A specific case is Roy Haynes's interaction with Sarah Vaughan during performances of "Shulie-A-Bop," in which Vaughan departs from her scat improvisation to introduce the other band members. The exchange that became a permanent feature of their rendition had its roots in an event during which, after hearing her acknowledge John Malachi and "Crazy" Joe Benjamin, Haynes decided that he would "set her up" for his own introduction. He anticipated the moment she would announce his name and, just ahead of it, played a loud kick on the drums. Then, hearing Vaughan call, "Roy," he interjected a few more kicks into the performance between "Roy" and "Haynes." Following her mention of his surname, he created an explosive drum response, ending, on their recorded version, with triplets that Vaughan immediately picks up to launch her own continuing vocal improvisation.[41]

Three recorded performances of "Moanin'" by the Jazz Messengers reveal comparable, arranged exchanges. In each performance, Lee Morgan concludes his solos with an identical phrase that Benny Golson adopts for the beginning of his own solos (ex. 13.17b). Moreover, during the group's third recording of the piece, pianist Bobby Timmons anticipates the same pattern in Morgan's solo and plays it in unison with him.[42]

What happens at one performance can eventually lead to radical revision of a composition that includes the development of new signals for its direction. Kenny Barron describes the transformation of one of his original pieces that "just began as a tune and some changes," he recalls,

> but evolved into a suite. The idea for the piece happened one time in Yusef Lateef's band when Yusef was soloing. For some reason the rest of the band just stopped, and Yusef continued soloing. Nobody said anything about that. Everybody just felt like stopping at the same time, and nobody started playing again until he had finished his solo.

Then we all came in and played the tune again. Then, when it was time for the next soloist, we all stopped and let him have it by himself. It eventually got to the point where everybody got a chance to solo. When soloing by ourselves we would take the music to many different places.

Sometimes, if I was getting into something on my solo, the bass player would accompany me very briefly on this particular thing. Maybe it was just a mood. Then the drummer might accompany me on another part of my solo when he felt like it, and when we had exhausted that together, he'd drop out, and I'd still have it by myself. Then I'd take it somewhere else, and they would join me for that. That's the way that piece worked. It was never discussed. It evolved to the point where we had little musical cues worked out to let the band know, "I'm ending my solo now. Everybody can come back in with the tune."

What I would do to signal the end of my long improvised solo was to start playing the bridge of the tune in time, over and over. Then, when they came in and joined me, we'd go back to the top and play the tune through together. Those were the only things that were the same from performance to performance. We could play the tune for a whole set.

Musical parts conceived through group interaction may even assume independent lives as compositions. Guitarist John McLaughlin and violinist Shankar, of Shakti, would record their informal improvising. After evaluating the taped sessions, they sometimes extracted the most cohesive segments to combine and reassemble into original compositions and arrangements.[43] As these representative cases demonstrate, collective interplay can lead players beyond the bounds of their initial plans and even cause them to invent new musical forms that subsequently serve as vehicles for the group's improvisations. Such practices, reminiscent of the genesis of tunes in solo invention, reveal the perpetual interplay between formerly composed ideas and those conceived in performance. It is this dynamic reciprocity that characterizes improvisation as both an individual and a collective music-making process.

# FOURTEEN

## When the Music's Happening and When It's Not

### Evaluating Group Performances

*Going out to hear musicians live is just like going to see some live drama. Either it's going to hypnotize you and cast a spell on you, or it makes you say, "This is not it. There's no magic here." When I go to listen to music, I tend to be antsy. When I run from club to club, I'm looking for those few minutes of magic. There is no constant magic, but I am hungry to witness as much as I can. Every now and then I get hypnotized. I'll plan to run from club to club to hear several different groups, but I'll get to one place and enjoy it enough not to leave.* —Don Pate

During collective improvising, the activities of creating, listening, and evaluating become integral parts of the same process. Outside of their performances, to refine their grasp of the abilities upon which improvisation depends, players constantly hone their skills as critics and expert listeners. When studying recordings or attending concerts by other players, they divide their attention among the individuals participating in a group's varied musical stream, evaluating the cogency and continuity of each part and following their interrelationships. "When I discovered the records Bill Evans made at the Village Vanguard," Fred Hersch says, "I especially appreciated that chamber music concept of real spontaneous give-and-take—that unity of direction established by a great solo, accompanied well." Bobby Rogovin articulates the views of many others when he asserts that "you can only really appreciate jazz if you listen to the whole group. The soloist's part by itself is just one line in a whole painting. In a lot of cases, the most interesting things are what the rhythm section is playing. It's what those cats are playing that makes the soloists sound as great as they do."

Early coaching, however subtle, guides the newcomer's appreciation of these distinctions and helps develop a sense of discrimination and taste. Some youngsters are initially surprised when a friend displays erudition by singing along with the bass player's or the drummer's performances on recordings instead of those of the featured soloist (BR). In other instances, veterans listening to records display their delight at high points in the individual performances of rhythm section players through spontaneous outbursts of laughter, or by miming the precise gesture, a pianist's unusual comping pattern or a drummer's kicks.

When Rufus Reid was in the air force, stationed in Tokyo, he frequently listened to recordings with an older drummer whose acute hearing and sensitive responses to the music were instructive. The drummer "wouldn't actually verbalize what was happening, but when something nice happened in the music, he would always say, 'See that?' and I would answer, 'Yes.' I didn't exactly know what had happened, but I did know that something special had happened at that particular time between the musicians." Another performer described a youngster of his acquaintance who had learned from his father, a professional musician, to make appropriate judgments about jazz and display his savvy according to the jazz community's convention. "It's really funny watching him listen to records. He shuts his eyes and snaps his fingers on 'two' and 'four,' and when something really hip happens in the music, he shouts, 'Yeah!' He's only eight years old, but he can already hear the music."

Youngsters gradually come to understand both the problems improvisers seek to avoid and the values that they wish to realize in performance. Listening to seasoned players animatedly recount stories about their successes and failures that chronicle the technical and experiential features of improvisation reinforces the student's growing awareness. So, too, does observing the selective processes by which artists choose material from their improvised interplay for arrangements and compositions.

### Ascending to the Music's Heights

Typically, the highest points of improvisation occur when group members strike a groove together, defining and maintaining a solid rhythmic ground for their musical explorations. "When you find a group that is rhythmically attuned to one another, it's the most beautiful thing that you would ever want to hear in your life" (BH). "Every jazz musician wants to be locked in that groove where you can't escape the tempo," Franklin Gordon declares. "You're locked in so comfortably that there's no way you can break outside of it, and everyone's locked in there together. It doesn't happen to groups every single night, even though they may be swinging on every single tune. But at some point when the band is playing and everyone gets locked in together, it's special for the musicians and for the aware, conscientious listener. These are the magical moments, the best moments in jazz."

The qualities of a group's groove, achieved through the masterful manipulation of musical elements, ultimately transcend the technical features of jazz to provide improvisers with a rich, varied experience, a dimension of which is distinctly joyful and sensual. With the precision of a skillful swimmer who, having synchronized movement with a powerful wave, surges to its crest to be carried effortlessly before its wake, the soloist sizes up the rhythm section's groove, entering its flow to ride forward on the passage of time. As soon as the artist releases a phrase, it seems to sail off, bobbing buoyantly atop the rhythm section's pulsating patterns. "When the rhythm section is floating, I'll float too, and I'll get a wonderful feeling in my stomach," Emily Remler says. "If the rhythm section is really swinging, it's such a great feeling, you just want to laugh."

Performers also liken their elated encounters to "gliding" across a ballroom in effortless tandem with a dance partner, or to the more intimate, pleasurable experience of lovemaking. "When you strike a groove, partner, it's delightful," a drummer says. "The first time I got the feeling of what it was to strike a groove, it was very similar to how your body is left after an orgasm; you really lose control. I remember that I was playing and grooving and it felt so good, I just started grinning and giggling."

Within the groove, improvisers experience a great sense of relaxation, which increases their powers of expression and imagination. They handle their instruments with athletic finesse, able to respond to every impulse. "The musicians I played with this Thursday hooked up so well, it just gave me a cushion for my own solos," Harold Ousley reflects. "They made it possible for me to put myself in a state of mind where I didn't block my ideas and was able to feel that freedom that we all strive for."

At such times, the facility artists display as individual music thinkers combines with their extraordinary receptiveness to each other. It is the combining of such talents in the formulation of parts that raises these periods of communal creativity to a supreme level. "When you're really listening to each other and you're performing together, it's like everyone is talking to each other through music," Curtis Fuller says. "When groups like Dave Brubeck's or Miles Davis's or Art Blakey's play, they have good conversations, group conversations.[1] When that's really happening in a band, the cohesiveness is unbelievable. Those are the special, cherished moments. When those special moments occur, to me, it's like ecstasy. It's like a beautiful thing. It's like when things blossom. When it's happening, it really makes it, man." For Lee Konitz, "relating fully to every sound that everyone is making not only keeps the improvising spirit going, but makes the experience complete. To hear it all simultaneously is one of the most divine experiences that you can have." Ronald Shannon Jackson asserts similarly that "this music is really about the relationships between all the players. When the relationship is happening, you don't hear piano, bass, and drums. . . . You hear the total communication of individuals."

The exceptional state of communication artists describe sometimes allows them to maximize the skills of musical interpretation discussed earlier and anticipate, phrase by phrase, idea by idea, the progress of another person's musical thoughts. "It's like when the soloist improvises a figure. Before he finishes his figure, I can almost telepathically know where he's going with his next idea," Keith Copeland explains.

> I can answer him halfway through his phrase while he's still creating it and know where he's going after that, so that we end up playing phrases together that match each other. It's like we're talking together at the same time. One example is Charlie Rouse. Charlie has that ability to make you hear one thing and play something else against it. He does this by the way in which he builds his solos. Ahmad Jamal has that gift too. He'll have you in the palm of his hand. He'll bring you to the point where you can actually sing what he's going to play next, and then, instead of playing that, he'll play something against it which complements what you're singing in your head.

Epitomizing this special rapport is an event Howard Levy recalls, in which a pianist and a guitarist confused the order of their solos and began their performances together by improvising "the exact same melody." Comparable occurrences are familiar to George Duvivier. "Playing jazz is a spontaneous thing," he says, "and I've experienced times in which it was almost like I've been able to read a soloist's mind. I'll play a phrase, like a descending passage, at the same time he does. We'll come down together in unison or maybe in harmony, and we'll hear it and react to it almost after the fact. After the thing is over, we'll say, 'Hey, man. Did you hear so and so?' [he laughs]. There are some things you just can't explain" (exx. 13.11d1–d2).

Within their heightened state of empathy, improvisers not only respond supportively to their cohorts, they also stimulate one another's conception of new ideas that grow directly out of the group's unique conversational interplay.[2] "Jazz musicians interact and learn from one another as they perform. That's what jazz is. Many times, I've listened to recordings I've made and said, 'Wow, I don't remember doing that! I never practiced that phrase before.' I played it because of what the other musicians were playing at the time" (RuR). Occasions when Fred Hersch played with Buster Williams are equally representative. "Buster's made me play complex chords like Herbie Hancock sometimes plays—that I couldn't even sit down and figure out now." Hersch attributes such remarkable inventions to "the effect of the moment and the effect of playing with Buster and really hearing everything, hearing all these figures."

Similarly, when Bob Moses and Emily Remler "play together, he always shows me different paths," Remler explains. "He can interpret things I play in the hippest way, hearing things in what I did that I never even thought of. For example, when I play a phrase, he'll play a rhythmic counterpoint to my rhythms that is very original. It will show me a different way of doing things and even push me to a point that I've never been before. I'll hear myself do something because of what he played and say, 'How did I ever think of that?' I just played the way I play, and he played his thing against it, and we came up with a new thing together."

In this connection, it is high praise for rhythm section players when their associates judge their creations to go beyond supportive accompaniments to stand on their own as independent parts. Larry Gray praises the richly varied textures in Herbie Hancock's accompaniment of Miles Davis on "I Thought about You" as characteristic, maintaining that together with the trumpet part, it could serve as a "double concerto"; alone, it could be "a piano prelude" (ex. 12.10b). Expressing a similar sentiment, Gil Evans once told Walter Bishop Jr. that from the "comping alone" on one recording of Bishop's he "could have made an arrangement" (WB). Another player says, "If you want to hear how it's possible to play exciting music with brushes, just listen to Elvin Jones on an album of Tommy Flanagan's called *Overseas*. Elvin plays nothing but brushes and, if Tommy weren't playing such brilliant piano, you could play that record over and over, just listening to Elvin's playing." By extension, artists appreciate successful collaborations for producing complex music in performance as cohesive as any produced by written composition.[3]

The experience of exceeding an artist's normal intellectual powers and creative abilities is also tied to exceptional emotional empathy and compassion, as when musicians exchange confidences "about how sad or lonely they feel, or how happy or angry."[4] Additionally, players express a keenly honed comic sensibility in shared playful expressions of musical humor.[5] Charlie Parker would tease fellow band members who had learned of their induction into the army by playing "a phrase which translated 'Bring enough clothes for three days.'"[6]

The intensity of impassioned performances can take on a religious quality, a "spirituality," evocative, for some players, of their early participation in African American church services. "The band I played in with Roy Haynes and George Adams was very spiritual," Don Pate says. "The energy was so intense and the spirits were up so high, the band was really hot. It was always a challenge to be a contributor to those high-energy situations." For Carmen Lundy as well, jazz recalls reverential aspects of church performance. She draws a focused analogy between them. "What I hear in jazz is also spiritual," she says.

> It involves that same kind of interaction, that ability of people to have this musical experience at the same time that they are actually participating in it. When you are in a congregation, everybody, not just the people in the choir, is part of the music—the person next to you, the people in front of you and behind you. You hear someone clapping this way, and someone else clapping another way. You feel this pulse

generating the rhythm, and the rhythm is getting stronger and stronger and more intense, and you feel this interaction between the people as the rhythm is going on. You are all beginning to clap more, and the spirit is getting more involved. There is some feeling coming through the music, and much of it has to do with rhythmic pulse.

In jazz, it's the same thing. No one in the group knows exactly what is going to be played next, so you all rely on your instinctive knowledge of music. It's that freedom of expression and expressiveness that comes through from a feeling you have of musical rapport with other people. It's something that you really can't touch, but you know when you are sharing it with another musician. That's the same thing that I shared with the person next to me when everybody was participating in the service. I can remember some unbelievable things from that time which I experience even now when I sing jazz. Sometimes, I really feel that I am just the vehicle, the body, and that something is really singing through me, like I am not controlling everything that I am singing. The last time I sang, I thought to myself, "Gosh, I feel like something is just singing through me." That's what I mean by the spiritual thing.

Such accounts harken back to those told earlier by soloists who, during the heat of their own part's conception, occasionally feel as if their creations come from outside themselves. The collective aspects of improvisation give a literal quality to these impressions, perhaps intensifying them by presenting an ongoing dichotomy between inside and outside sources of musical ideas, any of which can stimulate individual players.

At some moments, the rapid interaction of improvisers blurs these distinctions altogether. The effect is to dissolve the boundaries that normally separate musical imaginations, sensitizing artists to the "telepathic" receptivity mentioned earlier, thereby creating a deeply satisfying sense of unity within the group. "I don't know if I can describe it," Melba Liston says, "but I know it when I feel it. Just one night, everybody can feel what each other is thinking and everything. You breathe together, you swell together, you just do everything together, and a different aura comes over the room." Guided at such moments by the unspoken consensus, group members discard the hesitancy associated with more studied operations in pursuit of ever-emerging goals. Proceeding directly and easily, it is as if, as a collective unit, they no longer govern the performance. For many artists, the experience is like "being on automatic pilot" (DP). "With Miles," Buster Williams recalls, "it would get to the point where we followed the music rather than the music following us. We just followed the music wherever it wanted to go. We would start with a tune, but the way we played it, the music just naturally evolved."

Experiences heightened to a level of the mystical, in the minds of some artists, sometimes accompany these events. Ronald Shannon Jackson explains that

> with certain groups, like Albert Ayler, Cecil Taylor, Ornette Coleman, Blood, and now my own group, The Decoding Society, there is a level of playing which we try to reach which is the same thing that people do when they do transcendental meditation and yoga. They talk about "out of the body" experiences. That's what this music is. It's chanting; it's meditation; it's yoga. It's all these things. In order to play, something transcends. Something happens with the physical, the spiritual, and the mental state in which they combine, and their energy is turned free. It's a cleansing experience which in a religion they would say, "It's of another world." The state I'm talking about even transcends emotions. It's a feeling of being able to communicate with all living things.

Leroy Williams expresses a similar idea. From his perspective, there are many "hardships in this business, but I wouldn't give up anything for some of the experiences I have had playing this music. There's a feeling that you just can't buy," he declares.

> It's a beautiful, floating feeling that is hard to describe in words. It's a wonderful feeling, almost like getting out of your body. I never know when it's going to happen, but when everybody is there and it happens, it really happens. I'll get it playing with Barry Harris because we can really get into the music together. It's almost like there's a oneness. You and your instrument are one, there's no separation. And it's like a oneness with the music. It's like you're in tune with the universe.

Commenting self-reflectively on this matter, Paul Wertico states that he is "not necessarily a religious person, by and large, but there are many times," he admits, "where I'll play music and just kind of look up and say, 'Thank you.' And it's a real strange feeling. It's like I'm in touch with something so big and the joy is so incredible. And I don't even know why. It's not like I'm looking up and I know there's a heaven and a hell, but it's like I'm thanking the big picture for just the opportunity as a human being to feel this way—which is incredible."

Such exuberance also finds expression in the metaphor of love. Don Pate mentions that "love is another level of high feeling, high emotional intensity. I've often been described as being in love when I'm playing, being in love with playing or being in love with the music. When the music's happening, I'm in love with the bass—and I'm in love with life."

Love across its spectrum of emotions can also embrace group interaction, where it is revealed by the players' close attention to nuances and details in each other's musical personalities. According to Chuck Israels:

The more prevalent situation in a band is of the people really loving each other's playing, loving the music, and supporting each other. Recently [the National Jazz Ensemble] did a concert, and it was just electrifying. Everyone in the band was caught up in astonishment and pleasure at that. Every time Sal Nistico gets up to play, the band is ready to cry from the pleasure of the swing in the guy's playing. Tom Harrell shuffles modestly to the front of the band, and people are deeply touched by his playing. Bill Dobbins plays a piano solo, and people just get knocked out with that. Every once in a while, Joe Temperley will get up and play a baritone solo that's bubbling over with joy, and he'll get the whole band just romping. There's a great sense of mutual respect and appreciation in working together in any band that is functioning well. Those are the high points.

Journeying together through the medium of performance, musicians assist one another in entering an incomparably intense realm of human experience where thrive diverse overlapping domains of sensitivity and knowledge: intellectual and "intuitive"; aesthetic and emotional; physical, sensual, and spiritual; private and communal. Once touched by such experiences, improvisers retain them united as their principal goal, the standard for all performances. Trumpeter Herb Pomeroy explained it to me years ago: "One of the most wonderful benefits of this career is the feeling you're left with after an evening when the music is really happening," he said emphatically. "It's an incredibly warm feeling that you have, one that you've shared with the other musicians and you've shared with the audience. And when the evening's engagement is over, you still retain it. It fills you up inside, and you feel it like there's an aura all around you when you leave the club to go home. It's the kind of precious feeling that no other kind of career can give you."

In the aftermath of such euphoric states, improvisers commonly require a period of transition to ensure a successful return to the normal routines of life—which, in many respects, pale by comparison. Sometimes, band members socialize together over a meal in the early hours of the morning to reflect on the evening's events before going their separate ways. At other times, they choose to be alone directly after performances to harbor the profound sense of inner peacefulness.

Finally, some artists also endure wide swings of mood, and even deep melancholy, in the transition "back into reality." Paul Wertico has experienced this emotional intensity. "It happens on the road a lot," he reveals, "especially after a great gig. If we play a big city like New York—like musicians in the audience, and the band's burning, and you get back to your hotel room, and there you are with yourself again—it's not only just a loneliness; it's the feeling [that] you've broken the connection with that big picture you're able to relate to when you're playing. . . . You know," he says resignedly, "life's not like that all the time."

Just as musicians must deal with the high and low points of their transition from an exalted state to mundane existence, over the course of their musical journey, they must face low as well as high points of performance.

## Deficient Musicianship and Incompatible Musical Personalities

Although peak experiences improvising provide musicians their greatest professional rewards, it is not uncommon for problems to prevent musicians from fully realizing their goals. "Very few bands have everything perfect. It may look like things are perfect, and you may not be able to tell in the audience, but there is always some kind of conflict going on in the band" (GB). Some problems stem from deficient musicianship; others from incompatible styles. "Meeting people on the bandstand is just like meeting people and interacting with them in other aspects of life," Akira Tana remarks. "There may be certain idiosyncracies in their musical personalities that conflict. It doesn't mean that they're bad players. It's like, you get along well with some people, and you don't get along with others."

Don Pate agrees. "The chemistry between musicians is just not predictable," he observes.

> It is always a pleasant surprise when you play with a musician who's a stranger, and it happens automatically, the music really flows. But you never know until the actual performance situation whether the right combination is there.
>
> It's like love. Sometimes, you look at somebody and decide you're in love, but you find out differently later. The greatest things don't happen in bands often, because the chemistry between the combination of players doesn't lend itself to the most positive or highest level of music. It seems like it's a stroke of luck or genius when everyone is matched perfectly and the music's really happening.

A sample of the many difficulties that can plague a group more fully illuminates the demands of collective improvisation. Several problems, including "discrepancies in the way players interpret rhythm," are especially serious when they affect the rhythm section's fundamental interaction (BH). As in the case of soloists, some rhythm section players can represent the beat consistently, maintaining a particular interpretation of it or varying it with great control. Others cannot. "Rhythm sections are very fluid," George Duvivier says. "Some musicians rush, others pull back, and some do both."

These tendencies create various dilemmas for other members. Accommodating a weaker player might further destabilize the group. "Sometimes, the tempo doesn't stay where it should," Art Farmer points out. "If it gets too slow, the life goes out of the music. If it gets too fast, it just sounds amateurish." In an attempt to stabilize the group, strong members can try all the more to reinforce each other's performances and draw a weaker member into alignment.

When Gary Bartz sees "that someone's time isn't very good, I won't listen to them but will listen to whoever in the band is the strongest rhythmically, whether that be the bassist, the drummer, or the pianist." When such a tactic fails to correct an erratic performance, however, "you can get different tempos going in the group, and before long everybody's not on the same chord at the same time. That just adds to the distortion of the music" (HO).

In other instances, "you might end up at the same bar at the same time as the piano player or the bass player, and all your eight-bar phrases are ending up in the same places, but within that, the strong beats or downbeats are wishy-washy. When nobody is taking charge in laying down the time," Josh Schneider deplores, "it makes everybody's time sound funny." Unresponsiveness to normally acceptable time fluctuations within the group contributes to the problem. "Some people can only play metronomic time, and they're lost if the tempo changes," Rufus Reid complains.

A related concern would be failure to accommodate another's individual predilection for playing on different parts of the beat. "When the bass player or the drummer is right in the middle of a beat and the other is not, there's going to be a little tug, and you're going to feel it," Tommy Flanagan insists. Chuck Israels concurs. "If the relationship between the bassist and the drummer is not working, you know that right away. It's just painful if we can't agree."

Ultimately, significant disparity in individual preferences could threaten the entire group's foundation. "There are times when I am playing with a drummer who wants to play more on top of the beat than I do," Calvin Hill says. "I feel like he's rushing, so my reaction is to hold back. Since I like to play on top of the beat myself, if someone is playing even more on top of the beat, it usually means the tempo is going to pick up, so I have to step back and hold the beat down." For many, the pressures involved have physicality. One bass player likens his experience to steadying a boat's course on a rough sea by holding the mainsail taut against the wind.

Besides the problem of undermining the groove, other conflicts reflect a difference of personal taste surrounding a multitude of subtle issues, including dynamics. "Many drummers play too loud, and this can really do damage to a delicate acoustic instrument like the piano," Charli Persip explains. "There are many wars between pianists and drummers." Soloists also "have to deal with too much or too little volume from drummers at times" (AF). John McNeil admits that "it can be very discouraging to have a drummer just keep roaring right on through your solo. One drummer played so loud it was difficult for me to play. I didn't like to play that loud all the time, because after two or three tunes, I'd be wasted. I would have to force my sound just to be heard over him, and then the leader would say, 'Man, your sound is really brittle.' When you hear that enough, you begin to doubt yourself."

Whereas in the past the problem of excessive volume primarily centered on drummers, the increased role of amplification and the recent development of smaller, custom-made drum sets now occasionally shift the problem to bass players and pianists. "When you have bass players with amplifiers," Jimmy Robinson remarks, "the pianists and drummers get mad because they can't hear over the sound of the bass. Then when you go on a job, no one can adjust to the acoustics or hear anyone else, and it's just chaos." One bass player's assessment of the situation is particularly pointed:

> Amplifiers, pick-ups, and the fender bass have brought the level of the bass up to the point where it can be as loud as any drummer. The problem is that once you even begin to approach that volume, you lose the subtleties of dynamic shading. There is less difference between the loudest and softest thing you play. Among other things, what this has also done is to drown out the piano players, who need to use two microphones. The horn players also have to stick their horns into the microphones, and some pianists are forced to switch to electric piano just to be heard. This just electrifies the music in a negative way, robbing it of all its nuance.
>
> The other night, I went out to hear a friend's band, and the rhythm section was playing so loud, the music just started off screaming and screamed all night. I was out of work and went to the club wishing I was playing there, but I left feeling relieved that I wasn't.

Changes that amplification can bring about in the sound of an acoustic instrument, such as in its characteristic patterns of articulation, sometimes have negative ramifications for the group. Lonnie Hillyer says regretfully, "I don't know what's happened to bass players since they started using amplification. At times, it's indistinguishable where the beat is in their playing."

Improvisers also criticize problematic aspects of musicians' qualities of sound. Some perform "out of tune" or "with a rotten tone" that can grate on the ears of fellow players. Others perform with a too limited range of timbral colors. John Hicks describes one group that replaced acoustic piano with electric piano as having "very little contrast from one tune to the next because of the nature of their instruments. Even though," he concedes, "they're great musicians, there is a certain electric sound that doesn't lend itself to great variety." Kenny Barron finds that "there are very few drummers besides Ben Riley and the old masters like Max and 'Philly' Joe that I enjoy playing with when they use brushes. [The masters] are very smooth in the way they play, but other players can sound very scrapy. When they switch to brushes, it sounds like the whole bottom of the music has dropped out."

Indeed, new performance practices within the jazz tradition sometimes overshadow or supplant the old. "Brush work is almost a lost art today. There are not many players who know how to use brushes anymore, especially the younger players," Akira Tana rues. It may be that this trend reflects accommodation of the diminishing importance of ballads among young performers and the increased volume that amplified instruments emit, rendering brush work ineffective in many situations.

Improvisers cite other weaknesses among rhythm section players. John McNeil recalls "one bass player we had for a while who could play different rhythmic patterns, but whenever it came time for him to walk, four beats to the measure, he just played unaccented quarter notes. He couldn't throw accents around within that, doing the kind of things that make you want to dance. Even if what he did had been metrically perfect, which it wasn't, it felt horrible. It was a perpetual drone of quarter notes." Weakness in harmonic practice can be offensive, as Chuck Israels makes plain:

> Certain kinds of root motion belong in certain places in a bassist's harmonic phrase. There are rules for this that you can extract from common practice. The weakest kind of root motion is to move a third or sixth; the strongest is to drop a fifth or go up a fourth. In between those extremes are stepwise motions of all kinds. One of the perennial errors made by people who have not studied bass lines is to put too many movements by a third in there or to put them in the wrong places. Movements by thirds work in a very special and specific way when they're used. When they are used right, they are a beautiful thing. When they are used wrong, the sound is dumb and weak. I don't really know how to talk about this except to compare it to grammatical practice. If you put prepositions at the end of your sentences, I can still understand you, but it sounds weak. When players string together ungrammatical phrases and seem to wander into situations like that, unless they're trying to create purposeful mistakes for a deliberate effect, it simply vitiates the music for me.

Other violations concern conventions of repertory. James Moody was once "playing a simple blues line, just gutbucketing it, and when we got to the end of the progression, the bass player played some complicated, sophisticated turnback. Now, there's no need to have one of those hip turnbacks there. The bass player was trying to be intellectual on a funky, down-home blues. He ought to use a line like that on a different piece altogether." Art Farmer shares this concern:

> One piece is completely different from another. You shouldn't play two songs the same way. For example, if I play a show tune, I'm not playing that tune in order to be destructive. If I play a song like "Namely You" or "Here's That Rainy Day," then I want to hear the harmonic structure. Some piano players play those songs like they don't really want to play them, as if the songs were not hip enough. They alter the chords so much the song is barely recognizable. They obscure the form of it. Some of them play the chords the first chorus,

and then they just want to vamp, which has nothing to do with the song. They play the same chord over and over, even when they're supposed to be playing the harmonic form of the tune.

Related problems can arise in the rhythm section's collective assessment of the requirements of particular pieces. "On a tune like 'Giant Steps,'" John McNeil points out, "there are so many changes, and they move so quickly, all the rhythm section has to do is keep the rhythmic flow going and comp. But a slow tune like 'Little Sunflower' is different. If you have a rhythm section that is just laying there in an uninteresting way, you can't possibly play anything interesting over them and sustain it very long."

Musicians also describe their discontent with individuals who do not understand the performance conventions established by historic bands. "It can be frustrating to play certain ways unless the whole band context is suited for it," Max Roach declares. "Jo Jones played the way he did because Basie played the piano the way he did. Sidney Catlett played the way he did because Armstrong played the way he did. Elvin Jones played the way he did because he was playing with Trane." Young performers discover the importance of this matter when they first attempt to improvise in their mentor's style but lack the musical support that their mentor received. "After a few months playing with this group, I started feeling confined," one pianist recalls. "At the time, I was listening to Herbie Hancock and to a lot of rhythm sections and how they interacted. Since I was trying to play like Herbie Hancock, I was frustrated that I couldn't play with people like Ron Carter and Jack DeJohnette. I felt like I couldn't really get the music off."

As players contend with and work through individual challenges that occasional deficient musicianship or incompatibility of style present, they confront additional challenges in understanding the precise musical ideas of other group members.

## Problems Apprehending and Interpreting Musical Ideas

Probably the most basic concern within the realm of apprehending and interpreting the improvisations of fellow artists is uneven attentiveness to the music. "A drummer might set up a pattern that really swings, but if he's not listening to little things, like the way the piano player is comping, it's not going to complement the whole group," Leroy Williams explains. Ultimately, many leaders "chose individuals for their bands not because they are the best improvisers, but because they are the best listeners" (LH). In Charli Persip's opinion, "that's where the real artistry comes in." During the period in which the young Persip held a prestigious position with Dizzy Gillespie's big band, he was once "devastated" by the news that Miles Davis "couldn't stand" his playing. The remark made Persip aware that he had been concentrating mainly on himself during performances. It was as if "my father" had once more "thumped me painfully on the head," he recalls with laughter.

Inhibitions about extemporaneous invention and overreliance on prefigured patterns can exacerbate the problem of inattentiveness. "If the bass player is playing from something he heard somebody else play on a record, then there's always the time problem and other things that can go wrong," Ronald Shannon Jackson points out. "If the player is trying to play somebody else's licks, then the time doesn't get real settled, because he's thinking ahead of the notes, thinking of certain passages that somebody else played. But if he's thoroughly trained and relying totally on his own playing, then you have music, and you don't have to worry about the pulse, either." Don Sickler similarly recalls his early naivete concerning the risks of depending on complete precomposed solos within collective musical discourse. "Once, I copped another trumpet player's solo so that I'd sound really good when I played with an experienced band I was invited to play with. What I didn't count on was that they took the tune at a much faster tempo than on the record," he says, chuckling. "I could barely play the slow part of the solo, and when the double-time section of the solo came along, I fell apart completely. The other musicians just laughed. They seemed to know what had happened."

One pianist used a novel method to set up a student's skills in the flexible treatment of preplanned material, at the same time demonstrating the multiple levels of cognition that sympathetic improvisation requires. Initially, the pianist instructed the student to invent several phrases and practice them repeatedly in all keys until he had achieved "bodily mastery" over them. To demonstrate his progress at the next lesson, the student began improvising a solo based on the invented phrases. The teacher inquired loudly whether the assignment had posed any difficulty, insisting that the student answer him, thereby causing the student to lose control of the performance. "Now," the pianist said, "go home and don't come back until you learn those licks so well that you can use them in a solo while carrying on a conversation at the same time. When you play in a jazz group," the mentor advised, "you'll be too busy concentrating on everything else that's going on around you, for you to be able to think about what you're doing alone."[7] Barry Harris describes pianists for whom particular improvisational paths had become so routine, in fact, that they could literally carry on a conversation while performing.

The teacher's reference to conversation in the drill above is reminiscent of the term's use earlier as a common metaphor for improvisation, emphasizing the diverse demands that musicians formulate ideas with assurance and independence, at the same time interacting sensitively with their counterparts. Many eventually cultivate both skills; others, however, fail at the latter. "Some people only hear themselves when they play," James Moody observes. As a permanent feature of personality, self-absorption presents the same liabilities during performances as overdependence on precomposed material. "Playing is like speaking," Wynton Marsalis suggested during our interview. "As we are talking now, I only know what I'm going to say a second before I say it. People who don't do it like this can be the worst people to talk to. When you're talking, they're thinking about what they are going to tell you next, instead of listening to what you're saying."

Even for skilled listeners, however, the effort to anticipate the ideas of other players meets with variable results. "I have to be kind of hard on myself or I wouldn't develop," Leroy Williams confesses. "Some of the recordings I have made are okay, but I'm always so critical of my performances. I'll listen to myself and say, 'I could have done this; I should have done that. How could I have let that go by?'" Tommy Flanagan also describes the need for self-criticism in performance:

> Most of the people I've played with, from Coleman Hawkins to Ella Fitzgerald, give you the feeling that you've got to be on your toes all the time. Even though they are the ones in the spotlight, there is no room for you to underplay anything. There are always things that you could do that would take away from something marvelous that they played, and you would feel just terrible about it, like you had ruined a masterpiece. You always have to be careful. The problems have to do with not knowing a person well enough and maybe anticipating them wrong. You have to really get the feel of who you're playing for. You have to get a feeling for their phrasing and where they're going in order to be one hundred percent correct when you're anticipating what they're going to do.

Lack of rapport among musicians sometimes reflects their unfamiliarity with each other's melodic concepts. This extends to the stylistic bounds within which they create melodies and the logic that dictates their selection and development of motivic material. "In my experience with this one saxophone player, it was easier for me to get lost accompanying him than anyone else I ever played with," Ronald Shannon Jackson recalls.

> The challenge of playing with him was to play free and not free at the same time. He had such a raw sound that when he played the tune's head, it made you feel like he was playing free, but he really wasn't. He was in the conception of bebop. But when he got to the improvising portion, he was playing freely, really. The problem I had was following his improvisation and knowing where he was going to go next. I'd start off playing with him, and I'd hear one thing and start working on that, and by the time I got to developing and resolving that, he'd be resolving something else that he started midway after I got on the track of the thing I had first heard him doing.

Comparable confusion can arise over harmonic concepts. "Some bass players' choice of notes is just not good when they walk a line," Kenny Barron complains,"and it makes the particular chord voicing I'm using sound wrong. Or it just prevents whatever I'm using from sounding as good as it would if the bass player had chosen other notes." On the other hand, Chuck Israels asserts, "There are many approaches to improvisation that are very satisfying for people like pianists, but some of those ways drive me nuts as a bass player. If you take Art Tatum, for example," he continues,

> he was a genius who would stick close to the original melody while varying the harmonization from chorus to chorus. That could drive a bass player nuts, because there's no way of knowing where a piano player like that is going. Since his improvisation is in the harmony, you either had to play something that was so basic that almost any-thing would work with it, or you would have to play the melody, since that was the predictable part that you would play with him. Or you would have to be able to read his mind. These are the reasons why players like Tatum were often most successful as solo performers, al-though there may be sides of them that are sympathetic to playing with other musicians.

Yet other sources of conflict are rhythmic concepts, especially the imagi-native play of soloists in relation to the group's groove.[8] "As my time started getting pretty good, I would experiment with playing things against what the rhythm section was playing," Emily Remler recalls. "I would play against the rhythm with polyrhythms. When I did this, some guys would not trust me enough that I knew what I was doing, so they'd actually skip a beat to follow me, figuring that I had made a mistake." Roberta Baum has confronted the same problem.

> There was one group I played with, and I felt we were fighting each other very often. There were certain things that I would do that would throw the other musicians off, if they didn't know the way I sang and weren't able to anticipate those things. For example, I may have had some preconceived notion that jazz involved constant syncopation, so when the beat came down I was always a little ahead of it or behind it. When I was in the position of taking the lead with songs, and the musicians didn't know me, it seemed to them like I was coming in at some obtuse angle. They had no point of reference for where the beat was, or maybe they hadn't worked enough with singers to understand the ways I would phrase on a regular standard. I would very often phrase against the lyrics. I'd speed up a line or slow it down. I'd take a word and stretch it over a couple of measures. Or I might condense a whole phrase into one measure and make up my own melody. Often,

when I took those liberties, I felt the group wasn't really moving with me.[9]

As artists indicate, sluggish responses to musical maneuvers requiring split-second timing and mutual support can have drastic consequences for a performance. Curtis Fuller humorously compares these to the risks taken by trapeze artists. "If someone does something adventurous and the other person isn't there at the right place at the right time to catch him, it's like splatsville! [laughter]."

## Conflicting Notions of Tasteful Conversation

Once group members are familiar enough with each other's musical concepts to interpret ideas in another part correctly, anticipating its course, conflicts can arise over different notions of what is tasteful response. "If the music goes, 'da-dada-da-da' ['Pop Goes the Weasel'] and someone else answers, 'da-da.' ['pop, pop'], I feel, 'Well, damn, why don't you do something else?'" James Moody says. "I always like the subtle things, not the obvious. They are the hippest." Moody also avoids various other performance conventions that he regards as predictable or unoriginal. "I'll tell you something else that really gets on my nerves. It's when I hear a horn player who comes in playing the last phrase of someone else's statement. I never do that. That's that person's statement, he's got it. Let me do something else."

Comparable criticism applies to strict imitation between a member of the rhythm section and a soloist, what some deride as the "parrot school of jazz" (PW). "There might be times when you would play exactly what someone else plays, but you don't really like to do that," Leroy Williams contends. Rufus Reid agrees. "If you heard imitation all the time, it would be boring." Chuck Israels also condemns the practice. "If each time you say something in a musical situation, I repeat it back to you, it really kills conversation." John McNeil's discourse on imitation presents a model for appropriateness. "I want a drummer to listen to me, but not to play my stuff back to me. If I go 'fot do dot,' there are guys who will go 'flop ba ba, flop ba ba.' Some drummers and pianists will do that just to show that they're listening. If it happens once a night or so, that's fine, but sometimes guys will do that to you to the point that you're sorry you played the idea in the first place. I mean, I don't want to hear it three times. I just wanted to hear it the one time I played it. If *I* make a thing out of it, if *I* take a figure and play it over and over, then he can pick up on it and it's all right."

Also subject to critical evaluation is the particular balance the rhythm section maintains between supportive, responsive performance, on the one hand, and assertive, aggressive performance, on the other. Commonly, players charge accompanists who increase their own part's interest and complexity with doing so at the expense of the delineation of a piece's form and the complementing of soloists. A typical case would be the pianist's misuse of chord voicings and substitutions. "Since the piano player is the one playing the chords, the soloist has got to go with him. Some people try to lead you to places that you might not want to go," James Moody states. "Few pianists are hip enough to come in at just the right time, then to lay out enough to let you have the expanded harmony and then come in," Wynton Marsalis adds. "When you're playing something, some pianists will come in playing in the middle of what you're playing and play the wrong harmony." In Art Davis's opinion, as well, "pianists, or whoever is feeding the chords, can really do things that get on soloists' nerves. They're thinking about the harmony one way, and the other person is dealing with the chords a different way. The soloist may be thinking of a certain chord, and the pianist may play a substitute chord. That can constrain the soloist to the substitute chord when he wants to play something else. If he tries to play something else, it will sound like a clash."

Accompanying melodic figurations become a point of contention, at times. Lou Donaldson complains of harmful inconsistencies. "Some pianists put a lot of weird comping stuff behind you while you're playing," he says, "weird little figures and interludes. But when they get a solo, they don't play any of that stuff. They just play straight." Others object to undesirable rhythmic features of comping patterns. "An insensitive pianist can rush you. If the pianist isn't listening to you, you can't take a tune or a phrase and stretch it out in a relaxed way. You have to do it the way the pianist is doing it. That stifles your creativity" (VW). Some pianists, in particular, "bang and smash when they comp. They comp on top of the beat, behind the beat, all in the wrong places" (WM). At the other extreme, however, are weak players who "have a less rhythmic feel than others. They just seem content to play the chord on the first beat of every chord change" (AF).

Other differences concern the appropriate shape and complexity of the accompaniment. "From the horn player's point of view, if you don't give him room to establish his ideas first, then you can sabotage the whole solo," Lonnie Hillyer insists. "There may be a disagreement over how the piano player supports the soloists," Akira Tana explains. "He may be a very nervous, busy player, playing a lot of rhythmic figures and really jamming things in." Such density can be annoying to soloists, unduly challenging their creativity. "Whenever I play with this one cat, I never have any ideas," a trumpeter remembers.

> All I hear is his noodling around, filling up all the space. There's another piano player I worked with who would never leave any space between his figures. There were chords all the time, and I could very rarely play anything I wanted. From a horn player's point of view, I don't think he ever realized how much he tied your hands. Maybe

some guys need that kind of support, but I never did. If you give me too much support, I have a great deal of difficulty thinking of anything to play, because, if I want to outline the harmony and change the sounds around a bit, it's like all those sounds are already being played for me, and anything I do would seem sort of repetitious. What I have to do under those conditions is just to think more of very rhythmic punctuation or just playing high and loud to cut through all the comping. It becomes high intensity all the time.

Similar complaints are aimed at drummers and their capacity to dominate the group's musical texture. Walter Bishop Jr. condemns those drummers who "fill up all the space, making me feel like I have to fight to get my lines across." Curtis Fuller reasons that "things get out of hand, as they do with so many drummers, when they cease to be the accompanists and become the soloists themselves. When you're trying to develop something and the drummer takes away the rhythmic foundation," he concludes, "it can create a great deal of confusion."[10]

A comparable problem occurs when players emphasize the role of responsive interaction over essential time-keeping. "Some drummers are too influenced by what is going on in front," George Duvivier points out. "They try to catch every lick, to anticipate everything the orchestra or soloist will do, every syncopation, and they forget that they're the support for the whole thing. They're the ones that the soloist is leaning on. The soloist can do whatever he wants, as long as we, the rhythm section, remain constant. The rhythm section must be the foundation at all times. If you try to follow an erratic soloist when he goes off, then everyone's in trouble."

John Hicks warns of additional danger in "overplaying or overstating" a rhythmic concept after "picking it up from somebody else in the band." Illustrating his point, he dictated a rhythmic pattern for me to repeat, then performed a complementary interlocking pattern. "If the pattern I'm clapping is overdone and it becomes a statement on its own," he cautions, "it loses its complementary feeling. You've blocked the effectiveness of the original statement, the groove that's been set up." Among the transgressors are players who unilaterally double time their figures when neither the arrangement, nor a gesture in the soloist's part, nor a lull in the performance suggests the need for a radical change. Indeed, it can inadvertently destroy the music's mood.

On the other hand, musicians who weight their foundational responsibilities excessively may invite scorn. "Some drummers are too servile. They just play their limited thing, rarely responding to you," one pianist complains. Tommy Turrentine's good-humored lament is likewise telling: "The other night, the drummer was just playing 'tit-a-ting, tit-a-ting, tit-a-ting, tit-a-ting,' all night long. Now, what in the world can that generate?" He laughs. "Shoot, it was pitiful. This music is about listening and feeling and intensity. If the feeling ain't there, you got nothing." Curtis Fuller similarly implores drummers, "Don't leave me all exposed like that."

Lack of knowledge and experience sometimes lies at the root of deficient accompaniment. In Kenny Barron's early years, "there were good experiences, but many discouraging experiences as well. I still wasn't familiar with what was supposed to happen on the bandstand." Another pianist remembers her youthful puzzlement when, after a jam session, a disgruntled soloist advised her specifically, "You should really feed me more when you play." She had never heard that expression before and wondered what was expected of her beyond the accurate performance of the lead sheet's chords. "When you're still young, you're just figuring out what you're doing. You're more involved with expressing yourself than playing with other people. You don't really learn to feed other people ideas until you've been playing for a while and feel independent enough as a player," she reflects.

Differences reflect individual stages of artistic development and personal taste. In addition, disagreements described above commonly reflect strong allegiances to particular jazz idioms and their respective conventions of group interplay. Lou Donaldson sets forth the perspective of many bebop performers when he deplores aspects of the current jazz scene.

> I want the piano player to play as basic as he can. He should play the basic chords to the song and leave the improvisation to me. A lot of piano players talk about feeding me ideas, but I don't need no feeding. Jazz is very simple music. That's what makes it. You take a simple motive and you build from there, if you've got the talent. Also, in a small band there is nothing more important than the drummer, because you have to have your rhythm to make the band tight and to project to people. But a lot of drummers don't understand that.
>
> The toughest thing for any of them to do is just to play "one, two, three, four," just regular swing. It's not supposed to be this way, because playing swing should be as easy as turkey for a jazz drummer. But it's not, today. They're taught a lot of nonsense about improvising and doing stuff that they have no business doing. They get into those habits, and when they get into a spot where they have to swing, they can't do it. They play much too busy. When I was starting out, there wasn't any problem like this. If they didn't swing, they didn't have a job. You knew that if you called somebody they could do it, because it was a prerequisite for playing the music. Today, even if they can't swing, they can work. And they're stars!

Such views reflect, in part, the training that earlier generations of jazz musicians received in the context of dances. "You really learned the importance of rhythm then," Barry Harris recalls. "You had to keep steady time to swing and to make people feel like dancing."

In marked contrast to the traditionalists are musicians who champion the values of later performance trends. "You see, in the 1960s the beat was freed up. Tony Williams killed it," Wynton Marsalis says in admiration of Williams's trailblazing. Marsalis further outlines recent developments:

In the 1980s, drummers who have to keep going back to "one" don't have a feeling for the music. In the 1980s, drummers who have to keep playing the sock cymbal on two and four are corny. So are cats who have to keep playing the bass drum all the time. That's corny unless it's a drummer from the period in which they played that way. Today, a drummer has to keep the time, but the time now has a flow. It is no longer something locked in like a beat. Time is now something that just goes by. It still has structure, though. The purpose of the drummer is to keep the time flowing, not to keep steady time, "ONE, two, three, four, ONE, two, three, four." Now, the time is like, "one, two, three, four, five, six, seven, eight, nine, ten, eleven, etc." It's not 4/4 or 6/8. It's just a steady flow of pulses.

Band leaders whose group concept fuses the conventions of differing idioms sometimes face a diligent search for drummers with the requisite combination of skills. "It's hard to find a drummer who can keep a tempo and can swing," Art Farmer finds.

But even if you can get some of the older guys who play bebop who can do that, it's hard to get the balance you're looking for. That is, it's hard to find a drummer in the 1980s who's from the era that I came from who is not stuck in that period. Some of the older guys will sit down with you and play the same thing chorus after chorus, cha, cha, cha, cha, all night long. They're not flexible. They don't seem to be able to respond to you the way the younger players can. The younger players are into more spontaneity, which comes from the free jazz thing. They have been exposed to that type of playing, so they are not going to be content to sit there and play time all night long. They are not bound to that type of thing. Hopefully, they are going to be able to sit there and play time and to be able to respond to the moment. And if you play some pattern like five against four or three against four, they are going to be able to play something that goes along with it, instead of just doing the same thing regardless of what you play. The problem is that it's not easy to find young drummers who can twist and turn like that, and who can also play with a feeling of swing. They often don't have a good time-feel, so it's awkward to play with them. It's simply hard to find a drummer with the balance I'm looking for.

Comparable issues emerge from the soloist's interaction with bass players as they attempt to determine the desirable degree of musical activity within their respective parts. "When an insensitive bassist goes off in his own musical world, he can really kill the soloist's spirit," James Moody asserts. Similarly, Curtis Fuller finds that some bass players "undermine what you do as a soloist when they're trying to develop something else at the same time you're trying to develop something." Kenny Barron has also experienced the frustration of encountering this obstacle to a satisfying solo performance. "There is a way of playing more than bass notes without it becoming too much, but when it's overdone, it drives me up a wall. I was once playing with a bass player who's a fantastic technician, but we were playing a ballad and he was playing so much, I just stopped in the middle of my solo and let him play by himself."

Such conflicts have increased with the changing performance practices of jazz tradition. As a bebop player, Lou Donaldson recognizes that he has "to have walking bass. If I don't have that, I'll just put my horn up. If he's skipping and jumping all around and soloing while I'm soloing, then I'll just give it up." Donaldson gives an explanation for his attitudes: "There is a certain thing called a groove that the whole band should settle into at the beginning of the piece when we play the melody, and that needs to be maintained. If that groove is broken, then it's all over as far as I'm concerned. A lot of cats like bass players to do other things, but not me."

Art Farmer places such matters in historical perspective. "Today, with all their technique," he observes, "young players feel confined by limiting themselves to playing a good bass line and providing the root and foundation for the group. It doesn't give them enough of a challenge. They don't understand the value and the beauty of just playing bass. They want to play a thousand notes, all on top of the harmony. Mingus and LaFaro began to take it there, and then everybody started becoming freer in their playing. Now bass players become easily bored."

John McNeil's colorful imagery reflects the views of many improvisers:

> If we're playing a tune that requires a walking bass, and instead the bass player is sustaining notes, playing syncopations and complicated rhythmic figures, soloing is like trying to walk with an anvil tied to one leg and someone constantly trying to trip the other leg. A lot of young bass players don't understand the importance of having an on-going flow of time in the group. They hate to walk because they think it's not creative. If they can play other things besides regular walking lines and still keep the time going, then fine. The guy who plays quarter notes all the time is boring to listen to and boring to play with. But the chances are, if you do too many other things besides walking, you'll lose the time.
>
> Besides that, if you are really listening to my solo, there's no way that you can possibly play all that other stuff, because it stops me from playing. It stops me from achieving any ongoing sense of time when it goes against everything else that's being played.

We are all in this together, but as the soloist I am the leader of this particular musical expedition. I'm glad to listen to anyone else's suggestions as to what direction we should go in, but overall it's my safari, pal, and if I think we should go this way through the jungle, then we should go this way.

The role of the soloist continues to figure importantly in the group's negotiation of tasteful interplay.

## The Rhythm Section's Response to Criticism

Band members sometimes agree with the criticism they receive from soloists. The misappropriation of musical space or intrusive replication of roles that upset the soloist's flow of ideas sometimes also interfere with the formulation of parts within the rhythm section. "Some guitarists can absolutely smother the rhythm section by playing 'chunk, chunk, chunk, chunk,' four beats to every measure," George Duvivier remarks. "They should play occasional fills or break the line up, because you have a drummer and a pianist— so you don't really need everyone playing on the beat like this. What they are trying to do," he continues, "is to imitate Freddie Green with Basie's band, but there's an art to that. Freddie Green does it without getting in the way. He's supporting, not drowning out, the others. You can always hear the bass and drums when he plays." Another musician recalls a pianist who "played so much in the lower register that he was in the bass player's way—down there all the time. The bass player felt the bass was sort of extraneous in the group. His bass lines were just duplicating the pianist's left hand."

Common arguments surround two potential spoilers of invention: the performance of inappropriate material, generally, and the flaunting of technical ability specifically. Some drummers "try to get their own thing off, playing the stuff they practiced at home all day, not thinking about how it relates to what the rest of the guys are either capable or not capable of doing. A lot of guys just practice their technique on the bandstand" (KC). The problem is often one of inexperience. "The music of most of the drummers I hear, especially young drummers with amazing facility and dazzling technique, hasn't evolved as of yet," Charli Persip observes. Max Roach draws on years of experience when he reflects with understanding on the growth of musicianship. "Today, I don't have to prove my technique is together, so I can concentrate more on making the drums sound as musical as possible," he explains.

I don't have to say, "Well, if I do this, people will say I don't have good singles or don't have a good open or closed press roll, or don't have this or that." I don't have to worry about that now. As a young player, I was swayed by those considerations, at times. If you stay home and practice for hours, days, weeks, months in order to acquire your technique, the minute someone turns you loose, you try to crowd all that in at the moment. It can be disastrous at times. It ceases to be musical, and you can overwhelm people. I have heard a lot of people do it, pianists as well.

At the same time, however, rhythm section players argue that soloists should not necessarily dismiss the value of musical creation on the basis of "business" alone. "All the musical players like Elvin Jones and Jack DeJohnette who can play unbelievably busy are never going to play so busy that it gets in the way of the music," Keith Copeland asserts. "They are only going to play that busy when it fits." Fred Hersch allows that "there is such a thing as being too busy, just playing fluff, but," he contends, "there's also playing busy because you're excited, and you've got a lot to say, and you're trying to get it all out before it gets away."

With the shoe on the other foot, rhythm section members commonly lay responsibility for aspects of unsatisfactory performances upon the soloists themselves. Kenny Washington articulates this view when he observes that, "at times, the drummer is just a workhorse, playing chorus after chorus for horn players who can't play." Individuals for whom the normal need for support becomes, instead, an oppressive dependence attract special criticism. "It's sad to say, but many horn players use the rhythm section, they sap your energy," one pianist complains. "They want you to build them up." It is annoying that, "because they can't count for themselves," they expect the accompaniment to play "all the conventional patterns" behind them, supporting their "little prearranged things." One bass player considers himself "terribly taken advantage of by someone who can't keep track of the chords or the tempo by himself and needs my playing to do that for him. It's a physical thing. You can actually feel it happen, and you get tired of carrying another guy."

Such experiences lead some to defend themselves, countering that criticism from some soloists simply reflects the latter's own limited abilities. "Many musicians like less creativity in the beat," Charli Persip says contemptuously. "They just like me to play straight rhythms and a straight repetitive beat throughout their solos. Their feeble minds get confused when you play a lot of counterrhythms." Art Davis concurs. "Some players would get immersed in their playing, and they'd forget where the beat was, and they'd listen to the bass to get back to where they should be. If the bass wasn't playing the roots of the chords on the first and third beats or on 'one, two, three, four' of every measure, they'd get lost and say, 'This guy isn't good. We don't need him.'" Patti Bown has had similar experiences. "Some people don't want you to play too far out on piano," she says, "meaning that the chords are going to fight whatever their musical thing is, because they can only hear as far as the blues."

At the other extreme, however, talented but self-sufficient soloists who are indifferent to interplay can dampen an accompanist's performance.[11] "At one club, the gigs were like jam sessions, and the rhythm section was strictly utilitarian, like pumping oil for the featured players," a bass player recalls. Another adds, "There are some soloists for whom you can stand on your toes and nothing will happen." The experience can be deflating, as for one pianist who describes his disappointment after a concert with a renowned saxophonist: "I felt like I was hardly much use when I played with him."

### Circumstantial Problems Undermining Performances

Fundamental incompatibility between and among artists takes its toll. In other cases, unsatisfactory interplay reflects questions based on any number of circumstantial factors surrounding improvisations: Are musicians generally well practiced or out of shape? Are they well rested or tired? Are they warmed up or cold? Are their imaginations fertile or barren? Are they in the mood to extend themselves to other players or are they distracted by other matters? In one dramatic case that Patti Bown cites, a drummer who had "just split up from his wife" could neither set aside his preoccupations nor control his "terrible emotional problems." He improvised relentlessly and tastelessly "through everybody else's solos, trying to obliterate everyone on the bandstand." In some cases, temporary personal friction between individual band members can lead them to withhold the musical support they normally offer one another during performances.[12]

More commonly, a temporary attack of self-consciousness or unfamiliarity with pieces impairs improvisation. "If you are relaxed enough, you can listen to the other people you are playing with," Art Farmer says. "But if you're uptight, you're just trying to deal with the horn." Lee Konitz elaborates candidly:

> Frequently, at best, I can only relate to one person in the group at a time. At worst, I can't listen to anybody else during my solo. Nobody. And to me, that's really a danger sign. When my attention is so much on myself, I know that I'm in trouble. It has to start there, certainly. We have to get our own thing all balanced out before we extend ourselves to the next person. But if I'm just concerned with what I'm doing, I would tend to go into a more automatic kind of playing.

Konitz refers here to mechanical playing, not the positive experience of being on automatic pilot discussed earlier. "Many times," he continues, "I've felt I was squelching the possibility of my relating to the other musicians by just hammering away at my own thing, trying to keep up or doing whatever I thought I should be doing. No one said you have to keep playing without a break during a solo."

Within the fluctuating state of improvisation, intermittent problems that beset any part can potentially compromise the others. "Everybody's part is equally important," Wynton Marsalis states. "If you have one weak link, it doesn't happen, man." Chuck Israels sets forth an explanation for the effects of a typical off night: "If there is something wrong, it makes for a pulling back of our sensitivities. You have to defend against it in some way. This usually means you don't listen as sharply as you would ordinarily, and you're not as sensitive to what is going on around you. You just block it out and do your job."

In discussing some of the ramifications of losing one's sensitivity, Harold Ousley indicates the need for artists to work through the difficulty and attempt to take some responsibility for regaining equilibrium.

> Maybe the soloist is nervous and uptight and can't get his thing to-gether. Everyone else might really be able to do it, but the soloist is so tense, it makes everybody else tense to the point where nobody can find nobody else. It's just a matter of feelings. People can feel each other's tension. Like when a person is speaking, if the person is nice and relaxed, then everyone is relaxed when they listen to him. But if that person is nervous, sometimes you don't even want to watch some-one who's nervous, because it makes you so uncomfortable [laughter]. It works the same way with musicians.
>
> There was a time when the piano player might be playing the wrong chords, and as soon as I became aware of that, it got in the way of my own concentration and I began to fumble. Or I could forget a chord when I worried about those things. Whenever something was going wrong, I tended to go wrong with it. Fear used to do this to me. I wouldn't get completely immobilized, but I couldn't play my best all tensed up. Tension is one of the main reasons why things go wrong in a band. I've had to overcome that kind of sensitivity. I've had those moments when I could say, "Well, let me anchor everything," and I was strong enough to pull everything in that went astray.

There are instances when anxiety initially causes, or further aggravates, problems with a rhythm section player's timing, constraining, in turn, various aspects of invention within the group. "If the bass is not right," Ronald Shan-non Jackson observes, "I don't have the freedom to play whatever I want. I can't play different rhythms without clashing. I'm not at liberty even to think about playing different rhythms, because I will be trying too hard to keep the time together." Under these circumstances, polyrhythmic activity and the creation of cross-rhythmic effects by deliberately "turning the beat around," as described earlier, become risky business. "When I solo, I always know where I am, and I like to play with the time," Gary Bartz comments. "I might play a figure implying that I'm on 'one' when I know that it's not 'one,' just to fool some-body. If the other player's time is not good, they will think that I really am on 'one' and go with that and mess up everything for the whole band. So, I won't be able to do those kinds of things in my playing. It really makes me feel restricted when I solo."

Should an unstable and disruptive patch of performance result in major discrepancies in the rhythm section's interpretation of the beat, it can be disheartening for soloists. "When you have different guys in the rhythm section playing on different parts of the beat, they're going to be fighting each other constantly, and it's very difficult to solo against that." The focus of Jimmy Robinson's insights on this matter is that of long years in the tradition:

> Especially on fast tempos, if the rhythm section is not working together like a well-oiled machine, and I've got three different rhythms going on behind me, I can't relax in my playing. I can't concentrate on the tune and the chords when I've got to listen to what they're doing behind me and worry about their messing me up, making me sound bad if I play a certain phrase or something, even if I'm playing right.
>
> Some soloists have the attitude, "The tune goes this way, and this is the tempo," and they just keep playing their ideas that way. They don't care where the rhythm section is. It's up to the rhythm section to catch up to them or just fall by the wayside. I used to play like that when I had the chops and the endurance, but I'm not strong like that now, since I haven't been playing for a while. So now, I've got to depend on the rhythm section's cooperation. If things aren't right, it's going to pull me off.

## Group Interplay: A Comparative Perspective

The disruptive experiences cited above illustrate why musicians diligently cultivate sensibilities to group interplay on the bandstand. By necessity, the process is a gradual one. Excited by their discovery of jazz, students initially seek opportunities to improvise at every accessible performance venue and in any group that will have them. They are, in the beginning, less particular about the partners with whom they form musical relationships, because they have yet to appreciate the subtle dimensions of interpersonal communication and the intricate meshing entailed in successful improvisation. Many are not immediately attuned to the exceptional moments of performances, nor acclimated to the extramusical experiences that accompany them. "I remember the first time I experienced that floating, out-of-the-body feeling," Leroy Williams recalls. "It was a number of years ago, when I was playing in Chicago. At the time, I didn't know what it was. I said, 'What is this?' and I backed off it for a minute." Charli Persip reminisces along similar lines. "The first time I ever got the feeling of what it was like to strike a groove, I was pretty young. At the time, I didn't have enough sense to realize that it was one of the few times that I was playing smart. But I learned that later."

With growing sensitivity to the nuances of collective improvisation and a new perspective on earlier musical encounters, performers attach special significance to the support and emotional warmth they had formerly shared with players in particular bands. Over time, they increasingly discriminate in forming their associations. As in other kinds of human encounters, it is sometimes not until individuals have broken the bonds of one relationship to take up another that they appreciate how special were the qualities of the first. "There has to be a certain empathy among all the players in a group before the beauty in this music can really happen," Leroy Williams asserts. "In some situations, everybody is trying to outshine everybody else. Once you experience how beautiful this music can be, and then you play with musicians who aren't up to your level or who don't have the same chemistry, then things don't happen in the music, and it's bad. It's like when you're used to champagne, and you're given beer."

Similarly, for Lou Donaldson, "if it feels good in the band, you can keep playing all night, and it's a pleasure to go to work. If things are poppin' with the other musicians, and if they're really tight, we'll take chances on doing a lot of different things. But if somebody's lagging, we'll just stick to a routine to get through the job. It's just not right to try anything adventuresome under those conditions. You have to concentrate on the chords and make sure everything sounds right—and you're tired at the end of an evening."

Powerful performances by renowned groups keep the standard before artists, causing them to reflect upon their own experiences. "Sometimes," Chuck Israels recounts, "I remember the way Miles Davis interpreted 'Autumn Leaves' in his band with Cannonball Adderley, milking that song for everything it meant to him—autumn time, the falling of leaves, the ending of something, remembrance, and pathos. It makes me think of all the nondescript performances I have been involved in with other musicians playing that tune over the years."

Realizations of this nature highlight the enormity of the jazz musician's tasks and challenges. The thoughtful analysis of one player represents the attitude of many fine artists:

> It's difficult because it's a real intimate relationship to play music with people. It's very intuitive and visceral, very sensual. There are certain things you know right away about people by how they respond and how they feel in the music. The sensitivities involved are very much like sexual intuition, although I don't want to make too much of that comparison. But just as I don't need to make love for the sake of making love, anymore, I don't need to play for the sake of playing, anymore. Just as I've had all the empty sexual experiences when I was younger, finding myself just out of desperation with someone that I didn't want to be intimate with, I've had all the empty experiences

playing music that I needed in the past. Today, I have a wonderful relationship with a wonderful woman, and a family, and I'm not desperate anymore. The fact is, I'm not desperate to play, either. I've played in situations where music has really been made, and I'm not interested in anything else but that.

Such remarks reveal the intensely personal nature and complexities of collective improvisation. It puts into relief, as well, the occasional vulnerability of artists immersed in jazz performance.

# FIFTEEN

**The Lives of Bands**

Conflict Resolution and Artistic Development

*You really learn a lot about yourself on the road, and you get hurt a lot. You learn about how you react emotionally to different people telling you things that they feel aren't right about your playing, because you may have a different idea about what's right musically. You can reject what the other person said, or you can try to adjust according to the criticism you got. But in some cases you find yourself trying to adjust so much to accommodate another performer, it gets very confusing in terms of your own musical identity. You begin to wonder, "Well, exactly who am I?"*—Akira Tana

The configuration of musical personalities and talents within each band establishes its fundamental framework and determines its unique possibilities for invention. For those reasons, the leader's initial selection of personnel is itself a compositional act, requiring a special kind of sensitivity. Precise musical vision, knowledge of performance styles of prospective players, and prescient judgment of their potential as interacting improvisers profoundly affect the group's chances for success as an artistic enterprise.

As described earlier, despite the best intentions of their leaders, jazz groups may inadvertently include musicians with opposing tastes and incompatible skills. "When I hire the musicians, it's no problem," Gary Bartz says, "but when I work with other groups, I have no choice about who the other musicians are. When serious problems arise, it always amazes me why leaders of groups hire people who can't fit in." The obvious fault may rest with a leader's poor judgment or with misguided recommendations from other players, but given improvisation's demanding, capricious nature, even the most well informed employer may fail to anticipate subtle problems. For example, artists who, by individual reputation, share the same predisposition toward interpreting the beat sometimes discover significant disparity in their rhythmic concepts when they first perform together.

Identification and resolution of musical conflict remains a central issue over the careers of improvisers, an issue having immediate consequences for their groups' inventions and ongoing implications for personal artistic growth. Typically, handling problems depends not only on the specific problems a band encounters, but also on the group's political organization. Some bands are effectively leaderless, with all decisions about music potentially the result of more or less equal collaboration. Characteristically, however, band leaders exercise the greatest authority. Among supporting artists, veterans have more influence than newcomers; and composers, arrangers, or musical directors have greater power than do the other players. At the same time, these general power relationships are subject to myriad nuances and are constantly renegotiated and redefined by artists. Among the factors that determine the outcome of negotiation are the individual's sense of artistic identity and the values he or she attaches to collective improvisation as a form of social and musical interaction. Two common ideological positions represent opposite poles in this matter, the first focusing on the rights of the individual, the second on the welfare of the group.

### Power Relations and Musical Values: The Individual versus the Group

Characteristically, the jazz community emphasizes freedom of expression in music making. "Jazz is a democratic form of music," Max Roach declares.

> When a piece is performed, everybody in the group has the opportunity to speak on it, to comment on it through their performance. It's a democratic process, as opposed to most European classical music in which the two most important people are the composer and the conductor. They are like the king and the queen. In a sense, the conductor is also the military official who's there to see that the wishes of the masters—the composers—are adhered to, and as a musician your job may depend on how you conform to the conductor's interpretation of the composer's wishes. However, in a jazz performance, everyone has an opportunity to create a thing of beauty collectively, based on their own musical personalities.

Roach's hiring practices reflect these convictions, as does the way he delegates musical responsibility to showcase each player's unique talents. "For my bands, I look for musicians who have spent the time really developing themselves, trying to find their own individuality," he explains. "It always helps if a person knows his instrument as well as or better than anyone else around, but I also look for other qualities. Are the musicians as well rounded as possible?

Do they compose? Is their writing, the way they voice chords, as unique to them as their instrumental performance?"

Those who believe jazz should be democratic music maintain that they should always have the freedom to express themselves according to their own tastes, even as their professional affiliations change. In fact, this is often the experience of supporting players. "With Pharoah Sanders's group, the music is what you make of it. If he likes you, he gives you complete freedom to make up whatever you want and add it to the music" (CH). Walter Bishop Jr. has observed this repeatedly over his career. "When a person like Art Blakey, Miles Davis, or Charlie Parker hires you, that means one thing: you have what they want already. They have heard you with other bands, and they have heard you play on records. Bird never said, 'Comp this way or comp that way,' because he hired me to play the way I play. It's the same when I hire somebody. When I hire a drummer, it's because I have seen what he does with someone else. He knows that I know what he can do, and he can do the kinds of things I like a drummer to do behind me."

At the same time, the jazz community espouses a second view on freedom of expression, stressing the mutual interdependence of players and somewhat limiting individual freedom. For Leroy Williams, "playing jazz is like a team effort, the kind you find in basketball or baseball. Everybody has to do their specific job. That's the only way you're going to score. One guy can't take all the shots in basketball, for instance. He has to lay back at times. You have to give the ball to whichever player has the best shot. It's one big group effort, and when everybody's in harmony, that's when the best things happen. You have to sacrifice your own ideas at times."

In some organizations, a strong leader takes responsibility for regulating such interaction. "Whenever you have a group of people playing together, somebody has to lead and somebody has to follow," Wynton Marsalis explains. "If you get five people on the stand and they all play the way they want to, it sounds terrible. But if you get one person to show those five people what to play, they can sound great. . . . Everybody has to follow the leader's concept, but add everything they can to it." From the perspective of some artists, however, the leader's exercise of power brings the ideals of self-expression and group welfare into conflict and belies commitment to equality and the democratic process. "There are people who want you to do the robot thing. They're interested in controlling every note you play," Don Pate attests. John McNeil supports this observation. "I've played with some leaders that want what they want when they want it or bang, you're fired," he says. Comparable distinctions among leaders have shaped the nature of music making in jazz groups from its beginnings.[1]

Over the lives of bands, power relations are not necessarily static. Issue by issue, leaders differ in the limitations on expressive freedom that they impose upon supporting artists, just as the artists themselves differ in their compliance with authority. Eager apprentices who have yet to define their own musical values may readily conform to a leader's wishes. Experience and the maturation of their own styles increase assertiveness. One career drummer, for example, asserts his dislike for "musicians telling me how to play. It makes me hate myself," he claims, "because I feel that I've evolved to the point as a performer where they shouldn't have to tell me. It hurts a bit because I feel either they aren't really listening to me or I am still not as good as I should be. Of course, I will accept criticism from someone I respect, but it also depends how you lay it on me."

Calvin Hill reflects on the challenges he faced in the development of his individuality:

> Earlier in my career, when I was playing with Pharoah and McCoy and others, I played a certain way according to whoever I was playing with. I used to do this even more than the particular situation required. It was almost like not being Calvin Hill. If I played with, say, Joe Schmo on the piano, then I was playing more like Fred Schmo on the bass than Calvin Hill. I felt like I didn't have a personality of my own. Recently, I've been really starting to feel that I have an identity of my own, a sound of my own, and a personality of my own. I can play in any situation now and fulfill the requirements of the situation and still maintain my identity. I carry that wherever I go.
>
> For example, one of the things I've been interested in approaching in my playing is trying to bring more of an African influence into jazz. I got interested in this a few years ago when I heard an album of a guy from Burundi playing the bass zither. Since then, I've been trying to incorporate the feeling of what he was doing in my playing. I've been trying to have this influence come through in my playing with different groups, transcending the differences in their styles. With Max Roach, it's easy to do because he gives you so much freedom. It's a bit more difficult to do with [a certain bebop pianist], but there are ways of connecting some of the rhythmic patterns and little techniques I learned from the zither player with the bebop tradition's rhythmic patterns.

When disputes arise within bands, the forceful views of supporting players prevail, at times, over those of leaders. "There was one piece in which I wanted the drummer to solo over a melodic figure that the rest of the band played," John McNeil recalls, "and he just wouldn't do it. I asked him over and over because I wanted to hear what it sounded like, and he just refused to do it. We argued over it for a while, and when I asked him if he could give me one good reason why he wouldn't do it, he said, 'I just think it sounds terrible and I don't like it.' I said, 'Okay. We'll compromise. Since you think it sounds terrible and you're not going to want to play it very much, we just won't do it [laughter].'"

McNeil's clever joking resolved any tension that might have lingered in the wake of a clash of strong views.

Dissenting players can also set limits on a band's overall concept, or even redefine it. One leader's enthusiastic attempt to adopt African polyrhythmic settings for his group's entire repertory was thwarted by a particular member's threat to resign. The player liked the group's balance of "African-oriented and mainstream jazz" material and was uninterested in devoting more time to the former.

Despite differences in their power, leaders and group members typically strive to appreciate one another's viewpoints and to interact flexibly. "I have to be open-minded concerning what the other musicians might play," Fred Hersch concedes. "At times, I have to fight not to tell anyone else how to play. It might not be what I had in mind, but that's the whole point of playing jazz, to be open enough to accept what someone else has to say." Similarly, Rufus Reid has learned "through experience how to assess what is needed in different musical settings and how far I can go in my playing before I step beyond the boundaries of what people expect. You can see what different people's concepts are. Then you know how far you can stretch it and still give them what they want."

### Assessing and Accommodating Musical Situations

In a spirit of compromise, newcomers commonly size up the idiomatic requirements of their situations within groups and modify aspects of their personal styles accordingly. "You have to fit into the style of the band you're playing with," insists Red Rodney. "That's just professionalism. You can deviate a little, perhaps, as long as what you do fits in with the form and general style of the band. When a rhythm section is playing older music and older styles, it's hard to play the newer soloistic patterns and figures. They won't fit very well. So, I just try to stay in the style that I hear around me."

Likewise, when performing with the Heath brothers, whose "mainstream swing tradition calls for a straight-ahead mainstream swing beat," Akira Tana recognizes that "certain kinds of things come to mind that wouldn't really fit, or be tasteful, like playing with the soloistic concept of Tony Williams or Jack DeJohnette." In Tana's view, any player who performs with an artist of Percy Heath's stature should be prepared to "adjust to the era and tradition he's coming from and respect it. You're hired by people to make their music sound good and to complement them. The drummers in New York that I admire so much, like Al Foster, Billy Hart, and Ben Riley, are all people who can perform in many different settings. They are the ones who are always working. They can adjust and make other people's music sound good, and at the same time, they still contribute something of their own."

Within a group's idiomatic guidelines, the musical personalities of players dictate further adjustments. Meeting the needs of different individuals simultaneously with fulfilling multiple responsibilities can present dilemmas, however. Rhythm section players may discover that the approach to accompaniment favored by one of their counterparts conflicts with their own, and perhaps with the taste of a soloist, as well. This requires them to choose between adopting the other rhythm section player's approach as a constraint upon invention or following their own sense of appropriate interplay with soloists.

The situation is intricate, as Keith Copeland attests.

> In one group I played with, the bass player was a brilliant player, but he had a more laid-back way of playing that wouldn't allow me to take the kind of liberties I would with someone else. With that group, I had to play less, so that the bass player and I would lock up more and make the foundation of the band sound good. If I played too much off the bass figures and off the improvisation of the soloist, keeping a dialogue going with the soloist as well as keeping the time, it would be taking things too far. It would confuse the bass player, and he wouldn't feel as sure of the time as he would if I just tried to play along with him and let him dictate the kinds of embellishments that were going to happen for the rest of the band. If I played solely off of him, then I would play to whatever peak he would play to. If I went beyond that, it became too intense for him. He wasn't used to playing with that kind of energy level behind him, because the group he had played with for so many years was much more laid-back.
>
> I could have taken many more liberties in my playing if he had been accustomed to playing a different way. It would work if I was playing with a bass player who understood the way in which I like to play off the soloist, like the way Jimmy Garrison understood how Elvin Jones was playing off John Coltrane, or the way Jymie Merritt understood the way Art Blakey was playing off of Lee Morgan or Freddie Hubbard. But if the bass player doesn't feel comfortable about the way I'm taking liberties playing off the soloists, then it's better for me to play just to the level of the bass player, locking up with him, and let the rest of the guys play off of us. When I play with bass players like Sam Jones, it's very different. Sam plays so melodically and rhythmically that I can play things simultaneously with what he is playing and still enhance the soloist.

The sensitivity, understanding, and flexibility evidenced in Copeland's account are especially critical in musical contexts where arrangements are minimal and leaders offer little guidance in advance of performances. "I would go into the recording studio with Bud Powell and ask him for directions," Art Taylor recalls, "but he'd just tell me to hit. He'd say, 'You'll know what to do.' I had no choice but to go with it, but it could be very frustrating. I just had to trust my own instincts and musicianship." Under comparable circumstances, bands that depart from conventional performance practices compound the challenges for newcomers. Buster Williams remembers his experience performing with Miles Davis's quintet during the period, described earlier, "in which the group was playing way-out things like on the *E.S.P.* album. They had their own particular brand of stuff at the time, and nobody else had been doing it."

The group had no formal rehearsal before their first performance. Herbie Hancock, Tony Williams, and Wayne Shorter invited Williams to drop by the hotel where they were staying. They "ran through 'So What'" with him and simply pronounced "You got it." Williams laughs at the memory. It did not appear to concern them that he might face any difficulty with the music. "Because they were so relaxed," Williams says, "I thought I might as well be relaxed, too. That was the only way I was going to be able to play the music." He was, nevertheless, uncertain as to "what my precise role was supposed to be," he recollects, adding, "Nobody told me—and I was afraid to ask, because everybody took it so natural."

For the first few nights, the performances were unnerving for Williams, who describes the experience as "like trying to find my way through a maze." Davis consistently "opened up each set with 'Agitation,' the only thing that resembled a melody. From then on, it was out there. I listened to Tony, and when I found that I couldn't figure out anything from Tony, I listened to Herbie. But Herbie was laying out half the time. Wayne seemed to just float on the periphery of everything, and Miles would just make his statement and go to the bar. I didn't know what I was supposed to do, man, except play the bass. So, that's what I did. I played what I considered to fit in with what they were doing. Also, the guys were so beautiful, they adjusted to me," he concludes, in tribute to the fact of the group's inclusiveness and sensitivity: they were all listening to and accommodating him.

### Negotiating Musical Differences off the Bandstand

Should successful adjustments fail to occur during performances, musicians sometimes have post mortems, discussing problems afterwards, making requests, or expressing dissatisfaction with their own participation. Lonnie Hillyer had heard that Herbie Hancock "once told Miles, 'I don't know what to play behind you sometimes.' Miles answered, 'Then don't play anything' [laughter]. Guys like that will let a few bars at a time go by without playing." In Patti Bown's distant past, a saxophone player was equally direct. "He told me that I was playing too many things behind him. He said, 'Feed me, but don't get in the way.' I thanked him and heard afterwards what he was talking about. It made me stop and think, and I started listening very hard to what the soloists were doing."

Drummer Keith Copeland has received similar instruction. One pianist "asked me not to play too much because it confused him," Copeland recounts.

He was talking about volume and playing too many figures. He wanted me to play more simply, to play intensely, but softer because it was a trio. In a horn band, you tend to start soft, but you can build up to much higher levels of intensity and volume than you can with a trio. If I get too exuberant, I can cover the piano player up. So, I had to learn how to keep the intensity there, but to keep the volume down. I can get busy in the latter parts of his solos when I have an idea where he's going to go, but I can't start off that way. I have to give him a chance to build his solo and find out which way he wants to go. With other piano players, it's different. There's no way I can play too much because they're playing so much themselves, all kinds of ways rhythmically. I can't play as freely with this piano player. I have to play less busily or I'd get in his way, and he'd have to follow me.

Kenny Washington similarly recalls the invaluable counsel he received when performing with groups led by Lee Konitz, whom Washington considers to be "very special and different in terms of what he likes from drummers." At the time, Washington had been modeling his performance upon Louis Hayes, Art Blakey, and "Philly" Joe Jones. "All the cats in town who were about, bashing. You know, the 'hit it' cats." This approach held him in good stead within Konitz's nonet, but Washington "used to play too loud" in the settings of Konitz's quartets and trios. According to Washington, Konitz's advice was both supportive and specific—helpful at the time and over the long run:

"Listen, man, I love your playing and everything, but I want you to play softer, but with the same kind of intensity."
He told me that there was this record called *Motion* that he did with Elvin Jones and wanted to know if I was hip to that. I searched and searched until I finally found that record, and I could see what he was trying to tell me. Around the same time that Lee and Elvin did that album, Elvin was also playing with John Coltrane. When he was playing with Coltrane, he really had to hit it. It was intense. But when he got on the record with Lee, he was just tipping. He was playing the same stuff that he played with Coltrane, but playing much softer. It felt like a whole different way of playing, but the intensity was still there. He was playing the same polyrhythms and everything he played with Trane, but at a much lower level of volume. I heard this record and I couldn't believe it. Everything was surging ahead, but it was soft, pianissimo. When Lee told me to listen to this, he wasn't telling me to play like Elvin, but to play my way. But not loud.
Lee was also the first cat to turn me on to Mel Lewis. Lee called Mel up and said, "Listen, I've got this new drummer that's playing

with my band, and I want you to come down and talk to him"—because at that point, I hadn't begun to think about fitting into different situations. I didn't know anything about that until Mel started talking to me about it. He told me that you have to play according to whatever situation you're in. Like if it calls for playing loud, you go right ahead. But Lee is not into that kind of thing. Mel was very beautiful about that. He brought me up to his house and played me different records that he had done. Mel can fit into any situation.

As implied above, the criticism that performers receive within particular bands is commonly echoed within the jazz community's larger network, sensitizing performers to general weaknesses in their musicianship and to the requirements of different situations. After returning from a solo performance tour and participating in a few local sessions, one pianist was puzzled to find that his former friends were "always busy with other gigs" whenever he attempted to hire them. One evening when their wives were socializing with the pianist's girlfriend, the women diplomatically shared the view of their husbands that the pianist's "playing had gone down" during his tour. As a solo artist, he had become accustomed to taking unusual rhythmic liberties. Drummers subsequently regarded his time as unsteady. He experienced additional difficulties with bass players upon returning to ensemble work. Because he failed to readjust the densely textured style that he had developed to fill out his solo performance, bass players regarded him as "in their way." Upon receiving the women's kindly intentioned message, the pianist began practicing with a metronome and studying recordings of various bands' rhythm sections to reacquaint himself with the interaction of his favorite pianists. Achieving his former strength after several months, he regained the admiration of his friends.

When problems are elusive, improvisers sometimes require repeated trial and error before overcoming criticism they have received. Rufus Reid remembers the bass player who replaced him in Dexter Gordon's band telling a story that "just had me on the floor laughing." The bass player had previously performed with an artist who "liked things way up on the beat," and when he first joined the band,

Gordon would say, "Now, look, you sound real good, man, but just relax, lay back." Then, the next night, he would play more laid back, or what felt to him like more laid back, and Dexter would say, "Relax, man. Just let it flow." That kept happening until, one day, the bass player got sick of Dexter coming to him with this and decided he was really going to lay back to the point where there was going to be no doubt about his laying back. So, that night they were playing ballads, and he laid back so far that he knew [that] when he got off the bandstand and got into the dressing room they were going to say that it was too far back. He laid back so far that it hurt to do it, like he was becoming completely unglued with it. He knew they were going to have to say, "Not that much." So, he goes into the dressing room after the set, and everyone came into the room grinning from ear to ear. "That's it!" they said. "You got it now!" [Reid laughs.] He couldn't believe it.

In some instances, moreover, subtleties distinguishing different notions of tasteful interaction or the vague ways in which performers express disfavor make it difficult for performers to fathom their differences. A trumpeter remembers a group in which the pianist would set up an unvarying comping pattern, while insisting that the soloist

> not play anything off of it. You weren't supposed to play with it or even be inspired by it. If you started playing off his pattern, he'd change it and he'd tell you about it. That was a very weird concept to me because, in the first place, piano players rarely stick with one pattern long enough, and in the second place, when I go into a playing situation, I try to have an open mind to everything. And if I play off something that someone else is playing, I don't even think about it. I don't always specifically think about what the piano player is playing. I just try to hear all the stuff that the whole group is playing, and what the piano is playing is just part of that.
>
> Also, the piano player was always saying to me, "You've got to dig in more. You've got to play with fire. You've just got to try to dig in more and play with more fire." I wasn't about to tell him that that was what I thought I was doing already. He used to tell me about how much fire the former trumpet players with the group had. So, one day, I decided to get ahold of one of the group's earlier records, and I copped the trumpet player's solo on one of the tunes that had become a big hit. I changed it slightly, but I played the same thing basically when it came time for me to solo, and I just waited to hear the leader's reaction. He didn't know what I had done, and he came back saying, "Man, you've got to learn to play with more fire." After that point, I knew I'd never know what he was talking about, and I didn't take it so seriously because I considered the trumpet player whose solo I copped to be great.

Such points of contention may be fleeting in the relationship between players as they turn their attention to other issues, or they may remain nagging difficulties in their efforts to establish musical rapport.

## Negotiating Differences during Performances

Complementing the feedback artists receive off the bandstand is that which comes during actual performances, requiring them to make immediate adjustments in their playing. Due to the difficulties inherent in translating musical concepts into words and the awkwardness of confronting problems, some artists provide indirect or minimal commentary. "I hear you listening to me again tonight," a pianist once quipped at me in subtle derision in the course of an engagement. In his view, I had borrowed too much material from his accompaniment when formulating my solos. Leroy Williams recalls the reaction of Thelonious Monk to one of his performances when anxiety caused Williams to rush the music's tempo. "One thing that made a lasting impression on me took place during the first tune I played with Monk. We'd only gotten a few bars into it when Monk gets up from the piano and comes over to me and says, 'We have all night to play.' That's all he said, and then he went back to the piano. Wilbur Ware was playing bass, and he looked over at me and laughed. Monk was just telling me to relax."

Physical signs are also effective. Sonny Stitt once realized during a tour that young Buster Williams never took his eyes off the drummer's hi-hat cymbal, relying upon it as a visual prop to steady his performance. For the remainder of the engagement and during subsequent performances, he stood between the two musicians on the bandstand, deliberately blocking the view. As contrary as this may seem, the tactic eventually paid off. Williams agrees that, forced to depend on his own ears and cultivate his own sense of the beat, his "tempo started getting together from that time on." In another case, a bass player describes a renowned singer's stylized stroll to his part of the bandstand whenever she found fault with him and the trepidation he felt at the manner in which she "gaped" at him, until, heeding her stare, he altered his performance. It was similar for Keith Copeland when, as a teenager, he sat in with Barry Harris's group:

> If you tried some stuff on the gig that didn't work, like accents that didn't fit the head, or if you broke the flow, you'd get a dirty look from Barry. He had a way of looking at you that could scare you to death. He didn't have to say anything. Also, by the time I had a chance to play with Barry, I was listening a lot to "Philly" Joe Jones and a few other drummers from the hard bop period, and I was trying to do a lot of the things that they did. I wanted to drop all the bombs I had been practicing. But Barry would give me this funny look and say, "I need more bass drum. Give me some more foundation." It meant using the loud/soft technique, playing the bass drum on every beat and varying the dynamics and accents.

As described earlier, some leaders altogether eschew discussion about musical problems, leaving players to work out their differences through musical discourse in performance. "Whether people want less accompaniment or want you to play right along with them isn't necessarily discussed," Tommy Flanagan states. "With Sonny Rollins, it didn't need to be. You know when you feel like you're being crowded out [he laughs]. There's less room for you to play." With respect to the conversational aspects of jazz, Calvin Hill disdains "drummers who are like tape recorders. You play something, and then they imitate it," he bemoans. "Sometimes, I'll mess with cats like that. I'll just stop and wait for them to play the next thing. That forces them to play something of their own." Paul Wertico adopts the same tactic when uninspired soloists improvise continuously to the point of "self-indulgence, using you like Aebersold playalong records." Whereas poor soloists usually fall apart without the drummer's support, he adds, "heavy" players can take the music "to another level" by themselves, preparing the way for an even greater climax when the drums subsequently come back in.

Clever strategies come to their assistance when players strive to improve the level of conversation. In Fred Hersch's experience, "if you don't like what someone else is doing, there are little, polite musical ways of saying, 'I don't really want you to do that. It's lovely, but I would rather you did this.' I might do something musical with my left hand, the certain way I play a line," he explains. "Or, if Art Farmer plays some real unexpected stuff which makes what I'm playing behind him sound wrong, it means, 'Lay out!' You have to be able to communicate this way with the people you're playing with if you're going to play jazz." Sometimes, the titles of compositions serve as codes, as when soloists quote tunes like "I Got Rhythm" or "I Didn't Know What Time It Was" when the rhythm section begins to lose its coordination, destabilizing the beat.[2]

Of course, conveying through the language of music that you think other players have created a problem is one thing; convincing them of it and bringing it to resolution can be a complicated process. Various factors with consequences for collective invention affect this process, as the experiences of several artists attest.

The first time George Duvivier performed with one renowned singer, for example, he was initially very excited about the prospects "because I knew his band had some swinging arrangements. But unfortunately," he continues, "I discovered that some of the bass lines were terrible." From his point of view, "bass lines are generally a throwaway for many arrangers, who don't give them the same care they do horn voicings. I prefer to have them write out the chord changes and leave the bass lines to me."

Consequently, after reviewing the bass parts in the singer's arrangements, Duvivier started changing them. The singer was used to hearing the other lines, however, and he did not want bass players "to take too many liberties, because he felt it detracted from his own performance." Although not chastized directly, Duvivier eventually realized that the discrepancies were annoying the singer, and he returned to the original arranged bass parts. "Then everything was fine," Duvivier says, "except that I wasn't happy." When asked how he resolved the conflict, he replied simply, "Well, the gig ended and that was that." As in such instances, band leaders can constrain, if not stifle, the contributions of supporting artists, leaving them dissatisfied with their own role in the music.

There are times, however, when accommodating a leader can result in pleasing musical revelations for other players. Rufus Reid recalls occasions when Eddie Harris, in an effort to preserve the character of his own compositions, would instruct Reid "not to improve on" their bass parts. "I just hated them," Reid exclaims. Some nights, after playing one of the parts, Reid would alter the pattern "rhythmically a bit," which immediately drew Harris's attention. When Reid "fooled with the pattern again," Harris stopped playing the saxophone and gave Reid "a real dirty look. 'Oh, damn'," Reid said to himself, and he went back to the original pattern again. Several evenings later, Reid tired of the constant struggle and decided to play the pattern just as it was written in order to prove to Harris that the music would not "get off the ground that way." But to Reid's astonishment, "just the opposite thing happened. All of sudden, I got so involved with the pattern that the music just began to grow and grow and grow. The pattern became like a repeated chant." The music amazed Reid, making him realize that, not having appreciated what "Harris had wanted the music to achieve," he had inadvertently prevented the music from reaching its zenith. From that point on, the pieces presented "a different kind of challenge" to Reid. He adds that after this experience he approached conflicts with greater humility.

Fred Hersch recollects his own comprehensive adjustment to another artist's musicality. When he first played with Sam Jones as a duo at Bradley's in New York, he thought that of all the players on the music scene the two of them would be the "most mismatched." Hersch was much younger than Jones, who was, "at fifty-five, a legend. He's a beautiful cat, but he's got his opinions, and he's stubborn. He plays impeccable time and great changes. That's his thing. He lays it down, but he doesn't go with you." Their first performance fed into Hersch's apprehensions. Having become used to playing with active young bass players, Hersch found it frustrating to play with a bass player who just played steady bass lines and did not interact as, in Hersch's opinion, an Eddie Gomez would have, for example. However, on the second night of their engagement, he recounts,

> all of a sudden, I really started getting into his groove. And then it all opened up. I started to understand how you can be as free artistically within different parameters. I started realizing that Sam's playing is so classic and so subtle. Like, all his notes lie right under his fingers, and he always plays the right note for you. He plays the right notes, the right chord substitute, the right line—and the groove is just incredible. He's a rhythmic player, and it's just like playing with a whole rhythm section. Within a groove time, or within a standard tune, I

started feeling a new sense of freedom playing with Sam. I could go ahead and be melodic and not have to worry about playing all this textural pianistic stuff that people play. I could play bebop and play music just like Tommy Flanagan plays. It's very musical.

It was hard for me at first because I wanted to get my other thing off, my other way of playing. But then I really got into working the gig, learning something and satisfying myself. Just playing with Sam and coming to understand that way of playing was an incredible learning experience for me.

In other cases, direct challenges to another player's demands ultimately enrich the experiences of improvising. Don Pate recalls having had a conflict with Ahmad Jamal that was similar, initially, to the one between Reid and Harris, but it ran a quite different course. Jamal had composed bass lines for Pate

to play in certain places. I'd play the line for a while, and then, when it became too repetitive for me, I'd change the line and play something else. Then Ahmad would turn around at the piano, like the strict disciplinarian he is, and say, "Only play the line! Only play the line!" But being rebellious like I am, I would continue what I was doing. I would acknowledge the line and go in and out of it. I'd play the line to a point, but sometimes it's physically uncomfortable to play the same thing over and over. Eventually, Ahmad would give up his vocalizing, "Play the line!" and if you played something that he liked, he'd play your line back to you on the piano and smile. So, that was his way of compromising or giving. He still wanted you to play the line, but at the same time, if you took the risk and had the creativity to augment it, he was large enough to accept it.

Resistance to compromise within bands, on the other hand, does not always produce such favorable musical results. A musician describes the experience of being in the recording studio "with four people who were ready to play with one another and one guy who was not. [The trumpeter and saxophonist] were way ahead of me and possibly [the drummer], in terms of their abilities and skills at that point, but that did not prevent us from accompanying the others reasonably well. We had a fairly easy time of finding common ground." In his view, the pianist, whose style did not suit the others "harmonically or rhythmically," was the "odd man out. I don't think that [the drummer] and I listened to the pianist at all, because if we had, it would have destroyed whatever we did together. Nobody could listen to the pianist. We just blotted him out and went ahead and recorded the album." Following this event, the artists did not again record or perform together as their own group. In such cases, band members with irreconcilable differences coexist but tenuously, their performances achieving only minimal cohesion.

An incident involving a bebop quartet in San Francisco during the late

sixties epitomizes the problems that can arise when musicians downright refuse to compromise their differences. The dispute arose unexpectedly at a
nightclub when, unbeknownst to the group's conservative bass player, the saxophonist had decided to make his debut in the free jazz idiom during the engagement's second set. Rather than calling a particular piece's title, he merely
named a key and began improvising cascading modal patterns. In response,
the group's adventurous drummer immediately supported the soloist with free-
rhythmic waves of sound, and the trumpeter echoed fragments of the saxophonist's phrases. The bass player, scowling, seemed reluctant to join in. He
listened for the longest time without playing. Then, quite suddenly, he imposed
conventional walking bass lines and a strictly metered beat upon the music.
Surprised and indignant, the saxophonist shifted the mouthpiece to the far corner of his mouth, crying out, "No, man. Use your bow!" then continued his
solo. The bass lines ceased as suddenly as they had begun. Moments later,
bowed bass entered, appropriately supplying a sustained drone, ornamented
occasionally by melodic figurations of restricted range.

At the point when the group's interplay became cohesive, the bass player
withdrew from the performance a second time, uttering a derisive remark. Ignoring him, the saxophonist continued and eventually strove to bring his fluent
improvisation to a climax. At the solo's peak, however, the bass player plunged
into the music with his powerful metered beat again. Within an instant, the
bass hit the floor and the saxophone sailed into the air, as the two musicians
went after each other, fists flying, before an astonished audience. Although this
unfortunate occurrence prematurely terminated the engagement of the band,
the instruments were repaired, in time, as was the mutual friendship of the two
musicians. Nevertheless, the incident underscores the impassioned differences
improvisers sometimes develop regarding the aesthetic values of particular
jazz idioms and the personal violation players may experience when others
respond insensitively to intimate thoughts and feelings exposed through musical performance.

The varied machinations of conflict resolution described above illuminate
an aspect of the adage common among jazz musicians that they "play the way
they are," in other words, that the individual artists' personalities and their
"ways of being" form an inextricable part of their musical personalities. Correspondingly, collective improvisations are not only products of purely musical
concepts, tastes, and technical skills but also products of the group's distinct
modes of social interaction, power relations, and predispositions toward collegiality and compromise.[3] Within the social atmosphere of different bands, musicians sometimes finesse, sometimes hammer out, their differences. They
must acquiesce, at times, to another's demands or wishes, or hold on to their
own. Every outcome produces musical consequences. A supporting artist who
agrees in one group to interpret an arranged part as written may, in another

group, vary the part within limits tolerated by the leader and, in yet another group, ignore the composed part altogether, replacing it with improvised figures. This mix of options, deliberately and artfully taken, is typical. It sums up a unique and complex history of decision making and negotiation that underlies each player's offering within a group, contributing singularity to its creations.

## Musical Conflict and Economic Realities

Over the past few decades, the economic realities of the music business and the changing base of support for jazz have increased the potential for conflicts within bands. Although jazz maintained a substantial following as popular dance music into the early forties and commanded a serious listenership during the bebop and early hard bop periods, two developments subsequently challenged its position. During the sixties, the free jazz movement divided sentiment within the jazz community, alienating conservative listeners and sharpening competition for employment between mainstream and free jazz performers. Meanwhile, the sweeping success of rock captivated a generation of young listeners, drawing support away from jazz. Many nightclub owners who had previously hired jazz groups shifted their allegiances to cater to audiences for the new popular music.

In the aftermath of these developments, as rock has come to dominate the American commercial music market, jazz musicians have struggled increasingly to maintain their art in the face of chronic unemployment. Caught in the vise of a tightened market, performers find that seeking employment leads them in a vicious cycle. When initially organizing a group, it helps for leaders to be able to offer members the ready prospect of work, justifying the time required for rehearsals. Moreover, keeping a group together so that it can develop a reputation requires its steady employment. From the club owner's perspective, however, bands are in the strongest positions to secure work at an established nightclub after they have cultivated an identity and can draw patrons.

The recording industry, important in promoting musicians and ensuring their survival, represents another vexing dilemma for artists. As part of good business practices, some major labels, before offering a recording contract to new bands, require that they have established employment histories and can demonstrate their intention to retain their personnel status for their albums' promotion. Meanwhile, for equally sound business considerations, club owners prefer to hire bands who have already recorded albums that have radio airplay and visibility in record stores to assist in advertising club dates. In the face of this circularity, performers endeavor to break into the cycle of frustration at whatever point they can, pursuing those opportunities that first present themselves.

Some renowned bands manage to find regular or semi-regular work by touring within the national network of jazz clubs, participating in college and professional concert hall entertainment programs, and traveling on the international jazz festival circuit. Typically, new groups succeed in finding employment only sporadically. Some form to play a single engagement. Others disband between gigs, recombining several times a year when jobs materialize or for a few weeks of steady bookings. Musicians normally pursue simultaneous affiliations with different groups, trying to cobble together a living from a mix of opportunities while hoping that steady work eventually arises for a favored group, thereby enabling them to drop less satisfactory associations.

Unpredictable factors in the trials and tribulations of the music business sometimes thwart a musician's aspirations. Chance often determines which musician is to replace a major figure within a renowned band; for example, who is sitting by the telephone at the precise moment a leader, proceeding down a list of recommended prospects, calls? Chance likewise determines whether musicians are free to accept the most exciting job offers or whether, dishearteningly, they must decline them to meet other contractual agreements made recently with other groups. An older piano player once poignantly observed to Don Pate, "It's a strange life that we lead. Some of the people who we play the best with and that we love to play with the most, we may only get to play with them once, once every few years, or maybe once in a lifetime." Echoes of this come from Pate's own experience. "There are certain people that you have a special musical thing with, but it just isn't designed for you to hit together," he rues.

The economic instability of the jazz community makes it difficult for leaders to maintain bands long enough for players to become sufficiently acquainted with their band's material and each other's styles to realize their group's potential. Melba Liston's band was several months old when she first made the uncompromising appraisal that "the spirituality part of performing [had] only happened with my group a few times." She was aware, even then, that "to get more of it, more consistently," she explains, "you need lots of practice and lots of playing together."

The split affiliations of improvisers commonly undermine this goal, however. Many groups are limited to performing with scant musical arrangements and too little opportunity to reconcile differences outside of public concerts. Roberta Baum recalls working with a group that could only rehearse once or twice before an engagement. "That was just enough time to go through the charts and to make sure that the changes I had were the right ones. It was very sketchy in terms of what the intro and the endings were going to be like. We worked weekends in a club for a month together, and I felt we were fighting each other most of the time. It wasn't till the very end of the date that there was really a homogeneous thing happening, and after that," she says regretfully, "we never performed together again."

In Jimmy Robinson's experience, as well, "when you don't play together with the same group a lot, and you're playing with different musicians all the time, you don't develop the right feeling for one another. Each one goes his own way. When the musicians are out there just to play the gig and not to accomplish anything special, musically, you can't get that closeness that you need, that feeling for one another when you're playing. You just can't create, now, like you used to be able to." Curtis Fuller is only too aware of the multifaceted problems associated with inconsistent performance opportunities and their effect upon musicians across the board. "When you're not working regularly, inactivity makes you lose the inspiration to practice," Fuller laments.

> When people say to you, "You can play in this club this week only, not for the next six months," it's difficult. It's like, preparing for this gig that is coming up, there's not enough inspiration to really practice. Because when the gig is over, that's the end of the group. So, the musician's attitude is just, "All right, we'll play this gig, but it's just to get through it." It's frustrating to play under those conditions and with those attitudes.
>
> If we could only get back to the cohesiveness that I would really like to see come about. It's one of the injustices in jazz that, with only two rehearsals or so, we're supposed to walk out on the stage and sound like we've been playing together for five years. Like, "Hey, wait a minute! What do you want from me?" Somehow, it works because we make it work. And that, to me, is a blessing in disguise. But just think what the music would be like if a group could actually play together for any length of time.

As Fuller points out, the absence of steady work erodes morale and reduces incentive for performers to keep up the rigorous private practice routines that their roles within jazz groups require. Moreover, there are essential skills that performers can only cultivate and maintain in the context of bands. "You can't develop just by sitting at home and practicing so that you can gig once a month. You need to play with other musicians all the time in order to play well" (LH). Lack of work jeopardizes the physical endurance required to project an instrument's sound to audiences in club and concert hall settings. "Performing chops are a particular kind of chops," Lee Konitz asserts, "and sometimes you don't experience that until you're out on the stand, and then it's too late. I realized once that the only time I play at full volume was when I played on the job, and that's not the way it should be. That's when I get sore lips."

Similarly, in the practice room, improvisers can only partially contrive the strict mental discipline that they apply to public music creation, where, composing under the constant pressure of a passing beat, there is no stopping to revise ideas or correct errors. "Playing a gig is like running a marathon," Calvin Hill explains. "You can prepare for a marathon by training up to eighteen or twenty hours, but the final push is all psychological in the race itself. You can't really train for that. It's the same in playing a gig. The intensity with which you play is something that you can't practice by yourself. You wouldn't put yourself through that unless you had to," he says, laughing.

Finally, improvisers depend upon regular performance to remain sensitive to the conversational aspects of group interplay. "At first, I thought that the problem was the musicians I chose for the rhythm section," recalls a distressed artist following a disappointing recording session. "But then I realized that I was the one who had gotten out of shape. I just wasn't used to performing with top-notch rhythm section players and having them respond to me." Such situations reveal one limitation of practicing improvisation with recordings, however useful the exercise for learners. "Once musicians have played with a record a few times, they already know in advance what's happening," Lonnie Hillyer points out, "and it can't test their abilities the same way a live performance can." Although there are cases when an exceptional soloist's contributions compensate for conversationless interplay, effective conversation is so valued in the aesthetic system of jazz that artists typically strive to embody it in their performances, lest their playing be unworthy of the standards of their tradition.

## Irreconcilable Differences within Bands: Short-term Accommodation and Personnel Changes

When such imponderables as the artists' variable state of readiness for improvisation and circumstantial factors of hiring inadvertently produce groups whose members have fundamental problems, leaders can pursue various short-term solutions. Typically, they adapt their repertory and arrangements to accommodate the weaknesses of particular players. "We had a bass player who played great time and could play great groove tunes," a pianist recalls, "but he was not flexible in other ways. As long as he was in the band, there were certain things we couldn't play, such as real subtle, mood-oriented pieces like 'Nardis.'" In one of Cannonball Adderley's early groups, a bassist's inability to maintain a steady beat at fast tempos restricted the group to works well suited to medium and slow tempos until the bass player was replaced.[4] In yet another case, the limitations of a bass player restricted one band's repertory almost entirely to pieces with patterned bass parts. "He could play things like that because the same figures repeated over and over and the accents were written into the arrangement," the leader relates. "We almost never played a tune that had any walking in it, and when we did, we were restricted to medium tempos where he'd be more apt to put accents in. As soon as the tempos picked up, he'd lapse back into his drone of quarter notes."

If a player tends to overwhelm the performances of others and seems incapable of self-restraint, leaders adopt various strategies to offset the unwelcome consequences. They may restructure arrangements so that the incompatible individual periodically lays out during certain musical episodes or even through an entire piece. A saxophonist once requested the leader of a renowned group to "tell the piano player not to play behind me, because he would never really listen to what I was playing. I feel that what the piano player is doing now, playing solo concerts, is what he should be doing, because he doesn't listen to other people." Some artists are simply not very good group players. In other instances, improvisers may restrain themselves, adapting their playing to avoid dominating a cohort. One drummer recounts that "the bass player and I can take certain liberties up to the point at which we know it won't get in the way of the piano player. Also, he'll stroll every once in a while, and that will give us ample time to take things as far as we want to take them."

Ultimately, leaders change personnel when unabating problems permeate the group effort. "I wasn't with Miles for long," a musician recalls. "He kept the same bass player, but the piano chair and the drum chair kept changing." Another band leader once hired "a trumpet player who was not sensitive to the group's rhythmic or dynamic nuances. This very dominant voice didn't fit the way any of us felt it should." In yet another organization, "the piano player always made the tunes rush. Performing was like replacing a flat tire on a car with a tractor wheel and trying to drive. I knew it was the piano player because when another piano player came into the group, everything was all right."

Leaders may even alter a group's instrumentation when they are unable to fill every chair with suitable artists. "That's why Ornette never used a piano player," Wynton Marsalis asserts. "Nobody could play harmonically hip enough for what he was playing." At the extreme, they disband their entire organization and begin the effort to create, once again, a complementary union of artists. Leaders typically handle personnel changes discreetly, often indirectly. "A lot of people won't really tell you how they feel about your playing. Either they like it or they don't. And if they don't like the way you play, they just won't call you for another gig" (AT).

At the same time, supporting artists also switch group affiliations voluntarily as a result of their own grievances. Drawing attention to conversation within the music, a basic value of group coherence, an older musician once advised Fred Hersch, "You should be able to talk to other musicians in [the language of] this music. There are some people you can talk to and some people you can't." The oldtimer considered it better for musicians not to play at all than to play with people they "can't talk to" through the music. Musicians sometimes quit bands when they find that poor musical communication reflects a fundamental disparity between their own abilities and those of other players. "Compatibility is the name of the game. There are jobs that pay well that I'll turn down because I know who's in the rhythm section, and I'll take certain jobs for less money because I know who's in the rhythm section" (GD).

Lee Konitz has grappled with the dilemmas surrounding compatibility and appropriate conversation within the group. "When you play with a group of people, you're influenced by where they're at and you try to match where they're at." He adds good-humoredly: "Sometimes, when I would play with a certain band, someone would come up to me and say, 'How come you don't sound like you did when you played with Tristano?' I'd say, 'Because I'm not playing with Tristano, schmuck!' [he laughs]." His elaboration portrays the experience of a young player being drawn into more sophisticated communication than he had encountered previously.

> Basically, I tended to play simpler with this particular group than I would with Tristano. Playing with Tristano's band got me to try to play as intricately and as intensely as possible. I didn't have to be that intricate, but after Lennie and Warne Marsh got through with their solos, I felt a little funny playing simply. I would want to play my eighth notes and make them as intricate as theirs. And believe me, they really got intricate. When I was with Tristano, it became clear to me that I had to find a situation where I was really able to function best, because I felt that the music was way over my head.

There are instances when musicians simply tire of a band's repertory. "I liked one band's music, but I couldn't have spent five years playing it," a bass player maintains. "It was a lot simpler than other bands, that is, the rhythms and chord progressions." A pianist complains in a similar vein, "I've been in situations in which I've been terribly bored. I did one month on the road with a band where the music was all in C minor, and it was all modal, loud, and intense. Sometimes, you feel like that. But other times, it's nice to play something simple or something pretty or something with variety in it. I learned from that, that you don't put yourself in that kind of situation unless you really know that it's right for you, especially on the road. When the music is the only thing that you have to look forward to during the day and you don't look forward to it, it's really treacherous."

Intersecting matters of taste are such other repertory issues as the relative difficulty of pieces and the appropriateness of specific pieces to individual artists. Musicians desiring to present their own musical ideas in a flattering light are interested in the pieces' effectiveness as vehicles for their own improvisations. Dissatisfaction can also arise over features of arrangements. One saxophonist whose pieces contained extraordinarily elaborate bass parts could not convince local bass players that the value of his music warranted the time and effort required for its mastery. Eventually, he gave up the notion of maintaining a group to perform his compositions. Another saxophonist left a group because its tempos were uniformly fast, rendering the music uniformly "boring." A third player objected to his former group's dynamic level: "I wish that Miles had called me for one of his earlier bands because, during that period, everything in the band was electric. At first, I couldn't hear myself at all, and I'd come away some nights with my neck sore from trying to open up and get up over all the loud, electronic music." Other complaints portray the unsympathetic character of a leader who features his own protracted solos on every tune, "bogging the music down" and minimizing the opportunity for other players to solo. Also resented is the leader who features only sidemen as soloists when the group performs for unknowing audiences in small towns, thus preventing the other artists from gaining professional exposure for their own careers.

Improvisers also appraise the idiomatic bounds that bands adopt for collective interplay. "I sometimes get tired of groups using the old bebop school format," a pianist confesses. "A solo goes this way, a drummer plays brushes on one chorus, sticks on the next, the soloists trade fours, the group plays the head then tags out three times. Sometimes, it's musical to play that way, but sometimes, I want to play other ways." On the other hand, he admits, "I admire structural Western composers too much to get into jazz that's nonstructural embellishment, unless the music has the power of a John Coltrane or maybe a McCoy Tyner. Music needs something to compensate for the lack of form."

Finding a satisfying balance between these poles is not always a simple matter, as Roberta Baum's reflections on this problem indicate:

> One group was too conventional. The players weren't responding to me, and it really dragged me emotionally. The second group I sang with came a lot closer to having the kind of freedom that I wanted to have, since that was what they were doing in their own music. They were willing to take chances, creating a kind of anarchistic climax within the structure of the piece. But after a year of playing with the second group, I began to feel that playing outside was also a limitation. Sometimes, the other players didn't know where they were going. Other times, they became so busy that I couldn't get my ideas off. When things become too anarchistic, you can be overwhelmed by the sound. So, there can be different problems at each end.

Finally, conflicts within the overlapping domains of musical and interpersonal relationships require creative approaches to their resolution. Billing, salary, and status, for example, may become contested issues within groups. Other grievances are unfair compensation for, or lack of acknowledgment of, individual members' participation in and contributions to such collaborative music-making ventures as composing and arranging pieces.[5]

A musician's personality is another of the variables within the larger mix of conditions that can affect collective musicianship. "You have to be prepared to deal with the different musicians you come in contact with, because they're all different," Kenny Washington says. "So, you have to bend to be able to play with them, personality-wise, on and off the bandstand. Betty Carter would really be tough on the young musicians because she didn't want them to get into anything bad. Sometimes, she wanted to mother the band. Johnny Griffin was more or less a freestyle person. He used to say, 'If you don't have some fun, you can go out of your mind on the road.'"

Artists differ, indeed, in the kind of social relationships they cultivate within bands. Some confine their interaction with band members to the settings in which they rehearse and perform together. Others hold the ideal that a band should function much like an extended family. Curtis Fuller represents this view: "With the Messengers, we hung out together. It's like the group that hangs together, plays together. We didn't just meet on the bandstand. It was nothing to see Freddie Hubbard and Wayne Shorter and myself together all day long."

Such close relationships can work only among players who have compatible personalities and lifestyles. At the very least, there must be tolerance for each other's differences and mutual admiration for one another's musicianship. "Working with Max Roach," Calvin Hill recalls, "was not only important to me because of his music, but because of the tremendous dignity that he brought to the music, the respect with which he treated other people, and the respect they had for him." In contrast, a musician recalls his brief tenure with a group in which players did not share the same values: "I didn't go out with the others and hang out and get high. I remember the drummer once saying to me, 'Man. Why don't you ever hang out? You hold yourself apart.' I said, 'I have to play with you. That's my job. It doesn't mean I have to marry you and do what you do.' It's nice when everybody likes everybody in a group, but I'll be damned if I'm going to smoke dope and drink just so other people will think I'm nice."

Sometimes, the overlapping realms of music making and interpersonal relations combine in experiences that have musical ramifications for artists beyond the life of a band. When the intimate relationship between one member of a band and its singer went awry, the singer formed her own group, featuring a new repertory of original love songs. The texts were veiled commentaries, each dealing with different aspects of the soured affair. Gradually, as the performance of the new repertory assuaged her hurt, those songs assumed less prominence in her performances.

A personal tragedy left its mark on the repertory of Max Roach's bands. Roach recounted the details to me in a story already familiar through retelling within his groups. In the fifties, Roach formed a group together with prodigy Clifford Brown, a trumpeter of originality and virtuosity whose warmth and generosity of spirit matched his talent, winning the universal respect of the jazz world. Brown disarmed even the most ardent of his artistic rivals.

The Brown-Roach quintet was one of the most popular hard bop groups of its day. They frequently toured the country in exhausting bouts of night driving that linked sporadic club dates in a network of viable gigs. With an experienced leader's savvy, Roach had implemented an unwavering "cardinal rule" for his road bands, insisting that they travel in a "caravan," rotating shifts within each car: one member to drive, a second to stay awake and keep the driver from "dozing," the third to sleep in the back seat. With a certain job approaching in Chicago, however, Clifford Brown wanted to leave Philadelphia a day ahead of schedule so that he could stop en route to try out a new trumpet manufactured in Indiana. He pleaded with Roach, who repeatedly denied Brown the request. Worn down, at last, by Brown's ingenuous style of persistence, Roach relented, despite the vague feeling of uneasiness about the decision that stayed with him.

Brown left Philadelphia with pianist Richie Powell and Powell's bride, in a new car that had been her wedding gift. Late that night, they encountered a torrential rainstorm. Mrs. Powell, at the wheel, struggled to see clearly through thick glasses, her visual impairment compounded by the rain on the windshield. Taking a wrong highway exit, she made an impulsive turn to correct the error and drove the car into a deep ditch beside the lane, carrying all the occupants to instant deaths. Throughout the country, musicians mourned their community's tragic loss of talent. Clifford Brown was twenty-five years old; Richie Powell, twenty-four.

Roach was grief-stricken and haunted by an irrational sense of responsibility for the accident. The powerful emotion of the event reawakened his anger over related issues of racism in America, particularly the lack of economic support for African American music that requires jazz musicians to endure the risky life on the road.[6] The death of his good friend and colleague ushered in a long period of sadness for Roach. Only gradually did he free himself from his despondency. Ironically, the experience revisited Roach a few years later when Clifford Brown's replacement, Booker Little, an equally prodigious talent for whom Roach had also developed affection and respect, died of uremia at the unseemly age of twenty-three. The coincidental tragedies left Roach with a somewhat "superstitious" attitude that, as he sought to insulate himself from painful memories, temporarily influenced his hiring practices. For many years, his band's trumpet chair was often vacant, silencing the trumpet's voice in their music.[7]

In the face of wide-ranging personal and artistic factors that affect the inner workings of groups, many bands are fluid units. Some coalesce to enjoy limited success before disbanding, whereas others enjoy long lives by maintaining their identities in the face of continuous personnel changes.

### The Life Cycles of Bands and the Creative Process

Bands not only turn over personnel when players discover that they have irreconcilable problems; they also undergo changes when members have drawn what musical value they can from their mutual association. Although it is initially desirable for members of groups to work together extensively to develop the rapport upon which successful improvisation depends, typically there are limits to the ways in which any group of musicians can inspire each other over the longer term. "If you are working with a group of good players, then you can learn from them," Art Farmer explains. "But still, sometimes you find the music bogging down and you need to find other people. This is not to say that the players you are with are not good, but the whole thing has reached a stalemate as a unit. If you play the same songs night after night and year after year, and you find yourself playing in the same way, people get bored with it because there's no energy there. If you don't find some other way to break it, then you have to get somebody else into the band. You have to find some new songs or some new players."

Like many of his fellow artists, Lonnie Hillyer cannot tolerate the monotony of uninspired musicianship. "When I get bored playing the same old things all the time, as guys will do when they can't figure anything new to play, I like to jump on the bandstand and play with somebody in the band who I'm not familiar with. It forces me to think. That's what this music is all about. It's a thinking kind of music." Similarly, John McNeil extolls the stimulation that new musical components bring into routine playing.

> The groups I like to play with are the kind in which, if you changed one person, everything would be completely different. For example, I was playing a blues on my first album when Rufus Reid and Billy Hart got into this weird rhythmic thing that I never heard anybody do on an album before. It would be very hard to describe, but it's the kind of thing that wouldn't happen with any other bass player or any other drummer. It was just great and made me so excited I wanted to try all kinds of new things in my solo.

Such events often have ramifications beyond the performance for the musicians themselves, from group to group and through the enrichment of the pool of musical ideas throughout the jazz community. "I like to play with other people," Kenny Barron reports, "because you can bring some other things back to the guys you normally play with."

Over the lives of bands, then, personnel changes can be a normal consequence of the creative process. In a sense, they reflect, on the largest formal scale, improvisation's cyclical interplay of new and old ideas. Just as successful patterns initially improvised by one player and immediately complemented by the others can join a band's formal arrangement as fixed features for subsequent performances, additional facets of the band's interplay also can evolve gradually into routines, informally arranged over the group's life together. When their modes of interaction become increasingly predictable and artists begin to feel as familiar with the performance styles of other players as with their own, the band's collective ability to conceive new ideas in performance may diminish overall.

Within the chaotic world of the music business, as each group struggles for survival, its collective pattern of artistic growth and achievement, its evolving visibility and commercial success, and the respective needs of its members for creative renewal sometimes reinforce one another, contributing momentum to a unified musical undertaking. At other times, the pressures that such variables create pull players in different directions. One saxophonist describes his group's decision to disband just as their popularity reached its peak: "It was a shame in some ways, because we had just built enough of a following to be invited to record by a major label. But we reached the point where we were all tired of the music, and we wanted to follow different musical interests with other bands."

Similarly, within particular bands attrition commonly reflects the fact that individuals have outgrown their positions. With the leader's encouragement, many resign to join other groups where their responsibilities are greater or to form groups where they can devote full energy to their own ideas and compositions. The successive groups formed by Miles Davis epitomize the restless quest of some artists. Keith Jarrett smiles at his recollection of the difficulties Davis faced when combining the talents of jazz musicians with players whose background in rock had not prepared them for understanding the most basic conventions associated with playing ballads. He conjectures that Davis would rather have pursued new musical directions with a "bad band . . . playing terrible music" than remain complacent with former groups that had developed maximum cohesion within the bounds of his earlier musical interests. Moreover, Davis once shared with Jarrett the painful admission that the reason he had stopped performing ballads, a genre whose unique and masterful interpretation had gained him great distinction, was that he "loved playing them so much." Jarrett expresses admiration for such remarkable insight into the need to pursue new challenges, even when they go against an artist's "own natural instinct."[8]

Finally, as improvisers continue to define and redefine those musical areas that have the greatest meaning for them, their changing passions are sometimes influenced by matters of cultural and personal identity. Akira Tana's interest in cross-cultural musical matters finds much food for thought in Manhattan's international environment, where there is considerable opportunity for interacting with musicians drawn to the jazz scene from all parts of the world.

I've spoken with Japanese jazz musicians who are here in New York City searching for their own personal expression. They have worked with black and white musicians here and have come to the conclusion that they are different from them. The identity thing is very complicated. Things can get confusing, and you can have an identity crisis. As a Japanese American, I feel that parts of myself are very American and differ from the Japanese tradition. At times, I wonder if jazz can really express who I am fully. It's not the same for me as it would be if I were black and raised exclusively within that tradition.

My musical vision is a little broader than that of people who just hear and see jazz, because I've tried to learn so many different kinds of roles as a drummer—like studying classical orchestral percussion as well as jazz improvisation. Also, I sometimes feel a little dated playing the swing feeling, because a lot of musicians my age are playing funk and fusion. The funk thing is also very challenging for drummers, but the swing thing seems more conducive for a group playing jazz. Anyway, I believe in jazz, and for now I'm just trying to play meaningful music within the jazz field. But there are so many different ways of expressing yourself which have value. It's just a question of what you like.

### The Challenges of Different Bands

As musicians complete their tenure with particular bands and leave them to join others, they find each group to have contributed different aspects of their musicianship and knowledge. "Playing with each group is a formal education," Walter Bishop Jr. declares. "Each has a different feel and different repertory." Living with the compositions of some bands night after night, improvisers become fluent with complex chord progressions, perhaps, whereas the repertory of other bands may favor vamp tunes that artists use to create music from spare harmonic materials.[9] Musicians also gain experience playing different musical roles within the structures of various kinds of pieces. "It's true that in Bill Evans's band my function was pretty much to hold Bill's bass line through the duration of the performance," Chuck Israels says. "But I never felt it as a restriction, because the lines were so beautiful in all their detail. In other bands, the demands on me were much less specific and I had greater freedom." It was while sitting in with Barry Harris, Keith Copeland recalls, that he got his "loud/soft bass drum technique together, because I figured playing with Barry I didn't really have to drop all those bombs. It scared me to have to deal with this technique with Barry, but," he confesses, "it made me a better drummer."

Characteristic features of arrangements also have their influence on band members. "In Max Roach's band, some of the challenges were the tempos and the lengths of the pieces. You had to be able to play faster than you played in most groups, and you needed a lot of endurance" (AD). Kenny Washington reports a similar result from working with another strong player: "Johnny Griffin is known as the fastest tenor player in the world. One thing that working with Griff has really done for me is, it's made me physically stronger." In fact, before taking the position with Griffin, Washington had approached Louis Hayes, one of his mentors, for advice. Supporting the move and anticipating its demands, Hayes taught him specific technical exercises to strengthen his arms, wrists, and hands so that he could perform his role successfully.

The flexible programs of some bands encourage different players to try composing and arranging pieces. Kenny Barron remembers the excitement of having his first musical arrangement of a composition performed and recorded by Yusef Lateef's band.

Groups also place different emphases upon solo work. Whereas small bands feature artists as soloists, large bands tend to restrict individual soloing opportunity by distributing solo slots among many performers and by emphasizing ensemble work. Important distinctions do exist within small groups, however. Many limit the activity of drummers and bass players as soloists. From this perspective, Max Roach's group represented "a drastic change" for Calvin Hill because "the band was really into solos." It forced him to use all the knowledge formerly acquired with Betty Carter, Pharoah Sanders, and McCoy Tyner. "Suddenly I had to be an integral part of a group as a soloist," he recounts,

> and I wasn't playing in the background anymore. There was no piano, and Max put the four of us in a line on the stage. There was nobody in front and nobody in back, just four individuals. Max said, "I want everybody in this band to be long-winded," so we could play a tune for an hour and fifteen minutes. Soloing with Max was not a problem, because Max is a master accompanist.
>
> When I first joined the band, I was concerned about this, and he said, "Look, don't worry about anything. I've got the time covered, so you just play whatever you want. Just be free." He just lays everything down beautifully for you. You just go ahead and play. There is a lot of mutual feeling in the band. Everybody was on an equal level, and that's why it was so easy to solo in his band. You're not really out there by yourself.

The idiomatic conventions and instrumentation of different bands present unique challenges. To participate in every musical situation, players must negotiate within the group's timbral atmosphere and make the most of the aural palette at their disposal. In absorbing the blend of timbral colors, they derive a distinctive experience that stimulates their conception of ideas. Art Davis's professional affiliations depict the wide-ranging musical environments of jazz improvisers. When Davis joined Max Roach's band, the group comprised a pianoless hard bop quintet in which the unusual mix of bass and tuba accompanied the standard voices of trumpet and saxophone. Later, when performing with John Coltrane's *Ascension* band, Davis encountered an equally unusual combination of two basses. There, in the environment of a free jazz group whose eleven members included five saxophones and two trumpets, he intertwined his bass part with Jimmy Garrison.

Providing further contrast to these earlier experiences are the rhythm sections of some big bands. Count Basie's rhythm section of bass, drums, piano, and guitar embodied a classic swing feeling, whereas Dizzy Gillespie's rhythm section featured conga drums and an array of Latin percussion instruments, combining traditional Latin rhythms with those of jazz. Subsequently, Davis's tenure with saxophonist Arthur Blythe sometimes involved a standard quartet with piano, drums, and bass; at other times, an unconventional saxophone and bass duo. Other situations found Davis in the rhythm section of singers like Lena Horne and jazz pioneer Louis Armstrong. Altogether, Davis's affiliations spanned style periods from New Orleans jazz to the avant-garde. Another versatile artist, Don Pate, is "known as being open-minded by other musicians because," he asserts, "I feel there's a need for every kind of jazz: swing, bebop, free jazz, fusion. Each requires you to create different things. To me, playing with a different kind of jazz group is like going to a new city or a new country. I'll try anything once, for the experience."

Expounding on the incalculable value of such varied training, Benny Bailey tells of learning "how to develop a big sound in swing bands, how to phrase and blend with other musicians in a section." Sometimes, the precise conditions of each band's musical environment necessitate creative adaptation, inspiring new approaches to invention on an individual's part. Before the days of amplified music, Earl Hines developed the unusual stylistic trait of playing patterns in octaves in order to project his part better, "cut[ting] through the sound of the band," which had been, he felt, "drowning me out."[10] Similarly, Coleman Hawkins cultivated his dynamic range and characteristic "fullness of sound" in the context of groups that found him playing solos over "seven or eight other horns all the time."[11]

Kenny Barron describes Ron Carter's quintet, which, by contrast, featured the string bass as a solo instrument. "From that experience, we all learned to use dynamics and shading. I don't think that there was a band in the world that could play softer than us. Ron's music was also a lot more structured than some, and that accounted for the overall sound the band had." Art Farmer recollects his initial discomfort as a member of the group when "Gerry Mulligan's quartet was pianoless. It just had a baritone, trumpet, a bass, and drums. Basically, I missed the piano," he reveals.

> We had a few rehearsals, and then we went to work. The first night, I
> just felt like I didn't have any clothes on. I felt really exposed because

you didn't have any piano playing the chords to make what you're playing sound good. That was something that I had to learn to handle. It was a matter of being more careful. I learned to play lines that had musical value by themselves. Also, I learned to make an adjustment in volume because Gerry's style was much softer than others. The drummer was playing a lot with brushes, instead of bearing down with sticks, and so you couldn't go out there with your horn and start hollering and screaming.

In contemporary fusion bands such as the Pat Metheny Group and the Yellowjackets, musicians must learn to integrate their improvisations with the preprogrammed musical events of sequencers. They must, as well, pit their rhythmic skills against the mathematically precise and mechanical delineation of time provided by drum machines (PW).

A related characteristic distinguishing bands is their individual emotional atmospheres. It is the leader who usually sets up the feeling or the mood of the overall band, Melba Liston observes, and, as a member of the family, "you have to go that way, because if you don't, you don't fit in." Assessing the notion of a group's ambience, Liston brings up a virtual catalogue of legendary bands: In Dizzy Gillespie's band, players have a strong feeling "when you go on the bandstand, you're ready to burn. With Lady [Billie Holiday], you've got a laid-back kind of bluesy, sultry feeling. I mean, you've got to swing, but you're not going to holler, stomp, and carry on like you do with Dizzy's band. . . . Quincy Jones's band was sort of in between. It was . . . swinging, but still a little delicate. Not nearly as bluesy, kind of white collar. . . . Dizzy's hard hat [she laughs]. And Basie's band has its own different color—tone colors and feeling that's more organized and routine. You're going to stay about the same way all night long, whereas with other bands, you reach greater highs and lows."

Within the general emotional atmosphere of a band, subtle aspects of individual performance style and unique features of collective interplay further shape the experiences of musicians. "In each group, dealing with different musical personalities on the bandstand—just individual ways people had of expressing themselves—was a lesson in itself" (JH). Buster Williams elaborates on the variability in playing behind several individuals on the bandstand: "When you're playing with people who have their craft together, if you're wise enough, you just look and listen and learn. There is a special sensitivity that you learn from singers which is incredible. Sarah Vaughan has got perfect pitch, so you have to play perfectly in tune with her. Betty Carter's a real jazz stylist. Nobody's a stylist like her. When she does a ballad, she does a ballad softer and slower than anybody else I've ever experienced. So, I had to learn to play with a lot of space. It's always more difficult to play slow than it is to play fast. These are the kinds of things that really expanded my playing."

Close working relationships with the jazz community's renowned figures are commonly the high points of an artist's career. Composer/arranger Gil Evans praises Miles Davis's monumental achievement as a "sound innovator," recalling the excitement of being in his musical presence during their collaborations. "Like I told him one time, 'I sure am glad you were born!' "[12] Similarly, Elvin Jones beams in remembrance of John Coltrane and cites the combined qualities of inner peace, quiet determination, and superhuman control that enabled Coltrane to attain the ever-expanding artistic goals he set for himself. With deep religious conviction, Jones deliberates upon their association. "He was so calm and had such a peaceful attitude, it was soothing to be around him. And John, to me, has that spiritual context that he put into everything he did. It was something that everybody could recognize. . . . To me, he was like an angel on earth. He struck me that deeply. This is not just an ordinary person, and I'm enough of a believer to think very seriously about that. I've been touched in some way by something greater than life."[13] The inseparable mixture of Coltrane's personal and musical qualities had a remarkable effect on the musicians around him, urging them to extraordinary musical heights.

It is, perhaps, in guiding other artists to discover deep within themselves unique facets of their own sensitivities and talents, and in effecting creative inspiration that artists might otherwise never have realized by themselves, that jazz musicians share their greatest gifts as teachers. Betty Carter is "the kind of person who wants to hear you play to your ultimate," Buster Williams points out. "She has an incredible sense of swing, and the way she sings shows you who she is. When you see someone else like Betty putting everything that she has into the music, it makes you feel the responsibility to do the same. Like Miles, she has a way of bringing out your full potential."

Moving from band to band, performers strengthen various facets of their musicianship and deepen their knowledge of jazz, its idioms, conventional musical roles, and aesthetic values. Even when artists remain for an extended tenure with a band devoted to a particular idiom, the experience of improvising is seldom static. It changes constantly, in fact, with adoption of new repertory and arrangements, with developments in the individual styles of fellow players, and with turnover of personnel that dramatically alters the pool of musical personalities, bringing renewed enthusiasm to rehearsals and performances. Every constellation of musical talents and backgrounds alters the group's compositional materials as it fashions its collective artworks, and reestablishes its unique territory for invention.

In meeting the multiple challenges of a shifting mix of groups, artists sharpen technical skills as they continuously assert and evaluate their musical ideas, ultimately defining and refining their personal improvisation concepts. Bands are not simply an economic necessity for performers but are also fundamental forums for training and development. They are educational institutions indispensable to the sustenance and evolution of the jazz tradition.[14]

# PART IV

## Additional Factors Affecting Improvisation, and Epilogue

# SIXTEEN

## Vibes and Venues

### Interacting with Different Audiences in Different Settings

*Whether I exceed my own expectations in performance depends on a lot of different things—the piano, the sound, the audience. Sometimes, you play in big halls in which only five guys show up. Other times, you play in small clubs where guys are sitting in each other's laps. Some crowds are responsive and others are not. When you're on tour, every night presents a different situation: a different piano, a different sound, a different crowd.—*
Walter Bishop Jr.

Within the lives of bands, circumstances surrounding each performance introduce a bundle of variables that affect the art of improvisation. From nightclubs to concert halls to recording studios, the design and acoustics of a particular venue contribute to the "vibrations"—the general atmosphere—of music making, influencing the nature of musical invention. At every site, local management imposes unique conditions on the presentation of jazz, and correspondingly upon its formulation. Moreover, band members interact with different audiences whose responses may also guide the course of an improvisation.

Learning to adapt to changing performance conditions constitutes critical training for improvisers. Composing ideas in the tranquility of a practice room or rehearsal hall may be radically different from composing them before live audiences or live microphones. The unpredictable conditions of life on the road compound these challenges. "I was only nineteen when I went on the road with Dizzy," Kenny Barron recalls,

and I had never played that steadily before or under such different circumstances. If we had been traveling all night and hadn't been to bed, I had to be able to get off the plane and go right to the gig and play. I had to be able to perform well even though I was tired and

449

hungry. Also, I remember we once went to this small club in Cleveland, and when I went to sit at the piano, there were only about five keys that worked [he laughs]. It was one of those pianos! The point was, what was I going to do then? Was I going to feel sorry for myself and hold back, or was I going to go ahead and play? One of the things I learned with Dizzy's band was how to be consistent in my playing, how to play the best I could every night, no matter what the odds, no matter what the circumstances.

## A Venue's Acoustics

Foremost among the circumstances to which musicians must adapt is the acoustics of the performance location. Like an extension of the improviser's instrument itself, the physical characteristics of a venue have the capacity to mold and shape an artist's sounds. Improvisers derive great satisfaction from performing in a hall where natural amplification flatters the band's collective sound. In some settings, moreover, performers can play off the room with their instruments, imbuing improvisations with singular attributes. Performing on different parts of the stage and projecting sounds in different directions alter pitch colors and patterns of attack and decay. In especially reverberant halls, soloists sometimes create the impression of playing additional instruments. Playing these apparent duets with themselves, they may pause after each phrase just long enough to allow its shadowy echo to serve as its response. Or they may begin a new phrase before the sound of its antecedent has fully decayed, allowing the patterns to overlap. Alternatively, they may play rapid pitch sequences that melt together into chords or complex tonal clusters.

The success with which musicians exploit a hall's acoustics also depends on the group's size. A dry hall that thoroughly absorbs the sound of an individual performer, rendering it dull and lifeless, may provide perfect support for a large group. Conversely, a live hall that flatters a soloist or small group may devastate the sound of a larger one, causing its multitude of patterns to run together without definition. These issues are as critical to the audience as they are to musicians on stage. "It's the total sound that turns you on or turns you off. If the acoustics are strange and the sound is not right and musicians can't hear one another well, it creates great problems" (HO).

To mitigate these problems, musicians on stage try to situate themselves proximately enough to hear fellow players clearly without being overwhelmed by any one instrument. Recent practices combining acoustic instruments with electric instruments and synthesizers have increased the ordeal of balancing instruments of unequal volume and disparate qualities. As standard equipment, a performer of acoustic bass commonly uses a portable amplifier, a speaker, and pick-up microphone attached directly to the instrument. Many groups also adopt comprehensive sound systems to assist in achieving uniform sound.

Some groups purchase their own equipment, whereas others rent what is necessary for each event or rely upon management at performance sites to provide equipment.

Typically, individual musicians play into one or more microphones connected to a central mixing board in the hall's seating area. For each instrument, one or more technicians manipulate volume, tonal quality, and presence, striving to produce a particular acoustic sound approximate to the instrument's. The engineers then blend the sound with those of the other instruments to create a composite blend to be amplified through the room's speakers. The sound crew also arranges several speakers or monitors that stand on stage in front of improvisers and are connected to independent channels of the mixing board. Access to sophisticated equipment and an adequate number of monitors permits the technician to engineer a unique mix of the band's sound suited to the taste of an individual musician for that player's monitor. Sometimes, musicians request that their own instruments be brought into the foreground of sound on their personal monitors so that they can hear themselves more clearly amid the collective sounds on stage. Alternatively, a monitor's sound emission may favor the instrument whose beat provides the main rhythmic reference for the band, or it may simply duplicate the mix heard by the audience. It is when the acoustics are unfavorable on stage, or when cramped quarters require players to stand too close to one another or to a particular instrument's amplifier and speaker, that monitors are absolutely essential.

Engineers and band members experiment with such matters during rehearsals on the day of the engagement or during brief sound checks in the empty room shortly before the entrance of the audience. In the absence of a specialized sound crew, musicians operate the sound system themselves. "There is a whole different approach required in dealing with the electric aspect of music today," Max Roach explains, emphasizing the importance of attentiveness to the special acoustic characteristics of each instrument.

> During sound checks, you must listen to how the various textures of your instrument sound in the hall. You have to try out each part of your drum set with all the equipment that you use—brushes, mallets, and sticks. Its sound has to be checked by itself, and it has to be checked together with all the other instruments to see how they balance one another. And when everybody on stage is miked and you have monitors, you have to check thoroughly to see that what the audience hears is what you hear on the stage. A sound check shouldn't be taken lightly. As most professional musicians know, this can either make or break a performance.

Experimentation with sound in empty rooms requires musicians to anticipate a number of variables that subsequently affect the band's sound and to compensate for them by adjustment either prior to or during the performance. The actual size and seating arrangement of the audience can change the acoustical properties of a hall, altering its capacity for sound absorption and reverberation, in some instances throwing off the prepared mix. For this reason, individual players take periodic breaks during performances to appraise the sound from different parts of the room, and they adjust the sound system to suit the changing character of the room.

### Room Design, Audience Capacity, and Management Policy

The architectural design and management policy of venues also contribute to the distinct atmosphere, or vibes, of a performance space. Concert halls and nightclubs generally represent opposite poles in an improviser's experience; each has advantages and disadvantages. The concert hall, on the one hand, presents jazz in its the most formal setting as art music. Musicians expect a high standard of management. Engagements begin and end on time. Pianos are in tune. Typically, a band's concert hall performance of two to three hours begins at about eight in the evening and includes one short intermission. This format enables artists to build momentum from piece to piece throughout the event.

The size of different concert settings and audiences also influences improvisers. A large room with a small audience discourages, whereas a small room packed with listeners encourages. Of course, for improvisers, large concert halls can be as exciting as a festival's open arena when filled to capacity. With Miles Davis's group, Gary Bartz found it a moving experience "spiritually" merely to play for crowds of thousands, "people as far as you could see," he explains. Bartz had never played for audiences that large. Nevertheless, halls and arenas have the drawback of physically separating improvisers from their audience. The distance makes it difficult for artists to hear the nature of, and indeed may inhibit, audience response.

By contrast, nightclubs have the greatest potential for an intimate performer-audience relationship. Wynton Marsalis would "rather play in a great room with atmosphere than in Carnegie Hall. The shabbiest little room can be great," he continues, "if the people, the vibes, the feeling, the love is there." Another holds the view that "for this kind of music, we need the club so that we are close enough to one another to hear well and close enough to the audience to feel the energy going out and coming back." Nevertheless, for each club, there is the question of whether its particular features support or undermine the realization of these ideals. One club's excessively bright stage lights may prevent improvisers from viewing their audience, whereas another's diffused lighting may enable them to observe listeners clearly. One nightclub was "fixed up so formally, like a wedding reception, that it didn't allow the audience to be relaxed." Consequently, musicians found it difficult to establish audience rapport (BB). Another club's informal furnishings and spare, jazz-related decorations, consisting of album covers and enlarged photographs of great artists, present a more sympathetic atmosphere.

The general policies and attitudes of management in presenting jazz also differentiate clubs. In some establishments, the music's primary function is as entertaining background music. Its presence contributes an ambience for customers, justifying inflated costs for food and liquor, thus ensuring the club's economic survival. In such settings, performances typically begin at about nine in the evening and continue until one or two in the morning, up to seven days a week. Over an evening's course, clubs restrict performance sets to about forty-five minutes, alternating them with intermissions of similar duration. Often, especially for famous musicians, clubs clear the room at intermission, collecting door charges from each new audience.

Because few clubs provide dressing rooms for musicians where they can rest in seclusion, between sets musicians commonly visit other clubs or linger at the bar, fending off boredom. Periodically, patrons draw artists into socializing between sets, an activity that some artists may encourage, but others find tiring and distracting. Some performers partake of alcohol or drugs, rationalizing these practices in various ways: "It gives me something to do," or "helps me relax," or "gives me energy to play at one in the morning when I'm physically exhausted," or "helps me to concentrate on the music." In recent years, with increasing health awareness and other attitudinal changes, more and more artists have become "straight lifers" who avoid either or both of these substances.

As implied above, the conventional organization of performance sets at nightclubs can itself be troubling to improvisers. "It's hard to get the energy up to play when it's forty-five minutes on and forty-five minutes off. You know that as soon as you get cooking, you have to break. Then you lose the feeling and have to start up all over again" (BB). A common consequence of the evening's starts and stops is that artists devote the first few pieces of each set to unwinding physically and mentally to replicate an appropriate state of mind for creative interplay. In fact, bands sometimes take one or even two sets "to hit their stride." For this reason, musicians may wait until late at night before making the rounds of nightclubs as listeners, preferring to hear the second- or third-set performances of favored artists or friends.

In large part, the compromise that nightclubs strike between commercial concerns and artistic needs of musicians determines a club's atmosphere. Owners with a special affection for jazz—like the late Max Gordon of New York's Village Vanguard and Joe Segal of Chicago's Jazz Showcase—conduct business with minimal disruption to the music making and gain the reputation of "listening clubs" for their establishments. Many monitor audience behavior, requesting, when necessary, that audience members remain quiet during performances. In contrast, a musician describes the "terrible vibes" of a commercial club in which "the owner stands at the door, uptight about the door fee, and the waitresses hustle drinks like mad, constantly walking between the tables and the stage, blocking the audience's view of the musicians" (BR).

Management can also exercise power over a group's membership and musical arrangements. Sometimes, owners require that a group pare down its size to suit the capacity of a room or budgetary constraints. In other instances, to lessen the music's volume or to comply with local zoning regulations or outmoded "blue laws," they limit a band's instrumentation. Some laws prohibit drums or horns specifically because of their volume and potential for exciting the crowd, which, when combined with customer drinking, may become rowdy, disturbing the neighborhood. In other instances, management actually creates the groups that perform at its establishments, either unilaterally selecting musicians, or hiring headliners and inviting them to suggest supporting musicians from the area. Others maintain house rhythm sections, hiring renowned figures from the national, or even international, jazz community to be featured from week to week.

Management's role in combining the talents of local musicians with those of touring artists sometimes produces excellent musical groups whose members might not have performed together otherwise. Predictably, less sympathetic matches also result. Festivals can be problematic for the same reason. "Playing at a jazz festival is like an all-star baseball game," Red Rodney says. "When you put all stars together who haven't played together, it's never really that good. That's what I wish concert promoters would learn. For instance, the promoter at a major East Coast jazz festival is taking Ira [Sullivan] and me by ourselves this year, and we're going to have to use one of the festival's rhythm sections. I don't know who they are yet. They're all going to be stars with big names, but it's not going to be the same as playing with our own group."

Finally, the quality of the sound systems and musical instruments provided by management also impinges upon the experiences of improvising artists. Given the expense and the trouble of transporting large instruments, rhythm section players sometimes rely on those owned by nightclubs and concert halls or those that they themselves rent or borrow at different performance sites. Pianists must adapt to instruments in various states of repair with unfamiliar and sometimes undesirable playing action or sound quality. Even such apparently minute differences as the spacing of keys can be vexing initially. Bass players must adapt to instruments of different sizes with strings of varying gauge and tension, and drummers to combinations and physical arrangements of drum components that may differ significantly from what they regularly use. Such changes potentially alter both the motor aspects of musical conception and the artist's pitch and timbral palettes.

As discussed earlier, one measure of the prowess of great improvisers is their masterful exploitation of the idiosyncracies of instruments. In a legendary confrontation with a club owner, several musicians refused to begin their performance until he had tuned his piano. Bud Powell arrived at the club in the heat of the dispute and ran his fingers up and down the keyboard to identify the offending keys. He then proceeded to give a virtuoso performance in which he treated "the bad notes" as dissonances or special effects—like blue notes—integrating them perfectly with his solo. Dazzled by Powell's improvisation, the club owner refused to believe that there was anything wrong with the instrument, and the protestors lost their argument.[1]

Pianists who value acoustic qualities of sound may prefer, on tour, to use instruments provided by management, despite the instruments' shortcomings. Others, however, opt to own portable electric pianos, thus assuring themselves greater consistency from performance to performance. Similarly, bass players who travel without their own acoustic instruments, and who wish to avoid the risk of renting them on the road, commonly find that smaller, more durable electric instruments provide a practical solution to the problem. Like other circumstantial constraints artists face within their professional lives, those associated with travel can at times become the mother of invention, leading drummers, for example, to devise new equipment set-ups and fresh approaches to music making.[2]

Myriad conditional factors connected with a performance setting affect improvised performance. A cold room stiffens fingers, limiting rhythmic agility and, at times, the tempos at which bands interpret pieces. Conversely, in an excessively hot room or under the heat of stage lights, improvisers who perspire profusely must be alert to unanticipated musical events caused by a trumpet mouthpiece sliding from its embouchure or a drumstick slipping through fingers. The physical demands of extended programs also take a toll on improvisers, altering the motor aspects of performance. From touring with Pat Metheny's band, drummer Paul Wertico learned to adapt his musical ideas to a familiar progression of physical changes in his body. "At the beginning of a tour, my body is always fresh; it feels loose and flexible when I perform. But after a few months of steady playing, night after night, my muscles begin to get stiff and sore, and I'm not as flexible," he explains. By stretching exercises and massage, Wertico endeavors to mitigate such adverse effects of road life.

### Interacting with Different Audiences

The presence of an audience increases both the pressure and reward of performances, reminding improvisers of the irretrievability of their musical inventions and heightening their sense of being in the moment. At the same time, the artist-audience relationship is a dynamic and variable one, in part because, as improvisers well know, every audience is different. The composition of each audience depends, in turn, on many factors, including the performance center's location, admission fees, hours of business, taste in booking, and general management policy.

The most sophisticated audience members are, of course, other jazz musicians. Performers on stage commonly show appreciation for their attendance by introducing them to the larger audience and praising their abilities. Musician friends of featured artists may also bolster morale. Once, just before James Moody began a performance set at the Village Vanguard, a bass player in the audience offered warm greetings and added, "I heard that you were really burning on this gig. So, I thought I'd better come out and hear you before you burned the whole house down!" Pleased, Moody laughed, then graciously, as if shrugging off the compliment, said that he was just playing the "same old thing as always."

Other audience members are serious fans with ties to the jazz community. Regardless of their professions, many are inveterate record collectors, knowledgeable concerning such aspects of jazz as its history, its repertory, and the membership of different bands. Such enthusiasts do not necessarily share a technical knowledge of jazz, but they listen discerningly, following its intricate shapes and unfolding moods. Many also display an awareness of the basic conventions of audience behavior, which have their roots, like the music itself, in the African American cultural experience. In black neighborhood clubs, lively vocalized audience responses to performers reflect more general modes of interaction found within such group expressivity as a church congregation's testimonial responses to an inspired sermon or in the mutual banter between soul singers and their audiences.

Correspondingly, knowledgeable jazz audience members respond to exceptional improvisations with bursts of applause, shouts of praise, and whistle calls. Some join in the delineation of the beat by swaying, nodding, finger snapping and—when the style of jazz, the occasion, or room permits it—dancing. Others mark its course by singing silently to themselves or envisaging synchronous graphic images of the ongoing pulse. These subtler responses, more sensed by performers than visually observed, add to the spirit of the room, as audience members relax to the groove of the music and resonate sympathetically to the beat's compelling motion. At the very least, polite audience members listen attentively, typically offering applause after solos and at the conclusion of each piece.

In contrast to such individuals are assembled listeners who lack a serious interest in jazz but nevertheless appreciate it in nightclub settings. Without the inclination or training to focus on the details of the music, such listeners respond only to the most general features and moods of the music, distinguishing performances in such broad terms as *upbeat* or *mellow*. For some other listeners, the presence of jazz in a nightclub is strictly incidental. "Like the wall-paper," a musician once scoffed.

Although commonly dealing with mixes of all the different types of listeners described above, improvisers also perform for audiences that are clusters of one or two types. Some after-hours jam sessions are exclusively for musicians. Concert halls commonly attract audiences of dedicated jazz followers, as do renowned nightclubs and loft concert venues, the latter often rented by the artists themselves to promote their own music. "There are a few really special clubs around the country which have a special feeling because of the tradition associated with them," Keith Copeland explains, "like the Village Vanguard in New York. You know the history of the great players who have played there, and you know that the people who come there really come for the music and they understand it." For Benny Bailey, as well,

> playing at the Village Vanguard is not like playing at other clubs. It feels like a showcase. People from all over the world are always coming through, and you never know whether someone might hear you and other gigs will come from it. It's also not like playing in some small club somewhere, because other musicians will come out and sit in with you, like Woody Shaw came to sit in last night. A lot of musicians hang out together evenings and go from club to club. Also, out in the audience there were a lot of young players from the North Texas State Jazz Band Program. You're really exposed under those conditions.
>
> It's like that in New York. That's why the musicians are such nervous wrecks [he laughs].

With the increasing international appeal of jazz, serious fans abroad also have a special place in the hearts and memories of musicians. "One of the things that can be a pleasure about performing in Europe is that people do the research. They really know who you are, and they want you to play real jazz" (LD). George Duvivier's experience has been similarly gratifying: "In Europe and Japan, audiences are so conscious of what the artist is doing, their applause is always encouraging. They know your name and what you've recorded, and they acknowledge that when you're introduced. Backstage, you can sit for an hour after performances, just signing albums."

At the other extreme, improvisers perform for relatively homogeneous audiences who are ignorant of jazz and oblivious to the music. "Some of the jazz-dinner-drink places are just awful," Ira Sullivan exclaims. "There was one incident when Stan Getz was touring with our band in which there was a very noisy table right in front of the bandstand. A woman kept talking loudly about the mink coat her friend had just bought. After a while, the waiter came over and told her that she was disturbing another table of listeners. Then, the woman became indignant, 'What do you mean I should keep it down?' The waiter said, 'That's Stan Getz soloing.' She yelled back, 'Who's Stan Getz?'" [Sullivan laughs].

### Preparing for Audiences

The need to accommodate audiences is a fact of life for musicians that shapes their performances in different ways and in differing degrees. For many, the issue is a crucial one. "My father taught me about the audience a long time ago," Tommy Turrentine states. "It's a big factor. They're the ones who come to hear you, and they're the ones who buy your records. Without them, you don't have a living." Curtis Fuller also regards the audience as being "what it's all about. No audience, no conversation. If I wasn't concerned with the audience, I might as well stay in a room alone and practice."

Improvisers commonly take the tastes and anticipated responses of audiences into consideration when planning performance strategies. When Lou Donaldson "started out playing," he had many ideas about the music he wanted to play, and he wanted to present a great variety of things. The experience of working professionally, however, taught him to temper his music to each performance situation.[3] "I've developed a knack for feeling out a club or an audience over the years," Donaldson asserts. "For example, recently in Europe, I found out right away that the audience wanted a lot of swing music, and I just played a little touch of bebop. In the early days when Club Bohemia in New York was going, I knew I could stretch out and play 'Cherokee' and stuff like that all night. When I played in Harlem, I would stick to the blues and more funky stuff." Red Rodney has found that "it's important to develop a repertory of standards to keep audiences happy when you play commercial jobs. Since you're background and they're not really listening anyway," he admits, "you can get away with improvising if you play tunes they know. If you play standards, they will accept whatever you do with them."

In this regard, the conventional format of jazz arrangements serves the interests of listeners by reminding them of the structures on which artists base their intricate improvisations. Doc Cheatham always plays "the melody of each tune first before I improvise, so that the audience knows what I'm doing." Likewise, Vea Williams sings "songs straight the first time for the audience. Then I can take off on my own." By extension, repeating the melody at the close of a band's rendition encapsulates solos in familiar material, usually of a simpler lyrical nature, temporarily relaxing the demands upon listening and providing the rendition with a satisfying shape overall. Lee Konitz adds that repeated performance of the same pieces over the years allows serious fans to appreciate the uniqueness of the most recent version in relation to the history of past performances. "It sounds like he's improvising on that song," audience members observe. "I never heard him quite do it that way before."

In commercial clubs and at dances, groups also apportion material to accommodate their perception of the audience's appreciation for and tolerance of solo improvisation in relation to the ensemble's restatement of a piece's melody and its varied orchestration. For relatively unsophisticated audiences, bands may restrict soloists to short sporadic solos in order to increase the number of pieces performed over the evening. For more knowledgeable audiences, they increase opportunities for soloists within each piece. Performers also assure familiar melodic material a place within the flow of improvised lines by planning the use of common jazz vocabulary or quotations from popular tunes. For one improviser in Chicago, it became such a matter of musical gamesmanship to quote a favored song during solos within different pieces that his followers anticipated its clever adaptation in performances with the relish of filmgoers awaiting Alfred Hitchcock's passing appearances in his movies.

## Music Presentation as Drama

Every music performance is a dramatic presentation for listeners and improvisers alike. In a sense, both groups play interactive roles as actors from their respective platforms. Just as the design of the hall, the stage and the lighting frames the band's activity for the audience's observation, it also frames the audience's activity for the band to observe. Performers and listeners form a communication loop in which the actions of each continuously affect the other. Although sound serves as the principal medium binding improvisers to audience, the audience typically responds to the inseparable mixture of the music created by improvisers and their theatrical image or stage presence. "Sometimes, I think that you can't really understand how important this music is until you go into the clubs and watch the people play it," Benny Bailey once commented.

A fundamental part of the image of the individual artists is the display of their uniquely personal relationship to the act of music creation. At Bill Evans's memorial tribute, New York "jazz pastor" John Gensel remarked that it was necessary to see Evans arched over the keyboard in performance to appreciate fully the intense concentration of his artistry. "He was so totally absorbed in the music, so totally introspective." Possessing a markedly different stage presence is Ella Fitzgerald, who "always smiles and exudes a free joy when she's on stage. She's always bubbly and she looks happy to be singing" (CL).

Aware that performances are as much seen by audiences as heard, young musicians evaluate theatrical features of their peers and mentors in performance, at times emulating them in their own concerts. Vea Williams "learned early that the psychology of presentation is very important if you're going to earn your living by performing. Some people look for drama in performers, and you have to have a touch of that when you're presenting a song." Carmen

Lundy describes how "commanding" a performer's "aura can be. I have seen singers actually walk out on the stage and, without saying a word, convey to the audience, 'I'm a great singer and you are about to hear something great!'" Lundy adds that she herself has imitated Sarah Vaughan's "statuesque" stance. "Sarah looks like her back is giving her all this strength when she sings," Lundy says admiringly.

Improvisers also project images through their dress and demeanor. Although the early conventions associated with vaudeville and minstrelsy required musicians to assume clownish dress and stereotyped racial roles, such practices eventually ceased as the civil rights movement gained momentum and the status of jazz changed from entertainment to art. Subsequently, the stage personas of jazz musicians have reflected diverse personal values and individual tastes.

The choice of suit jackets and ties accords with a particular notion of dignity and professionalism, whereas the adoption of street clothes projects an image of naturalness and, in some instances, a rejection of perceived pretensions of classical music presentations. Alternatively, the adornment of skullcaps and dashikis expresses attachment to African cultural roots, whereas the assumption of a half-lotus position on stage symbolizes Eastern spiritual values. Young musicians commonly find less weighty matters equally compelling. Ronald Shannon Jackson and his peers emulated the "West Coast, sunglasses, cool style of play" embodied by veterans who passed through town. Among their most prized feats was the skill of keeping a steady beat on the drums with one hand while opening a matchbook and lighting a cigarette with the other. In another instance, a young drummer practiced playing with his chin held high, affecting the cool, detached posture that prevented his cigarette's smoke from irritating his eyes.

Learners also study the subtle dance moves with which artists support improvisations, the gestures imbuing their creations with rhythmic swing and sometimes dramatizing features of performance. Singers may use specific movement to guide their scat singing. Carmen Lundy periodically adopts Betty Carter's manner of "spelling out," with her right hand, the rhythmic patterns of her vocal improvisations. Other gestures enhance the delivery of song texts. "You have to use body movement with taste, treating it individually with each song as if it were just part of the flow of the song," Vea Williams says. "You shouldn't use body movements that are too abrupt. I received feedback about that from friends and musicians when I was just starting out. They'd say, 'Stop holding your hands like that,' and they'd show me how to hold my hands with the palms up when I sang. It looked better and it felt better. Different mannerisms like that are important to help you get your song across."

Lundy, too, recognizes the importance of body language and appreciates the attention of others in encouraging her awareness, development, and skills in this matter.

> Hands can be a great communicative device. People interested in my career pointed out to me how to use my hands when I sang and when not to use them. Hand gestures and every subtle thing you do is noticed on the stage, and you try to be less awkward and more graceful in your movements. The more relaxed I am on stage, the easier it is. When I became aware of how important posture was, I began taking dance. I learned to control my posture from ballet, modern dance, and stretch classes.
>
> Also, people would point out when not to overstress the lyrics, like singing with your eyes closed all the time. Sometimes, I still have to remember to do certain facial things, to furrow my eyebrows or to crease my forehead. There is so much concentration involved in a total, great performance.

Instrumentalists, too, may cultivate comparable aspects of performance. During a nightclub engagement, a young pianist threw periodic glances at the mirror across the room as he evaluated the pronounced facial expressions that accompanied changes in his music's intensity and mood. Other pianists track their explorations of different registers of the keyboard by swaying from side to side like a pendulum, or they lift their hands dramatically off the keys to highlight the ending of a long phrase. Horn players may crouch slightly or raise a foot off the floor when reaching for especially high pitches within a difficult passage. "There are ways of going about doing things on the drums that get a response from the audience," Kenny Washington discovered. "Most people want flash from a drummer. They're not checking out what you're playing, but how fast your hands are moving. Sometimes, I can play certain things around my whole drum set as a flash thing. I don't try to do this, but I realize that some things look fancy to the audience. Because the visual aspect of playing is important and a lot of people come for entertainment, drummers can sometimes get across by the ways they play things rather than by what they play."

These and other stylistic considerations intensify interaction with an audience. Vea Williams is "not a gimmicky kind of person." She appreciates, nevertheless, that "there is a kind of emotional thing you can get across through your eye contact with the audience." Carmen Lundy, too, is sensitive to the fact that at times she must "look at people or they feel you're withdrawing into yourself and they turn away from you. Looking into another person's eyes can be captivating. By watching other singers, I learned how important it is to keep a certain feeling when you are performing and to use the power of the eyes." Expressing appreciation for applause also reinforces audience involvement in the artist's performance.

Like their improvisation styles, the stage behavior of learners also develops from a fusion of their own ideas and those they copy from different idols. Youngsters constantly test and edit theatrical features of their performances. One singer stopped imitating Betty Carter's personal "choreography and energy" after failing to do so convincingly. "I just don't have that kind of movement when I sing," she concedes. "It doesn't fit with my personality or my repertory the way it fits Betty's." Similarly, a young saxophonist's exaggerated swaying drew criticism from other players, as did a singer's perpetual frown while performing and another's repetitious manner of "thanking audiences" after applause. Carmen Lundy herself once "used to try to tell jokes and be funny on stage because I thought that I should be entertaining in between songs. I used to think of things to say in those situations, because I watched other performers and admired the way they did this. But while they always made their jokes seem spontaneous, I never got a good response with mine. So, I stopped making that part of my act unless I thought of funny things that I really felt at the moment."

Improvisers ultimately evolve stage personalities that work with audiences and feel comfortable. Representing the profile of the artist at one extreme are band leaders, like Dizzy Gillespie and James Moody, who display great wit over an evening's course by entertaining audiences with ironic humor, fantastic stories, and good-natured social criticism. At the other extreme are leaders, like Miles Davis, too shy at times to address or acknowledge the audience directly, or even to announce pieces or introduce fellow band members. They prefer, instead, to allow their music to speak for them.[4] Artists may shape musical programs to suit their predispositions. Planning short breaks after every piece and limiting the length of renditions allow for regular exchanges with the audience. Conversely, extending performances of pieces and connecting them with musical segues produce continuous sets that minimize direct interaction, thus meeting the needs of those artists who prefer to speak to their audience primarily, or totally, through the music itself.

## Interpreting Behavior during Musical Events

As a fundamental part of music presentations, the spontaneous behavior of performers also aids audiences to assess musical events and interpret their subtleties. "You can watch Barry Harris and see how much delight he takes in suddenly coming across something new that's very exciting in his playing," an admirer observes. "His eyebrows go up and say, 'Wow! That was fantastic!'" Additionally, the appreciative responses of improvisers to one another's inventions can inspire players and observers alike. "Yeah, Vernel!" Clifford Jordan once exclaimed when Vernel Fournier played an effective rhythmic phrase in his drum accompaniment, and the two laughed together. "Come and stand next to me, man," the bass player beckoned soloist Jimmy Robinson at one point, thereby drawing his trumpet sound nearer. "I really like to feel you when you play."

Such player interaction is common. During a concert featuring saxophonist Frank Foster's group, guitarist Ted Dunbar built his solo to a peak of great intensity, then resolved it by strumming several chords on the downbeats of the final turnaround with pronounced, sweeping movements across the guitar's body. Smiling warmly, Foster nodded during his friend's definitive close, as if agreeing with his musical statement. Then, before beginning his own solo, he held his saxophone horizontally and mimed Dunbar's graceful strumming, raising laughter from Dunbar and the audience. As in this instance, displays of mutual admiration by improvisers put listeners at ease and draw them into the group's intimate musical discourse.

Conversely, displays of friction among improvisers reveal musical problems, affecting the audience's overall appreciation of the performance. Once, when a group's bass player concluded a solo with a sequence of sighing, glissando patterns, the violinist began his solo with the same patterns, stretching their intervals and, it would appear, inadvertently distorting their character. When he smiled back at the bass player, he drew an icy glare in return. In another instance, when an accompanying bass player lost his place, the group's unsympathetic pianist drew attention to the deficiency by loudly calling out the piece's chords. Moreover, one band's impatient leader routinely cut short the solos of other players in order to begin his own, and when the others improvised, he turned his back to them on stage and combed his hair. "There are ways in which musicians can sabotage a person's playing," Art Davis says. "Or, when one person is soloing, another can be talking loudly or looking elsewhere, obviously distracted. Also, jealousies sometimes arise within groups if a sideman is getting more praise than the leader. Things like that affect the whole group." Obvious dissension within bands also affects listeners, who typically share the discomfort of the abused parties, possibly dampening audience response to the music.

At the same time that the audience interprets the behavior of improvisers, improvisers interpret the behavior, or, one might profess, the performance of the audience, assessing its competence and relative sophistication. If the audience's verbal encouragement—or, for that matter, another artist's—is overdone or artificial, unrelated to the events at hand, it can be a distracting giveaway (PW). Additionally, listeners sometimes flaunt their ignorance by requesting only the most commercial jazz pieces or by displaying an overriding enthusiasm for the melodies of songs and their lyrics over instrumental improvisation. "In Europe, you don't have some guy coming up to you wanting to hear 'The Saints Go Marching In' and then complaining that there was no vocal," Lou Donaldson contends. In subtler terms, improvisers can determine how well an audience understands jazz from the particular events that inspire applause and from the appropriateness of the audience's body language in the context of the music.

An audience's performance may be energetic and supportive but nevertheless, in the artist's view, lack understanding. One player observes that "this audience was nice enough to applaud after each piece, but you could tell they weren't really listening." Another remarks during his group's intermission, "I see people out there tapping on two and four, but there is no two and four in the music we're playing. We're just playing a constant pulse." Yet another reflects on a recent tour: "Many audiences didn't seem to be able to tell whether the band was having a good night or a bad night. Sometimes, we'd play in ways we thought were awful and we'd still get a standing ovation. It made some of the musicians cynical about the audience, and they'd laugh about it after concerts."

In other instances, inappropriate responses reflect nothing more than unfamiliarity or discomfort with the norms of behavior on the part of jazz audiences. Listeners accustomed to the formality of classical music events may be inhibited or embarrassed about expressing their feelings vocally at performances. For improvisers accustomed to lively interaction with audiences, however, this can be dispiriting.[5] "Come on now. Come on now," an exasperated band leader once chastized his listeners. In an attempt to train them, he urged, "We need a hand for what we're doing up here. This is hard work and we need your encouragement." Turning to his band, he added beneath his breath, "I've heard of dead audiences, but this is ridiculous."

Sometimes, a dense screen of extramusical values filters audience perceptions of jazz presentations, feeding misguided responses. During one American tour, an interracial group periodically contended with hostile audience members who resented the sight of white and black performers collaborating respectfully in an African American music tradition. In another instance, a leader recalls his band's unsympathetic reception at a European event promoted by a "radical socialist group" for whom jazz served primarily as a political symbol. "They were critical of us because we were dressed formally and didn't move all around on the stage, giving black power signs. They really wanted some kind of avant-garde performance which was an angry demonstration of black revolution, and that's not what we were about. We're about making music."

As described earlier, audiences are typically most intrusive when their own performance consists of drinking and socializing, with jazz providing incidental accompaniment. Charles Mingus, like some other artists, occasionally dramatized such issues by chastizing audiences and club employees directly for their "noise" and demanding respect for his music.[6] The transitory nature of concert hall and jazz club engagements places musicians under fewer obligations to humor listeners than engagements in commercial clubs, where the length of a group's stay may depend on drawing back regular customers night after night.

## Musical Responses to Difficult Audiences

In the presence of inattentive listeners, improvisers pursue any number of options, each having its own ramifications for the performance. In the face of a boisterous dinner club audience, Lonnie Hillyer once concluded a delicate improvisation of a ballad with explosive, fiery lines whose unexpected character stilled the house for the next soloist. Approaching the microphone to exchange places with him, Hillyer's friend nodded in appreciation of the courtesy.

Many times, however, musical efforts to engage problematic audiences fundamentally undermine performances. One leader, unnerved by a small group of undemonstrative listeners scattered throughout a large auditorium, attempted to draw them out by increasing his performance's "energy." In the process, he inadvertently rushed the tempos. This, in turn, prevented his group from achieving a groove. "It's when you're not performing enough in public that an audience like that can really throw you," a member of the band remarked afterwards.

Other musicians may attempt to increase their appeal by self-consciously compromising their artistry.[7] "Some performers play worse when there's an audience than when they're alone, because they are so involved with the audience," one player asserts. "Their music takes the back seat. They might play down to the audience, playing some silly things that get over, but that don't mean anything musically. For example, I know [a string player] who wears bells on his feet and stomps around in a manner that has nothing to do with his playing. Other musicians can get across to the audience just by playing. There's a big difference."

Chuck Israels serves up a cautionary tale as he reflects on the potential for disrupting a soloist's musical growth that fawning can set in motion.

> There are players who, under the pressure of commerce and looking for acceptance, have lost their own voices. [There was a famous tenor player who] used to have an incredible way of coloring the sound of his saxophone. He had more colors, more timbres, than anyone, and you could identify him immediately from his sound alone. But now he seems to have decided to sound like a second-class imitation of a more commercially oriented tenor player. The tremendous invention that he used to employ all the time is now stifled in favor of really simple, repetitive music.
>
> If you stifle your creativity in order to try to appeal to a mass audience, and you get involved with pandering, you run the danger of not knowing the difference between what you're doing for yourself and what you're doing in order to please the audience. To me, an artist

is somebody who is deeply concerned with communicating what he believes to be his message and not what the audience wants to believe is his message. This is not to say that a true artist purposely cuts himself off from the audience. But his message has to be what he finds valuable. When people haven't followed that, I have only seen artistic disasters result.

Alternatively, musicians often attempt to ignore unresponsive audiences and play exclusively for themselves. Such conditions commonly take their toll, as well. Art Farmer plays "things that I feel according to the circumstances of the moment." When considering what to play under different circumstances, he says,

> I'm not thinking the same way. For example, if I hear noise and people talking, I know that they are not concerned with what I'm doing. An inattentive audience is very distracting. When I feel any tension or I feel ill at ease, my mind doesn't go out. Under those conditions, I play the most inside things, the safest things. I just don't think any other way. If I feel completely free and relaxed, like late at night with hardly anybody in the club, I'm just thinking other ways. The audience has a great deal to do with it. If you feel that what you are doing is well received, it frees you to go ahead and try for other things.

In light of the importance of these factors, it is a tribute to the creative powers of early musicians and their commitment to jazz that they overcame the distracting, even dangerous, conditions surrounding performance in speakeasies and other rough establishments that hired them. Jelly Roll Morton describes turbulent "gambling houses . . . ginmills and dancehouses" where he worked in New Orleans and Chicago. Beyond the sporadic violence of which musicians could be incidental victims, they were sometimes harassed by mobsters who operated the establishments. In Chicago, after changing managers, Louis Armstrong "was threatened with gangster violence" and had to hire bodyguards for protection.[8]

Contemporary musicians resign themselves to adverse performance conditions of another order, and occasionally even find redeeming features in them. "Sometimes, the informality of the club and the lack of absolute attention give you the freedom to try out things you might otherwise be hesitant to try" (CI). For Ira Sullivan,

> the dinner jazz clubs are what make the challenge of playing and trying to reach people even greater. Sometimes, I get tired of the prima donna attitudes of the younger players who get so bugged when you have to play in those places. They say, "What? I'm supposed to play for this noise?" One player thought that the solution was for him just to play louder. I said, "That's no good. They'll just talk louder."

People come here to meet old relatives and to talk and eat and have a few drinks. That can't be changed.

But every once in a while you play so strong and beautiful that suddenly you hush up an audience like that, and it's a great feeling of accomplishment you feel. Like you've given them something special even if they don't really recognize what it is you've done for them. You've reached them where they didn't know they can be reached.

Aptly illustrating Sullivan's remark is an event in which Barry Harris replaced a promising young pianist at a commercial club when he sat in with her group. Harris's masterful sense of rhythm instantly drew the bass player and drummer into a groove, elevating the group's performance from competent to outstanding. For the first time that evening, talkative audience members at the table in front of mine fell absolutely silent and began swaying unselfconsciously to the music. "I don't know what it is," one eventually exclaimed, "but he's *really* good, isn't he?" Because the sophisticated language of jazz limits the prospects for communicating with a general audience, improvisers sometimes adjust their expectations, taking satisfaction in modest accomplishments. A renowned musician more than once expressed his conviction that if only he had "reached one other human being" in the course of an event, it was enough to justify his performance.

### Responding to Knowledgeable Audiences

In contrast to unsophisticated listeners, knowledgeable audiences interpret the musical ideas of improvisers in light of the larger jazz tradition. "If I'm a mature artist and I'm playing to a mature audience, they can hear the reference to artists like Bird in my playing immediately," Arthur Rhames explains.

If it's done in a respectful way, not out of duplication directly, but placed in the right perspective, then everyone is able to relate to what I'm doing. There's an unspoken communication with the audience that way. I'm aware of my predecessors. I'm aware of this legacy. I'm aware of this tradition. It's a beautiful feeling because it's both nostalgic and has, at the same time, a very present feeling of joy, hearing these different lines, different turns, different mannerisms related in certain perspectives.

Moreover, sophisticated audiences respond consistently to a performance's most special moments—its "soul focal points," as composer Olly Wilson aptly describes them.[9] An exciting counterpoint within the rhythm section's interplay, a clever retort within the competitive exchanges of soloists trading fours, the climax in a musical idea's development, and the improvisation of phrases that are especially tasteful, poignant, or rich with historical meaning: all elicit a strong audience response.[10] "Look out now! Play it now!" cried listeners at one event when Lou Donaldson introduced a searing blues pattern into his solo. In another instance, Buster Williams fashioned a deeply moving solo around phrases with subtle speechlike inflections. Throughout, audience members filled the spaces between his phrases with such calls as "Yeah! I hear you!" and "Tell it, Buster," urging him to continue. These interactions recall the improviser's description of collective improvisation as a group conversation. In the metaphor's broadest sense, audience members enter into and broaden the base of the conversation, responding to the musical statements of band members as if they were literally speaking with them.

In turn, artists continue a spirited musical discussion with such an audience. Lou Donaldson will "play various types of pieces at the beginning of the evening, and from the audience's reaction, I'll know what to work on for the rest of the evening." Similarly, when Curtis Fuller catches "people in their little musical highs and little spiritual highs," and knows that he has "got them," this realization influences his next selection. "If I've got them going in this direction, on the next song I should play something in line with the first statement to enhance that high and take them even further. Also, I'll sometimes use dialogue and expressions in between numbers like, 'Here, the next song is going to be so and so.' I like to set up the audience, like, 'Hey [he laughs]. I'm getting ready to lay it on you!' I'll say something that will cause the audience to respond, 'Oh, yeah!' like a minister saying, 'Our text for today is so and so. Turn to page so and so.'"

Moreover, as Fuller describes in detail, musicians sometimes play off the audience's response throughout an improvisation:

> I feed on the audience when I play. You have to speak the language that the audience knows. I could draw on a familiar figure that even a layman would understand, something in front of a current hit or a blues lick that's soulful. If I play that and I see someone sway or someone says, "Yeah!" I'll stay right on this because they understand where I'm coming from, and I've got this going for me. Then he'll say, "Yeah, baby!" When I get that message, the guy in the audience is saying, "I'm still there. Come on, run it by me again" [Fuller laughs], you know? Sometimes, I'll keep the thing going there. I'll deal with that phrase and expand on that, develop that. Then you'll hear him say, "Yeeeaaaah!" or "Heeeyyyyy!" And when I see those little interests tapering off, I'll say, "All right now, come on. Let's try something else and take it another way." I'll put something else out there in my solo, and I flirt with it to feel them out to see what the response would be. It could be something melodic or rhythmic, something like a quotation, but not a gimmick. Just something that would stir up their interest. When I get that audience around that, they won't let me off the stage.

As implied above, various aspects of the experience shared by improvisers and audience within the realm of jazz are reminiscent of intense qualities of human relationship experienced "in real life," that is, off the stage. Tommy Turrentine, who generally enjoys joking and making other people laugh, says that "it's the same thing when I play. I feel good when I get a response." From Charli Persip's perspective, "there are divine moments when you receive feedback from audiences which make you feel sure that you're on the right road. The thrill of being liked and the pure adoration of fans is like falling in love."

For other artists, the expression of intimate feelings when improvising is itself like being in love with the audience. Musical banter sometimes grows out of this relationship. Roy Haynes recalls Charlie Parker offering musical commentary on the changing character of the audience through melodic quotations evoking the titles or lyrics of tunes. "He could see something happen and play about it on his instrument. Like he'd see a pretty girl walk in the club we're playing. He'd be playing a solo and all of a sudden he'd go into . . . 'A Pretty Girl Is Like a Melody,' wherever he was [in the piece]." Other times, he might weave into his improvisation patterns that mimicked the unusual behavior of an audience member. It was a function of his "fast mind, genius mind" that he could instantly absorb such material and make it "fit" within the context of his performance. Other Parker sidemen give comparable accounts.[11]

Similarly agile were the reactions of one drummer, who interacted playfully with a listener as she strolled in front of the stage. The drummer improvised patterns based on the rhythm of her swaying hips. In the context of dances, jazz musicians can derive rhythmic stimulation from the palpable pulse generated by an enthusiastic crowd, or the graceful movements of exceptionally skilled dancers.

The audience does not always affect musical events in such specific ways as eliciting particular phrases from an artist or influencing the development of these phrases into motives. It may rest, instead, on the periphery of the musician's consciousness, remaining, nevertheless, a powerful motivating force. The audience can energize improvisers amid the debilitating aspects of road life. There are times when he is on tour that Kenny Washington is "just tired from traveling." If he is tired when he enters a club, at first he may not "even want to play the drums. But," he says, "if I can feel the electricity from the audience, I can play well. In the Vanguard, I can feel the vibes of what the place will be like that night, just walking down the stairs. If the audience is attentive and excited, I can go to new horizons in my playing." For New Orleans veteran Johnny St. Cyr, as well, the "spirit" engendered by an "enthusiastic" audience stimulates his imagination; "with your natural feelings that way, you never make the same thing twice," he declares. "Every time you play a tune, new ideas come to mind and you slip that on in."[12]

Melba Liston remembers one Baltimore engagement that was "extraordinary because of the whole feeling in the air. It can be very contagious when you have a very enthusiastic audience clapping in between solos and after each composition. That night, the acoustics were terrible with echo, but the audience was so lovely, they made up for it. The band felt something special, not as individuals, but as a whole, as a unit." Chuck Israels recalls comparable events. "The highest points are when you have the concentration of everyone in the room. It's something that engulfs everyone. When you accomplish that without pandering, that is success. It's fulfilling and self-renewing. It's a real performer's high when you have that and don't let go of it. You can sense it sometimes just through the body language of the audience. It's electrical when you and everyone around you are paying rapt attention to the same thing—the actual transmission of musical thought in the air."

For artist and audience alike, it can be a profound transformational experience when the normal boundaries between them melts away, and they seem, as Denny Zeitlin puts it, to merge with the music, in effect, to "become the music." [13] From John Coltrane's standpoint, an audience member who was as deeply moved as the players was "like having another member in the group." Coltrane regarded listening itself as "an act of participation" in the music. [14]

Returning the affection and respect of improvisers, jazz audiences are fully aware that their responses may be contributing to the creation of an ephemeral musical masterwork. Privy to these events, they are part of a larger musical tradition from which they themselves draw inspiration. In the Village Vanguard, an elderly black man seated beside me at the bar listened intently to Lee Konitz's nonet perform arrangements from Miles Davis's *Birth of the Cool* album. At the close of the first set, he sighed audibly then spoke with deep satisfaction. "Look at those young cats in the band, playing that music. It makes me feel good to see it," he observed. "I know they could make more money playing rock today, the easy music. But they chose this instead, to carry on the tradition. It's a beautiful thing. Those sounds bring back memories from my youth, from the forties when they were originally played. And they're still here. The players come and go. Some die. But the music carries on."

Ultimately, knowledgeable audiences may influence the ongoing performance practices of improvisers. A bass player recalls that Betty Carter enjoyed challenging listeners with different arrangements of her repertory and eagerly anticipated their reaction. One evening, Carter introduced a new line of text within the body of an original song and used the line as the springboard for elaborate rhythmic, melodic, and timbral variations. Afterwards, she expressed pleasure at the audience's enthusiastic response and decided to add the text to the song's formal arrangement. [15] Ever mindful of the audience's importance, Barry Harris recalls the early encouragement of his young schoolmates, and their faithful attendance at dances where he and his peers developed their initial skills. "They were really the ones who made us what we are today," he insists.

Improvisers are also inclined to take criticism more seriously when it comes from listeners whom they perceive as sharing the jazz community's values. Lou Donaldson recalls that the customers at renowned clubs like Minton's Playhouse were not necessarily musicians, but they "knew their music" and could be very hard on artists whose performances were not up to their standards. In the face of obvious audience restiveness, artists may revise plans for the performance under way.[16] Carmen Lundy has learned that "certain things really worked with audiences, like my scat singing," but she has tried songs that "just didn't work and dropped them" from her repertory. Sophisticated listeners can even affect changes in a band's membership. Musicians have periodically approached Roberta Baum after performances to point out "weak links" in her groups and suggest replacements.

In light of this, the presence of great artists—and, at times, simply their association with particular venues and band positions—may create a special edge on the pressure of performances.[17] Many recall their initial panic and rush of adrenalin when, as aspiring players, they first looked out at an audience to discover their own idols seated before them. Moreover, when matters of competition and music ownership are at stake, the identification of particular musicians in the audience can lead improvisers to alter their repertory or solos.[18]

Fellow musicians, as insiders in the audience, often have freedom of movement in a nightclub, making it possible for more pointed exchanges of advice to occur in relative privacy. In such encounters, players may go so far as to challenge each other's fundamental values. For example, amid the turbulence of the sixties, as compelling ideas about social freedom, challenges to the status quo, and musical experimentation reinforced the interest avant-garde musicians in America had in extending the language of jazz, a debate intensified between them and bebop performers. Initial efforts at persuasion on either side were low-key at times. "Have you ever thought of playing free?" Ornette Coleman once quizzed another saxophonist after briefly surprising him in the wings of the stage on which he had just completed a performance set. The question seemed altogether cryptic to the saxophonist, who had yet to learn about the free jazz movement.[19]

Comparable encounters may eventually assume the pitch of religious fervor. From the back of one club where a conventional group performed, a few free jazz musicians spoke loudly and critically, disparaging the music—for its lack of energy—as "emasculated bebop." When a waitress complained about their disturbance, they raised their voices yet higher for the band's benefit. "If our talking is covering the music," one of them called out, "then how much music can be happening on stage?" An independent incident illustrates the opposite viewpoint. A pianist known among his followers as the "keeper of the flame of bebop" once arose from a nightclub audience and walked onto the stage, disrupting the performance of an avant-garde group. "Ladies and gentlemen," he passionately addressed the rest of the audience, "what these guys are trying to do here, they're not ready to do because they cannot even play conventionally. They can't even play bebop, and I'm going to prove that to you." With these opening remarks, he confronted the band members individually, demanding that each, in turn, perform "I Got Rhythm." When they failed in their efforts, he turned once again to the audience and said imploringly, "That's what I'm talking about!" (TT).

Other confrontations, revealing the overlapping spheres of social and musical change, spill over into the medium of music itself. At one club in San Francisco, a trio of African American musicians, dressed formally in suits and ties, played jazz standards. After a few pieces, they respectfully invited musicians in the audience to sit in with them. At once, a young trumpeter obviously steeped in the city's vast counterculture—judging from his large Afro and the slogans on the buttons adorning his buckskin jacket—accepted the trio's invitation. Joining the performance, he alternated his trumpet valves feverishly while blowing into the instrument with exceptional force, producing cascades of screaming patterns and superimposing them on the trio's accompaniment. Angered and contemptuous, the rhythm section stopped performing and walked abruptly off the stage. The soloist took no notice, however, and continued to play by himself. After several minutes, when the performance showed no signs of abating, the pianist ran back to his instrument, pounded the keys erratically and bombastically, and cried out in exasperation: "Can't you hear what you sound like, brother? This is what you sound like on your horn! Can't you hear how bad you sound?" Seemingly unperturbed, the trumpeter brought his solo to a close and marched back onto the street, no doubt seeking other conventional bands to challenge with his free jazz style.

Between the extremes represented by contentious experts, on the one hand, and indifferent dinner club guests, on the other hand, the composition of an audience and the improviser-audience relationship can change throughout the evening, bringing about corresponding changes in performance on stage. At the Jazz Showcase one night, a renowned pianist opened his first set before a small audience that listened politely at times but generally carried on a patter of conversation. The pianist, too, seemed distracted, his attention drawn from the keyboard by periodic bursts of laughter in the audience. At times, as he improvised, he would exchange brief glances with anonymous audience members seated around the room. Throughout the set, he seemed to be holding himself back, playing perfunctorily. His solos were relatively short, and he played many compositions.

By the third set of the evening, however, a fundamental transformation had occurred. The club filled to capacity. Fellow musicians in the audience had introduced themselves to the pianist in between the sets, and as listeners they were, as the saying goes, hanging on his every note. The pianist, in turn, had warmed up and committed himself fully to the performance. Arched over the keyboard, he never raised his eyes from his instrument, nor paused to wipe the sweat from his brow. His improvisations were long, intricate, intense. Another artist in the audience who had remained in the club from the first set expressed his astonishment: "I can't believe my ears. He's like a completely different musician. I have *never* heard playing like this before!"

## Recording Studios as Performance Settings

Opportunities to record enable groups to enhance their reputations by reaching a wider audience than through formal music events. In contrast to performance settings where improvisers interact with a live audience, recording studios present a characteristically severe atmosphere. However, with technological advances in recording, artists have potential to control the products of their performances before they reach listeners. In collaboration with studio and management personnel, improvisers manipulate the band's sound in countless ways. By recording each instrument with individual microphones and running its signal through equalizers attached to the main recording deck, engineers can alter the instrument's voice, rendering it, for example, richer and darker or thinner and brighter on the tape. They can also change the collective sound of a group by adding special effects like reverberation or manipulating the overall balance of separate recording tracks, possibly pulling back instrumental parts to highlight a singer's words within the music, or pulling back the singer's voice and treating it simply as another instrumental color.

In addition to its effect on the initial recorded performance, recording technology enables musicians to edit their taped material. They can overdub earlier performances, recording new parts and adding them to the music's texture. Or they can re-record multiple versions of the exact same part, superimposing them on one another to thicken its sound. Alternatively, they can create a composite version of repeated performances by splicing together excerpts of particularly successful phrases from different takes to create an optimal solo or by combining the best sections of an ensemble's renditions of a piece into a definitive version.[20] Under certain circumstances, they can fuse portions of studio recordings together with highlights of live recorded performances. Such devices even allow contemporary artists to produce performances that exceed their natural technical abilities. They might record separately extensive introductions or cadenzas that, in and of themselves, would tax endurance to the limit, then splice them to the main body of improvised choruses so that they appear to be part of the same performance. Moreover, studio technicians can remove performance errors to replace them with corrected versions of problematic passages.

Many performers and groups take advantage of the studio's editing capabilities because they recognize that the medium of recordings places them in a particularly vulnerable position as artists. Mistakes that passed unnoticed in the heat of live performances can detract from the music when subjected to repeated hearings. For all the value of such technological tools, however, improvisers are sometimes inclined to view them as crutches. Lou Donaldson never evaluates "musicians from their records. They are made under a different set of circumstances where they can make over what they don't like. You have to hear musicians in person to be able to judge them."

As a trade-off for the advantages they enjoy in the studio, players contend with numerous constraints that distinguish their performances from live events. Until relatively recently, the time constraints of a recording forced musicians to compress the length of presentations substantially. Lee Konitz recalls that the arrangements for Miles Davis's *Birth of the Cool* album "were between three and four minutes long. In those days, arrangements were written for one side of a 78 record." Similarly, Max Roach has sometimes limited his own solos to "two choruses" on recordings with his band.

The convention of restricted performances carried over to varying degrees from 78s to long-playing 78s and 33 rpm recordings. Although the space on 33 rpm LPs could be used for open-ended improvisations within the structure of a single piece, the recording industry—interested in reissuing earlier material and, perhaps, in keeping close to the conventional lengths of cuts for popular music—most often used the format to record an increased number of short renditions of pieces. In the thirties, experimental recordings of Duke Ellington compositions and recordings of jam sessions in extended performances proved notable exceptions to this practice.[21] Also unusual were such landmarks of the early avant-garde movement as Ornette Coleman's *Free Jazz* and John Coltrane's *Ascension,* whose continuous performances occupy the complete sides of albums.

Pressures of recording lead some improvisers to restrain other features of their performances than their length. George Duvivier recalls that outside the studio "you had plenty of liberty with Billie Holiday because she was that kind of a singer. She slid all around the changes. You could play almost anything behind her, as long as you didn't play a wrong note. A lot of the music was based on head arrangements, except when we went into the studio. Then, of course, we had written arrangements, which were different. If you listen to any of her recordings, you'll hear the bass is just basic playing—good, steady, and solid. I didn't play any flourishes or anything."

For a number of reasons tied to contracts and studio expenses, artists may adopt special performance strategies for recording sessions. When, as is commonly the case, a company absorbs the costs of recording studio operations and pays improvisers an hourly rate for sessions, it endeavors to limit each album's studio time. Should contracts stipulate that, beyond the initial session payment, a company pay band leaders (and in some instances supporting players) royalties on the basis of record sales, it commonly debits studio charges and numerous other expenses associated with the album's production from the musicians' accounts before allowing them to share in a recording's profits. Aware that performance errors may require recording multiple takes of pieces, each take having direct economic consequences, and aware, too, that they may not have the power to correct problems to their satisfaction in every part, musicians sometimes work out more formal improvisational sketches for recording sessions than for concerts. At the extreme, they occasionally compose complete models for solos and accompanying parts.[22]

Differing concerns about music ownership can influence recorded improvisation as well. Don Pate describes a bass player who refrained from introducing his "most advanced material" on recordings, fearing that others would copy them more easily than they could from his live performances. Pate himself does not share this anxiety. He views recordings, rather, as a useful medium for documenting the authorship of his most recent ideas. "If other people can cop my ideas from records and do more than I can with them," he adds with characteristic bravado, "they're welcome to them."

In response to the changing technology of recording over the years, improvisers have contended with a number of artificial conditions imposed on performances in order to enhance their recorded sound. During the era of acoustical recording from the late nineteenth century to the twenties of this century, groups arranged themselves in the studio so as to balance the single signal that the recording horn of early machines could receive. To achieve this, the musicians adapted to unfamiliar physical arrangements of instruments and, at times, even modified their instrumentation to accommodate the equipment's limits for mechanical reproduction and processing of particular instruments' sounds. "Tuba or bass saxophone or the pianist's left hand" commonly substituted for string bass. At times, drummers reduced their instrumentation to woodblocks, the rims of snare and bass drums, and cymbals, whose use they restrained. Moreover, brass players sometimes faced "the side wall of the studio" instead of playing into the recording horn so that the sounds of their instruments would overwhelm neither the recording equipment nor the music. These restrictions eased around 1925 with the advent of electrical recording techniques.[23]

Since the development in the fifties of two-track magnetic tape and multitrack recording, companies have favored other strategic practices in the studio. Engineers sometimes separate musicians with acoustic dividers so that the sound does not bleed from one microphone to another. The isolation of individual parts on different tape tracks maximizes the possibilities for subsequent editing and facilitates potential subtle adjustments in balancing the different parts when engineers transfer their signals and combine them, for the final master tape, on the two main channel tracks, right and left.

Acoustic dividers sometimes sacrifice the visual contact that normally assists interaction among improvisers, thus requiring players to use headphones to hear each other clearly. At an extreme, studios may even record band members separately. In such cases, individuals improvise their parts to the prerecorded performances of other players, or a mechanical click track that delineates the music's beat, or a combination of the two. Although such practices provide the cleanest isolation of parts, they also minimize the possibilities for musical interplay among artists. Moreover, the mechanical beat of the click track does not accommodate the subtle ebb and flow of time that is an important aspect of the rhythmic life of collective improvisations. Although they eventually oblige, young performers initially find such contrivances to be unnerving.

Some engineers regard the model of a clean sound favored by certain other studios as sterile. To achieve a more acceptable sound, they attempt to create as natural an environment in the studio as possible. Such technicians minimize the separation of musicians and balance instruments through the strategic placement of different microphones, creating the final mix during the actual recording. Correspondingly, they strive to capture the rich timbral blend of instruments typical in live performances, including the unique effect on the group sound of the original room's acoustics. Some engineers apply the same technique during a recording session that they use when recording a live performance for projected release to the public.

Engineers favoring a live or organic mix accept the limitations of the technique and its risks. If they wrongly place a performance mike, the resultant imbalance of the recording is difficult to change later. Organic mixes similarly reduce potential editing. Accepting this challenge, musicians take special pride in successful first-take performances, which are not only relatively flawless technically but possess a spirit of freshness that is difficult to maintain over the course of multiple takes. In fact, many improvisers and engineers prefer to live with minor performance flaws in order to realize their ideals for sound quality and spontaneous expression. The Blue Note recordings of the fifties and sixties remain a testament to the success of such ventures, having intelligently overcome the studio's normal obstacles to simulate the excitement of live performances.

Record companies differ in the control they exert over the content and production of albums. They exercise great power simply because they offer record contracts to a few groups among many within the jazz community. In some instances, a company actually creates bands, fashioning them according to budgetary concerns and the tastes of its producers. The company may maintain a house rhythm section, adding different soloists to create new bands. They may also rotate positions among a basic collection of artists, featuring different individuals as band leaders from album to album. Groups may also consist of a mixture that draws from performers under contract to the company, artists on contractual loan from other recording companies, and newcomers to the jazz community, including players at various stages of musical development. It can be a rude shock to a band leader who, having worked for years with the same players to cultivate a unique group sound, discovers that producers have the power to remake the band they invited to record, replacing any or all the other members of the original group.

Having put together a band or having contracted with an established one, companies afford improvisers various degrees of artistic freedom in the studio. Over the years, artists have typically had the most control when working with smaller independent companies such as Blue Note, Riverside, Contemporary, and Impulse! rather than major companies such as Victor, Decca, and Columbia.[24] Beyond general ideological differences distinguishing the major from the independent labels, the policies and procedures of individual companies, and the nature of the artistic productions they support, are influenced by numerous considerations, including, always, the fluctuating economy and changes in public taste, and, from time to time, such specific crises as the 1942 American Federation of Musicians' recording ban and shortages of raw materials for records.[25]

At one extreme, management may simply play a supporting role, relying upon artists to conduct and evaluate their own performances. More often, management interacts more directly with artists to dictate various terms for recordings and strike compromises between artist issues and commercial concerns. Company employees with overlapping spheres of influence, such as producers, musical arrangers, and those designated as artist and repertory (A and R) personnel, commonly play a role in developing material for recordings. In an effort to reach a broad commercial market, they sometimes require that artists choose compositions from a prescribed list of pieces with popular appeal, at times insisting on particular genres.[26] During the swing era, the vigorous efforts of music publishers to promote their latest popular song acquisitions were themselves an enticement for record companies to turn out recorded versions of commercially successful pieces, taking advantage of the publicity surrounding them.[27]

Also affecting decisions about repertory are legal considerations, a subject that has peppered artists' public and private accounts from the time they first began their associations with the industry to this very day. American copyright law requires record companies to pay royalties, on the basis of ongoing record

sales, to the copyright claimants, typically the composers and the music publishing houses associated with the pieces the record companies use.[28] For the
most part, the copyright law does not distinguish between a fully arranged
performance of a piece, in which, for example, a dance band treats the piece's
melody as an end in itself, and a performance in which a jazz group uses the
piece as a vehicle for its own invention. Correspondingly, the law fails to recognize as composition improvised solos and accompaniment, which characterize
the greater part of a jazz group's performance. Recording companies are not
compelled to make the same financial arrangements with improvisers that they
must with other composers.

As suggested earlier, small companies typically pay improvisers—band
leaders and supporting players—only once for their participation in the album's recording session, just as for dance band musicians. Precise practices
vary considerably from company to company, of course, and depend as well
on the reputation of artists. During the forties, "performance royalty payments
[were] a standard provision with the name bandleaders on the major labels."[29]
There have also been more recent cases of "'star' sidemen . . . insisting on a
royalty payment." According to Rachied Ali, John Coltrane was among the
first leaders to make such arrangements with companies on behalf of other
band members.[30]

Their increasing awareness of the implications of recording company
practices provided the impetus in the forties for many improvisers to begin
composing and recording original pieces.[31] Some, with legal assistance,
formed their own publishing companies to receive royalties from record companies. Many record companies also established their own publishing affili-
ates, subsequently requiring improvisers to sign over the publication rights of
their original pieces as part of the terms of recording contracts. This practice,
which continues today, includes the materials that a company sometimes encourages musicians to create extemporaneously and treats, for the purposes
of the recording, as original compositions: simple blues riff tunes, elaborate
improvised melodies, and transformed versions of popular songs falling within
the copyright law's permissible usage guidelines.[32] With publication rights to
a piece, a company can, in effect, pay itself royalties for the use of a piece, as
well as gain profit from its use by other recording companies.[33]

Companies implement various repertory strategies in accord with their
interests. At times, they may prefer to re-record new versions of pieces whose
publication rights they already own and release them on different albums rather
than record new pieces that obligate them to pay royalties. At other times, a
company's interest in increasing its inventory of different title offerings for
prospective listeners may lead it to select popular tunes that other musicians on
its label have not yet recorded. Whatever the rationale behind such repertorial
choices, decisions that defy the artist's sense of musical value can become the

basis for contention and even legal action on the part of musicians attempting to break their contracts (AT).

On the other hand, ideas originating with the production staff, even over an artist's initial objections, may produce positive results leaving a significant imprint on the jazz tradition. Incidents involving Coleman Hawkins bear this out. He related that he was not interested initially in either playing or recording "Body and Soul," an eventual jazz classic, and the idea for his innovative saxophone solo rendition of "Picasso" was greatly influenced by the record's producer. Also contributing to the jazz tradition are unexpected musical saves brought about by the pressures of studio recording that subsequently serve as influential models for other artists. There are accounts that attribute Louis Armstrong's invention of scat singing to his instantaneous improvisation of vocables when he forgot the words to a song during a recording session.[34]

As in the choice of repertory, studios differ in policy as to whether they encourage a group to arrange its own material or rely upon their own production staff to perform this function, factors that help define a group's sound and musical identity. Economic pressures on a company, such as a low operating budget, a narrow profit margin, or "small sales and limited distribution," can suggest a policy of simple, uniform arrangements requiring "little planning or rehearsal."[35]

When performers share the taste, and admire the skills, of staff arrangers who provide assistance, they benefit from the company's practices. So, too, do performers who have yet to develop strong musical personalities or who lack expertise sufficient for arranging music themselves. Others are less happy with this partnership. Should company producers insist upon arrangements that artists regard as displeasing, unaesthetic environments of sound, the situation undermines their ability to operate as creative inventors. Less damaging, perhaps, but disconcerting nonetheless, are such practices as studio personnel apportioning the events of arrangements to comply with management's emphasis upon tunes in relation to improvisation, dictating the number of pieces on an album, and restricting the time allotted for solos.

There are companies that allow musicians to determine such matters for themselves. "Even by today's standards, the albums we made with the Benny Golson–Art Farmer Jazztet would be great music," Curtis Fuller asserts in recognition of the appropriate conditions for recording that the management fostered. "The record company gave us a month to prepare that album and paid us a salary so that we could just work on it." Some of Fuller's other recording experiences, however, provide a marked contrast:

> In many companies today, you're pushed right into the studio, playing material that you may have never seen before, with musicians you have never played with before and no time to do anything. They say,

"You're a professional, aren't you? Shouldn't you be able to do that?" These guys just don't understand the music. They'll take the lamest rock group and pay them for a year just to rehearse and work on things, to come up with one lead tune. Our music is much more complex than that, and they push us into the studio to record on the spot. They're always telling me, "That was great, Curtis," even though I may not have even liked the track. They just don't care. They just want to get you in and out of the studio. Give us the time and backing, and we can come up with things as beautiful as we did with Benny Golson's group.

As Fuller attests, studio work can require improvisers who have never performed together to create music within the structure of unfamiliar, difficult pieces under the pressures of limited time. Because recordings reflect the conditions under which they are made, from the artist's viewpoint the results are predictable. "It takes a while [to develop] a sympathetic interplay between the members of the rhythm section to get the best out of everybody. It doesn't always happen right away," Tommy Flanagan observes. "I've made an awful lot of dates where I played with people for the first time or just a few times. . . . You're lucky when something like that comes out good. It would be interesting, but it might not be the best thing that could happen."

Under more favorable conditions, groups gain extensive experience performing together, deepening their grasp over repertory before recording. "I have some prospects for recording my new band, but I don't feel that we're ready yet. I don't want to rush it," Melba Liston explains.

We have two months ahead playing every Monday night at Sweet Basil's, and that should help tighten us up. You know, there's tight, and then there's TIGHT. We're alright as far as reading and playing together, but there is a spiritual thing that isn't there. And that's what I want to work on now. I'll have to see how I can get this thing developed in my band before I go into the recording studio. For my music, it's necessary. Sometimes, a steady tour on the road will bring that about in a group. It seems a shame that it takes that, but for all the steady series of hardships when I was on the road with Dizzy, when you come out of an experience like that, your band is together.[36]

Involvement with record production after the initial recording session can be an equally critical matter for artists. Some worry about the consequences of subsequent editing decisions by studio personnel whose expertise may lie primarily with recording technology, rather than music, or who may not share their personal artistic values. Within the jazz community, stories of negative studio experiences reinforce the artist's concern. One performer was dismayed when the engineers who produced his album removed his "best solo. The piece sounded lopsided with the solo cut out. If they had only consulted me and said there was too much material for that side of the record, there were all kinds of other places where it would have been more natural to cut." Another expressed frustration that a company had deleted the final chorus of his solo, inadvertently removing its "climax," thereby rendering the solo "nonsensical." Yet another objected to a company's practice of speeding up or slowing down slightly the original tempo of taped performances, thus shortening or lengthening them for a neater fit on the recording. In the process, however, the pitch was altered; by extension, so was the very mood of the performances. At one studio, an engineer whose aesthetic values were shaped by his specialization in rock added his equipment's maximum reverberation to the initial recording, depriving the music of its appropriate transparency.

Despite the possibility of such occurrences, other artists are content, after the initial recording session, to leave the remainder of the job to the recording company. Lacking an interest in the technical aspects of record production or simply accepting the limitations of their power in the studio, they take the subject of recording more lightly than their counterparts. Moreover, some hold different attitudes toward the goal of studio work and are less concerned with how faithfully the final product represents the original performance.[37] As suggested earlier, individuals may themselves adopt conservative improvisation practices under pressures of recording—or when concerned about others copying their material—that render albums, to varying degrees, unrepresentative of live performances. In fact, there is an example of one recording in release that is a deliberate musical put-on by artists, pointing up the deficient taste of the "recording manager."[38] Still other musicians appreciate the unique features of a recording studio as providing them a compositional medium distinct from live performance. Consequently, they work willingly with record producers to reshape the content and structure of recorded material for albums, in effect treating their group's improvisations as the "raw material for composition." Miles Davis's collaboration with producer Teo Macero at Columbia Records is such a case.[39]

From company to company, budgetary considerations can affect the characteristic sound quality of records. To economize on production costs, companies may contract with a second-rate record-pressing plant or select the lowest grade vinyl, resulting in a high ratio of noise to musical signal on the final product. Ultimately, decisions at every step of album production, from the preparation of the master tape to the cutting of the master disk to the actual pressing of the vinyl disks, can have major consequences. "On one recording date I did with a [vocal] chorus, [the recording engineer] got uptight when I asked him to allow me to be in the cutting room when they were doing the master," Max Roach recalls. "He said, 'Do I tell you how to do your business?' When the actual album was pressed, I was not even given a chance to hear it before it hit the stands. I was heartbroken when I heard it. The sound was so bad, so muddy. They undid all the careful work I had put into the music."

Record companies potentially wield additional power if they delineate idiomatic bounds within which improvisers work. The company's influence can guide artists along a conservative route, as when, in order to build on past success by promoting a consistent musical product, it persuades performers to continue creating music that has proved itself commercially. Artists can become "prisoners of their own success" in this regard (PW). "The problem," Curtis Fuller observes, "is that a lot of people get branded as doing only one thing when they really have talents in many different areas. Some people get caught up in the labels they're given by the record companies, and they get trapped there." Similarly, Lee Konitz recognizes that "I happen to have an identification from the time I played with Miles and a lot of people don't want to hear me playing differently. They just want a particular sound." Ironically, the same medium that helps to create the popularity of improvisers may also constrain their creative activities.[40] "Once I was standing next to Coltrane after he finished playing 'My Favorite Things' in a club," a renowned singer recalls. "He told me that he was so tired of audiences requesting the tune, he was sorry he ever recorded it in the first place."

On the other hand, record companies can provide the impetus for artists to explore a fuller range of expression. "My music has always evolved," Walter Bishop Jr. reflects.

> When the record companies told me that they wouldn't record bebop anymore and I was old hat, I found other areas to express myself in. If you've heard my albums on the Muse label, I have five albums which document my work through all the stages I went through, from bebop to avant-garde to fusion and back to bebop. The avant-garde affects everybody. Even if they're not playing free, they become more free in their playing. On my record *Call Keith,* I did a track which was sort of free, with a tonal center. I wanted to see what it felt like playing that music, and I learned a lot about playing free from that. You have to go on instinct, and everybody has to listen. With my fusion album, I was out to prove that I could be just as creative in the fusion area as I could in the bebop area. Since I get off on dancing myself, I could relate to this different beat. It was different from all my other albums. The challenge was to do it without losing my artistry.

Artists perceive adjustment in performances at the behest of recording company demands in various ways from creative challenge to inappropriate compromise. Idealists defer only minimally, or not at all, to such intrusions on their musical decision making. To pursue new interests, they risk disappointing fans whose tastes and expectations have been shaped by recordings and proceed with the hope that they can educate their former fans and develop a new base of support for their art. Similarly, they accept that their stance may force them to support themselves by other means than music or even impoverish them. "I can't get involved with music and the whole money thing," one artist explains, "people running around trying to get a hit. To me, this music is above all that. People need something beautiful in their lives that they can believe in, that's outside all the pressures of making money. If people want to make money, they should go into something other than jazz."

Betty Carter's position has a similar moral edge to it, winning her great admiration in the jazz community. When I asked her whether she had ever considered leaving bebop to perform more commercial music during the years in which she struggled with little recognition or financial success, she replied succinctly, "No. I like to sleep well at night." Recognizing that the pressures of pursuing materialistic values distract improvisers, sometimes fatally, from their artistic goals, Barry Harris advises students to avoid disruptive temptations and endure adversity. "Sometimes," he says, "it pays to scuffle, if you can."

Unless artists encounter individuals with a strong commitment to jazz and a personal interest in the music within recording companies that appeal to a mass market, such companies are the most precarious for improvisers. Of course, individual performers may enjoy increased power within a major company as their albums become financially successful and their reputations grow. The minority of musicians who attain superstar status commonly have considerable freedom and control in the recording industry's production laboratories.[41]

For many, the discouragement of collaboration with commercial companies leads them to work with smaller, independent labels with a specialized devotion to jazz and an eye on the connoisseur's market. Despite their restricted capacity for record production, distribution, and sales, such companies ordinarily provide the most sympathetic settings for jazz recording. Some improvisers learn enough about recording technology to develop their own recording studios, where they maintain complete control over their music's production and assist other musicians or groups in producing albums according to their satisfaction. Aspiring recording artists can rent studio time to produce their own master tapes and make independent agreements with small plants for limited pressings.[42] Following the lead of many small record companies and distributors, artist-producers generally advertise their records in trade magazines. They also sell them at performances and use them for promotion purposes when looking for performance work or other business opportunities. Today, more established independent companies find distributors in the mainstream of the record industry.

Like the bundle of variables, from a venue's general atmosphere to the character of the audience, that shape improvisations at live performances, the circumstances surrounding every recording session impose diverse conditions upon invention. Taken together, they contribute variety to the experience of improvising and increase the challenge of a jazz artist's career.

# EPILOGUE

## Jazz as a Way of Life

*The music is what sustains the player from beginning to end. That's where you get your life from. That's why you play jazz.* —Art Farmer

*You keep playing, keep studying, keep listening, keep learning, and you keep developing. Jazz is not a nine to one [A.M.] job, once or twice a week. It's a way of life. Some people develop in their twenties. Some people mature in their thirties. It took me to reach my fifties before I matured. It finally happened when a situation took place where I became more secure and much happier with myself. I wasn't satisfied then, but I was satisfied that I was finally heading in the direction that I really should have been heading in all along.* —Red Rodney

An unwavering commitment to learning and creativity characterizes the interrelated music specialties of jazz improvisers, their passionate pursuits. Jazz activities blend the composer's imaginative exploration of musical ideas with the performer's mastery of musical instruments, the theorist's penchant for analysis with the historian's curiosity about the development of musical tradition, the educator's concern for making musical language accessible to the nonspecialist with the concern all share with "passing it on."

The vastness of this field of study is not always apparent to observers outside the jazz community, nor to jazz learners, who themselves view improvisation initially as a finite ability. Lonnie Hillyer laughs as he recalls the most common question put to him by students. "'How long before I will be a player?' I tell them, 'How can I say how long it will take? Why, I'm still learning myself.'" Similarly, when Rufus Reid was a young player stationed with the air force in Japan, he once went to a nightclub to hear Ray Brown, who invited him to stop by his hotel. "When I got there, I was so surprised to see him practicing. At the time, I thought, 'A cat as great as he is, still practicing just like everyone else? Still trying to get better?'"

Because many learners first discover jazz through recordings, they also tend to venerate recordings as ends in themselves, attaching more significance to the products of improvisation than to its processes. Students modify such views as they gain experience. Eventually, like artists in other fields, they come to appreciate artworks as landmarks of personal development, as representations of ideas that occupy their creators over the course of particular projects at different periods, in some instances over their careers.

Literary and visual arts provide analogies. An author once quipped that he never completes a novel so much as abandons it when it is sufficiently rewritten for him to begin another. Similarly, a painter once told me that she does not regard any single painting as finished or finite in the sense that her buyers do. Rather, she views her cumulative paintings as a film's successive frames, each work representing a continuation of the preceding one. In totality, her paintings document her life's evolving artistic vision. Similarly, in the face of their own developing ideas and skills, many jazz improvisers maintain, with self-reflective humor, that they "can barely stand listening" to the last record they have produced (JH).

In this light, jazz improvisation is not merely a process by which musicians create a record album or an evening's performance. It is a particular artistic way of going through life. Seasoned improvisers commonly emphasize this point by advising learners that they must "live the life of a jazz musician" in order to perform jazz. Outsiders sometimes mistake such remarks as references to the night life of performers or to damaging social fads that have prevailed within the jazz community from time to time.[1]

In fact, when musicians speak of jazz as a way of life, they refer primarily to the unrelenting artistic demands of a jazz career and to a particular orientation to the world of musical imagination characteristic of jazz community members. They refer to the total immersion in the music's language that its rigors demand if players are to attain fluency as improvisers and enjoy continued artistic growth. Self-directed studies of jazz history, analyses of works by master improvisers, rigorous private practice routines, and interaction with other players in numerous bands continually sharpen abilities and replenish the artist's store of knowledge.

When performers speak of jazz as a way of life, they refer to the performer's constant preoccupation with musical ideas and notions of creativity, not only in the settings of practice rooms and concert halls, but outside of them, as well. They refer to Barry Harris's students continually reviewing music theory lessons while riding on the subway, envisioning the lettered names of chords and humming their pitches aloud amid surprised onlookers. They refer to Lee Konitz whistling new melodies to the beat of his footsteps as he walks his dog in the evening and to Calvin Hill jogging in Central Park, accompanied by the mental image of Max Roach's hard-driving cymbal pattern. They refer to musicians away from instruments thinking through the structures of new pieces and reflecting on their relationships to the historical literature of jazz.

When artists speak of jazz as a way of life, they also refer to the improviser's sensitivity to the soundscape, which can inspire composition in much the same way as the visual world inspires painters. Just as a painter finds material in an abandoned field, extrapolating images from its littered formations and borrowing features of their varied textures, shapes, colors, and qualities of light and shadow, flugelhornist Julius Ellerby ventures early in the morning to Golden Gate Park to perform with bird songs, copying elements of their rhythmic phrasing and crisply articulated melodies; saxophonists Rahsaan Roland Kirk and Paul Winter have intertwined improvisations with the songs of wolves. Additionally, Winter and his band once traveled to the floor of the Grand Canyon to explore its natural acoustics. On like searches, artists in New York City sometimes practice outside in deserted areas or near bridges where their performance is partially masked by late-night traffic, adopting the city's collective sounds—the rhythmic clatter of cars and trains, the mix of honking horns and sirens—as their accompaniment to improvisations. Regardless of the route of their arrival, such sounds sometimes find their way into formal arrangements, as when Max Roach's horn players mimic traffic in the group's rendition of "Parisian Thoroughfare."[2]

Patterns with musical implications, from the heartbeat to the rhythm of physical motion, are inherent in all aspects of the lives of improvisers. "Rhythm is all around us. You know?" Miles Davis conjectures. "If Tony [Williams] was walking down the street and stumbled, he might want to play that [rhythm]."[3]

Equally potent sources of musical material are human relationships and their varied traces within the soundscape. Duke Ellington's "Harlem Air Shaft" captures the cacophonous interweaving of the collective sounds of an apartment building's tenants—their "making love . . . intimate gossip . . . the radio . . . the janitor's dogs . . . people praying, fighting, snoring," the accidental breaking of a window, the emphatic rhythms of dancers in the apartment above, "every contrast" amplified by an air shaft.[4] John Coltrane's somber piece "Alabama," composed shortly after the infamous Klan bombing of 15 September 1963, at the height of the campaign for civil rights in the South, carries the full emotional weight of the incident. On that Sunday, a bomb exploded in Birmingham's Sixteenth Street Baptist Church during a children's Bible class, killing four girls ranging in age from eleven to fourteen and injuring many other innocent children.[5]

If in some instances the improviser's search for sounds with musical value steps over the boundary that conventionally distinguishes music and non-music, in others their search leads over the boundaries that normally distinguish jazz from other music systems and art forms to commingle their elements. Walter Bishop Jr. describes the influences of a diverse background characteristic in the jazz community. When Bishop studied canons at Juilliard, he wrote "jazz canons"; when he studied solfeggio, he selected melodies from its exercises for his composition of jazz pieces. "At one point, I learned to analyze and compose music like Gershwin's, seeing why it sounded so great," he recalls. Each of these activities provided Bishop with additional tools. "The more tools you have as an improviser, the better you can express yourself," he acknowledges.

Artists also constantly draw inspiration from the larger milieu where they grow up and earn a living. "We are called jazz musicians," Patti Bown says, "but, like other composers, we are influenced by everything we hear all around us. How could it be otherwise? We all listen to the radio. We all hear music on records, on television and on films, in the street and in concert halls." During the twenties, Louis Armstrong and his friends listened with relish to the latest musical theater songs, then went home immediately afterwards to work out jazz arrangements of the material.[6]

Jazz players commonly hold professional positions in different types of bands and orchestras. They perform in a large variety of settings, including concert halls, dance halls, churches, nightclubs, restaurants, and circuses, and in the venues of "general business jobs" like receptions for weddings and bar mitzvahs. The resulting experience introduces them to musical genres as diverse as classical, popular, and rock, and those of America's varied ethnic groups and religious congregations.

Correspondingly, the value that jazz musicians attach to innovation leads many to embrace a view of composition and music history that is global in its scope. "Music from many parts of the world" whets Patti Bown's "appetite, and I find myself drawing something from it," she explains. "I like Eastern music, Arabic music. Over the years, I've been in many different musical situations, and I feel it's all kind of universal." Max Roach elaborates on the extraordinary usefulness of such a perspective:

> In America, we haven't formulated so much of a musical tradition as in Europe, and we're still free to do different things. For example, I think Gunther Schuller is working on an opera with a jazz band in it. Before Charlie Parker died, he was talking about doing a double concerto with Yehudi Menuhin. It's not like India here, where traditionally you couldn't play an afternoon raga in the evening, or Africa, where a certain drum can only be played on a certain occasion. We have the freedom to try out a lot of things, and we're not set in our ways.

Artists' most expansive views and practices reflect an appreciation for the uniqueness of jazz within the broad sweep of the evolution of music. It is as if the world is seen rotating on its axis, holding an atmosphere close to its surface whose protective shield consists not simply of vapors but of the sounds of nature, which have nurtured the aesthetic side of humanity, offering since its earliest existence an inspiration for music making. Over the millennia, within the open arena of the world's soundscape, the cries of animals, the rhythm of thunder, the wind's play upon reeds, and the water's rippling over stone interact with the expressive human inventions they inspire. Language, song, and musical instruments, each with its own implications for composition, give rise to a diverse web of music systems and technological tools for their development.

From one part of the world to the next, such systems are rarely isolated or static. Like other elements of the earth's atmosphere, those comprising its soundscape have changed over time, sometimes subtly, at other times drastically. In every country, village, and household, individuals historically perform music inherited from their ancestors. Preserving many of its features and altering others, artists of each generation create new performance practices and repertory, eventually placing their cumulative tradition into the hands of the next generation. It is as if, within each society, its selected ancestral voices assume lives of their own, maintaining featured positions within the society's musical tradition as generations of singers, instrumentalists, and composers carry the ancient voices forward, even as they themselves join them.

Within the global network of music systems, contact among different societies stimulates change in the evolution of their respective traditions. In some instances, varied music systems born on two disparate continents join on yet a third continent, where they cross-fertilize one another, producing new stylistic fusions that eventually assert their independence from their parent traditions. The stage was set for such dramatic events in the birth of a new constellation of musical languages a few hundred years ago, when European expansionism and an African diaspora removed many European and African ancestral voices from their homelands. In the wake of patterns of trade, colonial domination, religious proselytism, and slavery, these voices dispersed to many parts of the world. In America, where European, African, and Native American ancestral voices mixed in the soundscape, African composers and their descendants created a unique family of musical traditions drawing from their heritage and the diverse elements of the international music culture around them. Jazz came forth from this family with its own affiliated conventions to develop through generations of creators, preserving and expanding upon contributions of the tradition's most significant composers and performers.

Just as jazz was born from an amalgam of African, European, and African American musical elements, it has continued the practice of absorbing different musical influences. Jazz remains a characteristically open music system capable of absorbing new traits without sacrificing its identity. Jelly Roll Morton incorporates the rhythms of popular Spanish and French dance music into his early compositions and improvisations in the twenties; Dizzy Gillespie incorporates Latin and African Caribbean rhythms into his music in the forties. John Coltrane and others experiment with blending elements of African rhythmic practices and Indian modal practices with jazz during the sixties. In the seventies, a recording of bass zither music from Burundi, Africa, inspires Calvin Hill, who adapts the zither's variation techniques to his own improvisations, and some of Roberta Baum's vocal mannerisms find their source in Middle Eastern women's ululation.

Reinforcing such trends, an increasing number of musicians outside of the United States, in an exercise of fusion, have learned the language of jazz, interpreting and reshaping its conventions according to the values of their own musical traditions. A Ghanaian highlife guitarist, Koo Nimo, pursues his goal to create an "Afro-jazz" by combining Charlie Christian and Wes Montgomery's chord voicings "with traditional [Ghanaian] rhythms." A British saxophonist applies John Coltrane's improvisational method within the framework of traditional English tunes. A Bulgarian group shapes its use of conventional jazz vocabulary to the asymmetrical meters of traditional Bulgarian music, and in St. Petersburg a group creates Dixieland-style polyphonic arrangements of Russian folk melodies. In the aftermath of the collaboration between Shankar and John McLaughlin in the group Shakti, other Indian artists adapt jazz to the complex classical system of rhythm and place raga improvisations in the setting of jazz piano accompaniment. In Puerto Rico artists present modal jazz improvisation within the conventional 2/4 rhythmic frameworks of folk music genres like *plena* and amid its reponsorial vocal exchanges. Haitian fusions of "big-band swing, *mereng,* and Vodou[n] rhythms" profit from the exciting interlocking patterns of three drums and other percussion instruments. In experiments of this nature, artists like Toshiko Akiyoshi of Japan, Gato Barbieri of Argentina, and Abdullah Ibrahim of South Africa, and others across the world, in endless variations, combine jazz elements with the timbral colors of indigenous instruments, traditional tuning systems, scales, melodies, rhythms, compositional forms.[7]

Within the jazz community's international network, direct exchanges among artists of different backgrounds replenish the pool of ideas favored by local communities. Students from Canada, Japan, Egypt, Israel, France, Italy, Holland, and Sweden attend Barry Harris's workshops in New York City. In their homelands, they subsequently share their recently acquired knowledge with other artists. Harris himself has given workshops in many of these countries, as well as in Spain and Denmark. In Harare, Zimbabwe, a small but impressive jazz community includes performers from different parts of Africa, some of whom have received training at the Berklee College of Music in Boston.[8] At Ahmadu Bello University in Zaria, Nigeria, Yusef Lateef has occupied the position of Senior Research Fellow, studying traditional Nigerian music and interacting with local musicians. Ghananian master drummer Gideon Alorwoyie has taken up permanent residence in Chicago, where he teaches traditional Ghanaian drumming to one group of American jazz musicians and collaborates with another group to create a fusion of pan-African musical styles with artists whose varied backgrounds include African American and African Caribbean musics. Patti Bown has "jammed with drummers from the Caribbean" and played with "Arabic highlife type groups" in Africa. "Everything is overlapping with everything else today," she observes.

As a result of diverse influences contributing to its tradition, jazz in performance reveals layered patterns of cultural history, which are as textured in meaning for the improviser as they are for the educated listener who interprets them. A soloist may, at one moment, adopt a personalized contemporary improvisation approach, using large intervals like fourths as the basis for a solo's melody, but fashion them in relation to the harmonic structure of the blues, one of the jazz tradition's most venerable vehicles. Further along the same evolving melodic line, the improviser may quote from a Louis Armstrong solo, paying momentary tribute to his genius and to the values of New Orleans jazz, then double up on the rhythm, improvising extended asymmetrical phrases that embody the conventions of the bebop period, or infuse an original pattern with the timbral marks of a particular idol from the swing period. Subsequently, the soloist may resolve the flight of fancy with a series of sustained pitches chosen from various chord substitutions—the legacy of nineteenth-century European harmonic practices—imbuing the pitches with microtonal bends that reveal the formative influence of traditional African musics. After a short rest, the performer may adopt an intricate phrase from the drummer's accompaniment as the template for the next melodic episode, utilizing Latin American rhythmic patterns that are the historical product of yet another fusion of African and European musical languages.

In carrying forth the jazz tradition's early voices within their improvisations, engaging their predecessors' ideas and uniting them with their own, contemporary performers sometimes have the sense of escaping the normal experience of time. Such performances can assume a spiritual quality in which improvisers draw strength from a symbolic link to the past, as if becoming joined to a long chain of expressive human history. Similarly, as music systems around the world provide jazz performances with additional sources of inspiration, improvisers may have the sense of participating in a global discourse among music thinkers, negotiating musical ideas that transcend cultural and historical boundaries.

Reinforcing such perspectives are yet other transcendental aspects of improvisation, the occasional out-of-the-body impressions and the sense of being part of a universal life force much larger than oneself. This occurs during moments when the conceptual boundaries between players disappear as they experience musical invention collectively, receiving ideas from outside themselves. The humility that envelops artists in the grip of such awe-inspiring aspects of creativity continually renews their sensitivity to life's spiritual qualities and great mysteries. They ask: What is the human imagination? Where do ideas actually come from?

## Improvisation as Composition

As their personal goals compel them to deepen their general understanding of music and to establish original voices within their own tradition, jazz improvisers fundamentally devote their lives to music composition. This remains true whether they store, edit, and revise musical ideas by ear, visual imagery, and instrument, or carry out similar procedures with the aid of writing or recording. It remains true whether the object of an artist's activity is to assemble ideas into a fixed composition, or to continually rework them into transient artworks with but fleeting identities. It remains true whether they confine their operations to inventing their own musical parts within groups, or also become involved with arranging parts for other instruments. It remains true whether they improvise within the conventional frameworks of standards or within the extended forms of original large-scale productions. It remains true whether they create music in the quiet of their studios or in the context of live audiences and halls. For jazz musicians, each situation simply imposes different kinds of compositional conditions on musical invention.

In this regard, the popular definitions of improvisation that emphasize only its spontaneous, intuitive nature—characterizing it as the "making of something out of nothing"—are astonishingly incomplete. This simplistic understanding of improvisation belies the discipline and experience on which improvisers depend, and it obscures the actual practices and processes that engage them. Improvisation depends, in fact, on thinkers having absorbed a broad base of musical knowledge, including myriad conventions that contribute to formulating ideas logically, cogently, and expressively. It is not surprising, therefore, that improvisers use metaphors of language in discussing their art form. The same complex mix of elements and processes coexists for improvisers as for skilled language practitioners; the learning, the absorption, and utilization of linguistic conventions conspire in the mind of the writer or speaker—or, in the case of jazz improvisation, the player—to create a living work.

Just as creative handling of jazz vocabulary bears analogy to language use, the methods by which improvisers cultivate their abilities bear analogy to language acquisition. Participants in renowned foreign language programs agree to confine discourse exclusively to the language under study and then immerse themselves in their subject, its vocabulary, grammar, and syntax, analyzing literature and practicing conversation during every social interaction.

Each activity reinforces the others, and as students work incessantly on their burgeoning skills, they gradually become more facile in manipulating the second language. Moments of natural usage—imagined, dreamed, or real—signal breakthroughs in their struggle toward fluency.

In study of comparable intensity, aspiring jazz performers peruse their music's multifaceted oral literature, acquiring and analyzing a repertory of compositions, classic solos, and discrete phrases, which embody the aesthetic values of jazz tradition and bring to light the underlying principles of improvisation. By contemplation of this repertory, students absorb the harmonic and melodic forms that guide invention and develop a storehouse of basic musical components from which they fashion their individual contributions to the group. The components include not only fully formed vocabulary patterns, but melodic and rhythmic cells, templates for rhythmic phrasing, fragments of theoretical materials, and the like.

Eager to use their knowledge, aspiring players privately practice creating their own solos by training themselves to conceive ideas in jazz phrases and to express them through their instruments. They put into effect the conventional principles they have absorbed for interpreting and transfiguring musical models, imagining and performing versions that are inflected and rephrased, slightly ornamented, more substantially varied, or radically altered. They practice combining musical components into credible statements and developing their elements motivically to create musical episodes. On a larger scale, players eventually acquire the ability to tell stories, shaping ideas into a structure that conveys, in the language of jazz, a beginning, middle, and end.

Amid practice sessions devoted to technical and theoretical studies, developing personal sounds, expanding repertories, creating melodic ideas, and experimenting with varied applications in solo construction, improvisers live at the threshold of new possibilities for invention, possibilities that expand dramatically with every discovery. Each requires disciplined drilling to ensure mastery over its use. "Just think of it this way," John Coltrane once advised Curtis Fuller when Fuller felt at a loss for new material. "If, every day, you come up with a new idea—whether it's just one new phrase or one new way of embellishing an old phrase—at the end of the year you'll have three hundred and sixty-five new things to deal with. After two years, you'll have over seven hundred new things to deal with, and so on." The implication of Coltrane's observation is that "new things" reach infinity when they are explored in relation to one another and a host of formerly mastered patterns.

Armed with this extraordinary sufficiency, within any twenty-four-hour day performers constantly make selective judgments about materials for study, pursuing those that seem most compelling at the time. They work on some pieces and not others, absorb some new phrases and not others, experiment with their use in some roles and not others, explore the cross-relationships among some theoretical materials and not others. Each decision, even on the most simple matter, has a direct impact on the performer's developing style of improvisation, further delineating the player's personal voice. It is in this sense that Walter Bishop Jr. regards improvisation as "the product of all that players have experienced, all the music they've studied, absorbed, deleted and refined. . . . This music is an evolutionary thing. You study and apply. Study and apply. It involves the intuitive and the intellectual—learning from within and from without." Analyzing the phenomenon, Chuck Israels explains that "the musical decisions that take place during improvisations are made instantly, but the work behind those decisions takes place over long periods of time—hours, days, weeks, months, and years spent considering all of the musical possibilities."

The perpetual pressure to increase understanding causes many an improviser to become a highly disciplined practicer. Each morning during Barry Harris's early years in New York City, he would "go to the studio, sit down at the piano, and play." When he raised his eyes again, "it was dark all around me and time to go home to bed. Every day was like that." It is not uncommon, moreover, while an artist sleeps, for aural dreams in the jazz idiom to reflect the player's waking passions. In John Coltrane's life, powerful dreams sometimes provided the inspiration for new ideas or encouraged his pursuit of innovative musical courses.[9] For learners, the dreams establish early landmarks in the absorption of their adopted language.

After seven to ten years of attention to the stringent routines typically required for basic competency in jazz improvisation, some musicians maintain their skills largely by performing.[10] "It's like after you've learned a new language," Charlie Mariano once explained to me. "You can basically keep it up by speaking it." At the same time, performers driven by ever-changing artistic goals retain their early discipline. Despite the demands of other personal and professional obligations, John Coltrane and Eric Dolphy practiced relentlessly during their waking hours—in their homes, in commercial studios, even in the back of touring band buses on the road and backstage at nightclubs and concert halls during intermissions. Not only does such intensive activity keep jazz vocabulary at the fingertips of improvisers, but it provides an ongoing forum in which they can "push the cutting edge of their interests and abilities."[11] In addition, their constancy accommodates the capricious nature of creativity. "There are drought periods," Barry Harris explains, "and then, all of a sudden, there's the oasis. Because you never know when the revelations will come to you," he cautions, "you have to practice every day, even when you're not inspired, so that you're at your instrument to receive the revelations when they do come."

Training in the collective aspects of jazz is equally essential. Students absorb a set of musical models associated with the arrangements of pieces, the roles of different instruments, and the conventions for player interaction. Aspirants seize every opportunity to converse with others through improvised interplay, whether at afternoon rehearsals or late-night jam sessions. As the practice routines and informal get-togethers of jazz musicians indicate, outside of formal events they work on perfecting every technical skill and compositional procedure that improvisation encompasses.

The pressures of professional engagements further test players' versatility with the operations of improvisation and finely hone their skills. Over the course of each piece's performance, they engage selectively in various "levels" or "intensities" of imaginative play, transforming to different degrees their melodic and harmonic models (LK). The design of the band's arrangement of a piece commonly dictates changes in each artist's selection of models and approach to invention. It may initially require a horn player to interpret the tune's melody with minor embellishments, while the rhythm section, guided only by a general prescription concerning the progression, improvises an accompaniment. Subsequently, the rhythm section may confine its action to embellishing a composed accompaniment, while the horn player improvises a solo melody.[12]

Within the realm of solo formulation, individuals may also, as a matter of personal taste, shift their focus among different kinds of models, changing their reliance on prefigured ideas and varying the intensity of their inventiveness. This adds variety to a musical creation and, at times, pushes out the boundaries of artistic daring, freeing the imagination. In certain segments of the progression, they may restrict themselves to ornamenting planned quotations from the tune, and in other segments radically transfigure prearranged vocabulary patterns. Alternatively, the players may choose to avoid the use of specific performance strategies or detailed melodic blueprints altogether. They commit themselves to pursuing the melodic ideas that occur to them in the heat of performance, whether formerly mastered phrases or unique conceptions unrelated to the tune or vocabulary store.

Characteristically, improvisation perpetually shifts between precomposed musical ideas and those conceived in the moment. Virtually every feature of the music models that players bring to a performance—comprising, at its outset, composed, prefigured, fixed, or known elements—can serve during the performance as a springboard for the conception of an altered version of the model or a new one that meets the same requirements. In either case, the invention may instantly join the artist's general storehouse of knowledge, where, in relatively fixed form, it awaits further use and transformation during the performance or at some later opportunity.

This cyclical process of generation, application, and renewal occurs at every level of music making from fashioning subtle details to executing radical changes. It pertains equally to musical ideas, whether simple or complex, short or long. Soloists may conceive new embellishments for a tune, then incorporate them within their maps as semi-permanent features that provide options for the tune's ongoing interpretation. Should the artist decide to apply the embellishments consistently, as originally conceived, they assume the role of orally composed, arranged elements. Alternatively, the artist may apply them improvisationally, varying their application within the composition or transforming them so that they spawn other embellishments. Similarly, spontaneous variations on a favored scale or vocabulary pattern, or chain of ideas, can produce tasteful new melodic shapes that, treated flexibly as compositional models, can generate additional ideas for the remainder of the event and during subsequent events.

Identical processes characterize various aspects of collective musical interplay. For example, at the initial stage of the cycle, an imaginative horn player extemporaneously deviates from an arrangement's unison melody to discover a new parallel harmony. Likewise, an exhausted bass player finds physical relief in a variation on a prescribed bass ostinato, creating a contrast to the overall accompaniment; or a group, with seeming intuition, by simultaneously shifting meters or sufficiently altering the harmony, invents a different form for the piece. Should musicians regard such unanticipated results of their interaction as successful, they can incorporate them into their formal arrangements as fixed or composed features, gaining new points of departure for their explorations.

From performance to performance, the particular balance achieved in any part between precomposed and freshly conceived ideas can differ considerably. This balance is affected not only by the dictates of specific arrangements, but by individual inspiration and the current state of each player's personal system of improvisation, including its latest practices of vocabulary usage. A musician who, at one point, improvises inventively within a certain piece's framework may begin, as a matter of performance habit, to favor increasingly consistent streams of vocabulary patterns or relatively fixed motivic episodes. Reworking particular linear arrangements of patterns may lead, in turn, to their consolidation into longer phrases with finalized identities, producing an entire accompanying part or a complete model for a solo. It may even produce the melody for a new composition, to serve, in turn, as a vehicle for additional invention.

Correspondingly, over many performances, a group may choose to preserve a greater number of details from successfully improvised musical exchanges by compiling them into a through-composed, or an almost through-composed, arrangement or suite, which later furnishes the basis for further improvisation. These operations illuminate the wide-ranging processes responsible for the production of jazz, as its composed and spontaneous elements continually stimulate each other within an ongoing cycle of generation, application, and renewal.

The compositional conditions under which jazz players create music provide insight into the special character of improvisation, distinguishing it by different degrees from composing that makes use of the written score.[13] The most obvious is the condition of juggling multiple tasks simultaneously to create art in real time. Improvisers constructing their parts in performance perpetually make split-second decisions about suitable materials and their treatment. As players strive physically to implement their flow of decisions, unexpected visions routinely complicate the artistic challenge to the interaction of mind and body. So do the discrepancies that inevitably arise between conceived and actualized ideas, requiring creative skill on the player's part to imagine and execute immediate solutions to compositional problems. Because the musical consequences of all actions are irreversible, the improviser must constantly grasp the implications of ideas at hand and work them into the flow of invention.

By extension, the operations of improvisation involving more than one person require the instant assimilation of ideas across the band's membership. Musical materials extemporaneously introduced in any of the parts can influence the others, potentially providing renewed inspiration for all. Consequently, band members endeavor to interact flexibly throughout a performance in order to accommodate one another; at times modifying their own ideas, occasionally even abandoning them for other ideas complementary to the group. The unpredictable quality of the band's musical negotiations is a fundamental ingredient in every performance, imbuing its creations with uniqueness. When jazz performances take place in public, any number of factors—from the ambience, acoustics, and management policies of a hall to the audience's response—can affect the course and outcome of an improvisation as a collective artwork. It is the combination of these conditions that typically defines improvisation as a unique creative undertaking.

To use one of the metaphors favored by musicians, improvisation is a musical conversation that the improviser enters on many different levels simultaneously. While shaping a part in relation to the underlying composition—conversing with its formal features—the player converses with predecessors within the jazz tradition, creating new ideas in relation to established improvisation conventions and previous interpretations of the composition known to the player. The inner dialogue by which individual band members develop the logic of their own specific parts comprises a conversation that they carry on with themselves. To the extent to which expression is shaped by idiomatic features of playing technique, or by idiosyncratic features of an instrument's responsiveness, the player converses with the instrument as well. Artists' conversations also have a historical dimension on a personal level: in each performance, the player's unfolding ideas grow, moment by moment, out of a cumulative lifetime of performance and musical thinking.[14]

As this takes place, interplay within the band projects another kind of con-

versation, a group conversation. On another level, so does the interaction between players and audience. Finally, at the highest level are extraordinary transcendental experiences in which players feel, if only momentarily, "in touch
with the big picture." Entering into another world of awareness and sensitivity,
they feel a deep sense of reverence for "all living things." In spiritual commu-
nion, they merge together in the shine of a universal life force—timeless,
peaceful, yet energizing and euphoric.

### The Musician's Odyssey

In the music culture of some Sufi groups, it is said that each ceremonial
performance is a musical pilgrimage, a symbolic miniature version of the performer's larger goal of traveling to Mecca to attain spiritual revelation.[15] Although this metaphor has its own subtle religious meanings within the context
of North African culture, it embraces, in agreeable comparison to a broader
landscape, universal images of life's journey that are similar to those invoked
by jazz musicians. For jazz players, a performance can also be likened to a
symbolic miniature version of their life's pilgrimage: their overriding musical
activities, creative processes, and life goals. Embarking on each musical journey, band members support each other, while striving to make a significant
personal contribution to the event. Periodically, individual players rest to reflect on their musical relationships and assess their inventions. Almost immediately, they isolate particular options from among the vast possibilities and determine where next to go in their development of ideas. At times, amid the
larger performance's fluid events, the travelers encounter turbulence. Differences arise over the precise course to take; major discrepancies develop in
interpretation of the beat or harmony. Improvisers may conceive new ideas
only with great difficulty or, once airborne, derive too little satisfaction from
them. At other times, the voyage is smooth. Travelers locked into a groove
receive exciting flashes of musical inspiration.

Similarly, over the longer course and with their larger community's support, improvisers spend their lives constantly probing more deeply into aural,
theoretical, physical, and emotional aspects of their understanding to discover
new ways of thinking about music and new ways of thinking in the language
of music. Ultimately, they strive to make a unique personal contribution to
their tradition. From one period to the next, musicians shift their precise routes
through all the possibilities. They may primarily devote some years to practicing, others to performing; some to learning from idols, others to developing
their own material. To refine their abilities, in the meantime, artists may continue to make occasional studies of different playing styles, learning how to
handle specific technical matters or probing musical concepts that are currently
of interest to them. In addition, artists may immerse themselves for a period

in such other systems as Latin American or Western classical music, adapting desirable features to their own use.

Throughout a jazz player's career, economic pressures and professional opportunities affect individuals' artistic pathways, continually marking their odyssey in often unpredictable ways. Intensely working within particular bands, repertory, and idioms, improvisers increase technical control over musical concepts favored by their current collaborators. Jazz musicians struggle to preserve time for practice amid the constant demands of extramusical jobs, band rehearsals, recording sessions, private students, road travel, and the ceaseless demand of marketing associated with music employment. Family life adds to an artist's responsibilities.

At times, tribulation throws performers off their route. Financial necessity may require them to divide their energies unfavorably between commercial music and jazz or devote themselves exclusively to the former for years at a time. Some eventually make a successful comeback within the jazz community, but others, discouraged by the prospects of economic hardship and little recognition, leave the music forever. "It can be depressing sometimes," confesses an advanced saxophonist in Barry Harris's workshop, "especially around holiday time when old friends that I went to school with return to the area to visit. After ten years, they've become successful lawyers and doctors. They have families and homes and respect and security. But I'm still in the same situation I've been in all along—still scuffling to pay the rent, still without any savings or health insurance, still trying to keep a band together, still trying to find places to play, still without any sense of the future."

Improvisers may experience periodic dry spells of imagination and drop out of the music world to recoup their creative energies. When asked about the several-year hiatus in his recording and performing career, Miles Davis remarked that, at one point, he found that he could no longer hear the music. "It just stopped and all of a sudden, I couldn't play anything."[16] In other instances, musicians may tire of invention within particular idiomatic frameworks, and take time off from performing to determine a new musical direction that has value for them. Subsequently, they reenter the field with renewed enthusiasm. Indeed, some careers are made up of successive periods of uniquely focused interest, each ultimately representing another leg of a restless artistic journey. "How many times in my life have I said to myself, 'If only?'" Walter Bishop Jr. muses. "If only I could play this passage? If only I could play that tune? If only I had the technique to do that? If only I could play with these musicians or those musicians? Only to discover that by the time I reached those goals, they had been replaced by other goals."

Over the years, vaguely imagined youthful prospects of unlimited possibilities and dreamlike aspirations give way to a history of finite accomplish-

ments. With age and maturity, many learn to assess their talents in the context
of the jazz tradition as they understand it, to make peace with themselves as
career artists. "I have felt quite deficient a number of times over the years, and
it's been quite embarrassing," Lee Konitz offers with characteristic candor.

> I keep thinking, "Jesus, why don't I have more of a vocabulary at my
> disposal so that I can just play fast tempos?" But at some point, I
> decided that that's the way it's going to be. I'm not going to get it all
> in, or be the best, or whatever. When I realized that Charlie Parker
> died at the age of thirty-four and I was going to be fifty-four, I realized
> that I probably won't live long enough to play as brilliantly as he did.
> But the fact is, I have never played that knockout kind of music that
> was obviously part of the bebop thing. That music was so intense in
> those dazzling tempos and lines that they played, that it made its im-
> pact that way. I have never been able to make it that way. For people
> who would like to hear a bit of an improvising attempt—sometimes
> even a walking on eggshells, if you will—I have a small audience,
> and it's enough for me.

Some artists take up new instruments or cultivate areas of musicianship
other than improvisation in order to make the most of their abilities and find
ways of distinguishing their voices from those of other experts. Such skills may
also help artists find commercial work—typically, producing musical scores
for television, radio, or film. "These days I am very concerned with developing
facility as a writer and an orchestrator," Konitz continues. "I can write lines
very easily, but I've not thought orchestrally so much in the past. Also, some
of the things which at one time were difficult for me, like the harmonic aspect
of jazz, I am much more in tune with now. I can handle the piano keyboard,
and I am much more aware of the harmonic aspects of music."

Some improvisers, for stimulation, change their allegiance from one jazz
idiom to another or turn their attention to precise musical fusions. As early
jazz groups borrowed elements from spirituals and blues, contemporary experiments include the fusion of jazz with toasts, a genre of narrative poetry some
consider "the greatest flowering of [African American] verbal talent," and with
hip-hop.[17] Imaginative fusions include the theatrical adaptation of a jailhouse
toast, "Honky Tonk Bud," for videorecording, and hip-hop recordings *Jazzmatazz* and *Doo-Bop* by Guru and Miles Davis respectively.[18]

Other remarkably varied mixtures of elements that Miles Davis created
late in his career also served as new textural settings for his "characteristic
articulation, phrasing and melodic figures." These mixtures encompass "the
electrified sounds of psychedelic rock, . . . the complex rhythm-guitar offbeats
of funk," and the "raw sound materials" provided by the "Brazilian and African
percussionists and the Indian musicians" with whom he collaborated.[19] Additionally, for concepts regarding the use of "rhythm and space" and the juxtapo-

sition of multiple, independent patterns, Davis acknowledges composers as different from each other as Bach, Stockhausen, and Ornette Coleman. Increasingly, he strove in his own group to achieve a "free association of musical ideas" around the rhythmic core provided by bass vamps.[20]

Ever experimenting with new sounds and new ways of organizing them, Davis sometimes reversed the conventional relationship between the top and the bottom of the ensemble. At times, rather than performing solos, the treble instruments repeated a simple melody or melodic fragment as the rhythm section instruments created "a thick web of simultaneous solos" and a multilayered fabric of ostinatos whose "static or repetitive harmonies" and "uncompromising metric framework" drew inspiration from "African and Brazilian polyrhythms and James Brown–style rhythm and blues."[21]

Davis explains his exploration of this fusion of jazz, rock, and world music in terms not only of its musical interest but also of its theatrical performance elements. His use of electric trumpet blends effectively with the band's other electric and synthesized sounds, allowing him freedom of movement to perform from any part of the stage, rather than having constantly to step out from the group's ranks as a soloist to play at a fixed microphone. Interweaving dramatic body language into the fabric of performance, Davis, in resplendent dress, poses momentarily at the side of the stage to interject sporadic musical commentary into the music. He continues his performance by stepping gracefully across the stage to the music's beat, stopping midway to make silent acknowledgment of the audience, then guides their attention from band member to band member as each delivers the subtle changes in performance his directing elicits. Davis's newfound stage demeanor underscores within the fusion idiom the attraction that extramusical features of performance hold for him.[22]

Max Roach, too, "is always in a state of experimentation." In recent years, he has been

working with strings. I hear strings as a percussive brass section, not saccharine. I've also been dealing with solo pieces with different forms. I hear pieces for large orchestras, too, not with the conventional string sections, but with banjos, mandolins, and guitars. All these things excite me. I like to deal with voices as well, and all kinds of different instrumental combinations. I've done duets with Archie Shepp, Cecil Taylor, Anthony Braxton, and [Abdullah Ibrahim]. I'm constantly working on new ideas. I'm interested in mixed media, film, dialogue, and dance, all together. These things keep me busy at home, experimenting with them, thinking about them, writing notes about them. And I love performing as well. So, I'm constantly trying to dream up ways to keep myself interested in what I'm doing, challenging myself in different ways and, hopefully, challenging the other musicians I have become involved with.

Whether improvisers choose to apply their skills within the bounds of varied idioms or whether they remain faithful proponents of a single style, the greatest satisfactions remain integrally tied to musical exploration and discovery, to artistic development. "It's amazing, but lately I've been suddenly feeling myself getting better and better each time I play," Barry Harris observes.

> I don't know why it's happening now, at this late stage of my career, but it is happening. I still feel like a little kid, a fifty-one-year-old kid, and it's beautiful. Every fifty-one-year-old should feel like I do about this, because it's a continual learning process. You can be doing this music till you're seventy, till you're one hundred, and just be learning all the time. If you could only do this till you were one hundred fifty or two hundred years old and learn all the time, just imagine the depth you could achieve. I must hope that I live long enough to solve more of the mysteries. I am solving some of the mysteries for myself, but I know that there are many more, and the thing is to keep at it and to solve them.
>
> I listened to some of the piano students who came to my class yesterday. About five of them played the same tune, but played it so differently! This thing we're involved with is so big that it's unbelievable what one can learn from so many people. I have such a ball in my classes, and I learn so much from my students. They probably don't realize that I come to school here, too. I'm just the oldest member of the class. I just wish everyone could experience the blessing of learning new things all the time.

In a similar spirit, octogenarian Doc Cheatham recalls his decision to leave the renowned big bands where he held the lead trumpet chair over most of his career to become the featured soloist and vocalist of a new quartet.

> We were well accepted when we opened at Sweet Basil, and I was so surprised, I just couldn't believe it—especially when I started singing. I started singing a few years ago. At first, I was worried that, at my age, I wouldn't be able to remember all the lyrics to the tunes. But I found that it wasn't any problem for me. So I said, "The heck with it, at seventy-five, I can't lose a darn thing, either people like it or they don't. If they don't, they don't have to hire me." But they accepted my singing and my soloing and everything, and they just love me. Everything is working out fine. So, instead of retiring, I'm being born into the business again. At a recent jazz festival in France, to be on the bandstand with Dizzy Gillespie, Clark Terry, and Bobby Hackett at the same time was one of the highlights of my whole entire life. I'll never forget it. I'm doing what I enjoy now. I play my solos and I sing my songs. And I try to learn new things all the time.

Paul Wertico observes an interesting pattern in his own maturation, and that of others, that reveals how musical expression reflects the major stages and landmarks of the artist's life experience. While in their youth, players bring unlimited energy to their improvisations, but their musical concepts are typically underdeveloped. With age, "your body slows down, but you acquire all this wisdom—all this taste." It is the blend of their technique and their cumulative "wisdom and experience" that enables jazz musicians to enjoy the continued artistic growth that "is so beautiful." Rufus Reid remembers a significant "turning point" in his understanding when he first performed on the same program with "early jazz musicians like Major Holley" who were in their sixties and seventies. "I had a great feeling when I saw them. I realized I would also be playing my whole life, and I had twenty or thirty years ahead of me to continue to improve."

Glimpsing the seasoned artist's perspective and experiencing the actual challenges and demands of jazz improvisation, newcomers soon lose their early naivete. They are not so much oblivious to the hardships of the career before them as they are optimistic in its opportunities and rewards. "What a satisfying life work as a jazz musician can be," reflects George Duvivier. "Where else do you have the freedom to play music which really expresses you—to be your own boss? Also, I still love to travel and to see new places. I especially love working in Europe and Japan."

Finally, for some, the commitment to jazz has a moral and ideological aspect. Improvisers embark on their personal odysseys with the conviction that they must share their talents with others, thus helping to maintain and ensure the survival of a unique, indispensable musical tradition. In so doing, they hope to make their mark on a world plagued by social conflict and preoccupied with materialistic values. Improvisers view performance as a positive force that can redress this imbalance, if only in a small way, by replenishing the earth's soundscape with music possessed of beauty and vitality, integrity and soul to remind listeners of these finer universal expressions of human aspiration.[23] "Music is a special gift from God to those who have it," maintains a performer at the threshold of his career. "And it's necessary for us to follow it through to the extent of our abilities, whatever they may be. That's what I live for. A friend of mine saw Kenny Dorham playing somewhere the night before he died. Kenny was playing on crutches," he recounts with admiration, "but he was playing right to the end. God willing, that's the way it will also be with me."

Over the years of this study, the jazz community has seen the passing of many important figures who forged, refined, and diversified the language of jazz, including Count Basie, Eubie Blake, Miles Davis, Billy Eckstine, Roy Eldridge, Bill Evans, Dizzy Gillespie, Charles Mingus, Thelonious Monk, Sun Ra, and Sarah Vaughan. Sadly, before the study's completion, participants George Duvivier, Lonnie Hillyer, Emily Remler, and Red Rodney also joined them.

Within the jazz community, players sometimes assuage feelings of loss with sensitive humor reaffirming their bond with musical ancestors and extending the metaphor of their tradition as an unbroken chain. "[Sarah Vaughan's] somewhere right now having a ball," singer Joe Williams muses affectionately. "She's in good company. . . . Somebody said when she died, 'Well, Basie needed a vocalist.' "[24]

# PART

# V

**Music Texts**

# MUSIC TEXTS

Most of part 5 consists of relatively short musical examples sampling improvised performances from a variety of different sources. Beginning with example 13.23, I present four large score segments of collective improvisations
based on "Bye Bye, Blackbird," "Softly, as in a Morning Sunrise," "I Thought
about You," and "Blues by Five." The top line of each large score segment
presents a conventional lead sheet of the composition, depicting the kind of
skeletal model that typically provides players with a framework for improvising and interpreting each other's improvisations. Following the first page of the
larger selections, italicized abbreviations in the left column identify the lead
sheet and instruments (*ml* for melody; *t*, trumpet; *ss*, soprano saxophone; *p*,
piano; *b*, bass; *d*, drum set), and measure numbers figured from the beginning
of each score segment provide reference points for analysis.

Interspersed with the short examples in the first part of part 5 are excerpts
from the large score segments. The titles of the compositions set these excerpts
apart from surrounding material, as do a number of graphic identifiers: measure numbers, time signatures, braces, and abbreviated instrumental identification. Chords appearing in brackets above each excerpt refer to the score's lead
sheet; harmonic analysis of greater detail appearing without brackets refers to
the total group harmonic sonority. Examples from the larger performances that
are not represented in the scores, and examples from other sources, typically
appear without measure numbers and time signatures. Unless otherwise indicated, they are in 4/4 meter.

The scores and other transcribed examples draw attention to different facets of jazz improvisation and include, accordingly, different degrees of musical
detail. Readers should consult examples I.1 and I.2 for a description of the
notational symbols that portray, in some transcriptions, subtle trumpet and saxophone timbral variations and pitch inflections and, in others, components of
drum set figures. To maintain a consistency of appearance with the original
transcriptions in this work, borrowed material from other authors' transcriptions notated for B♭ instruments appears transposed to C within the octave.
Additionally, I have made minor editorial changes with respect to articulation
marks, chord representation, and the like, and I have added such analytical
marks as boxes, circles, arrows, braces, and brackets to highlight particular
features within examples. Slight differences in notation among the examples
reflect peculiarities of the two music-writing programs used for the presentation, "Score" and "Finale."

In a rich, essentially oral tradition like jazz—whose language and forms
are not rooted in single, definitive written models—no feature of the music

is free from interpretation. Correspondingly, this work's transcriptions simply represent interpretations of selective features of the original recorded performances. In the preparation of the scores, individuals named in the acknowledgments took primary responsibility for translating into music notation the parts improvised by performers of the same instrument that the transcriber played. After compiling individual parts into scores, we invited other musicians to join us in comparing the transcriptions to the original recordings and suggesting revisions. The current versions, which represent the most recent collective interpretations of several artists, are the outcome of this process. As such, they reflect the mutual exchange of knowledge, the sharing of insights from different musical perspectives, and, in some instances, the spirit of compromise that underlie learning and musical understanding in the jazz community.

The process of score revision brought to light numerous factors that potentially distinguish interpretations of recorded performances. One is the sound quality of the original recording and its subsequent reproductions as records, cassettes, and CDs. Different pressings or reissues sometimes reveal substantial variance in the products' overall clarity or transparency, a function of such features as signal-to-noise ratio and the balance among the parts. Similarly, the individual qualities of sound systems (including, for example, record players, tape players, CD players, amplifiers, speakers, and headphones), play an obvious role in determining the information artists can glean from recorded performances. Transcribers found that some equipment revealed significant timbral variations and dynamic accents in an improviser's part—and, occasionally, entire gestures—that were inaudible or undecipherable on other equipment. The capacity of equipment for the isolation and replay of particular passages (recently facilitated with the advent of CD players and digital sampling equipment) also influences interpretation and analysis.

Even when transcribers work with the same recorded examples and the same playback system, their relative sensitivity to different features of music—harmony or rhythm or melody—distinguishes interpretations. Details that some players hear in the music simply elude other players. A related issue is the number of listenings over which artists study a recorded performance, each revealing slightly greater musical detail. The performances chosen for the large score segments are well known in the jazz community, and some of the transcribers had been listening to them repeatedly since their teens, acquiring an intimate knowledge of the music before trying their hands at transcription.

The instrument performed by the interpreter and the interpreter's physical characteristics can also be critical. Pianists commonly interpret the chords of other players in terms of how they themselves voice chords, in part a function of the size of their hands. Drummers commonly interpret the figures of another percussionist in terms of their own arrangement of drums and the sticking patterns that are comfortable for them.

Prior knowledge of the boundaries of an individual's improvisation style and of the performance conventions associated with particular jazz idioms also influences the interpretation of musical events. Especially when a recording lacks transparency, listeners tend to fill in a part's obscure details by assessing the likelihood of particular kinds of gestures occurring at particular points in an improvisation.

Along these lines, knowledge of the form of the composition is also essential. During one transcribing session, a highly skilled player was frustrated in his initial efforts to analyze the structure of a solo. He succeeded only after transcribing and analyzing the harmony of the recorded composition, which provided the key to understanding the soloist's elusive treatment of the form. Likewise, artists commonly interpret the accompaniment provided by rhythm section players as likely representations of the composition's structure, rather than inferring the structure from an analysis of individual bass line components or the pianist's isolated voicings alone. This is especially the case when performances feature incomplete chord voicings and bass lines in which arrival at periodic harmonic goals is more important than spelling individual chords.

The musical background and training of artists also distinguish interpretations. As expected, in the revision of the scores, musicians with the most experience writing music proposed especially elegant solutions to problems depicting elusive jazz rhythms. Likewise, training in musical analysis—whether acquired in the Western music theory classroom or from private study or from other players—influences the particular theoretical conventions improvisers favor for analyzing jazz harmony.

Typically, musicians adding chord symbols to the scores treated the symbols flexibly, applying them to suit different kinds of description and analysis. In part, their applications reflected the dynamic processes of listening within the group and the different models improvisers draw on when creating the music. At some points, for example, they labeled the harmony according to their own version of a lead sheet without feeling the need to account for greater detail or deviations in any of the individual parts. At other points, they derived chord labels from an analysis of the pitches emphasized by the soloist. At yet other points, their labels represented a detailed description of the pianist's precise voicings, or the bass player's line, or any combination of the options above. To provide a consistent sample of the possibilities for interpretation, the final scores present two basic chord lines, the first representing a skeletal lead sheet model, the second representing an analysis of the total group harmonic sonority.

The analysis of group harmonic sonority includes a representative sample of decorative and embellishing chords, but it largely emphasizes functional harmony, depicting chords whose placement and duration are structurally significant in relation to the underlying form. Similarly, it emphasizes the identification of tensions within chords that are structurally significant over those that provide harmonic color. Typically, in up-tempo performances such as "Softly, as in a Morning Sunrise," the fleeting notes of walking bass lines are not included in the analysis. Exceptions include structurally important bass ostinatos, pedal points, and notes representing an alternative interpretation of the harmony that create interesting harmonic effects.

In addition to their use of common schemes of chord labeling and analysis, the scores adopt the following alternative conventions within the jazz community: the sonority of a dominant seventh chord with a flatted fifth is labeled as a half-diminished seventh chord; the sonority including both the seventh and the thirteenth is labeled as a thirteenth chord, but if the seventh is omitted, it is labeled as a sixth chord; the dominant sonority including both a fifth and a raised eleventh is labeled as a raised-eleventh chord, but if the natural fifth is omitted, it is labeled as a dominant chord with a flatted fifth; a dominant chord including both a fifth and a flat thirteenth is labeled as a flat-thirteenth chord, but if the natural fifth is omitted, it is labeled as an augmented-fifth chord. The tension of a flat tenth, which typically functions as a blue note, is labeled as a raised ninth. Chords with upper tensions like thirteenths may include such lower tensions as the ninth and eleventh. Finally, some chord labels include the symbol *sus4* to indicate a harmonic suspension in which a pitch a fourth above the root substitutes for the third.

The extended harmonic practices of post-fifties jazz improvisation, including quartal voicings and other imaginative structures based on allusive or incomplete chords (in which interpreting harmony as listeners or improvisers does not necessarily require the presence of chord roots), can present challenges to conventional Western chord classification and reveal the limitations of conventional analysis for understanding the practices of jazz. To indicate musical inventions that are especially problematic for analysis, the scores use two devices. Parentheses appear around incomplete or implied chords at structural points in the music in which, for example, the piano is absent, or anticipations or delays in performing the harmony temporarily obscure the form. Braces appear around the analysis of harmonic structures open to multiple interpretations that defied consensus among transcribers.

Finally, all transcriptions, no matter how detailed, comprise reductive representations of the original recordings. Especially elusive are essential rhythmic and timbral features of jazz performance and the ever-changing blend of its composite harmonies, the complexities and subtleties of which staff notation can only portray to varying degrees. The jazz community typically uses the uniform rhythmic notation of even beat subdivision, leaving unnotated the subtle variations associated with swing, particularly the triplet swing feeling (ex. I.2d). This work largely adopts the same convention. The score to "I

Thought about You," however, endeavors to portray literally the performance's diverse rhythms and pronounced changes of time-feeling. Ultimately, the large score segments in this work and their captions are intended to serve as companions to the recorded performances, attuning readers to various facets of individual creativity and group interaction that seasoned jazz musicians appreciate in each other's improvisations.

## Example I.1    Trumpet and saxophone notation key

### a.    Normal timbre and timbral variations

1. pitch with normal timbre: full bodied, open sound

2. pitch with half-closed sound: partially muted, slightly compressed quality

3. pitch with closed sound: muted, compressed, nasal quality produced by half-valve or alternate fingering technique

4. harmonic: especially reverberant sound comprising two pitches produced simultaneously by saxophone alternate fingering technique

5. split attack: includes extraneous pitch or unpitched sound

6. pitch with raspy or buzzy sound

7. ghosted pitch: barely audible or implied sound

### b.    Other expressive devices

1. applied to individual pitches

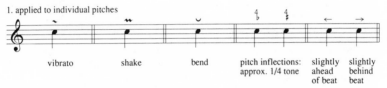

vibrato        shake        bend        pitch inflections:        slightly        slightly
                                                    approx. 1/4 tone        ahead        behind
                                                                            of beat        beat

2. applied prior to, between, or after individual pitches

rip        scoop        slide        bend        fall-off

3. changes within sustained pitches

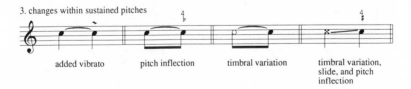

added vibrato        pitch inflection        timbral variation        timbral variation,
                                                                            slide, and pitch
                                                                            inflection

513

## Example I.2    Drum set notation key

### a.    Position of noteheads on staff

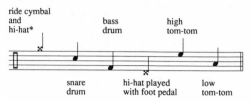

* when played with stick(s)

### b.    Abbreviations and symbols

rc = main body of ride cymbal struck by tip of drumstick, creating a ping sound (the closer the strike to the edge of the cymbal, the greater its sustained, ringing quality)

cup = raised center portion of cymbal struck by stick, creating a kang sound

hh = hi-hat cymbals struck by stick, creating a tick sound

+  = closed hi-hat: hi-hat cymbals struck together with foot pedal, creating a chick sound

○ = open hi-hat: hi-hat cymbals struck together with foot pedal but allowed to vibrate against each other, creating a sizzle sound

rs = rim shot: rim and head of drum struck simultaneously by stick, creating a kak sound

Z = multiple stroke or press roll: drum head struck by stick(s) bounced rapidly and repeatedly, creating a buzz sound

sh = ride cymbal struck by shoulder of stick (directly behind the tip), creating a pang sound

= snare drum played by brushes, creating a legato swishing sound; accent symbol over brush work indicates audible pulse

### c.    Sample drum part

* Abbreviations with a colon (to the left of the notehead) indicate an ongoing occurrence.
Abbreviations without a colon (directly above or below a notehead) indicate a single occurrence.

### d.    Rhythmic notation

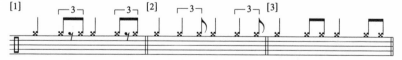

For ease of reading, the drum notation typically represents eighth notes phrased with a triplet swing feeling [1-2] as even eighth notes [3]. Three of this work's scores rely heavily upon this convention because of the relatively consistent swing feeling present in the drum set performances. In contrast, the score to "I Thought about You" endeavors to portray literally the performance's diverse rhythms and pronounced changes of time-feeling.

Example 3.1   Alternative representations of melody "Like Someone in Love"
(notated for B♭ trumpet)

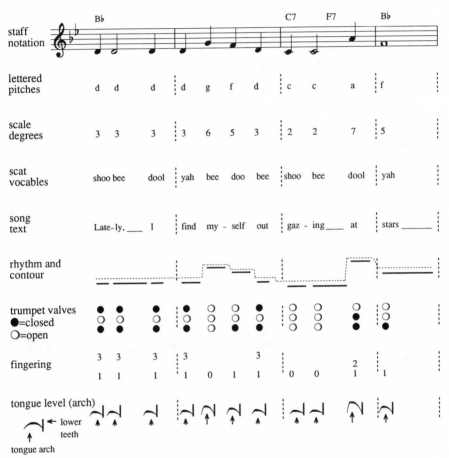

Example 3.2    Features of jazz vehicles

a.    Blues with single repeating figure
      Thelonious Monk, composer, "Monk's Point"

b.    Blues with AA'B melodic prototype
      Miles Davis, composer, "Blues by Five"

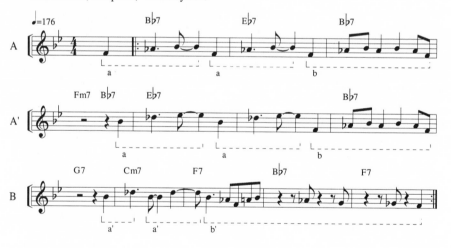

*Example 3.2 continued*

c.   Ballad with ABAC melodic prototype
     Jimmy Van Heusen, composer, "I Thought about You"

*Example 3.2 continued*

d.   Bebop composition with AABA melodic prototype
     Charlie Parker and Dizzy Gillespie, composers, "Anthropology"

Example 3.3    Various strategies in rendering melody

a.    Interpretive devices, including timbral changes, slides, fall-offs, and shaping melody
to speech rhythm
Miles Davis solo, "I Thought about You" (all excerpts ♩=54-56)

*Example 3.3 continued*

b. Transformation of single-phrase model through improvised introductory figures, rephrasing, and ornamentation

Clifford Brown solo, "What's New?"

*Example 3.3 continued*

c.  Comparing samples of artists' melody renditions
    John Coltrane, Kenny Dorham, Lee Morgan, and Booker Little solos, "Like Someone
    in Love"

This illustration presents excerpts from repeated statements of the melody by artists at the beginning and end of their respective group's performance (the former, labeled *hc* for head chorus; the latter, *oc* for out chorus). Scanning each vertical column reveals the players' individual approaches. Additionally, a comparison of different renditions by the same artist suggests that soloists alternate between exploring new possibilities for transforming the melody in performance and playing a personal version that they have composed previously—either before the recording session or during their first melody statement at the session—and retained as a model.

In bars 1–4, Coltrane displaces the initial melody phrase, whereas Morgan and Little approach it through short improvised introductory figures (M1, L1). Little's gesture features a distinctive mix of whole-tone and double-diminished scale degrees. Individual practices also include Coltrane's scalar fills between melody pitches (C2: bar 3), Morgan's consistent grace note ornamentation (M1, M2: bar 3), and Little's use of a recurring descending gesture to approach the concluding pitch of the melody phrase (L1, L2: bars 3–4). Also noteworthy are Little's octave transposition of the melody (L2: bars 1–2) and the exceptionally slow tempo and elastic rhythmic feeling with which he renders the L1 version.

In bars 13–16, Morgan and Little once again append the phrase with short introductory gestures (M1, L1). Pursuing his own approach, Coltrane repeats the same rhythmic displacement at the beginning of both versions, then, two bars later, departs from the melody to improvise figures that serve as responses to the preceding material (C1, C2: bars 15–16). Morgan features comparable grace note ornamentation (M1, M2: bars 13–14) and melody variants (bars 15–16) in his renditions, whereas Little fills in a static portion of the melody with his own gesture in one version (L1: bar 16), and in the other version departs radically from the melody to improvise complex phrases that periodically loop through pivotal melody pitches and include colorful harmonic alterations (L2: bars 13–16).

In bars 17–20, Morgan differentiates renditions by applying an ongoing triplet figure to prominent melody pitches in one instance (M2) and radically rephrasing the last two bars of both versions. Little transforms the melody through his unique use of octave displacement, grace note ornamentation, and radical rhythmic rephrasing, in one instance (L2) stretching out and developing his familiar descending A♭-to-E♭ gesture. Dorham's rephrasing of the melody is also individual (D1, D2: bars 17–18).

In bars 21–24, Dorham's versions illustrate the skillful use of ornamentation, subtle variation, and radical rephrasing to create different shapes from the same skeletal melody. Representing the opposite strategy, Morgan's versions are nearly identical to one another. The versions' consecutive use of grace note and upper neighbor embellishment and imitative leaps to melody notes also reveal the improviser's interest in the continuity and development of ideas, whether at the level of ornamentation or variation. Little's renditions follow a characteristic plan of their own, with the second rendition representing a simplification of the first.

*Example 3.3c continued*

*Example 3.3c continued*

*Example 3.3c continued*

*Example 3.3c continued*

*Example 3.3 continued*

d.  Expressive liberties within a complete melody rendition
    Miles Davis solo, "I Thought about You"

Davis's performance illustrates the soloist's diverse expressive options, even when remaining close to the melody overall. In bars 1–4, he rephrases the melody, characteristically, by anticipating or delaying the performance of phrase components, inserting rests between them, and compressing or stretching their rhythmic features. Pronounced timbral changes within pitches and an emphatic grace note animate Davis's first gesture; the second, he infuses with speechlike inflections and rhythmic shape. In bars 5–8, Davis takes liberties of another nature by varying the melody. He raises the arch of the initial phrase component, rests, then embellishes the second component with vocalizing slides and microtonal inflections. His concluding pitch, a tritone away from the chord root, is especially affective. Fall-offs at the end of this and previous phrases establish subtle continuity from one to the next. In bars 9–10, Davis rephrases the melody with dramatic rhythmic motion, flirting with double time and inflecting some pitches.

In bars 11–16, Davis departs from the melody, creating a new phrase reminiscent of earlier arch-like formulations. Its highly vocalized descent in bars 13–14 uses the reiterated melody pitch E and its octave displacement as a frame and includes other prominent melody pitches as well. In bars 15–16, Davis rephrases the first melody component, then varies the second. In bars 17–18, with a dynamic swell of sound, he applies his familiar technique of extending the arch of the melody, this time concluding the figure with a sixteenth-note gesture hinting at the group's impending shift to double time.

In bars 19–22, Davis reinforces the tempo change with a dramatic leap and emphatic quarter-note descent that once again adopts the octave displacement of a repeated melody pitch as a frame. Subsequently, he generates great rhythmic momentum by transforming the sustained melody pitch into a metrically displaced hemiola-like pattern, effectively highlighted by the use of fall-offs and increasing dynamics. In bars 23–25, Davis creates contrast through a series of climbing, scalar patterns that primarily avoid melody pitches and whose peaks form an ascending step progression. Then, in bars 26–28, he improvises a sequence whose peaks form a descending step progression spanning octave-transposed melody pitches. In bars 29–32, Davis continues the descending step progression by improvising a short melodic fill, which leads into a melody paraphrase reminiscent of his treatment of the same passage at the initial tempo in bar 9. (In the melody's last statement on the recording, his performance of a comparable figure suggests that it is a precomposed variant.) In bars 33–37, Davis uses an octave transposition of the repeated melody pitch as the frame for a powerful ascending gesture that probes the trumpet's upper register. Immediately, he develops the idea by probing even higher to create a dramatic climax of the solo (at nearly the same position at which the melody reaches its highest point) before resolving its tension through a scalar descent to the sustained melody pitch.

In bars 38–43, Davis explores another extreme by resting, then leading, through a radically rephrased variant of the melody, to his performance's longest sustained pitch, highly animated with vibrato, timbral changes, and inflections. In bars 44–50, Davis changes approaches yet again by improvising a series of short, bluesy call and response phrases whose off-beat, triplet phrasing imbues the performance with a strong swing feeling. In bar 51, Davis prepares to close his solo by recapitulating ideas introduced earlier in the performance. Two evocative cries, reaching once again into the high trumpet register, then descending with ever-diminishing dynamic levels, lead to the final phrase, whose expressivity recalls earlier gestures as much spoken as performed. The solo overlaps with the second chorus structure by five measures at the original tempo.

*Example 3.3d continued*

*Example 3.3d continued*

*Example 3.3d continued*

Example 3.4   Alternative representations of harmonic form

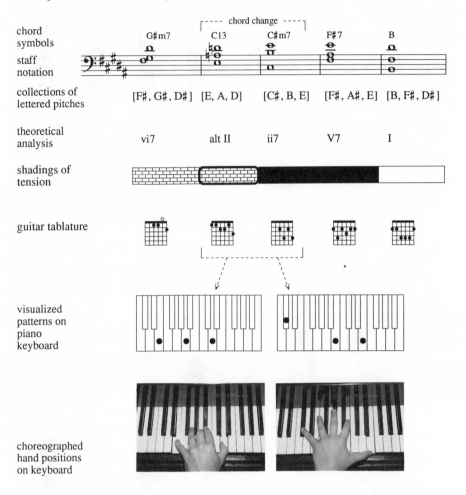

Example 3.5    Comparing harmonic movement within blues and AABA compositions

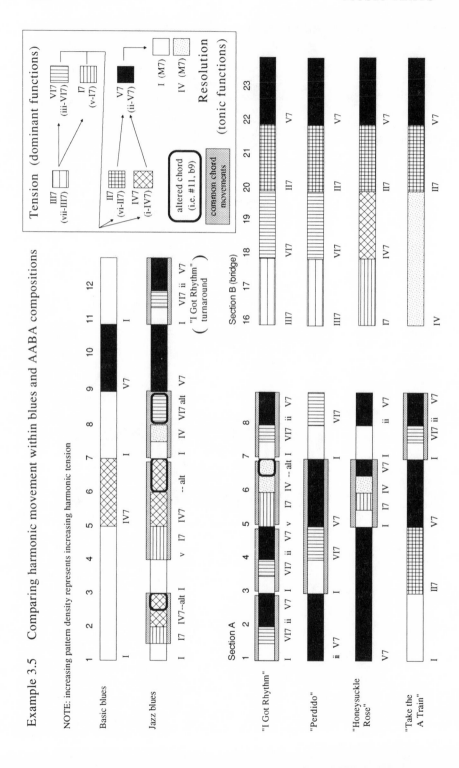

Example 3.6   A sample of chord voicings

Herbie Hancock accompaniment, "I Thought about You"

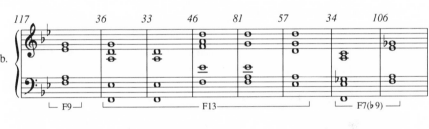

Red Garland accompaniment, "Blues by Five"

*Example 3.6 continued*

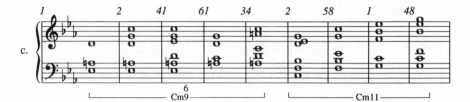

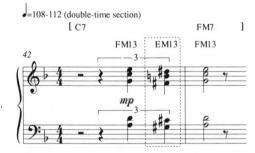

McCoy Tyner accompaniment, "Softly, as in a Morning Sunrise"

Example 3.7    Embellishing chords

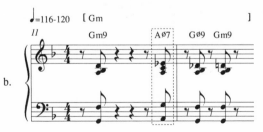

Herbie Hancock accompaniment, "I Thought about You"

Red Garland accompaniment, "Bye Bye, Blackbird"

Example 3.8    Substitutions: harmonic alteration chords
Red Garland accompaniment, "Blues by Five" (all excerpts ♩=176)

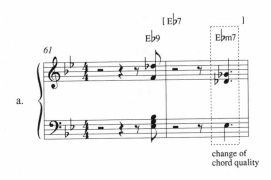

change of
chord quality

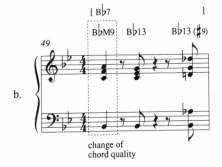

change of
chord quality

Example 3.9    Substitutions: chords having different roots

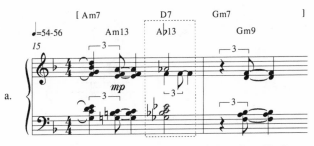

Herbie Hancock accompaniment, "I Thought about You"

*Example 3.9 continued*

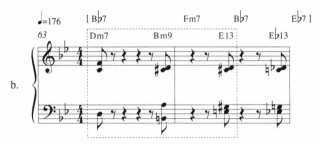

Red Garland accompaniment, "Blues by Five"

## Example 3.10     Substitutions: harmonic insertion chords

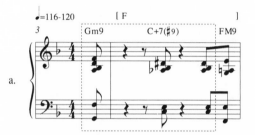

Red Garland accompaniment, "Bye Bye, Blackbird"

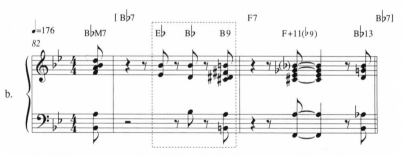

Red Garland accompaniment, "Blues by Five"

Example 3.11    Blues effects of substitute chords
Red Garland accompaniment, "Bye Bye, Blackbird"

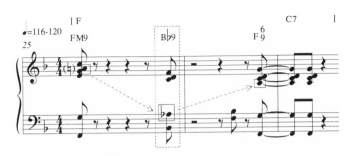

Example 3.12    Elastic interpretation of harmonic form
Red Garland accompaniment, "Blues by Five" (all excerpts ♩=176)

In relation to the regular recurring chunks of a model progression, pianists commonly alter the form's harmonic-rhythm subtly through delaying or anticipating chord changes by half a beat or more. Additionally, the relative rhythmic density of pianists' figures and their precise mixture of on-beat and off-beat accents can provide discrete chord areas or larger harmonic phrases with unique complexions. At one extreme, pianists may sustain a chord or play quarter notes on every beat to define the form. At the other extreme, they may treat the form allusively by withholding the performance of a chord altogether, or resting for most of its duration, or playing various kinds of chord substitutions: chords with different roots (cdr), harmonic insertion chords (hic), and harmonic alteration chords involving a change of chord quality (hac), to use Bill Dobbins's classification.

Interpreted in terms of these multiple operations, Garland's accompaniment sometimes underplays features of the conventional progression by introducing substantial rests into the performance (a1, a4), or simplifies its structure by continuing a particular chord's performance through the subsequent chord's area (a2). Alternatively, he adds complexity to the model through chord insertions and chords with different roots (a3), in some such instances producing unique effects by forming his part around a descending, linear, right-hand progression (a4), encasing alternating sixth and diminished chords within an octave-doubled, tonic pedal (b3), or harmonizing the ascending chromatic portion of a common blues figure (b4). In still other cases, he chooses to remain close to the original structure (b1, b2). Sometimes, he emphasizes off-beat phrasing (b2); sometimes, on-beat phrasing (b3); as often, he mixes the two (a1, a2).

*Example 3.12 continued*

a.  Blues samples, mm.1-4

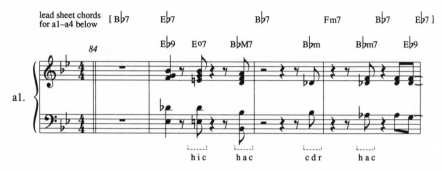

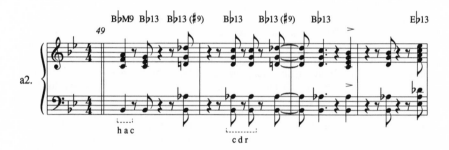

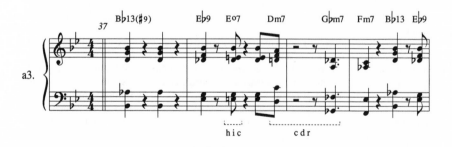

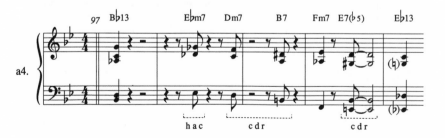

*Example 3.12 continued*

b.   Blues samples, mm.11-12

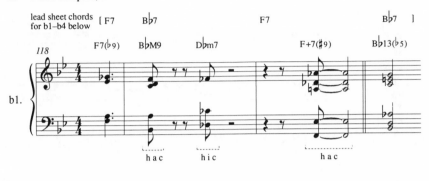

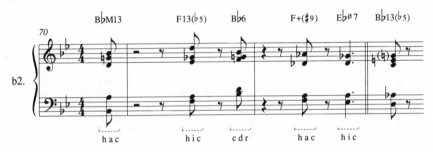

Example 4.1  Joe Oliver's "Dippermouth Blues" solo and its re-creations:
1923–1937
transcr. Witmer (rev. Kirkwood)

Joe Oliver solo, 6 Apr. 1923          Rex Stewart solo, 29 Apr. 1931
Louis Armstrong solo, 29 May 1925     Harry James solo, 6 Sept. 1937

Example 4.2  Diversity of jazz ideas or vocabulary patterns

Miles Davis solo, "Blues by Five," 26 Oct. 1956

*Example 4.2 continued*

Clifford Brown solo, "The Blues Walk," 23 Feb. 1955, transcr. Baker

Charlie Parker solo, "Card Board," Apr. 1949, transcr. Aebersold and Slone

Fats Navarro solo, "Lady Bird," 13 Sept. 1948, transcr. Slone

## Example 4.3   Sources of vocabulary

a.   Classic blues figures

Louis Armstrong accompaniment, "St. Louis Blues," 14 Jan. 1925

Joe Smith accompaniment, "Lost Your Head Blues," 4 May 1926

b.   Arranged shout pattern
Billy Eckstine band members, "Baby, Won't You Make Up Your Mind?" 18 Oct. 1946

*Example 4.3 continued*

c.  Common bebop figure
Dave Young solo, "Lullaby for Realville," 12 July 1956

d.  Compositional quotations

d1.

Booker Little solo, "Fire Waltz," 16 July 1961

d2.

Cannonball Adderley solo, "Somethin' Else," 9 Mar. 1958

d3.

Charlie Parker solo, "Cool Blues," 1949, transcr. Owens

*Example 4.3 continued*

e.   Quoting other soloists

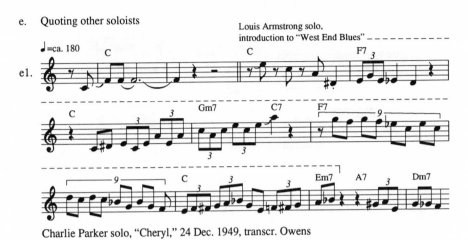

Charlie Parker solo, "Cheryl," 24 Dec. 1949, transcr. Owens

Charlie Parker solo, "Mohawk" (No. 1), 6 June 1950, transcr. Aebersold and Slone

Kenny Dorham solo, "Soft Winds," 11 Nov. 1955

Example 5.1   Dizzy Gillespie's complex approach to rhythm

Dizzy Gillespie solo, "Blues for Bird"

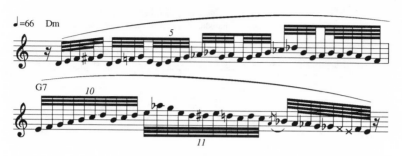

Example 5.2   Different approaches to melodic invention

a.   Vertical approaches

a1.

Coleman Hawkins solo, "Body and Soul," transcr. Tirro

a2.

John Coltrane solo, "Omicron," transcr. Sickler

b.   Horizontal approaches, both transcr. Porter

b1.

Lester Young solo, "After Theatre Jump"

b2.

Lester Young solo, "Honeysuckle Rose"

Example 5.3  Features of different vocabulary stores

a.  Common chromatic blues figure
    Kenny Dorham solo, "Soft Winds"

b.  Rhythmic tremolo patterns
    Lee Morgan solo (notated for B♭ trumpet), "Moanin'" (take 1)

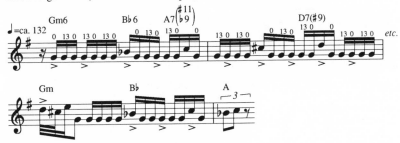

c.  Cadential figures in Kenny Dorham solos

"I Love You" (take 2)

"Soft Winds"

d.  Recurring cadential figure in Charlie Parker solos
    "Billie's Bounce," transcr. Aebersold and Slone

e.  Distinctive patterns in Booker Little solos

"Booker's Blues"

*Example 5.3e continued*

e2.

*accel.*

"Like Someone in Love"

f.  Common gesture serving as Booker Little signature pattern
    "Life's a Little Blue"

## Example 5.4    Approaches to invention for solo piano

a.  Horn-like linear approach
    Bill Evans solo, "Who Can I Turn To?" arr. Evans

b.  Orchestral or pianistic approach
    Art Tatum solo, "If I Had You," arr. Tatum

*Example 5.4 continued*

c. Block chord approach
Chick Corea solo, "Now He Beats the Drum, Now He Stops," transcr. Dobbins

Example 5.5    Approaches to invention for solo drums

a.    Horizontal or linear approach
"Philly" Joe Jones solo, "Gone with the Wind"

b.    Vertical approach
Max Roach improvised fours, "Jordu"

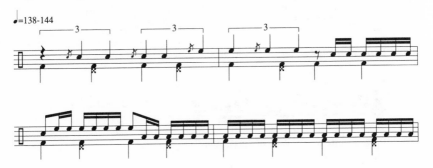

Example 5.6   Personalization of a vocabulary pattern

*Example 5.6 continued*

i.

Booker Little solo, "Life's a Little Blue"

j.

Booker Little solo, "Waltz of the Demons"

k.

Booker Little solo, "Waltz of the Demons"

Example 6.1   One-noting improvisations

Louis Armstrong solo, "Muggles"

Wilbur Hardin solo, "8540 12th Street"
(stoptime accompaniment: ensemble chords played at ♩)

Example 6.2 Rhythmic phrasing in relation to harmonic form
Charlie Parker solo, "Mohawk" (No. 1), transcr. Aebersold and Slone
(arr. author)

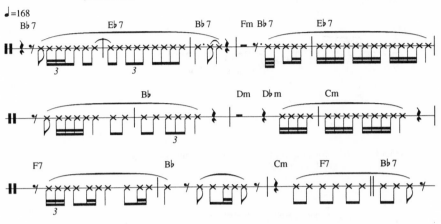

Example 6.3 Animating the features of phrases

a. Backbeat and off-beat accentuation schemes

Miles Davis solo, "I Thought about You"

Miles Davis solo, "Blues by Five"

*Example 6.3 continued*

b.   Gestural contour accented by rhythmic displacement
     Charlie Parker solo, "Mohawk" (No. 2), transcr. Aebersold and Slone

[underlying rhythmic pattern]

c.   Articulation transforming triplets into polyrhythmic groupings
     Lee Morgan solo, "Blue Train"

d.   Timbral variation and pitch inflection

d1.

     Miles Davis solo, "I Thought about You"

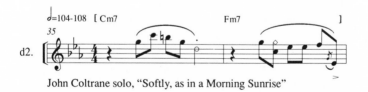

d2.

     John Coltrane solo, "Softly, as in a Morning Sunrise"

Example 6.4    Unpredictable, playful use of rests
Sonny Rollins solo, "St. Thomas"

Example 6.5    Elastic manipulation of rhythm
Joe Henderson solo, "Out of the Night," transcr. Sickler

Example 6.6    Melodic application of chord substitutions within blues structure

† basic harmonic motion
‡ performer's elaboration of harmonic motion through chord substitution

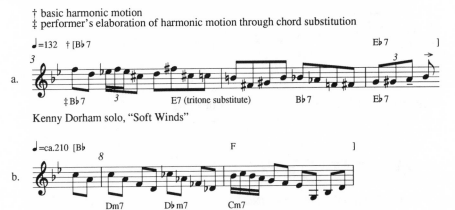

Kenny Dorham solo, "Soft Winds"

Charlie Parker solo, "Tiny's Tempo" (take 3), transcr. Owens

*Example 6.6 continued*

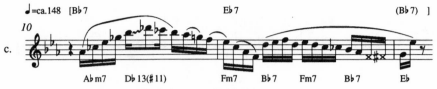

John Coltrane solo, "Blue Train," transcr. Sickler

Example 6.7    Barry Harris's dictation of scale transformation by chromatic and mordent ornamentation

C7th scale

Figure created by extending scale with chromatic embellishment between tonic and flatted seventh

c.    Figure embellished with inverted mordents

Example 6.8    Charlie Parker's practice of pivoting
both transcr. Aebersold and Slone

Charlie Parker solo, "Au Privave" (No. 1)

*Example 6.8 continued*

Charlie Parker solo, "Barbados"

## Example 6.9    Barry Harris's derivation of rules from Charlie Parker solo
"Sweet Georgia Brown," transcr. Harris

Deriving improvisation "rules" and exercises from his analysis of Parker's initial phrase, Harris recommends that students learn "the F minor arpeggio and the harmonic minor scale" by practicing the former's inversions and the latter's relative modal scales. Additionally, Harris interprets the descending phrase fragment in bars 25–26 as Parker "running an E♭7 scale to the third of a C7 chord" and suggests practicing the same maneuver. Next, Harris identifies a "D♭ major arpeggio" in bar 28, indicating that students should practice all major arpeggios and their inversions. The most important arpeggios used by jazz players, he adds, are "generally" those constructed on the root, the fifth, and the seventh of the underlying dominant seventh chord.

In bar 29, the recurrence of an "F minor arpeggio" reminds Harris of the importance of "practicing all scales in [intervals of] thirds," as well as mastering the triads found on each degree of the scale, in this case the A♭ major scale, which is related to the underlying chord. He goes on to identify Parker's ascending gesture in bar 30 as "a chord up from the third of F7 with a little hump in it." Correspondingly, players should "practice all chords on scale," in this case those built on each degree of the F7 scale. The first gesture in bar 31 illustrates once again the "importance of learning to chord up from the third," whereas the second suggests an important rule concerning the application of diminished chords. Students should practice arpeggiating "all the diminished chords" so that they can readily apply them to their related dominant seventh chords, that is, those chords whose third degree they share as a common tone.

Example 7.1    Blues structure of improvised phrases
Lee Morgan solo, "Blue Train"

Example 7.2    Sample of melody rendition and its subsequent quotation
Booker Little solo, "Old Folks"

### Example 7.3   Patterns combined with diverse harmonic backgrounds

a.   Combinations within a single solo performance

a1.   ♩=60

recurring pattern

Bill Evans solo, "My Romance," transcr. Smith

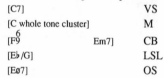

a2.   ♩=ca. 168

Charlie Parker solo, "She Rote" (No. 2), transcr. Aebersold and Slone

b.   Combinations within multiple solo performances

| [C7] | | VS |
|------|------|------|
| [C whole tone cluster] | | M |
| [F$^6_9$ | Em7] | CB |
| [E♭/G] | | LSL |
| [Eø7] | | OS |

♩=ca. 100

Booker Little solos, "Victory and Sorrow," "Matilda," "Chasing the Bird,"
"Like Someone in Love," "Opening Statement"

Example 7.4 Displacement and transposition of vocabulary within different compositions
all transcr. Owens

a.

Charlie Parker solo, "The Hymn" (take 2)

b.

Charlie Parker solo, "The Hymn" (take 2)

c.

Charlie Parker solo, "Thriving from a Riff" (take 1)

d.

Charlie Parker solo, "Billie's Bounce"

e.

Charlie Parker solo, "Out of Nowhere"

Example 7.5   Rhythmic transformations of an etude

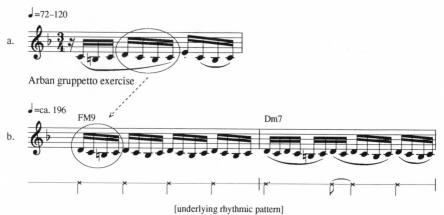

[underlying rhythmic pattern]

Clifford Brown solo (notated for B♭ trumpet), "I Can Dream, Can't I?" (take 1)

Example 7.6   Expanding networks within a community of ideas
Charlie Parker gestures, transcr. Aebersold and Slone, Owens (arr. author)

Gestures in adjacent columns adjoin
by fusion (1), or by fusion/pitch modification (2), or by direct coupling (3).

☐ skeletal frame for melodic exploration: harmonic pivot pitches D, B, E, A

Example 7.7   Interpretive extraction
Booker Little solo, "The Grand Valse"

Example 7.8   Truncation and contraction

a.   Truncation of phrase endings
Booker Little solo, "Opening Statement"

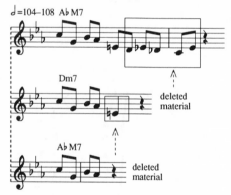

b.   Phrase contraction
Charlie Parker solo, "Tiny's Tempo," both transcr. Owens

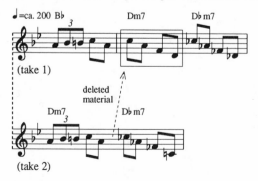

*Example 7.8 continued*

c.  Truncation and contraction combined with component substitution in the formulation
of complex phrases
Booker Little solo, "The Grand Valse"

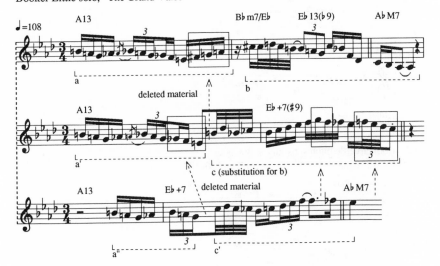

Example 7.9   Pitch substitution

a.   Charlie Parker pitch substitution practices
     Charlie Parker solo, "Tiny's Tempo," ♩=ca. 210, both transcr. Owens

(take 3)

(take 1)

b.   Booker Little pitch substitution practices
     Booker Little solo, "Minor Sweet," ♩=126–132

Example 7.10    Conservative rephrasing
all excerpts (♩=ca. 215) transcr. Owens

a.    Rephrasing without embellishing pitches
Charlie Parker solo, "Red Cross"

(take 2)

(take 1)

b.    Rephrasing with embellishing pitches

b1.    (take 1)

(take 2)

Charlie Parker solo, "Red Cross"

b2.    (take 1)

(take 2)

Charlie Parker solo, "Red Cross"

b3.    (take 2)

(take 3)

Charlie Parker solo, "Tiny's Tempo"

b4.    (take 2)

(take 1)

Charlie Parker solo, "Red Cross"

Example 7.11    Radical rephrasing

Booker Little solo, "Opening Statement"

Booker Little solo, "Minor Sweet"

Example 7.12    Radical rephrasing with rest fragmentation
Miles Davis solo, "Barbados"

Example 7.13    Expansion by interpolation
Booker Little solo, "Minor Sweet" (all excerpts ♩=ca. 126)

Example 7.14    Cadential extensions
Charlie Parker solos, "Mohawk" (Nos. 1 and 2)
all transcr. Aebersold and Slone (arr. author)

Example 7.15    Improvising from finger patterns
Miles Davis solo (notated for B♭ trumpet), "Motel"

1 = First valve pushed down (closed)
0 = First valve released (open)

Example 8.1    Repeating an idea while conceiving the idea to follow
Louis Armstrong solo, "Big Butter and Egg Man from the West"

Example 8.2    Running a figure into itself
Booker Little solo, "Who Can I Turn To?"

Example 8.3    Answering an idea by repeating it in a different octave
Louis Armstrong solo, "Struttin' with Some Barbecue," transcr. Tirro

## Example 8.4    Creating sequences

a.

Charlie Parker solo, "Anthropology," transcr. Owens

b.

Lee Morgan solo, "Like Someone in Love"

c.

Clifford Brown solo, "The Blues Walk"

## Example 8.5    Repeating an idea and extending it with a cadential figure

a.

Lester Young solo, "Pres Returns," transcr. Porter

b.

Miles Davis solo, "Blues by Five"

Example 8.6    Repeating an idea approached through an introductory figure

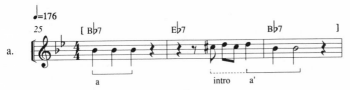

Miles Davis solo, "Blues by Five"

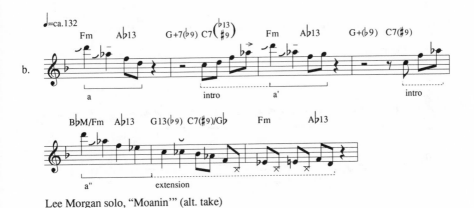

Lee Morgan solo, "Moanin'" (alt. take)

Example 8.7    Balanced call and response phrases with altered response
Charlie Parker solo, "Thriving from a Riff" (take 3), transcr. Owens

Example 8.8    Interpretive extraction generating consecutive ideas

a. Lester Young solo, "[Oh] Lady Be Good," transcr. Porter

b. Sonny Rollins solo, "Strode Rode"

(44 bars intervening material)

c. Clifford Brown solo, "The Blues Walk," transcr. Baker

Example 8.9    Developmental sections based on ostinatos

Louis Armstrong solo, "Struttin' with Some Barbecue"

Sonny Rollins solo, "Strode Rode"

Wes Montgomery solo, "Four on Six"

Example 8.10    Developing ideas through rhythmic variation
Louis Armstrong solo, "Tight Like This"

Example 8.11    Variations on complex rhythmic-melodic material
Booker Little solo, "Who Can I Turn To?"

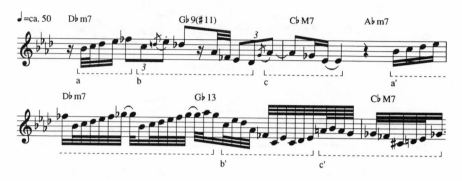

Example 8.12    Extensive call and response practices

Lester Young solo, "Pres Returns," transcr. Porter

Miles Davis solo, "Blues by Five"

Example 8.13 Multiple treatments of a Clifford Brown signature pattern

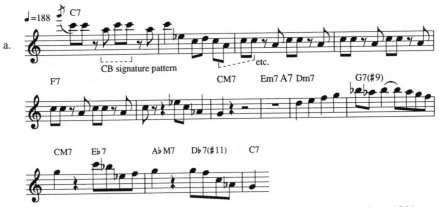

Rahsaan Roland Kirk composition, "A Quote from Clifford Brown," 16–17 Sept. 1964

Booker Little solo, "W. K. Blues," 2 Feb. 1960

Booker Little composition, "Memo: To Maurice," June 1958

Example 8.14    Forty-six years in the life of a lick: 1946–1992

a.

Billy Eckstine band members with Miles Davis in trumpet section, arranged ensemble shout figure, introduction, "Baby, Won't You Make Up Your Mind?" (take 1), 18 Oct. 1946

b.

Miles Davis solo, "Rifftide," 8–11 May 1949

c.

Bud Powell solo, "The Street Beat," 30 June 1950

d.
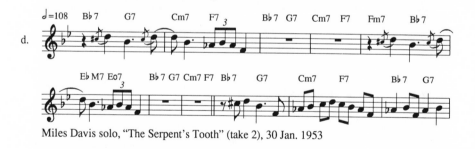

Miles Davis solo, "The Serpent's Tooth" (take 2), 30 Jan. 1953

e.
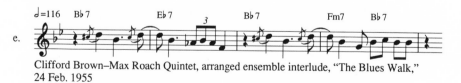

Clifford Brown–Max Roach Quintet, arranged ensemble interlude, "The Blues Walk," 24 Feb. 1955

*Example 8.14 continued*

Miles Davis and John Coltrane, part of Davis composition, "The Theme" (take 1), 11 May 1956

Dave Young solo (with the Sun Ra Arkestra), "Lullaby for Realville," 12 July 1956

Paul Chambers solo, "The Theme," 14 July 1957

Red Garland solo, "Billy Boy," 2 Apr. 1958

Ella Fitzgerald scat solo, "Stompin' at the Savoy," 25 Apr. 1958

*Example 8.14 continued*

Cannonball Adderley solo, "Love for Sale," 26 May 1958

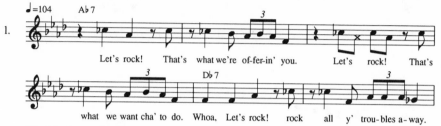

The Manhattan Transfer, part of Ray Charles composition, "Ray's Rockhouse"
(Jon Hendricks, lyrics), Fall 1985

John Scofield solo, "You Bet," Dec. 1991

Benny Green solo, "Billy Boy," 1992

Christian McBride solo, "Billy Boy," 1992

Example 8.15    Going away from and returning to a pattern
Booker Little solo, "Newport"

Example 8.16    Double-backing within an ongoing line

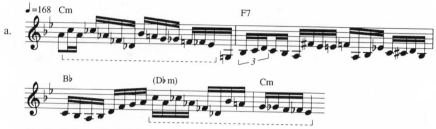

Charlie Parker solo, "Mohawk" (No. 1), transcr. Aebersold and Slone

Booker Little solo, "Opening Statement"

Example 8.17    Beginning a phrase with the last pitch of the previous phrase

Paul Chambers solo, "The Theme," transcr. Coolman

Blue Mitchell solo, "Sir John"

Example 8.18    Working within particular intervals

Booker Little solo, "Shirley"

Lee Morgan solo, "Blue Train"

Example 8.19    Balancing the phrase lengths of consecutive ideas
Lee Morgan solo, "Blue Train"

*Example 8.19 continued*

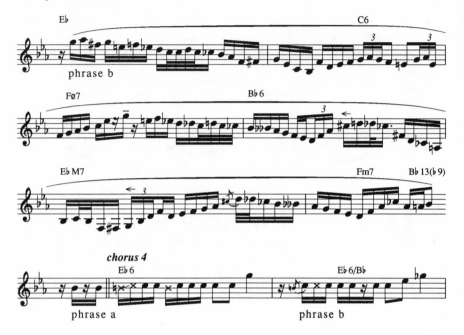

Example 8.20    Creating increasingly longer phrases
                John Coltrane solo, "Softly, as in a Morning Sunrise"

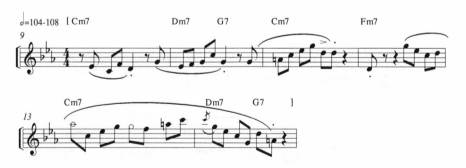

Example 8.21     Expanding the range of consecutive phrases
John Coltrane solo, "Softly, as in a Morning Sunrise"

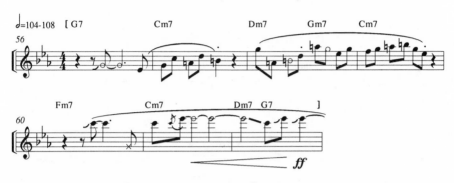

Example 8.22     Unfolding development of a chordal improvisation approach
both transcr. Sickler

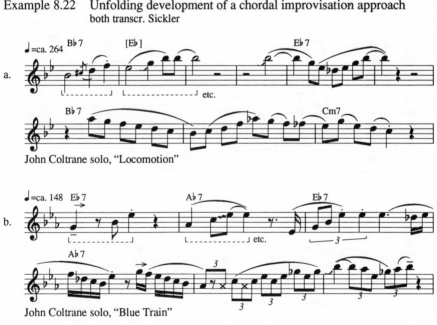

John Coltrane solo, "Locomotion"

John Coltrane solo, "Blue Train"

Example 8.23    Dynamic movements among different musical concepts

Miles Davis solo (notated for B♭ trumpet), "Motel"

Lee Morgan solo, "Git-Go Blues"

Example 8.24  Formulating a unique solo chorus from components of different
 choruses
 Miles Davis solo, "Blues by Five" (all excerpts ♩=176)

To create a new chorus, students could perform the first phrase of Davis's original solo,
as given in a, then choose between second-phrase options b1 or b2. Alternatively, they
could formulate new second-phrase call and response figures by combining the first
component of b1 with the second component of b2, or the first component of b2 with
the second component of b1, perhaps lengthening the rest between them. For the last
phrase of the chorus, they could select among options c1–c3 in their entirety, or try out
such combinations as substituting the first bar of c2 or c3 for that of c1, or substituting
the first bar of c1 for that of c2. Further diversifying their creations, students could
add short extensions to the model patterns or substitute altogether new ideas for any
of Davis's.

a.  First phrase

b.  Second-phrase options

c.  Third-phrase options

Example 8.25    Chorus designs for solos

a.   Break and first chorus
     Miles Davis solo, "Bye Bye, Blackbird"

Davis tells his story through unfolding, lyrical ideas that epitomize the spare, elegant improvisation style he cultivated between the late forties and early sixties. Adopting a moderate tempo for the performance and emphasizing quarter-note and longer rhythmic values in his formulations, Davis maintains a strong feeling of swing throughout. He uses space liberally, providing substantial rests between phrases and concluding phrases with sustained pitches. The performance excerpt begins with the last four bars of Davis's melody rendition. As the rhythm section approaches its break (suspended performance), Davis creates a striking segue to his solo by ascending the chord extensions to a high sustained pitch, then creating a sharp syncopated descent. Both components of the arch-like opening gesture establish characters or thematic material for the tale to come. Davis initiates the solo chorus in bars 1–2, for example, by extracting and rephrasing a fragment of the preceding pattern, then varying and developing it as a sequence. After resting and sustaining a low chord tone, he descends to the new chord, then, in bars 7–9, develops, through rephrasing and repetition, an ascending gesture that is an inversion of a component of the previous gesture. Subsequently, Davis plays a variant of the arch-like opening phrase, then generates tension by repeating an ornamented figure that anticipates the forthcoming chord change by two measures. In bars 17–20, he formulates distinctive call and response patterns whose overriding gesture recalls the descent of the opening phrase.

During the first twenty bars, Davis largely develops his idea from phrase to phrase, as if conversing with himself. At the same time, his figures periodically include important melody pitches (bars 1–2, 4, for example), correspondences that can be interpreted as a subtle conversation with the composition's melody or with chords sharing common tones with the melody. In bars 21–22, however, Davis performs a pronounced variation on the melody. Then, abandoning the strategy, he offers intense personal commentary through a distinctive burst of sixteenth notes. Highlighted by the surrounding rests and in marked contrast to the performance's conservative rhythmic nature, the figure represents a dramatic peak, as Davis leaves the bridge and approaches the last eight bars of the first chorus. From this point on, the story takes new turns while, at the same time, evoking earlier musical characters. In bars 25–28, Davis formulates the chorus's most elaborate unbroken phrase by leading, through an expansion of a familiar arpeggiation, to a new gesture whose peaks form an ascending chromatic step progression, then extending it with a rephrased melody quotation. He concludes the chorus by rephrasing and extending the melody pitches as in his opening phrase, then creating lyrical shapes reminiscent of his triadic formulations in bars 7–8. Limiting the store of materials with which he fashions the solo, Davis constantly generates interrelated ideas that display unique qualities. Within the framework of his simple storytelling style, nuances like the use of grace notes and sixteenth-note embellishments stand out prominently and reflect back on comparable expressions, contributing continuity to the tale.

*Example 8.25a continued*

*Example 8.25a continued*

b.  First and second choruses
    John Coltrane solo, "Softly, as in a Morning Sunrise"

Exploiting the fast tempo of the performance, Coltrane conveys a sense of urgency throughout his solo by emphasizing eighth-note formulations. His modal emphasis also characterizes the tale, demonstrating, like many of his sixties solos, the rich possibilities for fashioning ideas from restricted tonal material, in this instance based on the intervallic structure of the Dorian mode. Initiating the solo with three phrases reminiscent of blues storytelling technique, Coltrane introduces a two-part idea, varies it, then, in bars 5–7, provides contrasting material, which he develops sequentially. He contributes cohesion to the rapidly evolving tale and highlights the piece's form by beginning and ending the initial A section on the tonic and resting in bar 8. The first section's unfolding material reveals other rhetorical strategies as well. Coltrane often uses a particular rhythmic target, in this instance the third beat of the measure, for ending successive phrases, and he underscores their final pitches with special articulation devices. He also commonly formulates consecutive phrases (sometimes patterned on the contour of the first) that gradually increase in length and/or range, before resolving their tension through the opposite procedures. Coltrane applies the strategies throughout bars 9–16, concluding the second A section with a low chord root that recalls his phrase ending in bar 7.

The B section opens with a variant of the solo's second phrase that, in bar 17, creates the peak of the established solo. With this gesture, Coltrane prepares for the culmination of the first chorus: high sustained vocal cries in bars 19–20 that present the first prominent dissonance outside the mode. After treating the cry as a short sequence, he leads away from, then back to the cry through a twisting, dissonant line. Subsequently, in bar 23, he reduces the tale's tension through a short motive whose extension climbs down in range and ends on the familiar beat-three rhythmic target. The next phrase adopts the same target. In bars 29–32, Coltrane completes the chorus with a richly animated, ascending eighth-note figure that leads into a suspenseful syncopated riffing pattern overlapping the next chorus boundary. Over the first chorus, he sometimes applies his methods at different structural levels. Just as he marks off the first A section by beginning and ending ideas with the tonic, he marks off the larger chorus with the same design. Within the framework of the second A section, he creates a dramatic peak three-quarters of the way through the structure by improvising the highest and longest phrase thus far (bars 12–15). Similarly, he creates a climax approximately three-quarters of the way through the larger chorus structure (in the B section) by improvising vocal cries amid the highest and longest phrases of the chorus.

In the second chorus, Coltrane generates new phrases that follow the general strategies of the first. Beginning with short phrases of limited range, he gradually extends them in both respects, then reverses the procedure. Whereas the third beat of the measure serves as a common rhythmic target in the first chorus, Coltrane initially shifts the target to the fourth beat in the second chorus (bars 33–36), before returning to his original scheme (bars 39, 41, for example). At the chorus's close, Coltrane creates the

*Example 8.25b continued*

greatest climax of the evolving solo with an extended performance of searing vocal cries that reach high E♭ before returning to high C, framing his second chorus with a return to a tonic.

Contributing cohesion to the solo are recurring fragments of two eighth notes and a quarter note, a short figure and its variant serving as the response to longer improvisations (bars 26–27, 56–57), and specific gestures like wide leaps that answer one another as the cadential components of successive phrases (bars 45–46). Coltrane also establishes continuity at times by beginning and ending a phrase with the same pitch, then repeating it to initiate the following phrase (bars 3–4, 10–11). Providing variety in the context of Coltrane's predominantly modal solo are varied articulation, ornamentation, and timbral alteration devices. Also diversifying the performance are fleeting references to pitches outside the mode, typically to pitches A♭ and B♮ as if suggesting movement to an altered version of the piece's dominant chord (G7). One shift in Coltrane's approach to phrase construction contributes to the solo's development and intensification. After conforming to the composition's harmonic phrase structure in the repeated A sections of the initial chorus (bars 1–16), Coltrane subsequently creates phrases that routinely span the composition's formal sections. Although Coltrane does not appear to play off of the melody by quoting or varying its precise phrases, there are various points at which he begins or ends phrases with prominent melody pitches (see large score segment, ex. 13.24), reflecting, perhaps, a subtle conversation with the melody or with common tones shared by the mode and the melody.

*Example 8.25b continued*

*Example 8.25b continued*

c.   Complete three-chorus solo
     Booker Little solo, "W. K. Blues"

Little begins his tale with a short motive that he may have absorbed from the repeating, double eighth-note component of the composition's simple riff melody, or perhaps from the vocabulary of Clifford Brown, who influenced his style (see ex. 8.13). Throughout the first chorus, Little repeats, displaces, and varies the figure, at times applying different pitches to its rhythmic template (bars 1–2, 5), and at other times approaching the motive through improvised introductory figures (bars 3–4, 6–7). In bars 8–11, he provides contrast by creating the solo's first extended phrase, whose sequential and rhythmic expansion of the motive brings the chorus to a logical close. At the same time, he generates suspense by concluding with the ninth of the chord and a substantial rest.

Balancing elements of surprise and continuity in bars 12–13, Little, for the first time, begins an idea on the fourth beat of the measure and leads it over the bounds of the new chorus into a slight variant of the solo's initial motive. In bars 14–18, he answers himself by repeating the previous gesture, then transforming it with a mordent that initiates a long phrase extension. In bars 16–17, the extension includes interesting new shapes, such as a whole-tone scale fragment, and dissonant harmonic effects that ultimately resolve to a sustained chord tone in bar 18. With this passage, Little develops his story in numerous ways. Beyond the exploitation of harmonic dissonance, he increases the length of the phrase over earlier phrases and gradually expands the range of his ideas at the high and low end. Moreover, the solo's short pecking, dancelike motive gives way to lyrical ideas. From this point on, the tale evolves dramatically. In bars 19–21, Little generates excitement by shifting into double time with a burst of rhythmic energy, then markedly expands the solo's range. In bar 22, after climbing an octave through scalar patterns and leaps, he produces tension through a slightly dissonant offbeat descent. In bar 24, he begins his next phrase on the fourth beat and spans the chorus boundary, as he did at the conclusion of the first chorus.

In chorus 3, Little intensifies his exploration of ideas in the high trumpet register, ascending to the peak of the solo and improvising a segue to a restatement, in bars 26–27, of the preceding phrase's cadential component. Then he responds immediately with a short interjection, whose rapid rhythm and close intervals create the impression

*Example 8.25c continued*

of speechlike commentary. In bars 28–29, Little begins a gradual descent through a phrase comprising, in part, an octave-transposed and contracted variant of an earlier figure in the story (bars 15–17). Subsequently, in bars 30–31, he answers his variant phrase by reworking elements extracted from its cadential component and extending them. Finally, Little ends his tale with a striking gesture, the longest in the solo, which is an elaboration and extension of the closing passage of the previous chorus (bars 22–24). He makes his way back to the upper regions of his range, heightens harmonic tension by playing blues dissonance in relation to the prevailing harmony in bars 33–34, then reduces the tension through a descending line, embellished with lively rhythmic motion and chromaticism. Having produced such dynamism and variety over the performance, Little concludes his solo definitively with its lowest sustained pitch, the tonic of the piece. Minor recurring characters contributing continuity to Little's tale include a triplet upper mordent and its variants.

**chorus 1**

*Example 8.25c continued*

d.   Complete eight-chorus solo
     Miles Davis solo, "Blues by Five"

Davis's performance provides a model of storytelling method applied over multiple passes through the same harmonic structure. While developing ideas organically from
phrase to phrase, he reaffirms the larger blues design by resting during the last measure
of nearly every chorus. This strategy creates dramatic tension and, ultimately, frames
each chorus's ideas as a discrete episode in the tale. Moreover, it allows him time to
consider possibilities for each subsequent chorus. The opening character of the solo, a
repeating quarter-note figure, is one of Davis's simplest vocabulary patterns. Although
it is a neutral idea, in relation to which many following phrases would work well, Davis
chooses to develop it through a simple variation procedure, displacing the figure and
approaching it through a short introductory figure. Throughout the solo, characters
comprising on-beat quarter-note groupings of two or three repeated pitches, and variants compressing or expanding the original motive's rhythmic values, continually reappear, reflecting back on each other.

   Davis's initial formulation of short call and response phrases also represents a general rhetorical strategy for the story's construction, setting up expectations that new
ideas will be followed by ideas roughly equivalent in length and shape. Initially con-

*Example 8.25d continued*

forming to the plan, the solo assumes a lively breathing quality, as short imitative pairs of phrases in choruses 1 and 2 give rise to a pair of longer imitative patterns in chorus 3, before returning to short pairs again at the opening of chorus 4. Sometimes Davis works subtle references to the composition's melody into this scheme. He initiates chorus 2 with an emphasis on rhythmically displaced pitches that occur in the melody three bars earlier. Subsequently, at the beginning of chorus 3, he rephrases and extends melody pitches found in corresponding positions within the piece's form, then develops the idea according to the conventional AA'B blues design.

In chorus 4, the solo takes an unexpected twist when, after four short, imitative phrases of restricted range, Davis performs an expansive gesture, ascending through a stack of thirds to the highest pitch in the solo thus far and creating an initial climax. Davis then descends through the first chromatically embellished scalar gesture. Continuing to introduce new ideas into the story, he answers the descent with the first ascending scalar figure, followed by a lyrical pattern whose short imitative cadential components in bars 70–71 return to the solo's earlier rhetorical strategy for developing ideas. One of the subtle ways in which Davis creates variety over the first four choruses is by initiating the idea for each chorus on a different beat.

Chorus 5 builds upon the climactic gesture of the previous chorus by beginning in the high trumpet register and reworking a comparable idea. Richly animated, the figure includes a common Davis signature pattern in bars 75–76, a chromatically embellished descending step progression. After concluding the idea with a highly vocalized gesture, he rests, then creates a figure spanning the form's sixth and seventh bars, unique phrasing within the evolving solo. The chorus ends with a variant of the concluding figure in chorus 3 (bars 57–59), the variant's repeated pitch recalling the opening motive of the solo. Over the first five choruses, Davis displays his compositional control through the gradual expansion of the solo's range and the tendency to increase the size of the pitch set from which he formulates consecutive choruses.

In chorus 6, Davis introduces a sharp contrast into his story by applying his former call and response technique to displaced variants of the solo's opening motive—developing a pair of short ideas restricted in range and tonal elements. At the same time, the unique syncopated qualities and backbeat emphasis of his passages generate rhythmic tension and an intensified feeling of swing. Additionally, Davis creates variety by riding on the harmonically colorful blue third and by exploiting features of timbral change, microtonal inflection, articulation, and vibrato. The simplicity of the chorus's figures, with their blue-third and tonic emphasis, recalls comparable creations by early jazz players like Joe Oliver (see ex. 4.1).

Chorus 7 also introduces new material to the tale while recapitulating former elements. Its short opening patterns recall those of chorus 4. Subsequently, in bar 100, Davis initiates an extended line whose expansion of tonal materials leads through chromatically embellished scalar patterns to an imitative set of lyrical figures at the close of the chorus reminiscent of the final gestures of choruses 1 and 2. Davis exercises precise control over the cadential components of his figures in bars 104–7. Initially, he creates tension by playing an open tritone that ends with a dissonant flat-ninth pitch in relation to the conventional progression; he resolves the tension in his answering gesture by playing a perfect fourth that ends with a chord tone.

Chorus 8 contains two of the performance's longest and most elaborate phrases whose running eighth notes, constantly twisting contours, and varied rhythmic stress patterns create a heightened sense of swing. Balanced between the chorus's extended phrases is the solo's longest sustained pitch—a distinctive vocal cry—that is dissonant in relation to the changing chords of the conventional blues progression (bars 115–16). The cadential quarter-note component of the cry evokes the blue-third emphasis found in chorus 6 and elsewhere. The solo's concluding figure, too, resonates with associa-

*Example 8.25d continued*

tions. Its harmonic-rhythmic placement and contour is reminiscent of "harmonic syn-onyms" in comparable positions in choruses 3 and 5. In bar 119, the repeated tonic also recalls the solo's opening motive. Davis follows it with a precise variation on the mel-ody, thereby tying his own personal tale to the original story line and creating a sense of closure, as he turns over the performance to the next soloist. In a final surprise, Davis ends his variant with a suspenseful sustained pitch, a tritone away from the chord's root, during the first measure of the new chorus.

*Example 8.25d continued*

*Example 8.25d continued*

Example 9.1    Figure in different linear settings
both transcr. Aebersold and Slone

a.    Figure featured as a central idea
Charlie Parker solo, "Mohawk" (No. 1)

b.    Figure absorbed within a larger line
Charlie Parker solo, "She Rote" (No. 2)

Example 9.2    Different applications of an embellishing mordent

a.

Booker Little solo, "Stella by Starlight"

b.

Booker Little solo, "Memo: To Maurice"

Example 9.3    Different applications of a grupetto-like gesture
Clifford Brown melody rendition and solos, "I Can Dream, Can't I?"
(all excerpts ♩=ca. 196)

a.

melodic rendition (take 3)                    tune embellishment

b.

catalytic phrase component

solo rendition (take 3)

*Example 9.3 continued*

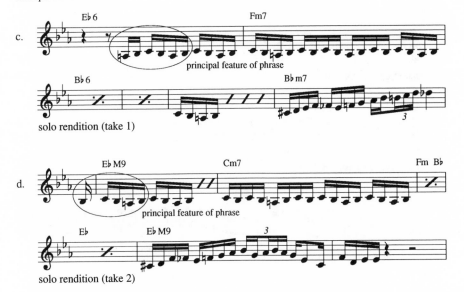

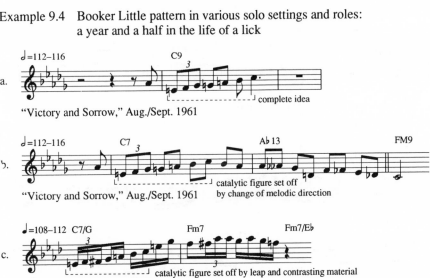

Example 9.4 Booker Little pattern in various solo settings and roles:
a year and a half in the life of a lick

*Example 9.4 continued*

d. "Far Cry," 21 Dec. 1960

catalytic figure blends into contour extension

e. "Far Cry," 21 Dec. 1960

expanded catalytic figure

f. "Opening Statement," 15 Apr. 1960

transitional bridge

g. "Forward Flight," Aug./Sept. 1961

cadential figure

h. "Victory and Sorrow," Aug./Sept. 1961     motivic expansion

i.

transitional bridge

cadential figure     catalytic figure

"Ode to Charlie Parker," 21 Dec. 1960

Example 9.5 Recurring vocabulary patterns within a single performance

a.

Miles Davis solo, "Miles Ahead," transcr. Washburn and Harbison

b.

Miles Davis solo, "Freddie Freeloader"

Example 9.6   Booker Little solo "Minor Sweet" model: long chain of vocabulary patterns (♩=126–132)

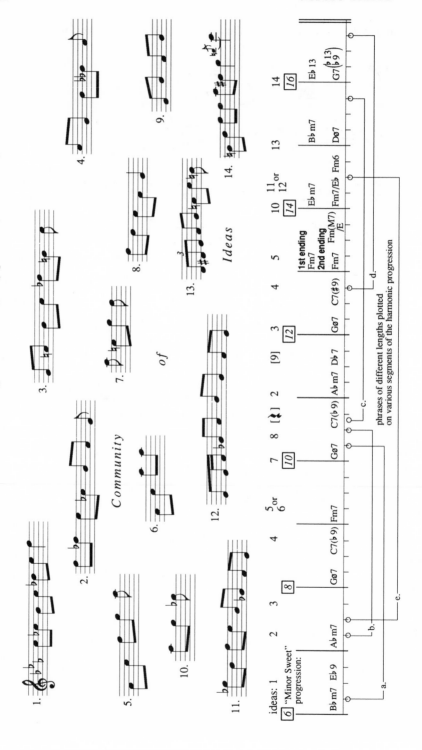

Example 9.7  Phrases derived from Booker Little solo "Minor Sweet" model

Example 9.8   Radical departures from Booker Little solo "Minor Sweet" model

Example 9.9    Artist's re-creation of own precomposed solo
Fats Navarro solo, two renditions, "Jahbero"

*Example 9.9 continued*

Example 12.1    Approaches to invention for bass accompaniment

a.    Walking bass line formulations

The bass accompaniment samples below illustrate changing performance conventions over a period of nearly twenty years and wide-ranging features of musical personality that distinguish individual players as accompanists. The excerpt of Russell's performance (a1) represents a comparatively conservative rhythmic accompaniment featuring largely scalar patterns with occasional skips and the frequent use of repeated pitches. Revealing a greater variety of expression is the excerpt of Heath's accompaniment (a2), which breaks up regular quarter-note performance with rhythmic embellishments and takes liberties with melodic shape, typically forming one- or two-bar figures within the boundaries of discrete chords. Chambers's sampled performance (a3) is more conservative rhythmically than Heath's, but adventurous in other ways. Lively melodic contours spanning different measure groupings constantly change directions with wide interval leaps and explore the upper register of the bass. Like Heath, Chambers builds phrases from short balanced components, but as the last four bars of the sample demonstrate, he often develops shapes extensively as motives. Whereas Russell's bass lines are largely diatonic, Heath and Chambers feature chromaticism in their parts.

Workman's approach sampled here (a4) is more conservative in range than the other players' but is the most adventurous rhythmically. Not only does he perform syncopated figures over the barline, but he occasionally stops the flow of his line with rests and wide interval leaps, creating, all together, a richly varied, unpredictable phrase structure. Finally, the accompaniment samples reveal different approaches to interpreting harmonic structure. Heath is relatively conservative in this instance, emphasizing root performance on the downbeats of new chord areas; Russell and Chambers mix root playing with the performance of other chord tones on downbeats. Workman takes the greatest liberties. He walks in the general tonality of the piece and is less concerned with describing each chord change.

Curly Russell accompaniment, "Ko Ko" (take 2), 26 Nov. 1945, transcr. Owens

Percy Heath accompaniment, design for complete chorus, "Bags' Groove" (take 1), 24 Dec. 1954

*Example 12.1a continued*

Paul Chambers accompaniment, design for complete chorus, "Blues by Five," 26 Oct. 1956

Reggie Workman accompaniment, "Softly, as in a Morning Sunrise," 2–3 Nov. 1961

b.   Diverse approaches incorporated with walking bass line formulations
     Ron Carter accompaniment, design for complete chorus, "I Thought about You,"
     12 Feb. 1964

Carter's part epitomizes contemporary trends in bass accompaniment, as well as the increased possibilities for expressive performance at a slow ballad tempo. His style displays a dynamic quality throughout, constantly presenting different kinds of ideas: expressive glissandos (bars 3–4), grace note embellishment (bar 5), double-stop ornamentation (bars 3–4, 9–12), and double pedal point effects (bars 11–12, 43–46). Equally diverse are the rhythmic and melodic features of his creations. At the original tempo and in the double-time section, he sometimes improvises in the two-beat feeling reminiscent of early jazz players (bars 13–15, 29–30); other times, he switches to a four-beat walking bass style (bars 47–56). Utilizing the full range of the bass, he builds some passages around virtuoso leaps (bars 19, 32–36); he develops other figures motivically (bars 6–7, 26–28). At the same time, his harmonic approach is conservative. Typically, he plays roots on the downbeats of chord changes and otherwise emphasizes thirds and fifths. Periodically, he decorates the conventional progression with tritone substitutions (bars 7–8, 15, for example) or creates tension by anticipating the chord changes (bars 30.33, for example).

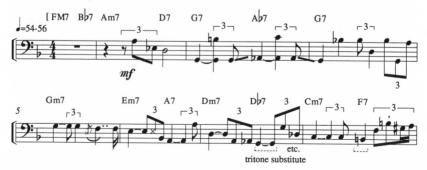

*Example 12.1b continued*

*Example 12.1b continued*

Example 12.2    Common bass vocabulary patterns

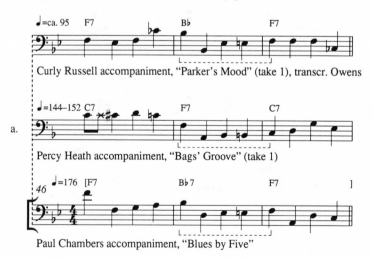

Curly Russell accompaniment, "Parker's Mood" (take 1), transcr. Owens

a.

Percy Heath accompaniment, "Bags' Groove" (take 1)

Paul Chambers accompaniment, "Blues by Five"

*Example 12.2 continued*

b.   Paul Chambers accompaniment, "Blues by Five"

Reggie Workman accompaniment, "Softly, as in a Morning Sunrise"

Example 12.3    The personalization of bass vocabulary patterns

a.   Paul Chambers variant patterns
    Paul Chambers accompaniment, "Blues by Five" (all excerpts ♩=176)

*Example 12.3 continued*

b.  Reggie Workman variant patterns
    Reggie Workman accompaniment, "Softly, as in a Morning Sunrise"
    (all excerpts ♩=104–108)

c.  Paul Chambers variant patterns
    Paul Chambers accompaniment, "Blues by Five" (all excerpts ♩=176)

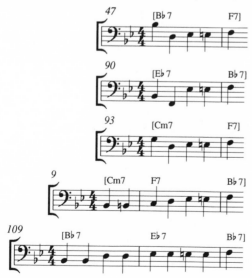

*Example 12.3 continued*

d. Percy Heath variant patterns
   Percy Heath accompaniment, "Bags' Groove" (take 1; all excerpts ♩=144–152)

model

Example 12.4 Recurring vocabulary chains in bass lines

a.     Paul Chambers vocabulary chains
       Paul Chambers accompaniment, "Blues by Five" (all excerpts ♩=176)

Example 12.4a continued

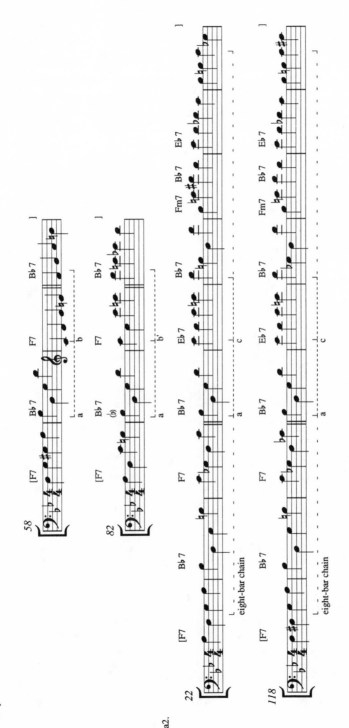

*Example 12.4 continued*

b.   Percy Heath vocabulary chains
     Percy Heath accompaniment, "Bags' Groove" (takes 1 and 2; all excerpts ♩=144–152)

Example 12.5    Ride cymbal and hi-hat time-keeping patterns: model and variants

Drummers can individualize the conventional bebop time-keeping pattern (a) through basic practices of component substitution, for example, replacing two eighth notes with a quarter note or vice versa (b1, b2), or replacing particular elements with rests (e2, e3). Such procedures alter the initial pattern's accentuation scheme. So, too, does tying elements together to elide one-bar figures (b2) or to create syncopation (c2, d1–d3). Changing a figure's orchestration and color also creates diversity. Drummers may alternate stick-driven hi-hat and ride cymbal performance (e3) or feature the ride cymbal exclusively (e1, e2). They may emphasize the ride cymbal's interplay with the foot-pedal-operated hi-hat (c3, e5), or the hi-hat struck with a stick (e4). Whether, after striking the hi-hat in open position with a drumstick, the player closes it with the foot pedal, or a hand, or both, also creates distinctive colors. Finally, whereas some drummers consistently phrase their eighth notes with a swing triplet feeling (b–d; see discussion in drum set notation key, ex. I.2), Williams's accompaniment varies such phrasing (e2, e3, e5) with the performance of even or straight eighth notes (e1) and tension-generating hemiola-like patterns (e4).

a.    Model bebop pattern

b.    Max Roach variants
      Max Roach accompaniment, "Jordu" (all excerpts ♩=138-144)

c.    "Philly" Joe Jones variants
      "Philly" Joe Jones accompaniment, "Bye Bye, Blackbird" (all excerpts ♩=116-120)

*Example 12.5 continued*

d.  Elvin Jones variants
    Elvin Jones accompaniment, "Softly, as in a Morning Sunrise" (all excerpts ♩=104-108)

e.  Tony Williams variants
    Tony Williams accompaniment, "I Thought about You"
    (all excerpts ♩=108-112 double-time section)

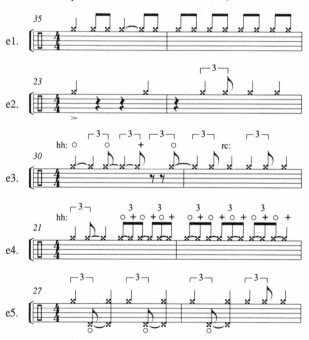

Example 12.6    Drum punctuations around time-keeping patterns
"Philly" Joe Jones accompaniment, "Blues by Five"
(all excerpts ♩=176)

Players can use their drums to accent different beats or portions of beats within each measure, creating varied schemes of on-beat or off-beat emphasis in relation to the time-keeping cymbal pattern (a1–a3). Multiple punches on the same drum cause figures of differing rhythmic density to emerge from the cymbal pattern (a4–a6); distributing punches between the voices of different drums produces patterns with melodic implications (a7–a8). Players can create longer drum phrases by repeating and varying simple ideas, such as accenting the second half of the fourth beat with the snare drum (b1) or accenting the fourth beat with repeated eighth-note snare punches or quarter-note bass drum punches (b2). Combining these procedures with such varied schemes as low-high-low or high-low tonal emphasis, for example, drummers can develop ideas of greater melodic-rhythmic complexity over an entire chorus (c).

a.    One-bar figures

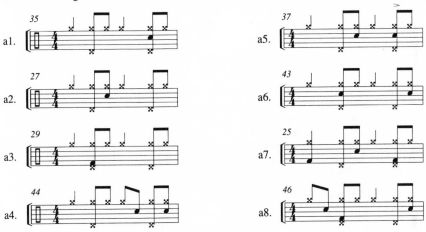

b.    Figures developing simple ideas

*Example 12.6 continued*

c.    Figures developing complex melodic-rhythmic ideas

Example 12.7    The personalization of drum vocabulary patterns

Revealing drummers' distinctive ways of orchestrating rhythmic patterns, Roach plays
a single-pitch bass drum version of a figure (a1) whose elements "Philly" Joe Jones
distributes between the snare and bass drums to create a descending melodic shape
(a2). Comparable versions of another figure suggest that players can alter a model pattern further by adding subtle rhythmic embellishments, distinctive accents, and syncopations to its basic frame, or by deleting selective elements from it (b1–b3). The varied
use of cymbals also plays a significant role in individualizing drum figures by encasing
them in unique textures of cymbal sound and reinforcing some of their elements over
others. In relation to Roach's figure (c1), for example, "Philly" Joe Jones's figure (c2)
withholds the hi-hat on beats two and four, and the ride cymbal on the last triplet drum
punch. It also deletes the initial punch of Roach's second triplet, transforming the five-
stroke pattern into a repeated double-stroke pattern. Elvin Jones's figure (c3) begins by
combining Roach's use of cymbals with "Philly" Joe Jones's manner of breaking up the
triplet figure. It goes on to substitute a punch on the middle triplet element of the third
beat for the original quarter-note punch and to syncopate the ride cymbal crash on the
second half of the fourth beat.

*Example 12.7 continued*

a.   Variant two-bar patterns

a1.

Max Roach accompaniment, "Jordu"

a2.

"Philly" Joe Jones accompaniment, "Blues by Five"

b.   Variant one-bar patterns with triple subdivision of beat three

b1.

Elvin Jones accompaniment, "Softly, as in a Morning Sunrise"

b2.

Elvin Jones accompaniment, "Softly, as in a Morning Sunrise"

b3.

"Philly" Joe Jones accompaniment, "Blues by Five"

*Example 12.7 continued*

c.    Variant one-bar patterns with triple subdivision of beats one and two

c1.

Max Roach accompaniment, "Jordu"

c2.

"Philly" Joe Jones accompaniment, "Blues by Five"

c3.

Elvin Jones accompaniment, "Softly, as in a Morning Sunrise"

## Example 12.8    Drum fills as structural markers

Players commonly use drum patterns or fills of relatively high density to indicate structural cadences within a composition's form, for example, at the end of four- or eight-bar harmonic phrases and the end of the chorus. Fills without triplet figures feature sixteenth-note patterns, or short accentuated patterns, or press rolls (a1–a4), whereas other fills feature repeated triplet figures (b1–b2). Artists may also develop ideas of greater complexity as structural markers by repeating or transforming their initial pattern's components or by generating a succession of contrasting rhythmic elements. In c1, for example, Jones establishes an off-beat punch idea, which he develops in the second measure by reinforcing the initial punch with the bass drum, adding a punch on the second half of beat two, and substituting off-beat triplet-eighth punches for their eighth-note counterparts on beats three and four. In c2, Jones establishes a largely triplet-eighth idea, which he varies in the second measure by omitting punches on beat one, then performing a displaced, altered version of the last component of the initial gesture. In c3, Williams develops a triplet idea, creating diverse polyrhythmic groupings by accenting different parts of the triplet with cymbal and drum punches. In the first bar, his syncopated ride cymbal initiates a hemiola-like pattern, while he performs a slightly displaced version of the conventional hi-hat pattern. He animates his figures further with constantly changing cymbal colors and an effective rim shot effect.

*Example 12.8 continued*

a.    Patterns without triplet figures

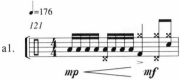

"Philly" Joe Jones accompaniment, "Blues by Five"

"Philly" Joe Jones accompaniment, "Blues by Five"

Elvin Jones accompaniment, "Softly, as in a Morning Sunrise"

Max Roach accompaniment, "Jordu"

b.    Figures stressing triplets

Max Roach accompaniment, "Jordu"

"Philly" Joe Jones accompaniment, "Bye Bye, Blackbird"

*Example 12.8 continued*

c.    Complex figures developing ideas through repetition and variation

Elvin Jones accompaniment, "Softly, as in a Morning Sunrise"

Elvin Jones accompaniment, "Softly, as in a Morning Sunrise"

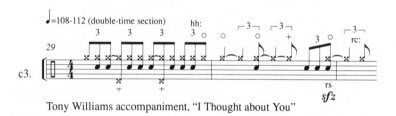

Tony Williams accompaniment, "I Thought about You"

Example 12.9    Chorus designs for drum accompaniment

a.    Designs delineating form through time-keeping patterns and structural markers

Providing a classic accompaniment model (a1) during the first chorus of Clifford
Brown's solo, Max Roach gradually increases the intensity of his performance, while
methodically marking the form of the composition and developing different ideas. At
the outset, he confines his part to simple variations on a cymbal time-keeping pattern
and first introduces drums to play a structural marker figure during the harmonic cadence in bar 8. Subsequently, he plays comparatively dense drum fills in the fourth and
eighth bars of harmonic phrases. Within areas delineated by his structural markers,
Roach's distinctive drum figures provide each section with a different character. In bars
9–16, he features a figure accenting beats two or four with the bass drum and the second
half of beats two or four with the snare drum. In bars 17–24, he divides the phrase into
two parts, the first featuring an isolated bass drum figure, and the second a repeated
eighth-note snare drum figure. The last eight-bar section is also unique but varies some
elements introduced earlier, such as the on-beat bass drum accent. Finally, Roach delineates the larger form with a powerful press roll in bars 31–32.

*Example 12.9a continued*

Max Roach accompaniment, "Jordu"

Elvin Jones's second chorus accompaniment of John Coltrane's solo (a2) also delineates four- and eight-bar phrases, and, from section to section, introduces distinctive figures. In bars 33–40, he features dense combined bass and snare drum figures that lead into contrasting structural markers, whereas in bars 41–48, he emphasizes spare off-beat snare punctuations and cymbal patterns before the extended cadential fill. In bars 49–56, Jones features highly active snare drum figures, in part continuing the previous structural marker's triplet idea. From his cadential figure in bar 56 forward, Jones rap-

*Example 12.9a continued*

idly builds intensity, initially renewing his bass drum emphasis, then creating linear combinations with bass and snare drums (bars 57–58), and, finally, playing both instruments simultaneously for maximum accentuation before leading into the chorus's climactic sixteenth-note fill in bar 64. Jones's chorus displays a higher level of drum activity overall than Roach's. Additionally, Jones constantly varies his cymbal patterns. Instead of the conventional beat-two-and-four hi-hat performance, he sometimes accents beat three (bar 64) or accents the second half of beats (bars 41, 61–63). He frequently plays syncopated ride cymbal patterns, sometimes eliding them with other patterns over the barline or combining them with complex drum figures. He also takes liberties by extending the intense drum activity of structural markers over the boundaries of harmonic phrases (bars 48–49, 56–57, for example).

*Example 12.9a continued*

Elvin Jones accompaniment, "Softly, as in a Morning Sunrise"   *concludes chorus*

b.   Design featuring the episodic development of ideas and dramatic changes in time-feeling
Tony Williams accompaniment, "I Thought about You"

Tony Williams's accompaniment of Miles Davis illustrates the expressive range of contemporary drummers within the framework of a ballad. Although situated in the piece's
formal structure, the accompaniment does not routinely provide regular structural
markers. Williams's virtuoso polyrhythmic fills, for instance, occur not only at predictable harmonic cadence points in the composition's form, such as bars 29–30 and 46 in
the double-time numbering system (that is, bars 24 and 32 at the original tempo), but
at less predictable points, such as bars 21–22 and 53–54 in the double-time numbering
system. For the most part, he develops his ideas organically, manipulating elements of
repetition and change within successive musical episodes as a function of his own internal conversation and his interaction with fellow band members discussed later in this
work. Similarly, Williams commonly varies his accompaniment through effective
changes in drum set emphasis and playing technique that are independent of major
structural cadences. For example, he initiates subtle textures of brush work on the snare
drum in the middle of bar 3, then creates suspense by introducing an extended rest in
bar 11. Subsequently, Williams changes instrumentation and technique to highlight the
group's dramatic shift to double time in bar 19, rather than at the beginning of the bridge
in bar 17.

Williams's diverse expression distinguishes the accompaniment throughout. His
vocabulary ranges from the elaborate figures mentioned above to various linear constructions alternating drum and cymbal sounds (bars 33–40) to march-like figures without cymbal accompaniment (bars 42–45). Over the course of the performance, he exploits accentuation, dynamics, timbral variation (bars 30, 37, 47), and the use of silence
(bars 11–18, 40–42). Compared to Roach and Jones, Williams emphasizes the colors
of the ride cymbal and stick-driven hi-hat over that of the foot-pedal-operated hi-hat,
playing the latter only sparingly (bars 25–29, 48–49). He frequently alternates the
voices of different cymbals (bars 19–23) and integrates them within the larger complex
of drum figures (bars 29–31, 50–54), rather than restricting their role to ostinato time-
keeping patterns. Also distinctive is Williams's creation of constantly shifting time-
feelings from straight eighths and sixteenths (bars 33–45) to swing eighths (bars
46–56).

*Example 12.9b continued*

*Example 12.9b continued*

Example 12.10    Chorus designs for piano accompaniment

a.    Block chord designs delineating form through structural markers and distinctive cadences

Red Garland's block chord accompaniment (a1) features a relatively low registral placement of chords. He primarily creates seventh and ninth chords with the root in the bass
whose open sounds emphasize sevenths and thirds in the left hand, and thirds and seconds in the right hand. To delineate the composition's form, Garland plays a recurring
rhythmic structural marker (first introduced in bar 8) and other markers of increased
rhythmic density (bars 4, 12) at the end of four-bar harmonic phrases. Within the
phrases, he improvises relatively spare off-beat patterns in which accenting the second
half of beat four is a common element. Sometimes, Garland creates a flow of nonrepeating rhythmic elements, but other times, he develops elements through repetition
and variation. In bars 1–4, for instance, he emphasizes off-beat punches on the second
half of beats two and four; in bars 5–8, he works with a repeated eighth-note figure. A
distinctive approach to the final cadence of the chorus highlights its larger form. In bar
30, Garland performs a displaced version of the recurring structural marker elided with
a unique figure containing the chorus's longest rhythmic values. Emphasizing sustained
on-beat punches, his right hand creates a descending upper voice line accompanied by
increased harmonic motion, while his left hand plays a C pedal emphasizing sustained
off-beat punches. As illustrated by the large score segment (ex. 13.23), Garland sometimes remains close to the simple conventional progression (bars 9–12); other times, he
ornaments the progression with chord substitutions (bars 21–24).

*Example 12.10a continued*

al.

structural marker

etc.

*Example 12.10a continued*

Red Garland accompaniment, "Bye Bye, Blackbird"

McCoy Tyner's block chord accompaniment (a2) places voicings higher in the piano's range than Garland's accompaniment and emphasizes quartal harmony, sometimes omitting the chord root or relegating it to other voices than the bass (bars 1–5). Indicating the piece's structure, Tyner performs a recurring rhythmic structural marker (bar 1) or its syncopated variant (bars 4–5) at the beginning of four-bar phrases. Like Garland, Tyner emphasizes off-beat punches within phrases, but he distinguishes his accompaniment through increased rhythmic density, a greater diversity of rhythmic values, and a predilection for tying figures over the barlines. Marking off the chorus's final cadence (bars 31–32), Tyner performs rhythmically dense off-beat figures and especially high, expansive six-element chords, whose tension he resolves with a sustained chord on the downbeat of the new chorus. To highlight the form further, Tyner adopts a different harmonic approach for the composition's major components. As illustrated by the large score segment (ex. 13.24), he typically simplifies the A section's standard progression by emphasizing Cm⁶ or Cm11 chords voiced in fourths (bars 1–8) but elaborates the progression of the bridge (bars 17–24) with occasional substitutions. Moreover, he gives the bridge a unique color by diversifying his quartal voicings with comparatively conservative tertian voicings. The latter feature stacks of thirds in the left hand, rather than the sevenths characteristic of Garland's accompaniment.

*Example 12.10a continued*

*Example 12.10a continued*

McCoy Tyner accompaniment, "Softly, as in a Morning Sunrise"

b. Design characterized by diverse textural effects and dramatic changes in time-feeling
   Herbie Hancock accompaniment, "I Thought about You"

Differing markedly from Garland's and Tyner's performances is Herbie Hancock's diverse "pianistic" or "orchestral" accompaniment, created initially at a slow ballad
tempo. Overall, Hancock's voicings are higher in range than those of the other pianists,
with his right hand periodically venturing nearly an octave higher than Tyner's voicings
for dramatic effect (bars 53–55). Additionally, Hancock does not outline the form with
repeating structural markers but generates a constantly changing accompaniment in
which he develops his ideas organically and responds to the musical events taking place
in the other parts. Hancock's performance encompasses a tremendous range of colors,
gestures, and textural effects. At one moment, he adopts the conventional block chord
approach (bars 41–43); at another, he creates a soloistic melodic phrase (bars 10, 12),
or a subtle inner voice melody (bar 6), or an unusually wide leap (bar 32), or he suddenly rests for a measure or two (bars 23–24). His formulations range from simple
close-voiced dyads (bar 18), stacks of thirds (bar 39), and blues-ornamented structures
(bar 11) to complex clusters (bar 35) and characteristically hard-biting, six- and seven-
note voicings with octaves on top (bars 53–55). Throughout, Hancock varies the rhythmic values of his comping figures and their registral placement as well. He enjoys exploring the extremes.

*Example 12.10b continued*

*Example 12.10b continued*

*Example 12.10b continued*

Example 13.1    Rhythmic tension among the accompanying parts
McCoy Tyner, Reggie Workman, and Elvin Jones,
"Softly, as in a Morning Sunrise" (all excerpts ♩=104-108)

Example 13.2    Balancing expressions of freedom and constraint between bass
                player and drummer
                Ron Carter and Tony Williams accompaniment, "I Thought about You"

a.    Bass player intensifies activity while drummer limits activity

b.    Drummer intensifies activity while bass player limits activity

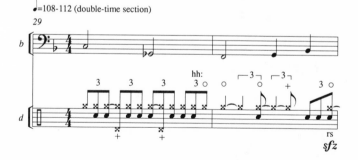

Example 13.3    Exchanging patterns between drummer and pianist

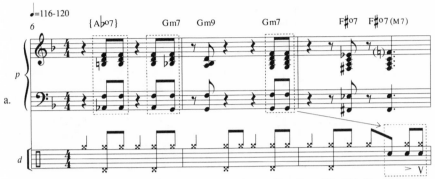

"Philly" Joe Jones and Red Garland accompaniment, "Bye Bye, Blackbird"

"Philly" Joe Jones and Red Garland accompaniment, "Blues by Five"

"Philly" Joe Jones and Red Garland accompaniment, "Blues by Five"

Example 13.4    Intensified interplay between drummer and pianist

a.    Increasing density of coordinated punches
      Elvin Jones and McCoy Tyner accompaniment, "Softly, as in a Morning Sunrise"

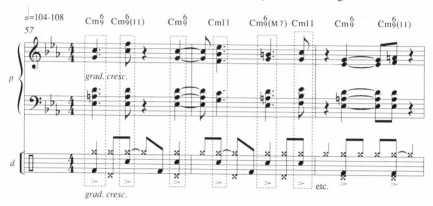

b.    Developing ostinato shout patterns
      "Philly" Joe Jones and Red Garland accompaniment, "Blues by Five"

(lh=hi-hat played with left-hand stick)

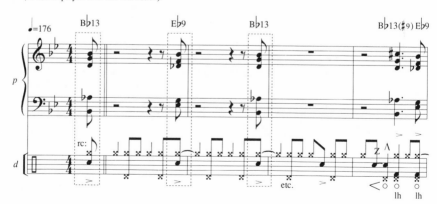

*Example 13.4b continued*

Example 13.5    Composite representation of chord by bass player and pianist

The bass player and pianist sometimes create, in musical time and space, a composite interpretation of a progression that is close to a conventional lead sheet representation. Performing simultaneously on the downbeat of the chord change, the bass player may articulate the root and fifth of the chord, while the pianist performs a selection of chord tones and extensions, perhaps sustaining the structure for a few beats (a). As often, the pianist anticipates the chord change by half a beat, while the bass player leads a line toward the root (or other chord tones) on the subsequent downbeat (b). Taking slightly greater liberties, the pianist may sustain a chord through the downbeat of the next chord's area, mixing the sound of the first chord with the new root articulated by the bass player before changing chords and resolving the dissonant effects (c1, c2). The pianist can also create varied colors by altering the harmonic quality of a chord, for example, from a dominant quality to a minor quality, while the bass player maintains the root (d).

*Example 13.5 continued*

a.   Simultaneous downbeat performance of chord
     Reggie Workman and McCoy Tyner accompaniment, "Softly, as in a Morning Sunrise"

b.   Pianist anticipates chord changes while bass player sounds chord tones on downbeats
     Paul Chambers and Red Garland accompaniment, "Bye Bye, Blackbird"

c.   Pianist sustains previous chord color while bass player sounds new root

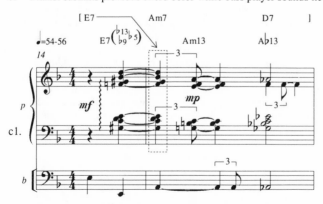

Ron Carter and Herbie Hancock accompaniment, "I Thought about You"

*Example 13.5c continued*

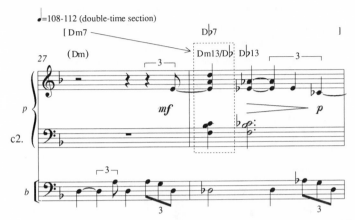

Ron Carter and Herbie Hancock accompaniment, "I Thought about You"

d.   Pianist alters chord quality while bass player sounds root
     Ron Carter and Herbie Hancock accompaniment, "I Thought about You"

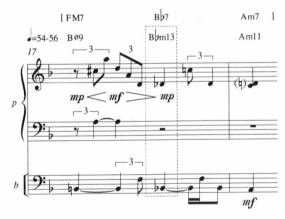

Example 13.6   Bass player and pianist interrelating different harmonic
               pathways

The bass player and pianist commonly interrelate different harmonic pathways to vary
their mutual representation of form, contributing diversity to the music's changing composite harmony. In a, while the bass player subtly alters the conventional progression
through his line's ii–V–ii downbeat emphasis, the pianist plays chord substitutions that
initially complement the bass part, then deviate from it. The parts converge harmonically on the next downbeat. In b1, the musicians begin by representing the progression
faithfully; then they create dissonant effects, which they subsequently resolve. In b2,
the pianist remains close to the progression while the bass player adopts an unexpected
course, emphasizing the upper tensions of chords and playing fifths on the downbeat
of chord changes, before returning to root performance. The musicians can both take

*Example 13.6 continued*

harmonic liberties at times, creating unique colors and playful ambiguity in their portrayal of form. In c, as the bass player largely avoids performing roots on downbeats, the
pianist embellishes the progression with substitute chords. Shortly after, the musicians
converge on the form. Finally, d illustrates another common device for creating diverse
colors: pedal point technique. Typically, one instrument sustains or reiterates the tonic
or fifth of the key—sometimes with imaginative rhythmic motion—amid changing harmonic features in its own part or the other part.

a.    Harmonic liberties on piano
      Paul Chambers and Red Garland accompaniment, "Bye Bye, Blackbird"

b.    Harmonic liberties on bass

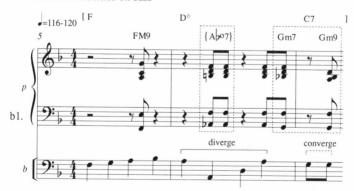

Paul Chambers and Red Garland accompaniment, "Bye Bye, Blackbird"

*Example 13.6b continued*

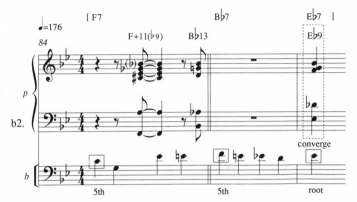

Paul Chambers and Red Garland accompaniment, "Blues by Five"

c.  Harmonic liberties on bass and piano
    Paul Chambers and Red Garland accompaniment, "Blues by Five"

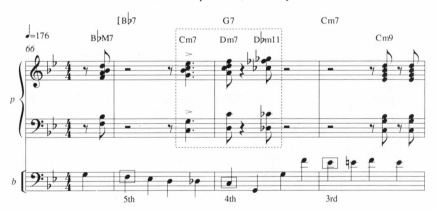

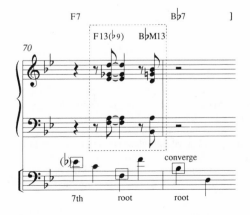

*Example 13.6 continued*

d.   Pedal point effects

Paul Chambers and Red Garland accompaniment, "Bye Bye, Blackbird"

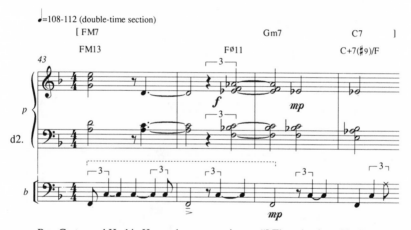

Ron Carter and Herbie Hancock accompaniment, "I Thought about You"

Example 13.7   Exchanging melodic-harmonic ideas between bass player
               and pianist
               Paul Chambers and Red Garland accompaniment, "Blues by Five"
               (all excerpts ♩=176)

Within the accompaniment's multilayered musical fabric, the bass player and pianist commonly respond to each other's suggestions. In a, the bass player's insistent performance of a pitch outside the piece's form prompts the pianist to transform the progression with a related chord substitution. In b, the pianist takes the lead in altering the form with chord substitutions, concluding with a tritone substitution that influences the bass player's choice of pitches. Artists' exchanges can also involve melodic gestures. In c1, the pianist introduces a fragment of a common blues figure, while the bass player performs an independent idea; subsequently, in c2, the artists perform the figure together, and in c3, they develop it motivically.

*Example 13.7 continued*

a.  Responding to the bass player's suggestions

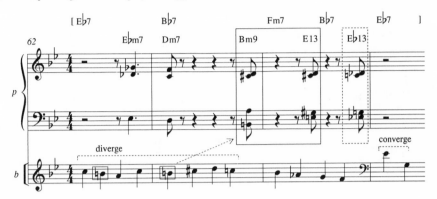

b.  Responding to the pianist's suggestions

c.  Setting up ideas for mutual performance

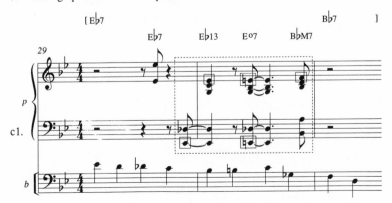

*Example 13.7c continued*

Example 13.8    Melodic-rhythmic interplay between bass player and pianist

In a, the bass player departs momentarily from walking bass patterns to reinforce an off-beat fragment of the pianist's comping patterns, and in b, the bass player engages in imitative call and and response with the pianist. As illustrated in c, artists can alternate such diverse operations with creating interlocking figures or contrapuntal patterns that converge on the downbeat to delineate the form.

Reggie Workman and McCoy Tyner accompaniment, "Softly, as in a Morning Sunrise

*Example 13.8 continued*

Ron Carter and Herbie Hancock accompaniment, "I Thought about You"

Ron Carter and Herbie Hancock accompaniment, "I Thought about You"

Example 13.9    Interplay between bass player and drummer

In a, the bass player momentarily abandons his walking bass line to reinforce two drum kicks, then imitates a third immediately after hearing it. In response, the drummer plays on-beat punches that reinforce the bass player's return to a walking bass pattern. One part's subtle phrasing shift, for example, from an even quarter-note and eighth-note feeling to a triplet swing feeling, can result in a near simultaneous fleeting shift in the other part, or, as in b, initiate subtle call and response exchanges between players. In c, an intensified feeling of swing in the drummer's part leads to comparable intensification in the bass part that progresses from straight to swing patterns and, finally, to triplet figures.

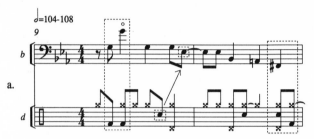

Reggie Workman and Elvin Jones accompaniment, "Softly, as in a Morning Sunrise"

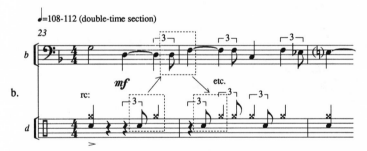

Ron Carter and Tony Williams accompaniment, "I Thought about You"

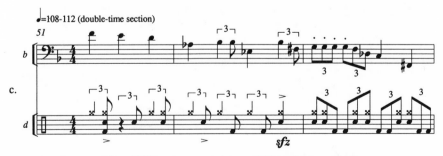

Ron Carter and Tony Williams accompaniment, "I Thought about You"

Example 13.10    Interplay between soloist and drummer

In a1, the drummer responds to the soloist's leap by creating analogous leaps from the snare drum to the hi-hat, filling in the backbeats between the soloist's pitches with accented cymbal colors. In a2, the soloist plays a rapid rhythmic passage, then rests while the drummer answers him with an intense drum fill. In b1, the drummer's on-beat quarter-note kicks inspire the soloist to begin his performance with a simple quarter-note pattern, which he develops as a motive. In b2, the soloist's creation of a metrically displaced hemiola-like pattern invites the drummer to adopt a comparable idea for his part. In c1, the drummer rests after accenting the first beat of the rhythm section break at the close of the initial melody rendition. Then, on the basis of recurring elements in the soloist's break passage, he returns to reinforce its concluding pitch with him. As illustrated in c2, a drummer accompanying a melody rendition sometimes highlights important phrase components with kicks; in c3, the drummer applies the same procedure to the solo line, successfully predicting its important features, in effect playing the soloist's line together with him.

a.    Filling open beats in solo part

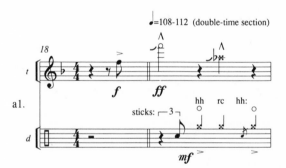

Miles Davis and Tony Williams, "I Thought about You"

Miles Davis and "Philly" Joe Jones, "Bye Bye, Blackbird"

*Example 13.10 continued*

b.  Exchanging precise rhythmic ideas

Miles Davis and "Philly" Joe Jones, "Blues by Five"

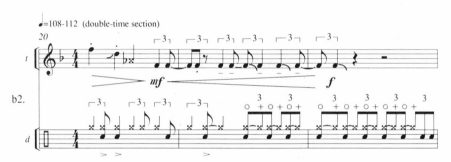

Miles Davis and Tony Williams, "I Thought about You"

c.  Reinforcing rhythmic features of melody rendition and solo part

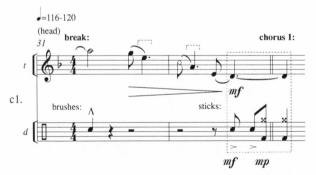

Miles Davis and "Philly" Joe Jones, "Bye Bye, Blackbird"

*Example 13.10c continued*

Red Garland and "Philly" Joe Jones, "Blues by Five"

Miles Davis and "Philly" Joe Jones, "Blues by Five"

### Example 13.11    Melodic interplay between soloist and pianist

As illustrated in a1–a2, the top voice of the pianist's block chord accompaniment or any of the inner voices can potentially perform a subtle melodic function, suggesting discrete pitches for the soloist's adoption. Conversely, the pianist can adopt prominent pitches from the solo for chord voicings. Melodic interaction is commonly more extensive. In b, the pianist helps maintain the performance's momentum and supports the soloist by filling the spaces between his phrases with independent figures. Such procedures can lead to imitative call and response exchanges. In c1, while the soloist rests, the pianist feeds him an idea in the form of a four-bar vamp pattern. The soloist immediately performs a transposed version of the pattern, then rests again, before conceiving a contrasting idea for the solo's continuation. In c2, the pianist answers a soloist's phrase with a harmonized variant, prompting the soloist to answer, in return, by performing his own variation on the pianist's version before extending it in another direction. Finally, there are exceptional moments of near-simultaneous conceptualizing of figures between soloist and pianist shown in d1 and d2. The intimate knowledge players have of each other's improvisational styles and precise vocabulary patterns enhances such events. The soloist's descending phrase in d1, for example, appears to be a precomposed melody variant, whose periodic recurrence assists the pianist in predicting its performance. (A comparable phrase appears later in the first chorus, as shown in ex. 13.19b,

*Example 13.11 continued*

and in the final statement of the melody on the recording.) In d2, the pianist may have set up the possibility of their coordinated interplay by feeding the soloist a transposed version of the same phrase, one of the soloist's own signature patterns, as an earlier melodic fill (see b above, bars 30–31).

a.   Interrelating through block chord accompaniment
     Miles Davis and "Philly" Joe Jones accompaniment, "Blues by Five" (all excerpts ♩=176)

b.   Adding melodic figures between solo phrases
     Miles Davis and Herbie Hancock, "I Thought about You"

*Example 13.11 continued*

c.   Imitative exchanges

Booker Little and Mal Waldron, "Aggression"

*Example 13.11c continued*

Booker Little and Don Friedman, "Booker's Blues"

d.    Near simultaneous conceptualizing of figures
      Miles Davis and Herbie Hancock, "I Thought about You"

*Example 13.11d continued*

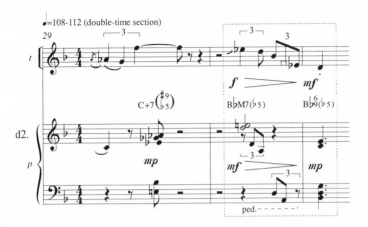

Example 13.12    Rhythmic interplay between soloist and pianist

In a1, amid his accompaniment's short eighth-note punches, the pianist fleetingly imitates the longer rhythmic values of the soloist's gesture. In a2, the pianist suggests a figure to the soloist for their mutual development. Rhythmic interplay does not only consist of exchanging specific patterns. At times, it involves regulating general features of parts like rhythmic density to create similar or complementary designs. In b, the soloist initially improvises short lyrical phrases accompanied by sustained piano patterns, but when the pianist shifts to rhythmically dense melodic commentary, it prompts the soloist to follow suit, improvising intricate linear patterns, to which the accompanist, in turn, responds by simplifying his part. Rhythmic reinforcement is another form of interaction. In c1, the pianist predicts the soloist's off-beat accentuation scheme, creating a satisfying routine that the players re-create later in the performance in c2.

a.    Imitative exchanges

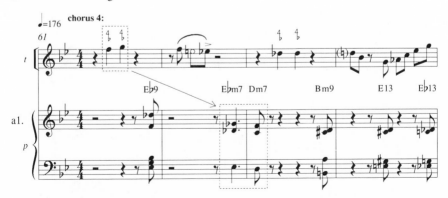

Miles Davis and Red Garland, "Blues by Five"

*Example 13.12a continued*

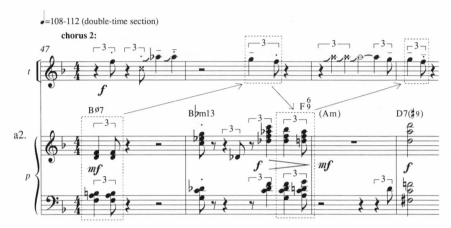

Miles Davis and Herbie Hancock, "I Thought about You"

b.   Alternating schemes of rhythmic density
     Booker Little and Jaki Byard, "Ode to Charlie Parker"

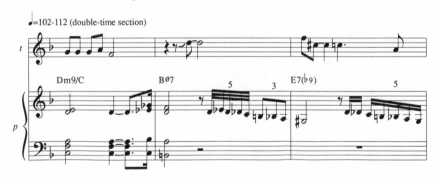

*Example 13.12b continued*

c. Reinforcing rhythmic features of solo part
Miles Davis and Red Garland, "Bye Bye, Blackbird" (all excerpts ♩=116-120)

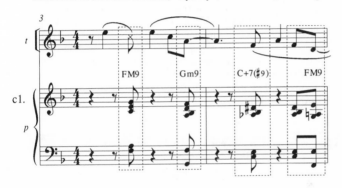

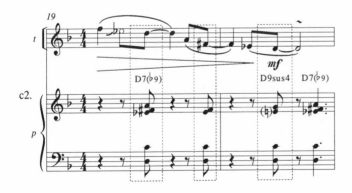

Example 13.13    Harmonic interrelationships among pianist, bass player, and
                 soloist

In a, the pianist and bass player portray a segment of a composition's structure explicitly, while the soloist, adopting a comparable approach, arpeggiates the underlying chord. More typically, as illustrated in b, the soloist creates ideas comprising imaginative mixtures of chord tones and non-chord tones, while the accompanists embellish the progression. Should the soloist emphasize non-chord tones or ignore a particular chord change within the progression—as in c, by remaining on the initial chord of the blues form—the bass player and pianist may follow suit, continuing their own performance of the initial chord through the next chord's area. In other cases, such as d, artists strive to create polychordal effects. The pianist performs a highly altered version of the progression's chords, while the soloist improvises from the materials of a Cm⁶₉ chord and the bass player walks generally in the key of C minor. Alternatively, as illustrated in e, when the solo becomes highly chromatic and harmonically ambiguous, the pianist may choose to rest temporarily while the bass player performs the roots of the progression, creating an open musical texture for the soloist. After sizing up the soloist's gesture, the pianist supports its ending with a comparable harmonically ambiguous chord. In f, musicians create imitative patterns of melodic-harmonic tension and release. As the soloist embellishes the melody with affective chromatic slides, the bass player and pianist respond, in part, with a series of chromatic gestures of their own. At the same time, they exchange harmonic ideas with a tritone emphasis. The accompanists replace the progression's D♭7 chord with a tritone substitution, the soloist concludes his phrase with a pitch a tritone away from the Cm7 chord root, and the accompanists replace the following chord with another tritone substitution.

a.    Mutual reinforcement of chord
      Miles Davis, Red Garland, and Paul Chambers, "Bye Bye, Blackbird"

*Example 13.13 continued*

b. Soloist mixes chord and non-chord tones while accompanists remain close to harmony
Miles Davis, Red Garland, and Paul Chambers, "Blues by Five"

c. Accompanists follow soloist in simplifying progression
Miles Davis, Red Garland, and Paul Chambers, "Blues by Five"

*Example 13.13 continued*

d.   Group members create polychordal effects
     John Coltrane, McCoy Tyner, and Reggie Workman, "Softly, as in a Morning Sunrise"

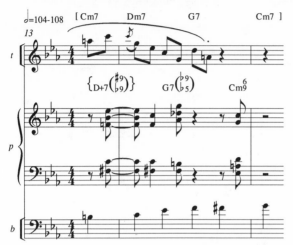

e.   Pianist rests while soloist plays harmonically ambiguous gesture
     Miles Davis, Herbie Hancock, and Ron Carter, "I Thought about You"

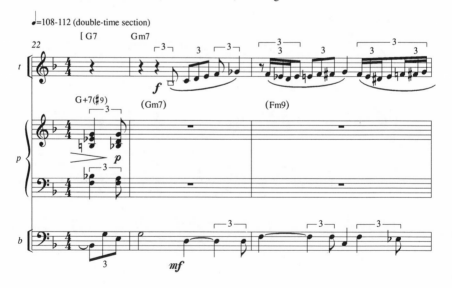

*Example 13.13e continued*

f.  Alternating melodic-harmonic tension and release
    Miles Davis, Herbie Hancock, and Ron Carter, "I Thought about You"

Example 13.14    Melodic-rhythmic interplay between soloist and bass player

In a1, the soloist adopts the rhythm and gestural shape of the bass player's figure to embellish the solo's sequential idea, and in turn, the bass player performs a slight variation on his original gesture. In a2, the accompanist departs from walking bass patterns to respond to the soloist's extended triplet passage, then returns to his former groove. There are also moments of near-simultaneous conceptualization between soloist and bass player. In b, the bass player's prediction of the soloist's idea likely reflects familiarity with the gesture as a precomposed melody variant. (The soloist repeats the gesture on the recording's final melody statement.)

a.    Triplet exchanges

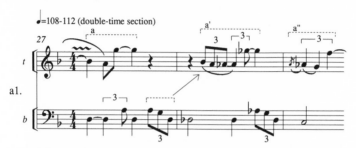

Miles Davis and Ron Carter, "I Thought about You"

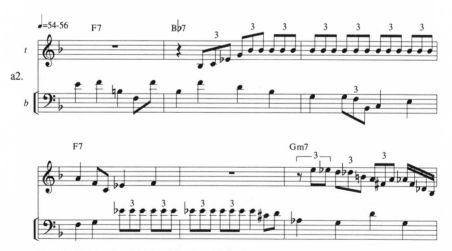

Freddie Hubbard and Richard Davis, "Blues for Duane," transcr. Monson

*Example 13.14 continued*

b. Near simultaneous conceptualizing of figure
Miles Davis and Ron Carter, "I Thought about You"

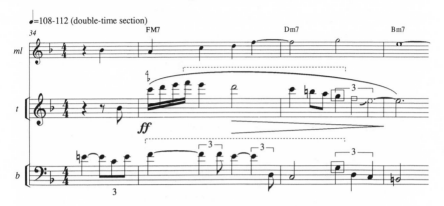

Example 13.15    Intensified conversation across all the parts
Miles Davis, Red Garland, Paul Chambers, and "Philly" Joe Jones,
"Blues by Five" (all excerpts ♩=176)

In a, intensified conversation takes the form of imitative responses to a single idea, the soloist's emphatic on-beat accent. In b, it involves a concentration of different kinds of exchanges: the near-simultaneous conceptualization of a melodic idea between the soloist and bass player, and the sharing of identical or otherwise complementary pitches among soloist and accompanists as the players alter the progression. In contrast to choruses in which performers create relatively independent complementary lines or in which exchanges are fleeting, some choruses, as illustrated in c, are deeply embedded with responsive exchanges among different combinations of players. From the onset of the chorus, a recurring rhythmic component of the soloist's motive invites the pianist and drummer to perform a related, ongoing fill together. Meanwhile, the bass player sets up a blues figure in bar 90, then plays a variant of it in bar 93, prompting the pianist to absorb a prominent component of the figure into the lower voice of the piano part, rephrasing and harmonizing it. Subsequently, the soloist adopts the rhythm and gestural shape of the pianist's figure to create a variation on the cadential portion of his previous solo phrase. Finally, the pianist responds by combining the rhythm and tonal center of the soloist's idea (in the outer voices of the piano part) with a slight variant of the bass player's previous blues figure (in the inner voice of the piano part) to produce a fitting chorus cadence.

*Example 13.15 continued*

*Example 13.15 continued*

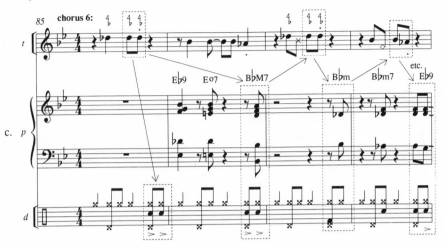

*Example 13.15c continued*

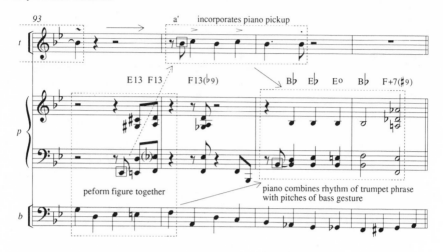

## Example 13.16  Responding to ideas introduced in the previous solo prior to its final phrase

a.  Adoption of previous soloist's recurring gesture
    Miles Davis and Sonny Rollins consecutive solos, "My Old Flame"

*Example 13.16 continued*

b.   Adoption of previous soloist's tune quotation
     Cannonball Adderley and Miles Davis consecutive solos, "Somethin' Else"

repeats melody transformation

## Example 13.17   Responding to the previous soloist's final phrase

In a, Rollins adopts Brown's final gesture as a model, rephrasing it radically and extending it with a cadential figure. In b, Golson adopts Morgan's figure as a model, rephrasing it slightly and altering its concluding interval, then answering it briefly in call
and response fashion. In c, reacting in rapid succession to the last element of Davis's
solo, Garland harmonizes it, and Coltrane expands it melodically and rhythmically, before using his variant's concluding pitch to begin his next phrase. In d, Adderley adopts
Davis's concluding gesture as a skeletal frame, instantly filling it in with scale degrees,
then developing it sequentially and extending it with an elaborate cadential improvisation. As in such instances, musicians commonly use the last component of the previous
soloist's phrase as the initial component for their own ideas. Alternatively, they can
improvise a gesture that leads into a restatement of the previous soloist's idea. In e,
Rollins plays an extended blues figure that concludes with a rephrased version of Davis's idea. Similarly, in f, Coleman improvises a short introductory figure to a variant of
the final component of Davis's phrase, then develops the idea motivically before going
on to others.

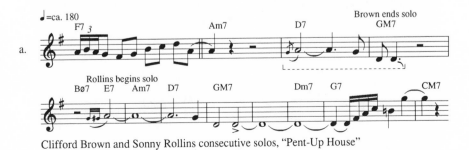

Clifford Brown and Sonny Rollins consecutive solos, "Pent-Up House"

*Example 13.17 continued*

Lee Morgan and Benny Golson consecutive solos, "Moanin'" (take 1)

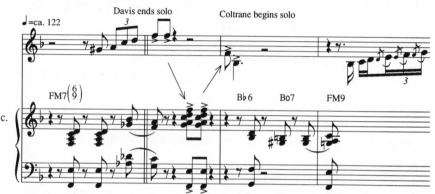

Miles Davis and John Coltrane consecutive solos, Red Garland accompaniment, "When the Lights are Low"

Miles Davis and "Cannonball" Adderley consecutive solos, "Fran Dance"

Miles Davis and Sonny Rollins consecutive solos, "Bluing"

*Example 13.17 continued*

Miles Davis and George Coleman consecutive solos, "I Thought about You"

## Example 13.18  Soloists trading fours and other short phrases

a.   Exchanges of simple one-bar ideas at moderate tempo
     Miles Davis and "Cannonball" Adderley, "Somethin' Else"

b.   Exchanges of complex four-bar ideas at fast tempo
     Charlie Parker and Fats Navarro, "The Street Beat"

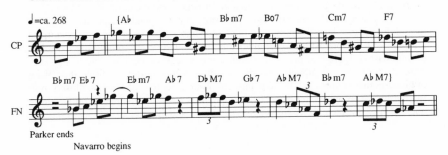

Parker ends
     Navarro begins

*Example 13.18 continued*

c.   Exchanges combining independent motive development with absorption of ideas across
     parts
     Clifford Brown and Harold Land, "The Blues Walk" (♩=ca. 138)

Example 13.19    Range, voicing, and contour during group interplay

In a1, the pianist extends his part into the piano's upper register when performing the
melody, doubling it with octaves and harmonizing it with wide intervals and distinctive
mixtures of chord tones and non-chord tones. With the soloist's entrance in a2, however,
the pianist moves the accompaniment to a lower octave and creates less dissonant voicings emphasizing thirds and other close intervals. In b, the pianist responds instantly to
the soloist's octave leap by harmonizing a comparable gesture in the accompaniment.
Subsequently, the pianist moves dramatically into a high octave, prompting the soloist
to improvise a figure that probes the high trumpet register, creating one of the solo's
peaks. In turn, the accompanist absorbs the soloist's concluding pitch into the voicing
of his responsive chord. In c1, the pianist follows the contour of the solo closely, reinforcing its shape, while the bass player improvises a line in contrary motion. Subsequently, in c2, the bass player shifts approaches to match the general contour of the solo.

*Example 13.19 continued*

a. Adopting different strategies for melody harmonization and solo accompaniment
   (all excerpts ♩=176)

a1.

Red Garland, "Blues by Five"

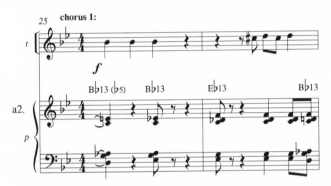

a2.

Miles Davis and Red Garland, "Blues by Five"

b. Responding to changes in range
   Miles Davis and Herbie Hancock, "I Thought about You"

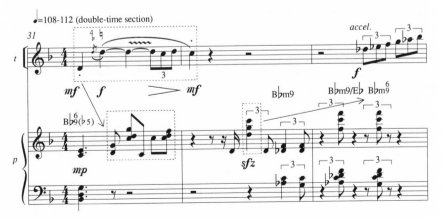

*Example 13.19b continued*

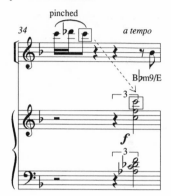

c. Creating contrapuntal schemes
   John Coltrane, McCoy Tyner, and Reggie Workman, "Softly, as in a Morning
   Sunrise" (all excerpts ♩=104-108)

Example 13.20    Accompaniments defining structural cadences through
increased activity

a.   Concluding a four-bar phrase
Miles Davis, Red Garland, Paul Chambers, and "Philly" Joe Jones, "Bye Bye, Blackbird"

b.   Concluding an eight-bar phrase
John Coltrane, McCoy Tyner, Reggie Workman, and Elvin Jones, "Softly, as in a
Morning Sunrise"

*Example 13.20 continued*

c.  Concluding a chorus
    Miles Davis, Red Garland, Paul Chambers, and "Philly" Joe Jones, "Blues by Five"

Example 13.21    Collaborative changes in mood, texture, and time-feeling
                 Miles Davis, Herbie Hancock, Ron Carter, and Tony Williams,
                 "I Thought about You"

While the drummer rests, the pianist initiates exchanges with the bass player in bar 17. Meanwhile, amplifying the dynamic swell of the pianist's figure, the soloist creates a gesture whose sustained pitch creates tension in relation to the active accompaniment, then resolves through rapid motion, reinforced by the bass player, that hints of the change to come. Responding to his counterparts, the pianist accelerates toward the downbeat of bar 19, which the soloist accentuates by leaping into the high trumpet register—dramatizing the group's formal shift into double time. With this change, the bass player and pianist modify their former melodic-rhythmic activity and settle into a more conventional accompaniment style, the pianist initially imitating the soloist's leap and descent. Compelled by events to rejoin the performance, the drummer also imitates the soloist's dramatic gesture, creating analogous leaps between drum set components and intensifying the music's new swing groove through backbeat accentuation.

*Example 13.21 continued*

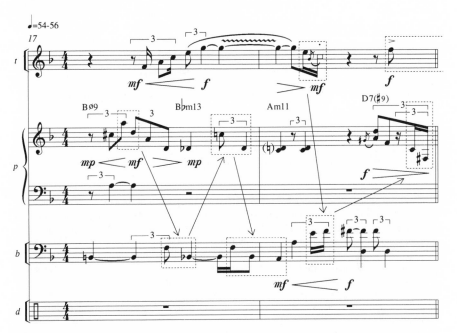

Example 13.22  Musical save
Booker Little solo, "If I Should Lose You"

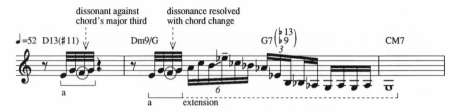

Example 13.23   Miles Davis Quintet large score segment: "Bye Bye, Blackbird"; Miles Davis, trumpet; Red Garland, piano; Paul Chambers, bass; "Philly" Joe Jones, drum set

*General solo accompaniment characteristics.* At the performance's medium tempo, the bass player improvises a steady walking bass line, while the drummer improvises spare, tasteful drum punches around a time-keeping pattern characterized by regular hi-hat kicks on beats two and four and a constant, lightly textured, wash of ride cymbal color. The piano player performs characteristically short, drum-like, off-beat punctuations, including a recurring rhythmic structural marker at the end of four-bar harmonic phrases (first introduced in bar 8), and he embellishes the composition's spare conventional progression throughout.

*Conclusion of head (bars 29–32).* As the soloist departs from the melody to improvise a segue to his solo, the rhythm section concludes its two-beat melody accompaniment with an arranged break. The drummer switches from brushes to drumsticks and punctuates the soloist's figure, setting up the subsequent change to a four-beat solo accompaniment.

*Bars 1–4 (solo chorus 1).* The pianist embellishes the progression with repeated ii–V chord substitutions (see also bars 15–16). Meanwhile, in the following bar, the drummer reinforces the off-beat piano punch with a combined ride cymbal and snare drum kick. In bar 3, the soloist creates a phrase developing the off-beat emphasis, which the pianist reinforces with off-beat and double eighth-note punches.

*Bars 5–8.* Between the soloist's phrases, the pianist adds a short punctuating kick, and the drummer immediately responds with a colorful cymbal accent. The pianist then develops his former double eighth-note figure. This elicits an imitative response, first from the bass player, next from the drummer, who includes it in the cadential fill with which he punctuates the pianist's structural marker, signaling the A section's close. At the same time, the group creates an interesting scheme of tension and release, beginning with the bass player's dissonant pitches in bar 6 and resolving with the musicians' harmonic convergence on the downbeat of bar 9.

*Bars 9–12.* While the pianist provides a spare accompaniment that remains close to the static harmony of this segment of the piece, the bass player walks a steep four-bar phrase implying an alternating ii–V cadence, and the soloist suddenly increases his part's range through a rhythmically embellished version of his opening segue figure. In bar 12, the pianist and drummer respond with interlocking figures of increased range and rhythmic density, marking the close of the four-bar harmonic section, and recalling in the drum part the rhythm section's previous double eighth-note comping figure.

*Example 13.23 continued*

*Bars 13–16.* Following the drummer's on-beat accents in bar 12, the soloist develops an ornamented on-beat quarter-note idea, building tension through repetition and anticipation of the chord change in bar 15. Meanwhile, as the drummer increases his activity, inserting punches between those of the spare piano accompaniment, the bass player, in bar 14, responds to the pianist's voicing of a C7♭9 chord by absorbing its chromatic alteration into the bass line.

*Bars 17–20.* The soloist formulates call and response phrases with an increasing off-beat emphasis (reminiscent of earlier descending gestures), which the pianist and drummer reinforce with punches. Meanwhile, the pianist and bass player reinforce each other's alteration of the progression in bar 17. In bars 18–19, however, they take divergent courses. The pianist anticipates the D7 chord, while the bass player presents a subtle surprise by leading an ascending chromatic gesture to the pitch F instead of D on the downbeat, before outlining the Cm6 chord. The F reinforces the soloist's pitch, a blue third in relation to the preceding piano chord. Subsequently, the soloist colors his descending figure with an E♭ pitch, derived, perhaps, from the underlying chord in the conventional progression, or from the preceding piano voicings that feature the pitch as a common tone. The players converge on the same harmonic area in bar 20.

*Bars 21–24.* The soloist paraphrases the melody, then, after resting, creates an exciting high point through the most rapid commentary of the chorus. Responding to the soloist and highlighting the close of the bridge, the drummer plays his accompaniment's most active fill and the pianist performs his structural marker. In bar 23, the group's mutual transformation of the conventional progression (repeated during subsequent choruses on the original recording) suggests that the D♭7 sonority was an arranged chord substitution. In bar 24, the pianist, developing the harmonic motion he created in the preceding bar, embellishes the progression with a tritone chord substitution that resolves to the subsequent chord by a half step.

*Bars 25–28.* Initiating his longest, most elaborate eighth-note phrase, the soloist leaps again to the highest pitch of his improvisation, then ornaments his descending gesture with a prominent blue-third grace note, which prompts the pianist to interject a bluesy chord containing the flatted third into the progression. Meanwhile, as the bass player walks into the upper register, the soloist, in bar 26, absorbs and expands upon an ascending chromatic fragment of the bass line initiated on beat three of the previous bar. Throughout, the drummer and pianist create largely interlocking figures that sometimes simultaneously reinforce an element within the solo part. The pianist initially plays sparingly while the drummer plays dense rhythmic punches. Then, in bar 27, the two players switch strategies, the drummer withholding drum kicks but performing a unique variation on the ride cymbal and hi-hat time-keeping pattern.

*Bars 29–32.* The soloist concludes the chorus with a variant of his opening segue figure, and the rhythm section alters its accompaniment dramatically to highlight the chorus ending. The bass player increases his rhythmic embellishment of the walking bass line and, with striking leaps and flamboyant flat-ninth dissonance (bar 30), follows the soloist's general contour. Previously, he has often created contrary motion (bars 1–4, 7–8, for example). The pianist instantly seizes the flat ninth for his voicing, while also imitating the soloist's gesture—leaping, then creating a descending line in the upper voice of his distinctive C pedal cadence. In bar 32, the pianist creates a blues effect by inserting augmented chords between the preceding and following major chords, as the soloist extends his phrase over the chorus boundary.

*Example 13.23 continued*

*Example 13.23 continued*

*Example 13.23 continued*

*Example 13.23 continued*

*Example 13.23 continued*

*Example 13.23 continued*

*Example 13.23 continued*

*Example 13.23 continued*

Example 13.24   John Coltrane Quartet large score segment: "Softly, as in a Morning Sunrise"; John Coltrane, soprano saxophone; McCoy Tyner, piano; Reggie Workman, bass; Elvin Jones, drum set

*General accompaniment characteristics.* At the performance's fast tempo, the rhythm section creates a powerful, densely textured accompaniment that reflects innovative musical practices of the sixties. The drummer does not restrict cymbals to an ostinato time-keeping role. Sometimes, he withholds hi-hat performance on beat two or four (bars 1, 9); other times, he withholds its performance for a measure or more (bars 20–21). Yet other times, he accents beat three (bar 64) or accents the second half of beats (bars 31–32, 41). He frequently plays syncopated ride cymbal patterns, sometimes eliding them with other patterns over the barline or combining them with complex drum figures. At one point, he leaves a beat silent in the accompaniment (bar 7). Additionally, he does not limit drum figures to brief punctuations but offers a relatively constant commentary on the performance through extended fills created from diverse elements. Some fills serve as structural markers delineating four- and eight-bar phrases, but they commonly extend slightly over harmonic section boundaries or merge with subsequent passages of intense drum expression.

Throughout, the bass player and pianist transform the piece's conventional structure to provide a varied harmonic setting for the solo, which is based largely on the intervallic structure of the Dorian mode. The pianist adopts two general approaches to differentiate components of the piece's AABA form. He tends to simplify the A section's progression, featuring quartal Cm$^6_9$ or Cm11 chord voicings as a kind of harmonic drone, with occasional embellishing V or ii–V chord substitutions. He adopts a more conservative approach to the B section, mixing or alternating tertian voicings with quartal voicings and elaborating the progression with various chord substitutions. The rhythm section's accompaniment scheme also includes a few recurring figures. Generally, at the beginning of four-bar phrases, the pianist plays a rhythmic structural marker pattern (bar 1, beats one and two) or its syncopated variant (bars 4–5). At the beginning of four-bar phrases in the A section, the bass player commonly performs an inverted arch gesture alternating tonic to dominant root movement (bars 1–2), which represents a slightly simplified version of the conventional progression. Sometimes, he varies and displaces the gesture (bars 6–7).

*Bars 1–8 (chorus 1).* The soloist initiates his performance with a pair of call and response gestures, followed by a contrasting gesture. The first and third of these figures begin and end with prominent melody pitches. At the same time, in bar 1, the bass player performs his inverted arch gesture and the pianist introduces his rhythmic structural marker, accentuated by the drummer. Subsequently, the drummer places drum kicks primarily between the piano kicks until bar 4, where his final accent reinforces the start of the pianist's variant marker. In bars 5–6, repeated elements in the soloist's descent invite rhythmic reinforcement across the rhythm section. During the first eight bars, the upper voice of the piano part complements the general contour of the first and third solo gestures, while the bass line begins with contrary motion, then matches the soloist's general ascent and descent. The pianist and bass player simplify the progression, with the bass part initially alternating tonic to dominant movement in relation to the form, then displacing the gesture in bar 6. Shortly after, the soloist's rest, a comparatively high, sustained piano voicing, and a drum fill mark the end of the first A section.

*Example 13.24 continued*

*Bars 9–16.* As the soloist creates a series of climbing figures that land on a beat-three rhythmic target, the pianist and drummer leave the third beat relatively open in their accompaniment. The soloist answers his third figure with a short staccato punch as if accompanying himself. Meanwhile, in bar 9, an unusual, coordinated bass and drum punch reinforces the initial component of the soloist's figure, and in the next bar, the syncopated bass kick inspires the drummer to feature syncopation in his ongoing ride cymbal part. In bars 11–12, the pianist substitutes altered ii–V chords for the conventional progression's Fm7 chord, and the soloist begins an extended, highly embellished phrase, whose cadential Cm$^6_9$ gesture creates polychordal effects with the pianist's altered voicings. The soloist subsequently resolves the tension in his part by reducing the range of his figures markedly and coming to rest on a low sustained pitch, the tonic of the chord in bar 16.

In the second A section, the drummer does not reinforce the pianist's structural marker, but at the end of bar 13, he catches the piano punch and, in the next bar, reinforces the concluding pitch of the soloist's phrase. The bass player creates considerable excitement during these events. Through his striking leap and off-beat improvised introductory figure in bar 9, he displaces by one bar, a version of his recurring gesture, before climbing gradually to the high register of his instrument. In bar 13, the soloist plays his first note outside the predominant mode. Over the course of the solo, such fleeting pitches (principally A♭, B♮, D♭, and E♮) add color and tension to the soloist's figures. In some instances, the pitches allude to an underlying chord in the conventional progression. In other instances, appearances of A♭ and B♮ seem to represent a whimsical flirtation with movement to an altered version of the piece's dominant chord (G7), displaced from its position within the form.

*Bars 17–24.* Perhaps influenced by the bass player's upper-register exploration, the soloist ascends to the upper saxophone register, where he performs a variant of his solo's second gesture, then creates the chorus's high point with improvised vocal cries. Meanwhile, differentiating treatment of the bridge from the A section, the pianist elaborates the composition's progression, mixing conventional tertian voicings with quartal voicings, while the bass player largely emphasizes the conventional structure. While still in the high register in bar 19, however, the bass player introduces a prominent altered pitch, D♭, which the soloist instantly adopts for his climactic vocal cry—the first sustained venture outside the solo's mode—and the pianist reinforces with his C7♭9 chord voicing.

In bar 20, the bass player performs a colorful tritone substitution beneath the cry. Then, as the rhythm section converges harmonically in the next bar, the soloist acknowledges the chord change with a passing A♭ pitch. Subsequently, the pianist and bass player both perform a diminished chord substitution, whose ambiguity the soloist exploits with a climbing chromatic gesture. As the soloist reiterates his vocal cry with the piece's tonic, distinctively inflected, the bass player reinforces the pianist's syncopated punch. Next, the soloist emphasizes the A♭ pitch once again, which the pianist instantly adopts for his voicing of an A♭ chord insertion. The group converges on the conventional harmony on the downbeat of bar 24, with the soloist responding to the pianist's altered G7 chord voicing by weaving B♮ and A♭ pitches into the solo line. Accompanying these developments to the conclusion of the bridge are intensified drum commentary and a piano part whose upper voice leaps high with the soloist's vocal cry in bar 22, then follows its general descent, as does the bass line.

*Example 13.24 continued*

*Bars 25–32.* As the soloist completes, then answers, his previous figure with a short response, the pianist repeats his previous accompaniment design of a leap and descent. Meanwhile, the bass player plays his tonic-to-dominant gesture, then, in bar 28, complements the pianist's recurring altered ii–V substitution for the Fm7 chord. Subsequently, the soloist brings the chorus to a close with an animated, extended line beginning and ending with melody pitches; it rises to the upper register, then climbs down to a tonic riffing pattern, emphasizing the same pitch on which he began the chorus. In bar 30, the solo line includes the A♭ pitch, perhaps responding to the pianist's preceding altered Dm7 chord. Throughout the section, the drummer provides support by improvising two four-bar phrases, each gradually increasing in intensity and often reinforcing the pianist's punches. The second phrase ends with distinctive hi-hat color and combined snare and bass drum kicks, while the pianist expands his voicings' registral placement dramatically. At the same time, he features substitutions, which the bass player reinforces with a high D pitch before beginning his descent. The collective events highlight the close of the first chorus and propel the musicians into the next.

*Bars 33–40 (chorus 2).* Although beginning with a familiar design of short ascending, then descending, figures, the soloist shifts the rhythmic target of his figures to beat four before reverting to the former target in bar 39. Meanwhile, the drummer continues to create commentaries of complex four-bar phrases. Initially, the bass player and piano player descend together in bars 33–35; then they move in contrary motion. The accompanists remain relatively close to the conventional progression throughout the new A section, but in bar 36, they perform the same chord substitution together, reacting, perhaps, to the soloist's allusion to the dominant chord in the previous bar.

*Bars 41–48.* Here, the rhythm section plays an especially dramatic role in intensifying the music by introducing polyrhythmic tension, then resolving it. On the downbeat of bar 41, the pianist reiterates his structural marker figure without the drummer's reinforcement, then continues to create patterns emphasizing dotted-quarter-note groupings, while the drummer initiates, on the second beat, patterns emphasizing groupings of three quarter-notes. Meanwhile, the bass player departs from walking bass lines to create wide leaps and a broken syncopated figure whose initiation coincides with the second drum kick. Amid this instability, the soloist reacts to the rhythm section's altered dominant chord by ending his phrase with a B♮ pitch. Subsequently, as the soloist sets up striking call and response patterns with wide leaps in bars 45–46, the rhythm section suddenly changes the music's texture again. The pianist drops out, the drummer reduces his part to cymbals, and the bass player returns to a lower range to perform an off-beat, syncopated variation on his recurring gesture. Two bars later, when the soloist rests, the pianist rejoins the performance, rapidly expanding the registral placement of voicings, the bass player develops an ascending walking line, and the drummer introduces an intense fill. All together, the rhythm section players drive toward the temporary release of tension on the downbeat of the bridge.

*Bars 49–56.* Perhaps inspired by the rhythm section's previous ascending figures, the soloist again creates a series of patterns climbing into the upper register. In contrast, the pianist reduces the range and rhythmic density of his accompaniment or comping figures markedly, returning to the strategy of mixing tertian and quartal voicings and elaborating the conventional progression. The bass player and pianist follow the same general plan, with occasional deviations and exchanges. In bar 51, the bass player emphasizes the E♮ pitch from the conventional harmony for the first time, which the

*Example 13.24 continued*

pianist, after playing a substitution, includes in his delayed performance of an altered C+7 voicing. Reacting to the changing harmonic complexion of the accompaniment, the soloist, in bar 52, weaves the pianist's augmented-fifth pitch and the bass player's prominent flat-ninth pitch into his line, then, in the next bar, plays an E♮ pitch for the first time. Subsequently, the bass player and pianist collaborate on diminished substitutions, prompting the soloist to venture momentarily outside the mode again. Such interplay, like that of the flat-ninth exchange above, is reminiscent of the improvisers' interplay during the previous B section. Meanwhile, the drummer begins the bridge by playing the accentuation pattern associated with the pianist's structural marker figure, but without piano reinforcement. Later, responding to the soloist's extended phrase and emphatic ending in bar 56, he closes the bridge with a strong fill that features the bass drum and reinforces some of the piano punches. The last piano punch includes a prominent B♮ in the upper voice that resolves the raised-ninth tension in the preceding sustained voicing.

*Bars 57–64.* Against the background of the pianist and drummer independently hinting at the structural marker figure, and their most recent coordinated punches above, the two accompanists set up another musical intensification episode in bar 57. Not only do they coordinate their performance of the marker, as they did initially in bar 1 of the solo, but they develop its dotted-quarter-note element together. Increasing the density of their coordinated punches, they superimpose upon the underlying meter a polyrhythmic scheme, which the drummer accentuates further with combined snare and bass drum punches. At the same time, the bass player creates tension by moving into the extreme high register and shifting his eighth-note embellishment of the walking bass line, before gradually reducing range. Meanwhile, in bar 57, the soloist concludes his short answering phrase with a B♮ pitch, possibly in response to the pianist's preceding dominant chord voicing, then continues to use the pitch in his next phrase, accompanied by similar harmonic flirtations in the bass and piano parts. Finally, increasing the range and length of his ideas, he rides the crest of the rhythm section's wave to create the chorus climax: performing his highest sustained wailing figures over the accompaniment. The soloist reduces his intensity only slightly by returning to the tonic at the close of the chorus, which the drummer marks with a powerful distinctive drum fill.

*Example 13.24 continued*

Example 13.24 continued

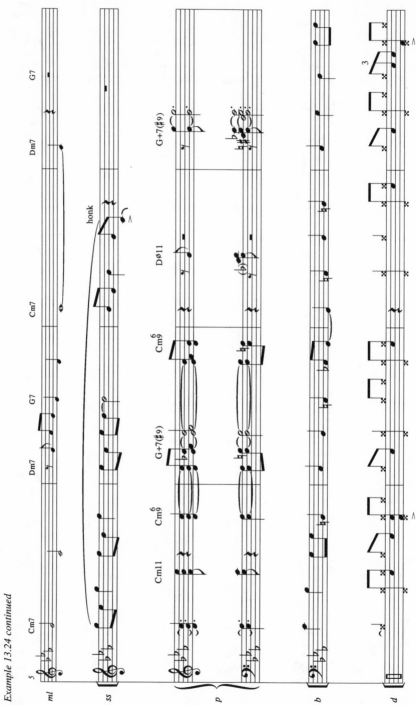

*Example 13.24 continued*

*Example 13.24 continued*

*Example 13.24 continued*

*Example 13.24 continued*

*Example 13.24 continued*

*Example 13.24 continued*

Example 13.24 continued

*Example 13.24 continued*

*Example 13.24 continued*

*Example 13.24 continued*

*Example 13.24 continued*

*Example 13.24 continued*

*Example 13.24 continued*

*Example 13.24 continued*

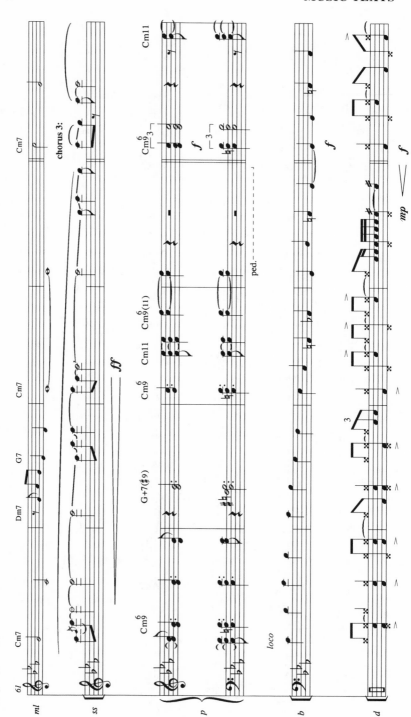

Example 13.25    Miles Davis Quintet large score segment: "I Thought about You"; Miles Davis, trumpet; Herbie Hancock, piano; Ron Carter, bass; Tony Williams, drum set

*General accompaniment characteristics.* The group's performance illustrates the expanded role and expression of the sixties rhythm section, even when creating jazz within the structure of a conventional progression. There is constant interplay among the musicians. From moment to moment, different individuals take initiative for the music's direction, respond to their counterparts (overtly absorbing material from them or offering complementary support), recede into the group's musical texture, or temporarily drop out of the performance. Operating within the piece's ABAC form and a rich emotional atmosphere created by the soloist's affective melody rendition, the band members sometimes take great liberties. They shift unexpectedly into double time in bar 19, rather than at the beginning of a major harmonic section; the soloist extends his performance into the second chorus structure, rather than concluding at the end of the first chorus (bar 47 in the double-time numbering system). Throughout, the artists interpret rhythm with endless nuances. In relation to the original or subsequent tempo, the band members sometimes double up on the time or play at the slower rate, establish a two-beat or a four-beat feeling, or emphasize even eighth-note and sixteenth-note subdivisions or, to varying degrees, swing them. Amid the group's fluid rhythmic shifts, the players sometimes juxtapose different grooves, increasing tension; other times, they converge on the same groove, resolving tension.

Just as the soloist remains close to the melody in his rendition, the bass player and pianist remain close to the composition's conventional progression. Occasionally, they embellish it with tritone substitutions or alter the quality of chords for coloristic effect. For the most part, the bass player drives the group with a highly rhythmically embellished, two-beat style. Articulating pitches with a distinctive singing quality, he provides a solid harmonic foundation emphasizing chord roots and fifths, with periodic double stops combining roots and thirds. This approach frees the pianist from the necessity of providing complete, root-based chord voicings. Rather, he emphasizes texturally and rhythmically diverse structures with striking harmonic alterations, which he alternates with periodic melodic commentary. Meanwhile, the drummer creates an inventive part whose rhythmic figures, instrumentation, color, and dynamics are ever changing. He rarely creates separate layers of ostinato time-keeping patterns and drum punctuations. Instead, he creates unique linear ideas featuring individual instruments, or pairs of instruments, or various combinations in integrated, constantly unfolding gestures of drum and cymbal sound.

*Bars 1–4 (chorus 1).* The soloist rephrases the standard melody, leaving a substantial rest between phrase components, which the bass player and pianist fill together with a nearly identical gesture. The gesture establishes the tempo and creates an embellished two-beat feeling as the drummer enters with soft brush strokes. Amid the dense texture of the pianist's appoggiatura-like figures, the bass player's double stops and slides, and imitative triplet motion across the parts, the soloist completes his melody phrase with a highly vocalized, speech-inflected delivery. Subsequently, the bass player creates a fill with strong rhythmic motion over the barline to the root on the downbeat, an approach he favors throughout the performance.

*Bars 5–8.* The pianist reduces activity during the soloist's initial statement, then responds to the bass player's triplet chromatic gesture by creating inner-voice piano movement, which in turn inspires the soloist's affective chromatic slides and timbral changes when varying the melody. In bars 7–8, the bass player and pianist develop the

*Example 13.25 continued*

triplet gesture further, the pianist initially absorbing the soloist's melody pitches into the right-hand voicing and creating distinctive patterns of descending parallel fourths. At the same time, the group converses through a scheme of alternating harmonic dissonance. The rhythm section embellishes the progression with tritone substitution chords, and in between its alterations, the soloist concludes his melody variant with a pitch that is a tritone away from the root of the prevailing harmony. In bar 8, the bass player's rhythmic motion over the barline to the subsequent chord root resolves the dissonance.

*Bars 9–11.* The music's mood changes unexpectedly as the artists intensify their conversation. The pianist, predicting the soloist's double-time variation on the melody, plays it in near unison, then, while the soloist rests, performs a rapid interlocking fill with the bass player. In turn, the pianist rests and the bass player reduces activity while the soloist continues with a melody variant. Responding to the variant, the pianist and bass player perform melodic fills in contrary motion. This propels the soloist's ascent to a sustained pitch, which generates tension in relation to the active accompaniment. Meanwhile, in bar 11, the bass player reacts to the pianist's grace note by creating a similar effect within an off-beat double-pedal figure, and the drummer suddenly drops out of the performance.

*Bars 12–14.* The pianist and bass player create coordinated contrapuntal patterns over the barline, reestablishing a clear two-beat feeling with a rhythmically spare, harmonically lush accompaniment in relation to the fluid vocalized solo phrase.

*Bars 15–18.* In bar 16, the group's rhythmic activity heats up again with rapid downward gestures in the soloist's and bass player's parts. The bass player's development of the descending gesture elicits an imitative response in the next bar from the pianist, while the soloist creates contrary motion with a melody variant, which expands upon the dynamic swell in the pianist's gesture. Amid the group's melodic-rhythmic commentaries, triplet and sixteenth-note activity builds in intensity across the parts until, in bar 18, near-simultaneous sixteenth-note gestures by the soloist and bass player and a hard-driving, bluesy piano fill inspire the soloist to leap dramatically to the high trumpet register on the downbeat of the next measure.

*Bars 19–22.* The soloist's leap reinforces the group's formal change to double time. Instantly, the drummer rejoins the performance to complement the change, using sticks to create an analogous leap from the snare drum to cymbals and generating a strong sense of swing by accenting the open backbeats in the solo part with hi-hat punches. Meanwhile, the pianist, switching to a conventional block chord comping style, also imitates the soloist's gesture with a leap and descent in the top line of his chord voicings, as the bass player creates a swinging, highly rhythmically embellished, two-beat accompaniment. After descending, the soloist intensifies the music's swing by creating a metrically displaced, hemiola-like pattern whose blues inflections elicit a bluesy grace note response in the piano part, and whose rhythm inspires a comparable pattern in the drum part, supported by the bass player's and pianist's triplet figures. In relation to this section's simple lead sheet model, the group's elaborate harmonic, melodic, and rhythmic creations underscore the extent to which compositions serve jazz musicians as vehicles for their own inventions.

*Example 13.25 continued*

*Bars 23–25.* In bar 23, the group dissolves its new groove as suddenly as it established it. To allow space for the soloist's new idea, the pianist drops out, and the drummer and bass player simpify their parts. As the bass player outlines a descending step progression, the soloist improvises a rhythmically fluid, harmonically ambiguous, climbing chromatic gesture, whose concluding pitch the pianist reinforces with a comparably ambiguous altered chord. In bar 25, the bass player responds with a chromatically embellished fill over the barline, and the drummer provides a short punctuating press roll.

*Bars 26–29.* The music's complexion changes once again as the drummer develops a rhythmically intense idea that combines different cymbal sounds and spare drum punches, the pianist plays a unique melodic-rhythmic fill, and the soloist introduces a new ascending gesture, perhaps imitating the leap in the piano part. Meanwhile, the bass player, supported by the drummer's overlapping figures, develops a descending gesture, whose triplet eighth-note ornament, in bar 27, the soloist instantly seizes for the sequential development of his figure. Reminiscent of the bass line in bars 23–25, the peaks of the soloist's sequence create a descending step progression, which leads into the melody pitch in bar 29. In bar 29 (bar 24 at the original tempo), the rhythm section marks the conclusion of the bridge with an intense drum fill and tritone substitute root movement to the following chord.

*Bars 30–34.* In bars 30–31, the soloist performs a descending signature pattern— reinforced, in part, by the drummer's kicks and a similar piano gesture—which leads to a familiar, near-simultaneous performance of a melody variant by the soloist and pianist. (The pianist's earlier performance of the soloist's signature pattern in bars 10–11 may have suggested its subsequent use to the soloist.) In bars 32–33, the rhythm section fills in the rest in the solo part with exciting motion. Creating wide leaps, the bass player flirts momentarily with a four-beat pattern before returning to lively, embellished two-beat figures. Meanwhile, the pianist leaps to the upper register and expands the registral placement of his voicings, and the drummer intensifies his commentary by shifting to a predominantly off-beat, straight eighth-note groove—juxtaposing this with the ongoing swing triplet feeling of his counterparts. The changing accompaniment prompts the soloist's ascent to the upper trumpet register through rapid triplet motion. At the same time, in bars 32–34, the pianist and bass player create harmonic tension, in part by anticipating or delaying their respective performance of the conventional chord changes.

*Bars 34–37.* In bar 34, the pianist's adoption of the soloist's concluding pitch for the upper voice of an answering chord inspires the soloist to leap yet higher, before descending through a floating vocalized phrase that lands on a prominent melody pitch. Meanwhile, in bar 35, the pianist and bass player resolve their previous tension by converging on the harmony at a culminating point in the solo. At the same time, the bass player performs a fragment of the soloist's gesture in near unison, the pianist creates an analogous melodic shape with increasingly simplified comping patterns that match the gesture's rhythmic quality, and the drummer simplifies his commentary, concluding with distinctive cymbal color. The soloist's gesture creates a dramatic climax at the approximate point where the composition's melody reaches its highest peak.

*Example 13.25 continued*

*Bars 38–41.* The group gradually simplifies its musical texture to provide another contrast. While the soloist plays a vocalized pattern in the middle trumpet register, generating suspense with his longest sustained pitch, the rhythm section follows a familiar accompaniment design. It initially increases, then reduces, the range and complexity of its parts, with the drummer eventually dropping out of the performance. In bar 40, the soloist's movement to a pitch a tritone away from the chord root prompts the accompanists to adopt a related chord substitution.

*Bars 42–46.* The music's mood and rhythmic complexion change radically in bar 43, with four bars remaining before the close of the first chorus. At the end of his phrase, the soloist falls off to a pitch that the pianist adopts for the upper voice of his next chord, altering the conventional harmony chromatically. Against the slower motion of the pianist's comping figures, the bass player shifts from his typical time-keeping role to perform a syncopated double-pedal figure, which creates increasing tension in relation to the changing harmony of the other parts. Meanwhile, the drummer rejoins the performance, stirring up rhythmic activity with a march-like, predominantly off-beat, straight eighth-note figure, to which the soloist responds with an ascending triplet gesture. The soloist's ascent, supported by the drummer's cadential press rolls and the bass player's shift to a four-beat walking bass line, brings about a convergence of the players' distinct grooves upon a unified swing groove at the onset of the new chorus.

*Bars 47–49 (chorus 2).* While the soloist initiates a series of relatively high, call and response phrases, the rhythm section, in bar 47, releases the tension created by the bass player's previous double pedal by converging on the same chord substitution. Subsequently, it remains close to the conventional progression, altering the quality of one chord and inserting another into the progression. At the same time, the accompanists build tension through a climbing bass line, an increasingly active drum part, and a burst of rhythmically dense piano punches with markedly expanded registral placement.

*Bars 50–56.* Spurred on by the bass player's upper register excursion and the drummer's intensified fills, the soloist makes one last striking ascent, delivering, for the final climax, two vocal cries reinforced by the pianist's comping patterns, then descending. The accompanists answer the soloist's descent with powerful drum fills, a rhythmically embellished bass line, and high, hard-biting, six- and seven-note piano voicings. The soloist concludes his improvisation with an affective phrase, as much sung or spoken as performed, while the rhythm section reduces its activity to prepare the way for the next soloist.

*Example 13.25 continued*

*Example 13.25 continued*

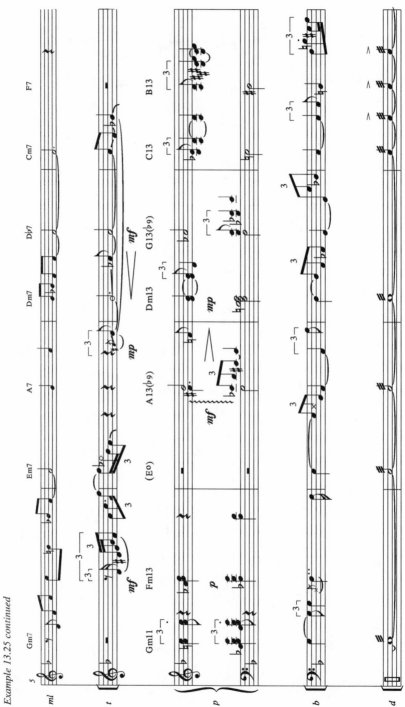

*Example 13.25 continued*

*Example 13.25 continued*

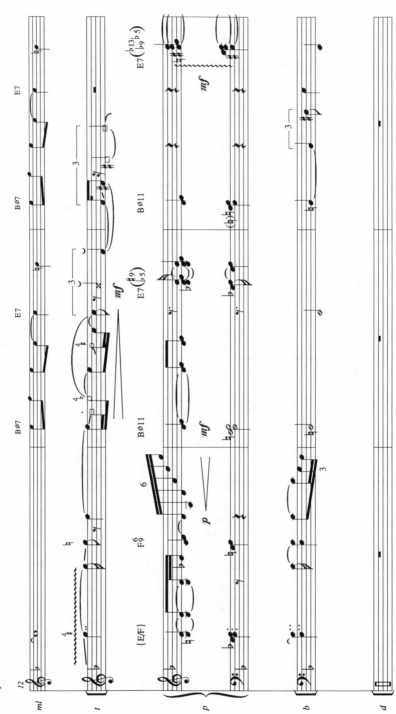

*Example 13.25 continued*

*Example 13.25 continued*

*Example 13.25 continued*

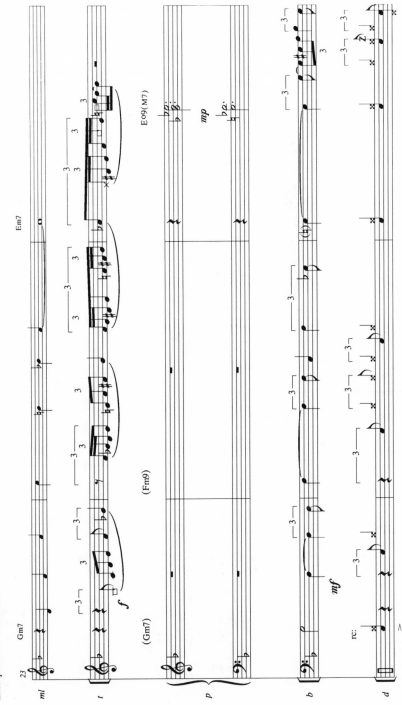

*Example 13.25 continued*

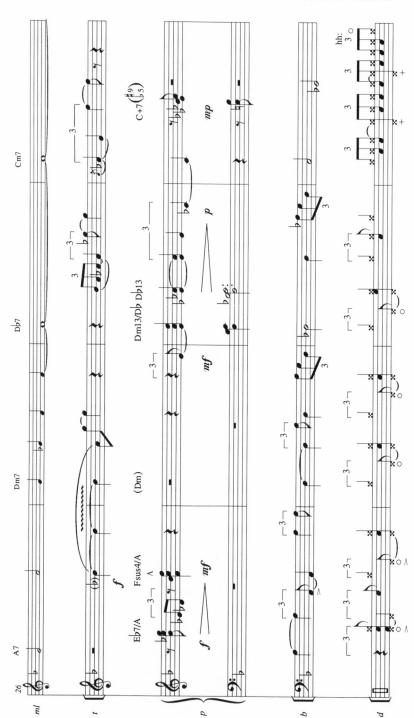

*Example 13.25 continued*

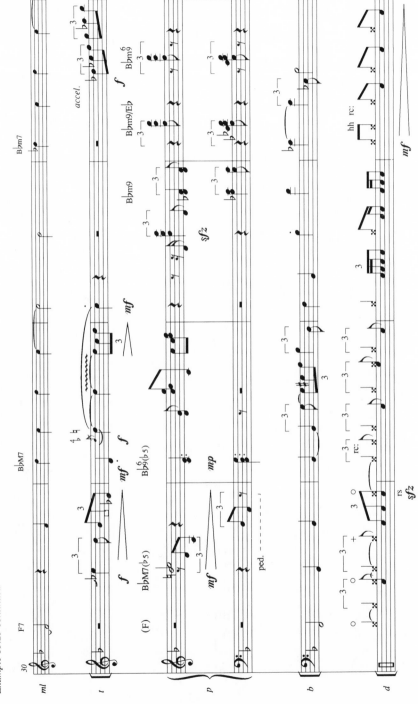

*Example 13.25 continued*

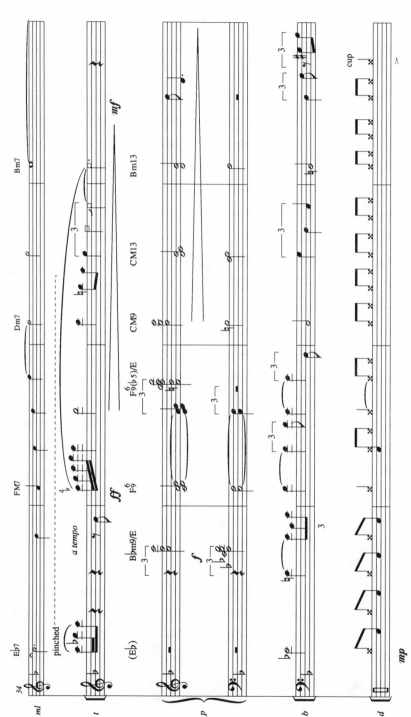

*Example 13.25 continued*

*Example 13.25 continued*

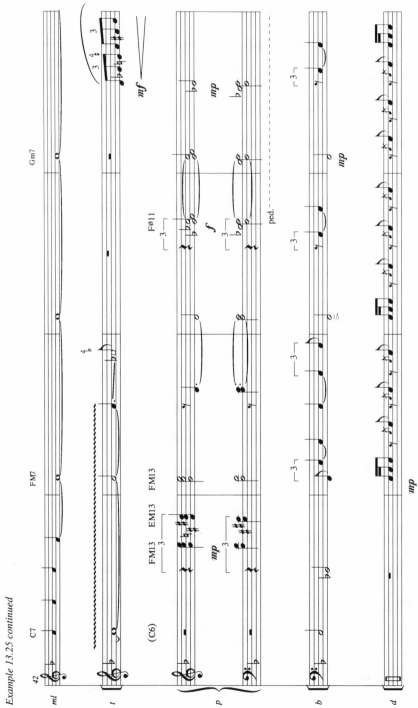

Example 13.25 continued

*Example 13.25 continued*

*Example 13.25 continued*

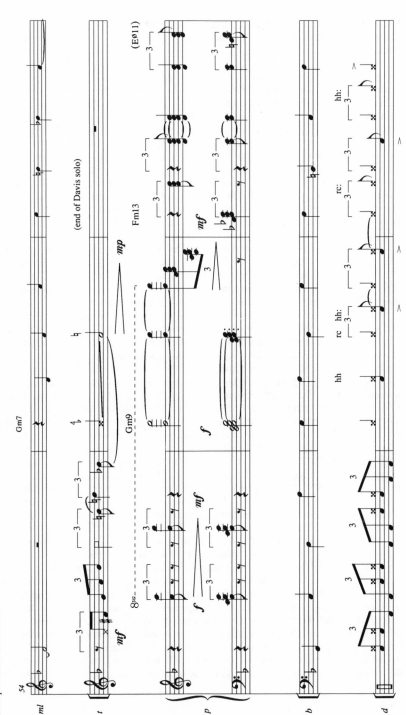

Example 13.26    Miles Davis Quintet large score segment: "Blues by Five";
Miles Davis, trumpet; Red Garland, piano; Paul Chambers, bass; "Philly" Joe Jones,
drum set

*General solo accompaniment characteristics.* Complementing the soloist's strategy of
resting in the last bar of each chorus to highlight the blues form, the rhythm section
increases its activity during the final cadence of each chorus. Typically, in various
combined maneuvers, the drummer plays distinctive fills, the pianist switches to denser
or more sustained rhythmic patterns and increases his harmonic embellishment of the
progression, and the bass player changes the direction of his melodic gestures, for
example, reducing range to ascend from the tonic on the downbeat of the new chorus.
Over their accompaniment's course, the players ornament or transform particular
segments of the conventional progression with a number of recurring chord
substitutions. In bars 2 and 5–6 of the basic blues form, they sometimes insert an E°7
chord between the E♭7 and B♭7 chords; in bars 11–12, they insert E♭7 and E°7 chords
before the B♭7 chord. For further variety, they change the B♭7 chord to a B♭M7 chord
or replace it with a Dm7 chord. Such operations periodically create a prominent step
progression, E♭–E♮–F, in the bass player's line or in one of the voices of the pianist's
part. In bars 8–9 of the basic blues form, they occasionally replace the conventional
G7–to–Cm7 movement with a Dm7–to–D♭m7–to–Cm7 movement, which, in some
instances, creates a prominent step progression, F–F♭–E♭, in the upper voice of the
pianist's part. In bar 9, they sometimes add a tritone chord substitution.

*Bars 1–24 (head).* Featuring relatively high voicings, the pianist doubles the
melody in octaves with open fifth or sixth intervals in the right hand, and in the left
hand outlines a seventh, frequently omitting the chord root in the bass. The parallel
movement of the pianist's hands generates distinctive, dissonant harmonic colors
throughout. Meanwhile, the bass player follows the convention of root performance on
the downbeats of chord changes in bars 1–4. Subsequently, he fashions a harmonically
adventurous bass line by emphasizing fifths on downbeats, before returning to his
former practice to initiate the new chorus in bar 13. Supporting the thickly textured
block chord melody rendition, the drummer performs emphatic melodic-rhythmic drum
fills whose kicks reinforce the melody's accents and whose component shapes
selectively and occasionally add punctuation between melody figures. He combines
these strategies with the performance of ostinato time-keeping patterns, which he varies
in conjunction with drum kicks, frequently producing syncopation in the cymbal part.
In bars 1–4, he diversifies his performance with rests, different hi-hat colors, and the
change from hi-hat to ride cymbal. At the head's close in bar 24, the drummer sets
up the solo with strong on-beat accents, inspiring the soloist's initial on-beat quarter-
note motive.

*Bars 25–36 (solo chorus 1).* With the onset of the solo, the pianist lowers the
registral placement of his chord voicings, and the drummer gradually reduces the
rhythmic density of his activity. Together, they create a series of interlocking punches
in bars 25–29, as the soloist introduces simple ideas of restricted range. Meanwhile, the
bass player improvises a highly melodic counterpart climbing into the upper register, as
if exchanging roles with the soloist. Subsequently, the soloist continues to develop
simple ideas, and the rhythm section simplifies its accompaniment. The bass player
winds down in range, the pianist provides sparer, sustained patterns, and the drummer
switches largely to cymbal time-keeping patterns. An interesting exchange of roles
occurs in bar 30, when the pianist plays especially low voicings that extend well into
the bass's upper register and the bass player takes increasing harmonic liberties. To

*Example 13.26 continued*

mark the end of the chorus in bars 35–36, the pianist plays a harmonized version of a chromatic cadential blues figure, concluding with an accented, sustained piano kick that the drummer punctuates with a subtle fill.

 *Bars 37–48 (chorus 2).* In bar 37, the soloist and drummer exchange on-beat accents. Amid the chorus's predominantly interlocking scheme of piano and drum punctuations, the drummer increases his activity, developing a high-low, snare-to-bass-drum idea. Meanwhile, the bass player formulates a characteristically varied line, beginning with a three-bar chromatically embellished scalar pattern that he initiates on the tonic in bar 37. Subsequently, he creates vertical one-bar patterns that lead, through unexpected changes of melodic direction and leaps, to the upper bass register, then descend through sequential figures to the tonic on the new chorus downbeat. In bars 43–46, when the piano player and bass player venture into each other's range again, the latter leaps to a high descending chromatic gesture, initially imitating, then reinforcing, the top voice of the pianist's chords. In bars 47–48, they coordinate their performance of a version of the conventional blues pattern discussed above, variants of which each player has performed alone previously (the bass in bars 33–34 and the piano in bars 35–36, for example). Subtle exchanges between the soloist and the pianist occur in bar 41, where the pianist absorbs the soloist's accented pitch into the top voice of the subsequent chord, and in bar 46, where the soloist picks up the top voice of the piano chords for a subsequent melodic figure.

 *Bars 49–60 (chorus 3).* When the soloist creates an extended pair of call and response phrases, the pianist and drummer reinforce some of their rhythmic elements with coordinated punches, and they highlight the conclusion of each phrase with imitative on-beat accents. At the same time, the artists engage in harmonic interplay. In bar 50, the pianist and bass player follow the soloist in remaining on the B♭ chord, ignoring the conventional form, and in bar 54, the bass player plays a prominent E♮ outside the key, instantly prompting the pianist to insert a complementary chord into the progression. In bars 56–58, the pianist and drummer develop a routine of coordinated punches on the second half of beat four, leading to heightened cadential activity, which the bass player intensifies through his imposing ascent to the high register.

 *Bars 61–72 (chorus 4).* In response to the bass player's dramatic climb, the soloist begins with the highest pitches of his previous chorus, then, after a few short imitative patterns—when the bass player descends—soars to an extended climactic phrase. Alternating courses of high register exploration is a recurring feature of the two artists' interplay. During these events, the pianist punctuates the soloist's phrases sparingly, while responding to the bass player's persistent performance of a high, dissonant B♮ pitch in bars 61–63 by performing related tritone substitution chords in bars 63–64. Subsequently, the pianist and drummer coordinate their punches. The soloist changes strategies in bar 68, initiating a lyrical phrase whose rhythmic features the drummer accents selectively, in part with syncopated ride cymbal kicks, used sparingly since his melody accompaniment. In response, the soloist works syncopation and off-beat accentuation into his evolving part, which the drummer and pianist reinforce together in bars 69–71. At the same time, the pianist adopts some of the soloist's pitches for the upper voice of his chords. Meanwhile, the bass player ascends again in bars 68–71, in this instance following and expanding upon the contour of the soloist's phrase before working his way down through angular constructions to the tonic on the downbeat of the new chorus.

*Example 13.26 continued*

*Bars 73–84 (chorus 5).* The soloist re-creates the climactic peak of the previous chorus, then gradually descends, while the bass player climbs upward through an elongated version of the conventional blues pattern discussed earlier, setting up the piano's complementary chord insertion in bar 74. Developing a punctuating routine at the onset of the chorus, the drummer accents beat four with the bass drum and the pianist accents the second half of beat four. Subsequently, the drummer switches to snare drum kicks on the second half of beat four, which the pianist reinforces over the next several bars. The band members deepen their melodic-harmonic interplay in bar 78, as the bass player predicts, and performs in near unison, the soloist's initial phrase component. Shortly after, the pianist takes up the concluding pitch of the soloist's phrase for the upper voice of a substitute chord, initiating a descending progression whose top line the bass player fashions into a variant for his bass part and whose final upper voice the soloist adopts for the start of his next phrase. In bar 83, the soloist concludes with a repeated tonic reference to the solo's opening motive, and the pianist answers him by developing the idea in the upper voice of his chords.

*Bars 85–96 (chorus 6).* As the soloist develops short figures of restricted range that reiterate the blue third of the key, the pianist and bass player instantly absorb the pitch into their parts in bar 86, the pianist continuing its performance over the next few bars. At the same time, the pianist and drummer generate tremendous swing through a coordinated routine of beat-four eighth-note punches that answer the repeated eighth-note component of the soloist's motive. In bar 89, percussive piano punches penetrate well into the bass's range. Subsequently, in bars 90–91 and 93–94, the bass player sets up the common blues figure for interaction with the pianist, who, in the latter instance, rephrases and harmonizes it with an eighth-note pick-up in the lowest voice of his chords. The conversation among the players intensifies as the soloist immediately adopts the pick-up to create a variation on his own previous phrase ending. Then, in bars 95–96, the pianist creates a cadential phrase that masterfully combines a variant of the bass player's previous blues figure (in the middle voice of the piano chords) with the rhythm of the soloist's phrase and its emphasis on the tonic (in the outer voices of the piano chords).

*Bars 97–108 (chorus 7).* The soloist returns to short call and response patterns with an off-beat and backbeat emphasis, initially prompting the drummer to respond with a fill and syncopated cymbal kicks, whose off-beat accentuation the pianist imitates, then reinforces in bar 98. In the next bar, the two accompanists accentuate the soloist's concluding pitch, the pianist adding emphasis with a dissonant chord substitution. In bar 100, the soloist sustains a syncopated pitch a tritone away from the conventional chord root, which the pianist reinforces with a related substitution. Subsequently, while the pianist and drummer provide predominantly interlocking punches, the soloist ornaments a figure with a prominent grace note, which elicits a comparable emphatic response from the bass player two bars later. When the soloist closes the chorus with short imitative gestures in bars 105 and 108, the drummer answers each with a fill.

*Bars 109–20 (chorus 8).* At the start of his last chorus, the soloist creates an extended swinging line, and the pianist and drummer gradually increase their coordinated punches. At the same time, in bars 111–12, the pianist imitates the soloist's descending pitches in the top line of his chords and, on the last beat, predicts the soloist's precise figure. Next, the soloist rests, then seizes the upper voice of the

*Example 13.26 continued*

intervening chords for his vocal cry, which he sustains against the changing harmony before concluding it with a blue-third quarter-note figure. In response, the pianist plays a related tritone chord substitution, and when the soloist ascends again, the pianist adds momentary tension with a comparable substitution. Working his way down from the peak of his phrase, the soloist makes reference to the solo's opening motive in bar 119. Then he extends the phrase with a variant of the composition's melody, whose initial pitch the pianist adopts for the top voice of his next chord. To highlight the end of the solo, the soloist sustains a suspenseful dissonant pitch, which the pianist absorbs into his chord voicing, the bass player probes his instrument's high register, and the drummer plays a forceful distinctive fill.

*Example 13.26 continued*

*Example 13.26 continued*

*Example 13.26 continued*

*Example 13.26 continued*

*Example 13.26 continued*

*Example 13.26 continued*

*Example 13.26 continued*

*Example 13.26 continued*

*Example 13.26 continued*

*Example 13.26 continued*

*Example 13.26 continued*

*Example 13.26 continued*

*Example 13.26 continued*

*Example 13.26 continued*

*Example 13.26 continued*

*Example 13.26 continued*

*Example 13.26 continued*

*Example 13.26 continued*

*Example 13.26 continued*

*Example 13.26 continued*

Example 13.26 continued

*Example 13.26 continued*

*Example 13.26 continued*

*Example 13.26 continued*

*Example 13.26 continued*

*Example 13.26 continued*

# APPENDIX A: HOUSE
# CONGRESSIONAL RESOLUTION 57

Whereas, jazz has achieved preeminence throughout the world as an indigenous American music and art form, bringing to this country and the world a uniquely American musical synthesis and culture through the African-American experience and—

(1) makes evident to the world an outstanding artistic model of individual expression and democratic cooperation within the creative process, thus fulfilling the highest ideals and aspirations of our republic,

(2) is a unifying force, bridging cultural, religious, ethnic and age differences in our diverse society,

(3) is a true music of the people, finding its inspiration in the cultures and most personal experiences of the diverse peoples that constitute our Nation,

(4) has evolved into a multifaceted art form which continues to birth and nurture new stylistic idioms and cultural fusions,

(5) has had a historic, pervasive, and continuing influence on other genres of music both here and abroad, and

(6) has become a true international language adopted by musicians around the world as a music best able to express contemporary realities from a personal perspective; and

Whereas, this great American musical art form has not yet been properly recognized nor accorded the institutional status commensurate with its value and importance;

Whereas, it is important for the youth of America to recognize and understand jazz as a significant part of their cultural and intellectual heritage;

Whereas, in as much as there exists no effective national infrastructure to support and to preserve jazz;

Whereas, documentation and archival support required by such a great art form has yet to be systematically applied to the jazz field; and

Whereas, it is in the best interest of the national welfare and all of our citizens to preserve and celebrate this unique art form: Now, therefore be it

Resolved by the House of Representatives (the Senate concurring), that it is the sense of the Congress that Jazz is hereby designated as a rare and valuable national American treasure to which we should devote our attention, support and resources to make certain it is preserved, understood and promulgated.

Proposed by Congressman John Conyers Jr., 1st District/Michigan: March 3, 1987
Passed by the House of Representatives: September 23, 1987
Passed by the United States Senate: December 4, 1987

# APPENDIX B: LIST OF ARTISTS INTERVIEWED

| NAME | INITIAL CODE | INSTRUMENT | PLACE OF BIRTH | DATE OF BIRTH, DEATH |
|---|---|---|---|---|
| Bailey, Benny | (BB) | trumpet | Cleveland, OH | 13 August 1925 |
| Baker, David | (DB) | trombone, cello | Indianapolis, IN | 21 December 1931 |
| Barron, Kenny | (KB) | piano | Philadelphia, PA | 9 June 1943 |
| Bartz, Gary | (GB) | tenor sax | Baltimore, MD | 26 September 1940 |
| Baum, Roberta | (RB) | voice | New York, NY | 21 February 1950 |
| Bishop, Walter, Jr. | (WB) | piano | New York, NY | 4 October 1927 |
| Bown, Patti | (PB) | piano | Seattle, WA | 26 July 1931 |
| Copeland, Keith | (KC) | drums | New York, NY | 18 April 1946 |
| Cheatham, "Doc" Adolphus | (DC) | trumpet | Nashville, TN | 13 June 1905 |
| Davis, Art | (AD) | string bass | Harrisburg, PA | 5 December 1934 |
| Donaldson, Lou | (LD) | alto sax, voice | Badin, NC | 1 November 1926 |
| Duvivier, George | (GD) | string bass | New York, NY | 17 August 1920– 11 July 1985 |
| Farmer, Art | (AF) | trumpet, flugelhorn | Council Bluffs, IA | 21 August 1928 |
| Flanagan, Tommy | (TF) | piano | Detroit, MI | 16 March 1930 |
| Friedman, Don | (DF) | piano | San Francisco, CA | 4 May 1935 |
| Fuller, Curtis | (CF) | trombone | Detroit, MI | 15 December 1934 |
| Gray, Larry | (LG) | bass, piano, guitar | Blue Island, IL | 26 June 1954 |
| Harris, Barry | (BH) | piano | Detroit, MI | 15 December 1929 |
| Hersch, Fred | (FH) | piano | Cincinnati, OH | 21 October 1955 |

| NAME | INITIAL CODE | INSTRUMENT | PLACE OF BIRTH | DATE OF BIRTH, DEATH |
|------|--------------|------------|----------------|----------------------|
| Hicks, John | (JH) | piano | Atlanta, GA | 21 December 1941 |
| Higgins, Patience | (PH) | tenor sax | Greenville, SC | 12 June 1954 |
| Hill, Calvin | (CH) | string bass | Bridgeport, CT | 27 June 1945 |
| Hillyer, Lonnie | (LH) | trumpet | Monroe, GA | 25 March 1940– 1 July 1985 |
| Israels, Chuck | (CI) | string bass | New York, NY | 10 August 1936 |
| Jackson, Ronald Shannon | (RSJ) | drums | Fort Worth, TX | 12 January 1940 |
| Johnson, George V., Jr. | (GJ) | voice | Washington, DC | 20 December 1950 |
| Konitz, Lee | (LK) | alto sax | Chicago, IL | 13 October 1927 |
| Liston, Melba | (ML) | trombone | Kansas City, MO | 13 January 1926 |
| Levy, Howard | (HL) | piano | New York, NY | 31 July 1951 |
| Langdon, Greg | (GL) | tenor sax | New York, NY | 16 November 1951 |
| Lundy, Carmen | (CL) | voice | Miami, FL | 1 November 1954 |
| Marsalis, Wynton | (WM) | trumpet | New Orleans, LA | 18 October 1961 |
| McNeil, John | (JMc) | trumpet | Yreka, CA | 23 March 1948 |
| Moody, James | (JM) | tenor sax, flute, voice | Savannah, GA | 26 February 1925 |
| Ousley, Harold | (HO) | tenor sax | Chicago, IL | 23 January 1929 |
| Pate, Don | (DP) | string bass | Chicago, IL | 8 October 1948 |
| Persip, Charli | (CP) | drums | Morristown, NJ | 26 July 1929 |
| Reid, Rufus | (RuR) | string bass | Sacramento, CA | 10 February 1944 |
| Remler, Emily | (ER) | guitar | New York, NY | 18 September 1957– 3 May 1990 |
| Rhames, Arthur | (AR) | piano, guitar, tenor sax, voice | New York, NY | 25 October 1957 |

| NAME | INITIAL CODE | INSTRUMENT | PLACE OF BIRTH | DATE OF BIRTH, DEATH |
|------|--------------|------------|----------------|----------------------|
| Roach, Max | (MR) | drums, percussion | New Land, NC | 10 January 1924 |
| Robinson, Jimmy | (JR) | trumpet | Yakima, WA | 1932 |
| Rodney, Red | (RR) | trumpet | Philadelphia, PA | 27 September 1927 |
| Rogovin, Bobby | (BR) | trumpet | New York, NY | 10 January 1946 |
| Schneider, Josh | (JS) | alto sax | Stamford, CT | 26 November 1954 |
| Tana, Akira | (AT) | drums | San Jose, CA | 14 March 1952 |
| Turrentine, Tommy | (TT) | trumpet | Pittsburgh, PA | 22 April 1928 |
| Washington, Kenny | (KW) | drums | New York, NY | 29 May 1958 |
| Williams, Buster | (BW) | string bass | Camden, NJ | 17 April 1942 |
| Williams, Leroy | (LW) | drums | Chicago, IL | 3 February 1937 |
| Williams, Vea | (VW) | singer | Pittsburgh, PA | 1950 |
| Wertico, Paul | (PW) | drums | Chicago, IL | 5 January 1953 |

# SOURCES

## Figures

**3.1** Oral tradition, the jazz community.

**3.2** Composer, George Gershwin, copyright 1930 New World Music Corp. Version based on oral tradition, the jazz community.

**3.3** Transcribed from rec., Parker 1951. "She Rote" harmony based on Richard Whiting's "Beyond the Blue Horizon" copyright 1930 Famous Music Corp.

**3.4** Composed by Bronislau Kaper; copyright 1947 Leo Feist, renewed 1975 Metro-Goldwyn Mayer. Version based on composite of progression in Aebersold 1984, 1, and in performance provided on accompanying record.

**3.5** a. Composed by Jimmy Van Heusen; copyright 1949 (renewed 1971) by Burke and Van Heusen, now Bourne Co. and Dorsey Bros. Music. Version taken from Aebersold 1980, 4; b. Composed by Ray Noble; copyright 1938 by the Peter Maurice Music Co., Ltd., London; U.S.A. copyright renewed and assigned by Shapiro, Bernstein & Co., Inc. Version taken from *The Real Book,* 83; c. Composed by Dave Brubeck; copyright 1955, 1956 Derry Music Co. Version based in part on Sher 1991, 158; d. Composed by John Coltrane, copyright 1974 Jowcol Music. Version taken from Strunk 1988, 494.

**3.6** Baker 1968, 1.

**3.7** a. Oral tradition, jazz community; b. Sher 1988, 146; c. *The Real Book,* vol. 2, 174.

**3.8** Version described to me in personal conversations with Harold Ousley, Winter 1983, and Barry Harris, Summer 1991.

**4.1** Harris workshop, Jazz Cultural Theatre, New York City, Winter 1982.

**5.1** Based on sketch provided by John McNeil, Sept. 1993.

**6.2** Harris workshop, Jazz Cultural Theatre, New York City, Winter 1983.

**13.1** Rec., Davis 1956b.

## Music Texts

**3.1** Lead sheet sample taken from Aebersold 1980, 4. Jimmy Van Heusen, composer; copyright 1949 (renewed 1971) by Burke and Van Heusen, now Bourne Co. and Dorsey Bros. Music.

**3.2** a. Melody and harmony transcribed from rec., Jordon 1988; b. Melody and harmony transcribed from rec., Davis 1956c; c. Copyright 1939 (renewed 1969) Lewis Music Publishing Co. and 20th Century Fox Music; melody taken from Sher 1988, 146; harmony, common basic progression, oral tradition, jazz community; d. Copyright: 1946 (renewed) by Consolidated Music Publishers, a Division of Music Sales Corp. (ASCAP) and Criterion Music Corp.; melody and chords taken from *The Real Book,* 24.

**3.3** a1–a2. Rec., Davis 1964; b1–b5. Composer: Bob Haggart; copyright 1939; arrangement cited in example, copyright 1984 Warner Bros., Inc., Limerick Music Corp., and Marke Music Publishing Co., Inc.; lead sheet sample, Sher 1988, 337;

performance transcribed from rec., Brown 1955a; c. Lead sheet source and copyright information same as 3.1 above. Coltrane and Dorham on rec., Coltrane 1958; Morgan on rec., Blakey 1960; and Little on rec., Dolphy 1961a, vol. 2; d. Lead sheet source and copyright information same as 3.2c above; performance transcribed from rec., Davis 1964.

**3.5** "I Got Rhythm" by George Gershwin, copyright 1930, New World Music Corp.; "Honeysuckle Rose" by Thomas Waller, copyright 1927, Andy Razaf, Pub., Des and Chappell and Co.; "Perdido" by Juan Tizol, copyright 1942 Tempo Music, Inc.; "Take the A Train" by Billy Strayhorn, copyright 1941 (renewed 1969) Tempo Music, Inc. Progressions presented in example based in part on oral tradition, jazz community, and on versions of "Honeysuckle Rose" and "Perdido" in Sher 1991, 134 and 287.

**3.6** a. Rec., Davis 1964; b. rec., Davis 1956c; c. rec., Coltrane 1961.

**3.7** a. Rec., Davis 1964; b. rec., Davis 1956b.

**3.8** a–b. Rec., Davis 1956c.

**3.9** a. Rec., Davis 1964; b. rec., Davis 1956c.

**3.10** a. Rec., Davis 1956b; b. rec., Davis 1956c.

**3.11** Rec., Davis 1956b.

**3.12** a–b. Rec., Davis 1956c.

**4.1** Kirkwood, unpublished manuscript containing transcriptions by Robert Witmer, revised by Kirkwood. Oliver's original "Dippermouth Blues" solo can be heard on rec., Oliver 1923a. Numerous re-creations of Oliver's solo appear on different recorded versions of the related composition "Sugarfoot Stomp." The three illustrated here are Armstrong's on rec., Henderson 1925; Stewart's on rec., Henderson 1931; James's on rec., Goodman 1937b. Additionally, Oliver's re-creation of his own solo as "Dippermouth Blues" can be heard on rec., Oliver 1923b.

**4.2** a. Rec., Davis 1956c; b. Baker 1982, 50, line 7 from top; c. Aebersold and Slone 1978, 93, line 14; d. Slone 1977, 48, line 1 (spelling of "Ladybird" corrected to "Lady Bird").

**4.3** a1–a2. Louis Armstrong and Joe Smith, respectively, accompanying Bessie Smith on rec., Smith 1925, 1926; b. rec., Davis 1946 (original recording session under singer Earl Coleman's name); c. rec., Sun Ra 1956; d1. rec., Dolphy 1961a, vol. 1; d2. rec., Adderley 1958; d3. Owens 1974, vol. 2, 358, 13-7; e1. Owens 1974, vol. 2, 360, 7-1; e2. Parker in Aebersold and Slone 1978, 39, lines 9–10; Dorham on rec., Blakey 1955.

**5.1** Rec., Gillespie 1956.

**5.2** a1. Tirro 1977, 368, line 8 from top; a2. Sickler 1979, 19, bar 25; b1–b2. Porter 1985b, 94, A9; 72, example 31.

**5.3** a. Rec., Blakey 1955; b. rec., Blakey 1958a; c1. rec., Dorham 1953; c2. rec., Blakey 1955; d. Aebersold and Slone 1978, 81, lines 12–13; e1. rec., Little 1961b; e2. rec., Dolphy 1961a, vol. 2; f. rec., Little 1960.

**5.4** a. Evans n.d.; b. Tatum n.d.; c. Dobbins 1988.

**5.5** a. Rec., Evans 1967. b. rec., Brown 1954b.

**5.6** a. Oral tradition, jazz community; b. rec., Davis 1964; c, f, h, i; rec., Little 1960; d–e. rec., Coltrane 1957; g, j, k: rec., Strozier 1960.

**6.1** a. Rec., Armstrong 1928b; b. rec., Lateef 1957.

**6.2** Aebersold and Slone 1978, 38, lines 4–6.

**6.3** a1. Rec., Davis 1964; a2. rec., Davis 1956c; b. Aebersold and Slone 1978, 41, line 9; c. rec., Coltrane 1957; d1. rec., Davis 1964; d2. rec., Coltrane 1961.

**6.4** Rec., Rollins 1956b.

**6.5** Sickler 1968, 21, top line.

**6.6** a. Blakey 1955; b. Owens 1974, vol. 2, 137, last two lines; c. Sickler 1979, 21, bars 10–12.

**6.7** a–c. Barry Harris workshop at the Jazz Cultural Theatre, New York City, winter 1984.

**6.8** a–b. Aebersold and Slone 1978, 25, line 9; 71, line 7.

**6.9** Barry Harris, private lesson, Spring 1992.

**7.1** Rec., Coltrane 1957.

**7.2** a–d. Composition by Willard Robison, copyright 1938 Remick Music Corp.; transcribed performances from rec., Roach 1959.

**7.3** a1. Smith 1983, 210; a2. figure: Aebersold and Slone 1978, 37, lines 9 and 13; harmony: rec., Parker 1951; b. VS, M: rec., Little 1961b; CB: rec., Little and Byrd 1960; LSL: rec., Dolphy 1961a, vol. 2; OS: rec., Little 1960.

**7.4** a–e. Owens 1974, vol. 2: 141, B3–7; 140, B2–7; 176, A3a2–3; 242, A3–8; 428, 1b2–7.

**7.5** a. Arban, 95, grupetto exercise #9; b. rec., Brown 1953.

**7.6** Top line of example based in part on recurring vocabulary chain in transcriptions by Aebersold and Slone (1978, 35, line 9; 37, lines 9 and 13); other figures sampled from various solos in Aebersold and Slone 1978 and in Owens 1974, vol. 2. Harmony taken from rec., Parker 1951.

**7.7** a–b. Rec., Little 1960.

**7.8** a. Rec., Little 1960; b. Owens 1974, vol. 2: 135, A3–8; 136, B4–8; c. rec., Little 1960.

**7.9** a. Owens 1974, vol. 2: 137, C4–10; 135, A5–10; b. rec., Little 1960.

**7.10** All Owens, 1974, vol. 2. a: 174, B2b–3; 173, A2b–3; b1:173, A2a2–6; 174, B2a2–6; b2: 173, A2b–8; 174, B2b-8; b3: 136, B5–7; 137, C5–7; b4: 174, B2b–5; 173, A2b–5.

**7.11** a–b. Rec., Little 1960.

**7.12** a–c. Rec., Parker 1948.

**7.13** a–b. Rec., Little 1960.

**7.14** a–g. Aebersold and Slone 1978: a: 39, line 14; b: 38, line 4; c: 38, line 7; d: 39, line 13; e: 39, line 9; f: 40, line 8; g: 39, line 11.

**7.15** Rec., Davis 1957.

**8.1** Rec., Armstrong 1926.

**8.2** Rec., Little 1960.

**8.3** Tirro 1977, 366.

**8.4** a. Owens 1974, vol. 2, 182, 3a1–8; b. rec., Blakey 1960; c. rec., Brown 1955b.

**8.5** a. Porter 1985b, 97; b. rec., Davis 1956c.

**8.6** a. Rec., Davis 1956c; b. Blakey 1958a.

**8.7** Owens 1974, vol. 2, 178, C3a3–1.

**8.8** a. Porter 1985b, 90; b. rec., Rollins 1956b; c. Baker 1982, 49, line 4; 50, lines 6–7.

**8.9** a. Rec., Armstrong 1927; b. rec., Rollins 1956b; c. rec., Montgomery 1960.

**8.10** Rec., Armstrong 1928b.

**8.11** Rec., Little 1960.

**8.12** a. Porter 1985b, 97, line 7; b. rec., Davis 1956c.

**8.13** a. Rec., Kirk 1964; b. rec., Strozier 1960; c. rec., Roach 1958a.

**8.14** a. Rec., Davis 1946 (original recording session under singer Earl Coleman's name); b. rec., Davis 1949 (original recording session under Tadd Dameron's name); c. rec., Parker 1950; d. rec., Davis 1953a; e. rec., Brown 1955b; f. rec., Davis 1956a; g. rec., Sun Ra 1956; h. rec., Chambers 1957; i. rec., Davis 1958a (original recording session under Red Garland's name); j. rec., Fitzgerald 1958; k. rec., Davis 1958b; 1. rec., The Manhattan Transfer 1985 (copyright: "Ray's Rockhouse," Progressive Music Pub. Co., Inc., 1958, 1963); m. rec., Scofield 1991; n–o. rec., Green.

**8.15** Rec., Hampton 1959.

**8.16** a. Aebersold and Slone 1978, 39, lines 15–16; b. rec., Little 1960.

**8.17** a. Coolman 1985, 41, lines 5–6; b. rec., Mitchell 1960.

**8.18** a. Rec., Roach 1958b; b. rec., Coltrane 1957.

**8.19** Rec., Coltrane 1957.

**8.20–8.21** Rec., Coltrane 1961.

**8.22** a–b. Sickler 1979, 32, bar 1; 24, bar 85.

**8.23** a. Rec., Davis 1957; b. rec., Mobley 1958.

**8.24** a–c. Rec., Davis 1956c.

**8.25** a. Tune composed by Ray Henderson, copyright 1926 (renewed) Warner Bros.; lead sheet model taken from fake book, *Volume 1 of Over One Thousand Songs,* 40; Davis performance on rec., Davis 1956b; b. rec., Coltrane 1961; c. rec., Strozier 1960; d. Tune composed by Miles Davis, lead sheet melody and solo transcribed from rec., Davis 1956c.

**9.1** a–b. Aebersold and Slone 1978, 39, line 9; 36–37, lines 8–9.

**9.2** a–b. Rec., Roach 1958a.

**9.3** a–d. Rec., Brown 1953.

**9.4** a–b, g, h: Rec., Little 1961b; c. rec., Dolphy 1961a, vol. 2; d–e, i: rec., Dolphy 1960; f. rec., Little 1960.

**9.5** a. Washburn and Harbison 1980, 14, lines 2, 4, 8; 15, line 2; b. rec., Davis 1959.

**9.6–9.8** Rec., Little 1960.

**9.9** Rec., Navarro 1948, vol. 2.

**12.1** a1. Owens 1974, vol. 2, 214; a2. rec., Davis 1954 (chorus 3 of Davis solo); a3. rec., Davis 1956c; a4. rec., Coltrane 1961; b. rec., Davis 1964.

**12.2** a. CR: Owens 1974, vol. 2, 145; PH: rec., Davis 1954; PC: rec., Davis 1956c; b. PC: rec., Davis 1956c; RW: rec., Coltrane 1961.

**12.3** a, c. Rec., Davis 1956c; b. rec., Coltrane 1961; d. rec., Davis 1954.

**12.4** a1–a2. Rec., Davis 1956c; b. rec., Davis 1954 (take 1: chorus 4 of Monk solo; take 1: chorus 9 of Davis solo; take 1: chorus 6 of Jackson solo; take 2: chorus 3 of Jackson solo).

**12.5** a. Common bebop pattern, jazz community; b1–b2. rec., Brown 1954b; c1–c3. rec., Davis 1956b, d1–d3. rec., Coltrane 1961; e1–e5. rec., Davis 1964.

**12.6** a–c. Rec., Davis 1956c.

**12.7** a1, c1. Rec., Brown 1954b; a2, c2. rec., Davis 1956c; b1–b2, c3. rec., Coltrane 1961.

**12.8** a1–a2. Rec., Davis 1956c; a3. rec., Coltrane 1961; a4, b1. rec., Brown 1954b; b2. rec., Davis 1956b; c1–c2. rec., Coltrane 1961; c3. rec., Davis 1964.

**12.9** a1. Rec., Brown 1954b; a2. rec., Coltrane 1961; b. rec., Davis 1964.

**12.10** a1. Rec., Davis 1956b; a2. rec., Coltrane 1961; b. rec., Davis 1964.

**13.1** a–c. Rec., Coltrane 1961.

**13.2** a–b; Rec., Davis 1964.

**13.3** a. Rec., Davis 1956b; b–c. rec., Davis 1956c.

**13.4** a. Rec., Coltrane 1961; b. rec., Davis 1956c (choruses 4–5 of Coltrane solo).

**13.5** a. Rec., Coltrane 1961; b. rec., Davis 1956b; c–d. rec., Davis 1964.

**13.6** a, b1, d1. Rec., Davis 1956b; b2, c. rec., Davis 1956c; d2. rec., Davis 1964.

**13.7** a–c. Rec., Davis 1956c.

**13.8** a. Rec., Coltrane 1961; b–c. rec., Davis 1964.

**13.9** a. Rec., Coltrane 1961; b–c. rec., Davis 1964.

**13.10** a1, b2. Rec., Davis 1964; a2, c1. rec., Davis 1956b; b1, c2–c3. rec., Davis 1956c.

**13.11** a1–a2. Rec., Davis 1956c; b. rec., Davis 1964; c1. rec., Dolphy 1961a, vol. 2; c2. rec., Little 1961b; d1–d2. rec., Davis 1964.

**13.12** a1. Rec., Davis 1956c; a2. rec., Davis 1964; b. rec., Dolphy 1960; c1–c2, rec., Davis 1956b.

**13.13** a. Rec., Davis 1956b; b–c. rec., Davis 1956c; d. rec., Coltrane 1961; e–f. rec., Davis 1964.

**13.14** a1, b. Rec., Davis 1964; a2. Monson 1991, 121.

**13.15** a–c. Rec., Davis 1956c.

**13.16** a. Rec., Davis 1951; b. rec., Adderley 1958.

**13.17** a. Rec., Rollins 1956a; b. rec., Blakey 1958a; c. rec., Davis 1956c; d. rec., Davis 1958b; e. rec., Davis 1951; f. rec., Davis 1964.

**13.18** a. Rec., Adderley 1958; b. rec., Parker 1950; c. rec., Brown 1955b.

**13.19** a1–a2. Rec., Davis 1956c; b. rec., Davis 1964; c1–c2. rec., Coltrane 1961.

**13.20** a. Rec., Davis 1956b; b. rec., Coltrane 1961; c. rec., Davis 1956c.

**13.21** Rec., Davis 1964.

**13.22** Rec., Little 1961b.

**13.23** See 8.25a above for lead sheet melody source, composer and copyright information. Performance transcribed from rec., Davis 1956b.

**13.24** Melody composed by Sigmund Romberg, copyright 1928 Harms, Inc. Lead sheet version taken from *The Real Book,* vol. 2, 333. Performance transcribed from rec., Coltrane 1961.

**13.25** See 3.2c above for lead sheet melody source, composer and copyright information. Performance transcribed from rec., Davis 1964.

**13.26** Performance of original Davis composition and solo transcribed from rec., Davis 1956c.

# NOTES

## Introduction

1. *Webster's New World Dictionary,* 3d college ed. New York: Simon and Schuster, 1988.

2. Original and revised music dictionary definitions in Apel 1969; Randel 1986. Randel provides a revision of the definition appearing in Apel, replacing that cited in the text with ethnomusicologist Bruno Nettl's more neutral definition, "the creation of music in the course of performance." Nettl's entry also adds mention of the complexity of the subject in light of the varied practices of Western art music and of various music cultures around the world.

3. Cheatham's, Duvivier's, and Washington's statements, and quoted passages that follow, are from my interviews, described further later in this chapter.

4. Music critics are sometimes inclined to treat their own personal tastes as the measure of the value of jazz, without understanding artists' goals and values, or "the attitude . . . philosophy . . . the complete human context" of the "people" who produce the music. My hope is that allowing artists to articulate the subtleties of their art can help redress these problems in the literature cited here as identified by Amiri Baraka (1970, 13, 14, 16).

5. The recording, a fusion of jazz and music from Zimbabwe and other parts of the world, is *The Sun Rises Late Here,* Flying Fish Records, 1979.

6. John Coltrane (Kofsky 1973, 242) expresses exasperation at the initial response of critics to his groups' creations. "I couldn't believe it. . . . It just seemed so preposterous . . . absolutely ridiculous, because they made it appear that we didn't even know the first thing about music—the first thing." Against the backdrop of familiar slights, musicians are often skeptical of what praise they do receive, in particular when the flattery is at the expense of the larger community from which the artists themselves draw inspiration. "What is he *saying?*" a renowned pianist once asked me rhetorically—and with some irritation—after reading a description of himself in the liner notes to an album in my collection as an "unusually thoughtful pianist." "Is he saying that my colleagues *aren't* thoughtful?"

In another instance, according to Martin Williams's editorial note to Schuller 1962 (239), Rollins was put off by the article Schuller wrote analyzing (and praising) Rollins's improvising and said that he "never intended to read his notices again." The article praises Rollins's "Blue Seven" solo as exceptional in relation to improvisations deemed "less inspired" because certain aspects of their diversity and their independence from surrounding material (that is, the solos of other band members and the composed sections of the composition) do not conform to a particular Western art music model of "thematic and structural unity." Schuller asserts that "the average improvisation is mostly a stringing together of unrelated ideas," and that improvisers may "create pure improvisations which are meaningful realizations of a well-sustained over-all feeling [but] the majority of players are perhaps not temperamentally or intellectually suited to do more than that." Ibid., 240–41. See also note 4 above.

7. *The Soul of Mbira,* Nonesuch Records H-72054, 1973; *Shona Mbira Music,* Nonesuch Records H-72077, 1977.

8. For an elaboration of the collective aspects of art production, see Becker 1982.

9. The findings of this work do not support the conclusion of a former study asserting that the "jazz musician remains relatively illiterate in respect to the verbal expression of his own art." Merriam and Mack 1960, 216.

10. The key to performers' initials, arranged alphabetically by family name, is in appendix B at the back of the book.

11. See *Passing It On,* videorecording, for an introduction to Harris's work as a pianist and teacher. Citations to videorecordings and films refer readers to items listed in the videography at the back of the book. All future references to jazz videorecordings, television programs, and films in notes are cited using the abbreviation *video,* the artist's name, and date.

12. As far as I know, three music dissertations, Owens 1974, Kernfeld 1981, and Monson 1991, and an article, Stewart 1986, contain transcribed samples of group interplay, including rhythm section parts. For reference to transcriptions of accompaniments by individual rhythm section players, see chapter 12, note 7.

13. Views of numerous artists on the issues addressed by this work are presented in *Jazz Is Our Religion* (video compilation, 1986) and Evans, video 1991. Complementary data can also be glimpsed in interview excerpts presented in most of the works selected for the videography.

14. See appendix A for the full text of U.S. Congressional Resolution 57.

15. For a sample of the work of ethnomusicologists on improvisation from a comparative standpoint, see Nettl 1974, Nettl 1991, and Lortat-Jacob 1987; for a sample of cross-cultural work on musical learning, see Merriam 1964, 145–64. Of importance as well are Lord 1970, Bennett 1980, and the overview provided by Campbell 1991, 186–206.

16. Many musicians view the approach in formal education of "putting the cart" of music theory "before the horse" of practice as problematic. They refer, in fact, to certain graduates of college jazz programs by ridiculing their deficient artistry as "school jazz." The implication, elaborated upon later in the study, is that, despite the students' obvious instrumental virtuosity, they lack understanding of the jazz tradition and fail to appreciate fundamental creative processes and aesthetic values integral to jazz as an expressive language. See also chapter 7, note 17.

## 1. Love at First Sound

1. The idea of the newborn's first dance and song is a popular Ghanaian view, as expressed by Ghanaian dancer Victor Clottey as part of a lecture and demonstration he gave for my world music class at Northwestern University, winter 1986. Similarly, in Nigeria, "it is believed that the musical training of the vocal-music composer starts from the womb. . . . The pregnant mother who participates in musical activities is believed to introduce the unborn baby to rhythmical movements of all categories of music. After the baby is born, he gradually becomes acquainted with musical sound through the lullabies sung to him, and through his mother's continuous musical involvement while he is firmly strapped to her back." Agu 1984, 13–14. The popular media in America

has made frequent reference to similar notions in mentioning such contemporary child-birthing practices as encouraging women to hear, while pregnant, only those types of music they prefer.

2. The role played by these inventions of the music industry differs, of course, from person to person, community to community, and from one period to the next. For commentary on technological tools, see Fraser 1983, 38; although live performance appears to have had the most profound effect on initiating the interest of the older jazz players in his study, the radio and record player assumed a greater role in attracting learners of more recent generations to jazz.

3. It was not uncommon for youngsters to develop skills on a variety of instruments. Coleman Hawkins studied piano and cello, as well as tenor saxophone; Lester Young studied violin, trumpet, and drums with his father, and later learned clarinet, as well as baritone, alto, and tenor saxophones; Clifford Brown could play piano, vibraphone, and drums, as well as trumpet. Various considerations, from personal taste to the needs of different bands and the relative opportunities for acquiring one kind of instrument over another, ultimately influenced artists' decisions as to performing on a variety of instruments and switching instruments during their careers. Hawkins in Shapiro and Hentoff 1966, 208; Young in Porter 1985b, 4–6; Brown in Gardner 1961, 20.

4. Shapiro and Hentoff 1966, 92–93. Similarly, as a youngster, Coleman Hawkins "used to sit up and practice [instrumental lessons] . . . all day long. Then when I was through . . . I would play jazz all the rest of the day. . . . I also used to go to all the classical concerts." Ibid., 208.

5. Beiderbecke in Sudhalter and Evans 1974, 27; Armstrong described by Kid Ory in Shapiro and Hentoff 1966, 49.

6. Gillespie 1979, 31. Regarding comparable aspects of musical training and models in the African American community, Pops Foster describes the members of a Holiness church as playing "some great jazz on those hymns." Foster 1971, 21. Milt Jackson says, "My blues comes from church music." Balliett 1971, 167. T. Bone Walker reaches back in his memory to early childhood when he relates that "the first time I ever heard a boogie-woogie piano was the first time I went to church. . . . [It] was a kind of blues," he recalls, adding, "The preacher used to preach in a bluesy tone sometimes." Shapiro and Hentoff 1966, 250.

In the face of the ideological tensions between black religious and secular musical genres that sometimes complicate their learning courses, often youngsters absorb the essential elements of African American music from alternative sources, or adopt clever ploys of musical code switching to disguise their objectives. "Mama and them were so religious," Nina Simone maintains, "that they wouldn't allow you to play boogie-woogie in the house, but would allow you to use the boogie-woogie *beat* to play a gospel tune. . . . Our music *crosses* all those lines." Fraser 1983, 75. Doc Cheatham described his participation in an early church band where he and his young friends would experiment with jazz until they caught sight of the dean, then quickly switch to hymns as he passed by. One day, the dean found the musicians out, and became "so angry that he broke up the group." For an elaboration on the aesthetic values common to different African American musics, see Burnim and Maultsby 1987. Scenes of lively church music performance appear in Jones, video 1991, and Zardis, video 1993.

7. Gillespie 1979, 31. Aspiring white jazz musicians like Bud Freeman and his friends also attended services of Chicago's African American churches, drawing great inspiration from the music. Freeman 1989, 17–18.

8. Fraser 1983, 61.

9. Bix Beiderbecke was alleged to have frustrated his piano teacher ("the Professor") by playing back the demonstrated pieces "with improvements." Sudhalter and Evans 1974, 30. As youngsters, Joe Venuti and Eddie Lang "slipp[ed] in some improvised passages" amid the mazurkas and polkas they performed at dances. Shapiro and Hentoff 1966, 272–73. At times, circumstantial features of performance bring the student's special talents to light. Earl Hines recalls an early public recital in which he temporarily forgot the music and improvised "fourteen bars" of his "own ideas until I caught up with the music again." Dance 1977, 15. Other artists whom I interviewed describe their experiments, as youngsters, with varying such material as classical music themes and marching band parts (FH, GB, and BB).

10. Levine (1977, 294) notes the powerful "conversion" experiences of young white musicians discovering the music of African American jazz artists in Chicago during the twenties. The unnamed Japanese musician told his story, in Japan, to Ralph Samuelson, who repeated it to me in New York City during a personal conversation, fall 1982.

11. Stan Getz refers to contributing to his family's income as a youngster, explaining that "the openness of jazz was so intriguing." He adds, "Besides, I needed the money, for my family. My father was a mostly out-of-work printer and at that time in the 30s they didn't allow Jews into the printer's union, so we had a hard time." Hooper 1991, 76.

12. For an elaboration on the theme of small-town bigotry, see Gillespie 1979, 30. Danny Barker discusses the jazz career as one of the few alternatives to domestic and manual labor jobs for blacks in New Orleans in Zardis, video 1993.

13. Related issues concerning the "attractions of a jazz identity" are discussed in Cambor, Lisowitz, and Miller 1962, 7–8.

## 2. Hangin' Out and Jammin'

1. *Community* is used here in the sense of a "community of interest" that transcends geographic boundaries, where people "participate to some extent in the occupational role and ideology of the professional jazz musician. They learn and accept at least some of the [jazz musician's] norms . . . regarding proper and improper language, good and bad music, stylish and unstylish clothing, acceptable and unacceptable audience behavior and so on." Merriam and Mack 1960, 211. For additional sociological studies elaborating upon this notion, see Becker 1951 and 1963 and Cameron 1954.

2. Similar devotion to idols has characterized the behavior of jazz learners over the music's history. Young Rex Stewart "tried to walk like [Louis Armstrong], talk like him, eat like him, sleep like him." Shapiro and Hentoff 1966, 206. Jimmy and Percy Heath admit that, two generations later, they "followed [Dizzy Gillespie's] band around. We were even wearing his costume, berets and thin artist ties." Watrous 1992.

3. For numerous accounts by musicians of "cutting contests" in the early jazz and swing periods, see Shapiro and Hentoff 1966, 24–25, 128, 172, 194, 284; for a sociologist's perspective on the jam session, see Cameron 1954.

4. Becker (1953, 22–25) describes the essential role of such networks in the jazz musician's search for employment.

5. For discussion of these famous jam sessions, see Patrick 1983, Shapiro and Hentoff 1966, 335–70, and Davis 1990, 51–82.

6. My recollection of an interview with Armstrong during a televised portion of the 1970 Newport Jazz Festival.

7. Konitz, video 1990. For an elaboration of Tristano's teaching method and philosophy, see McKinney 1978.

8. Hooper 1991, 76.

9. Shapiro and Hentoff 1966, 76.

10. Davis, video 1986.

11. Dave Bomberg told me of the Coltrane and Dolphy incident in a personal conversation, fall 1984.

12. Learner responsibility is a common feature of occupational apprenticeships in many trades. Becker 1972, 94–95.

13. For reference to male competitive bonding routines in African American culture, see Abrahams 1970b, 32–39.

14. Harsh methods by which jazz artists test each other's abilities—especially during transitional, innovative periods in the history of the music—are well documented. Kenny Clarke and Dizzy Gillespie describe devising and performing compositions with unusual, difficult chord progressions to repel players who might otherwise have tried to sit in with their bands. Feather 1980, 9; Stearns 1956, 222.

15. Former students like Patience Higgins fondly recall not only the modest fees that Harris charged them, but exciting classes that extended from the evening into the early hours of the morning, until finally the exasperated landlord forced them out of the building where Harris had rented the classroom space. "Barry's a giving, loving person," Higgins explains. "It's one of his purposes in life to pass the music on to our generation, the younger generation, to keep this music alive."

16. Classical music influence noted in Schuller 1968, 146. The practice of musicians with varied training interacting extends back to the early days of jazz in Storyville, New Orleans, where Jelly Roll Morton experienced the sharing of "musical knowledge" and musical "gifts" among African Americans of distinct social classes, each providing its artists with different kinds of training. Lomax 1950, 84.

17. Carter (1986, 12) credits Bowden in particular for his contribution as a pioneering instructor of dance band music at Tuskegee Institute in 1919, and at Georgia State College, now Savannah State College, in 1926.

18. The Berklee School of Music became the Berklee College of Music. Berk 1970, 29, 46. Reference to Lenox in Carter 1986, 10–11, 12. For a description of other early American degree programs in related areas such as "Commercial Music" at Los Angeles City College, 1946, and "Dance Band" at North Texas State University, 1947, see Branch 1975, 22. Discussions of the growing trends in jazz education are also in Bowman 1988, Briscuso 1974, and Suber 1976.

Attaining respect within the dominant culture is a problem of long standing for African American artists in every media. In the case of jazz, a number of interrelated attitudes have contributed, over the years, to the resistance artists have faced from the mainstream public and America's music institutions. One fundamental problem has been racism. As early as their 1901 national meeting, members of the American Federation of Musicians pledged "to play no ragtime, and to do all in their power to counteract the pernicious influence exerted by 'Mr. Johnson.' 'My Rag-Time Lady' and others of the negro school." Berlin 1980, 41. By 1947, the only local musicians' unions in America that were integrated were those of New York and Detroit (Lewis 1947, 1), and many remained segregated until the early sixties. See also the discussion by Merriam (1964, 241–44) of the portrayal of jazz as a symbol of evil, and Gioia's apt critique of "The Primitivist Myth" (1988, 19–49).

Other disparaging views owe to the confusion between jazz as an art form and the venues at which jazz has been performed, especially those promoting illicit activities. For musicians, the most offensive of these lingering associations concerns the alleged origin of jazz in New Orleans houses of prostitution. Sidney Bechet (1960, 53–54) attacks this misrepresentation, pointing out that, although such establishments hired solo ragtime pianists, they rarely hired jazz bands. Jazz musicians largely earned their livings by playing for parties, picnics, or balls. Bechet sees the stereotypes surrounding New Orleans jazz as prurient projections on the part of jazz's critics, and observes wryly, "If people want to take a [jazz] melody and think what it's saying is trash, that ain't the fault of the melody" (54). Related associations damaging to the reputation of jazz concern substance abuse in the lives of some musicians. See discussion in chapter 17, note 1.

Beyond the confusion of jazz as an art form with the extramusical issues described above are fundamental misunderstandings rooted in differences that distinguish jazz from the dominant music culture epitomized by Western art music. Many of the music's detractors have neither understood nor appreciated the stylistic, formal, and aesthetic components of jazz that delineate it as a unique musical language. See discussion in notes 4 and 6 to the introduction.

Equally problematical have been outsiders' perceptions of the processes of learning, transmitting, and producing jazz. The emphasis that the Western art music community places on formalized education and the written symbols of musical knowledge—from notation systems to music degrees—has made it difficult for members to recognize and appreciate, as a learned system, the knowledge that improvisers transmit through alternative education systems and through alternative forms of representation, some oral, some altogether nonverbal. Naivete and ignorance have frequently led to belittling stereotypes about jazz artists as "unschooled" or "illegitimate" musicians.

Correspondingly, the importance that the Western art music community attaches to music literacy and written composition has obscured recognition of the actual skills required by improvisation. Although improvisation has had its own rich history in Western art music—contemporaries of Beethoven considered his some of his improvisations equal, if not superior, to some of his written compositions (Sonneck 1927, 15, 22)—improvisation has, with the exception of isolated practices of the avant-garde and church music, all but disappeared from the training of classical musicians and from their performances. Lacking experience with improvisation in their own music tradition, many fail to appreciate it as a rigorous compositional activity in other music traditions. To this day, jazz musicians feel that they must be prepared, outside their own community, to deal with any or all of the attitudes discussed above.

19. Brief discussion of jazz programs in Kernfeld 1988d, passim.

20. It was Benjamin Bloom's study of prodigious development in other areas of creativity—among world-class tennis players and Olympic swimmers, outstanding research mathematicians and neurologists, sculptors, and classical piano virtuosos—that suggested to me the possibility of distinctive learning courses for jazz musicians. Although the backgrounds and educations of jazz musicians differ considerably from those of Bloom's subjects, his work contains some useful points of comparison and contrast for this study. Bloom kindly shared the preliminary findings of his research with me as I began writing this book. He has since published the conclusions of his study in Bloom 1985, 507–49.

21. Like the written score, the record presents the artist with fixed representations of music; like a live performance, it remains an aural representation. For the advantages that these hybrid qualities offer musicians, the recording has become a primary vehicle for music learning and transmission in many aural/oral music traditions—both popular and classical. See Bennett 1980, 140–45, and Shelemay 1991.

### 3. A Very Structured Thing

1. Reference to various jazz standards in Witmer 1988c and Crawford and Magee 1992.

2. Sargeant (1976, 197) describes "the hot improviser build[ing] his spontaneous variations" on the jazz tune's "harmonic pattern." "Jazz historians generally agree that jazz changed from an ensemble to a solo art during the third decade of this century. . . . The front-line instruments no longer played all or at least most of the time, and the music consisted of a series of 'choruses' (solos) accompanied by the rhythm section. . . . How this change of style evolved and developed is one of the important questions for the future." Wang 1988, 110–11. For Pops Foster's account of this change, see Foster 1971, 75–76.

3. Owens describes popular songs from the musical theater as commonly including two sections: a nonrepeating introductory verse; and a refrain or chorus, the main repeating theme. He observes that, whereas early jazz players sometimes used the two-section model in performances, since the twenties musicians have largely adopted the refrain alone as the song form or vehicle for invention. Owens 1988, 396.

4. Melrose Bros. Music Co. in Chicago published original jazz compositions such as "The Jelly Roll Blues" by Jelly Roll Morton as early as 1915. Lomax 1973, 292. Legal fake books, which musicians regard as providing more consistently accurate chord changes, have also appeared on the market in recent years. See Hyman 1986, Sher 1988, and Sher 1991. One of the inadvertent consequences of the production of fake books may be the weighting of pieces according to their alphabetical listings. As one artist I spoke with good-humoredly offered, "One thing you can always depend on now is that every player knows 'Blue Bossa,' because it's in the front of the book." For an elaboration of the conventions of notation adopted by the jazz community, see Witmer 1988b.

5. By the forties, learning to read music was part of the training of most jazz musicians. Embarrassment at not reading music or reading poorly is a common theme in early artists' accounts. Lester Young (Porter 1985b, 5–6) and Eddie Barefield (Driggs 1960, 20) describe their own comparably humiliating experiences.

6. My discussion of Konitz's views here combines features of my interview and Balliett's interview with Konitz (Balliett 1982).

7. Davis's ghosted note technique in McNeil 1993, 42.

8. In an early account of techniques for achieving myriad tonal effects, Lieutenant James Reese Europe says: "This 'jazzing' appeals to [the African American] strongly. It is accomplished in several ways. With brass instruments we put in mutes and make a whirling motion with the tongue [growling technique], at the same time blowing full pressure. With wind instruments, we pinch the mouthpiece and blow hard. This produces the peculiar sound which you all know." He went on to describe the "jazz effects" produced by his musicians as exotic and remarkable to the ears of French musicians, so much so that, until they "examined" the musicians' instruments for themselves, they thought "special instruments" had produced them. Anon. 1919, 28. The value attached to timbral variety has remained an essential part of the jazz tradition. Features of Lester Young's style include playing saxophone with a "pinched sound," a "fuzzy tone quality," and swallowed notes after their articulation. Byrnside 1975, 232–34. One source characterizes Ornette Coleman's notion of "human pitch" and sound "vocalization" as a commitment to the idea that sounds of the same pitch should be richly varied from performance to performance. Jost 1975, 53.

9. Various techniques are discussed in Maxwell 1982, 18–27. These wide-ranging techniques have sometimes formed the basis for misunderstanding in the classical music world. For example, I often hear classical musicians misinterpret the expressive jazz improvisers' deliberate avoidance of uniform tonal quality and articulation as indicating that improvisers lack the control necessary to achieve such uniformity.

10. Lomax 1950, 92–93.

11. I include this brief sample of Africanisms merely to indicate the larger historical context in which American musics operate, a vast subject in and of itself. Within a large body of scholarship that concerns itself with questions of origins, influences, and family resemblances among musics within the African diaspora, see Courlander 1963; Epstein 1973, 1975, 1977; Evans 1978, 1987; Kubik 1993; Logan 1984; Oliver 1970; John Storm Roberts 1972; Stuckey 1987; and Waterman 1948, 1963, 1967. For a broader discussion of these influences within the complex matrix of Western art music, Anglo-American folk music, and other musical genres in America, see Van Der Merwe 1989.

12. On instruments functioning as surrogate speech, see Nketia 1974, 90, and Nketia 1971.

13. Southern (1971, 311–12) writes about African Americans developing their own "institutions and culture." For reference to preservation and adaptation of African elements in African American religious music, see discussion of such Africanisms as the ring shout—the "fertile seed for the bloom of new forms" in Stuckey 1987, 16. For an interpretation of the shout's rich characteristics as embodying "all the defining elements of black music . . . ," and discussion of how "call-and-response, blue notes and elisions, pendular thirds, etc." came to be "part of the black-idiom-informed musical genres that emerged from the shout, so that all Afro-American musical products become models to be revised through a continuing Signifyin(g) process," see Floyd 1991, 268, 8–9.

14. One scholar details the interrelationship of religious music and jazz in the African American community. "Rhythmic syncopation, polyphony, and shifted accents,

as well as the altered timbral qualities and diverse vibrato effects of African music were all used by the Negro to transform most of the 'white hyms' into Negro spirituals. . . . The first instrumental voicings of New Orleans jazz seem to have come from the arrangement of the singing voices in the early Negro churches, as well as the models for the 'riffs' and 'breaks' of later jazz music. The Negro's religious music contained the same 'rags,' 'blue notes,' and 'stop times' as were emphasized later and to a much greater extent in jazz." Baraka 1963, 47. Mutt Carey recalls that "Joe Oliver was very strong. He was the greatest freak trumpet player I ever knew. He did most of his playing with cups, glasses, buckets, and mutes. He was the best gut-bucket man I ever heard. I called him freak because the sounds he made were not made by the valves, but through these artificial devices. . . . Joe could make his horn sound like a holy-roller meeting; God, what that man could do with his horn!" Shapiro and Hentoff 1966, 42. For an elaboration of such themes as the flexible boundary between speech and song in African American church services and its implications for jazz performance, see Daniels 1985, 317–18, and Porter 1985a, 613–19.

15. Comment on appending grace notes, etc., in LaPorta 1968, 13.

16. Dorham, rec. 1959. In notes, citations to this and all future recordings use the abbreviation *rec.*, referring readers to items listed in the discography at the back of the book.

17. By placing improvisation at the end of his continuum, Konitz reveals common features of the jazz community's definition of the term. In the context of a tune's delivery, improvisation is the process by which players radically alter portions of the melody or replace its segments with new creations bearing little, if any, relationship to the melody's shape. Many artists make distinctions comparable to those along Konitz's continuum, describing varied degrees of transformation of musical models. The precise terms used by musicians (e.g., *ornamentation* in place of *embellishment*) may differ. Artists also may differ as to where they draw the precise boundary between categories, such as where increasingly elaborate variation becomes improvisation.

Providing space for improvisation during melodic form is commonly the case for AABA pieces like "Oleo" in which the bridge remains open for the improvisation of a melody with each rendition. See also chapter 16, notes 32 and 35.

A claim by Sadik Hakim to have improvised the theme to "Jumpin'," generally attributed to Young, is cited in Porter 1985b, 110; for Parker's improvisation of themes, see Patrick 1975, 13–15.

18. The artist's variable exploitation of the wide-ranging possibilities described here has been noted by a number of analysts. Kernfeld (1983, 60) describes two John Coltrane versions of the ballad "'Round Midnight" in which "an embellished paraphrase of Thelonious Monk's theme is recognizable at times, but at other times, notes extracted from it serve only as signposts for complex elaborations." Porter (1985b, 41–42) reports a similar range of Lester Young's treatments of tunes. Moreover, in handling the material of a melody, jazz musicians' practices range from (as observable in an analysis of Coleman Hawkins, Hodeir 1961, 144) the "consistent melodic variation of a theme as a whole" (Kernfeld 1983, 8) to the motivic treatment of quoted ideas from the tune or from its introduction (as in analyses of Sonny Rollins, Fats Waller, and Louis Armstrong, respectively, in Schuller 1962, 243–48; Hodeir 1961, 169–76; and Austin 1966, 281–83).

19. Warren Kime, personal conversation, fall 1989. Additional transcriptions demonstrating the treatment of tunes by such artists as Lester Young, Benny Goodman, Coleman Hawkins, Roy Eldridge, and Chu Berry are in Byrnside 1975, 232–34, and Kernfeld 1988b, 556–57.

20. Gushee (1981, 151) aptly observes that it is the rhythm section's expression of the underlying harmony of the piece that serves as a "timing cycle which guides, stimulates and limits jazz solo playing."

21. Miles Davis describes Dizzy Gillespie's role in guiding his education in this regard; in an independent interview, Gillespie likewise recalls his advice to Davis, explaining that the keyboard can assist single note players in visualizing "all the possibilities" for chord arrangements and pitch choices. Davis, video 1986.

22. Mid-1920s manuals for ragtime and stride piano styles provided basic chord theory instruction and directions for inventing stride bass lines and breaks, "broken chord patterns used to fill in static points in popular songs." Smith 1983, 68. Western classical music theory books have been available to jazz musicians since the late nineteenth century. Although Turrentine did not recall the title, it was probably Goetschius 1889.

Because of the differences that distinguish jazz and Western classical music, analysts and musicians alike find Western concepts of functional harmony limited in their helpfulness to artists seeking an understanding of all the harmonic features of jazz, features which have themselves changed from one period to another. Among the music's features that pose challenges to outside analysts is the blurring of the distinctions between consonance and dissonance, since sometimes non-chord tones are treated by improvisers as chord tones. Others are the emphasis placed upon flatted-seventh chords, which may substitute for major seventh chords and play dual roles within progressions as chords of either instability or resolution; the appreciation for parallel motion; and the formal design of pieces that mix diatonic movements with those following "another, usually contrapuntal, logic." Strunk 1988, 485–92. See also Kernfeld 1983, 12–16.

For an excellent critical analysis of more recent jazz method books, see Witmer and Robbins 1988, 7–29.

23. One scholar views the jazz community's preference for naming this tension as a raised ninth, rather than a flatted tenth—as would be more common with conventional analysis—as reflecting the jazz community's preference for describing upper chord tensions as odd numbers. Witmer 1988b. Furthermore, thinking in terms of flatting and sharping a single element like the ninth is simply more efficient for improvisers than thinking of manipulating two tensions. James Dossa suggests that this practice may also reflect the jazz musician's adoption of the shorthand methods of arrangers and sheet music copyists who worked speedily to produce written arrangements and fake book lead sheets. Personal conversation, summer 1992.

24. Strunk 1988, 491–92. For harmonically sensitive jazz musicians, the concept of key change encompasses a wide range of possible emphases, including not only sustained ventures from the tonic into another key with a firm emphasis on the new tonality, but fleeting allusions to change created by subtle movements such as ii–V chord patterns borrowed from other keys, commonly known as secondary dominants.

25. Sudhalter and Evans 1974, 35; Shapiro and Hentoff 1966, 228.

26. Demonstrating tunes at a music store was one of Lil Armstrong's first professional jobs as a young pianist when she came to Chicago from Memphis. Shapiro and Hentoff 1966, 92; Foster 1971, xii, 92.

27. Tirro 1976. See also reference to the jazz musician's "borrowed-harmony" technique in Patrick 1975 and Patrick's liner notes to Parker, rec. 1948.

28. Dobbins (1984, 1:24) describes such gestures as I7–vi7–IV7 (in C: CM7–Am7–FM7), whose roots descend in thirds; and iii7–IV7–V7 (in C: Em7–FM7–G7), whose roots ascend in scale steps. This and the discussion that follows owes much to Dobbins's excellent overview of the rules guiding the jazz artist's formulation of chords and transformation of progressions. For an elaboration of the conventions sampled in this chapter, see Dobbins 1984, vols. 1 and 2. See also demonstrations in Bishop, video 1987, and Evans, video 1991.

29. Ross (1989, 31–35) elaborates upon the interrelationships of the constituent elements of chord progressions associated with different jazz compositions.

30. Dobbins 1984, 1:20.

31. For an elaboration of the generative principles underlying jazz harmony and its transformation, see Steedman 1984; Martin 1980, 1988; Strunk 1979, 1988; and Winkler 1978.

32. Strunk 1988, 490.

33. Dobbins 1984, 1:24.

34. Ibid., 46–47.

35. Sample alternative bridges for "Rhythm" and richly embellished versions of blues progressions are in, respectively, ibid., 2:50–51; and 1:49 and 2:41.

36. Bowen 1990; for a description of his composition and flexible use of such structures for renditions of different tunes mentioning other artists who have borrowed and expanded upon his inventions, see Gillespie 1979, 489–90.

37. This is apparent in published versions of Kenny Dorham's compositions arranged for piano (Walter Davis Jr. 1983).

38. For his argument that the original melody associated with a chord progression subsequently adopted by other tunes can continue to suggest material to improvising soloists within the frameworks of the other tunes or serve as basis for their conception of new tunes as countermelodies, see Tirro 1967, 326–27, 329; for his description of Benny Harris writing a countermelody to "How High the Moon," which "became quite a thing with bebop musicians," see Gillespie 1979, 207.

39. Experimentation with the fundamental design of compositions has blossomed since the early days of jazz. In contrast to the diverse structures described in this section, about half of the Basie band's repertory in the late 1930s consisted of thirty-two-bar AABA popular song forms, a quarter comprised other thirty-two-bar forms, and the remaining quarter, twelve-bar blues. Porter 1985b, 38; discussion of "Giant Steps" is in Strunk 1988, 494.

40. Discussion of the merits of the term *vamp* over *modal* in connection with Miles Davis's performance style of the sixties is in Kernfeld 1981, 158–60; elaborating upon various repertorial trends sampled below in useful overviews are Owens 1988, Strunk 1988, and Gridley 1985, 377–86, 421–23.

41. Reference to Coleman in Tirro 1974, 292; "Ode to Charlie Parker" is on Dolphy, rec. 1960.

42. For information on "Carolina Moon," see Feather 1960, 64; for listening to his unique compositions and arrangements, see Little, rec. 1961a; the Roach and Rollins album is cited in Blanq 1977, 51–52.

43. Jabbo Smith described the story behind his piece at a 1981 midwinter concert I attended in New York City.

44. Golson describes "want[ing] to write something that would sound similar to or synonymous with [Clifford Brown] and also to serve as a reminder to all of us who knew him and those would come to know of him, of his greatness." Crawford 1961, 22–23. Jon Henricks subsequently composed lyrics for Golson's piece. In a similar spirit, Max Roach describes "memorializ[ing]" Brown in his compositions "Tender Warriors" and "Praise for a Martyr." Gardner 1961, 21.

45. See Nat Hentoff's liner notes to Roach, rec. 1960.

46. The naivete of some contemporary jazz learners surprises veterans in this regard. One saxophonist recalls his astonishment at a young pianist at a jam session who accused him of playing the "wrong chords" to a piece when the saxophonist deviated from its basic fake book model to perform interesting chord substitutions.

47. In a discussion of Billie Holiday's artistry, one scholar argues appropriately that "it is not possible to so thoroughly recompose and improvise upon that many songs without knowing them completely. You can only intelligently deviate from something—perform variations on it—if you know it deeply." Schuller 1989, 541. The same must be said of the improvisers' mastery over all the musical components of jazz, if artists are to access them instantly in performance and apply them flexibly and creatively. One dissertation refers to this mastery as "internalization." Smith 1983, 90.

## 4. Getting Your Vocabulary Straight

1. Coker 1975, 3.

2. "Whenever a new Bix or Louis record came out we would have a party. Some guy would serve wine and food at his parents' home and we would discuss the record. . . . We talked about phrases. We would sing a phrase and play it over and over. . . . This is what we did for years on end," recalls Freeman (1989, 17).

3. Disheartening experiences are common for learners who grapple seriously with this process, only to discover suddenly how vague is their grasp over ostensibly familiar material. One scholar-pianist reports, "Particularly with respect to the rapid passages, I found that, when singing along with a Charlie Parker recording, for example, I had been glossing the particularities of the notes in many of my hummings, grasping their essential shape perhaps but not singing them with refined pitch sensitivity. . . . What had I in fact been listening to as a jazz fan all these years?" Sudnow 1978, 17.

4. My recollection of a tape-recorded Gillespie anecdote played for Roy Eldridge and conferees at the New York Brass Conference for Scholarships (Charles Colin, organizer) at session honoring Eldridge, March 23, 1981, New York City. Another autobiographical version of the story with a slightly different twist appears in Gillespie 1979, 53–54.

5. A transcription of this "Body and Soul" solo appears in Tirro 1977, 368–70.

6. Tucker 1988, 546.

7. Ibid.

8. A transcription of Coltrane's "Giant Steps" solo appears in Tirro 1977, 381–86.

9. The original "September Song" Clifford Brown solo is on Vaughan, rec. 1954b; the Marsalis performance is on Vaughan, video 1984. According to producer Bill Cosel, the choice of "September Song" for the Pops program was itself the result of Marsalis's enthusiastic recollection of Brown's original solo and his interest in paying homage to Brown. Personal conversation, December 19, 1991.

That there is a significant history behind such practices is suggested by Witmer and Kirkwood's transcriptions and an analysis of different groups' recordings of Joe Oliver and Louis Armstrong's "Dippermouth Blues"—recorded also under the names of "Sugarfoot Stomp" and "In De Ruff"—between 1923 and 1937 that Witmer kindly shared with me. (This material samples that of an ongoing research project that Witmer and his student Kirkwood intend to publish in the future.) The recordings reveal that, to varying degrees, Oliver re-created the same solo in performance, as subsequently did many players who wished to pay homage to him, including Louis Armstrong, Sharkey Bonano, Benny Morton, Rex Stewart, Bobby Stark, J. C. Higgenbotham, and Harry James. Moreover, musical allusions to the original 1923 recording appeared decades later in the music of Charles Mingus and fellow band members. Priestly 1982, 119.

As for Armstrong and Oliver's relationship, the transmission and performance of solos associated with particular pieces sometimes become part of a band's performance tradition. The Bubber Miley solo on Ellington's "Black and Tan Fantasy" was passed "over a period of many decades" among successive Ellington trumpet soloists from Miley to Cootie Williams to Ray Nance to Cat Anderson. Schuller 1989, 95; see also Schuller's general discussion of such practices during the swing era, 162, 307–8.

With regard to instrumental section re-creations, Henry "Red" Allen recalls Horace Henderson writing out his successful improvisations on "Yeah Man" for the Fletcher Henderson brass section to perform. Balliett 1977, 10. Recordings of "Singin' the Blues" by the Fletcher Henderson orchestra in which the saxophone section re-created Frankie Trumbauer's original solo recorded in 1927 are described in Porter 1985b, 34. The citation of a Henderson arrangement of "Singin' the Blues" featuring the Bix Beiderbecke recorded solo is in Feather 1960, 76. He also recalls the Lionel Hampton band's arrangement of "Flyin' Home," in which the entire saxophone section performed Illinois Jacquet's renowned two-chorus solo, and Quincy Jones's elaborate orchestration of the Clifford Brown solo on "Stockholm Sweetenin' "; Feather cites, as well, Jones's regard for it as "a stimulating, inspired composition." Tommy Turrentine mentions the current group Super Sax, whose performances include harmonized renditions of Charlie Parker solos, as a contemporary example of these practices in the jazz community. See Jacquet, video 1993, and Konitz, video 1990, for discussion and re-creation of famous solos including "Flyin' Home."

10. Jimmy McPartland expresses the same view; his young friends copied every feature but the solos of recorded arrangements of Wolverines records. Shapiro and Hentoff 1966, 144.

11. Chick Corea and Herbie Hancock had different approaches to copying their idols, as revealed by a portion of the program notes for a 1978 concert featuring the two artists. Corea describes "taking the creators I got attracted to, and just duplicating their art form as much as I desired—their techniques. I would consciously try to sound like them for a period. . . . I'd become McCoy. I'd become Herbie [Hancock]. . . . I used to sit down with Bud Powell records and copy his solos. . . . [Afterwards] I used

to play along with the record for hours until I couldn't hear the difference between [myself and] the way he did it. And then I'd say, 'Okay, I've got that now' [laughs]." Hancock responds, "I never did it quite that far, not the whole solo. I'd take some little thing I liked, and work on that for hours, or even days, in the beginning." Silvert 1978. I am indebted to Thomas Owens for sharing this data from his collection of concert program notes.

12. This can be as problematic for the scholar as analyst, as for the learner. From the improviser's operational standpoint, the model for a musical idea or any of its components is the particular version of it that the improviser happens to call up in performance at the time. For a discussion of the usefulness for jazz analysis of the concept of musical formulae, as well as the problems surrounding its application to jazz, see Kernfeld 1983, 10–18, and Smith 1983, 142–215, 1991. The concept is borrowed from the influential study of Lord (1970).

13. As Pee Wee Russell explains: "What notes to make and when to hit them—that's the secret. You can *make* a particular phrase with just one note. . . . It's like a little pattern." Balliett 1977, 89. A simple three-quarter-note idea, comparable to that in ex. 4.2a with which Davis opens his solo, is also used by Gerry Mulligan to initiate his "Sunday" solo (see Byrnside 1975, 239, 241) and by the first tenor saxophone soloist (Al Cohn or Zoot Sims) to initiate his "For Adults Only" solo (Davis, rec. 1953b). See also the discussion of musical ideas or licks in Kernfeld 1988b, 558. The term *lick* is also used by artists to refer to new ideas improvised during a performance, as in "That's a nice lick."

14. "Stereotyped phrases are always to be found, as every mature musical language has its idioms. These idioms play a particularly important part in jazz improvisation, in playing of an ad hoc nature." Gonda 1971–72, 198. A sample of a "common stockpile of [jazz] figures used over a period of years, sometimes decades, and on almost all melody instruments" is presented in Robert Brown 1981, 25–26.

15. For a description of Parker's practice of quoting from the arrangements of jazz compositions, including the "beginning of the clarinet obligato from the trio section of the well-known Dixieland piece 'High Society'" and Louis Armstrong's "famous introduction to 'West End Blues,' which dates from 1928," see Owens 1974, 1:29–30.

16. Early references to salient ingredients of characteristic patterns in the styles of great improvisers appear in Hodeir 1961, 106–7; and Schuller 1968, 90; subsequent scholarship offers extensive treatment of the language of individual artists. See studies of Charlie Parker by Owens (1974) and Koch (1974–75); of Lester Young by Gushee (1981), Porter (1985b), and Gottlieb (1959); of John Coltrane by Kernfeld (1981), Porter (1983), and White (1973–78); of Bill Evans by Smith (1983); of Sonny Rollins by Blanq (1977); of Charlie Christian by Spring (1980); of Wes Montgomery by Van Der Bliek (1987); of Miles Davis by Kerschbaumer (1978).

Free jazz players like Albert Ayler, too, draw upon their own distinct vocabulary as the construction components for solos, including such "recurring formulas [as] leaps over wide intervals, rapid, unmeasured, sweeping lines of undistinguished pitches, freely placed vocalistic exclamations in extreme high or low registers." Kernfeld 1988b, 558.

17. Borrowed patterns have been passed from player to player over the history of jazz. Some derive from complete solos that artists master for their own practice and

study, complementing those mastered for performance (see note 9, chapter 4). Just as Lester Young and many of his contemporaries memorized Frankie Trumbauer solos, Charlie Parker subsequently memorized Lester Young solos. Hentoff 1956, 9; Zwerin 1968, 19; Gottlieb 1959, 190; Owens 1974, 1:24. According to Lee Konitz, "at one time, Charlie Parker played exactly like Lester Young." He also recalls hearing Parker play Young's famous "Shoe Shine [Boy]" solo "about twice as fast as the record." Katz 1958, 47–48. Similarly, one scholar attributes several of Lester Young's favored vocabulary patterns, describing them as musical formulas, to Louis Armstrong, whose records Young apparently "owned and admired." Among them is an ascending blues pattern. Porter 1985b, 36, 62. The ascending blues pattern is a variant of what became an "ultimate swing era cliché" (Schuller 1989, 347) and subsequently featured prominently a music generation later in solos by Parker and his friends (Owens 1974, 1:20). Kenny Dorham, for example, used the same pattern repeatedly in performance—as is discernible in my transcription, ex. 5.3a.

18. For an interpretation of musical quotations in jazz in light of current theories regarding "intertextuality" and "metanarrative," see Beeson 1990.

19. Taylor 1982, 13.

20. Tony Scott reports, "When Bird and Diz hit The Street regularly . . . everybody was astounded and nobody could get near their way of playing music. Finally, Bird and Diz made records, and then guys could imitate it and go from there." Shapiro and Hentoff 1966, 360. According to Mutt Carey, "Freddie [Keppard] really used to play good. He could have been as big as Louis [Armstrong], since he had the first chance to make records, but he didn't want to do it because he was afraid that other musicians would steal his stuff." Ibid., 45.

Rudi Blesh notices that recordings rarely captured bassist Pops Foster building inventive countermelodies to those of horn players—a common practice of his in live performances. Foster 1971, xix. Similarly, there are no recordings portraying Dizzy Gillespie's early experimental work with bebop in the Earl Hines band of 1943. DeVeaux 1988, 137.

21. Drums in Sheridan 1988, 358; performance alterations in Tallmadge 1979, 68. For an opposing view of recording limitations, see chapter 16, note 23. See also Tirro 1977, 80–81, and Porter 1985b, 110–11, n. 4.

22. Lester Young commonly used alternate fingerings to muffle the tone and lower the pitch of approach notes leading to their targets, producing a "wah-wah" effect, which he sometimes exaggerated by manipulating his embouchure. Porter 1985b, 52–53.

23. It is an important asset for learners when they develop the ability to apprehend sophisticated jazz phrases in terms of an instrument's layout. With respect to the piano keyboard, for example, they learn to interpret each phrase "not in its note-for-noteness, but [in] the pattern of its location as a configuration emerging out of the broader visual field of the terrain." Subsequently, a mentor's improvised lines reveal "gestalt looking courses." Sudnow 1978, 9, 25.

24. Sheridan 1988, 359.

25. "I found over the course of several months of listening to and watching Jimmy Rowles . . . that in order to get the sound of a song to happen like his, his observable bodily idiom, his style of articulating a beat, served as a guide. In the very act of sway-

ing gently and with elongated movements through the course of playing a song, the lilting, stretching, almost oozing quality of his interpretations could be evoked. It was not that I could imitate his intonations and phrasing with fine success, capture the full richness of his way of moving and pacing and caretaking . . . but I found that I could get much of his breathing quality into a song's presentation by trying to copy his ways," Sudnow 1978, 83; for his elaboration, providing rich detail on this point, see also 86–89, 115, 118–19, 139–40.

Equally instructive concerning the integral relationship between body movement and performance is Chick Corea's experience: "When I was doing Bud Powell [recreating his recorded solos], I found myself with my body at a certain angle at the piano, and having my emotions and attitude be a certain way." Corea later had the opportunity to observe Powell in performance, and he recalls his reaction: "I was amazed, because the guy looked just like I would look at the piano when I'd be playing his shit. It wiped me out," Silvert 1978.

26. David Bomberg, personal conversation, 1986.

27. Henderson and Nichols in Shapiro and Hentoff 1966, 219, 275; Hubbard in Gillespie, video 1988.

28. Foster 1971, 142. See also chapter 13, note 20.

29. Cannonball Adderley and Miles Davis trading phrases throughout the blues head of "Somethin' Else" is heard on Adderley, rec. 1958.

30. Leo Vauchant recalls that in the twenties, he "analyz[ed] a bit what the guys [in Louis Mitchell's band] were doing—just by hearing them play . . . I knew the tunes they were playing. I could hear the phrases and I was trained. I knew the names of the intervals and the degrees of the scale. If you look at a chord as a question they were giving the answers by playing a certain phrase." Goddard 1979, 261–62. At performances of Joe Oliver, and years later at the famous jam sessions at Minton's, neophytes whose recall was perhaps not as developed as Vauchant's transcribed bits and pieces of music "on their cuffs" or "on the tablecloth" to aid them. Preston Jackson and Mary Lou Williams in Shapiro and Hentoff 1966, 99, 350.

31. Coker 1975, 17.

32. One cognitive scientist discusses the wisdom of this "redundancy of description." Ultimately, it allows the player "maximal flexibility of path selection, so that whatever creative impulse presents itself as an intention, and whatever attentional loadings may be set up, some means of cognitive organization and corresponding motor realization will be available within the limiting constraints of real-time processing. . . . Control of event production is heterarchical, and may potentially shift rapidly from one cognitive control area to another. Indeed this must be considered the most effective strategy for improvisation." Pressing 1988, 159, 161.

33. Davis 1990, 70.

34. Dance 1977, 18.

35. Joan Wildman, School of Music, University of Wisconsin, Madison, private conversation, summer 1991.

36. W. C. Handy (1941, 150) praises in his characteristic way the contribution of "new technique[s] . . . acquired by outstanding composers and instrumentalists" in the African American tradition. According to one account, these techniques had their origin in the "clown[ing]" of self-taught musicians who produced "notes . . . by false fingering

and incorrect lipping [with the clarinet]." Jess Stacy in Balliett 1977, 108. Like the techniques of many great artists from Dizzy Gillespie to Thelonious Monk, Bix Beiderbecke's technique (his cornet and piano fingerings) was said to be "unorthodox." Sudhalter and Evans 1974, 36.

37. For reflections on the role of such specialists, I am indebted to my former trumpet teacher, Natalo A. Paella, Music Department, University of Lowell (Lowell, MA).

## 5. Seeing Out a Bit

1. Milt Hinton tells the story in Shapiro and Hentoff 1966, 405.

2. Louis Armstrong reports that when Joe Oliver arrived in New York City from Chicago, having been preceded by other trumpeters who "were playing him," Oliver found that there were no professional opportunities left for him. Stories abound regarding the artist's ambivalence over related issues. According to Mutt Carey, fear "that other musicians would steal his stuff" was behind Freddie Keppard's turning down the opportunity to make the first jazz recording. Shapiro and Hentoff 1966, 187, 45. Equally poignant are accounts of Joe Oliver's and Lester Young's responses to stylistic imitators. Buster Bailey recounts that Oliver "was a jealous guy. . . . Some of the musicians . . . [would] write down the solos, steal like mad, and then those ideas would come out on *their* records. . . . We'd call them alligators." Young, too, sometimes viewed such musicians as "picking [my] bones while the body is still warm." Shapiro and Hentoff 1966, 96–97; Porter 1985b, 29. On one occasion, Young remarked ironically that he did not "know whether to play like me or like Lady Q [Paul Quinichette], because he's playing so much like me," and on another occasion responded to an imitator's recording, "He's trying to be me. If he's going to be me, then who can I be?" Hentoff 1956, 9–10; Kessel 1979, 22.

3. As a label for this period, the term *swing* is used in a restricted sense; in a larger sense, it refers to an essential rhythmic aspect of jazz performance that cuts across different jazz idioms.

4. Owens 1974 1:14–15.

5. Porter 1985b, 33.

6. For a reference that distinguishes "at least five" different effects produced by this "slap-tongue style," ranging from a "violent slap" when the air is finally released into the mouthpiece to "a legato caress," see the dissertation on Clifford Brown by Stewart (1973, 7).

7. Owens 1974, 1:11, 13.

8. Russell 1959, xx.

9. Ibid. Similarly, a description of improvisation that "glides . . . on the outer surface of the harmony . . . more concerned with . . . the tendencies of the harmonic progression" than with "the individual chords" is in Gonda 1969, 196.

10. Gushee (1981, 165–66) observes that whereas Lester Young's performances are "vague from the standpoint of functional analysis," he finds Young's system to be "concrete with reference to the instrument," featuring such idiomatic gestures as particular arpeggios and intervallic chains that are compatible with the piece's harmony.

11. Russell 1959, xviii–xix.

12. T. Dennis Brown 1988, 312. An introduction to teaching basic rudiments is found in Bruce Roberts 1991.

13. A range of drum patterns is demonstrated and discussed by drummer Baby Dodds, rec. 1946.

14. For a discussion of the rhythmic patterns that distinguish individual artists, see the analysis of Ornette Coleman by Heckman (1965a, 15; 1965b, 16) and of Charlie Parker by Koch (1974–75, part 1, 81–85).

15. For description and illustration of Parker's virtuosic practice of quoting compositions, including such wide-ranging repertory as jazz pieces ("High Society"), popular songs ("I'm in the Mood for Love"), older traditional tunes ("Oh Come, All Ye Faithful"), and classical and semi-classical compositions by such composers as Bizet, Chopin, Stravinsky, Grieg, Rossini, Wagner, and Grofé, see Owens 1974, 1:29–30.

16. Roché is featured with Duke Ellington and his orchestra on Roché, rec. 1952.

17. Initially rooted in ragtime orchestra and string band performance in the 1890s, the bass was used by early jazz groups. During the "era of acoustic recording," however, it was commonly replaced by tuba, possibly because of the tuba's "great carrying power." With the introduction of "electrical recording techniques" in the mid-twenties, it became possible to record the bass with greater clarity, contributing to its renewed popularity. Shipton 1988, 301–2.

18. Ibid, 302. The following historical sketch combines the observations of artists in my study with the useful overview of Shipton. (See discussion and demonstration of changing bass performance conventions in Zardis, video 1993.)

19. Shipton 1988, 302.

20. Blanton's solo is on Ellington, rec. 1940.

21. Shipton 1988, 303.

22. Koch 1988, 309. For historical information in this section, I am indebted to the helpful synopsis of Koch.

23. Ibid., 311.

24. Ibid., 309–10.

25. Ibid, 311–14.

26. Rinzler (1983) elaborates upon Tyner's use of pentatonicism and modality, describing various features of his improvisation's grammar and syntax.

27. Koch 1988, 315.

28. Ibid., 312.

29. Gene Krupa's featured improvisation on the 1937 performance of "Sing, Sing, Sing" with Benny Goodman's band, the first extended drum solo on a recording, inspired many others to exploit comparable practices. T. Dennis Brown 1988, 313. Krupa's performance is on Goodman, rec. 1937.

30. Billy Taylor praises Sid Catlett "as the first drummer I'd heard who would play regular choruses—like thirty-two or sixty-four bars . . . the way a piano or a horn might. He thought very musically. . . . He was a really advanced drummer in his concern with a melodic approach to the drums." Shapiro and Hentoff 1966, 363–64. For a description of Max Roach's use of this approach—rhythmically re-creating the harmonic phrasing of a blues progression during his solo to "Blue Seven" on the Sonny Rollins album *Saxophone Colossus*—see T. Dennis Brown 1988, 314.

31. Ibid.

32. Ibid. Elvin Jones describes vivid color imagery associated with the sounds of

individual cymbals and their mixture that influences his use of them in Jones, video 1991.

33. My own experimentation in performing trumpet with a wider separation between the jaws than is conventional has enabled me to reproduce Fruscella's sound, but with the consequence of a severely restricted range.

34. See McNeil (1993, 26–27) for a discussion of the relationships depicted in fig. 5. An excellent portrayal of this lineage is shown on *Trumpet Kings* (video compilation, 1985).

35. Lawrence, video 1986.

36. On avoiding players of his own instrument as models, Odean Pope realized at one point "that you never get any recognition if you played too much like someone else. I became very frustrated and my solution to this was just to take all the saxophone records out of the house and stop buying saxophone records. I tried to come up with some other concept, so I started to listen to piano players. I wondered what it would be like if I could play my horn like Hassan or Art Tatum or Scott Joplin, Jelly Roll Morton, or Bill Evans. I'm pretty happy with the results because dynamically, harmonically, and melodically, I think I got a tremendous amount of knowledge from that experience." Woessner 1983, 46.

Mention of Young's interest in different instrumentalists is in Young interview with Hentoff (1956, 9); see also Porter 1985b, 35.

37. For this interpretation, I am indebted to saxophonist Aaron Horne, lecturer in the Department of African American Studies at Northwestern University, spring 1990. According to Jimmy Heath, Young also used alternate fingerings as a technique for imitating speech. Daniels 1985, 317. One scholar suggested that Jimmy Dorsey's special effects—created by alternate fingerings—may have also provided a model for Young's experimentation. Like many others, Young constantly sought to expand his expressive horizons by drawing inspiration across instrumental lines, "develop[ing] my saxophone . . . make it sound like a alto, make it sound like a tenor, make it sound like a bass, and everything, and I'm not through working on it yet." Porter 1985b, 35, 45.

38. For Coltrane's observation, see Kofsky 1973, 237–38.

39. Hines recalls, "After I learned the piano and got into jazz, the idea came to me to do on the piano what I'd wanted to do on cornet. That went into my style, too, [together] with this [pianist's] left hand and that [pianist's] right hand, until I got to the stage where I began to feel myself." Hines also "marveled at [Louis Smith's] style, and wanted to play [on piano] what he played on trumpet. It gave me a lot of new ideas." Dance 1977, 20.

40. Smith interview with Fraser (1983, 218).

41. One trumpet student who wished to imitate Miles Davis bemoaned the fact that after years of effort he still could not figure out the subtle ways in which Davis manipulated his tongue, jaw, and oral cavity when performing to produce particular timbral effects on the trumpet, nor approximate the emotions Davis engendered through them.

42. Rose 1979, 146–47.

**6. The More Ways You Have of Thinking.**

1. Hardin performs his solo on Lateef, rec. 1957. This technique has been described as "one-noting" in Lester Young solos. It is a device that also featured prominently in the earlier improvisations by Louis Armstrong, Joe Oliver, and others. Porter 1985b, 36, 87.

2. For a description of these and other features of African music throughout the African Diaspora, see Waterman 1967.

3. Elaborations of the complexity of African music are in Jones 1959, Chernoff 1979, Locke 1987, and Kubik 1962.

4. Anon. 1919, 28.

5. For the characterization of the dual accentuation scheme, I am indebted in part to the discussion concerning the equality of strong and weak beats in jazz and its " 'democratization' of rhythmic values" in Schuller 1968, 6–8.

6. Coltrane 1960, 27.

7. Bud Scott remembers: "Each Sunday, Bolden went to church and that's where he got his idea of jazz music. They would keep perfect rhythm there by clapping their hands. I think I am the first one who started four-beat for guitar, and that's where I heard it." Shapiro and Hentoff 1966, 37. Bud Freeman also describes going "to the black churches to hear the singing and to hear the most wonderful beat in music, the most inspired jazz I've ever heard." Freeman 1989, 17.

8. Gillespie 1979, 31.

9. Jazz pianist and composer Joan Wildman, Music Department, University of Wisconsin, Madison, personal conversation, summer 1991.

10. Wynton Marsalis recalls Tony Williams cautioning him against keeping time with his foot when performing with other musicians, because it amounted to "setting up" a potentially conflicting rhythm section of his own. Goodman 1983, 36.

11. Gillespie explains that because "the body keeps the tempo . . . it helps to be able to dance . . . any little simple step; it helps your rhythm." Fraser 1983, 203–4. The association of rhythm and dance expresses itself most dramatically in the context of African American tap dancing, which made strong impressions on learners from Bud Freeman (1989, 18) to Miles Davis (1990, 132); the latter likens tap dancers to drummers and recalls watching "tap dancers dueling each other. . . . You can learn a lot from just listening to the rhythms they get from their taps." An excerpt of "jazz tap percussionist" Baby Lawrence trading improvisations with a drummer is presented on Lawrence, video 1986.

12. Waterman 1967, 211.

13. Coltrane adopted this approach in part as a function of his experimental efforts with harmony that involved playing the scales of three chords superimposed over each one in the progression. "I found that there were a certain number of chord progressions to play in a given time, and sometimes what I played didn't work out in eighth notes, sixteenth notes, or triplets." Asymmetrical patterns "like five and seven" provided a means to "get them all in." Coltrane 1960, 27.

14. A description of Armstrong's tapping twice the tempo, then, in his singing and playing, "stress[ing] accents *around and between* the taps of his foot" is in Stearns 1972, 5.

15. For an account of such events "operat[ing] at the rhythmic level of the eighth note or the quarter note," see Porter 1985b, 81.

16. Miles Davis praises Lee Konitz for his ability to "break [up] phrases" in different ways, to "play 7- or 11-note phrases . . . and they swing" in Hentoff 1955, 14.

17. Herb Pomeroy shared this memory with me in a private improvisation lesson, Summer 1968.

18. Davis describes Charlie Parker's finely honed practice of eliding the forms of compositions, in this case "start[ing] on the 11th bar" of the blues, in Hentoff 1955, 14.

19. Regarding comparable features of the rhythmic life of Ghanaian music, Chernoff (1979, 56, 98) describes musicians "not so much moving along with a pulsation as . . . *pushing* the beat to make it more dynamic"; he also praises Richard Waterman's insights into the "notion of [the artist's] *deliberate* pressure on the continuity of time."

20. Fraser 1983, 182. Regarding the varied sources of Gillespie's ideas, Billy Eckstine describes his borrowing some patterns from Kenny Clarke's drum licks. Shapiro and Hentoff 1966, 349. In a discussion I had with Gillespie, he described rhythmic vocabulary patterns he learned from Cuban drummer Chano Pozo's performances, New York City, winter 1984.

21. Although this is the experience of all the interviewees in my study, some recall periodically encountering exceptional players on the bandstand who, they had the impression, had never learned theory.

22. Typically, Gillespie recalls that from experimentation with the flatted fifth, "I found out that there were a lot of pretty notes in a chord that were well to hold, instead of running over them . . . and that has governed my playing ever since. And that's one of the things that's distinctive about Miles Davis, that he learned form me, I'm sure. Because I showed him on the piano the pretty notes in our music. There are a lot of pretty notes in a chord, and if you hold them for an extended time, it adds a hue . . . to your solos. He really went for that." Gillespie 1979, 92.

23. Elaborating on inventive harmonic mixtures, Coltrane (1960, 27) describes his development of a "three-on-one chord approach," and Kernfeld (1983, 14) notes that Coltrane "consistently introduces a further embellishment . . . [by] accentuat[ing] the change from the tonic to subdominant [in the blues, bars 4–5] by using pitches from extreme flat keys." Porter (1985b, 70) describes Coleman Hawkins as "often insert[ing] connecting arpeggios between chords that were not in the original progression." Similarly, Parker "sometimes superimposed one familiar harmonic sequence (implying it in his melodic line) on another familiar harmonic base," while at other times he abruptly shifted "harmonic accents" within a designated harmonic area, for example, reinterpreting the progression Am7–D7 as Am7–D7–Am7–D7 or D7–Am7–Am7–D7. Koch 1974–75, part 1, 79, 85.

24. Gillespie (1979, 92) recalls his initial discovery of such concepts when playing a ballad arrangement by Rudy Powell for Edgar Hayes's band that included "this weird change, an E-flat chord built on an A. . . . I heard this A Concert going up a scale, and I played it, and I played it again. . . . I said, "Damn! Listen at this shit! . . . That's when I first became aware that there was a 'flatted fifth.' " Gillespie says that he then "started using it in my solos. My solos started taking on a quality where there were long runs and points where the playing was sort of behind the beat." To this day, artists like Jimmy Rowles pass on comparable scalar approaches to students directly, advising at times

that "with this particular chord you can get a characteristic sound by playing this particular scale." Sudnow 1978, 18.

25. Although older musicians spoke to me about "blue notes" and "blues licks," some question the notion that there is a particular "blues scale." To the extent that younger musicians speak about "the blues scale," their concept may represent a construction of more recent jazz pedagogy, which, in turn, reflects the terminology of analytical writing about jazz. As early as 1938, there is a discussion of a "purely Negroid musical scale" that may be inferred from "the system of intonations to which these passages of hot jazz respond" and for which "there is no European precedent. . . . For convenience, and because it is associated with the performance of the blues as well as with hot jazz proper, we will call it the blues scale." The same author likens it to a major scale in which the third and seventh can function as blue notes whose intonation may "range through an infinite number of gradations in pitch," typically "sliding up and down" between the third and the flatted-third or the seventh and the flatted-seventh degrees. Other pitches are also "frequently subject to distortions of intonation, particularly by jazz trumpeters." Sargeant 1976, 158, 160–61, 169. More recently, one scholar describes various heptatonic, hexatonic, and pentatonic blues scales, concluding, "There is no single 'blues scale' but many blues scales." Additionally, he describes singers regularly using pitches between the major-sixth and minor-seventh degrees. Evans 1982, 24. Beyond describing blues tonalities in terms of the inflected pitches and interval configurations of particular scales, artists discuss the importance of their harmonic context. It is when played in relation to chords containing the raised counterparts of the flatted tonalities of blue notes that their effects become especially pronounced.

26. Russell 1959.

27. Stephen Ramsdell told me of Cheatham's instruction in a personal conversation, summer 1991.

28. For Miles Davis's early bebop training, see Stearns 1972, 229.

29. It is with Harris's kind approval that this discussion is presented for illustrative purposes. Although Harris continues to make his ideas public through workshops, I am hopeful that one day he will publish an elaborate work devoted to his method. In the meantime, the reader can glimpse comparable approaches in the method of his student and collaborator in his early study groups, Yusef Lateef. See Lateef 1979.

30. For illustrations of these practices, see exx. 5.3d, 6.8, 6.9, 8.4b–c, and 8.23b.

31. Suber 1976, 367; Carter 1986, 12.

32. Slonimsky 1947, i. Donald Byrd, personal conversation, New York City, summer 1986. Several different jazz musicians recommended Slonimsky's book to me during my travels to both coasts in 1967. All artists were not equally enthusiastic about the work, however. Walter Bishop Jr. found it to be overrated. Apart from its catalogue of theoretical materials, the transformational techniques it describes were already well known within the jazz community, Bishop contends.

33. Stephen Ramsdell, a student in Cheatham's workshops, personal conversation, summer 1991.

34. In addition to others cited in the text, popular published examples of method books include Coker 1964; Cheatham 1960; Russell 1959; Nelson 1966; Bishop 1976;

Lateef 1979; Farmer 1984; Ricker 1976; Baker 1969. Multifaceted resources include Aebersold's "Jazz Aids" catalogue, available at P.O. Box 1244, New Albany, IN 47150, and the Advance Music catalogue, available from Caris Music Services, RD7–Box 7621G, Stroudsburg, PA 18360. An example of a teaching videorecording is Bishop, video 1987, in which he demonstrates numerous applications of his theory of fourths to jazz improvisation.

### 7. Conversing with the Piece

1. Balliett 1977, 10.

2. According to Robert O'Meally (1991, 13), Holiday trained in Baltimore's "good-time houses" during the Depression by singing along with records or "trading choruses" with the piano player.

3. Mingus (1971, 69) recalls early advice on practicing with the radio in this fashion.

4. Gillespie (1979, 21, 29) received direct instruction in such practices from his first teacher, who would "jazz" up popular tunes on the piano—demonstrating how to "put that jazzing part in there," so that Gillespie could follow, imitating her patterns with the trumpet.

5. Some of the varied improvisation practices elaborated over the next two chapters are discussed in Byrnside 1975 and Kernfeld 1988b. See also Bill Evans's discussion and demonstration of improvising in relation to form in Evans, video 1991.

6. Other musicians confirm the importance of this approach. Milt Jackson keeps "the melody in mind. I always remember the melody and then I have something to fall back on when I get lost, and with the human element I do get lost, but I've always been able to find my way back." Similarly, when Connie Kay performs a drum solo, he "think[s] of the tune I'm playing. I try to fit what I'm playing into the composition rather than do just twelve bars of rudiments. The melody goes through your mind and you go along with it, fitting yourself to it." Balliet 1971, 167.

7. For many instrumentalists, such feeling for phrasing reflects a deep understanding of a piece's words. Young himself once explained, "A musician should know the lyrics of the songs he plays, too. . . . Then you can go for yourself and you know what you're doing. A lot of musicians that play nowadays don't know [them]. . . . They're just playing the changes. That's why I like records by singers when I'm listening at home.'" Hentoff 1956, 10.

8. See ex. 8.19 for the elaborate third chorus of Morgan's solo.

9. Drawing cleverly on various conventions for producing and resolving harmonic tension, Lester Young sometimes played the same figure repeatedly over the changing chords, whereas at other times, when the harmony was static, he transposed the figure with each repetition, producing chromatic sequences. Porter 1985b, 66, 71–72. Based on a similar observation in Bill Evans's improvisations that "an identical series of pitches can be harmonized in different ways," Smith (1983, 210) questions whether "the repetition of a given series of tones has more to do with its particular keyboard configuration, or the interval it outlines, than with its harmonic setting." See also Gushee's reflections on Young in note 10, chapter 5, of this work.

10. The importance of practicing away from the instrument for improvisers ap-

pears to be missing from the literature on improvisation, although as Pressing (1988, 140) mentions, the method is widely recognized as a part of skill development among performers of written music.

11. Parker, video 1987.

12. In light of the changing formal conventions of jazz, even accomplished artists must at times retrain their perceptions along such fundamental lines. Drummer Dave Tough, a newcomer to bebop, described his initial reaction to the Gillespie-Pettiford quintet: "These cats snatched up their horns and blew crazy stuff. One would stop all of a sudden and another would start for no reason at all. We never could tell when a solo was supposed to begin or end. Then they all quit at once and walked off the stand. It scared us." Stearns 1972, 224–25.

13. Reflecting on his own five-year development, Sudnow (1978, 146) describes learning the language of jazz "as my instructable hands' ways—in a terrain nexus of hands and keyboard whose respective surfaces had become known as the respective surfaces of my tongue and teeth and palate are known to each other."

14. It is appropriate to maintain that "the performer's own knowledge of the structure allows him to plan excursions whilst retaining markers which tell him exactly when he must arrive at a particular musical event." Sloboda 1989, 141.

15. Shapiro and Hentoff 1966, 47.

16. Ibid., Mutt Carey interview. Sudnow (1978, 95–6,149–50) describes his appreciation of comparable advice: after eventual breakthroughs in linking his "head's aimings for sung sounds" with an evolving "partnership" between his hands and the keyboard's terrain, he experiences "the awesomeness of an altogether new coupling . . . between my vocalizations and my fingerings." Scenes of Charles Mingus composing phrases vocally at the piano are in Mingus, video 1987.

17. A review of contemporary jazz method books aptly notes that, beyond introductory lessons on traditional devices such as "repetition, transposition, sequence, inversion, and so forth," little insight is provided on how to turn theoretical materials "into melodic gold." Smith 1983, 79–80.

Along similar lines, many veterans are critical of graduates of university jazz programs that emphasize theoretical approaches to improvisation. While acknowledging the impressive instrumental virtuosity of the graduates, Melba Liston remarks, "They don't know a thing about jazz really . . . no style in the traditional way. You don't feel the jazz thing, you feel the mechanical thing. Jazz is feeling, and I worry about this. I really advise them to study as much of the history of jazz as possible—not by book or by transcription—but by ear. . . . If they listened back to Louis Armstrong, Lester Young, the swing days, the forties, early Trane and Miles, and loved it, it would influence the way they play." Gary Bartz adds, "I've never been able, for myself, to get anything out of trying to apply this scale to this chord. I've never been able to get anything that's really musical that way, even if it sounds right. The young players don't know what to do with their [unbelievable technique]. Sounds like they're playing computer music; it doesn't sound like ideas. It's all fast and furious." George Duvivier's critique of the contemporary jazz scene is, perhaps, the most most poignant of all. "The music's still here," he remarked to an associate, "but the voices are gone."

18. Walter Bishop Jr. demonstrates this process with regard to "fourths" and other materials on Bishop, video 1987. Jazz musicians with classical music training liken

some of their methods for transforming and embellishing chords—such as appoggiatura and échappée—to those used by Baroque musicians and composers. Barron 1975.

19. Robert Lowery, Clifford Brown's teacher, provides insight into the theory and instruction that lay behind the practices Cheatham observes. According to Lowery's pedagogical theory of "'active and inactive notes, . . . active [notes] are notes that are played around the principal notes that you want to get to. . . . Inactive notes are notes that are like a solid foundation. And the active notes are the notes that you use to color those inactive notes. You play around those notes to make them sound like you want them to sound." Quoted in Fraser 1983, 109.

20. Similarly, analysis of Charlie Parker solos shows that "in many cases, the distinguishing motives [i.e., vocabulary patterns] for each group occur only when the harmonic context is unique to that group, and . . . there is a high degree of motive crossover from one group to another whenever the harmonic context is the same." Owens 1974, 1:113, 119.

21. The categorizations that follow are based, in part, on such complementary methods as interview data, my own experiences improvising during formal performances, and reflective experiments recalling, altering, and developing musical ideas from a set of known models in the practice room—training myself according to the methods described by interviewees. In turn, this data has influenced my interpretation, as an analyst, of the musical models and transformational processes underlying solos by other artists. When interpreting another player's improvisation, of course, the researcher can only infer the artist's unvoiced models and transformational procedures from a comparison of related, recurring ideas in different parts of a solo and in different solos.

Moreover, because of the interrelated nature of the processes discussed in this section, multiple interpretations are possible concerning the actual processes at work. When one is interpreting an observed pattern in a solo, for example, one is aware that it may have been conceived as an entity, produced by contracting a larger related idea, or it may be an interpolation of a smaller related idea. The process behind the conception and performance of the same idea may differ from player to player, just as players may conceive of the basic components of the language of jazz differently. Moreover, in my experience, the processes can differ from an individual's standpoint from performance to performance. As mentioned earlier, "the" model for a particular idea that the improviser performs or transforms is the version of it that the improviser calls up at the time of the performance.

22. These processes are partially responsible for the complex interrelationships among improvised figures noticed by jazz scholars, who have shown that related musical ideas appearing in the solos of individual jazz artists form dense, overlapping networks of melodic cells and patterns. Owens 1974; Kernfeld 1981, 1983.

23. Concerning Bill Evans's extensive practice of rephrasing ideas in his solos, Smith (1983, 199) mentions that "the number of patterns repeated verbatim, with the same rhythmic profile . . . is very small."

24. Whereas the distinction between phrase expansion and its opposite, phrase contraction (described earlier), is an obvious one from the operational and experiential standpoint of one's own performance, it remains a matter of conjecture when one is interpreting another artist's improvisation.

25. Described in Sawyer 1991, 8.

26. Balliett 1977, 13.

27. Other scholars have also noted this capacity. With respect to lute performance in Afghanistan, "the spatiomotor mode can be regarded as a legitimate and commonly used mode of thought, used to instigate and to control musical performances, and just as creative as the auditory mode, for creativity in music may often consist of deliberately finding new ways to move on the instrument, which are then . . . assessed, and further creative acts, guided by the aesthetic evaluation of the resultant novel sonic patterns." Baily 1985, 257–58. Similarly, from his own theoretical standpoint, Pressing (1988, 161) views "the motor enactment of novel combinations of values of array components" as a "common source of behavioral novelty." Analogous features of dance improvisation have relevance for the physical dimensions of thought in improvised music. For discussion of "kinetic intelligence," "thinking in movement," and a "fundamental creativity founded upon a body logos, that is, upon a mindful body, a thinking body," see Sheets-Johnstone 1981, 406, and for a larger study of dance improvisation, see Blom and Chaplin 1988.

28. Porter (1985b, 75) speculates that physical comfort lay behind particular Lester Young triplet eighths and sixteenth-note patterns that Gottlieb (1959, 194) describes Young favoring in solos regardless of their key. At the same time, physical ease in negotiating musical ideas with respect to an instrument is itself only one variable contributing to the shape of artist's conceptions. Owens (1974, 1:18, 23) maintains that Charlie Parker often emphasized particular patterns over others of comparable difficulty and, at times, emphasized gestures that were more difficult than their counterparts in alternative keys. Moreover, as mentioned earlier, musicians commonly pursue ideas they find attractive in the solos of other instrumentalists, despite the technical difficulties they encounter adapting them to their own instruments.

## 8. Composing in the Moment

1. Perlman and Greenblatt (1981, 169) have also been intrigued by this notion and state that the improviser's "specific harmonic and melodic constraints . . . are in many ways analogous to the syntactic and semantic constraints of natural language and that playing an improvised solo is very much like speaking sentences."

2. Players often use *motivic* and *thematic* interchangeably, rather than reserving the latter, as some analysts do, for the manipulation of material from the melody of the piece. Kernfeld (1988b, 559–61) provides a useful discussion of the motivic improvisation approach, distinguishing it from others and clarifying some of the confusion created in the jazz literature as a result of the inconsistent application of analytical terms borrowed from Western classical music scholarship. For an analysis of various techniques of motivic development in the solos of markedly different improvisers whose styles range from early jazz to free jazz, see Byrnside 1975, 238–43; Schuller 1962; Gottlieb 1959, 189; Koch 1974–75, part 2, 73–77; Stewart 1979, 141; Porter 1985b, 82–86; and Jost 1975, 48–50, 59.

3. Study of Western classical music reinforces the understanding of some jazz musicians. "It's the same way that Bach started out with a melody and did variations on a theme. You can take a two- or three-note phrase, maybe a phrase from the melody, and develop it rhythmically, or you can depart from the original phrase and go back to

it later and take it in another direction" (CL). Bach's "Inventions," in particular, illustrate "how you can change around a phrase in many ways, maybe repeating it and inverting certain parts of the structure" (PB). At the same time, jazz musicians define motivic development according to their own conventions, typically avoiding "the kind of systematic repetition and transposition heard in classical music." Exceptions to this are in such works as Coltrane's suite "A Love Supreme," whose first movement is built upon the constant repetition of a motive, "eventually transposing it into all 12 keys." Kernfeld 1988b, 559.

4. Although some improvisers derive such compositional methods from their own interpretations of classical music, they may face challenges in applying the methods that differ in degree from those confronting classical music composers. Scholars such as Sloboda (1985, 138–39, 148), Johnson-Laird (1988, 209), and Alperson (1984, 22) speculate that whereas composers who fix their ideas in writing can subsequently review musical scores and revise them, by considering their ideas' possibilities for variation and development at leisure, real-time composition greatly constrains the improviser's possibilities for conceiving and processing new ideas, that is, reflecting on, revising, and developing them over the larger performance. At the same time, as this work shows, the imaginative field of improvisers is far richer, and their processing capabilities far greater (both in terms of developing their own ideas and in responding to those of other artists within the group), than scholars have allowed. During practice routines, jazz musicians routinely subject their ideas to procedures comparable to those of written composition without the use of musical scores. Furthermore, with respect to revision in particular, they may revise ideas from one improvisation to another, as well as over the duration of a single performance.

5. One insightful phenomenological account describes the improviser's "perceptual field . . . [which] includes not only perception of external tonal events, but the perception of internal images, as well as states of consciousness aroused by these images." The field "contains within itself the potential structure of future fields," and the artist may at times "immediately glimpse the future horizons of the embryonic jazz idea." Ultimately an "original image can be repeated, or permuted in various ways." Pike 1974, 89–90. An elaboration upon these ways under the rubric of "a generalized caretaking throughout play, to do things with things formerly done" is in Sudnow (1978, 145–46), who views the processes as an inherent aspect of formulating melodies, or "melodying."

In the most comprehensive psychological model of these processes, one scholar describes "continuous aural and proprioceptive feedback, which allows continuous evaluation, on the basis of which the current ideas are either repeated, developed or discarded. In this way a long-term improvisation can be built up." In another study the same scholar elaborates on "the cognitive structures of processing and control" involved with the moment-to-moment progression of events in improvised musical behavior, decomposing aspects of musical ideas into "three types of analytical representation" that can be taken up by the improviser as the basis for development or "improvisational continuations." The analytical representations include specific "objects" such as a set of pitches; their more general "features" or shared properties such as melodic motion; and "processes," that is, "descriptions of changes of objects or features over time." Pressing 1984, 353; 1988, 154–66.

6. For a description of the widespread use of ostinatos in jazz and other black improvised musical genres, see Logan 1984.

7. In his solos and compositions, Thelonious Monk often adopted such a motivic approach, repeating a simple figure, while displacing it and subtly compressing or stretching its rhythmic values. See transcription in Kernfeld 1988b, 560. An early discussion of displacement and other rhythmic features of jazz is in Sargeant 1938, 99–102.

8. Such techniques have been observed over the history of jazz. For an interpretation of "Armstrong's single line . . . [as] incorporating fragmentary antiphonal answers to its own leading ideas," see Austin 1966, 283. A description of Coltrane's "self-dialogue" procedure, in which he rapidly alternates "related phrases, two, and sometimes three octaves apart," is in Jost 1975, 100.

9. For an analysis of Coltrane's piece, see Porter 1985a, 593–621.

10. Perlman and Greenblatt (1981, 180) likewise contend that the "phrases in a jazz solo do have meaning. . . . The meaning of a phrase is its history, that is, where it comes from." For an illustration of a gesture recurring in different players' solos, where it is transformed in various ways—suited to different time signatures, different keys, and different tempos, and adjoined to different material—see exx. 7.7a (entire thirty-second-note figure), 8.14g (last two bars), and 8.19 (end of bar 4 and first half of bar 5).

11. A version of the pattern in a Clifford Brown solo appears in ex. 8.8c; it also provides the basis for a short developmental section during Booker Little's solo on "Old Folks" in ex. 7.2d.

12. Just as Sudhalter (cited in Porter 1985b, 34) attributes the ending of Lester Young's composition "Tickle Toe" to a phrase from Bix Beiderbecke's solo on "When," Gottlieb (1959, 190) maintains the first phrase of Charlie Parker's composition "Ornithology" was borrowed from Lester Young's solo on "Shoe Shine Boy." Schuller (1968, 163) also identifies a particular phrase not only used by early soloists such as Oliver, Armstrong, and Bechet but appearing as one of the themes in James P. Johnson's "Yamekraw" and the standard "Copenhagen."

Patrick (1975, 3–11) elaborates upon the similar melodic materials that comprise jazz compositions, improvised solos, and arranged background riffs, attributing them to both the artist's self-conscious borrowings and to the common vocabulary with which jazz musicians worked. Gillespie (1979, 489–90) describes some of the composed features of his own arrangements that have been taken up by other arrangers and transformed in various ways.

13. For a description of comparable processes in the free jazz context, where, in John Tchicai solos, the "motive derived from the theme has more the function of an anchor, serving as a fixed point of reference throughout his whole improvisation," see Jost 1975, 91.

14. Jimmy Knepper interview in Jeske 1981, 67.

15. Quoted material is from Coker 1964, 13.

16. Illustrations of this practice appear in exx. 6.4 and 8.22b (bars 1–4).

17. Additional illustrations of this practice appear in exx. 8.9a and c.

18. Floyd (1991, 273) regards swing as "a dance-related legacy of the ring shout" and appropriately asserts that "the power of swing is such that even in the absence of

motivic and thematic ideas, its presence creates a sense of eventful continuity in a work of music."

19. For a discussion of "syncopation on the level of harmonic rhythm" in jazz and the resolution of dissonance created by conflicts between melody and harmony, see Winkler 1978, 16. Lester Young's and Sonny Rollins's performances provide typical examples of the improviser's practice of anticipating chord changes. Porter 1985b, 72; Schuller 1962, 250. For an elaboration on the "continuous fluctuation of dissonant and consonant events" in Bill Evans's improvisations that contributes to the music's "maximum forward propulsion," see Smith 1983, 212–13.

20. These qualities may include "timbral continuity or a characteristic personal timing with respect to the rhythm section. The piece is already so strongly connected in its rhythmic order that a time-span of four measures may be perceived as linked to a preceding one merely by virtue of a note-group, or even a single pitch, played in the equivalent metrical position. Pitch-centered or motivic analysis will often not take this sufficiently into account. Also, such connections, clearly as they may be *heard* in performance, lose much of their force when *viewed* in a transcription." Gushee 1981, 159.

21. That actually transcribing solos also cultivates these abilities in learners is suggested by Coker (1964, 34–35).

22. The challenges of shaping stories over various spans of time have changed over the history of jazz. Gushee (1981, 159) reports that "the welding of two choruses into a whole may seem a modest achievement by today's standards, [but] it was not at all usual in 1936, with few players being given that much time on an approximately three-minute recording."

23. Floyd (1991, 277) elaborates on the concept of the "non-verbal semantic content of musical phrases," which owes in part to his interpretation of the work of Murray and Gates.

24. Gushee 1981, 168.

25. Armstrong reportedly told Wingy Manone: "The first chorus I plays the melody. The second chorus I plays the melody round the melody, and the third chorus I routines." Sudhalter and Evans, 1974, 192. Lawrence Gushee interprets *routines,* in this case, to mean the formulation of high-note riffing patterns. Personal conversation, 25 January 1992. Sidney Bechet's advice to Bob Wilber and Lester Young's praise of Frankie Trumbauer reveal comparable approaches. Balliett 1977, 243; Hentoff 1956, 9.

26. Neil Tesser, Chicago jazz critic, observed this in Gordon's performances at the Jazz Showcase, personal communication, Fall 1991. The versatility of many instrumentalists as vocalists is demonstrated in Jacquet, video 1993; Kirk, video 1988; and Zardis, video 1993.

27. Similarly, Sidney Bechet reports: "All that happens to you makes a feeling out of your life and you play that feeling. But there's more than that. There's the feeling inside the music too. And the final thing, it's the way those two feelings come together." Bechet 1978, 123.

28. Morgan's rendition of "I Remember Clifford" is on Blakey, rec. 1958b.

29. A musician explains, "Within the past few months I was listening to Miles, and I remember noticing that I started playing things that sounded like his patterns. But it wasn't something I was trying to do. But it would be on a song that would sound like something he would play." Sawyer 1991, 11.

30. A number of works provide additional transcriptions and analyses of such issues as large-scale melodic continuity and coherence in the stories of outstanding soloists. For Louis Armstrong, see Schuller 1968, 102–5; 1989, 161–64; Austin 1966, 281–83. For Lester Young, see Gushee 1981; Porter 1985b, 60, 90, 93–94, 97. For Charlie Parker, see Koch 1974–75, part 2, 77–85. For Cannonball Adderley and John Coltrane, see Kernfeld 1981, 96–102, 270–77; 1983, 46–59.

31. Pike (1974, 90–91), also portrays the "affective reactions" that accompany the soloist's musical creations, and astutely reports, "As his improvisation grows successfully, his pleasure flows from the pleasure of its creation, its appropriateness, and the shaping of its destiny. Phenomenally subjective terms (such as *expectation, satisfaction, disappointment, tension-release*) may be used to describe the various affective phases of his creative jazz experience." Sudnow (1978, 146) describes his own internal "nudgings."

32. Coltrane 1960, 21.

33. Keith Jarrett spoke on "ecstatic states" at the School of Music, Northwestern University, Evanston, IL, October 19, 1987.

34. Personal conversation, Northwestern University, Evanston, IL, July 15, 1983.

35. Raising comparable issues in his analysis of a solo on "Blue Seven," Schuller (1962, 245) conjectures "that Rollins had some fingering problems with the passage, and his original impulse in repeating it seems to have been to iron these out. However, after six attempts to clean up the phrase, Rollins capitulates and goes on to the next idea." See also the same scholar's discussion of Dizzy Gillespie's masterful saves (1989, 434). Similarly, John Lewis explains that when "things go wrong . . . many times you find a nice way of getting out of a phrase that is better than the original way you were going." Balliett 1971, 166. As in such cases, "musicians often characterize 'mistakes' . . . [as performing] a valued function of interrupting the pre-arranged ideas and forcing an innovative alternative." Sawyer 1991, 14.

36. My recollection of Maxwell's remarks at the New York Brass Conference for Scholarships (Charles Colin, organizer) at session honoring Roy Eldridge, March 23, 1981, New York City.

37. Zwerin 1982, 18.

38. Similarly, Jim Hall explains that "if a solo is going well, is developing, I let it go on its own. Then I've reached that place where I've gotten out of my own way, and it's as if I'm standing back and watching the solo play itself." Balliett 1977, 223.

39. Issues of the mystique of jazz are as intriguing for analysts as for improvisers. On the one hand, experiences of automaticity reported above are common among players. According to one musician, sometimes an idea "just comes out, it falls out of my mouth." Sawyer 1991, 8–9. Henry "Red" Allen experiences it as if "somebody [is] making your lip speak, making it say things he thinks." Balliett 1977, 13. From the standpoint of cognitive psychology, one technical explanation involves the "change from *controlled* processing to *automatic* motor processing . . . [a stage of developed skill in which artists] completely dispense with conscious monitoring of motor programmes, so that the hands appear to have a life of their own, driven by the musical constraints of the situation." Pressing 1988, 139.

On the other hand, it can be argued that at such moments artists are, in fact, operating on different levels simultaneously, consciously creating music, while standing outside themselves and observing a process so rapidly and successfully under way in the language of music that it simply precludes the possibility or necessity of reflexive verbal intervention and redirection. As Pike (1974, 90–91) maintains, the improviser "is pursuing a definite musical goal and is engaged in a highly differentiated and precise act. . . . This behaviour is based on a conscious inner perception . . . a rational creative process." That is, the artist is "not behaving in terms of unconscious causes but in terms of sharply differentiated present perceptions of various musical ideas." The precise relationship between such features of improvisation remains a matter for speculation. Hargreaves and associates (1991, 53) interpret the artists' experience of automaticity as an indication that they are "consciously aware of playing detailed figures or 'subroutines' at a relatively peripheral or unconscious level, with central conscious control reserved for overall strategic or artistic planning." Sawyer (1991, 9, 15) suggests that there is a complex interaction between the artist's conscious and unconscious creative processes, likening the latter to the "*intuitive* creativity" discussed by Simonton or Martindale's "*primordial* cognition," and the former to Simonton's "*analytical* creativity" or Martindale's "*conceptual* cognition." See also Bill Evans's reflections in Evans, video 1991.

## 9. Improvisation and Precomposition

1. This famous quotation reappears in many works, including Shapiro and Hentoff (1966, 354) and Owens (1974, 1:109), who attributes the original source to Levin and Wilson (1949). Upon reading the original, I was surprised to find the quotation to be partly in the third person and not exclusively in the first person. The oft repeated variation seems consistent with Parker's intention, however.

2. For a description of McCoy Tyner's practice of "improvising mode changes" and alternating between improvisations inside and outside of a composition's designated mode, see Rinzler 1983, 122, 133.

3. Schuller 1961, [2–3], 10–11.

4. A music dissertation provides an important account of various aspects of the behavior of approximately one hundred vocabulary patterns [the dissertation uses the term *motives*] in Charlie Parker's improvisational language. Short vocabulary patterns commonly form a part of longer pattern-complexes. Altogether, they are distinguished not only by frequency of use, but by the roles they assume and the musical contexts in which they make appearances. Some always or usually occur in a particular key or in the setting of particular chords. Others arise "almost exclusively" within the boundaries of a particular composition, or within a discrete group of compositions, and do not arise in other compositions. Some characteristically occur within a particular segment of a harmonic form, where they may begin a blues chorus, for example, or serve "primarily as a coda." Within the contexts of larger musical statements, some patterns are typically found at the "beginnings of phrases," and so on. Owens 1974, 1:17–18, 24–25, 92, 102, 113. See also Koch 1974–75, part 2, 77–85.

So, too, do Porter (1985b) and Gushee (1981, 160–64, 166, 168) analyze the varied functions of formulas used by Lester Young, with Gushee enumerating Young's predilections for degree progressions, pitch repetitions, and oscillations, particular arpeggios with an emphasis on selected pitches, blues clichés, and idiomatic saxophone expressions "such as false fingerings, rips upward to the palm keys, dramatic bombs in the extreme low register, chains of thirds." See also the discussion of formulas with regard to John Coltrane's improvisations in Kernfeld 1983, and with regard to Bill Evans's improvisations in Smith 1983 and 1991.

As this work shows, developing a base of vocabulary patterns is an integral part of the jazz musician's learning process, and using them is an integral part of the improvisation process. At the same time, identifying precise vocabulary patterns (or "formulas" or the "formulaic system" underlying the production of individual formulas—terms adopted by jazz analysts influenced by Parry's and Lord's [Lord 1970] important study), and determining their function in a musical language that is not text bound presents numerous difficulties and continues to be a controversial matter. See Gushee 1981, 160; Kernfeld 1983, 9–18; Smith 1983, 137, 144, 154, 160–62, 204–6, 208, 210; and Sawyer 1991, 10.

5. Floyd (1991, 277) elaborates upon the "non-verbal semantic value of instrumental music" and cites Murray's (1973, 86) discussion of the Ellington band, whose soloists manage to create the analogue of verbal expressions, conveying precise moods and attitudes and engaging in rhetorical interplay. The soloist does not simply perform, but rather "states, asserts, alleges, quests, requests, or only implies, while the trumpets in the background sometimes mock and sometimes concur, as the 'woodwinds' moan or groan in the agony and ecstasy of sensual ambivalence and the trombones chant concurrence or signify misgivings and even suspicions (which are as likely to be bawdy as plaintive) with the rhythm section attesting and affirming."

6. Gushee (1981, 160, 164) also observes Young's varied application of formulas, noting that patterns comprising "physically the same kind of gesture" serve as "a penultimate element of an eight-measure section" in one instance, and "as traditional between the first and second four-measure sections" in another. Similarly, a particular formula "which might appear to function to give LY time to think of what to do next . . . also serves as a formal element in an over-all repetition scheme." Porter (1985b, 59, 61) states that whereas one formula of Young's consistently occurs at phrase endings, another "may begin on any beat and occurs at phrase endings as well as during the middle of phrases." Owens (1974, 1:112) observes that in some Parker performances the "same introduction also serves as a coda."

7. In the language of music, "ideas" themselves may be specific or general, or comprise a combination of specific and general properties. As suggested earlier, improvisers sometimes draw upon general musical features or principles to generate specific versions of patterns, while at other times they generalize from the details they appreciate in specific patterns and formulate larger principles from them that subsequently serve as guidelines. The precise circumstances of performances affect this process, of course, for artists must ultimately contend with whichever representation of an idea occurs to them in the moment, whether specific or general.

8. In such instances, it can be argued that "each improvisation has a history of similar, related performances. . . . [Although] no two performances will be exactly alike, one must include a consideration of past events that act as preparation for a present event." Tirro 1974, 296, 298.

9. For interview with Clark Terry, see Beach 1991, 12.

10. For the properties of the pentatonic scale, see Benward and Wildman 1984, 89.

11. Ellington 1980, 47.

12. In his analysis of Lester Young's solos from a "schematic" point of view,

Gushee (1981, 165) also describes the ways in which improvisers can explicitly indicate the structure of the piece in their solos. Young commonly marked eight-bar units strongly "by long silences, statements of tonic harmony or both," and subtly articulated four-bar units "by changes in direction or indefinite ('ghost') pitches." With respect to the "contrastive character and sequential harmony" of the bridge, Young produced "strongly similar renditions of the 'underlying' chord progression." Porter (1985b, 46, 49, 67) adds that Young used "honks" to end eight-bar sections, and tended to distinguish his improvisation over a piece's bridge by emphasizing high notes and adding special harmonic color to the section's final seventh chord.

13. John Lewis adopts the approach of building on the concluding idea of each chorus to establish "a link" with the following chorus. Porter 1988, 27. Jim Hall (Balliett 1977, 223) and Jimmy Knepper (Jeske 1981, 67) describe their use of comparable compositional techniques, introducing a single idea and then developing it motivically "throughout a solo" or creating successive motivic sections over a solo's course.

14. A description of Coltrane's exploitation of range is in Porter 1985a, 620.

15. Sonny Rollins's solo on "St. Thomas," Rollins, rec. 1956b.

16. Wes Montgomery's solo on "West Coast Blues," Montgomery, rec. 1960. For an elaboration of Montgomery's techniques for organizing solos, see Van Der Bliek 1987.

17. Gushee 1981, 167. Other schemes mentioned by Gushee involve building each chorus of a two-chorus solo "in very much the same way," or fashioning solos according to a "single-minded dramatic 'ride-out' of mounting intensity, much favored by trumpeters at this time."

18. Porter 1985b, 96.

19. The listener's familiarity with the specific vocabulary patterns of an artist is germane here. It "allows the listener to follow a solo with great insight into the creative process taking place," noting the unique ordering and mixture of patterns, as well as their modification "by augmenting or diminishing [them], by displacing [them] metrically, or by adding or subtracting notes." Owens 1974, 1:17, 35.

20. Little's quotations are sampled in ex. 7.2. Dorham's solo, "I Love You (take 2)," appears on Dorham, rec. 1953.

21. Dorham's cadential figure appears in ex. 5.3c1. A transcription of "Giant Steps" appears in Tirro 1977, 381–86. See further discussion of this issue with regard to Coltrane's various improvisation approaches in Kernfeld 1983 and Porter 1983 and 1985a.

22. The design of Parker's phrases is illustrated in ex. 7.14.

23. A comparably elaborate model also guides multiple solo choruses on Little's piece "Opening Statement," found on the same album, Little, rec. 1960.

24. Two takes of Lee Morgan's solo on "Moanin'" were recorded on 30 October 1958 and appear on the studio recording. Blakey, rec. 1958a. The third recording of Morgan's solo was made during the group's live performances in Paris, 17 December. Blakey, rec. 1958b.

25. Navarro's catalytic phrase appears in ex. 4.2d; Davis's, in ex. 7.12; Brown's motivic figure, in ex. 9.3; a portion of Parker's recurring "Tiny's Tempo" phrase, in ex. 6.6b. Transcriptions of complete versions of different takes of the Parker solos on "Red Cross" and "Tiny's Tempo" are in Owens 1974 (2:173–74, 135–37). See also Parker,

rec. 1944. Owens (1:112) describes other Parker performances that were "partly composed and partly improvised," and observes, in the case of Parker's interpretation of the chords to "Cherokee," that "a number of phrases in this solo are literal or varied excerpts" from earlier solos. Another example of a recurring chain of Parker ideas—performed during two takes of "She Rote"—is shown on the top line of ex. 7.6 of this work. See also Parker, rec. 1951. Gushee 1981 provides transcriptions of multiple versions of Lester Young's solos on "Shoe Shine Boy" and an analysis of their resemblances.

26. The opening and closing events of Morgan's solo on "Moanin'" are given in exx. 8.6b and 13.17b; Davis's long blues crip is given in ex. 8.25d, chorus 6. It can also be heard in Davis's solo on "Trane's Blues" and the improvised melody to "The Theme (take 1)," Davis, rec. 1956a. Similarly, in his extensive work on Davis, Kerschbaumer (1978, 32) reports that a succession of figures found in Davis's solo on "Billie's Bounce" comprises more than half of his improvisation on "Ornithology," recorded four months later, indicating that Davis had not substantially modified his repertory of figures over that period. Such findings call into question Martin's assertion (1986, 116) that Davis put "little reliance on previously composed licks."

27. Heard on Navarro, rec. 1948, vol. 1.

28. Analysis that Robert Witmer has kindly shared with me concerning recorded solos on Joe Oliver's and Louis Armstrong's "Dippermouth Blues" (also recorded under the names of "Sugarfoot Stomp" and "In De Ruff") reveals that, to varying degrees, Oliver re-created the same solo in performance three times between 1923 and 1926, as did, subsequently, Rex Stewart, in paying homage to Oliver on three recordings in 1931. Schuller's (1989, 173–76) transcription and analysis of multiple takes of Louis Armstrong's solo on "Star Dust" reveal that he had previously worked out their "over-all" design and had plotted the use of "certain identical" phrases. See Schuller's general discussion of such practices during the swing era (ibid., 162, 307–8).

29. For a discussion of comparable practices, concerning blues melodies and texts, that involve the improviser's creation of music from a storehouse of basic construction materials, see Evans 1982, 145, and Titon 178–93, respectively, and regarding music cultures in various parts of the world, see Nettl 1974, 13–15, and Lord 1970, passim.

30. Tucker 1988, 546. Artists' inclinations differ with regard to these practices. With a sense of irony, Coleman Hawkins (1955, 18) recalled his intention to try to learn his own solo on "Body and Soul" from the recording because it was requested by audience members, and he knew it would increase his commercial appeal. In the end, his creative instincts prevailed, however; he couldn't bring himself to do it. "To this day I never play 'Body and Soul' the same way twice."

31. Similarly, in reference to his experience with the relationship between improvisation and written music, John Lewis reports, "My writing and my playing are connected. I can take ideas I have written or maybe not written down yet—ideas just floating around back there. I can take those ideas or written things and expand on them each time I improvise, so in that way the pieces I write are never finished, never complete. The reverse—taking an idea or a phrase from a solo of mine and letting it inspire a new composition—is trying to happen to me for the first time." Balliett 1971, 169.

32. Correspondingly, the products of artists' improvisations on the same composition can preserve the "contour and many details" (as on Louis Armstrong's "two re-

cordings of the same tune . . . released as 'S.O.L. Blues?', Col. 35661, and 'Gully Low Blues?', OK 8474," recorded 13 and 14 May 1927) or be "startlingly different" (as on Charlie Parker's "two takes of 'Embraceable You,'" recorded on 28 October 1947, Dial 1024). Kernfeld 1988b, 562. See Armstrong, rec. 1927, and Parker, rec. 1947.

33. In the most general terms, Gioia (1987, 593–94) distinguishes the improviser's "blueprint method," in which details are planned in advance "of the work of art before beginning any part of its execution," from the "retrospective method," in which "each new musical phrase can be shaped with relation to what has gone before." Regarding the mediation between these two approaches, Hargreaves and his associates (1991, 53) have found in their preliminary study that the formulation and flexible application of overall improvisation strategies or plans are fundamental abilities distinguishing expert improvisers from novices.

## 10. Getting There

1. One analyst elaborating upon the qualities of syncopation and forward motion uses such terms as "vital drive" and "rhythmic fluidity." Hodeir 1961, 207. For a description of the essential "tension generated by a complex relationship between rhythm and meter," see Keil 1966, 341. Sudnow's (1978, 24), teacher, Jimmy Rowles, urged him "get the phrasing more syncopated." Stu Katz describes Young's growing interest in "how much variety one could get out of few notes. He'd play one note or a three to four note phrase and play with it, vary it rhythmically, as [Sonny] Rollins now does" in Porter 1985b, 103. For further discussion of these attributes, see Byrnside 1975, 230–32.

2. Bobby Tucker in Shapiro and Hentoff, 1966, 200.

3. As one scholar suggests aptly, "The rhythmic excitement of [some] phrases depends on the tension created between the articulation of the line and the fairly square metre of the changes." Cases in point are Lester Young's "metric suggestion of 3/4" for two measures within the framework of a 4/4 meter, and Lennie Tristano's creating "rhythmic interest . . . by temporarily superimposing a new metre on the square [4/4] meter of the changes . . . a very deliberate use . . . of a repeated 11/8 pattern followed by 3/8 patterns." Newsom 1973, 402, 404–5.

4. Fraser 1983, 176.

5. Ibid., 192.

6. Like Konitz, Sudnow (1978, 90) recognizes the importance in mature playing of intentionality in the ongoing selection of melodic goals, "each and every next sounding place expressly aimed for and arrived at." From John Lewis's perspective as well, "you have to be a musician first and an instrumentalist second. It's more important to be a master of the music than a master of an instrument, which can take you over." Balliett 1971, 166–67.

7. Hancock's account is in Pareles 1983.

8. For the artist, as for the analyst, the assessment of these matters is never free from interpretation and varies with the aesthetic values and training of the observer. As early as 1938, Sargent (1976, 168, 174) describes such unique African American musical practices as the cultivation of blue notes and the harmonic ambiguity that surrounds their application. The blue (flatted) third or seventh "often appeared simultaneously with a chord that is completely out of harmony with it according to the European notion

of harmonization," a chord containing a natural third or seventh, for example. In Bessie Smith's performances, "the sureness and consistency of her deviations from European usage carry with them their own artistic justification. And the effect is undeniably satisfactory." In a similar light, Kubik (1959, 449–50) explains the discrepancies between early New Orleans soloists' pitch choices and the underlying harmony in terms of practices of "bitonality," but Schuller (1968, 83) refers to some such discrepancies as "flaws." At the heart of such differing interpretations are methodological problems associated with applying to jazz "a traditional analysis of functionality in Western art music," and the challenges presented by issues as basic as inferring the improviser's actual harmonic model and defining dissonance and consonance. Kernfeld 1983, 12–17.

9. Davis 1990, 103.

10. Sudnow 1978, 146.

11. I overheard the advice on scat singing backstage at a concert of Betty Carter's quartet at Pick-Staiger Auditorium, Northwestern University, Evanston, IL, December 5, 1978.

12. The remark concerning "inappropriate" harmonic tension is from my discussion with pianist Billy Taylor on the occasion of a concert he gave at Northwestern University, Evanston, IL, July 8, 1983.

13. A jazz trumpeter in New York described reading about this interaction between Wynton Marsalis and Art Blakey in an article about Marsalis which had appeared in a jazz magazine. Personal conversation, winter 1986.

14. "Lester sings with his horn; you listen to him and can almost hear the words." Holiday 1969, 59. Other artists elaborate on Young's special ability in Daniels 1985, 317–18. Gene Ramey describes Parker's practices in Reisner 1979, 186–87. Similarly, Porter (1985a, 613–17) discusses Coltrane's solo during "Psalm" on his *A Love Supreme* album, as a "wordless recitation of [Coltrane's composed] poem, one note to each syllable. Each section of several lines has an arched shape . . . [which Porter interprets] as [grow]ing out of formulaic procedures used by preachers in black churches." The rhythmic and melodic implications of language for jazz artists, as well as the latitude for personal interpretation, are demonstrated by Louis Armstrong's, Roy Eldridge's, and Dizzy Gillespie's respective performances of a poetic line suggested to them for a musical experiment by Feather 1960, 68–69.

15. Tiny Parham comments on Joe Louis's soulfulness in Shapiro and Hentoff 1966, 210.

16. Pee Wee Russell comments on committing oneself to each solo as if it were one's last appear in Balliett 1977, 89.

17. Davis's youthful distinction between white and black swing bands is from Davis, video 1986.

18. Golson on Brown is from Crawford 1961, 23.

19. For a discussion of the importance of the music's "idiomatic rhythmic emphasis that generates a dance-step response," see Murray 1976, 144.

20. Ellington in Shapiro and Hentoff 1966, 238.

21. Handy in ibid., 252.

22. Ellington in ibid., 238.

23. Included under the rubric of "verbal signifyin(g)" is "marking, loud-talking,

testifying, calling out (of one's name), sounding, rapping, playing the dozens and so on." Gates 1988, 52. Gates interprets intertextuality in jazz as a form of signifyin(g). Ibid., 63–64. Building on Gates's interpretation, Floyd (1991, 271, 277) proposes that the jazz artists' "calls, cries, hollers, riffs, licks, overlapping antiphony, and the various rhythmic, melodic and other musical practices" dating from the early ring shout serve "as Signifyin(g) *musical* figures . . . used to comment (Signify) on other figures, on the performances themselves, on other performances of the same pieces, and on other and completely different works of music." Toward such ends, improvisers transform borrowed material by "using it rhetorically or figuratively—through troping, in other words. . . . Signifyin(g) is also a way of demonstrating respect for, goading, or poking fun at a musical style, process, or practice through parody, pastiche, implication, indirection, humor, tone- or word-play, the illusions [*sic*] of speech or narration, and other troping mechanisms. . . . Such practices *are* criticism—perceptive and evaluative acts and expressions of approval and disapproval, validation and invalidation through the respectful, ironic, satirizing imitation, manipulation, extension, and elaboration of previously created and presented tropes and new ideas."

24. The order of soloists is not included on the album, but I believe that the trumpeter is Clark Terry. The incident is part of a sequence of trading fours at a jam session with Dinah Washington, Clifford Brown, and Maynard Ferguson on the piece "I've Got You under My Skin." Washington, rec. 1954.

25. The Mingus-Dolphy exchange is on Mingus, rec. 1960.

26. Charlie Parker especially favored such practices in live performances, where they served the function of facilitating communication with the audience, providing them with familiar material amid his improvisations. At times, they provided the basis for creating humor. Parker quoted "familiar melodies out of context as a musical joke" in live recorded performances where they can be heard to raise laughter from the audience. Contributing to the humorous linear juxtaposition of materials were "harmonic clash[es]" that Parker sometimes created in a quotation's application or its deliberate melodic or rhythmic "disfiguration." Owens 1974, 1:29, 99.

27. Pee Wee Russell similarly states that "when I play the blues, mood, frame of mind, enters into it. One day your choice of notes would be melancholy, a blue trend, a drift of blues notes. The next day your choice of notes would be more cheerful." Balliett 1977, 90. Percy Heath quoted in Balliett 1971, 182–83.

28. Keith Jarrett made the point about overplaying in a lecture, School of Music, Northwestern University, Evanston, IL, October 19, 1987.

29. Trumpeter and band leader Johnny Cappolla made the remark during a private improvisation lesson in San Francisco, spring 1968.

30. I heard various versions of this story from different musicians in New York.

31. Gil Evans praises Davis in Davis, video 1986.

32. Thad Jones's comment on Eldridge described to me in a personal conversation with a musician who was an associate of Thad Jones, New York City, winter 1982.

33. Eldridge on Armstrong is quoted in Eldridge's obituary, Wilson 1989.

34. Gillespie is quoted in Fraser 1983, 143.

35. Description and illustration of similar features of "large-scale melodic continuity" in Coltrane's solo on "So What," are in Kernfeld 1983, 50–54. With respect to Coltrane's performance on the suite "A Love Supreme," see Porter 1985a.

36. Such advice typifies the kind of wisdom attributed to Miles Davis that, during my research, I frequently heard quoted by other artists for one another's benefit.

37. Sudnow (1978, 57) also describes such turning points in his development. "From a virtual hodgepodge of 'phonemes' and approximate 'paralinguistics,' there was a 'sentential structure' slowly taking shape . . . themes starting to achieve cogent management."

38. As is the case for many others, Jim Hall likes his "solos to have a beginning a middle and an end. I like them to have a quality that Sonny Rollins has—of turning and turning a tune until eventually you show all of its possible faces." Balliett 1977, 223.

39. Pee Wee Russell also describes his own objective as a soloist to "write a little tune of your own." Balliett 1977, 90. Here artists refer to the cogency and coherence of their creations rather than a single model of a "tune." As mentioned earlier, tunes within the jazz repertory run the full gamut from those comprising short repetitive phrases to those comprising extended intricate lines with little repetition. In fact, as Gushee (1981, 160) suggests, soloists typically avoid extensive or too literal repetition of four- and eight-bar phrases in their improvisations which may be "immediately labelled as 'composition,'" that is, the kind of repetition found in many popular tunes and considered suitable as a vehicle—encapsulating the larger performance—but requiring contrasting, expansive ideas during solo invention to sustain interest throughout a performance.

40. Lester Young's witty remark is in Porter 1985b, 58.

41. Lester Young anecdote is in Balliett 1971, 174. Heath's recollection of Gillespie is in Watrous 1992. Making comparable distinctions for early jazz players, Pops Foster (1971, 77) describes some early New Orleans trumpeters who "really played beautiful tones, but they wouldn't make their breaks off the melody like the hot trumpet players would. If they had to play a break, it had to be written for them."

42. Analysts, too, have remarked on the incredible pressures of composing at the tempos negotiated by jazz improvisers since the bebop period. For example, at such tempos, ideas are commonly conceived and executed at a rate of "six-and-one-half eighth notes (or thirteen sixteenth notes)" a second and at extremes, over a third faster, at a tempo of one quarter-note = 310 or even 355. Owens 1974, 1:35, 112; Kernfeld 1983, 60.

43. Robert Witmer mentioned the ascription "two-chorus player" to me in a personal conversation, fall 1985.

44. The effects of negotiating "rapidly changing harmonies" are speculated on in Kernfeld 1983, 59.

45. At one extreme, a scholar describes a Coltrane solo as "dominated" by a short vocabulary pattern of four or five pitches whose "formulaic" use recurs "thirty-six" times and appears "only three times in unique surroundings." In contrast, other Coltrane improvisations create "a flexible relationship between the recurring melodies and the beat; they appear ahead of or behind a pulse, and Coltrane compresses them into untranscribable groups." Contributing to his ability to disguise "excessively repetitive appearances of formulas" was Coltrane's eventual cultivation of "timbral contrast . . . [as] an established stylistic device" and his "rhythmic fluidity," the result of radical advances in saxophone technique that enabled him to perform eighth-note formulas at twice their initial speed. Kernfeld 1983, 18, 45, 60.

46. The two takes of "Bee Vamp" appear on Dolphy, rec. 1961a, vol. 1, and 1961b, respectively. My interpretation is that the shorter of the two takes—released as an outtake years after the release of the first—was the initial recorded performance of the piece.

47. Ken McIntyre mentioned "musical gems" to me during a private improvisation lesson, Wesleyan University, CT, fall 1969.

48. Cecil Taylor comparing Joe Gordon to Idres Sulieman in Spellman 1966, 59.

49. Descriptions of changes in tone, articulation, ornamentation practices, expressive devices, harmonic approach, dynamics, emphasis on different formulas and intervals, treatment of rhythm, and the like are in Porter 1985b, 55, 65–68, 75, 78, 82, 86–88.

50. Insightful portraits of Davis at various stages in his career and the changing musical values that defined each are provided by Kerschbaumer (1978), Carr (1984), and Davis (1990).

51. For a discussion of Coltrane's stylistic development between 1960 and 1967, see Porter 1983, and for a massive compilation of transcribed Coltrane solos documenting his work, see White 1973–78.

52. Kirk performs the reed instruments simultaneously on Kirk, video 1988.

53. The "Prof" Buster Smith anecdote is in Parker, video 1987.

54. In their transcriptions and analyses of solos, Feather (1960, 62–72) and Wang (1973, 545) detail the core conventions generally distinguishing swing and bebop players. In part, as Wang points out, "swing phrases are more uniform in length, more symmetrical in shape, and more congruent with the harmonic phrase than those of bebop; . . . bebop, on the other hand, is more complex, full of greater contrasts, has more rhythmic subtleties, and makes greater and more expressive use of dissonance."

55. Mary Lou Williams quoted in Shapiro and Hentoff 1966, 294–95.

56. In part, Konitz refers to the group's 1949 improvisations on "Intuition" and "Digression" appearing on Tristano, rec. 1949.

57. Gillespie bandstand evaluation of Hinton is recounted in Shapiro and Hentoff 1966, 344–45.

58. Jimmy Knepper, when asked by Leonard Feather (for his *Encyclopedia of Jazz* entry) which were his best recorded solos, replied simply "No Good Solos." Jeske 1981, 15.

59. Haynes on Navarro is in Crouch 1977. Benny Golson praises Clifford Brown, whose performance style was in many ways an extension of Navarro's, in almost precisely the same terms point for point in Crawford 1961, 23.

## 11. Arranging Pieces

1. McPartland in Shapiro and Hentoff 1966, 102–21, 144.

2. Written method books were available to artists in the mid-thirties, including such early texts as Norbert Bleihoof's *Modern Arranging and Orchestration* and a *Down Beat* column devoted to the subject. Carter 1986, 11.

3. Collier 1988, 63.

4. An Armstrong-Hines duet on "Weather Bird," Armstrong rec. 1928a; Eldridge-Bolling duets on "Fireworks" and "Wildman Blues" are heard on Eldridge, rec. 1951.

5. Descriptions of various precursors to unaccompanied solo improvisation by

horn players, as well as such well-known performances as Hawkins's solo on "Picasso," are in Guralnick 1987, 24–27; and Rollins's solo on "Body and Soul," Rollins, rec. 1958; Rollins actually recorded his first unaccompanied solo performance on "It Could Happen to You," Rollins, rec. 1957.

6. Distinctions for arrangements are in Schuller 1988, 32–33.

7. The references to etiquette are from Becker n.d.

8. For a discussion of practices of "verbal framing in jazz," see also Beeson 1990, 9–10.

9. The string bass doubling reference is from Shipton 1988, 301–2.

10. Morton quotation is in Lomax 1950, 63. In the use of riffs, contemporary players sometimes plan "send-off choruses" in which a repeated riff introduced at the end of each solo carries over into the first chorus of the next soloist, who, in turn, delays entering the performance for a few measures or overlaps with the horns to create excitement. Ingrid Monson, personal conversation, Spring 1992.

11. A brief discussion of such arrangements is in Schuller 1988, 35, 38. For the most part, my study confines the discussion of arrangements to small group practices. An elaborate analysis of the extended works by large jazz ensembles and orchestras such as Duke Ellington's is provided by Tucker 1991 and Schuller 1989.

12. "The Prophet" is on Dolphy, rec. 1961a, vol. 1.

13. Reference to Dodds is in T. Dennis Brown 1988, 312. See also Dodds, rec. 1946.

14. Wells quoted in Balliett 1977, 143.

15. Drummer Dannie Richmond reports that Charles Mingus also requested specific kinds of piano accompaniment, including, for example, particular chord voicings, reinforcing the melody of the piece with the right hand, or playing a counterpoint to the melody. Priestly 1983, 77–78.

16. Morton quoted in Lomax 1950, 63.

17. Although a common model for early jazz groups was for individual players to be featured during a break, Armstrong remembers his duet breaks with Joe Oliver as an exciting innovation, just as Edgar Hayes describes his band's unique breaks featuring three trumpets, with Dizzy Gillespie as section leader. At the same time, Lawrence Gushee observes that early dance bands in New York City (preceding the Oliver and Armstrong recordings) commonly featured duet breaks—some with trumpets playing parallel thirds or sixths, as part of their written arrangements. Armstrong in Shapiro and Hentoff 1966, 104; Hayes in Gillespie 1979, 93; Gushee, personal conversation, winter 1992.

18. Four renditions of "Like Someone in Love" can be heard on Baker, rec. 1956; Blakey, rec. 1960; Coltrane, rec. 1958; Dolphy, rec. 1961a, vol. 2.

19. Pops Foster describes Jelly Roll Morton dictating to a transcriber the details of arrangements for recording dates. Band leaders also sometimes hired individuals with extraordinary abilities for music apprehension and recall to transcribe another band's material so they could perform it. One such individual "could copy down any arrangement he heard once." James P. Johnson's skill was also spectacular. Foster says that in studio sessions devoted to composing and arranging compositions with Fats Waller, Johnson could transcribe a chorus of Fats Waller's performance as "fast as Fats would play it." Foster 1971, 146, 142, 150. Similarly, Lil Armstrong could take instant

dictation from Louis Armstrong, writing down the tunes he composed with the trumpet "as fast as Louis played." Preston Jackson in Shapiro and Hentoff 1966, 102. Glimpses of rehearsals in Jacquet, video 1993, and Monk, video 1990, provide insight into collaborative aspects of creating and transmitting arrangements.

20. Louis Bellson recalls Duke Ellington's use of programmatic imagery in providing instruction, suggesting that he play a drum solo "imitat[ing] thunder and lightning. . . . He knew how to explain things; he knew how to put everything in its certain context so that you were always aware of what was going on." Clark 1977, 12.

21. Europe quoted in Anon. 1919, 28.

22. St. Cyr quoted in Lomax 1950, 194–95.

23. Holiday reference to Basie and her own directions for arrangements in Holiday 1969, 61–62, 59.

24. Ellington quoted by Richard Boyer in Austin 1966, 287.

25. Ellington quoted in Shapiro and Hentoff 1966, 225.

26. Golson's account is in Blakey, video 1987.

27. Holiday describes her practice in *The Sound of Jazz* (video compilation 1957).

28. "You Are My Everything" is on Davis, rec. 1956d.

29. Whereas Chuck Israels recalls extensive plans for chord progressions—as well as the beginning, middle, and ending of pieces—when he performed with Evans, Evans informs Gregory Smith (1983, 59–60) that his regular trio rarely rehearsed for recording sessions, but would "lay out a routine" at the studio and perform an extemporaneous arrangement. Similarly, although some artists recall the importance of detailed instructions during rehearsals when performing with Miles Davis, "Philly" Joe Jones reported that "we'd call a rehearsal but we never rehearsed all those years. We'[d] talk about the tunes at rehearsal but never play them." Mansfield interview, cited in Stewart 1986, 187.

30. Roach on Gillespie is in Gillespie 1979, 398.

31. For a discussion of Coltrane's directing role on the album *Ascension,* see Jost 1975, 88.

32. Wells on Young is in Wells 1971, 62.

33. Mention of Mingus's verbal practices of directing is in Priestly 1982, 80.

34. Byard quotation is in Monson 1991, 253–54, 257.

35. For a detailed analysis of Morton's arrangements, see Schuller 1968, 134–74. An analysis of multiple recorded renditions of pieces by the Creole Jazz Band indicates that the "content and form" of the front line's "distinct but strongly interrelated polyphonic lines" represent largely fixed features of head arrangements with little improvisation or "spontaneous creation of 'new' material." Rather, "frequent small scale variation occurs, with details changing while functions and essential structures remain the same." Robert Bowman 1982, v. This is congruent with Johnny St. Cyr's recollections of Oliver: "See, Joe, he got on the strictly legitimate side when he got to recording. It had to be just so with him and that cause the men to be working under a tension and they couldn't give vent to their feelings, as they would like to." Lomax 1950, 195.

36. Count Basie arrangements discussed in Porter 1985b, 40.

37. In the context of this study, I am using the term "*Ascension* band" to refer to the group of musicians with whom Coltrane recorded his album *Ascension.* Coltrane, rec. 1965.

38. Practices in Charles Mingus's bands similar to Lateef's are described by Priestly 1982, 59.

39. For an elaboration of the diverse practices of avant-garde jazz composition and improvisation, as well as the concepts behind them, see Such 1985, Radano 1985, Guralnik 1987, Jost 1975, and Wilmer 1977.

## 12. Adding to Arrangements

1. Although featured in early jazz groups and in those of the late twenties, the bass was commonly replaced by the tuba in the early twenties during the "era of acoustic recording." Subsequently, the development of "electrical recording techniques" enabled the bass to be heard more clearly on recordings, contributing to the instrument's resurgence of popularity. Shipton 1988, 302. Bassist Paul Barbarin recollects the tuba coming into jazz in 1922 (Barbarin interview transcript, page 14, Tulane Jazz Oral History Project, William Ranson Hogan Jazz Archive, Tulane University, New Orleans. This data is from the research of Ingrid Monson). The bass's subsequent popularity was also the consequence of the growing taste for a "new kind of swing" that the instrument could produce with its lighter sound. Zardis, video 1993. Finally, within the variable constitution of early jazz bands, the choice of bass or tuba was also obviously influenced by the overall instrumentation of the group (i.e., a brass band would cover the sound of the string bass) and the nature of the social functions for which it performed (e.g., whether it was a stationary group performing for parties and dances or a marching group performing for funerals or parades).

2. Shipton 1988, 302.

3. Quotations on slap-bass technique from Bertram Turetzky in Foster 1971, xvi.

4. Ibid., 76.

5. Rudi Blesh's observations on Foster's countermelodies in ibid., xix.

6. Reference to Mingus and the changing role of the bass is in Shipton 188, 302. Milt Hinton demonstrates various styles of bass accompaniment in Zardis, video 1993.

7. Examples of method books for bass by jazz musicians are Reid (1977, 1983) and Davis (1976). Examples of transcribed bass lines, piano comping parts, and drum accompaniments can be found in the Jamey Aebersold and Advance Music catalogues (addresses provided in chapter 6, note 34).

8. Reference to nineteenth-century antecedent of drum sets is from Brown 1988, 308.

9. Ibid., 310.

10. Ibid., 311–12.

11. Ibid., 312. In the passages that follow, I give a synopsis of Brown's useful overview. For an elaboration of the early history of jazz drumming, see also Brown 1976.

12. Quotation regarding fills is from Witmer 1988a, 375.

13. Brown 1988, 313.

14. Gridley 1985, 91.

15. Brown 1988, 314.

16. Carvin quoted in Monson 1991, 146, 151.

17. Ibid., 152–53. Monson reports that two-beat drum fills, taught to her as the

drummer's "bread and butter," commonly conclude with the "strong articulation of the downbeat of the measure it leads into."

18. Figures used for this purpose are also known as "set-up figures" by some drummers. In rarer instances, I have heard drummers refer to them as turnaround figures (RSJ) because of their association with the turnaround sections of pieces' forms.

19. One aural analysis of group interaction describes drummer Bill Goodwin "reserv[ing] a heavier fill using bass drum and tom-toms to accent the end of the larger formal unit, the chorus." Rinzler 1988, 158.

20. Gillespie describes this in his conversation with pianist Walter Davis Jr. in Blakey, video 1987.

21. Kay quotation from Balliett 1971, 166.

22. Quotations on "Philly lick" in Davis, 1990, 199.

23. The piano's role elaborated in this chapter is, in some groups, fulfilled or reinforced by another chording instrument such as vibraphone, banjo, or guitar. The variable place of the piano with respect to the latter two instruments in early jazz rhythm sections reflected such factors as the type and size of different groups, the particular contexts in which musicians performed jazz, the changing tastes of the public, the role of the recording industry, and social attitudes toward particular instruments. Some accounts by New Orleans players suggest that the piano was initially featured as a solo instrument in the red light district of Storyville, then gradually found its way into ensembles where it became an integral part of the rhythm section. Bassist Paul Barbarin recalls the piano joining the more conventional rhythm section of drums, guitar, and bass around 1915. Beyond the new musical challenges of accommodating the piano, Barbarin was uncomfortable with the new change because of the piano's association with the red light district. Guitarist and banjo player Johnny St. Cyr remembers a recording session date in which the record company requested piano instead of guitar or banjo.

Guitarist, mandolin and banjo player Clearance "Little Dad" Vincent reports that the piano was only used for indoors performances; orchestras that performed for popular events like outside parties favored guitar and banjo. He relates that some male players had an aversion to the piano because it was considered a women's instrument and a "sissy" instrument, one associated with homosexuality on the part of male performers. It was not uncommon for wives of the musicians to play the instrument as an addition to the group. With respect to the role of the banjo within the rhythm section, Vincent asserts that neither he nor St. Cyr wanted to play the instrument, but that they did so to meet the public demand for it. For this rich data, I am largely indebted to the research of Ingrid Monson. The source for interviews with players mentioned above is the Tulane Jazz Oral History Project, William Ranson Hogan Jazz Archive, Tulane University, New Orleans. See also Zardis, video 1993.

24. Koch 1988, 313.

25. Ibid., 314.

26. Ibid., 313.

27. Performance recalled by Jones is on Coltrane, video 1985.

28. Byrd shared his view of rock drummers with me in a conversation in New York City, Summer 1986. See also Byrd's collaboration with hip-hop vocalist Guru on Guru, rec. 1993.

29. Hawkins's remarks recalled by Budd Johnson in Gitler, 1985, 122.

30. Over the history of jazz, particular pieces have served as exceptionally flexible vehicles, providing the framework for improvisations in styles that preceded and followed the style in vogue when the piece was composed. "What Is This Thing Called Love?" has served as the basis for improvisations ranging from solo stride piano to swing, bebop, and free jazz. Kernfeld 1988b, 555.

31. Transcription and analysis of the band's comparatively conservative interplay on "I Thought about You" appears later in this work. See ex. 13.25. For insightful accounts of this historic group, see also Carr 1984, 134–68 and Davis 1990, 271–80.

32. Michael Carvin's observation of the innovative drumming concepts introduced by Tony Williams in Miles Davis's band is in Monson 1991, 148.

33. Hancock quotation is on Davis, video 1986.

34. Miles Davis recalls asking Red Garland to play like Ahmad Jamal at times, that is, using space and performing spare rhythmic patterns. Williams 1962, 166.

35. Gillespie's comments on Blakey, video 1987.

36. This can be a sensitive issue unless artists are inclined to absorb the influences of their predecessors. When Lester Young followed Coleman Hawkins in the Fletcher Henderson band, he resisted the pressure he faced from the other members and from Henderson's wife to "play like [Hawkins] did," and was eventually replaced by a "Hawk man," Ben Webster. Hentoff 1956, 9.

37. Eckstine quotation is in Feather 1984.

38. Davis's comments on Davis, video 1986. Wayne Shorter and Art Blakey recall the egg-scrambler story on Blakey, video 1987.

39. These are matters of taste, of course. Although Billy Taylor once described to me his adherence to this principle, others describe deviating from it. Barry Harris does not try to avoid the piano's lower register. In fact, Coleman Hawkins used to request that Harris provide "more bottom" in his comping when they performed together.

40. Morton quotation in Lomax 1950, 63.

41. Byard discusses his view in Monson 1991, 253.

## 13. Give and Take

1. Only a few works have been devoted to the important features of group interaction in jazz improvisation. The most valuable is research presented in Monson's dissertation (1991), an ethnomusicological study based in part on interviews with fourteen professional jazz musicians. Monson's findings complement my own, providing rich data that amplifies the musical roles of the rhythm section instruments and the nature of collective improvisation. She situates her analysis within the framework of relevant issues in anthropology and interactional sociolinguistics. Other relevant works include articles by Keil (1966b), Rinzler (1988), and Stewart (1986). The last includes useful scores of group interplay, as do the dissertations of Owens (1974, 2:142–54, 207–31, 256–71, 279–306) and Kernfeld (1981, 270–77, 298–302). The subject has also been noted in Schuller 1968, 110; Schuller 1989, 234–35; Tirro 1974, 278–88; Jost 1975, 15–16; Gridley 1985, 26; Gushee 1981, 159; and Porter 1985a, 606–7.

2. Striking a groove is also known as playing "in the pocket" (DF). For an early discussion of the importance of such matters as the rhythm section's "build[ing] a groove or track for the soloist to get into," see Keil 1966b, 341. A recent dissertation

elaborates upon the concept of 'groove' and its emotional impact—emphasizing its qualities as a rhythmic pattern "collectively put forth by the individual parts played by the rhythm section instruments." The concept has broad application with reference to distinct repertory genres (swing grooves vs. Latin grooves), as well as "to certain bands or individuals." Monson 1991, 111, 166–69.

3. Keil (1966b, 343–44) suggests models for the complementary meshing of parts by drummers and bass players that encompass different approaches to the beat's interpretation. An example of playalong records for rhythm section instruments is Music Minus One's 1970 production, *Modern Jazz Drumming* (MMO 4001), which includes Jim Chapin's early drum manual (1948) as its accompanying booklet.

4. Monson 1991, 237.

5. Ibid., 151.

6. See also ex. 13.13 for bass player and piano player harmonic interaction in relation to the soloist.

7. For a documentation of similar interaction, describing Alan Dawson's anticipating and reinforcing soloist Tucker's "continuing triplet rhythms . . . by playing a triplet-based fill between the snare, tom-toms and bass drum," see Monson 1991, 238. A description of Bill Goodwin responding to Phil Woods's use of double time in his solo by temporarily switching to double-time patterns in the accompaniment is in Rinzler 1988, 158.

8. Concern with such features of drumming extend back to early players like Baby Dodds, who "was a percussionist more than a drummer. He thought of drums in terms of colors, and how to mix them. He was fanatical about tuning his drums, and he'd be on the stand a half-hour before showtime, tightening and tapping." Bob Wilbur in Balliett 1977, 245. For a discussion of the sensitivity of contemporary drummers to the peculiar tonal and timbral qualities of the drum set instruments and their blend with features of the group's melodic and harmonic musical fabric, see Monson 1991, 156–58. One analyst describes "Philly" Joe Jones's imitative idiomatic response to a melodic phrase by Miles Davis, in which Jones initially "moves from the high-pitched instruments of his drum set to the low." Then he transforms the pattern by eliminating particular rhythmic elements and reorchestrating others among the drum set's instruments, which he gradually reduces to ride cymbal and snare drum. Stewart 1986, 188.

9. Freddie Greene quoted in Shapiro and Hentoff 1966, 305.

10. Monson 1991, 123.

11. The quotation is from a musician in Sawyer 1991, 9. A description of one pianist's development as a listener within a group aptly likens the challenge of carrying on multiple operations in this context to Charlie Chaplin's hilarious misadventures on the assembly line depicted in the film *Modern Times*. Sudnow 1978, 30.

12. These can reappear in different players' solos or across the parts. An example is the shout pattern that recurs on different Miles Davis albums during the forties, fifties, and early sixties, not only in Davis's solos and in a version of the group's piece "The Theme," but in solos by other group members such as Red Garland and Paul Chambers (ex. 8.14). See also discussion in main body of text and example commentary surrounding exx. 13.4a, 13.10b1, 13.11d2, and 13.17b.

13. Roland Hanna quotation is in Monson 1991, 139.

14. Ibid., 252.

15. Terence Blanchard quotation in Blakey, video 1987.

16. Bobby Watson in ibid.

17. Floyd (1991, 277) discusses the "semantic" aspects of phrases in connection with "the values, sensibilities, and cultural derivations of the ring [shout]."

18. One scholar describes ironic humor created through harmony by Eric Dolphy's dissonant solo over "consonant rhythm changes" and the musical incongruity created during Rahsaan Roland Kirk's parody of avant-garde composer Edgar Varese. Kirk "count[s] the band in with castanets" after breaking a glass in his composition, borrowing a sonority from Varese's "Poeme electronique." She appropriately observes that, for analysts, the meaning in such musical events can only be appreciated by analyzing "intermusical relationships" that are potentially "communicated through the full sonic range of the ensemble: rhythm, harmony, melody, timbre, groove, phrasing and gesture of all the participating musicians." Monson 1991, 214–15, 219, 221.

19. Freddie Green commented about Basie in Shapiro and Hentoff 1966, 305.

20. For transcriptions and discussions of the "connecting" phrase as a fleeting transition and other such exchanges in which the "pianist seizes upon Mulligan's last utterance, repeats it, adds to it something of his own, and uses that as his initial idea," see Byrnside 1975, 242. Within the same performing context, practices like this allow for the absorption of ideas across generational lines. See reference to Red Norvo using the last phrase of Gillespie's preceding chorus as recurring theme, unifying his own solo, Wang 1973, 541–42.

21. Pee Wee Russell explains, "In lots of cases, your solo depends on who you're following. The guy played a great chorus, you say to yourself. 'How am I going to follow *that*? I applaud him inwardly, and it becomes a matter of silent pride. Not jealous, mind you. A kind of competition. So I make myself a guinea pig—what the hell, I'll try something new." Balliett 1977, 90. The interest in variety may also suggest that successive soloists adopt different strategies for their treatment of the melody, for example, avoiding direct quotations of the melody if the previous soloist has exploited this approach. Kernfeld 1988b, 557.

22. The concern with balancing continuity and change can play itself out in endless ways between musicians. In one performance, Sonny Rollins returned to his earlier thematic material after the contrast provided by Max Roach's solo, "build[ing] a kind of frame around the drum solo," and subsequently Roach used thematic material from his drum solo within the context of his accompaniment of Rollins's ongoing solo performance. Schuller 1962, 244, 248.

23. For a penetrating analysis of these interactive and collaborate aspects of performance leading to musical intensification, see Monson 1991, 230–62.

24. Rinzler 1988, 157.

25. For a discussion of preparing for "phrase completion" and artists driving in unison to enhance rhythmic intensity at the end of a chorus, see Monson 1991, 241, 245, 252. In fulfilling such common objectives, artists use "widely different musical techniques idiomatic to [their] particular instrument. . . . The soloist may play faster rhythms, the pianist may use special voicings or a longer comping phrase with a repeated rhythm, the bassist may play more angularly or in a higher range than normal, and the drum may fill or accent certain beats." Rinzler 1988, 157. For a description of a climax in Young's solo in which, as he plays "shorter note values and heightened

volume and vibrato," Jo Jones performs the drums with greater force and Basie "begins to play the chords on every beat in guitar style instead of leaving spaces," see Porter 1985b, 92.

26. Keil (1966b, 345–47) appropriately stresses the importance of the feeling engendered in performance by the ongoing resolution of "pulse-meter-rhythm" tensions and the essential features of "swing" that contribute to the cohesion and logic of melodic ideas—"holding our attention and increasing our involvement."

27. There is considerable precedent for such practices in jazz. Preston Jackson reports that Joe Oliver "never had to call the number he was to play. He would play two or three bars of whatever number he was going to play, stomp twice, and then everyone would start playing the same tune as if they had been told." Shapiro and Hentoff 1966, 102.

28. "Soft Winds" on Blakey, rec. 1955.

29. Jones quoted on Coltrane, video 1985.

30. Quotation on Davis, video 1986.

31. Ibid.

32. Errors are often made "in places that suggest the importance of eight-measure units in terms of memory encoding. In an AABA structure, a performer may forget the second A section (or play the bridge too soon, however you wish). Another related error is to play the wrong bridge, or to forget the correct one." Gushee 1981, 159.

33. Quotation on Davis, video 1986.

34. Herbie Hancock also recalls an incident in which, at one of the quintet's performance peaks, he "played a chord that was so wrong that I winced. . . . [Instantly,] Miles found some notes that made my chord right." The experience left Hancock "so stunned," he explained to one writer, "that he was unable to play for a couple of choruses." Shipp 1991.

35. "If I Should Lose You" on Little, rec. 1961b.

36. For a detailed description of the musical maneuvers through which Jaki Byard's band members reestablish "a consistent chorus structure" after the bassist inadvertently adds two extra beats to his part, see Monson 1991, 246ff. The example documents "the way in which a band can collectively remedy a mistake in performance while at the same time generating an exceptionally rich musical intensification."

37. Buster Bailey and Louis Armstrong in Shapiro and Hentoff 1966, 103–4.

38. In comparing multiple versions of "Shoe Shine Boy," one scholar also observes that Young's improvisation on the bridge had become "something of a routine, with a fixed drum part accentuating [Young's] phrases." Gushee 1981, 165.

39. ["Philly" Joe Jones] *knew* everything I . . . was going to play [Davis writes]; he anticipated me, felt what I was thinking. Sometimes I used to tell him not to do that lick of his *with* me, but *after* me. And so that thing that he used to do after I played something—that rim shot—became known as the 'Philly lick,' and it made him famous, took him right to the top of the drumming world. After he started doing it with me, guys in other bands would be telling their drummers, 'Man, give me the Philly lick after I do my thing.'" Davis 1990, 199.

40. Jones quotation from Mansfield interview cited in Stewart 1986, 187. Davis describes his own directions to Tony Williams and Herbie Hancock in his autobiography (1990, 274–75).

41. Haynes interview on Vaughan, video 1991. A version of "Shulie-A-Bop" appears on Vaughan, rec. 1954a.

42. Two takes of Lee Morgan's solo on "Moanin'" appear on Blakey, rec. 1958a; the third solo appears on Blakey, rec. 1958b.

43. Shankar describes this same creative process within the context of the musical life of the many classical Indian performance groups he has performed with and in such popular music groups as his current rock band, the Epidemics. Personal conversation, winter 1991.

## 14. Evaluating Group Performers

1. One scholar analyzes comparable language metaphors, derived from interviews with other improvisers, interpreting the metaphors in light of anthropological and sociolinguistic theory. She also relates features of group interaction to other forms of social interaction in the African American community such as the relationship between preacher and congregation and various forms of verbal dueling. Monson, 1991, ch. 5.

2. One musician reports to another scholar that "by talking to people up on stage through your music, you can start working on stuff you've never heard and never done. . . . You need people to play with. . . . When I do it, I'd find that there are these things coming out of myself, which I didn't even know were there, I'd never heard them, I didn't know where they came from. . . . But playing with others triggers it. So maybe consciously or subconsciously you'll hear that thing that you're trying to find . . . by listening to what other people have to say, and by talking to them about it." Sawyer 1991, 6.

3. Expressing the general feelings of many jazz musicians, Dave Brubeck says of the success of one record, "Almost everyone who has heard this album (including Joe and Gene, our own rhythm section) has had difficulty separating the composed from the improvised sections. I take this to be a real compliment, because good jazz composition sounds as though it were really improvised, and good improvisation should sound as though it was as well thought out as a composition." Brown 1981, 31.

4. Musician's quotation is in Sawyer 1991, 6.

5. Sometimes, humor includes interaction with other members of a larger musical production. Dizzy Gillespie recalls routines with comedian "Johnny Hudgins, the Wah-Wah King, whose otherwise silent act depended upon an ironic inconsistency in timing between Hudgins' pantomime gestures . . . and Gillespie's playing the Wah-Wah phrase." Fraser 1983, 161.

6. Gene Ramey in Reisner 1962, 187.

7. I am indebted to Richard Keeling, Department of Ethnomusicology, UCLA, for sharing this story with me. Personal conversation, spring 1981.

8. Miles Davis (1990, 101) gives his legendary account of the disorientation Charlie Parker initially caused rhythm section players with his experimentation with innovative phrasing and rhythmic displacement "to turn the rhythm section around." Musicians also commonly describe the effect as turning the beat around.

9. Embedded in the differences that some artists face in these and similar experiences may be preconceptions that operate in such social contexts as race, gender, sexual preference, and religion.

10. In some circumstances "rhythmic interactiveness—which generates excite-

ment and contributes to the overall intensification of the music—can also be seen as an aesthetic and interpersonal struggle for control of the musical fabric." Monson 1991, 180.

11. One scholar distinguishes quality and nature of interaction in terms of whether artists are generating their own parts by "merely following the rules of the game with little or no creative impulse," or "creatively fulfilling their own individual musical function but not interacting with fellow musicians," or else "creatively interacting with other musicians in the group." He also describes the difficulties that analysts may have in determining whether seeming aspects of subtle interplay simply represent coincidental occurrences in different parts. Rinzler 1983, 156, 158.

12. In his autobiography Miles Davis describes one such incident within his rhythm section (1990, 280).

## 15. The Lives of Bands

1. James Reese Europe describes the necessity of frequent rehearsals in order to limit his band members' creative contributions to band arrangements in Anon. 1919, 28. Similarly, Johnny St. Cyr contrasts Joe Oliver's restrictive practices in the recording studio with Jelly Roll Morton's flexible interaction with his sidemen in Lomax 1950, 194–95.

2. Larry Gray made this observation after hearing Booker Little quote the melody of "I Got Rhythm" during his solo on "Runnin'" just after the rhythm section "got a little shaky." Little's solo can be heard on Strozier, rec. 1960.

3. As Monson (1991, 294) also concludes: "In music that is created in performance relationships between musical parts are at the same time relationships between specific people."

4. Adderley 1960, 12.

5. According to some of Lester Young's friends, he was not properly credited with inventing riffs that became the themes of compositions associated with the Basie band. Porter 1985b, 19, 39.

6. For Roach's references to issues of racism, hardships on the road, and Clifford Brown, see Gardner 1961, 21.

7. The painful adjustment to the tragic loss of collaborative jazz artists is a poignant theme with musical consequences in the jazz community. In terms similar to Max Roach's experience, Jaki Byard changed the emphasis of his art after the deaths of several close musical friends: "That's when I really concentrated on . . . solo piano work and I disregarded all trios and all forms of orchestration because the guys were dying." Monson 1991, 266.

8. Jarrett quoted on Davis, video 1986.

9. Similarly, because ballads were largely reserved for singers in the Basie band, it was not until Lester Young played in small recording groups with Billie Holiday and formed his own recording groups that he could feature himself as a ballad performer. In his own groups, he also increased his emphasis on blues repertory. Porter 1985b, 38–39.

10. For Hines reference, see Dance 1977, 26.

11. Hawkins quoted in Shapiro and Hentoff 1966, 209.

12. Evans quoted on Davis, video 1986.

13. Jones quoted on Coltrane, video 1985.

14. Veterans like George Duvivier who are critical of the level of skill and understanding of the youngest generation of jazz musicians ascribe their problems, in part, to the lack of thorough immersion in the music that was formerly characteristic of jazz training. This includes constant opportunities to learn from mature improvisers by performing together with them in bands and at jam sessions. Economic factors like exorbitant door fees at some jazz clubs also discourage attendance by aspiring players and limit their absorption of ideas from live performances by jazz masters. Moreover, as Betty Carter recently informed me, some club owners in New York City have shifted the burden of their financial losses to the performing artists themselves, at the extreme requiring them to rent the nightclub performance space. "It's much harder for young musicians to start out today than it was for our generation," she commented.

## 16. Vibes and Venues

1. I am indebted to Chicago pianist Jodie Christian for sharing this account of Bud Powell's prowess with me. Personal conversation, summer 1984.

2. Jo Jones describes the genesis of some of his unique approaches to drumming. "The way I use cymbals and the hand-drum solo, I've been doing for twenty-three years. It all happened almost unconsciously, through the bare necessities I had to work with at the time I was learning drums—in carnivals. When I was traveling with a carnival, I didn't travel with much. . . . With this limited amount and kind of equipment I had to do something." Hentoff and Shapiro 1966, 306.

3. For additional discussion of the ways in which jazz groups regulate their precise mix of musical features to accommodate the tastes of different audiences, see Becker 1982, 318–20; and Schuller 1989, 406.

4. Dizzy Gillespie's interpretation of Miles Davis's stage behavior on Davis, video 1986.

5. Unfamiliar audience environments also undermine the normal "self-criticizing process" that "operates spontaneously where performers sing and play in contact with their cultural base. [The process] cannot function the same way when . . . jazz . . . [is] performed for audiences whose behavior is governed by the customs of the European concert hall." Floyd 1991, 276.

6. A re-creation of his admonitions is on Mingus, rec. 1960.

7. From this standpoint, audience approval can even become a liability at times. In Denny Zeitlin's experience, "An audience's excitement as the music unfolds presents [the] . . . challenge [of using] . . . that energy to lift your music to a higher level without becoming seduced by their approval into grandstanding or overusing that material." Milano 1984, 30.

8. Morton in Lomax 1950, 91–92, 140, 183. Armstrong in Shapiro and Hentoff 1966, 131. For an account of contemporary violence, see Davis 1990, 306–7.

9. His comments on sophisticated audience response are from an oral presentation (Olly Wilson 1990).

10. Perlman and Greenblatt (1981, 180) distinguish knowledgeable jazz listeners on several bases, including their skill to follow solos closely, "note by note and phrase by phrase . . . comprehend[ing] what is happening, both structurally and historically." Similarly, in all the forms it can take, the improviser's practice of "Musical Signifyin(g)

... elicits response and interaction from a knowledgeable and sensitive audience." Floyd 1991, 275.

11. Haynes's observations of Parker are on Parker, video 1987. According to Gene Ramey, "Bird kept everybody on the stand happy, because he was a wizard at transmitting musical messages to us, which made us fall out laughing. All musicians know certain musical phrases that translate themselves into 'Hello Beautiful' or, when a young lady ambles to the powder room, 'I know where you're going.' Well, Bird had an ever-increasing repertoire of these. . . . If he was in the act of blowing his sax, he would find something to express and would want you to guess his thoughts. . . . Sometimes on the dance floor, while he was playing, women who were dancing would perform in front of him. Their attitudes, their gestures, their faces, would awaken in him an emotional shock that he would express musically in his solos. As soon as his tones became piercing, we were all so accustomed to his reactions that we understood at once what he meant. . . . He could look elsewhere, but soon as he repeated this phrase, we all raised our eyes and grasped his message." Reisner 1979, 186–87.

12. St. Cyr in Shapiro and Hentoff 1966, 20.

13. Zeitlin explains, "Very often I get into an altered state of consciousness where I feel that I'm really part of an audience, and that we're all listening to the music. In fact, we've *become* the music—everything has merged. And an audience can be tremendously helpful in reaching that ecstatic state if they supply the energy and the willingness. . . . You can sure feel it when you're up on stage. It's really quite magical when that happens—when we're *all* listening to the music." Milano 1984, 25.

14. Coltrane interview in Kofsky 1973, 226.

15. Betty Carter concert at Pick-Staiger Auditorium, Northwestern University, Evanston, IL, July 15, 1983.

16. Murray (1973, 87) describes the "confusion, annoyance, boredom and . . . indifference" with which listeners respond to "inept performances." According to Denny Zeitlin, such responses "certainly can [affect which road you go down]. . . . I've experienced an audience's restlessness with certain musical material; when you sense that, there is a tendency to scuttle the direction you're taking, or to prolong it out of stubborn defiance. It's a challenge to be peripherally aware of their reaction without derailing yourself. To be willing to alter your course if the audience is truly 'telling you something' that alters your esthetic judgement. Maybe the music *has* gotten boring, too abstract, *et cetera.*" Milano 1984, 25, 30.

17. One account by a musician attributes the failed debut performance of a fine trumpet player at the Village Vanguard to the venue's "vibes. . . . Coltrane, Miles, Coleman Hawkins . . . cats who've left their vibes here . . . [the trumpet player] didn't belong in that company. The vibes scared the hell out of him." Gordon 1980, 96–97. In a related story, Rex Stewart describes his trepidation at taking over the chair of his idol, Louis Armstrong, with Fletcher Henderson's orchestra. He quit the position not long after having accepted it because he "couldn't stand the pressure." Shapiro and Hentoff 1966, 208.

18. Buster Bailey reports that Joe Oliver would hold back particular tunes and alter his ideas as a soloist when he noticed musicians in the audience who he felt were inclined to steal from him; bebop innovators like Thelonious Monk and Dizzy Gillespie

would perform "complex variations on chords . . . to scare away the no-talent guys" who might otherwise be inclined to sit in with them during performances. Shapiro and Hentoff 1966, 96, 337.

19. Ornette Coleman spoke to Chicago saxophonist Bunky Green; personal conversation, fall 1984.

20. For reference to creating definitive versions through studio editing, see Kernfeld 1988c, 363.

21. On experimental recordings of the thirties, see Sheridan 1988, 358, 362–63. Extended jam session performances involving Dizzy Gillespie, Harry Edison, and Roy Eldridge are found on "Steeplechase" and "Tour de Force," Gillespie and Eldridge, rec. 1955.

22. One saxophonist explained to me that he regarded himself as a "less spontaneous" soloist than the other members in his group. He described writing out and memorizing the solos for his first album. Concerned about how this practice might be regarded by other jazz musicians, he asked to remain anonymous in reference to this matter.

23. On the brass facing away from the recording horn and discussion of early recording techniques, see Sheridan 1988, 358. On the other hand, the evidence for the technological limitations of early recording equipment appears to be mixed. Robert Witmer suggests that, because some early jazz records, such as by the Original Dixieland Jazz Band, James Lent, and James Reese Europe, display intense drum and cymbal work, the variability may reflect different technical abilities of different recording engineers, and the musical preferences of individual musicians, who, in some instances, may have wished to re-create woodblock drumming styles from the minstrelsy era. Personal conversation, summer 1991. Similarly, Jasen (1973, 9) dismisses the common notion that the piano's sound was too soft to be picked up by acoustic recording techniques and points out that "prior to 1912," piano accompaniment on vocalists' records could be heard clearly. He agues that the low payment offered early ragtime pianists by record companies discouraged many from making records. They could simply earn more by making piano rolls. He also suggests that the artists who toured the vaudeville circuit were concerned about their material becoming overexposed through records.

24. For an elaboration of distinctions between independent and major labels, see Gray 1988, 21–36. Regarding independent companies like Theresa Records, their "independent status is also a product of the ideologies, organization, and meanings that the members construct for themselves, their music, their audiences, and their artists. . . . Theresa's experience suggests that independent labels are not just smaller versions of Columbia Records, but that they represent a different sensibility in making records." Ibid., 36, 88.

25. For an insightful elaboration of important issues regarding economic, social, and political factors influencing company policies, see DeVeaux 1988.

26. Jay McShann recalls that although his band "had a fantastic book . . . [it] never got a chance to record but very little of that stuff because the record companies were in business to sell records." He describes company management at Decca Records allowing the band to record some of their pieces only as a trade-off for the blues and boogie-woogie pieces it was pushing them to record. Gitler 1985, 65–66. Similarly, Earl

Hines reports that "one time, when we went to record, and we had all those beautiful arrangements on ballads for [Billy Eckstine] to sing, the A and R man said, 'Don't you have any blues?'" Dance 1977, 241. Eckstine also complained of having to write and impose two choruses of "some little dumb blues . . . lyric" on instrumental numbers because the record company required his voice as a signature for his band's recordings. Gitler 1985, 129.

27. DeVeaux 1988, 135.

28. For a more complete description of copyright procedures and a discussion of their actual application in the context of Charlie Parker's agreements with record companies, see Patrick 1975, 16–19.

29. The one-time fees paid artists are often only minimum union scale, but depending on their reputations and on the competition among companies for their services, band leaders can negotiate much higher rates, and the fee for their sidemen can rise to as much as double the union scale. DeVeaux 1988, 154, and Wilmer 1977, 237. DeVeaux cites union scale in 1944 as being thirty dollars per person for "three hours, four tunes. And double for the leader." Wilmer reports that minimum scale went up from sixty dollars for a three-hour session in 1965 to ninety-five dollars in 1975.

30. Ali in Wilmer 1977, 237.

31. Gillespie and Roach describe the economic impetus to compose and record original pieces in Gillespie 1979, 207–9.

32. Patrick (1975, 11) attributes the jazz musician's technique of borrowing harmonic and melodic fragments for creating new compositions, in part, to the policies of record companies and the pressures of studio work. Tommy Potter recalls of Charlie Parker that "on record dates he could compose right on the spot. The A and R man would be griping, wanting us to begin. Charlie would say, 'It'll just take a minute,' and he'd write out eight bars, usually just for the trumpet. He could transpose it for his alto without a score. The channel of the tune could be ad libbed. The rhythm section was familiar with all the progressions of the tunes which were usually the basis of originals." Reisner 1979, 183. Such practices sometimes included the spontaneous invention of song texts, as well. Billie Holiday (1969, 59) recalls periodical improvisation of lyrics for original blues compositions when they were "one side short on a [recording] date."

33. The precise contractual arrangements companies made with artists who contributed compositions to records varied considerably. "By acting as publishers, record companies were often able to acquire a percentage of composers' royalties in exchange for an advance against future sales." DeVeaux 1988, 154–55. "Parker was paid a flat fee for his compositions recorded for Savoy," and Dial "guaranteed Parker two cents per side (the maximum rate) for all records sold using his compositions." Patrick 1975, 18.

In the face of the complexity of the legalities involved with the copyright law, and the uncertainty this generates as to their rights to music ownership, there is a lingering feeling of bitterness among many artists concerning exploitation on the part of record companies. Typically, Bud Freeman writes, "Tommy Dorsey said, 'Bud, don't give those choruses away to publishers. They're going to steal them. . . . Give it a title and have it published under your own name.' . . . I took all of my improvised choruses on given themes and gave them different titles. . . . Even when I did give the tune a name and published it I ended up with practically nothing. . . . I don't receive all the royalties I should. . . . Suppose I did want to make a case of it, what could I get? Even if I won, by the time I got through paying the lawyers I wouldn't have anything." See notes to "Selected Discography" in Freeman. The cynical manipulation of artists by unscrupulous record company management is also portrayed in Feather 1945, 82.

34. Hawkins describes his lack of interest in "Body and Soul" in Hawkins 1955, 18. Another source cites James Maher's reporting that "it was Norman Granz's idea to let Hawkins play alone." Guralnik 1987, 27, 29. Joe Glaser and Kid Ory recount Louis Armstrong's scat debut on "Heebie Jeebies" in Shapiro and Hentoff 1966, 108–9.

35. When "money for composer fees, rehearsals, studio time, and engineering was scarce . . . [small companies] . . . often [pursued] a cheap and convenient way to record 'new' material with a minimum of rehearsals, retakes, and composer fees . . . [and favored such routines as an] . . . improvised piano introduction, unison statement of theme by saxophone and trumpet, improvised saxophone solo for the B section of thirty-two measure AABA themes," and so on. Patrick 1975, 11–13.

36. In the context of my interview with Melba Liston, she spoke of bad road experiences on tour with both Billie Holiday's and Dizzy Gillespie's bands. She was referring, in part, to her experiences with racism in the South, and the "hygenic difficulties of being the only woman on a touring road bus."

37. George Wettling says of Joe Oliver and his renowned Creole Jazz Band, "Unless you were lucky enough to hear that band in the flesh you can't imagine how they played and what swing they got." Ibid., 100.

38. Jimmy McPartland tells of the genesis of "Shirt Tail Stomp" in the musicians' clowning, "playing as corny as possible," in Shapiro and Hentoff 1966, 279.

39. References to Davis's and Macero's collaboration are in Kernfeld 1988c, 363, and Chambers 1985, 222.

40. Regarding this common dilemma, Lester Young, too, reported, "I get all kinds of insults about . . . 'You don't play like you played when you were with Count Basie.' . . . They get all trapped up, they go, '*Goddamn,* I never heard him play like this!' That's the way I *want* things, that's modern—dig?" Postif interview cited in Porter 1985b, 102.

41. John McLaughlin was given "complete freedom" in the recording studio at a stage in his career after his previous records had become popular. Shankar, personal conversation, 1983. From contract to contract such liberties can change considerably. According to Ross Russell, Charlie Parker was "responsible for the selection of all material recorded by Parker-led groups for Dial, although this privilege was not granted to certain other jazzmen." Subsequently, however, when Parker signed a contract with Norman Granz, he found himself under pressure to record popular songs—"pretty tunes written by good writers"—rather than the blues alone. Patrick 1975, 22, 19.

42. For a description of the endeavors of several artists, including Charles Mingus, Dizzy Gillespie, Max Roach, Duke Ellington, Stanley Cowell, Betty Carter, and Sun Ra, to establish their own independent labels over the years, see Gray 1988, 88. For an elaboration on the experiences of free jazz musicians with independent labels, see Wilmer 1977, 227–40.

### Jazz as a Way of Life

1. Over the years, the media's focus on issues such as substance abuse within the jazz community has contributed to the mistaken impression that drugs and alcohol play a significant role in the creative process of jazz. In fact, they are independent features

of the lives of some players, serving some—and not others—as a means of occasional relaxation or stimulation to energize themselves during the strenuous demands of late hour performances. Some artists in this study who at one time had drug habits attributed them to the influence of Charlie Parker, and their own naive notion, as youngsters, that if they imitated their hero in every respect, they would be able to achieve the same kind of inspiration he did in his own performance. Others were drawn into drug use in the face of social pressures by other musicians who were addicts. Parker himself felt desperately trapped by his addiction and tried often, in vain, to discourage his followers from pursuing the same course. Shapiro and Hentoff 1966, 379. Artists frankly discuss the problem of drugs in the jazz community in ibid., 371–82; and in Hentoff 1978, 75–97. See also chapter 2, note 18.

2. Roach's horn players mimic traffic on Brown, rec. 1954a. Improvisation with Wolf song on Winter, rec. 1978, and Kirk, video 1988.

3. Davis discusses Tony Williams on Davis, video 1986.

4. Discussion of "Harlem Air Shaft" in Shapiro and Hentoff 1966, 224–25. The composition can be heard on Ellington, rec. 1940.

5. The recording "Alabama" was made on November 18, 1963, and has been included on Coltrane, rec. 1963.

6. Armstrong comments on the inspiration of popular music in Shapiro and Hentoff 1966, 204.

7. For a sample of these trends, inspired by international music, see studies for jazz in Africa by Collins (1987, 188); for jazz in India and Puerto Rico, by Pinckney (1989–90, 48, 50; 1989, 245); for jazz in Haiti, by Averill (1989, 217); and for jazz in the Soviet Union, by Slobin (1984, 201) and Starr (1983).

8. During a return trip to the country in the summer of 1986, it was my pleasure to interact with seasoned artists and aspiring players such as pianist John Nyathi, saxophonists Vukeeley Judge and Biddy Partridge, trumpeter Nigel Samuels, and many others.

9. Of the dreams Coltrane discussed with friends, one exposed him to a "beautiful droning sound." In another, during the period in which he was experimenting with intricate chord substitution schemes, Charlie Parker actually appeared and counseled him to "keep on those progressions cause that's the right thing to do." Simpkins 1975, 58, 60.

10. A seven- to ten-year range I have commonly heard described in the jazz community. In Lennie Tristano's pedagogical method, a minimum apprenticeship of eight years was necessary for students to develop an appropriate base from which to develop their own individuality. McKinney 1978, 182.

11. Ken McIntyre of the Music Department at Wesleyan University, CT, personal conversation, Winter 1970.

12. Another scholar also suggests that different improvisation approaches can occur simultaneously in different ensemble parts. "The saxophonist might paraphrase the theme and then invent a new, fast-moving formulaic melody, while the pianist maintains the harmonic structure, though with his own local variations, the double bass player creates a formulaic walking bass line from the given harmony, moving in quarter-notes from chordal root to chordal root, and the drummer plays strings of rhythmic patterns, including variations on swinging cymbal rhythms and irregularly placed bass-drum beats (or bombs)." Kernfeld 1988b, 561.

13. There is some speculation about instances of comparable real-time composition in the abilities of prodigious composers like Mozart, Chopin, and Schubert, who are said to have written music as quickly as they conceived it with minimal revision. Nettl 1974, 10. See also chapter 8, note 4.

14. Other scholars have also commented on various historical dimensions of improvisation. "No one can genuinely improvise outside an existing tradition with which he is intimately familiar," maintains Donington (1970, 11). Gates (1988, 63–64) interprets improvisers' references to earlier styles and earlier versions of pieces in the most general sense as a "Signifyin(g)" process whose features of "repetition and revision," of respectful extension and of "intertextuality" are analogous to those found in "Afro-American formal literary tradition." "Every jazz performance is an interpretation of the history of the tune," according to Bowen (1990). An artist "cannot escape his own musical habits, his previous musical experiences, his personal performance facility and compositional procedures." Byrnside 1975, 224. "The conversation or interaction between jazz musicians takes place *over* time as well as *in* time. . . . [Artists] reveal themselves to be self-conscious participants in musical history" through their adoption of wide-ranging features of performance from the use of traditional repertory, or a particular groove, to the use of particular mutes that "invoke reference" to individual trumpeters who favored them. Monson 1991, 206–7.

Elaboration on "the dialogical, conversational character of black music" and, drawing on Gates's theory of African American literary criticism to interpret improvisation as "Signif[ying] on (1) the structure of the piece itself, (2) the current Signifyin(g)s of the other players in the group, and (3) the players' own and others' Signifyin(g)s in previous performances," is in Floyd 1991, 277, 279–80. Artists pay tribute to their musical predecessors in Jacquet, video 1993, and Zardis, video 1993.

15. Comments on the music culture of some Sufi groups are based on the findings of ethnomusicologist Philip D. Schuyler, University of Maryland/Baltimore County, who shared them with me in a personal conversation, spring 1992.

16. Davis quotation from Davis, video 1986.

17. Abrahams 1970a, 97. For a complete discussion of the subject, see ibid., 97–172.

18. "Honky Tonk Bud" is the result of a collaboration among lyricists John Toles-Bey and David Smith, composer Edward Wilkerson Jr., and producer-director Scott Laster. Toles-Bey and Wilkerson, video 1986.

19. For an insightful analysis of Davis's rock fusion period, see Tomlinson 1991, 257–63. Davis's own discussion of his changing interests is in Davis 1990, 311–32.

20. Davis's interest in Coleman in particular represents an interesting shift in his former ideas and tastes, for he had dismissed the value of Coleman's music during the sixties. Davis also acknowledges the influence of British composer Paul Buckmaster on his music (1990, 322).

21. For reference to Davis's experimentation, see Tomlinson 1991, 257.

22. For presentation of Davis's stage demeanor, see Davis, video 1986.

23. Coltrane explains this view, stating that he "know[s] that there are bad forces, forces put here that bring suffering to others and misery to the world, but I want to be the force which is truly for good." Kofsky 1973, 241. Similarly, Abdullah Ibrahim re-

gards music as "a healing force . . . [that] transcends all political, social and ethnic barriers because it speaks directly to the heart. . . . I do not think of myself as a pianist or a composer. My talent is a medical formula handed down from the creator. I am a dispenser of medicine." Zwerin 1982, 18.

24. Williams's quotation is on Vaughan, video 1991.

# DISCOGRAPHY

This list provides the recording session dates and names of the original companies associated with selected recordings cited in this work, emphasizing those that provide the basis for its original transcriptions. In some cases in which the original albums are no longer in print or are difficult for readers to obtain, it mentions reissues. Part 1 arranges compositions chronologically by session date under the names of featured artists. Part 2 follows the same basic scheme but lists those albums or CDs whose citation in this work does not include reference to specific compositions. For further information, see comprehensive jazz discographies by Bruyninckx (1980), Kraner (1979), Lord (1992), and Rust (1978).

## 1. Listing by Artist and Composition Titles

ADDERLEY, JULIAN "CANNONBALL"
"Somethin' Else," March 9, 1958. *Somethin' Else,* Blue Note BST-81595.

ARMSTRONG, LOUIS
"Big Butter and Egg Man from the West," Nov. 16, 1926. *The Smithsonian Collection of Classic Jazz* (compilation), CBS, Inc., CD Edition RD 033 A5 19477.
"S.O.L. Blues" and "Gully Low Blues," May 13 and 14, 1927; "Struttin' with Some Barbecue," Dec. 9, 1927. *The Louis Armstrong Story,* Columbia CBS 66427.
"Weather Bird," Dec. 5, 1928a. *The Smithsonian Collection of Classic Jazz* (compilation), CBS, Inc., CD Edition RD 033 A5 19477.
"Muggles" and "Tight like This," Dec. 12, 1928b. *The Louis Armstrong Story,* Columbia CBS 66427.

BAKER, CHET
"Like Someone in Love," July 30, 1956. *Let's Get Lost,* Capital/Pacific Jazz CDP 7 92932 2.

BLAKEY, ART
"Soft Winds," Nov. 11, 1955. *The Jazz Messengers at the Cafe Bohemia, Volume 1,* Blue Note CDP 7 46521 2.
"Moanin'" (original and alternate take), Oct. 30, 1958a. *Moanin',* Blue Note CDP 7 46516 2.
"I Remember Clifford," Nov. 22, 1958b; "Moanin'," Dec. 17, 1958b. *Jazz Messengers 1958—Paris Olympia.* Fontana 832 659-2.
"Like Someone in Love," Aug. 7, 1960. *Like Someone in Love,* Blue Note CDP 7 84245 2.

BROWN, CLIFFORD
"I Can Dream, Can't I?" (takes 1–3), Oct. 15, 1953. *The Clifford Brown Quartet in Paris,* Prestige OJCCD-357-2.
"Parisian Thoroughfare," Aug. 2 and 14, 1954a. *The Immortal,* Limelight LM2-8201.
"Jordu," Aug. 2, 1954b. *Jordu,* EmArcy MG 36036.

"What's New?," Jan. 18, 1955a. *Clifford Brown with Strings,* EmArcy 814 642-2.

"The Blues Walk," Feb. 24, 1955b. *More Study in Brown,* EmArcy 814 637-2.

CHAMBERS, PAUL

"The Theme," July 14, 1957. *Bass on Top,* Blue Note BST-81569.

COLTRANE, JOHN

"Blue Train" and "I'm Old Fashioned," Sept. 15, 1957. *Blue Train,* Blue Note CDP 7 46095 2.

"Like Someone in Love," Oct. 13, 1958. *Coltrane Time,* United Artists Jazz UAJ 14001 (originally issued as: Cecil Taylor, *Stereo Drive,* United Artists UAS 5014).

"Softly, as in a Morning Sunrise," Nov. 2–3, 1961. *"Live" at the Village Vanguard,* MCA/Impulse! MCAD-39136.

"Alabama," Nov. 18, 1963. *Live at Birdland,* Impulse! AS-50.

DAVIS, MILES

"Baby, Won't You Make Up Your Mind (take 1)," Oct. 18, 1946. *Bopping the Blues,* Black Lion BLCD 760102.

"Rifftide," May 8–11, 1949. *The Miles Davis/Tadd Dameron Quintet In Paris Festival International de Jazz,* Columbia JC34804.

"My Old Flame" and "Bluing," Oct. 5, 1951. *Dig,* Prestige P-24054.

"The Serpent's Tooth" (take 2), Jan. 30, 1953a. *Collectors' Items,* Prestige OJCCD-071-2.

"For Adults Only," Feb. 19, 1953b. *Dig,* Prestige P-24054.

"Bags' Groove" (takes 1 and 2), Dec. 24, 1954. *Bags' Groove,* Prestige OJCCD-245-2.

"The Theme" (take 1) and "Trane's Blues," May 11, 1956a. *Workin',* Prestige VDJ-1521.

"Bye Bye, Blackbird," June 5, 1956b. *Round about Midnight,* Columbia CK 40610.

"Blues by Five" and "When the Lights Are Low," Oct. 26, 1956c. *Cookin',* Prestige VDJ-1512.

"You Are My Everything," Oct. 26, 1956d. *Relaxin',* Prestige 7129.

"Motel," Dec. 4, 1957. *Ascenseur pour l'echafaud (Lift to the Scaffold),* Fontana 836 305-2.

"Billy Boy," April 2, 1958a. *Milestones . . . ,* Columbia CL1193.

"Fran Dance" and "Love for Sale," May 26, 1958b. *58 Sessions,* Columbia/Legacy CK 47835.

"Freddie Freeloader," March 2, 1959. *Kind of Blue,* Columbia CL 1355.

"I Thought about You," Feb. 12, 1964. *My Funny Valentine,* Columbia PC9106.

DOLPHY, ERIC

"Far Cry" and "Ode to Charlie Parker," Dec. 21, 1960. *Far Cry,* New Jazz OJCCD-400-2.

"Bee Vamp," "Fire Waltz," "Like Someone in Love," and "The Prophet," July 16, 1961a. *At the Five Spot, Volumes 1 and 2,* Prestige VDJ-1525, VDJ-1504.

"Bee Vamp," July 16, 1961b. *Dash One,* Prestige MPP-2517.

DORHAM, KENNY

"I Love You (take 2)," Dec. 15, 1953. *Kenny Dorham Quintet,* Debut Records OJC-113.

"Alone Together," Nov. 13, 1959. *Quiet Kenny,* Prestige VDJ-1535.

ELDRIDGE, ROY
"Fireworks" and "Wild Man Blues," March 29, 1951. *I Remember Harlem,* Inner City Records IC7012.

ELLINGTON, DUKE
"Jack the Bear" and "Harlem Air Shaft," Feb. 14 and July 22, 1940. *At His Very Best,* RCA LPM 1715.

EVANS, BILL
"Gone with the Wind," Aug. 17–18, 1967. *Jazz-Club Drums* (compilation), Verve 840 033-2.

FITZGERALD, ELLA
"Stompin' at the Savoy," April 25, 1958. *Ella in Rome: The Birthday Concert,* Verve 835 454-2.

GILLESPIE, DIZZY
"Blues for Bird," Jan. 12, 1956. *Cross Currents,* Verve VE-1-2533.

GILLESPIE, DIZZY, AND ROY ELDRIDGE
"Steeplechase" and "Tour de Force," Nov. 2, 1955. *Diz and Roy,* Verve VE-2-2524.

GOODMAN, BENNY
"Sing, Sing, Sing," July 6, 1937a. *The Complete Benny Goodman, Volume 4,* RCA VVAXM2-5537.
"Sugarfoot Stomp," Sept. 6, 1937b. *This Is Benny Goodman,* RCA Victor VPM-6040.

GREEN, BENNY
"Billy Boy," 1992. *Testifyin'!,* Blue Note CDP 7 98171 2.

HAMPTON, SLIDE
"Newport," late 1959. *Slide!,* Strand SLS 1006.

HAWKINS, COLEMAN
"Body and Soul," Oct. 11, 1939. *Body and Soul,* RCA LPV 501.
"Picasso," July/Aug. 1948. *The Essential Coleman Hawkins,* Verve 2304-537.

HENDERSON, FLETCHER
"Sugarfoot Stomp," May 29, 1925. *Jazz, Volume 7: New York 1922–34* (compilation), Folkways FJ 2807.
"Sugarfoot Stomp," April 29, 1931. *The Complete Fletcher Henderson,* RCA AXMZ-5507.

JORDON, MARLON
"Monk's Point," Dec. 1988. *For You Only,* Columbia CK 45200.

KIRK, RAHSAAN ROLAND
"A Quote from Clifford Brown," Sept. 16–17, 1964. *I Talk with the Spirits,* Limelight LM 82008.

LATEEF, YUSEF
"8540 12th Street," Oct. 9, 1957. *Jazz and the Sounds of Nature!,* Savoy MG 12120.

LITTLE, BOOKER

"Minor Suite" and "Life's a Little Blue," April 13, 1960; "Opening Statement," "The Grand Valse," and "Who Can I Turn To?," April 15, 1960. *Booker Little*, Bainbridge BCD1041.

"Quiet Please," March 17, 1961a; "Strength and Sanity" and "Moods in Free Time," April 4, 1961a. *Out Front*, Candid CD 9027.

"Booker's Blues," "Forward Flight," "If I Should Lose You," "Matilda," and "Victory and Sorrow," Aug./Sept. 1961b. *Victory and Sorrow*, Bethlehem BCP-6034.

LITTLE, BOOKER, AND DONALD BYRD

"Chasing the Bird," 1960. *The Third World*, TCB 1004 (originally *Soul of Jazz Percussion*, Warwick 5003).

THE MANHATTAN TRANSFER

"Ray's Rockhouse," Fall 1985. *Vocalese*, Atlantic 7 81266-2.

MINGUS, CHARLES

"What Love," Oct. 20, 1960. *Presents Charles Mingus*, Candid CD 9005.

MITCHELL, BLUE

"Sir John," Aug. 24–25, 1960. *Blue's Moods*, Riverside OJC-138.

MOBLEY, HANK

"Git-Go Blues," Feb. 9, 1958. *Peckin' Time*, Blue Note CDP 7 81574 2.

MONTGOMERY, WES

"Four on Six" and "West Coast Blues." Jan. 26, 28, 1960. *Incredible Jazz Guitar,* Riverside OJCCD 036-2.

NAVARRO, FATS

"Jahbero" (original and alternate take) and "Lady Bird" (original and alternate take), Sept. 13, 1948. *The Fabulous Fats Navarro, Volumes 1 and 2*, Blue Note 81531, 81532.

OLIVER, JOE

"Dippermouth Blues," April 6, 1923a. *Louis Armstrong and King Oliver,* Milestone M-47017. Also, *The Smithsonian Collection of Classic Jazz* (compilation), CBS, Inc., CD Edition RD 033 A5 19477.

"Dippermouth Blues," June 23, 1923b. *The Smithsonian Collection of Classic Jazz* (compilation), CBS, Inc., LP Edition P6 11891.

PARKER, CHARLIE

"Red Cross" (takes 1 and 2) and "Tiny's Tempo" (takes 1–3), Sept. 15, 1944. *The Complete Savoy Studio Sessions,* Savoy S5J 5500.

"Embraceable You" (takes 1 and 2), Oct. 28, 1947. *Bird on Dial,* Spotlite 104.

"Barbados" (takes 1, 3, 4), Sept. 18, 1948. *The Complete Savoy Studio Sessions,* Savoy S5J 5500.

"The Street Beat," June 30, 1950. *One Night in Birdland,* Columbia 34808.

"She Rote" (original and alternate take), Aug. 8, 1951. *Swedish Schnapps,* Verve V6-8010.

PARKER, CHARLIE, AND DIZZY GILLESPIE
"Mohawk" (original and alternate take), June 6, 1950. *Bird and Diz,* Verve 831 133-2.

ROACH, MAX
"Stella by Starlight" and "Memo: To Maurice," June 1958a. *Max on the Chicago Scene,*
    EmArcy MG 36132.
"Shirley," June 6, 1958b. *Standard Time,* EmArcy 814 190-1.
"Old Folks," Nov. 25, 1959. *Award-Winning Drummer,* Bainbridge BCD1042.

ROCHÉ, BETTY
"Take the A Train," June 30, 1952. *Hi-Fi Ellington Uptown,* Columbia CCL 830.

ROLLINS, SONNY
"Pent-Up House," March 22, 1956a. *Sonny Rollins plus 4,* Prestige VDJ-1524.
"St. Thomas" and "Strode Rode," June 22, 1956b. *Saxophone Colossus,* Prestige
    OJCCD 291-2.
"It Could Happen to You," June 11–12, 1957. *The Sound of Sonny,* Riverside RLP 241.
"Body and Soul," July 10, 1958. *Brass/Trio,* Verve UMV 255.

SCOFIELD, JOHN
"You Bet," Dec. 1991. *Grace under Pressure,* Blue Note CDP 7 98167 2.

SMITH, BESSIE
"St. Louis Blues," Jan. 14, 1925. *The Smithsonian Collection of Classic Jazz* (compila-
    tion), CBS, Inc., CD Edition RD 033 A5 19477.
"Lost Your Head Blues," May 4, 1926. *The Smithsonian Collection of Classic Jazz*
    (compilation), CBS, Inc., CD Edition RD 033 A5 19477.

STROZIER, FRANK
"Runnin'," "Waltz of the Demons," and "W. K. Blues," Feb. 2, 1960. *Fantastic Frank
    Strozier,* Vee Jay LP 3005.

SUN RA
"Lullaby for Realville," July 12, 1956. *Sun Song,* Delmark DD-411 (originally issued
    on Transition TRLP 10).

TRISTANO, LENNIE
"Intuition" and "Digression," May 16, 1949. *Crosscurrents,* Capital M11060.

VAUGHAN, SARAH
"Shulie-A-Bop," April 2, 1954a. *Swingin' Easy,* EmArcy MG 36109.
"September Song," Dec. 18, 1954b. *Sarah Vaughan,* EmArcy MG 36004

WASHINGTON, DINAH
"I've Got You under My Skin," Aug. 14, 1954. *Dinah Jams,* EmArcy MG 36000.

WINTER, PAUL
"Wolf Eyes" and "Trilogy," 1978. *Common Ground,* A&M Sp-4698.

## 2. Listing by Artist and Album Titles

COLEMAN, ORNETTE
*Free Jazz,* Dec. 21, 1960, Atlantic SD 1364.

COLTRANE, JOHN
*A Love Supreme,* Dec. 9, 1964, Impulse! A-77.
*Ascension,* June 28, 1965, Impulse! A-95.
*Expression,* Feb. 15 and March 7, 1967, Impulse! AS-9120.

DAVIS, MILES
*Birth of the Cool,* Jan. 21 and April 22, 1949, and March 9, 1950, Capital T762.
*E.S.P.,* Jan. 20–22, 1965, Columbia CS 9150.

DODDS, BABY
*Talking and Drum Solos,* Jan. 10, 1946, Folkways FJ2290.

FLANAGAN, TOMMY
*Overseas,* Aug. 15, 1957, Prestige 7134.

GURU
*Jazzmatazz,* vol. 1, 1993, Chrysalis 0946 3 21998 2 9.

KONITZ, LEE
*Motion,* Aug. 29, 1961, Verve MGV 8399.

ROACH, MAX
*Jazz in 3/4 Time,* March 18–21, 1957, EmArcy MG 36108.
*We Insist! Max Roach and Oscar Brown Jr.'s Freedom Now Suite,* Aug. 31 and Sept. 6, 1960, Candid CJM 8002.
*Drums Unlimited,* Oct. 14 and 20, 1965, and April 25, 1966, Atlantic 1467.

# VIDEOGRAPHY

BISHOP, WALTER, JR.
*A VHS Master Class Featuring Walter Bishop Jr.* Walter Bishop Jr. and Bret Primack. Video Production Center. Video, 58 mins. 1987. Available from Jazzvideo International.

BLAKEY, ART
*Art Blakey: The Jazz Messenger.* Dick Fontaine and Pat Hartley. Grapevine Pictures, Central Independent Television and Channel Four (UK). Film, 78 mins. 1987. Available as video from Rhapsody Films, Inc., #8016, 1988.

CARTER, BETTY
*But Then, She's Betty Carter.* Michelle Parkerson. Eye of the Storm Productions. Film, 53 mins. 1980. Available as video from Women Make Movies.

COLTRANE, JOHN
*The Coltrane Legacy.* Burrill Crohn. Jazz Images, Inc. Video, 61 mins. 1985. Available from Video Artists International, Inc., #69035.

COMPILATIONS
*Jazz Is Our Religion.* John Jeremy. Silverscreen Productions, Ltd. Film, 50 mins. 1972. Available as video from Rhapsody Films, Inc., #8033, 1986.
*The Sound of Jazz.* Robert Herridge. CBS Studio 58. "The Seven Lively Arts" televison program, 58 mins. Dec. 8, 1957. Available as video from Vintage Jazz Classics, Ltd., #2001-4, 1990.
*Trumpet Kings.* Burrill Crohn. Jazz Images, Inc. Video, 72 mins. 1985. Available from Video Artists International, Inc., #69036.

DAVIS, MILES
*Miles Ahead: The Music of Miles Davis.* Mark Obenhaus and Yvonne Smith. WNET/Thirteen and Obenhaus Films, Inc., in association with Channel 4 Television, London. "Great Performances" public television program #1303, 60 mins., Oct. 17, 1986. Available as video from BMG Music, 1993 (forthcoming).

EVANS, BILL
*The Universal Mind of Bill Evans.* Helen Keane. Charter Oak Telepictures, Inc. Film, 45 mins. 1966. Available as video from Rhapsody Films, Inc., #9015, 1991.

GILLESPIE, DIZZY
*Wolf Trap Salutes Dizzy Gillespie: An All-Star Tribute to the Jazz Master.* John T. Potthast. Maryland Public Television in association with WNET/New York and Wolf Trap Foundation for the Performing Arts. "Great Performances" public television program #1419, 90 mins., Feb. 26, 1988.

HARRIS, BARRY

*Passing It On (featuring Barry Harris).* David Chan and Kenneth Freundlich. Weatherbird Film Productions. Film, 23 mins. 1984. Available as video from Rhapsody Films, Inc., #8018, 1986.

JACQUET, ILLINOIS

*Texas Tenor: The Illinois Jacquet Story.* Ronit Avneri and Arthur Elgort. Arthur Elgort Productions, Ltd. Film, 81 mins. 1991. Available as video from Rhapsody Films, Inc., #9021, 1993.

JONES, ELVIN

*Different Drummer Elvin Jones.* Edward Gray. Edward Gray Films, Inc. Film, 30 mins. 1979. Available as video from Rhapsody Films, Inc., #9014, 1991.

KIRK, RAHSAAN ROLAND

*Sound??* Dick Fontaine and Mike Hodges. ABC Television (UK). Film, 27 mins. 1967. Available as video from Rhapsody Films, Inc., #8056, 1988.

KONITZ, LEE

*Konitz (Lee Konitz): Portrait of an Artist as Saxophonist.* Robert Daudelin. Les Films du Crepuscule International (Canada). Film, 83 mins. 1988. Available as video from Rhapsody Films, Inc., #8041, 1990.

LAWRENCE, BABY

*Jazz Hoofer: Baby Lawrence.* Bill Hancock, H-D Productions. Film, 28 mins. 1981. Available as video from Rhapsody Films, Inc., #8030, 1986.

MINGUS, CHARLES

*Mingus (Charles Mingus)—1968.* Thomas Reichman. William B. O'Boyle Productions. Film, 58 mins. 1968. Available as video from Rhapsody Films, Inc., #8046, 1987.

MONK, THELONIOUS

*Thelonious Monk, Straight No Chaser.* Charlotte Zwerin and Bruce Ricker; Clint Eastwood. Warner Bros., Inc. Film, 90 mins. 1988. Produced as video by Warner Home Video, Inc., #11896, 1990. Available from Rhapsody Films, Inc.

PARKER, CHARLIE

*Celebrating Bird: The Triumph of Charlie Parker.* Toby Byron. Toby Byron/ Multiprises. Video, 59 mins. 1987. Available from Kultur International Films, Ltd., #1293.

TOLES-BEY, JOHN, AND EDWARD WILKERSON JR.

*Honky Tonk Bud.* Scott Laster. Urban Legend Films. Film, 12 mins. 1985. Available as video from Rhapsody Films, Inc. (in compilation, *Jazz Shorts,* #8034), 1986.

VAUGHAN, SARAH

*Evening at Pops* (featuring Sarah Vaughan and Wynton Marsalis). Bill Cosel. WGBH and Boston Symphony Orchestra, Inc. "Evening at Pops" public television program #6002, 60 mins. July 9, 1984.

*Sarah Vaughan: The Divine One.* Toby Byron and Richard Saylor. Toby Byron/ Multiprises in association with Taurus Film, Munich, Video Arts, Japan, and

Thirteen/WNET. "American Masters" public television program #604, 60 mins. July 29, 1991. Available as video from BMG Music, 1993 (forthcoming).

ZARDIS, CHESTER

*Zardis: The Spirit of New Orleans.* Preston McClanahan. PM Films, Inc. Video, 88 mins. 1989. Available from Rhapsody Films, Inc., #9026, 1993.

# BIBLIOGRAPHY

Abrahams, Roger D. 1970a. *Deep Down in the Jungle.* New York: Aldine.

———. 1970b. "Toward a Black Rhetoric: Being a Survey of Afro-American Communication Styles and Role-Relationships." *Texas Working Papers in Sociolinguistics* no. 15. Austin: University of Texas.

Adderley, "Cannonball" Julian. 1960. "Paying Dues: The Education of a Combo Leader." *Jazz Review* 3, no. 5 (May): 12–15.

Aebersold, Jamey. 1980. *One Dozen Standards,* vol. 23. New Albany, IN: Jamey Aebersold.

———. 1984. *Jam Session,* vol. 34. Booklet and recording. New Albany, IN: Jamey Aebersold.

Aebersold, Jamey, and Ken Slone. 1978. *Charlie Parker Omnibook (Transposed for B-flat Instruments).* New York: Music People, div. of Music Books.

Agu, Daniel C. C. 1984. "The Vocal-music Composer in a Nigerian Traditional Society and His Compositional Techniques." *Pacific Review of Ethnomusicology* 1:13–28.

Alperson, Philip. 1984. "On Musical Improvisation." *Journal of Aesthetics and Art Criticism* 43:17–29.

Anon. 1919. "A Negro Explains 'Jazz.'" *Literary Digest,* April 26:28–29.

Apel, Willi. 1969. *Harvard Dictionary of Music.* 2d ed., rev. and enl. Cambridge: Belknap Press of Harvard University Press.

Arban, Joseph Jean Baptiste Laurent. 1982 (1894). *Arban's Complete Conservatory Method for Trumpet.* Ed. Edwin Franko Goldman and Walter M. Smith. New York: Carl Fisher.

Austin, William W. 1966. *Music in the Twentieth Century from Debussy through Stravinsky.* New York: W. W. Norton.

Averill, Gage. 1989. "Haitian Dance Bands, 1915–1970: Class, Race, and Authority." *Latin American Review* 10, no. 2 (Fall/Winter): 203–35.

Bailey, Derek. 1980. *Musical Improvisation: Its Nature and Practice in Music.* Ashbourne, Eng., and Englewood Cliffs, NJ: Prentice-Hall.

Baily, John. 1985. "Music Structure and Human Movement." In *Musical Structure and Cognition,* Ed. Peter Howell, Ian Cross, and Robert West. London: Academic.

Baker, David. 1968. *Turnbacks: Techniques of Improvisation.* Vol. 3 of *Music Workshop Publications.* Chicago: Maher.

———. 1969. *Jazz Improvisation.* Chicago: Maher.

———. 1982. *The Jazz Style of Clifford Brown.* Hialeah, FL: Studio P/R.

Balliett, Whitney. 1971. *Ecstasy at the Onion: Thirty-One Pieces on Jazz.* Indianapolis: Bobbs-Merrill.

———. 1977. *Improvising.* New York: Oxford University Press.

———. 1982. "Jazz: Ten Levels." *New Yorker,* August 16:76–83.

Baraka, Amiri [LeRoi Jones]. 1963. *Blues People: Negro Music in White America.* New York: William Morrow.

———. 1970. *Black Music.* New York: William Morrow.

Barron, William, Jr. 1975. "Improvisation and Related Concepts in Aesthetic Educa-
tion." Ph.D. dissertation, University of Massachusetts.
Beach, Doug. 1991. "Clark Terry and the St. Louis Trumpet Sound." *Instrumentalist*
(April): 9–12, 80.
Bechet, Sidney. 1978. *Treat It Gentle: An Autobiography.* New York: Da Capo. Orig.
pub. New York: Twayne, 1960.
Becker, Howard S. 1951. "The Professional Dance Band Musician and His Audience."
*American Journal of Sociology* 57 (September): 136–44.
———. 1953. "Some Contingencies of the Professional Dance Musician's Career." *Human Organization* 12, no. 2 (Spring): 22–26.
———. 1963. *Outsiders: Studies in the Sociology of Deviance.* New York: Free Press.
———. 1972. "A School Is a Lousy Place to Learn Anything In." *American Behavioral
Scientist 16* (September/October): 85–105. Rpt. in idem, *Doing Things Together.*
Evanston, IL: Northwestern University Press, 1986.
———. 1982. *Art Worlds.* Berkeley and Los Angeles: University of California Press.
———. n.d. "The Etiquette of Improvisation." Unpublished article.
Beeson, Ann. 1990. "'Quoting Tunes': Narrative Features in Jazz." *Collectanea* 1
(Summer): 1–15.
Bennett, H. Stith. 1980. *On Becoming a Rock Musician.* Amherst: University of Massa-
chusetts Press.
Benward, Bruce, and Joan Wildman. 1984. *Jazz Improvisation in Theory and Practice.*
Dubuque, IA: Wm. C. Brown.
Berk, Lee. 1970. "The Jazz School: Berklee at Twenty-five." *Musical Journal* 28, no. 9
(October): 29, 46–47.
Berlin, Edward A. 1980. *Ragtime: A Musical and Cultural History.* Berkeley and Los
Angeles: University of California Press.
Berliner, Paul F. 1978. *The Soul of Mbira: Music and Traditions of the Shona People of
Zimbabwe.* Berkeley and Los Angeles: University of California Press. Rpt. Chi-
cago: University of Chicago Press, 1993.
Bishop, Walter, Jr. 1976. *A Study in Fourths.* New York: Caldon.
Blanq, Charles C., III. 1977. "Melodic Improvisation in American Jazz: The Style of
Theodore 'Sonny' Rollins, 1951–1962." Ph.D. dissertation, Tulane University.
Blom, Lynne Anne, and L. Tarin Chaplin. 1988. *The Moment of Movement: Dance
Improvisation.* Pittsburgh: University of Pittsburgh Press.
Bloom, Benjamin S., ed. 1985. *Developing Talent in Young People.* New York: Bal-
lantine.
Bowen, José A. 1990. "Jazz, Utterance, and Tradition: Finding the Tune in ''Round
Midnight.''" Paper delivered at the AMS/SEM/SMT annual meetings in Oakland,
CA, November 10.
Bowman, Robert. 1982. "The Question of Improvisation and Head Arrangement in
King Oliver's Creole Jazz Band." Master's thesis, York University, Toronto, On-
tario.
Bowman, Wayne. 1988. "Doctoral Research in Jazz Improvisation Pedagogy: An Over-
view." Council for Research in Music Education Bulletin, no. 96 (Spring): 47–76.
Urbana: School of Music, University of Illinois.

————, ed. 1987–88. "Research in Jazz Education," parts 1 and 2. Council for Research in Music Education Bulletin, nos. 95, 96 (Winter 1987; Spring 1988). Urbana: School of Music, University of Illinois.

Branch, London G. 1975. "Jazz Education in Predominantly Black Colleges." Ph.D. dissertation, Southern Illinois University.

Briscuso, Joseph James. 1974. "A Study of Ability in Spontaneous and Prepared Jazz Improvisation among Students Who Possess Different Levels of Musical Aptitude." In *Experimental Research in the Psychology of Music: 9,* ed. Edwin Gordon. Iowa City: University of Iowa Press.

Brown, Robert. 1981. "How Improvized Is Jazz Improvisation?" In *Proceedings of NAJE Research,* vol. 1, ed. Charles T. Brown. Manhattan, KS: NAJE Publications.

Brown, T. Dennis. 1976. "A History and Analysis of Jazz Drumming to 1942." Ph.D. dissertation, University of Michigan.

————. 1988. "Drum Set." In *The New Grove Dictionary of Jazz.* See Kernfeld 1988d.

Bruyninckx, Walter. 1980. *Sixty Years of Recorded Jazz 1917–1977.* Mechelen, Belgium: Bruyninckx.

Burnim, Mellonee V., and Portia K. Maultsby. 1987. "From Backwoods to City Streets: The Afro-American Musical Journey." In *Expressively Black: The Cultural Basis of Ethnic Identity,* ed. Geneva Gay and Willie L. Baber. New York: Praeger.

Byrnside, Ronald. 1975. "The Performer as Creator: Jazz Improvisation." In *Contemporary Music and Music Cultures,* ed. Charles Hamm, Bruno Nettl, and Ronald Byrnside. Englewood Cliffs, NJ: Prentice-Hall.

Cambor, C. Glenn, Gerald M. Lisowitz, and Miles D. Miller. "Creative Jazz Musicians: A Clinical Study." *Psychiatry* 25, no. 1 (February): 1–15.

Cameron, William B. 1954. "Sociological Notes on the Jam Session." *Social Forces* 33:177–82.

Campbell, Patricia Sheehan. 1991. *Lessons from the World: A Cross-cultural Guide to Music Teaching and Learning.* New York: Schirmer Books.

Carr, Ian. 1984. *Miles Davis: A Biography.* New York: Quill.

Carter, Warrick L. 1986. "Jazz Pedagogy: A History Still in the Making." *Jazz Educators Journal* 18 (3): 10–13, 49–50.

Chambers, Jack. 1985. *Milestones 1 and 2.* New York: Beech Tree Books (William Morrow).

Chapin, Jim. 1948. *Advanced Techniques of the Modern Drummer.* Sag Harbor, NY: Jim Chapin.

Cheatham, "Doc" Adolphus. 1960. *Ad-lib Chord Reading.* London: B. Feldman.

Chernoff, John Miller. 1979. *African Rhythm and African Sensibility.* Chicago: University of Chicago Press.

Clark, C. E. Frazer, Jr., managing ed. 1977. *Conversations with Jazz Musicians,* vol. 2. Detroit: Gale Research.

Clarke, Herbert L. 1934 (1912). *Technical Studies for the Cornet.* New York: Carl Fisher.

Coker, Jerry. 1964. *Improvising Jazz.* Englewood Cliffs, NJ: Prentice-Hall.

————. 1975. *The Jazz Idiom.* Englewood Cliffs, NJ: Prentice-Hall.

Collier, James Lincoln. 1978. *The Making of Jazz: A Comprehensive History.* Boston: Houghton Mifflin.

————. 1988a. "Bands." In *The New Grove Dictionary of Jazz.* See Kernfeld 1988d.

————. 1988b. "Jazz." In *The New Grove Dictionary of Jazz.* See Kernfeld 1988d.

Collins, John Edmund. 1987. "Jazz Feedback to Africa." *American Music* 5, no. 2 (Summer): 176–93.

Coltrane, John. 1960. With Don DeMichael. "Coltrane on Coltrane." *Down Beat* 27, no. 20 (September 29): 26–27.

Coolman, Todd. 1985. *The Bass Tradition: Past, Present, Future.* New Albany, IN: Jamey Aebersold.

Courlander, Harold. 1963. *Negro Folk Music, U.S.A.* New York: Columbia University Press.

Crawford, Marc. 1961. "Benny Remembers Clifford." *Down Beat* 28, no. 21 (October 12): 22–23.

Crawford, Richard, and Jeffrey Magee. 1992. *Jazz Standards on Record, 1900–1942: A Core Repertory.* Chicago: Center for Black Music Research, Columbia College.

Crouch, Stanley. 1977. Liner notes for recording, *Fats Navarro,* Milestone M-47041.

Dance, Stanley. 1977. *The World of Earl Hines.* New York: Charles Scribner's Sons.

Daniels, Douglas Henry. 1985. "Lester Young: Master of Jive." *American Music* 3, no. 3 (Fall): 313–28.

Dauer, Alfons M. 1960. "Improvisation: Zur Technik der spontanen Gestaltung im Jazz." *Jazzforschung/Jazz Research* 1:113–32.

Davis, Arthur. 1976. *The Arthur Davis System for Double Bass.* Crugers, NY: K.M.V. Enterprises.

Davis, Miles. 1990. With Quincy Troupe. *Miles: The Autobiography.* New York: Touchstone. Orig. pub. New York: Simon and Schuster, 1989.

Davis, Walter, Jr. 1983. *Thirty Compositions by Kenny Dorham Arranged for Piano.* Ed. Don Sickler. New York: Second Floor Music.

DeMichael, Don. 1962. "John Coltrane and Eric Dolphy Answer the Critics." *Down Beat* 29, no. 8 (April 12): 20–23.

DeVeaux, Scott. 1988. "Bebop and the Recording Industry: The 1942 AFM Recording Ban Reconsidered." *Journal of the American Musicological Society* 41, no. 1 (Spring): 126–65.

Dobbins, Bill. 1984. *The Contemporary Jazz Pianist.* 4 vols. New York: Charles Colin.

————. 1988. *Chick Corea: Now He Sings, Now He Sobs.* Rottenburg, Germany: Advance Music.

Donington, Robert. 1970. "Improvisation." *Encyclopaedia Britannica.*

Driggs, Frank. 1960. "Eddie Barefield's Many Worlds." *Jazz Review* 3, no. 6 (July): 18–22.

Ellington, Edward Kennedy "Duke." 1980. *Music Is My Mistress.* New York: Da Capo. Orig. pub. Garden City, NY: Doubleday, 1973.

Epstein, Dena J. 1973. "African Music in British and French America." *Musical Quarterly* 59, no. 1 (January): 61–91.

————. 1975. "The Folk Banjo: A Documentary History." *Ethnomusicology* 19, no. 3, (September): 347–71.

————. 1977. *Sinful Tunes and Spirituals: Black Music to the Civil War.* Chicago: University of Chicago Press.

Erlmann, Veit. 1985. "Model, Variation and Performance: Ful'be Praise Song in Northern Cameroon." *Yearbook for Traditional Music* 11:88–112.

Evans, Bill. n.d. *Bill Evans Plays Five Original Compositions plus "Who Can I Turn To?"* Ft. Lauderdale, FL: TRO Songways Service.

Evans, David. 1978. "African Elements in Twentieth-century United States Black Folk Music." *Jazzforschung: Jazz Research* 10:85–109.

———. 1982. *Big Road Blues.* Berkeley and Los Angeles: University of California Press.

———. 1987. "The Origins of Blues and Its Relationship to African Music." In *Images de l'africain de l'antiquité au XXe siècle,* ed. Daniel Droixhe and Klaus H. Kiefer. Bayreuther Beiträge zur Literaturwissenschaft, vol. 10. Frankfurt am Main: Verlag Peter Lang.

Farmer, Art. 1984. *The Art of Art Farmer.* New York: Charles Colin.

Feather, Leonard. 1945. "The Rhythm Section." *Esquire* 24, no. 3 (September): 82.

———. 1960. *The Encyclopedia of Jazz.* New York: Horizon.

———. 1965. *The Book of Jazz: A Guide to the Entire Field.* New York: Horizon.

———. 1980. *Inside Jazz.* 2d ed. New York: Da Capo. Orig. pub. as *Inside Be-bop.* New York: J. J. Robbins and Sons, 1949.

———. 1984. *The Fabulous Fats Navarro.* Liner notes, Blue Note BST 81531.

Feather, Leonard, and Ira Gitler, eds. 1976. *The Encyclopedia of Jazz in the Seventies.* New York: Horizon.

Floyd, Samuel A., Jr. 1991. "Ring Shout! Literary Studies, Historical Studies, and Black Music Inquiry." *Black Music Research Journal* 11, no. 2 (Fall): 265–87.

Foster, Pops. 1971. With Tom Stoddard. *The Autobiography of Pops Foster.* Berkeley and Los Angeles: University of California Press.

Fraser, Wilmot Alfred. 1983. "Jazzology: A Study of the Tradition in Which Jazz Musicians Learn to Improvise." Ph.D. dissertation, University of Pennsylvania.

Freeman, Bud. 1989. *Crazeology.* Urbana: University of Illinois Press.

Gardner, Barbara. 1961. "The Legacy of Clifford Brown." *Down Beat* 28, no. 21 (October 12): 17–21.

Gates, Henry Louis, Jr. 1988. *The Signifying Monkey: A Theory of Afro-American Literary Criticism.* New York: Oxford University Press.

Gillespie, Dizzy. 1979. With Al Fraser. *To Be or Not to Bop: Memoirs.* Garden City, NY: Doubleday.

Gioia, Ted. 1987. "Jazz: The Aesthetics of Imperfection." *Hudson Review* 39, no. 4 (Winter): 585–600.

———. 1988. *The Imperfect Art: Reflections on Jazz and Modern Culture.* New York: Oxford University Press.

Gitler, Ira. 1985. *Swing to Bop.* New York: Oxford University Press.

Goddard, Chris. 1979. *Jazz away from Home.* New York and London: Paddington.

Goetschius, Percy. 1889. *The Material Used in Musical Composition: A System of Harmony.* 2d ed. New York: G. Schirmer.

Gonda, Janos. 1971–72. "Problems of Tonality and Function in Modern Jazz Improvisation." *Jazzforschung/Jazz Research* 3–4:194–205.

Goodman, George W. 1983. "Jazz Artists Recall Their Summer of European Festivals." *New York Times,* October 9.

Gordon, Max. 1980. *Live at the Village Vanguard.* New York City: St. Martin's.

Gottlieb, Louis. 1959. "Why So Sad, Pres?" *Jazz* 3 (Summer): 185–96.

Gray, Herman. 1988. *Producing Jazz.* Philadelphia: Temple University Press.

Gridley, Mark C. 1985. *Jazz Styles.* Englewood Cliffs, NJ: Prentice-Hall.

Guralnik, Tom. 1987. "Contemporary Improvised Solo Saxophone Performance and Recording Activity." Master's thesis, Wesleyan University.

Gushee, Lawrence. 1981. "Lester Young's 'Shoeshine Boy.'" In *Report of the Twelfth Congress, Berkeley 1977,* International Musicological Society, ed. Daniel Heartz and Bonnie Wade. Kassel: Bärenreiter.

Haggart, Bob. n.d. *Bass Method.* Hialeah, FL: CPP Belwin.

Handy, W. C. 1941. *Father of the Blues: An Autobiography.* New York: Macmillan.

Hargreaves, David J., Conrad A. Cork, and Tina Setton. 1991. "Cognitive Strategies in Jazz Improvisation: An Exploratory Study." *Canadian Journal of Research in Music Education* 33, Special ISME Research Edition (December): 47–54.

Harrison, Max. 1980. "Jazz." In *The New Grove Dictionary of Music and Musicians,* vol. 9, ed. S. Sadie. London: Macmillan.

Hawkins, Coleman. 1955. "Almost Didn't Record 'Body, Soul,' Hawk Says." *Down Beat* 22, no. 1 (January 12): 18.

Heckman, Don. 1965a. "Inside Ornette Coleman." *Down Beat* 32, no. 19 (September 9): 13–15.

———. 1965b. "Inside Ornette, Part 2." *Down Beat* 32, no. 26 (December 16): 20–21.

Hentoff, Nat. 1955. "Miles." *Down Beat* 22, no. 22 (November 2): 13–14.

———. 1956. "Pres." *Down Beat* 23, no. 5 (March 7): 9–11.

———. 1978. *The Jazz Life.* New York: Da Capo. Orig. pub. New York: Dial, 1961.

Hodeir, André. 1961 (1956). *Jazz: Its Evolution and Essence.* Tr. David Noakes. New York: Grove.

Holden, Stephen. 1991. "Holiday Biographies." *New York Times,* "The Pop Life" column, May 22.

Holiday, Billie. 1969. With William Dufty. *Lady Sings the Blues.* New York: Lancer Books. Orig. pub. New York: Doubleday, 1956.

Hooper, Joseph. 1991. "Stan Getz: Through the Years." *New York Times Magazine,* June 9.

Hyman, Dick. 1986. *Professional Chord Changes and Substitutions for One Hundred Tunes Every Musician Should Know.* Katonah, NY: Ekay Music.

Jasen, David A. 1973. *Recorded Ragtime 1897–1958.* Hamden, CT: Shoe String Press (Archon).

Jeske, Lee. 1981. "Jimmy Knepper." *Down Beat* 48, no. 1 (August): 14–17, 66–67.

Johnson-Laird, Philip N. 1988. "Freedom and Constraint in Creativity." In *The Nature of Creativity,* ed. R. J. Sternberg. Cambridge: Cambridge University Press.

Jones, A. M. 1959. *Studies in African Music,* vols. 1 and 2. London: Oxford University Press.

Jones, LeRoi. *See* Baraka, Amiri.

Jost, Ekkehard. 1975. *Free Jazz.* Graz; Vienna: Universal Edition.

Katz, Steven. 1958. "A Conversation with Two Jazz Musicians." *Northwest Review* 1, no. 3 (Spring): 40–66.

Keil, Charles. 1966a. *Urban Blues.* Chicago: University of Chicago Press.

―――. 1966b. "Motion and Feeling through Music." *Journal of Aesthetics and Art Criticism* 24:337–49. Rpt. in *Rappin' and Stylin' Out: Communication in Black Urban America,* ed. Thomas Kochman. Urbana: University of Illinois Press, 1972.

Kernfeld, Barry Dean. 1981. "Adderley, Coltrane, and Davis at the Twilight of Bebop: The Search for Melodic Coherence (1958–59)." Ph.D. dissertation, Cornell University.

―――. 1983. "Two Coltranes." *Annual Review of Jazz Studies* 2:7–66.

―――. 1988a. "Blues Progression." In *The New Grove Dictionary of Jazz.* See Kernfeld 1988d.

―――. 1988b. "Improvisation." In the *The New Grove Dictionary of Jazz.* See Kernfeld 1988d.

―――. 1988c. "Recording (II, 4, 7–8)." In *The New Grove Dictionary of Jazz.* See Kernfeld 1988d.

―――, gen. ed. 1988d. *The New Grove Dictionary of Jazz,* vols. 1 and 2. London: Macmillan.

Kerschbaumer, Franz. 1978. *Miles Davis.* Graz: Akademische Druck-u. Verlagsanstalt.

Kessel, Barney. 1979. "Lester Young, Part 2." *Guitar Player* (January): 22, 97.

Kirkwood, Kenny. 1986. "Dippermouth Blues/Sugarfoot Stomp: Thoughts on an Oral Tradition." Unpublished paper prepared for Robert Witmer's course, Music 5080.03, York University, Toronto, Ontario.

Koch, Lawrence O. 1974–75. "Ornithology: A Study of Charlie Parker's Music (Parts 1 and 2)." *Journal of Jazz Studies* 2, no. 1 (December 1974): 61–87; 2, no. 2 (June 1975): 61–85.

―――. 1988. "Piano." In *The New Grove Dictionary of Jazz.* See Kernfeld 1988d.

Kofsky, Frank. 1973 (1970). *Black Nationalism and the Revolution in Music.* New York: Pathfinder.

Kraner, Dietrich H. 1979. "Booker Little Discography." *Journal of Jazz Discography* (South Wales, U.K.), no. 5 (September): 2–8.

Kubik, Gerhard. 1959. "Archaischer und moderner Jazz." *Neue Zeitschrift für Musik* (September): 448–51.

―――. 1962. "The Phenomenon of Inherent Rhythms in East and Central African Instrumental Music." *African Music* 3 (1): 33–42.

―――. 1993. "Transplantation of African Musical Cultures to the Americas." In *Slavery in the Americas,* ed. Wolfgang Binder. Würzburg, Germany: Königshausen and Neumann.

LaPorta, John. 1968. *A Guide to Improvisation.* Boston: Berklee.

Lateef, Yusef. 1979. *Method on How to Improvise Soul Music.* Amherst, MA: Fana.

Lerdhal, Fred, and Ray Jackendoff. 1983. *A Generative Theory of Tonal Music.* Cambridge: MIT Press.

Lewis, Marjery. 1947. "Get Those Coloured Boys off the Bandstand." *Melody Maker,* June 28, 1.

Levin, Michael, and John S. Wilson. 1949. "No Bop Roots in Jazz: Parker." *Down Beat* 16, no. 17 (September 9): 1.

Levine, Lawrence W. 1977. *Black Culture and Black Consciousness.* New York: Oxford University Press.

Locke, David. 1987. *Drum Gahu.* Crown Point, IN: White Cliffs Media.

Logan, Wendell. 1984. "The Ostinato Idea in Black Improvised Music: A Preliminary Investigation." *Black Perspective in Music* 12, no. 2 (Fall): 193–215.

Lomax, Alan. 1973 (1950). *Mister Jelly Roll: The Fortunes of Jelly Roll Morton, New Orleans Creole and "Inventor of Jazz."* Berkeley and Los Angeles: University of California Press.

Lord, Albert. 1970. *The Singer of Tales.* New York: Atheneum, 1970. Orig. pub. Harvard Studies in Comparative Literature, no. 24. Cambridge: Harvard University Press, 1960.

Lord, Tom. 1992–. *The Jazz Discography.* Vols. 1–5 (A–Dz) completed; forthcoming volumes four to six per year. Redwood, NY: Cadence Jazz Books.

Lortat-Jacob, Bernard, ed. 1987. *L'Improvisation dans les musiques de tradition orale.* Ethnomusicologie-4. Centre National de Recherche Scientifique du Ministere de la Culture (Direction de la Musique) et de la Maison des Sciences de l'Homme; Selaf-Paris.

McKinney, John Francis. 1978. "The Pedagogy of Lennie Tristano." Ph.D. dissertation, Fairleigh Dickinson University.

McNeil, John. 1993. *The Art of Jazz Trumpet,* vol. 1. New York: Gerard and Sarzin.

Mansfield, Horace, Jr. 1985. "The Survivors." *Be-bop and Beyond* 3, no. 1 (January/February): 24–32.

Martin, Henry. 1980. "Jazz Harmony." Ph.D. dissertation, Princeton University.

———. 1986. *Enjoying Jazz.* New York: Schirmer Books.

———. 1988. "Jazz Harmony: A Syntactic Background." *Annual Review of Jazz Studies* 4:9–30.

Martindale, Colin. 1990. *The Clockwork Muse.* New York: Basic.

Maxwell, Jim. 1982. *The First Trumpeter.* New York: Charles Colin.

Meadows, Eddie S. 1981. *Jazz Reference and Research Materials: A Bibliography.* New York: Garland.

Mehegan, John F. 1959. *Jazz Improvisation: Tonal and Rhythmic Principles,* vol. 1. New York: Watson-Guptill.

Mensah, Atta Annan. 1971–72. "Jazz—The Round Trip." *Jazzforschung/Jazz Research* 3–4:124–37.

Merriam, Alan P. 1964. *The Anthropology of Music.* Evanston, IL: Northwestern University Press.

Merriam, Alan P., and Robert J. Brenford. 1954. *A Bibliography of Jazz.* Philadelphia: American Folk-lore Society. Rpt. New York: Da Capo, 1970.

Merriam, Alan P., and Raymond W. Mack. 1960. "The Jazz Community." *Social Forces* 38 no. 3 (March): 211–22.

Milano, Dominic. 1984. "Jazz Pianist and Psychiatrist Denny Zeitlin on the Psychology of Improvisation." *Keyboard* 10, no. 10 (October): 25, 30–35.

Mingus, Charles. 1971. *Beneath the Underdog.* New York: Alfred A. Knopf.

Monson, Ingrid T. 1991. "Musical Interaction in Modern Jazz: An Ethnomusicological Perspective." Ph.D. dissertation, New York University.

Moorman, D. L. 1984. "An Analytical Study of Jazz Improvisation with Suggestions for Performance." Ph.D. dissertation, New York University.

Mumma, Gordon, with Chris Sheridan and Barry Kernfeld. 1988. "Recording (I)." In *The New Grove Dictionary of Jazz.* See Kernfeld 1988d.

Murray, Albert. 1973. *The Hero and the Blues*. Columbia: University of Missouri Press.

———. 1976. *Stomping the Blues*. New York: McGraw-Hill.

Nelson, Oliver. 1966. *Patterns for Improvisation*. New Albany, IN: Jamey Aebersold.

Nettl, Bruno. 1974. "Thoughts on Improvisation: A Comparative Approach." *Musical Quarterly* 60, no. 1 (January): 1–19.

———, ed. "New Perspectives on Improvisation" issue. *World of Music* 33, no. 3 (1991). Wilhelmshaven, Germany: Florian Noetzel Edition.

Newsom, Jon. 1973. "Jazz: Aspects of Melodic Improvisation." In *Music in the Modern Age*, ed. F. W. Sternfeld. New York: Praeger.

Nketia, J. H. Kwabena. 1971. "Surrogate Languages of Africa." *Current Trends in Linguistics* 7:699–732.

———. 1974. *The Music of Africa*. New York: W. W. Norton.

Oliver, Paul. 1970. *Savannah Syncopators: African Retentions in the Blues*. New York: Stein and Day.

O'Meally, Robert. 1991. *Lady Day*. New York: Arcade; Little, Brown.

Owens, Thomas. 1974. "Charlie Parker: Techniques of Improvisation." 2 vols. Ph.D. dissertation, University of California at Los Angeles.

———. 1988. "Forms." In *The New Grove Dictionary of Jazz*. See Kernfeld 1988d.

Pareles, Jon. 1983. "Celebrating Miles Davis at Music Hall." *New York Times,* November 4.

Patrick, James. 1975. "Charlie Parker and Harmonic Sources of Bebop Composition: Thoughts on the Repertory of New Jazz in the 1940s." *Journal of Jazz Studies* 2, no. 2 (January): 3–23.

———. 1983. "Al Tinney, Monroe's Uptown House, and the Emergence of Modern Jazz in Harlem." *Annual Review of Jazz Studies* 2:150–79.

Pearson, Nathan, Jr. 1987. *Goin' to Kansas City*. Urbana and Chicago: University of Illinois Press.

Perlman, Alan M., and Daniel Greenblatt. 1981. "Miles Davis Meets Noam Chomsky: Some Observations on Jazz Improvisation and Language Structure." In *The Sign in Music and Literature,* ed. Wendy Steiner. Austin: University of Texas Press.

Pike, Alfred. 1974. "A Phenomenology of Jazz." *Journal of Jazz Studies* 2, no. 1 (December): 88–94.

Pinckney, Warren R., Jr. 1989. "Puerto Rican Jazz and the Incorporation of Folk Music: Analysis of New Musical Directions." *Latin American Review* 10, no. 2 (Fall/Winter): 236–66.

———. 1989–90. "Jazz in India: Perspectives on Historical Development and Musical Acculturation." *Asian Music* 21, no. 1 (Fall/Winter): 35–77.

Porter, Lewis. 1983. "John Coltrane's Music of 1960 through 1967: Jazz Improvisation as Composition." Ph.D. dissertation, Brandeis University.

———. 1985a. "John Coltrane's 'A Love Supreme': Jazz Improvisation as Composition." *Journal of American Musicological Society* 38, no. 3 (Fall): 593–621.

———. 1985b. *Lester Young*. Boston: Twayne.

———. 1988. "John Lewis." In *The New Grove Dictionary of Jazz*. See Kernfeld 1988d.

Pressing, Jeff. 1982. "Pitch Class Set Structures in Contemporary Jazz." *Jazzforschung/ Jazz Research* 14:133–72.

———. 1984. "Cognitive Processes in Improvisation." In *Cognitive Processes in the Perception of Art,* ed. W. Ray Crozier and Antony J. Chapman. Amsterdam: Elsevier.

———. 1988. "Improvisation: Methods and Models." In *Generative Processes in Music,* ed. John A. Sloboda. Oxford: Clarendon.

Priestly, Brian. 1983 (1982). *Mingus: A Critical Biography.* New York: Da Capo.

Radano, Ronald Michael. 1985. "Anthony Braxton and His Two Musical Traditions: The Meeting of Concert Music and Jazz." Ph.D. dissertation, University of Michigan.

Randel, Don Michael, ed. 1986. *The New Harvard Dictionary of Music.* Cambridge: Belknap Press of Harvard University Press.

*The Real Book.* 2d ed. Illegal fake book, no credits.

*The Real Book,* vol. 2. Illegal fake book, no credits.

Reed, Ted. 1958. *Progressive Steps to Syncopation for the Modern Drummer.* Clear Water, FL: Ted Reed.

Reid, Rufus. 1977. *Evolving Upward: Bass Book 2.* Teaneck, NJ: Myriad.

———. 1983. *The Evolving Bassist: Exercises and Solos.* Teaneck, NJ: Myriad.

Reisner, Robert George. 1959. *The Literature of Jazz: A Selective Bibliography.* New York: New York Public Library.

———, ed. 1979. *Bird: The Legend of Charlie Parker.* New York: Da Capo.

Ricker, Ramon. 1976. *Pentatonic Scales for Jazz Improvisation,* Hialeah, FL: Studio 224, Columbia Pictures Publications.

Rinzler, Paul. 1983. "McCoy Tyner: Style and Syntax." *Annual Review of Jazz Studies* 2:109–49.

———. 1988. "Preliminary Thoughts on Analyzing Musical Interaction among Jazz Performers." *Annual Review of Jazz Studies* 4:153–60.

Roberts, Bruce. 1991. "Teaching the Seven Fundamental Rudiments." *Instrumentalist* 45, no. 9 (March): 74–77.

Roberts, John Storm. 1972. *Black Music of Two Worlds.* New York: Praeger. Rpt. New York: William Morrow, 1974.

Rose, Al. 1979. *Eubie Blake.* New York: Schirmer.

Ross, Thomas W. 1989. "Improvisatory Models in Two Cultures: Todi and Rhythm Changes." *Asian Review* (Fall): 30–38.

Russo, William. 1968. *Jazz Composition and Orchestration.* Chicago: University of Chicago Press.

Russell, George A. 1959. *The Lydian Chromatic Concept of Tonal Organization for Improvisation.* New York: Concept.

Rust, Brian. 1978. *Jazz Records 1897–1942.* 4th ed. New Rochelle, NY: Arlington House.

Sargeant, Winthrop. 1976. *Jazz: Hot and Hybrid.* 3d ed., enl. New York: Da Capo. Orig. pub. New York: Arrow, 1938.

Sawyer, Keith. 1992. "Improvisational Creativity: An Analysis of Jazz Performance." *Creativity Research Journal* 5 (3): 253–63.

Schillinger, Joseph. 1946. *The Schillinger System of Musical Composition.* New York: Carl Fisher.

Schuller, Gunther. 1958. "Sonny Rollins and the Challenge of Thematic Improvisation." *Jazz Review* 1, no. 1 (November): 6–11, 21.

———. 1961. *Ornette Coleman.* New York: MJQ Music.

———. 1962. "Sonny Rollins and Thematic Improvising." In *Jazz Panorama,* ed. Martin Williams. New York: Crowell-Collier. Rpt. of Schuller 1958.

———. 1968. *Early Jazz: Its Roots and Musical Development.* New York: Oxford University Press.

———. 1988. "Arrangement." In *The New Grove Dictionary of Jazz.* See Kernfeld 1988d.

———. 1989. *The Swing Era: The Development of Jazz 1930–1945.* New York: Oxford University Press.

Shapiro, Nat, and Nat Hentoff. 1966. *Hear Me Talkin' to Ya: The Story of Jazz as Told by the Men Who Made It.* New York: Dover. Orig. pub. New York: Rinehart, 1955.

Sheets-Johnstone, Maxine. 1981. "Thinking in Movement." *Journal of Aesthetics and Art Criticism* 39, no. 4 (Summer): 399–407.

Shelemay, Kay Kaufman. 1991. "Recording Technology, the Record Industry, and Ethnomusicological Scholarship." In *Comparative Musicology and Anthropology of Music,* ed. Bruno Nettl and Philip V. Bohlman. Chicago: University of Chicago Press.

Sher, Chuck, ed. 1988. *The New Real Book,* Musical ed. Bob Bauer. Petaluma, CA: Sher Music.

———. 1991. *The New Real Book, Volume 2.* Musical ed. Bob Bauer. Petaluma, CA: Sher Music.

Sheridan, Chris. 1988. "Recording (II, 1–3, 5–6)." In *The New Grove Dictionary of Jazz.* See Kernfeld 1988d.

Shipp, E. R. 1991. "Fans Recollect the 'Eternal Music' of Miles Davis." *New York Times* obituary, October 7.

Shipton, Alyn. 1988a. "Double Bass." In *The New Grove Dictionary of Jazz.* See Kernfeld 1988d.

———. 1988b. "Piano." In *The New Grove Dictionary of Jazz.* See Kernfeld 1988d.

Sickler, Don. 1978. *The Artistry of Joe Henderson.* Ed. Bobby Porcelli. New York: Big 3 Music.

———. 1979. *The Artistry of John Coltrane.* Ed. Bobby Porcelli. New York: Big 3 Music.

Silvert, Conrad. 1978. "A Conversation with Chick Corea and Herbie Hancock." Interview appeared on program notes for a concert featuring the two artists in northern CA, February. No information available to me on its earlier publication.

Simonton, D. K. 1988. *Scientific Genius: A Psychology of Science.* Cambridge: Cambridge University Press.

Simpkins, Cuthbert Ormond. 1975. *Coltrane: A Biography.* Perth Amboy, NJ: Herdon House.

Sloboda, J. A. 1989 (1985). *The Musical Mind: The Cognitive Psychology of Music.* Oxford: Clarendon Press.

Slobin, Mark. 1984. "Europe/Peasant Music-Cultures of Eastern Europe." In *Worlds of Music,* gen. ed. Jeff Titon. New York: Schirmer Books.

Slone, Ken. 1977. *Twenty-eight Modern Jazz Trumpet Solos*. Ed. Jamey Aebersold. Lebanon, IN: Studio 224.

Slonimsky, Nicolas. 1947. *Thesaurus of Scales and Melodic Patterns*. New York: Coleman-Ross.

Smith, Gregory Eugene. 1983. "Homer, Gregory, and Bill Evans? The Theory of Formulaic Composition in the Context of Jazz Piano Improvisation." Ph.D. dissertation, Harvard University.

———. 1991. "In Quest of a New Perspective on Improvised Jazz." *World of Music* 33 (3): 29–52.

Sonneck, Oscar, comp. and trans. 1927. *Beethoven: Impressions of Contemporaries*. London: Humphrey Milford; Oxford University Press.

Southern, Eileen. 1971. *The Music of Black Americans: A History*. New York: W. W. Norton.

Spellman, A. B. 1966. *Four Lives in the Bebop Business*. New York: Pantheon.

———. 1970. *Black Music: Four Lives in the Bebop Business*. New York: Schocken. Rpt. of Spellman 1966.

Spring, Howard. 1980. "The Improvisational Technique of Charlie Christian." M.F.A. thesis, York University, Toronto, Ontario.

Starr, Frederick S. 1983. *Red and Hot: The Fate of Jazz in the Soviet Union 1917–1980*. New York: Oxford University Press.

Stearns, Marshall W. 1972 (1956, 1970). *The Story of Jazz*. London: Oxford University Press.

Steedman, Mark J. "A Generative Grammar for Jazz Chord Sequences." *Music Perception* 2, (1): 52–77.

Stewart, Milton Lee. 1973. "Structural Development in the Jazz Improvisational Technique of Clifford Brown." Ph.D. dissertation, University of Michigan.

———. 1979. "Some Characteristics of Clifford Brown's Improvisational Style." *Jazzforschung/Jazz Research* 11:135–64.

———. 1986. "Player Interaction in the 1955–1957 Miles Davis Quintet." *Jazz Research Papers* 6:187–210.

Strunk, Steven. 1979. "The Harmony of Early Bebop: A Layered Approach." *Journal of Jazz Studies* 6, no. 1 (Fall/Winter): 4–53.

———. 1988. "Harmony." In *The New Grove Dictionary of Jazz*. See Kernfeld 1988d.

Stuckey, Sterling. 1987. *Slave Culture: Nationalist Theory and the Foundations of Black America*. New York: Oxford University Press.

Suber, Charles. 1976. "Jazz Education." In *The Encyclopedia of Jazz in the Seventies*, ed. Leonard Feather and Ira Gitler. New York: Horizon.

Such, David. 1985. "Music, Metaphor and Values among Avante Garde Jazz Musicians Living in New York City." Ph.D. dissertation, University of California at Los Angeles.

Sudhalter, Richard M., and Philip R. Evans. 1974. *Bix, Man and Legend*. New Rochelle, NY: Arlington House.

Sudnow, David. 1978. *Ways of the Hand: The Organization of Improvised Conduct*. Cambridge: Harvard University Press.

Tallmadge, William H. 1979. "Equipment Failure and Audio Distortion in the Acoustical Recording and Remastering of Early Jazz." *Journal of Jazz Studies* 5, no. 2 (Spring/Summer): 61–75.

Tatum, Art. n.d. *The Genius of Art Tatum Piano Solos.* Miami: CPP Belwin.

Taylor, Billy. 1982. *Jazz Piano: A Jazz History.* Dubuque, IA: Wm. C. Brown.

Tirro, Frank. 1967. "The Silent Theme Tradition in Jazz." *Musical Quarterly* 53, no. 3 (July): 313–34.

———. 1974. "Constructive Elements in Jazz Improvisation." *Journal of the American Musicological Society* 27, no. 2 (Summer): 285–305.

———. 1977. *Jazz: A History.* New York: W. W. Norton.

Titon, Jeff. 1977. *Early Downhome Blues: A Musical and Cultural Analysis.* Urbana: University of Illinois Press.

Tomlinson, Gary. 1991. "Cultural Dialogics and Jazz: A White Historian Signifies." *Black Music Research Journal* 11, no. 2 (Fall): 229–64.

Tucker, Mark. 1988. "Transcription." In *The New Grove Dictionary of Jazz.* See Kernfeld 1988d.

———. 1991. *Ellington: The Early Years.* Urbana and Chicago: University of Illinois Press.

Ulrich, John Wade. 1977. "The Analysis and Synthesis of Jazz by Computer. In *Proceedings of the Fifth International Joint Conference on Artificial Intelligence,* 865–72. Los Angeles: William Naufmann (distrib.).

Van Der Bliek, Robert. 1987. "Wes Montgomery: A Study of Coherence in Jazz Improvisation." Master's thesis, York University, Toronto, Ontario.

Van Der Merwe, Peter. 1989. *Origins of the Popular Style: The Antecedents of Twentieth-century Popular Music.* New York: Oxford University Press.

*Volume 1 of Over One Thousand Songs.* Fake book, no credits.

Wang, Richard. 1973. "Jazz circa 1945: A Confluence of Styles." *Musical Quarterly* 59 (4): 531–46.

———. 1988. "Researching the New Orleans–Chicago Jazz Connection: Tools and Methods." *Black Music Research Journal* 8 (1): 101–12.

Washburn, Dick, and Pat Harbinson. 1980. *Miles Davis Transcribed Solos.* New Albany, IN: Jamey Aebersold pub. no. JA1300.

Waterman, Richard A. 1948. "'Hot' Rhythm in Negro Music." *Journal of the American Musicological Society* 1 (1): 24–37.

———. 1963. "On Flogging a Dead Horse: Lessons Learned from the Africanisms Controversy." *Ethnomusicology* 7, no. 2 (May): 83–87.

———. 1967. "African Influence on the Music of the Americas." In *Acculturation in the Americas: Proceedings and Selected Papers of the Twenty-ninth International Congress of Americanists,* ed. Sol Tax. New York: Cooper Square.

Watrous, Peter. 1992. "Dizzy Gillespie Stays Put, but Not for Long." *New York Times,* January 7.

Welburn, Ron. 1987. "James Reese Europe and the Infancy of Jazz Criticism." *Black Music Research Journal* 7:35–44.

Wells, Dicky. 1971. As told to Stanley Dance. *The Night People: Reminiscences of a Jazzman.* Boston: Crescendo.

White, Andrew. 1973–78. *The Works of John Coltrane.* Washington, D.C.: Andrew's Music.

Williams, Martin T. 1958. *Jazz Panorama*. New York: Crowell-Collier.

———. 1967. *Where's the Melody? A Listener's Introduction to Jazz*. New York: Funk and Wagnalls.

———. 1970. *The Jazz Tradition*. New York: Oxford University Press.

Wilmer, Valerie. 1977. *As Serious as Your Life*. London: Quartet.

Wilson, John. 1989. "Roy Eldridge, 78, Jazz Trumpeter Who Spanned Music's Style, Dies." *New York Times* obituary, February 28.

Wilson, Olly W. 1990. "Musical Analysis of African American Music." Paper delivered at the Preconference Symposium of the Society for Ethnomusicology, Oakland, CA, November 7.

Winkler, Peter K. 1978. "Towards a Theory of Popular Harmony." *In Theory Only* 4, no. 2 (May/June): 3–26.

Winter, Keith. 1979. "Communication Jazz Analysis." *Jazzforschung/Jazz Research* 11:93–132.

Witmer, Robert 1988a. "Fill." In *The New Grove Dictionary of Jazz*. See Kernfeld 1988d.

———. 1988b. "Notation." In *The New Grove Dictionary of Jazz*. See Kernfeld 1988d.

———. 1988c. "Standard." In *The New Grove Dictionary of Jazz*. See Kernfeld 1988d.

Witmer, Robert, and James Robbins. 1988. "A Historical and Critical Survey of Recent Pedagogical Materials for the Teaching and Learning of Jazz." Council for Research in Music Education Bulletin, no. 96 (Spring): 7–29. Urbana: School of Music, University of Illinois.

Woessner, Russell. 1983. "Odean Pope." *Down Beat* 50, no. 3 (March): 46–47.

Zinn, D. B. 1981. *Theory*. Vol. 1, *The Structure and Analysis of the Modern Improvised Line*. New York: Excelsior Music.

Zwerin, Michael. 1968. "Dues Paid." *Down Beat* 35, no. 3 (February 8): 18–21, 40.

———. 1982. "Abdullah Ibrahim." *International Herald Tribune*, October 27.

# INDEX

Language (*continued*)
   tions, sending messages through; Musical
   logic; Storytelling
La Roca, Pete, 337
"Last Time I Saw Paris, The," 176
Lateef, Yusef, 140, 313, 385–86, 490–91
Latin American music, 94, 204, 224–25, 233,
   254, 292, 297–98, 324, 344, 444, 490–91,
   500
Lawrence, Baby, 139, 788n.11
Laying out, 299, 311, 338, 341, 366, 373,
   375–76, 382, 385–86, 404, 422, 427, 435
Lead sheets, 64, 74–75, 82, 171, 356
Learning methods, 16, 27, 144–45, 770n.16;
   apprenticeships, 38, 39–41, 143; bands, 49–
   50, 65, 81–82, 320, 329–30, 442–46,
   818n.14; churches, 23–25; formal training,
   117–18, 149–50, 174, 784n.36; other artists,
   37, 136, 249, 290–91, 303; performances
   and demonstrations, 37, 44–46, 73, 81, 83,
   89, 93–94, 99, 107–11, 189, 227, 282–83,
   320, 333, 350, 783nn. 23, 25, 791n.4; recordings, 58, 64–65, 95–97, 101–2, 104–7,
   123, 158, 166, 170, 173, 177, 188, 199,
   237–40, 289–90, 321, 330, 331, 350, 387–
   88, 780nn. 2, 3, 781n11, 782n.12, 783n.20,
   801nn. 19, 25, 802nn. 26, 28; relatives, 22,
   27, 47; schools, 25–27, 37, 771n.3. *See also*
   Colleges; Conservatories; Developmental
   breakthroughs/revelations; Method books;
   Mentors; Playalong records; Schools; Technology (jazz practices and); Universities
Lenox School of Jazz, 56
Lent, James, 820n.23
Levy, Howard, 32, 89, 93, 223, 224, 247, 257,
   352, 390
Lewis, John, 56, 73, 247–50, 359, 798n.35,
   801n.13, 802n.31, 803n.6
Lewis, Mel, 423–24
Licks, 102, 104, 116, 196, 227–30, 254, 270,
   782n.13, 799n.4, 800nn. 5–7. *See also* Jazz
   vocabulary
Liebman, David, 56
"Like Someone in Love," 300–301, 521
Lincoln, Abbey, 92
Lincoln University, 56
Lindsay, John, 130, 315
Linear concept, 134, 161, 184–85, 265, 327.
   *See also* Horizontal concept
Listening, 55, 92–94, 291, 362–63, 470. *See*

*also* Ear, jazz and; Recordings, learning
from; Scores, live performances as
Liston, Melba, 24–26, 28, 37–38, 46, 49, 58,
   73, 96, 97, 109, 123, 149, 159, 207–8, 282,
   290, 392, 432, 445, 470, 480, 822n.36; mu-
   sical development of, 24, 25, 26, 28
Literacy. *See* Musical literacy
Little, Booker, 11, 44, 53, 91, 117, 126–29,
   136, 191, 196, 233–34, 238–39, 265–66,
   271, 297, 300–301, 308, 382–83, 439, 521,
   591–92, 807n.46, 817n.2
"Little Sunflower," 233, 399
Locked hands block chord approach, 133
Lofts, 43, 457
Logic. *See* Musical logic
Lomax, Alan, 4
Lord, Albert, 4
Loud/soft technique, 329–30, 442
Louis, Joe, 255
Love, jazz and, 31, 40–41, 45, 91, 100, 109,
   256, 389, 393–95, 432, 438, 441, 452, 469,
   487. *See also* Sensuality, jazz and
"Lover," 159
"Lover Come Back to Me," 78
"Love Supreme, A," 195, 794n.3; album, 30,
   804n.14
Lowery, Robert, 793n.19
Lunceford, Jimmie, 32, 313
Lundy, Carmen, 24–25, 66, 71–72, 83, 92,
   103, 104, 125–26, 149, 152–53, 158, 266,
   391–92, 459–62, 471, 794n.3
Lyricism, 201, 231, 234, 247–48, 266–67,
   279, 367, 458
Lyrics, 40, 64, 66, 90, 99–101, 103, 125, 135,
   171–72, 176, 196, 203–4, 255, 283, 293,
   304, 308, 358, 360, 402–3, 438, 460–61,
   463, 470, 473, 479, 502, 791n.7, 821n.32.
   *See also* Musical quotations; Singing;
   Vocalese

Macero, Teo, 481
Mack, Raymond W., 4, 770n.9
Major labels (recordings), 477–78, 483,
   820n.24
Mallets, 298, 324, 343, 451
Mambos, 94
Mangelsdorff, Albert, 347
"Manteca," 297
Manuals, jazz and instrument pedagogy. *See*
   Method books